HANDBOOK OF PSYCHOTHERAPY
CASE FORMULATION

Handbook of Psychotherapy Case Formulation

Edited by
TRACY D. EELLS

THE GUILFORD PRESS
New York   London

Library of Congress Cataloging-in-Publication Data
Handbook of psychotherapy case formulation / Tracy D. Eells, editor.
   p. cm.
  Includes bibliographical references and index.
  ISBN 1-57230-216-X
  1. Psychiatry—Case formulation. 2. Psychiatry—Differential
therapeutics. I. Eells, Tracy D.
  [DNLM: 1. Psychotherapy—methods. WM 420 H23232 1997]
RC473.C37H46 1997
616.89'14—dc21
DNLM/DLC
for Library of Congress   97-3394
                                                            CIP

To my mother and father,
and to Bernadette, Elias, and Aidan

Contributors

Dawn Bennett, BSc, MSc, Central Manchester Health Care Trust, Manchester Royal Infirmary, Manchester, England

Franz Caspar, PhD, University of Bern, Bern Switzerland, and Psychiatric Hospital Sanatorium Kilchberg, Zurich, Switzerland

John T. Curtis, PhD, Department of Psychiatry, University of California School of Medicine, and San Francisco Psychotherapy Research Group, San Francisco, CA

Tracy D. Eells, PhD, Department of Psychiatry and Behavior Sciences, University of Louisville, Louisville, KY

Stephanie H. Friedman, MA, Doctoral Candidate, Department of Clinical and Health Psychology, Allegheny University of the Health Sciences, Philadelphia, PA

Rhonda Goldman, PhD, Department of Psychology, York University, North York, Ontario, Canada

Leslie S. Greenberg, PhD, Department of Psychology, York University, North York, Ontario, Canada

Stephen N. Haynes, PhD, Department of Psychology, University of Hawaii at Manoa, Honolulu, HI

William P. Henry, PhD, Department of Psychology, University of Utah, Salt Lake City, UT

Mardi J. Horowitz, MD, Department of Psychiatry, University of California School of Medicine, and the Center on Stress and Personality of the Langley Porter Psychiatric Institute, San Francisco, CA

Kelly Koerner, PhD, Psychology Department, University of Washington, Seattle, WA

Hanna Levenson, PhD, Department of Psychiatry, University of California School of Medicine, VA Medical Center, California Pacific Medical Center, and the Levenson Institute for Training in Brief Therapy, San Francisco, CA

Marsha M. Linehan, PhD, Department of Psychology, University of Washington, Seattle, WA

Lester Luborsky, PhD, Department of Psychiatry and Center for Psychotherapy Research, University of Pennsylvania, Philadelphia, PA

John C. Markowitz, MD, Department of Psychiatry, The New York Hospital–Cornell Medical Center, New York, NY

Stanley B. Messer, PhD, Department of Clinical Psychology, Graduate School of Applied and Professional Psychology, Rutgers University, Piscataway, NJ

Arthur M. Nezu, PhD, Department of Clinical and Health Psychology, Allegheny University of the Health Sciences, Philadelphia, PA

Christine Maguth Nezu, PhD, Department of Clinical and Health Psychology, Allegheny University of the Health Sciences, Philadelphia, PA

J. Christopher Perry, MD, Institute of Community and Family Psychiatry, Jewish General Hospital, Montreal, Quebec, Canada

Jacqueline B. Persons, PhD, Center for Cognitive Therapy, Oakland, CA

Anthony Ryle, DM, FRCPsych, CAT Office, Munro Clinic, Guy's Hospital, London, England

George Silberschatz, PhD, Department of Psychiatry, University of California School of Medicine, San Francisco, and San Francisco Psychotherapy Research Group, San Francisco, CA

Hans H. Strupp, PhD, Distinguished Professor of Psychology, Emeritus, Vanderbilt University, Nashville, TN

Holly A. Swartz, MD, Department of Psychiatry, The New York Hospital–Cornell Medical Center, New York, NY

Michael A. Tompkins, PhD, Center for Cognitive Therapy, Oakland, CA

David L. Wolitzky, PhD, Department of Psychology, New York University, New York, NY

Preface

If asked, most psychotherapists would probably agree that case formulation is an important, and even basic, clinical skill. They would agree that a therapist should be guided by a set of ideas about what has caused and is perpetuating a patient's interpersonal, intrapsychic, or behavioral problems, and what that patient needs to feel better. They might even agree that therapy patients would benefit more if the clinician developed and consistently adhered to a case formulation. Yet, if asked whether they routinely construct comprehensive case formulations for their patients, my guess is that most clinicians would acknowledge that they do not. I am not alone in this belief. Sperry, Gudeman, Blackwell, and Faulkner (1992) recently described case formulation as a poorly defined and undertaught clinical skill. Perry, Cooper, and Michels (1987) lament, as psychotherapy supervisors, that a comprehensive formulation "is seldom offered and almost never incorporated into the written record" (p. 543).

Why do clinicians not routinely construct case formulations for their patients? One reason may be that clinicians do not feel well trained in case formulation. Three surveys conducted in the last several years indicate that most psychiatry residency training programs view case formulation as important but do not clearly define the term nor provide guidelines for how to construct formulations (Ben-Aron & McCormick, 1980; Fleming & Patterson, 1993; Friedman & Lister, 1987). I suspect that training programs in other mental health disciplines would report similarly. Perry et al. (1987) cite five "misconceptions" that might also explain why most clinicians do not routinely construct case formulations: (1) the belief that case formulation is indicated only for patients in long-term psychotherapy; (2) the view that case formulation is primarily a training experience and therefore unnecessary for experienced therapists; (3) the belief that case formulation is an elaborate and time-consuming process; (4) the view that a loosely construed formulation "in one's head" is sufficient; and (5) the worry about becoming so invested in a formulation that one will not hear or accept patient communications that do not fit the formulation. Perry et al. counter these misconceptions by arguing that case formulations (1) are just as important for short-term treatments as for longer ones; (2) are best used routinely by all practitioners, regardless of experience; (3) need not be laborious or time-consuming; (4) are best in written form; and (5) facilitate rather than hinder the therapist's understanding of therapy events that may not fit the formulation. These experts conclude that a need exists for therapists to improve their formulation skills.

The purpose of this *Handbook* is to provide explicit definitions and guidelines to help clinicians improve their case formulation skills. Each chapter is conceived as a "manual" to help therapists think in new and systematic ways about their patients. Fortunately, the field of psychotherapy is well equipped to provide interested clinicians with sophisticated training in case formulation. Recent years have seen a surge of interest in psychotherapy case formulation. This interest is shown by the appearance of special issues in scholarly journals devoted to the topic (Luborsky & Barber, 1994; Messer, 1996; Persons, 1995); it is also reflected in the recent publication of books on case formulation written by practitioners of different therapy orientations (Caspar, 1995; Horowitz, 1997; McWilliams, 1994; Persons, 1989) and, further, by scientific developments in which psychotherapy case formulations are treated psychometrically (Barber & Crits-Christoph, 1993). Luborsky and colleagues (1993) identified 15 different methods that have been developed in recent years, although most were developed for research purposes. These new formulation methods are potentially of great value to practicing clinicians, although the gap between psychotherapy research and psychotherapy practice leads me to think that few nonresearcher clinicians are aware of them. Another goal of this *Handbook*, therefore, is to present a sampling of these new methods of psychotherapy case formulation to a broader and primarily clinical audience.

OVERVIEW OF THE CHAPTERS

The choice of chapters was governed by two primary considerations. The first was to invite individuals who had developed case formulation methods primarily for research purposes to translate their approach into a format useful for day-to-day clinical work. The chapters that fit this description are those by Luborsky (3); Levenson and Strupp (4); Curtis and Silberschatz (5); Perry (6); Horowitz and Eells (7); Henry (9); and Caspar (10). Since many of these researchers work within a psychodynamic framework, the reader will note that psychodynamic methods are more heavily represented than other major orientations. Although there was some concern about excessive overlap among these chapters, this seems not to have been borne out. As Chapter 2 by Messer and Wolitzky illustrates, contemporary psychodynamic thought is diversified into three camps: ego psychology, object relations theory, and self psychology. The psychodynamically oriented chapters vary in their relative emphases in these suborientations. A number of them are also influenced by streams of thought outside of psychodynamics. For example, Horowitz's Configurational Analysis method credits cognitive psychology as a significant influence.

The second consideration in the choice of chapters was diversity of theoretical orientation, although no attempt was made to be comprehensive in this respect. In addition to psychodynamic perspectives, the *Handbook* has chapters written from the cognitive-behavioral (Persons & Tompkins, 12), behavioral (Nezu, Nezu, Friedman, & Haynes, 14), dialectical–behavioral (Koerner & Linehan, 13), interpersonal (Henry, 9; Markowitz & Swartz, 8), and process–experiential (Goldman & Greenberg, 15) standpoints. Chapter 2 by Messer and Wolitzky is a presentation of case formulation from the traditional psychodynamic approach, independent of the research considerations of the other psychodynamically based chapters. In addition, two chapters represent the integrationist trend in the field of psychotherapy. Chapter 11 by Ryle and Bennett integrates psychodynamic and cognitive approaches. Caspar's approach in Chapter 10 is influenced by cognitive psychology, interpersonal theory, and learning theory, as well as dynamic approaches. An additional criterion for selection of chapters was to focus on individual psychotherapy of adults.

Following the successful efforts of Crits-Christoph and Barber (1991, 1995), each chapter in this *Handbook* follows a standard format. The reasons for that format are to facilitate comparisons among the methods, to ensure that similar categories of information are provided for each method, and to increase the book's ease of use. All contributors were asked to organize their chapters according to the following headings: historical background of their approach, conceptual framework, inclusion/exclusion criteria, steps in case formulation construction, application to psychotherapy technique, case example, training, and research support for the approach. The following sections describe what was asked of each author.

Historical Background of the Approach

In this section, authors describe the historical and theoretical origins of their case formulation approach.

Conceptual Framework

The goal of this section is to present *what* is formulated and *why*. Authors were asked to consider the following questions: What assumptions about psychopathology and healthy psychological functioning underlie the approach? What assumptions about personality structure, development, self-concept, affect regulation, and conflict (if any) are made? What are the components of the case formulation and what is the rationale for including each component? How are treatment goals incorporated into the model? Does the formulation predict the course and outcome of therapy, including obstacles to success? If so, how?

Inclusion/Exclusion Criteria

Contributors were asked to present the type and range of problems for which their method is suitable. Which patients are appropriate and inappropriate for formulation with the method?

Steps in Case Formulation Construction

The goal of this section is to provide a detailed, step-by-step description of *how* to construct a case formulation with the method under discussion. After reading this section, readers should be able to make an attempt at constructing a case formulation using that method. Questions authors were asked to address included the following: How much time is required to formulate the case? What materials are used (e.g., interviews, questionnaires, progress notes)? Does the patient participate in constructing the formulation? Is a structured interview format or other special procedure required to make the formulation? What provisions are made for evaluating, amending, or correcting the formulation? What form does the final product take?

Application to Psychotherapy Technique

This section addresses how the therapist might use the formulation in therapy. For example, is the formulation shared directly with the patient and, if so, in what form?

Case Example

A concrete case example is presented to illustrate the method. Authors were encouraged to present actual materials used in case formulation, for example, interview transcripts, questionnaires, or diagrams. (All names used are pseudonyms.)

Training

This section addresses how individuals are best trained to use the case formulation method. The reason for including this section was to provide interested readers with concrete steps that may be taken in order to learn the method described.

Research Support for the Approach

This section summarizes scientific evidence for the reliability and validity of the method. The decision to include this section was based on the assumption that a case formulation method can be treated as a psychometric instrument and therefore is subject to similar empirical scrutiny.

REFERENCES

Barber, J., & Crits-Christoph, P. (Eds.). (1991). *Handbook of short-term dynamic therapies.* New York: Basic Books.

Barber, J. P., & Crits-Christoph, P. (1993). Advances in measures of psychodynamic formulations. *Journal of Consulting and Clinical Psychology, 61,* 574–585.

Barber, J., & Crits-Christoph, P. (Eds.). (1995). *Dynamic therapies for psychiatric disorders (Axis-I).* New York: Basic Books.

Ben-Aron, M., & McCormick, W. O. (1980). The teaching of formulation: Facts and deficiencies. *Canadian Journal of Psychiatry, 25,* 163–166.

Caspar, F. (1995). *Plan analysis: Toward optimizing psychotherapy.* Seattle, WA: Hogrefe & Huber.

Fleming, J. A., & Patterson, P. G. (1993). The teaching of case formulation in Canada. *Canadian Journal of Psychiatry, 38,* 345–350.

Friedman, R. S., & Lister, P. (1987). The current status of psychodynamic formulation. *Psychiatry, 50,* 126–141.

Horowitz, M. J. (1997). *Formulation as a basis for planning psychotherapy.* Washington, DC: American Psychiatric Press.

Luborsky, L., & Barber, J. (1994). Perspectives on seven transference-related measures applied to the interview with Ms. Smithfield. *Psychotherapy Research, 4,* 152–154.

Luborsky, L., Barber, J. P., Binder, J., Curtis, J., Dahl, H., Horowitz, L., Horowitz, M., Perry, J. C., Schacht, T., Silberschatz, G., & Teller, V. (1993). Transference-based measures: A new class based on psychotherapy sessions. In N. E. Miller, L. Luborsky, J. P. Barber, & J. P. Docherty (Eds.), *Psychodynamic treatment research: A handbook for clinical practice* (pp. 326–341). New York: Basic Books.

McWilliams, N. (1994). *Psychoanalytic diagnosis: Understanding personality structure in the clinical process.* New York: Guilford Press.

Messer, S. (1996). Special section on case formulation. *Journal of Psychotherapy Integration, 6,* 81–137.

Perry, S., Cooper, A. M., & Michels, R. (1987). The psychodynamic formulation: Its purpose, structure and clinical application. *American Journal of Psychiatry, 144,* 543–550.

Persons, J. B. (1989). *Cognitive therapy in practice: A case formulation approach.* New York: Norton.

Persons, J. B. (1995). Special issue on case formulation. *In Session: Psychotherapy in Practice, 1.*

Sperry, L., Gudeman, J. E., Blackwell, B., & Faulkner, L. R. (1992). *Psychiatric case formulations.* Washington, DC: American Psychiatric Press.

Contents

HANDBOOK OF PSYCHOTHERAPY
CASE FORMULATION

1

Psychotherapy Case Formulation: History and Current Status

TRACY D. EELLS

Tracing the history of the psychotherapy case formulation requires excursions into general medicine, psychiatry, and psychology. A review of this breadth is necessary if one views a psychotherapy case formulation as both a clinical and a research tool for psychotherapy and as lying at an intersection of diagnosis and treatment, theory and practice, science and art, and etiology and description. I will begin with a working definition, then review major historical and contemporary influences on the form and content of a psychotherapy case formulation. Next, I will propose five tensions that influence the psychotherapy case formulation process. Finally, I will discuss the psychotherapy case formulation as a tool for scientific study.

The primary goal of this chapter is to provide a historical and contemporary framework from which the subsequent chapters on specific case formulation methods can be viewed. A second goal is to encourage the reader to view a case formulation as a necessary conceptual tool in psychotherapy, one that facilitates organizing and synthesizing information about a patient, and further, a tool with considerable untapped potential for research. First, a note on terminology: Although I use the term "formulation" throughout the chapter, it is used analogously with "assessment," "explanation," or "hypothesis."

A WORKING DEFINITION

A psychotherapy case formulation is essentially a hypothesis about the causes, precipitants, and maintaining influences of a person's psychological, interpersonal, and behavioral problems. A case formulation helps organize often com-

1

plex and contradictory information about a person. It should serve as a blue-print guiding treatment, as a marker for change, and as a structure enabling the therapist to understand the patient better. A case formulation should also help the therapist anticipate therapy-interfering events and experience greater empathy for the patient.

As a hypothesis, a case formulation may include inferences about predis-posing or antecedent vulnerabilities based on early childhood traumas, a patho-genic learning history, biological or genetic influences, sociocultural influences, currently operating contingencies of reinforcement, or maladaptive schemas and beliefs about the self or others. The nature of this hypothesis can vary widely depending upon which theory of psychotherapy and psychopathology the cli-nician applies. Psychodynamic approaches focus primarily on unconscious mental processes and conflicts (Messer & Wolitzky, Chapter 2, this volume; S. Perry, Cooper, & Michels, 1987); a cognitive therapy formulation might focus on dysfunctional thoughts and beliefs about the self, others, the world, or the future (e.g., J. S. Beck, 1995; Freeman, 1992; Persons, 1989); in con-trast, a behavioral formulation does not focus on intrapsychic events but on environmental contingencies, the individual's learning history, and inferences about stimulus–response pairings (Haynes & O'Brien, 1990; Wolpe & Turkat, 1985). Biological explanations might also be interwoven into a case formula-tion. Some experts advocate pursuing rigorous causal connections between a psychopathological condition and its determinants (Haynes, Spain, & Oliveira, 1993), whereas others stress achieving an explanatory narrative that may not have a factual basis in "historical truth" but is nevertheless therapeutic (Spence, 1982).

Viewed more broadly, a psychotherapy case formulation also includes *descriptive information* on which the hypothesis is based and *prescriptive rec-ommendations* that flow from the hypothesis (Sperry, Gudeman, Blackwell, & Faulkner, 1992). The *descriptive* component lays out the central "facts" of a person's life and current problems. Although the selection of "facts" can never be free of the influence of theory or perception, there is usually no attempt to interpret or infer meaning in this section; instead, the emphasis is on providing a reliable information base. Descriptive information usually in-cludes the presenting problem and its history, additional psychosocial stres-sors, previous episodes of psychological problems and treatment, the indi-vidual's developmental and social history, a medical history, and the results of a mental status examination. The *prescriptive* component of a case formulation should flow directly from the earlier descriptions and hypotheses, and should propose a plan for treating the individual. It may include details such as the type of therapy recommended, the frequency and duration of meetings, therapy goals, obstacles toward achieving these goals, a prognosis, and a referral for adjunctive interventions such as pharmacotherapy, group therapy, substance abuse treatment, or a medical evaluation. Alternatively, a form of treatment other than psychotherapy, or no treatment at all, might be recommended.

HISTORICAL AND CONTEMPORARY INFLUENCES

In this section I will review five influences on the psychotherapy case formulation. These are the medical examination and case history; models of psychopathology and its classification; models of psychotherapy; psychometric assessment; and case formulation research.

The Medical Examination and Case History

The major influences on the form and logic of the psychotherapy case formulation are the medical examination and case study, which have their roots in Hippocratic and Galenic medicine.[1] The rise of Hippocratic medicine in the fifth century B.C. marked a repudiation of polytheism and mythology as sources of illness or cure. It also signaled an embrace of reason, logic, and observation in understanding illness, and the conviction that only natural forces are at play in disease. The Hippocratic physicians believed that diagnosis must rest on a firm footing of observation and employed prognostication as a means of corroborating their diagnoses. They took a holistic view of disease, viewing the patient as an active participant in his or her cure. Foreshadowing contemporary physicians who propound "wellness" and psychotherapists advocating a focus on patients' "problems in living," the Hippocratics viewed disease as an event occurring in the full context of the patient's life. Their treatment efforts were aimed at restoring a balance of natural forces in the patient.

Working within erroneous theoretical assumptions involving humoral interaction, vitalism, and "innate heat," the basic task of the Hippocratic physician was to determine the nature of a patient's humor imbalance. Toward this end, a highly sophisticated physical examination developed in which the physician, using all five senses, sought objective evidence to determine the underlying cause of the observed symptoms. According to Nuland (1988), Hippocratic case reports included descriptions of changes in body temperature, color, facial expression, breathing pattern, body position, skin, hair, nails, and abdominal contour. In addition, Hippocratic physicians tasted blood and urine; they examined skin secretions, ear wax, nasal mucus, tears, sputum, and pus; they smelled stool; and observed stickiness of the sweat. Once they had gathered and integrated this information, they used it to infer the source of humoral imbalance and how far the disease had progressed. Only then was an intervention prescribed. The main point to be appreciated is the empirical quality of this examination. Symptoms were not taken at face value, nor were they assumed to be the product of divine intervention; instead, objective evidence of the body's ailment was sought.

The focus on observation and empiricism by Hippocrates and his students laid the foundation for physical examinations performed today. It also serves as a worthwhile credo for the modern psychotherapy case formulation. Importantly, the Hippocratics also provide modern psychotherapy case formulators with the caveat that even concerted efforts at objectivity and empiricism can fall prey to an overbelief in a theoretical framework into which observations are organized.

Before it could be described as modern, the Hippocratic ethos required two additional ingredients: a focus on anatomic (and subanatomic) structure and function as the foundation of disease, and the establishment of planned experimentation as a means of understanding anatomy and disease. These ingredients were supplied more than 500 years after Hippocrates by another Greek physician, Galen of Pergamum. Before Galen, a detailed knowledge of the body's anatomy and how disease disrupts it was considered ancillary information in medical training, at best. Galen's emphasis on anatomy and structure can be seen as a precursor to current psychological theories that posit central roles for mental structures. These include psychodynamic concepts of id, ego, and superego, as well as self-representations, or schemas, which both cognitive and some psychodynamic theorists and researchers emphasize (Segal & Blatt, 1993).

Galen was the first to prize experimentation as a method for understanding anatomy. In a series of simple and elegant experiments, he proved that arteries contain blood and that arterial pulsations originate in the heart. Consistent with this Galenic spirit, experimentation to test formulations about the "psychological anatomy" of individual psychotherapy patients has been proposed by psychodynamic (Edelson, 1988), behavioral (Barlow & Hersen, 1984), and process–experiential (Goldman & Greenberg, Chapter 15, this volume) psychotherapy researchers (see also Carey, Flasher, Maisto, & Turkat, 1984).

Another significant advance in medical science with regard to diagnosis occurred many centuries after Galen. This was the publication, in 1769, of Giambattista Morgagni's *De Sedibus et Causis Morborum per Anatomen* (*The Seats and Causes of Disease Investigated by Anatomy*). Morgagni's work is a compilation of over 700 well-indexed clinical case histories, each linking a patient's symptom presentation to a report of pathology found at autopsy and any relevant experiments that had been conducted. *De Sedibus* was a remarkable achievement in that it firmly established Galen's "anatomical concept of disease." Although we now understand that illness is not only the product of diseased organs but also of pathological processes occurring in tissues and cellular and subcellular structures, the reductionist concept of disease still maintains. An 18th-century physician using *De Sedibus* to treat a patient could use the index to look up his patient's symptoms, which could be cross-referenced to a list of pathological processes that may be involved. Morgagni's credo that symptoms are the "cry of suffering organs" parallels the guiding assumption of some psychotherapy case formulation approaches that symptoms represent the "cry" of underlying psychopathological structures and processes.

A second accomplishment of Morgagni is his foundation of the clinico-pathological method of medical research, in which correspondences are examined between a patient's symptoms and underlying pathology revealed at autopsy. Although there is no psychological equivalent of the conclusive autopsy, the advent of the clinicopathological method foreshadowed an emphasis on obtaining independent, corroborating evidence to substantiate hypothesized relationships in psychology. Morgagni's *De Sedibus* also demonstrated how advances in medical science can occur on a case-by-case basis and how the integration and organization of existing information can advance a science.

By extending the reach of our five senses, the tools and technologies of medicine have also added immensely to diagnostic precision; in doing so, medicine has provided a model for psychotherapy case formulations. Examples of developments in medicine that aided diagnosis include René Laënnec's invention of the stethoscope in the early 19th century, Wilhelm Roentgen's discovery of X rays, and recent developments in brain imaging techniques. If parallels exist in psychology, one might cite Sigmund Freud's free association, B. F. Skinner's demonstration of the power of stimulus control over behavior, the technology of behavior genetics, and the advent of psychometrics. Each of these "technologies" has added to our understanding of individual psychological and psychopathological functioning. Later in this chapter, I shall discuss the potential for structured case formulation methods to serve as research tools.

As this review of the medical examination and case study has shown, the structure and logic of a traditional psychotherapy case formulation are modeled closely after those aspects of medical diagnosis. Specific aspects that are borrowed include an emphasis on observation; the assumption that symptoms reflect underlying disease processes; experimentation as a means of discovery; an ideal of postmortem (or posttreatment) confirmation of the formulation; and an increasing reliance upon technologies to aid in diagnosis.

Models of Psychopathology and Its Classification

A clinician's assumptions about what constitutes psychopathology and how psychopathological states develop and are organized will frame how that clinician formulates cases. These assumptions impose a set of axiological constraints about what the clinician views as "wrong" with a person, what needs to change, how possible change is, and how change might be effected. Although an extended discussion of the nature and classification of psychopathology is beyond the scope of this chapter, three themes that underlie ongoing debates on this topic are relevant to case formulation. For an expanded discussion, see Blashfield (1984), Kendell (1975), or Millon (1996).

Etiology versus Description

Throughout its history, psychiatry has oscillated between descriptive and etiological models of psychopathology (Mack, Forman, Brown, & Frances, 1994). The tension between these approaches to nosology reflects both dissatisfaction with descriptive models and the scientific inadequacy of past etiological models. During the 20th century, this trend is seen as Emil Kraepelin's descriptive psychiatry gave way to a psychosocial focus inspired by Adolf Meyer and Karl Menninger, as well as a Freudian emphasis on unconscious determinants of behavior. A focus on description to the virtual exclusion of etiology was revived in 1980 with the publication of DSM-III. With etiological considerations relegated to the background at present, a conceptual vacuum has been created that case formulation attempts to fill, perhaps as an interim measure until a more empirically sound etiological nosology is established.

Categorical versus Dimensional Models

Just as psychopathologists have oscillated between etiological and descriptive nosologies, so have they debated the merits of categorical versus dimensional models of psychopathology. The categorical or "syndromal" view is that mental disorders are qualitatively distinct from each other and from "normal" psychological functioning. The categorical approach expresses the "medical model" of psychopathology, which, in addition to viewing diseases as discrete pathological entities, also adheres to the following precepts: (1) diseases have predictable causes, courses, and outcomes; (2) symptoms are expressions of underlying pathogenic structures and processes; (3) the primary but not exclusive province of medicine is disease, not health; and (4) disease is fundamentally an individual phenomenon, not social or cultural. The categorical approach to psychopathology is traceable in recent history to Kraepelin's "disease concept" and is embodied in DSM-III and its successors. In recent years it has exerted a pervasive influence on psychopathology and psychotherapy research and clinical practice (Garfield & Bergin, 1994; Wilson, 1993).

Those advocating a dimensional approach claim that psychopathology is better viewed as a set of continua from normal to abnormal. Widiger and Frances (1994) argue that dimensional approaches help resolve classification dilemmas, especially regarding "poorly fitting" cases; that they retain more information than categorical models about "subclinical" functioning; and that they are more flexible in that cutoff scores can be used to create categories when clinical or research goals require them.

In terms of case formulation, what difference does it make whether a nosology is dimensional or categorical? Three factors can be identified: potential for stigmatization, goodness of fit to one's view of personality organization, and ease of use.

Compared to dimensional models, categorical approaches may be more prone to stigmatize patients due to a greater tendency to reify what is actually a theoretical construct. For example, being told that one "has" a personality disorder can produce or exacerbate feelings of being defective, especially when proffered as an explanation of one's condition. This "formulation" can also have an unnecessarily demoralizing effect on the therapist. Dimensional approaches may be less prone toward stigmatization because dimensions are assumed to vary from normal to abnormal ranges and are not assumed to represent discrete psychological conditions.

When expressed in experience-near, functional, and context-specific terms, a case formulation can serve as a therapeutic adjunct to a categorical system, thus reducing the potential for stigmatization. For example, instead of labeling a person as having a personality disorder, the therapist might offer formulation-based interventions such as, "Could it be that when threatened by abandonment, you hurt yourself in an attempt to bring others close; but instead, you only drive them away?" or "I wonder if you are letting others decide how you feel, instead of deciding for yourself."

The dimensional–categorical debate also has implications for the case formulator's frame of reference in understanding personality. If one views personality in an intraindividual context (Valsiner, 1986, 1987), that is, as an internally organized system of interconnecting parts, then the categorical approach is a closer fit. This view of personality is consistent with those offered by Allport (1961) and Millon (1996), among others. The categorical approach assumes that signs, symptoms, and traits cluster together, forming a whole that constitutes an organization greater than the sum of its parts. Thus, from the intraindividual standpoint, if a patient exhibits grandiosity in an interview, suggesting narcissistic personality disorder, the case formulator might examine more closely for interpersonal exploitativeness or entitlement, which are other features of this disorder. Reaching beyond DSM-IV to other accounts of narcissism, the interviewer might also prepare for sudden fluctuations in the individual's self-esteem, for depressive episodes that come and go quickly, or might examine for evidence of using others as "selfobjects" (Kohut, 1971, 1977, 1984).

On the other hand, the dimensional approach is the better fit if one views individual personality in an interindividual frame of reference (Valsiner, 1986, 1987), that is, as an array of traits that do not necessarily interrelate and which are best understood according to how they compare with their expression in other individuals. Dimensional approaches such as the five-factor model (Costa & Widiger, 1994) are built on the assumption that the dimensions are not correlated. Thus, an individual's "score" on the trait "agreeableness" would not help one predict his or her degree of "conscientiousness." A clinician working from an interindividual frame might propose a set of cardinal traits as constituting the core of a case formulation.

Ease of use is another consideration relevant to case formulation, since practically a case formulation must often be done quickly. As Widiger and Frances (1994) note, the categorical approach is better adapted to clinical decision making, which usually involves discrete decisions, such as to treat or not, to make intervention A or intervention B, and so on. Since the case formulation process involves a similar style of decision making, it may be more compatible with a categorical system. Categories may also have greater ease of use in helping a therapist and patient "name" experiences. For example, a patient's salient "states of mind" might be incorporated into the case formulation and introduced into the therapy at an appropriate time (Horowitz & Eells, Chapter 7, this volume).

Normality versus Abnormality

Related to the issue of dimensional versus categorical models of psychopathology are decisions as to what is and what is not "normal." These decisions are central to the task of psychotherapy case formulation. They not only guide the structure and content of the formulation but also the clinician's intervention strategies and goals for treatment. Several criteria can help in making this decision. First, as Millon (1996) notes, it is important to recognize that all conceptions of psychopathology are social constructions, at least to some extent. They reflect culturally derived, consensually held views as to what is to be considered abnormal and what is not. Other criteria include the following: statistical deviation from normative behavior; personal distress, causing distress in others; violation of social norms; deviation from an ideal of mental health; personality inflexibility; poor adaptation to stress; and irrationality (e.g., Millon, 1996; Widiger & Trull, 1991). These criteria provide a baseline and a context against which the patient's behaviors and experiences can be compared. They enable the case formulator to better understand patients by comparing their responses to stress to normative stress responses, and to assess the separate contributions of dispositional versus situational, cultural, social, and economic factors to a patient's clinical presentation. The case formulator does not act as judge of the patient's experiences but uses knowledge about consensual views of "normality" and "abnormality" to help the patient adapt.

In sum, the content and structure of a psychotherapy case formulation is inextricably linked to the therapist's implicit or explicit views on issues regarding the etiology of emotional problems, the dimensional versus categorical debate about mental disorders, and assumptions about what is normal and abnormal in one's psychological functioning.

Models of Psychotherapy

The therapist's approach to psychotherapy will, of course, greatly influence the case formulation process. In this section, I will review four major models of psychotherapy with a focus on their contributions to case formulation. These approaches are psychoanalytic, humanistic, behavior, and cognitive therapies.

Psychoanalysis

Psychoanalysis has had at least three major influences on the psychotherapy case formulation process. The principal contribution is that Freud and his successors developed models of personality and psychopathology that have significantly shaped our understanding of normal and abnormal human experience and behavior. Among the most significant psychoanalytic concepts are psychic determinism and the notion of a dynamic unconscious; the over-determination, idiogenesis, and symbolic meaning of symptoms; symptom production as a compromise formation; ego defense mechanisms as maintainers of psychic equilibrium; and the tripartite structural model of the mind. Beginning with the early formulation that "hysterics suffer mainly from reminiscences" (Breuer & Freud, 1893/1955, p. 7), psychoanalysis has provided therapists with a general framework for understanding experiences that patients report in psychotherapy. More recent formulations by object relations theorists (e.g., Kernberg, 1975, 1984) and self psychologists (Kohut, 1971, 1977, 1984) have added to our understanding of individuals with personality disorders.

A second contribution of psychoanalysis to case formulation relates to an expanded view of the psychotherapy interview. Before Freud, the psychiatric interview was viewed similarly to an interview in a medical examination. It was highly structured and focused on obtaining a history and mental status review, reaching a diagnosis, and planning treatment (Gill, Newman, & Redlich, 1954). Since Freud, therapists have recognized that patients often enact their psychological problems, and especially interpersonal problems, in the course of describing them to the therapist. The interview process itself has become an important source of information for the formulation. That is, the manner in which patients organize their self-presentations and thoughts, approach or avoid certain topics, and behave nonverbally has become part of what the therapist formulates.

A third contribution of psychoanalysis to formulation is its emphasis on the case study. Although the value of the case history continues to be debated (e.g., Runyan, 1982), there is little question that Freud elevated the method's scientific profile. The case study was the principal vehicle through which Freud presented and supported psychoanalytic precepts.

Interestingly, psychoanalysis has not traditionally incorporated the concept of a medical diagnosis into a formulation (Gill, Newman, & Redlich, 1954). Freud's own disinterest in diagnosis is revealed in the index of the *Standard Edition* of his complete works, which shows no entries for "diagnosis" or "formulation," although a few under "anamnesis." Pasnau (1987) and Wilson (1993) argue that psychoanalysts' lack of emphasis on diagnosis contributed to the "demedicalization" of psychiatry earlier this century. These writers contend that the "disease concept" was not seen as compatible or relevant to psychoanalysts' focus on unconscious psychological determinants of symptoms as opposed to organic determinants, nor to an emphasis on motivational states, early life history, or interpersonal relationship patterns.

Along with its contributions to case formulation, psychoanalysts have also been criticized for applying general formulations to patients when they do not fit. One prominent example may be Freud's case study of Dora (see Lakoff, 1990). Psychoanalytic formulations have also been criticized for being overly speculative (Masson, 1984) and for exhibiting a male bias (Horney, 1967).

Humanistic Therapy

Proponents of humanistically oriented psychotherapies have traditionally taken the view that case formulation, or at least "psychological diagnosis," is unnecessary and even harmful. According to Rogers (1951, p. 220), "psychological diagnosis . . . is unnecessary for [client-centered] psychotherapy, and may actually be detrimental to the therapeutic process." Rogers was concerned that formulation places the therapist in a "one up" position in relation to the client and may introduce an unhealthy dependency into the therapy relationship, thus impeding a client's efforts to assume responsibility for solving his or her own problems. In Rogers's words, "There is a degree of loss of personhood as the individual acquires the belief that only the expert can accurately evaluate him, and that therefore the measure of his personal worth lies in the hands of another" (1951, p. 224). Rogers also expressed the social philosophical objection that diagnosis may in the long run place "social control of the many [in the hands of] . . . the few" (1951, p. 224). While Rogers's criticisms serve as a caveat, they also seem based on the assumption that the practice of "psychological diagnosis" necessarily places the therapist and patient in a noncollaborative relationship in which the formulation is imposed in a peremptory fashion rather than reached jointly and modified as necessary. It is also noteworthy that contemporary exponents of phenomenological therapies are less rejecting of formulation than was Rogers but tend to emphasize formulation of the moment-to-moment experiences of the client rather than proposing global patterns that describe a client (Goldman & Greenberg, Chapter 15, this volume).

Contributions of humanistic psychology to case formulation include its emphasis on the client as a person instead of a disorder that is treated, its focus on the here-and-now aspect of a human encounter rather than an intellectualized formulation, and its view of the therapist and client as equals in their relationship. Humanistic psychology also takes a holistic rather than a reductionist view of humankind. Methodologically, humanistic approaches have also contributed techniques that facilitate insight and a deepening of experience, and therefore add to the formulation process. These include role playing and the "empty chair" technique. Taken as a whole, these influences have tempered what some have viewed as the potential dehumanizing effects of case formulation.

Behavior Therapy

Behavior therapists have historically tended to neglect assessment (Goldfried & Pomeranz, 1968) and to criticize the concept of diagnosis. They view diagnosis as emphasizing unobservable mental entities or forces, as focusing unnecessarily on classification per se, and as lacking utility in helping individuals (Hayes & Follette, 1992). These therapists prefer to focus on a "functional analysis" of behavior, which involves identifying relevant characteristics of the individual in question, his or her behavior, and environmental contingencies or reinforcement, then applying behavioral principles to make alterations. Some behaviorists have acknowledged limitations in the functional analysis approach to case formulation, primarily due to difficulties in replicability and resulting problems in studying patients scientifically (Hayes & Follette, 1992).

Notwithstanding these criticisms, behaviorists have made at least three major contributions to the case formulation process. First is an emphasis on symptoms. Behaviorists have strived to understand the "topography" of symptomatology, including relevant stimulus–response associations and contingencies of reinforcement. In contrast to dynamic thinkers who view symptoms as *symbolic* of a more fundamental problem, behaviorists focus on symptoms *as* the problem and aim directly at symptom relief. Second, more than other practitioners, behaviorists have emphasized environmental sources of distress. As a consequence, greater attention has been placed on changing the environment rather than the individual. A formulation that is more balanced in attributing maladaptive behavior to the individual and his or her environment is less stigmatizing. Third, behaviorists have emphasized empirical demonstrations to support the effectiveness of their approaches. These include measuring symptomatology, isolating potential causal variables, and systematically varying them and examining the effects on behavior. This tradition dates back to John B. Watson's demonstration with Little Albert that specific phobias can be produced and extinguished according to principles of classical conditioning.

Cognitive Therapy

In a series of influential volumes, A. T. Beck and his colleagues have set forth general formulations about the causes, precipitants, and maintaining influences in depression (Beck, Rush, Shaw, & Emery, 1979), anxiety disorders (Beck, Emery, & Greenberg, 1985), personality disorders (Beck, Freeman, & Associates, 1990), and, most recently, substance abuse (Beck, Wright, Newman, & Liese, 1993). These formulations emphasize a set of cognitive patterns, schemas, and faulty information processes, each specific to the type of disorder. Depressed individuals, for example, tend to view themselves as defective and inadequate, the world as excessively demanding and as presenting insuperable obstacles to reaching goals, and the future as hopeless. The thought processes of depressed individuals are described as revealing characteristic errors, including making arbitrary inferences, selectively abstracting from the specific to the general, overgeneralizing, and dichotomizing. In contrast, formulations of anxious individuals tend to center around the theme of vulnerability; and those of substance-abusing individuals may focus on automatic thoughts regarding the anticipation of gratification and increased efficacy when they are using drugs, or symptom relief that will follow such drug intake.

Until recently, cognitive psychologists tended to focus on general formulations for these disorders, rather than individualistic variations constructed for a specific patient (Persons & Tompkins, Chapter 12, this volume). Since Persons (1989) published her book on case formulation from the cognitive-behavioral perspective, there is increased focus on individualized formulations. As she and Tompkins note in this volume, the jury is still out on whether individualized formulations have a differential impact on the outcome of cognitive-behavioral therapy than when generalized formulations are used.

Psychometric Assessment

Among clinical psychology's contributions to understanding psychopathology are the development of reliable and valid personality tests, standards for constructing and administering these tests, and a statistically informed "way of thinking" about assessment. The influence of these developments on psychotherapy case formulation has been indirect, however, and not what it potentially might be. One reason may be a tendency among many clinical psychologists to see psychotherapy and psychometric assessment as separate, and perhaps incompatible, enterprises. Secondly, questions have regularly arisen about the practical value of psychological assessment for psychotherapy (e.g., Bersoff, 1973; Hayes, Nelson, & Jarrett, 1987; Korchin & Schuldberg, 1981; Meehl, 1958). In fact, very little research has examined the incremental benefit of psychological assessment on treatment planning, implementation, and outcome, despite the availability of research strategies for addressing this issue (Hayes, Nelson, & Jarrett, 1987).

What are the potential contributions of psychometrics and psychometric thinking to psychotherapy case formulation? First is the use of validated personality and symptom measures themselves in the case formulation process. As the reader of this volume will see, several authors routinely use symptom measures as part of their case formulation method. Other authors have discussed psychotherapy applications of frequently used measures, including the Minnesota Multiphasic Personality Inventory–2 (Butcher, 1993), the Rorschach technique (Aronow, Rezinikoff, & Moreland, 1994), and the Thematic Apperception Test (Bellak, 1993). In addition, Widiger and Sanderson (1995) advocate the use of semistructured interviews to assess the presence of personality disorders more reliably. Quantitative approaches to evaluating life history events might also provide a powerful means of understanding a patient's dynamics, as suggested by Meehl (1958) and developed by Bruhn (1995) with regard to early memories.

A second potential contribution to case formulation relates to the "way of thinking" that is associated with psychometric assessment. An awareness of concepts such as reliability, validity, and standardization of administration of a measure may increase the "accuracy" of a case formulation. For example, just as standardized administration of psychological tests is important for a reliable and valid interpretation of the results, so might it be important for the therapist to adopt a standard approach in an assessment interview so as to understand the client more accurately and empathically. In accomplishing this goal, the therapist need not be rigid or wooden, or refuse to accommodate specific needs of a patient. Rather, the therapist might strive to be close enough to the patient but also sufficiently distant as to remain a reliable instrument for assessing the patient's problems, including the possible expression of those problems in the therapy relationship. Maintaining such a stance is particularly important during the psychotherapy interview since it is the most frequently used "measure" for assessing psychotherapy patients and is also highly subject to problems with reliability (Beutler, 1995).

Case Formulation Research

Until recently, very little was known about either the interrater reliability or the predictive validity of psychotherapy case formulations. Interrater reliability here refers to how well clinicians can independently construct similar formulations based on the same clinical material; it can also refer to the extent to which they agree as to how well an already-constructed formulation or its components fit a particular set of clinical material. Predictive validity refers to how well the formulation predicts psychotherapy process events or outcome.

Philip F. Seitz, a Chicago psychoanalyst, published a paper in 1966 detailing the efforts of a small research group to study what he termed "the consensus problem in psychoanalytic research." For 3 years, the group of six psychoanalysts independently reviewed either detailed interview notes from a single case of psychotherapy or dreams taken from several psychotherapy cases. Each formulator wrote an essay-style narrative addressing the precipitating situation, focal conflict, and defense mechanisms at play in the clinical material. The participants also reported their interpretive reasoning and evidence both supporting and opposing their formulation. After the formulations were written, they were distributed to each of the group members, who then had the opportunity to revise their own formulations in light of clues provided in the formulations of others. The group met weekly to review its findings. Despite the group's initial enthusiasm, the results were disappointing, even if predictable. Seitz reported that satisfactory consensus was achieved on very few of the formulations.

The primary value of Seitz's (1966) paper is that it alerted the community of psychotherapy researchers and practitioners to the "consensus problem." If psychotherapy research aspired to be a scientific enterprise, progress had to be made in the consistency with which clinicians describe a patient's problems and way of managing them. Seitz's paper is also valuable for its presentation of why the clinicians had difficulty obtaining agreement. A general reason was the "inadequacy of our interpretive methods" (p. 214). One of these inadequacies was the tendency of group members to make inferences at an overly deep level, for example, making references to "phallic–Oedipal rivalry" and "castration fears." Seitz also recognized that the group placed "excessive reliance upon intuitive impressions and insufficient attention to the systematic and critical checking of our interpretations" (p. 216). These remarks foreshadowed those of current researchers who have identified limitations and biases in human information-processing capacities (Kahneman, Slovic, & Tversky, 1982; Turk & Salovey, 1988).

Seitz's paper achieved its stated purpose and sparked research efforts to improve the reliability and validity of psychotherapy case formulations. As of this writing, over 15 structured case formulations methods have been proposed in the literature (Luborsky et al., 1993). Although most of these methods were developed within a psychodynamic framework, methods from behavioral, cognitive-behavioral, cognitive-analytic, and eclectic/integrative schools have also been proposed. The reliability and validity of several have been tested (Barber & Crits-Christoph, 1993). A sampling of these methods includes the Core Conflictual Relationship Theme (CCRT; Luborsky, 1977; Luborsky & Crits-Christoph, 1998), the Plan Formulation method (Curtis, Silberschatz, Sampson, & Weiss, 1994), the Role Relationship Model Configuration method (M. J. Horowitz, 1989, 1991) the Cyclic Maladaptive Pattern (Johnson, Popp, Schacht, Mellon, & Strupp, 1989; Schacht & Henry, 1994), the Idiographic Conflict Formulation method (J. C. Perry, 1994; J. C. Perry, Augusto, & Cooper, 1989), the Consensual Response Formulation method (L. M. Horowitz, Rosenberg, Ureño, Kalehzan, & O'Halloran, 1989), cognitive-behavioral case formulation (Persons, 1989, 1995), and Plan Analysis (Caspar, 1995).

Since many of the methods just named are described in this volume, it will suffice here to describe similarities among many of these methods. According to Luborsky and colleagues (1993), the following four features characterize these methods: they focus on relationship interactions expressed in psychotherapy sessions; they identify core relationship conflicts based on the frequency with which patterns are conveyed in therapy; they rely on clinical judgment rather than a patient's self-report alone; and they include provisions to assess interclinician agreement as to the inferred underlying mechanism. Three additional features can also be identified. First, they emphasize levels of inference that remain close to observable statements or behaviors of a patient. One fortunate consequence of this emphasis on low-level inferences is the relative absence of jargon and heavily theory-laden terminology in formulation statements. Second, the goal of achieving a comprehensive formulation is approached by separating the formulation into components, each of which can be evaluated individually for reliability. For example, Luborsky's CCRT method identifies three components of a "relationship episode," which is a narrative about an interpersonal interaction. These are wishes of the self with regard to another person, expected and actual responses of the other, and the responses of the self. Once these elements are identified, they can be assessed individually for interclinician agreement. Finally, a psychotherapy integration trend pervades many of the methods. For example, several methods incorporate elements of both cognitive and dynamic framework, particularly with regard to the notion that enduring maladaptive cognitive representations, or schemas, are implicated in many psychological disorders. An important feature of these methods is that they have been demonstrated to be reliable measures of patients' core problems, as well as to predict psychotherapy process and outcome (Barber & Crits-Christph, 1993).

In this section, I have traced historical and contemporary influences that have shaped the process and content of the psychotherapy case formulation to what it is today. As reviewed, its form and structure originated in Hellenic days and are deeply embedded in medicine but have also been altered in significant ways by psychoanalytic, humanistic, behavioral, and cognitive psychology. Psychotherapy case formulation has also been influenced by how psychopathology is understood; by the development of psychometric assessment; and by recent research in which the reliability and validity of a case formulation has been examined.

TENSIONS INHERENT IN
THE CASE FORMULATION PROCESS

We will now examine five tensions that must be handled in developing a comprehensive case formulation. Each tension represents competing and incompatible goals faced by the clinician in attempting to understand a patient. The clinician must reconcile each of these tensions if the case formulation is to achieve its goal of serving as an effective tool for psychotherapy.

Immediacy versus Comprehensiveness

The task of case formulation is foremost a pragmatic one. From the first hour of therapy, the clinician needs to develop an idea of the patient's symptoms, core problems, goals, obstacles, coping or defense mechanisms, interpersonal style, maladaptive behavior patterns, life situation, and so on. For this reason, a case formulation is needed relatively early in treatment. At the same time, the more comprehensive a case formulation is, without loss of clarity or focus, the better it will serve the clinician and patient. The priority given to practicality necessarily exacts a cost in comprehensiveness.

Some writers have advised that a case formulation should be completed in a single hour session with a patient (Kaplan, Sadock, & Grebb, 1994; Morrison, 1993). It may be unrealistic, however, to produce a sufficiently comprehensive case formulation on the basis of a single hour. Nevertheless, it is worth noting that experienced physicians begin to entertain and rule out diagnostic possibilities from the earliest minutes of medical interviewing (Elstein, Shuylman, & Sprafka, 1978). The same may be the case for experienced psychotherapists.

Another aspect of the tension between immediacy versus comprehensiveness is that the clinician observes a restricted behavior sample in a relatively controlled interview context. This may promote a selection bias and obscure a patient's capabilities and limitations that in other contexts would be apparent.

In sum, as the therapist seeks to balance the goals of immediacy and comprehensiveness, he or she must efficiently identify what is needed to help the patient and avoid areas that may be intriguing or interesting but which have little to do directly with helping the patient get better.

Complexity versus Simplicity

One can construe the case formulation task in relatively simple or complex terms. If an overly simple construction is offered, important aspects of the person's problems may go unformulated. If overly complex, the formulation may be unwieldy, too time consuming, and impractical. In addition, the more complex a case formulation method, the more difficult it may be to demonstrate its reliability and validity. Thus, a balance between complexity and simplicity is an important aim in case formulation construction.

Of course, even the most complex of formulations falls far short of the complexity of the actual person one interviews. As the writer Robertson Davies (1994, p. 20) asks, then answers, "How many interviewers, I wonder, have any conception of the complexity of the creature they are interrogating? Do they really believe that what they can evoke from their subject is the whole of their 'story'? Not the best interviewers, surely."

Clinician Bias versus Objectivity

A third tension in the case formulation process is between a therapist's efforts at accurate understanding of a patient and inherent human flaws in every therapist's ability to do so. There is a long tradition of research demonstrating the limits of clinical judgment, inference, and reasoning (Kahneman, Slovic, & Tversky, 1982; Kleinmuntz, 1968; Meehl, 1954; Turk & Salovey, 1988). These errors include heuristic biases, illusory correlation, neglecting base rates, and "halo" and recency effects. Meehl's (1973) paper, "Why I Do Not Attend Case Conferences," is filled with examples of logical and statistical errors that can undermine clinical judgment. These include the following: either over-pathologizing patients on the basis of their "differentness" from the clinician or underpathologizing them on the basis of their "sameness"; presuming merely on the basis of the coexistence of symptoms and intrapsychic conflict that the latter are causing the former; conflating "softheartedness" with "softheadedness"; and treating all clinical evidence as equally good.

Psychoanalysts have also long been aware of how distortions in a therapist's understanding of a patient can affect the therapy. This awareness is reflected in terms such as "countertransference," "projection," and "suggestion." (See also Meehl, 1983.)

Observation versus Inference

Fourth, all case formulations are built upon both observation and inference about psychological processes that organize and maintain an individual's symptoms and problematic behavioral patterns. If a clinician relies too heavily on observable behavior, he or she may overlook meaningful patterns organizing a patient's symptomatology. If the clinician weights the formulation excessively on inference, the risk of losing its empirical basis increases. Thus, a clinician must achieve a balance between observation and inference. The clinician should be able to provide an empirical link between psychological processes that are inferred and patient phenomena that are observed. It may aid the clinician to label inferences according to how close to or distant from observable phenomena they lie.

Individual versus General Formulations

A case formulation is fundamentally a statement about an individual and is thus tailored to that specific individual's life circumstances, needs, wishes, goals, blind spots, fears, thought patterns, and so on. Nevertheless, in arriving at a conceptualization of a patient, the therapist must rely upon his or her general knowledge about psychology as well as past experiences working with other individuals, especially those who seem similar to the person in question. The goodness of fit from the general or theoretical to the specific or individual is never perfect.

When attempting to balance the individual and the general in constructing case formulations, two kinds of errors are possible. First is the error of attempting to make a patient "fit" a generalized formulation that really does not fit. As mentioned earlier, Freud's analysis of Dora has been criticized on this point. Examples are not restricted to psychoanalysis. In the cognitive-behavioral realm, for example, attributing a patient's panic symptoms entirely to catastrophic interpretations of bodily sensations may neglect significant life history events or relationship patterns that also contribute to the onset and maintenance of the symptoms, as well as to the meaning they have for the patient. Overgeneralizing can also result from stereotyping patients on the basis of ethnicity, age, gender, appearance, socioeconomic background, or education.

A second kind of error is to overindividualize a formulation, neglecting one's knowledge of psychology, psychopathology, and past work with psychotherapy patients. If each patient is taken as a complete tabula rasa with experiences that are so unique that the therapist must throw away all previous knowledge, then the therapist is doing the patient a disservice.

Thus, a balance must be reached between an individual and general formulation. Humility is an asset in this respect. The "match" between any model and any individual is inherently imperfect, and the formulation is never more than an approximation of the individual in distress.

CASE FORMULATION AS A SCIENTIFIC TOOL

Earlier, I discussed how psychotherapy case formulations have become *objects* of scientific study. The success of these reliability and validity investigations opens the possibility that a case formulation might also serve as a *tool* of science, that is, as a means through which knowledge about individual psychological functioning might be advanced. Although case study research in psychology has traditionally been viewed as within the discovery rather than the confirmation context of science, other scientific disciplines and even some within psychology have benefited from the aggregation of individual case studies. Notable examples include medicine (Nuland, 1988), ethnography (Rosenblatt, 1981), and neuropsychology (Shallice, 1989). Within psychotherapy and psychopathology research, a number of epistemological questions arise as one considers the possibility that a case formulation might serve as a tool in both the discovery *and* confirmation phases of science. For instance, how might the use of case formulations as research tools affect the nature of the scientific knowledge that subsequently accumulates? A complete answer to this question depends on many factors, not the least of which is the ingenuity, structure, design, comprehensiveness, reliability, and validity of the specific case formulation method in question. Nevertheless, there may be two classes of psychological knowledge for which a structured case formulation method would be particularly well suited.

One of these is knowledge about intraindividual psychological functioning. As noted earlier, the intraindividual frame of reference focuses on the individual as an internally organized system of interconnecting parts. Since a case formulation focuses on one person and how the internal organization of that person has gone awry to produce distress, research designs based on case formulations may permit the study of individuals while preserving the systemic nature of those individuals. Such an approach would diverge from the dominant research strategies in psychology, which Valsiner (1986) describes as based on an interindividual frame of reference. According to Valsiner (1986, p. 396), the interindividual frame involves "comparison of an individual subject (or samples of subjects) with other individuals (samples) in order to determine the standing of these subjects relative to one another." Statements such as "The experimental group scored higher on variable X than the control group" or "John obtained a WAIS-R [Wechsler Adult Intelligence Scale–Revised] IQ of 112, which is at the 79th percentile" reflect an interindividual frame of reference. These conclusions provide comparative information but do not address intraindividual issues such as how variable X interacts with variables Y or Z within any individual; nor do they address John's preferred problem-solving strategies, or how well his intelligence, affective style, or motivations are integrated. In sum, although useful for answering questions about differences *between* systems, the interindividual frame does not address variation *within* the systems that are compared, except as error variance.

The distinction between the intraindividual and interindividual frames of reference is particularly important in light of a growing body of literature addressing epistemological problems that arise when one conflates these two frames (Eells, 1991; Hilliard, 1993; Kim & Rosenberg, 1980; Kraemer, 1978; Lewin, 1931; Sidman, 1952; Thorngate, 1986; Tukey & Borgida, 1983). In clinical psychology, this conflation typically takes the form of a mismatch between the research questions and the means used to answer them. In an informal review, Eells (1991) found that most articles in a prestigious psychology journal framed research questions in terms of intraindividual psychological functioning, analyzed these questions from the interindividual frame, then returned to the intraindividual frame of reference when interpreting the results. At first glance, this incongruity between hypothesis, method, and interpretation may appear innocuous, since interindividual methodologies such as analysis of variance and correlational analysis dominate the research training of most psychologists and hence we are in the habit of "thinking interindividually" even about intraindividual problems. However, a variety of studies suggest harmful consequences of such mismatches (e.g., Kim & Rosenberg, 1980; Kraemer, 1978; Tukey & Borgida, 1983). Each of these studies explored a research question from within the interindividual frame, then explored the same question from the intraindividual frame using the same sample of individuals. In each study, the results produced from each frame were staggeringly divergent! The logical basis for this divergence has been discussed by Sidman (1952), Thorngate (1986), Valsiner (1986), and others.

Although a psychotherapy case formulation can facilitate the construction of hypotheses at the intraindividual level of analysis and can provide a framework for the interpretation of results, there is also a need to apply methodologies that are appropriate for analyzing data at the level of the individual. Several such methods have been developed, proposed, or demonstrated (e.g., Bakeman & Gottman, 1986; Barlow & Hersen, 1984; Eells, 1995; Eells, Fridhandler, & Horowitz, 1995; Fonagy & Moran, 1993; Gottman, 1980; Jones, Cumming, & Pulos, 1993; Rosenberg, 1977; Rudy & Merluzzi, 1984).

The second class of psychological knowledge for which the use of case formulations as research tools might be well suited is that growing from an "individual–socioecological" frame of reference (Valsiner, 1986). According to Valsiner, this frame emphasizes individuals in transactions with others, focusing on how assistance from one individual influences problem solving that emerges when two individuals interact. Problems are viewed as both created and constrained by the structure of the interpersonal environment and by the goals of the individual in question. "In this reference frame, an individual's actions and thinking to solve a problem that has emerged in the person–environment transaction is not a solitary, but a social event" (Valsiner, 1986, p. 400). One example of research from the individual–socioecological frame is L. S. Vygotsky's "zone of proximal development" (Van der Veer & Valsiner, 1991; Wertsch, 1985).

The development of a case-formulation-based program of research from the individual–socioecological frame may be particularly helpful in improving our understanding of the therapeutic alliance, which is one of the most powerful predictors of outcome (Horvath & Greenberg, 1994). Such a program could also help us better understand individual change processes in psychotherapy and how processes such as imitation, introjection, identification, and role reversal may create conditions for both psychopathology as well as psychological health.

CONCLUSIONS

At the outset of this chapter, I described psychotherapy case formulation as lying at an intersection of diagnosis and treatment, theory and practice, science and art, and etiology and description. To conclude the chapter, we return to this point. With respect to diagnosis and treatment, a case formulation provides a pragmatic tool to supplement and apply a diagnosis to the specifics of an individual's life. It also serves as a vehicle for converting a diagnosis to a plan for treatment, both in terms of general treatment strategies and tactics with respect to one's choice of specific interventions. With respect to theory and practice, a psychotherapy case formulation provides a link between theories of psychotherapy and psychopathology, on the one hand, and the application of these theories to a specific individual, on the other. The case formulation reflects a transposition of theory into practice. As both science and art, a case formulation should embody scientific principles and findings, but also an appreciation of the singularity and humanity of the person in question. In sum, a psychotherapy case formulation is an integrative tool. In the hands of a psychotherapist who knows how to construct and use it, a case formulation is indispensable.

NOTE

1. Much of the material in this section is based on Nuland (1988).

ACKNOWLEDGMENTS

I appreciate the comments of John Schwab, Bernadette Walter, and Janet Woodruff-Borden on an earlier draft of this chapter.

REFERENCES

Allport, G. W. (1961). *Pattern and growth in personality*. New York: Holt, Rinehart & Winston.
Aronow, E., Rezinikoff, M., & Moreland, K. L. (1994). *The Rorschach technique: Perceptual basics and content analysis*. Needham Heights, MA: Allyn & Bacon.

Bakeman, R., & Gottman, J. M. (1986). *Observing interaction: An introduction to sequential analysis.* Cambridge, England: Cambridge University Press.

Barber, J. P., & Crits-Christoph, P. (1993). Advances in measures of psychodynamic formulations. *Journal of Consulting and Clinical Psychology, 61,* 574–585.

Barlow, D. H., & Hersen, M. (1984). *Single case experimental designs: Strategies for studying behavior.* New York: Pergamon Press.

Beck, A. T., Emery, G., & Greenberg, R. (1985). *Anxiety disorders and phobias: A cognitive perspective.* New York: Basic Books.

Beck, A. T., Freeman, A., & Associates. (1990). *Cognitive therapy of personality disorders.* New York: Guilford Press.

Beck, A. T., Rush, A. J., Shaw, B. F., & Emery, G. (1979). *Cognitive therapy of depression.* New York: Guilford Press.

Beck, A. T., Wright, F. D., Newman, C. F., & Liese, B. S. (1993). *Cognitive therapy of substance abuse.* New York: Guilford Press.

Beck, J. S. (1995). *Cognitive therapy: Basics and beyond.* New York: Guilford Press.

Bellak, L. (1993). *The Thematic Apperception Test, the Children's Apperception Test and the Senior Apperception Test in clinical use* (5th ed.). Needham Heights, MA: Allyn & Bacon.

Bersoff, D. N. (1973). Silk purses into sow's ears: The decline of psychological testing and a suggestion for its redemption. *American Psychologist, 28,* 892–899.

Beutler, L. E. (1995). The clinical interview. In L. E. Beutler & M. R. Berren (Eds.), *Integrative assessment of adult personality* (pp. 94–120). New York: Guilford Press.

Blashfield, R. K. (1984). *The classification of psychopathology: Neo-Kraepelinian and quantitative approaches.* New York: Plenum Press.

Breuer, J., & Freud, S. (1955). On the psychical mechanism of hysterical phenomena: Preliminary communication. In J. Strachey (Ed.), *The standard edition of the complete psychological works of Sigmund Freud* (Vol. 2, pp. 1–17). London: Hogarth Press. (Original work published 1893)

Bruhn, A. R. (1995). Early memories in personality assessment. In J. N. Butcher (Ed.), *Clinical personality assessment: Practical approaches* (pp. 278–301). New York: Oxford University Press.

Butcher, J. N. (1993). *Use of the MMPI-2 in treatment planning.* New York: Oxford University Press.

Carey, M. P., Flasher, L. V., Maisto, S. A., & Turkat, I. D. (1984). The a priori approach to psychological assessment. *Professional Psychology: Research and Practice, 15,* 515–527.

Caspar, F. (1995). *Plan analysis: toward optimizing psychotherapy.* Seattle, WA: Hogrefe & Huber.

Costa, P. T., & Widiger, T. A. (Eds.). (1994). *Personality disorders and the five-factor model of personality.* Washington, DC: American Psychological Association.

Curtis, J. T., Silberschatz, G., Sampson, H., & Weiss, J. (1994). The plan formulation method. *Psychotherapy Research, 46,* 197–207.

Davies, R. (1994). *The cunning man.* New York: Penguin Books.

Edelson, M. (1988). *Psychoanalysis: A theory in crisis.* Chicago: University of Chicago Press.

Eells, T. D. (1991, August). *Single subject research: An epistemological argument for its scientific value.* Paper presented at the meeting of the American Psychological Association, San Francisco, CA.

Eells, T. D. (1995). Role reversal: A convergence of clinical and quantitative evidence. *Psychotherapy Research, 5,* 297–312.

Eells, T. D., Fridhandler, B., & Horowitz, M. J. (1995). Self schemas and spousal bereavement: Comparing quantitative and clinical evidence. *Psychotherapy, 32,* 270–282.

Elstein, A. S., Shuylman, L. S., Sprafka, S. A. (1978). *Medical problem solving: An analysis of clinical reasoning.* Cambridge, MA: Harvard University Press.

Fonagy, P., & Moran, G. (1993). Selecting single case research designs for clinicians. In N. E. Miller, L. Luborsky, J. P. Barber, & J. P. Docherty (Eds.), *Psychodynamic treatment research: A handbook for clinical practice* (pp. 62–95). New York: Basic Books.

Freeman, A. (1992). Developing treatment conceptualizations in cognitive therapy. In A. Freeman & F. Dattilio (Eds.), *Casebook of cognitive-behavioral therapy* (pp. 13–23). New York: Plenum Press.

Garfield, S. L., & Bergin, A. E. (1994). Introduction and historical overview. In A. E. Bergin & S. L. Garfield (Eds.), *Handbook of psychotherapy and behavior change* (4th ed., pp. 3–18). New York: Wiley.

Gill, M., Newman, R., & Redlich, F. C. (1954). *The initial interview in psychiatric practice.* New York: International Universities Press.

Goldfried, M. R., & Pomeranz, D. M. (1968). Role of assessment in behavior modification. *Psychological Reports, 23,* 75–87.

Gottman, J. M. (1980). *Time-series analysis: A comprehensive introduction for social scientists.* Cambridge, England: Cambridge University Press.

Hayes, S. C., & Follette, W. C. (1992). Can functional analysis provide a substitute for syndromal classification? *Behavioral Assessment, 14,* 345–365.

Hayes, S. C., Nelson, R. O., & Jarrett, R. B. (1987). The treatment utility of assessment: A functional approach to evaluating assessment quality. *American Psychologist, 42,* 963–974.

Haynes, S. N., & O'Brien, W. H. (1990). Functional analysis in behavior therapy. *Clinical Psychology Review, 10,* 649–668.

Haynes, S. N., Spain, E. H., & Oliveira, J. (1993). Identifying causal relationships in clinical assessment. *Psychological Assessment, 5,* 281–291.

Hilliard, R. B. (1993). Single-case methodology in psychotherapy process and outcome research. *Journal of Consulting and Clinical Psychology, 61,* 373–380.

Horney, K. (1967). *Feminine psychology.* New York: Norton.

Horowitz, M. J. (1989). Relationship schema formulation: Role-relationship models and intrapsychic conflict. *Psychiatry, 52,* 260–274.

Horowitz, M. J. (Ed.). (1991). *Person schemas and maladaptive interpersonal patterns.* Chicago: University of Chicago Press.

Horowitz, L. M., Rosenberg, S. E., Ureño, G., Kalehzan, B. M., & O'Halloran, P. (1989). Psychodynamic formulation, consensual response method and interpersonal problems. *Journal of Consulting and Clinical Psychology, 57,* 599–606.

Horvath, A. O., & Greenberg, L. S. (1994). *The working alliance: Theory, research, and practice.* New York: Wiley.

Johnson, M. E., Popp, C., Schacht, T. E., Mellon, J., & Strupp, H. H. (1989). Converging evidence for identification of recurrent relationship themes: Comparison of two methods. *Psychiatry, 52,* 275–288.

Jones, E. E., Cumming, J. P., & Pulos, S. M. (1993). Tracing clinical themes across phases of treatment by a Q-set. In N. E. Miller, L. Luborsky, J. P. Barber, &

J. P. Docherty (Eds.), *Psychodynamic treatment research: A handbook for clinical practice* (pp. 14–36). New York: Basic Books.

Kahneman, D., Slovic, P., & Tversky, A. (1982). *Judgment under uncertainty: Heuristics and biases.* New York: Cambridge University Press.

Kaplan, H. I., Sadock, B. J., & Grebb, J. A. (1994). *Kaplan and Sadock's synopsis of psychiatry: Behavioral sciences, clinical psychiatry* (7th ed.). Baltimore: Williams & Wilkins.

Kendell, R. (1975). *The role of diagnosis in psychiatry.* Oxford: Blackwell Scientific.

Kernberg, O. (1975). *Borderline conditions and pathological narcissism.* New York: Aronson.

Kernberg, O. (1984). *Severe personality disorders.* New Haven, CT: Yale University Press.

Kim, M. P., & Rosenberg, S. (1980). Comparison of two structural models of implicit personality theories. *Journal of Personality and Social Psychology, 38,* 375–389.

Kleinmuntz, B. (1968). The processing of clinical information by man and machine. In B. Kleinmuntz (Ed.), *Formal representation of human judgment* (pp. 149–186). New York: Wiley.

Kohut, H. (1971). *Analysis of the self.* New York: International Universities Press.

Kohut, H. (1977). *Restoration of the self.* New York: International Universities Press.

Kohut, H. (1984). *How analysis cures.* New York: International Universities Press.

Korchin, S. J., & Schuldberg, D. (1981). The future of clinical assessment. *American Psychologist, 36,* 1147–1158.

Kraemer, H. C. (1978). Individual and ecological correlation in a general context. *Behavioral Science, 23,* 67–72.

Lakoff, R. T. (1990). *Talking power: The politics of language.* New York: Basic Books.

Lewin, K. (1931). The conflict between Aristotelian and Galileian modes of thought in contemporary psychology. *Journal of General Psychology, 5,* 141–177.

Luborsky, L. (1977). Measuring a pervasive psychic structure in psychotherapy: The core conflictual relationship theme. In N. Freedman & S. Grand (Eds.), *Communicative structures and psychic structures* (pp. 367–395). New York: Plenum Press.

Luborsky, L., Barber, J. P., Binder, J., Curtis, J., Dahl, H., Horowitz, L., Horowitz, M., Perry, J. C., Schacht, T., Silberschatz, G., & Teller, V. (1993). Transference-based measures: A new class based on psychotherapy sessions. In N. E. Miller, L. Luborsky, J. P. Barber, & J. P. Docherty (Eds.), *Psychodynamic treatment research: A handbook for clinical practice* (pp. 326–341). New York: Basic Books.

Luborsky, L., & Crits-Christoph, P. (1998). *Understanding transference: The CCRT method.* (Rev. ed.). Washington, DC: APA Books.

Mack, A. H., Forman, L., Brown, R., & Frances, A. (1994). A brief history of psychiatric classification: From the ancients to DSM-IV. *Psychiatric Clinics of North America, 17,* 515–523.

Masson, J. M. (1984). *The assault on truth: Freud's suppression of the seduction theory.* New York: Farrar, Straus & Giroux.

Meehl, P. E. (1954). *Clinical versus statistical prediction.* Minneapolis: University of Minnesota Press.

Meehl, P. E. (1958). Some ruminations on the validation of clinical procedures. *Canadian Journal of Psychology, 13,* 102–128.

Meehl, P. E. (1973). Why I do not attend case conferences. In *Psychodiagnosis: Selected papers* (pp. 225–302). New York: Norton.

Meehl, P. E. (1983). Subjectivity in psychoanalytic inference: The nagging persistence of Wilhelm Fliess's Achensee question. In J. Earman (Ed.), *Minnesota studies in the philosophy of science: Vol. 10. Testing scientific theories* (pp. 349–411). Minneapolis: University of Minnesota Press.

Millon, T. (1996). *Disorders of personality: DSM-IV and beyond.* New York: Wiley.

Morgagni, G. (1824). *The seats and causes of disease, investigated by anatomy: Containing a great variety of dissections and accompanied with remarks* (W. Cooke, Trans.). Boston: Wells and Lilly. (Original work published 1769)

Morrison, J. (1993). *The first interview.* New York: Guilford Press.

Nuland, S. B. (1988). *Doctors: The biography of medicine.* New York: Vintage Books.

Pasnau, R. O. (1987). The remedicalization of psychiatry. *Hospital and Community Psychiatry, 38,* 145–151.

Perry, J. C. (1994). Assessing psychodynamic patterns using the Idiographic Conflict Formulation method. *Psychotherapy Research, 4,* 239–252.

Perry, J. C., Augusto, F., & Cooper, S. H. (1989). Assessing psychodynamic conflicts: I. Reliability of the Ideographic Conflict Formulation method. *Psychiatry, 52,* 289–301.

Perry, S., Cooper, A. M., & Michels, R. (1987). The psychodynamic formulation: Its purpose, structure and clinical application. *American Journal of Psychiatry, 144,* 543–550.

Persons, J. B. (1989). *Cognitive therapy in practice: A case formulation approach.* New York: Norton.

Persons, J. B. (1995). Interrater reliability of cognitive-behavioral case formulations. *Cognitive Therapy and Research, 19,* 21–34.

Rogers, C. R. (1951). *Client-centered therapy: Its current practice, implications, and theory.* Boston: Houghton Mifflin.

Rosenberg, S. (1977). New approaches to the analysis of personal constructs in person perception. In A. W. Landfield (Ed.), *Nebraska Symposium on Motivation: Vol. 24. Personal construct psychology* (pp. 179–242). Lincoln: University of Nebraska Press.

Rosenblatt, P. C. (1981). Ethnographic case studies. In M. B. Brewer & B. E. Collins (Eds.), *Scientific inquiry and the social sciences: A volume in honor of Donald T. Campbell* (pp. 194–225). San Francisco: Jossey-Bass.

Rudy, T. E., & Merluzzi, T. V. (1984). Recovering social-cognitive schemata: Descriptions and applications of multidimensional scaling for clinical research. In P. C. Kendall (Ed.), *Advances in cognitive-behavioral research and therapy* (Vol. 3, pp. 61–102). New York: Academic Press.

Runyan, W. B. (1982). In defense of the case study method. *American Journal of Orthopsychiatry, 52,* 440–446.

Schacht, T. E., & Henry, W. P. (1994). Modeling recurrent patterns of interpersonal relationship with the Structural Analysis of Social Behavior: The SASB–CMP. *Psychotherapy Research, 4,* 208–221.

Segal, Z. V. (1988). Appraisal of the self-schema construct in cognitive models of depression. *Psychological Bulletin, 103,* 147–162.

Segal, Z. V., & Blatt, S. J. (Eds.). (1993). *The self in emotional distress: Cognitive and psychodynamic perspectives.* New York: Guilford Press.

Seitz, P. F. (1966). The consensus problem in psychoanalytic research. In L. Gottschalk & L. Auerbach (Eds.), *Methods of research and psychotherapy* (pp. 209–225). New York: Appleton-Century-Crofts.

Shallice, T. (1989). *From neuropsychology to cognitive neuroscience.* Hillsdale, NJ: Erlbaum.

Sidman, M. (1952). A note on functional relations obtained from group data. *Psychological Bulletin, 49*, 263–269.

Spence, D. P. (1982). *Historical truth and narrative truth.* New York: Norton.

Sperry, L., Gudeman, J. E., Blackwell, B., & Faulkner, L. R. (1992). *Psychiatric case formulations.* Washington, DC: American Psychiatric Press.

Thorngate, W. (1986). The production, detection, and explanation of behavioral patterns. In J. Valsiner (Ed.), *The individual subject and scientific psychology* (pp. 71–93). New York: Plenum Press.

Tukey, D. D., & Borgida, E. (1983). An intrasubject approach to causal attribution. *Journal of Personality, 51*, 137–151.

Turk, D. C., & Salovey, P. (Eds.). (1988). *Reasoning, inference, and judgment in clinical psychology.* New York: Free Press.

Valsiner, J. (Ed.). (1986). *The individual subject and scientific psychology.* New York: Plenum Press.

Valsiner, J. (1987). *Culture and the development of children's action.* New York: Wiley.

Van der Veer, R., & Valsiner, J. (1991). *Understanding Vygotsky: A quest for synthesis.* Cambridge, England: Blackwell Scientific.

Wertsch, J. V. (1985). *Vygotsky and the social formation of mind.* Cambridge, MA: Harvard University Press.

Widiger, T. A., & Frances, A. J. (1994). Toward a dimensional model for the personality disorders. In P. A. Costa & T. A. Widiger (Eds.), *Personality disorders and the five-factor model of personality* (pp. 19–39). Washington, DC: American Psychological Association.

Widiger, T. A., & Sanderson, C. J. (1995). In J. N. Butcher (Ed.), *Clinical personality assessment: Practical approaches* (pp. 380–394). New York: Oxford University Press.

Widiger, T. A., & Trull, T. A. (1991). Diagnosis and clinical assessment *Annual review of psychology, 42*, 109–133.

Wilson, M. (1993). DSM-III and the transformation of American psychiatry: A history. *American Journal of Psychiatry, 150*, 399–410.

Wolpe, J., & Turkat, I. D. (1985). Behavioral formulation of clinical cases. In I. D. Turkat (Ed.), *Behavioral case formulation* (pp. 5–36). New York: Plenum Press.

2

The Traditional Psychoanalytic Approach to Case Formulation

STANLEY B. MESSER
DAVID L. WOLITZKY

In this chapter we present an account of psychoanalytic case formulation as it is used clinically in conjunction with psychoanalytic treatment. Because it was developed in a clinical context, it is less formal and systematic than other approaches in this volume that are research based. For example, the psycho-analytic clinician does not typically record sessions, prepare verbatim transcripts, or have a panel of judges formally rate such material. At the same time, the psychoanalytic case formulation implicitly includes many of the concepts reviewed in other chapters, such as the Core Conflictual Relationship Theme (CCRT) and cyclical maladaptive behavior.

For present purposes we may define the psychoanalytic case formulation as a hierarchically organized set of clinical inferences about the nature of a patient's psychopathology and, more generally, about his or her personality structure, dynamics, and development. These inferences, which are generated in the course of the psychoanalytically informed interview, include the pre-sumed reasons for (or "causes" of) the patient's experience and behavior such as symptoms, dreams, fantasies, and maladaptive patterns of interpersonal relationships. For example, the clinician might observe that whenever the patient begins a new emotional involvement with a woman he experiences an upsurge in claustrophobic symptoms. Specifically, the patient might express anxiety about being in a crowded elevator and its getting stuck between floors. The "causal" explanation for the inference that there is an association between the patient's level of emotional intimacy with women and the intensity of his claustrophobic symptoms might be that the nature and timing of these symptoms are manifestations of an unconscious fear of being trapped in a relationship that may lead to a loss of a sense of personal identity.

The inferences and the interpretations that follow from them in the course of therapy often will include the therapist postulating a probable sequence of historical events and the meanings assigned to them by the patient, many of which have continued to be unavailable to the latter's awareness. The nature of the evidence and clinical reasoning that lead to such clinical inferences, and the means of attempting to validate interpretations based on them, will be addressed below.

HISTORICAL BACKGROUND OF THE APPROACH

The clinical case history method originated with Sigmund Freud, and his early case studies continue to be taught as models of psychoanalytic thinking. Although other theorists such as Morton Prince (1905) also used the case study method, it was Freud's extensive reliance on this method and the insights it yielded that leads us to emphasize his key role in its development. It is interesting to note Freud's own, rare statement about the case history approach. In his discussion of Elisabeth von R., Freud wrote, "It still strikes me as strange that the case histories I write read like short stories and that, as one might say, they lack the serious stamp of science. I must console myself with the reflection that the nature of the subject is evidently responsible for this, rather than any preference of my own. . . . [A] detailed description of mental processes such as we are accustomed to find in the works of imaginative writers enables me, with the use of a few psychological formulas, to obtain at least some kind of insight into the course of that affliction" (i.e., hysteria; Breuer & Freud, 1893–1895/1955, p. 160). And, Freud continued, the case histories provide "an intimate connection between the story of the patient's suffering and the symptoms of his illness" (p. 160).

The history of efforts at psychodynamic case formulation began with Freud's search for treatment methods more effective than rest, hydrotherapy, and faradic stimulation (the application of low-voltage electrical stimulation to afflicted areas of the body). Freud began experimenting with hypnosis and eventually came to prefer the method of free association in which he directed the patient to say everything that came to mind. As we now know, this method became central to the evolution of psychoanalysis. Freud was searching for the most efficacious way to facilitate the recall of so-called pathogenic memories. The theory he was developing was that the onset of symptoms coincided with a disagreeable experience that the patient forgot, that the quota of affect associated with this experience was "converted" to symptoms, and that the recovery of this experience and its associated affects was essential to the alleviation of the symptom. The experience was both wished for and simultaneously dreaded in that it violated the person's moral code. As is well known by now,

Freud came to the idea that hysterics suffer from reminiscences connected to unacceptable sexual wishes.

From the start Freud tried to present plausible accounts of why and how the patient's symptoms developed and were ameliorated. Faced with a stream of seemingly disconnected, often bizarre sequences of verbal associations, Freud wanted to construct a meaningful explanation of the patient's often irrational behavior. He was particularly struck by gaps in the patient's memory, by the patient's tendency to avoid certain material, and by the inexplicable nature of the patient's symptoms. The assumptions of psychic determinism and unconscious motivation were central to his attempts at a rational explanation of the patient's difficulties. The subsequent development of psychoanalytic theory showed an increasingly complex and subtle understanding of human experience, particularly from the perspective of unconscious, intrapsychic conflict, a core notion of Freudian theory. The major tenets of the theory can be found in Brenner (1973).

Rapaport and Gill (1959), two important later figures who contributed to the structure of psychoanalytic case formulation, argued that a comprehensive case formulation would have to include the following multiple perspectives: dynamic, structural, genetic, adaptive, topographic, and economic. That is, corresponding to the order of the preceding terms, the formulation would have to address the patient's major conflicts (dynamic: e.g., wishes, and defenses against those wishes), those aspects of the patient's personality involved in the conflicts (structural: e.g., id vs. superego), the historical and developmental etiology of the conflicts (genetic), the adaptive and maladaptive compromise formations involved in the patient's defensive and coping strategies (adaptive), the conscious versus unconscious status of the conflicts (topographic), and the "economic" consequences of the preceding factors, not in the original sense of the distribution of "mobile" and "bound" cathexes but in the more descriptive sense of how constricted and brittle the patient's adjustment is by virtue of the excessive "energy" invested in his or her defensive maneuvers. Although contemporary case formulations generally contain less metapsychological language than in the past, with the exception of the economic viewpoint, they do attempt to cover the perspectives just outlined.

CONCEPTUAL FRAMEWORK

There are three major conceptual models in contemporary, mainstream psychoanalysis in North America—traditional Freudian, object relations, and self psychology.[1] Each model makes different assumptions about human beings and their core motivational dynamics. Some clinicians elect to adopt a multimodel approach in which they bring to bear each theoretical perspective with every patient (e.g., Silverman, 1986). Others use whichever model seems to fit a given case best, wheras some therapists stick to one of the models for most cases. Pine (1990) argues that each of the models refers to an important domain of human experience and each has a place in a comprehensive, multifaceted understanding of the patient. Unfortunately, we do not have a body of empirical evidence concerning the relative clinical utility of the different formulations offered by the several models. Nor do we know whether using any particular model or some combination of models is better than using no model at all beyond a commonsense, implicit personality theory. Clearly, these are issues for empirical study, as we note in the research section at the end of the chapter.

Following are the core propositions of the different models, focusing on what is formulated and why (for a more detailed account of each model, see Greenberg & Mitchell, 1983). According to the *Freudian drive/structural model*, human behavior is determined by sexual and aggressive drives, which have four attributes: a source, an aim, an impetus, and an object. The *source* of the drives is somatic processes that make a demand on the mind. The *aim* of the drive is gratification through discharge, and the *impetus* is the drive's intensity. The *object* of the drive is the most variable aspect; gratification could be sought through an inanimate object, another person, or a part of one's body. The system operates according to the pleasure principle; that is, people's goals are to reduce tension to an optimal level, maximize drive gratification, and minimize unpleasure. The person's major motivational thrust is to seek satisfaction of the wishes that are the psychological derivatives of the instinctual drives. Wishes are attempts to reinstate "perceptual identity" with the memories of past gratifications (Freud, 1900/1953). Obstacles to the immediate or long-term gratification of wishes are inevitable, creating intrapsychic conflicts. That is, the person seeks to gratify the wish but simultaneously avoids seeking gratification when wishes threaten to give rise to anxiety, guilt, or fear of external punishment. In brief, Freudian theory conceptualizes human behavior from the perspective of intrapsychic conflict.

In the tripartite, structural model of id–ego–superego, the id is the repository of the drives, the superego represents the internalized standards and prohibitions of the parents and the culture, and the ego modulates drive discharge by automatically instituting defenses. Defenses are activated by "signal anxiety" based on the ego's appraisal that the awareness or expression of certain wishes is apt to lead to traumatic anxiety. The principal anxieties, or danger situations of childhood, are loss of the object, loss of the object's love, castration anxiety, and superego anxiety (Brenner, 1982). These anxieties correspond to the psychosexual stages of oral, anal, phallic, and genital development. These key Freudian concepts are part of the larger, complex structure of interlocking concepts that constitute the framework for organizing the clinical material. A formulation based on these concepts that takes account of the metapsychological points of view listed above will focus principally on the patient's repetitive reenactments of core unconscious conflicts and fantasies, their defensive, adaptive, and developmental aspects, and their influence on character styles and object relationships (Perry, Cooper, & Michels, 1987; Weisman, 1959).

A key feature of a Freudian formulation is an emphasis on unconscious fantasy, the conflicts expressed in such fantasy, and the influence of such conflicts and fantasies on the patient's behavior both within and outside the consulting room. A corollary assumption is that the current unconscious fantasies are based on core conflicts originating in childhood. Current maladaptive behavior is seen to be largely motivated by unconscious fantasies, even if patients experience their behavior as lacking a sense of personal agency or as attributable primarily to external circumstance. Indeed, a significant aspect of the interpretive work in the course of treatment is to help patients realize the nature and extent of their intentional, though not conscious, disavowal of motives and affects that clash with their conscious values and attitudes.

In general terms, Freudian analysts emphasize the importance of unresolved oedipal conflicts whereas adherents of object relations theories and of self psychology stress the significance of preoedipal issues. Stated very briefly, preoedipal issues refer to anxieties arising in the first 2–3 years of life in relation to concerns about loss of the "object" (i.e., the principal caretakers) and the loss of the object's love, anxieties which correspond, respectively, to the oral and anal Freudian psychosexual stages of development. These anxieties are potentially present throughout life, and the fear of their full-blown eruption is what triggers defensive reactions. The principal anxiety of the next psychosexual stage, the phallic stage, is castration anxiety, which is said to arise in relation to the boy's oedipal complex, i.e., his wish to destroy the rival for his mother's love and affection, namely, his father. For the models presented below it is issues of trust, safety, self-esteem, cohesion and preservation of self, and conflicted ties to parental figures who have also been significant sources of psychic pain that are seen as relatively more important than oedipal conflicts in the development and maintenance of psychopathology.

From an *object relations perspective* (and for present purposes we combine the different theorists who represent this approach) the emphasis is on the internalized mental representations of self and other and their interactions, particularly the affective coloring of these interactions. This approach emphasizes the tendency to split self and other representations into "good" versus "bad" and the difficulty of integrating these representations. Concepts of introjective and projective identification figure prominently in these formulations. Many clinicians find these concepts especially useful in describing the difficulties people diagnosed with borderline personality disorder have in internalizing a stable, soothing introject and in establishing a differentiated, integrated sense of self. In contrast to traditional Freudians, object relations theorists stress human relatedness rather than drive discharge as human beings' central motivational aim. Correspondingly, their developmental formulations place relatively more weight on preoedipal experience, for example, the absence of "good enough" mothering and other environmental failures.

Case formulations based on this perspective will of course draw upon concepts central to one or another version of object relations theories, principally those proposed by Klein (1948), Fairbairn (1952), Winnicott (1965), or Guntrip (1971), to mention only the more popular proponents of this point of view. Because this perspective stresses the patient's difficulty integrating "good" and "bad" mental representations of self and other, case formulations can be expected to focus on the patient's splitting off and disavowal of rage against parental figures in order not to threaten one's tie to the object on whom one also depends. As part of this defensive effort the patient may present a facade of "good" behavior (e.g., appear to conform to the parents' values and standards) along with a tendency to project onto others aspects of one's "bad self." The fully developed case formulation in this or any theoretical perspective emerges in the course of acquiring an in-depth knowledge of the patient in an intensive, exploratory psychotherapy.

The *self psychology model*, developed originally by Kohut (1971, 1977, 1984), centers on the development and maintenance of a cohesive self and the factors that promote healthy versus pathological narcissism. Kohut's self psychology focuses on the failure of parents to provide the experiences necessary for the child to form a cohesive sense of self and to actualize joyfully its ambitions and ideals. A key notion for Kohut is the parents' failure in empathic responsiveness, a failure that does not allow the child to use the parents as idealized selfobjects or as mirroring selfobjects. Observations of transference patterns are crucial to formulating the patient's narcissistic problems and the manner in which the patient has attempted to compensate for his or her self-defects. Although Kohut's theory is closer in some respects to Carl Rogers's views than to Freud's, his work has remained in the mainstream of American psychoanalysis.

The concept of selfobject refers to a generally unconscious mental representation in which one person regards another as an extension of the self to be used to regulate aspects of his or her own sense of self (e.g., sense of cohesion or self-esteem). The two major classes of selfobjects are mirroring selfobjects and idealized selfobjects (Kohut, 1971, 1977). Both enhance the self by the self leaning on the perceived qualities contained in the mental representation of others, especially their perceived power, strength, and reliability. In the case of a mirroring selfobject, the person can have an experience such as "You admire me, and therefore I feel affirmed as a person of worth." In the case of an idealized selfobject, the schematic equivalent would be "I admire you; therefore my sense of self and self-worth are enhanced by my vicarious participation in your strength and power." An everyday example of a mirroring selfobject experience is the young child's observation of the attentive, joyful gleam in its mother's eye, as might occur when the child masters a new skill. A common example of an experience of an idealized selfobject is the vicarious sense of power the young child feels when sitting on the shoulders of a parent.

For Kohut these kinds of experiences are reflections of parental empathy regarding the child's needs and constitute crucial building blocks in the development of a firm, cohesive sense of self, or what he would call the development of healthy narcissism. It is only the excessive reliance on selfobject needs that is associated with pathology of the self. An essential emphasis in the

Kohutian approach to treatment is to provide patients with the missing selfobject experiences on the assumption that this will help repair the self-defects that are said to originate from the parents' failure to serve as phase-appropriate selfobjects. For therapists operating from this vantage point, the emergence of the mirroring and idealizing transferences will provide vital data for an eventual case formulation specific to a particular patient.

Clinicians who prefer one or another of the aforementioned theories will make different psychodynamic formulations both at the outset of treatment and as the treatment progresses. For example, sexual difficulties are apt to be seen by the Kohutian in terms of disturbances in a cohesive sense of self, while in Freudian theory the notion of a fragmented self is more likely to be formulated as a derivative expression of castration anxiety. What the Kohutian takes at face value is for the Freudian merely manifest content suggestive of a "deeper" meaning, and vice versa.

Perry et al. (1987) state that a psychodynamic formulation, like a clinical diagnosis, has as its "primary function . . . to provide a succinct conceptualization of the case and thereby guide a treatment plan" (p. 543; but see McWilliams, in press, for a contrast of DSM and psychoanalytic diagnoses). Such a formulation, *based on whatever theoretical perspectives one prefers*, "concisely and incisively clarifies the central issues and conflicts, differentiating what the therapist sees as essential from what is secondary" (p. 543). They point out five misconceptions regarding the psychodynamic formulation: (1) that it is indicated only for long-term cases; (2) that it is of value only for inexperienced clinicians in training; (3) that it must be complete and comprehensive rather than tentative and partial; (4) that it need not be written; and (5) that the clinician will cling to it in the face of new and contradictory evidence. Thus, they urge that following any initial evaluation clinicians should write out at least a brief dynamic formulation (i.e., 500–750 words) as a working guide to understanding and treating the case. The formulation, as they conceive of it, should focus on patients' current problems in light of their individual histories and current situations; sketch the dynamic and other factors that seem to explain the clinical picture; offer surmises about patients' individual backgrounds; and predict the likely impact of the above factors on the process and outcome of therapy. We will follow such a plan in the example given below.

The Nature of Psychoanalytic Inference

Before turning to a discussion of how the psychoanalytic clinician goes about formulating an actual case, it is useful to consider the process of clinical inference that undergirds case formulations. In line with the recognition that we can no longer speak of *the* theory of psychoanalysis, we have the increasingly accepted notion that, when formulating a case, the clinician creates a narrative structure.[2] This structure is an attempt to provide a coherent, comprehensive, plausible, and hopefully accurate account of the individual's personality development and current functioning that is based on the life history of a particular patient as that history is told, lived, and retold by the patient in the course of the psychoanalytic encounter. However, there is no single, definitive, unchanging narrative to be told (Schafer, 1992). Implicit in this view is that there is no such thing as a psychoanalytic fact when we are talking about the reading of intentionality and meaning in patients' behavior and experience. There are observations of overt behavior from which inferences are drawn concerning the multiple psychological meanings of what is observed. Furthermore, what is observed (i.e., what is attended to selectively), stored, and retrieved from memory to arrive at a case formulation at a given point in time is influenced by the nature of the patient–therapist interaction and the evolving narrative structure into which it is placed. In other words, observation as well as inference is theory saturated (Messer, Sass, & Woolfolk, 1988). It is no wonder that Freudian patients are found to have Freudian dreams, and Jungian patients Jungian dreams.

The higher the level of inference in case formulation, the stronger the influence of the particular narrative structures through which the material is being conceptualized. Theoretical concepts can be thought of as a series of lenses through which the data of observation are filtered. For example, if a patient's first response to Card I of the Rorschach Inkblot test is "a mask," clinicians would probably agree that the response connotes "concealment." However, once we go beyond the inference of "concealment" to hypothesize what it is that is being concealed and why, we are increasingly guided by our preferred theory. As suggested earlier, traditional Freudian theory posits that adaptation to the environment requires that the id be socialized, renounce its unrealizable aims, and instead secure for the individual as much instinctual gratification with as little pain as possible. This developmental narrative of "the beast within that needs to be tamed" is consonant with the idea that the pleasure principle has to accommodate to the reality principle if the organism is to survive and adapt adequately. As Schafer (1992) points out, Freud's other major narrative structure was that of the organism as a machine in which behavior is strictly determined through shifts in the quantity of psychic energies.

Freudian analysts will formulate case material from these (and related) Freudian perspectives at various degrees of distance from the clinical data. That is, one can speak in experience-distant terms of transformations of psychic energies and/or on a more experience-near level in terms of wishes, fears, and conflicts. Thus, for the Freudian, the inference of "concealment" is likely to generate hypotheses about defense against sexual and/or aggressive wishes. For an object relations theorist influenced by Winnicott (1965), the same inference will likely lead to formulations in terms of the "true self" and the "false self." As another example, whether we create a narrative in which idealization is seen primarily as a defense against hostility (i.e., a reaction formation) or whether it is regarded as stemming mainly from the search for an idealized selfobject to shore up one's sense of personal cohesiveness and strength would partly depend on whether we prefer Freud's or Kohut's theory. Those adopting a multimodel approach (e.g., Silverman, 1986) would more freely entertain both inferences.

In connection with case formulation, Perry et al. (1987, p. 546) state that "The aim is to find a small number of pervasive issues that run through the course of the patient's illness and can be traced back through his or her personal history." We need to emphasize, however, that what are considered observations or issues, let alone what inferences we draw from them, are inevitably shaped by the dominant models we use to understand human behavior. If we find, for example, a man repeatedly snatching defeat from the jaws of victory, what does his undermining of his own bid for success mean? From a traditional Freudian perspective, he is punishing himself, undoing his guilt over oedipal wishes, and warding off retaliation (or castration). From the perspective of Weiss's (1993) psychodynamic theory, which emphasizes "survivor guilt," the person may hold the "pathogenic belief" that his success is tantamount to his father's defeat and demise and he would, out of loyalty, devotion, and love, not want to do anything that would mean harming his father.

The clinician brings to the analytic situation not only one or more psychoanalytic frameworks within which to order and organize the clinical data but other cognitive frameworks that interact with the psychoanalytic lenses through which the clinical material is viewed. It is useful, following Peterfreund (1976), to think of a *series* of "working models" that are brought to bear on the material. First, is our *commonsense working model* of psychological functioning, or what might be called our implicit theories of personality. Included here are such everyday notions as: if mother favors one sibling over another, the less favored sibling is apt to feel hurt, unlovable, and angry; reality is often more disappointing than the wishful fantasy would suggest; and past experiences have a psychological impact on future behavior.

Second, we have a *working model of ourselves* based on both the commonsense model noted above and on one or more *psychoanalytic models* through which we have come to understand ourselves. The *commonsense* and *psychoanalytic models* influence the *model of ourselves*, and these three models interact to influence our beginning understanding of the patient. A fourth model that influences our understanding of a particular patient is based on *the aggregate of one's experiences with previous patients.* Thus, the multiple, overlapping working models we employ include a commonsense model, a preferred theoretical model, a model of ourselves based on these, and a model based on experience with previous patients.

It is particularly the model of ourselves that serves as the basis of empathy. By empathy we mean our sense of cognitive/affective comprehension of the patient's mode of experiencing him- or herself and the world, based on our partial, transient identification with the patient. Grasping the patient's phenomenological world is the first basis for the construction of an initial psychoanalytic understanding that will ultimately include much more than the patient's conscious experience.

In formulating a case the analyst seeks to extract a few core organizing themes from the vast amount of material provided by the patient. One useful way of understanding how the analyst processes information is to view the patient as repeatedly telling a variety of what we might call "relationship episodes," or stories of interpersonal encounters. In explicating this perspective, we shall draw on Edelson's (1992) recent conceptualization of the analytic process as involving the telling and enacting of stories by both patient and analyst.

The analyst's stories are retellings of the patient's stories. The repeated revisions and elaborations of the stories told by both participants lead ideally to a shared, coauthored story that includes an understanding of the transference–countertransference configurations that inevitably arise and are enacted in the course of analysis. The later stories in the treatment are more complex, comprehensive, and complete. They bring to light previously hidden, implicit, and conflicted elements that are present in a variety of single or partial stories. One winds up with what Edelson calls a "master story." The word "story" in this account should not be taken to mean that one seeks an aesthetically pleasing, convenient fiction, as some accounts might suggest. In fact, one assumes that the patient suffers in part because the stories with which he or she begins the treatment contain significant elements of self-deception and hidden conflicts. The aim is to tell as veridical a story as is possible under the circumstances.

The telling of psychoanalytic stories by the analyst is one way of talking about the process of a psychodynamic case formulation. Psychoanalytic stories have a certain narrative structure. They assume that there is a manifest and a latent content to most significant emotional stories. The master story includes an explication of the manifest and the latent content, why and how they are connected to one another, and why there has to be a latent and a manifest content in the first place. This latter point is another way of stating that the patient has conflictual wishes, and defenses against such wishes, and that there is a desire to express and to conceal these mental contents.

In general, one could say that the telling and retelling of narratives is a means of situating the protagonist in relation to his or her mental life. In terms of Schafer's (1976, 1992) action language conception, this would mean attempting to develop a coherent, plausible narrative in which the patient comes to an "appropriate" appreciation of his or her role as the author of and actor in the script that is being enacted. From this perspective, behaviors that are initially understood as merely "happenings" are retold as intentional actions. Alternate theoretical models with their different etiological emphases would yield different story lines, even though they all share a recognition of the adverse impact of childhood trauma. For example, in the Freudian story line, one would tend to emphasize the operation of defense as a kind of disclaimed action and, in general, see the patient as responsible for his or her emotional dilemmas. By contrast, Kohutian story lines probably tend to cast the patient in the role of victim. At the extremes, Freudians could be seen as "blaming" the victim whereas Kohutians could be seen as "blaming" the parents. In turn, these perspectives could result in subtle differences in one's sense of personal responsibility for who one has become and for one's future.

Aside from what we may call the preferred story line, analysts share certain assumptions about how the mind works. These assumptions guide clinical listening and the evolving psychodynamic formulation. To explicate them all would require at least a chapter-length treatment. Therefore, we will confine ourselves to the major assumptions, which include psychic determinism, unconscious motivation, the ideas of displacement and symbolic equivalence, and the principles of convergent and divergent causality.

Psychic determinism refers to the assumption of lawful regularity in mental life. That is, significant psychological events do not occur on a chance basis. Thus, if the patient switches the topic in the course of the session, a working hypothesis that guides the psychodynamic formulation is that the shift is not random but is likely to be dynamically linked to the earlier topics. This assumption operates at the clinical level in terms of the principle of contiguity. For example, suppose the patient says, in the first session, that she is afraid that if she starts to speak freely she will not be able to contain herself and will lose emotional control. She pauses momentarily, then asks where the women's bathroom is located. The clinician assumes that these two seemingly disparate topics are dynamically linked, as expressed in the following hypothesis: "The patient makes an unconscious equation between the control of thoughts and feelings and the control of bowel and bladder functions."

A corollary set of assumptions that leads to this hypothesis include the notions of displacement from below to above—specifically, that a person can and often does treat the contents of their mind in a manner analogous to the way they regard the contents and functioning of their bodies. This notion rests on the more fundamental one that the ego, as Freud noted, is first and foremost a "body ego." There is the further assumption that it usually is easier (i.e., less anxiety laden) to express thoughts and feelings about one's mind than about one's body, even though similar conflicts and issues pertain to both (e.g., shame or humiliation). Thus, the hypothesis advanced above actually entails all the assumptions enumerated—psychic determinism, unconscious motivation, displacement and symbolic equivalence, and convergent causality. The latter refers to the proposition that the patient's question about the location of the bathroom and her concern about not being able to control her emotions both stemmed from an unconscious conflict between a desire to express herself or let go and her fear of humiliation if she were to do so.

The working hypothesis one might hold regarding unconscious motives at play in this example could include the patient's desire to expose herself in conflict with a wish to avoid humiliation based on the fear that her body is defective and her self, inferior. It is further assumed that these hypothesized possibilities are outside the patient's awareness at the beginning of treatment. The clinician would store these inferences in his or her memory and scan them periodically for their "fit" with other aspects of the evolving working model of the patient. If evidence emerged that these inferences were relevant to an understanding of the patient's core issues, the therapist could offer interpretations based on them. For example, "I notice that when you started getting teary just now you quickly tried to hold back your feelings. Recently you recalled how as a young girl you were afraid you might wet your pants if you were upset, and that if you did so, you would feel mortified. I wonder whether you're afraid that crying here would make you feel the same way." The nature of the patient's associations to such an interpretation, including what other childhood memories might be recalled, would be among the criteria a psychoanalytic clinician would use to evaluate the accuracy of the interpretation and its clinical utility.

It needs to be emphasized that this is merely an example of how a psychoanalyst might arrive at a particular clinical inference that could become part of a dynamic formulation. We do not mean to suggest that this clinical hypothesis is necessarily a valid explanation for the contiguity of these two particular ideas in the patient's associations. Only further supportive clinical material, uncontaminated by any suggestive interpretation of the kind offered above, could increase one's confidence in the original hypothesis. It also should be noted that we are not implying that the analyst is necessarily aware of the implicit "rules of clinical evidence" that he or she is using, but only that there is an underlying "clinical logic" to what might otherwise be seen as pure intuition.

INCLUSION/EXCLUSION CRITERIA

There are no exclusion criteria for a psychoanalytic case formulation. The approach described here can be used with all patients, although the richness, detail, and comprehensiveness of the formulation will depend on how self-disclosing the patient is willing and able to be. The patient's free associations as elicited in psychoanalytic sessions are the main source of information. The formulation, however, can also be based on interviews with someone who knows the patient or on psychological test data.

The psychodynamically based case formulations also takes into account other information about the patient. For example, in patients with organic or biological factors that contribute significantly to the patient's pathology, unconscious conflict will play a more modest role in the overall case formulation. Nonetheless, the psychoanalytic clinician will look carefully at the premorbid factors in such patients' psychological makeup that place a unique stamp on how their psychopathology is expressed. Thus, one will not rush to infer that an Alzheimer patient's growing disorientation with regard to time, place, and sense of personal identity has dynamic meaning. At the same time, selective confusions and distortions often are understandable as reflecting long-standing conflicts and personality styles. At a similar stage of dementia, not all patients will express guilt over burdening their children or deny that they were ever married to their spouse of many years. Similarly, even if there is a genetic basis for schizophrenia or depression, it still leaves us with the necessity of explaining the particular content of the schizophrenic's delusional system or the psychotically depressed patient's view of his or her "sins." This way of looking at pathology has characterized psychodynamic approaches since Freud's observations of individual differences in reaction to traumatic events.

PSYCHOANALYTIC CASE FORMULATION CONSTRUCTION

In contrast to the research-based approaches described in this volume, traditional psychoanalytic case formulation does not follow a standardized protocol. Nor is there a uniform format used to obtain the clinical material on which it is based. Nevertheless, there is enough commonality among psychoanalytically oriented psychotherapists in both spheres of endeavor to allow us to set out a framework of concepts typically drawn upon in case write-ups, as well as to suggest how an interview should be conducted to elicit the information on which the formulation relies. This will be followed by a case example illustrating how the theoretical concepts and the framework are applied in practice. Based upon the psychoanalytic concepts described above, we will now outline how they are covered in a case formulation. In doing so, we have drawn upon Friedman and Lister's (1987) useful format.

What Is Formulated

Structural Features of Personality

Structure refers to those aspects of psychological functioning that are fairly stable and enduring. There are four areas covered under this heading:

Autonomous Ego Functions. These include disruptions in basic biological, perceptual, motoric, or cognitive functions, including language. Of special import here is the adequacy of the patient's reality testing.

Affects, Drives, and Defenses. This refers to the person's characteristic ways of experiencing impulses and feelings and containing them. Questions regarding drives and affects to be considered in the formulation include the following: Is the person able to tolerate a range of feelings without overly suppressing some or feeling overwhelmed by others? Is there one predominant affect that colors wide areas of the person's functioning? Are closely related affects such as anger, hate, irritation, and jealousy sufficiently differentiated or are they all subsumed under rage? How flexibly does the person respond on an emotional level to diverse circumstances?

Defenses are the intrapsychic mechanisms that allow us to manage difficult external events and internal turmoil. What are the characteristic defenses that the person employs? Are these successful in allowing him or her sufficient emotional response without experiencing strong anxiety or depression? How mature or primitive are the defenses (e.g., intellectualization vs. denial or splitting)? Are the defenses interfering with or restricting the person's enjoyment of life?

Object-Related Functions. These refer to the person's basic modes of relating to others, including their internal representations of self, other, and the links between self and other. Is the person able to be trusting, intimate, and at the same time autonomous? Can he or she sustain disappointment, disillusionment, and loss without becoming incapacitated? In relationships is the person overly controlling?—too submissive?—self-defeating?—demanding?

Self-Related Functions. These refer to the person's ability to maintain the coherence, stability, and positive evaluation of the self. They also include issues of the individual's identifications, identity, ideals, and goals. Are the person's values stable? Do ambitions match desires and talents? Is the person overly susceptible to shame and humiliation, inflation of self or deflation of self? That is, how susceptible is the individual to precipitous drops in self esteem?

Dynamic Features of Personality

"Just as the structural viewpoint examines the *form* of psychological functioning, the dynamic viewpoint examines its *content*. . . . The focus is consistently on meaning and motive" (Friedman & Lister, 1987, pp. 135–136; italics in original). The psychoanalytic case formulation responds to the following questions in this sphere: What is the meaning of the symptom understood psychoanalytically? What motivates the person to act in particular ways? What are the person's major areas of conflict, be they intrapsychic or interpersonal? Within psychoanalytic theory, conflict and ambivalence are considered to be ubiquitous in human affairs.

What is the nature of the conflict among various motives such as wishes, fears, impulses, and needs? Does the patient effect some compromise among them that actually obscures the nature of the conflict? These wishes, fears, and conflicts are often of a sexual, dependent, or aggressive nature. For example, a woman may wish to enjoy sex more freely but feel morally remiss and guilty were she to do so. A man may wish to have an intimate relationship with a woman but at the same time fear being controlled or engulfed by her or overly dependent on her. A woman may wish to speak up and express herself in a group but fear being shamed or humiliated. Any of these conflicts can lead to the formation of symptoms, anxiety, or inhibitions.

Sometimes the wishes are particularly disturbing, taking the form of homicidal fantasies, ego-alien sexual fantasies (e.g., of incest), or primitive urges to merge with the object. For example, a person may feel angry and want to express it, but then fear losing control and having the anger emerge as murderous rage. Typically, there are layers of motive, meaning, and conflict, only some of which will be apparent in the initial interviews. In this part of the formulation, the object is to describe the various areas of motive and conflict, both intrapsychic and interpersonal, that may operate on conscious or unconscious levels.

Developmental Antecedents

Preceding and underlying the structural and dynamic facets of a patient's personality and psychopathology are earlier events that take on particular meaning depending on the developmental (or, in psychoanalytic parlance, "genetic") phase in which they occurred. These may include traumatic events such as physical or emotional abandonment, sexual or physical abuse, surgery, or parental psychosis or drug abuse; or more moderate stresses such as the birth of a sibling, parental discord, or school failure. The meaning and impact of these events will be influenced by their timing, namely, the psychosexual and psychosocial stage of development that the person was going through when they occurred. In this way, the formulation takes account of the stages of infancy, childhood, and adolescence as these have affected the patient's current psychological functioning.

Adaptive Features: Assets and Strengths

Because there tends to be an (understandable) emphasis in the case formulation on patients' deficiencies and maladaptive ways of interacting, it is important not to neglect noting their strengths. What are their accomplishments? Do they have intellectual strengths?—mechanical aptitudes?—artistic talents? Are they able to get along with others? Can they assert themselves appropriately? And so forth.

The Psychoanalytic Interview

The most usual source of information on which the case formulation is based comes from a skillfully conducted, psychoanalytically informed interview. In some settings, initial demographic information, or even more extensive descriptions of the person's complaints and background, are obtained by having the patient fill out a data sheet or life-history questionnaire. Objective tests such as the Minnesota Multiphasic Personality Inventory (MMPI) or the Millon Scales, which are completed by the informant, may be used. In special circumstances, where the interview leaves considerable uncertainty regarding diagnosis and treatment recommendations, a full battery of tests is employed that includes projective techniques. The latter can be especially useful in addressing the structural and dynamic areas of the case formulation.

The interview can be thought of as having *content* and *process* features (MacKinnon & Michels, 1971), the first referring to the information to be gathered through the patient's words and cognitive style, and the second, to the manner in which the interviewer and patient relate to each other.

Content of the Psychoanalytic Interview

Identification of the Patient. This includes the patient's age, sex, ethnicity, socioeconomic status, education, marital status, occupation, means of referral, and living situation.

Chief Complaints/Symptoms. This is what the patient usually wants to talk about, and it is important to get a clear picture of each symptom or complaint. What stresses or events precipitated the present episode? Were there previous occurrences and, if so, under what circumstances did they occur, and how were they resolved?

Personal History. As time permits, one wants to get a history of each period of the person's life—infancy, childhood, adolescence, and adulthood. The object is to discern the personality patterns the person has developed in the process of responding to the environmental forces that have been formative. One may ask for the patient's earliest memories, as these can often shed light on dynamic issues. One particularly notes difficulties that have arisen and instances of psychopathology that were apparent at any phase of development.

Family History. This includes a description of the parents and siblings in the patient's family of origin and the way that he or she felt about and interacted with them in childhood and more recently. Included are the names, ages, occupations, economic and social status, marital relationship, and history of physical and emotional illnesses of the most significant family members. One pays special attention to the occurrence of psychological problems such as depression, psychiatric hospitalization, suicide, alcoholism or other drug addiction, and mental retardation.

Optimally, one would conduct several interviews to be able to gather this much information and to observe the patient over a period of time. Typically, in the press of clinical practice, only one or two hours are available for this purpose, and one must curtail the gathering of a full personal history and family history, which are then combined in one section of the narrative. If the patient continues on to psychotherapy, one can then fill in the gaps as therapy proceeds.

Process of the Psychoanalytic Interview

Observing the Patient. In addition to gathering information from the patient, the interviewer notes the patient's behavior in the course of the interview. The traditional psychiatric way of referring to these observations is the *mental status* exam. This is a description of the patient's current emotions, behavior, thought processes, thought content, and perceptions. It includes appearance, general attitude (cooperative, withdrawn, seductive?), mood and affect (depressed, anxious, flat?), speech (coherent, relevant?), thought (grandiose, delusional, suicidal?), perceptions (hallucinations, derealization?), cognitive functions (memory, intelligence, judgment, and insight), and sensorium (orientation as to time, place, and person). This kind of information will also help establish a formal DSM diagnosis.

It is important to observe precisely to what dynamic themes and what events the patient shows affect, as these will tend to be the most significant. One also strives to follow patients' associations, that is, to note the sequence in which themes are presented. This is in keeping with the psychoanalytic dictum that the order of a person's verbal production is partly determined by inferred underlying psychic forces, as described earlier.

One takes note of the development of transference, countertransference, and resistance. Patients may reveal, even in initial interviews, the way in which they regard the interviewer, based on their relationship to parental figures. There may be an exaggerated need for gratification of dependency needs, for example. The interviewer may experience a countertransference pull to gratify such needs, which alerts him or her to the nature of the transference. Regarding resistance, one notes how and when the patient expresses defense in sidestepping the recognition of certain feelings or thoughts, including those pertaining to the interviewer.

We turn now to consideration of a general approach that will enable the interviewer to obtain the information on which the formulation is constructed.

Optimal Stance of the Interviewer. The interviewer should show an interest in the patient as a whole person, and not merely as an object of clinical focus. This includes attending to patients' assets as well as deficiencies. One is interested not solely in patients' diagnosis, symptoms, or complaints but in their total life functioning (work and love relations) in the context of their life history.

Even if one does not approve of what the patient does, it is important to try to accept the patient unreservedly. One attempts to maintain a certain degree of professional detachment, but this should not be construed as indifference. Nor should interviewers allow their own emotions to interfere with their judgment. Knowing their own emotional makeup and vulnerabilities will help them to predict those areas where they are most likely to lose objectivity.

The clinical information should not be collected in a lockstep manner but along the way where it seems to fit the flow of the individual's presentation. One line of thought often leads the patient to another, and if one has the above format in mind much information can be obtained without the interview becoming a question-and-answer session. In fact, one of the advantages of an interview over a paper-and-pencil questionnaire is that it allows the interviewer to observe the flow of information, affect, and behavior, and to follow up on areas of special import.

The most general guideline we can offer about the psychoanalytic interview is that one should try to listen without interrupting too frequently. Following are the circumstances when the interviewer would want to intervene:

1. *One wants to know more about something than the patient is offering spontaneously.* One can simply lean forward expectantly, say, "Uh-huh," "I see," or something similar. If this isn't sufficient, one can say, "I'd like to hear more about that."

2. *The patient's anxiety level is too high or too low.* One can say, in the former case, "Go ahead, You're doing fine," or "Something makes it hard for you to talk to me about this matter. Can you tell me what it is?" In the case of low anxiety, one may need to be more probing and challenging to stir up some feeling.

3. *One wants to encourage emotional expression.* Pressing patients for details of an emotion-laden event often gets them to relive it partially and can yield a clearer picture of the dynamics.

4. *One needs to control irrelevance and chitchat.* Since time is limited, one has to keep control of the interview and deflect patients from irrelevancies. One should also try to understand the defensive function served by excessive or trivial verbiage.

5. *One wishes to channel the interview.* One can ask questions that tactfully steer the patient back toward significant areas already touched on or to matters that have not been brought forward. One should not confuse tact with timidity; that is, if one asks questions firmly, not hesitantly, one is more likely to get a useful answer.

The above is a very condensed set of guidelines for the psychoanalytic interview. For a fuller exposition of content and process of the interview see Sullivan (1954), and for a deeper psychoanalytic understanding of personality structure as it derives from the clinical process we recommend McWilliams (1994).

CASE EXAMPLE

Presentation of the Patient

Identification

Jim is a 24-year-old, white, married, Catholic man in his first year of college, majoring in computer science. He is currently on leave from the U.S. Army, which is financing his college education, upon completion of which he will owe 4 years of service as a computer programmer. He and his wife, Audra, to whom he has been married for 5 years, have recently returned from a military base overseas. Jim was self-referred to the college counseling center, and this is his first contact with psychological services.

Presenting Problem

In taking an exam in a computer hardware course, Jim said he "blanked out." Although the professor had a reputation for being tough, Jim had felt confident going into the exam. However, when he looked at the first question, he could not think clearly, got confused, and said to himself, "I can never do this. I don't know this." After he left the exam and sought the help of a tutor, it became clear that he did know the material and could have done well had he taken the exam.

Jim reported a similar sequence of events occurring twice before when he was taking college courses in the Army. In both cases, he knew the work well enough to have gotten a high grade had he followed through with the exam. He did not experience this specific problem taking exams in high school, although he described himself as being perfectionistic about his work. For example, as a youngster he did excellent written and artistic work that the teachers admired but which he would crumple up and throw away as not being good enough. Although he could have had a career as a graphic artist, he prefers fields that are "sensible, logical, and orderly."

Personal and Family History

Jim's family consists of his father and mother and three younger siblings—Scott (22), who is 1 year younger, Michelle (21), 3½ years younger, and Warren (16), who is 8 years younger. They are living together in Arizona. Jim's father is an auto mechanic, and his mother is an office administrator.

Jim described his father as a man who had a very difficult childhood due to his own father dying when he was six and having been left with his mother whom he described as "a bitch." In Jim's mind his father was "a madman" who couldn't tolerate his children's mistakes and would swear, scream, or smack them if their behavior did not meet his expectations. He broke furniture and dishes when he was in a rage. If Jim was visibly upset, his father would call him a baby or a girl. He forced his children to address him as "Sir" and stated, "I'm God and this house is my castle. You follow my laws."

When Jim was seven, he witnessed his father "lay out" a man who had tried to cheat him. The man cracked his head on the cement, and Jim had to clean up the blood. Jim decided at that moment that he would never fight his father and would always walk away from arguments. This resolution was reinforced on several other occasions when his father beat up other men. Jim handled his father's demands by saying, "O.K., Dad, whatever you say." He added that he hated his father and wanted to tell him to shut up, but held in his feelings, felt "totally tense," and kicked and punched walls instead (but not in his father's presence). He and Scott also rebelled silently by purposely not trying harder to improve their performance after father's scoldings and admonishments. When Jim was little he had looked up to his father, who was affectionate to him, but after the age of six he never agreed with his father. His father was frequently unemployed and the family in debt, with father passing bad checks. He also stole money from the children that came from their newspaper routes, birthdays, and gifts from relatives.

Jim described his mother as warm, affectionate, and encouraging, and believed himself to be her favorite child. As a young child, he would often get into bed with his parents, on his mother's side of the bed, and she would put her arm around him. His father brought an end to this when Jim was six. Jim said there were times when his mother would sit with his father at the kitchen table and send Jim and Scott outside "like dogs." He always felt his father vied with him for his mother's attention "like another child," and it bothered him when she would attend to his father and shut him out. He had a recurrent dream from the age of four in which the family was away, leaving him alone with his mother who was dressed up as she would be to go out with his father. There were also times when his mother would say, "I wish I hadn't had you kids."

The relationship between his parents was stormy, and the children asked their mother to divorce their father. When she would threaten to do so, Jim's father was contrite, cried, and "the whole matter blew over." She would say that she feared that, if she left, his father would blow his brains out, which Jim believes would have been the case. His mother worked from the time Jim was 11, leaving him to care for his siblings. During this time, there was often no phone, electricity, or food in the house. Jim found respite in music, art, and books.

As a teenager, Jim hated all authorities such as principals, teachers, and policemen. He wrote sexual, angry, and violent poetry at this time. He said his sex education consisted of his father's saying, "If you want to fuck somebody, go jerk off." He was exposed to pornographic movies and magazines that his father left around the house, which Jim viewed while masturbating.

Jim's "breaking point" came at age 16 after his father broke Scott's nose when he had resisted being locked in the cellar for some minor misdemeanor. Jim began screaming and swearing at his father, telling him not to lay a hand on Scott. He said he was too angry to be scared and his father did not hit him. He told his father that he was leaving home and would never return. He then began spending his daytime hours at his girlfriend Audra's house, feeling close to her parents. He and Audra got engaged but broke the engagement briefly over fights about her being extremely possessive. They married 5 years ago when she was 17 and he was 19. The last two times Jim saw his parents were at the wedding and a year later (4 years ago) before he left for the service.

Jim described his wife in very positive terms, adding that although they fought while overseas, they argue very little now. While abroad, he came to feel that he had never been free to have responsibility for himself alone and considered leaving Audra. He felt pressure to be her ideal and discussed this with a close Army friend, Bill, who told him to be who he wanted to be. When Jim and Bill were put on separate shifts, Jim encouraged Bill to use their house when he wasn't there. Bill then had an affair with Audra and, when Jim found out, they tried for several weeks to have an "open" marriage. Bill was told by a supervisor to stay away from Audra, and she and Jim straightened things out. Jim felt betrayed by Bill and was afraid he would beat up Bill and kill him.

Currently, Jim feels good about his marriage, but he and Audra do have a conflict over his being turned on by pornography. They enjoy sex, but at times he is stimulated by sexual advertising, buys *Playboy* or *Penthouse* magazine and masturbates, or goes to porno houses and views movies.

So far Jim has been able to avoid any direct conflict with officers of higher rank, but he fears that he may one day react to an abuse of authority by, for example, laughing in the general's face during inspection. He hates what the Army stands for and hates the President, who, he feels, does not "wish to take care of us, but only wants to go down in history." Jim would like to leave this country and live abroad or in the hills away from people.

Mental Status

Jim is an average-looking man who came to one interview dressed neatly and to another looking wrinkled and unshaven. His affect was usually appropriate and wide ranging, but he sometimes smiled while recounting upsetting events. In this connection, when asked to examine what he is experiencing, he backs off from his affect by minimizing, rationalizing, or focusing on others' feelings or motives. He does not appear depressed, nor is he suicidal, but there is a heaviness and seriousness to his mood. He is afraid of the intensity of his anger and will not fight for fear of hurting someone as his father did. He showed no evidence of thought disorder, severe acting out, or other serious psychopathology. He is very intelligent and has good judgment.

Case Formulation

For didactic purposes, we present a formulation using the headings described above. However, it should be recognized that clinical formulations are typically written as a continuous narrative that interweaves structural, dynamic, developmental, and adaptive aspects of the case. In the case formulation below, we draw only on the initial interviews because clinical cases are typically formulated at this juncture. Nevertheless, it is important to realize that a formulation may change as more is learned about the patient during the process of psychotherapy.

Structural Features of Personality

Autonomous Ego Functions. Jim's cognitive functioning is severely hampered when taking exams. He gets confused, blanks out, and is convinced that he is unable to proceed. That is, Jim's ego is overwhelmed by anxiety in this circumstance, leading to a highly dysfunctional response. Otherwise, his ego functioning, including reality testing, is largely unimpaired.

Affects, Drives, and Defenses. Jim has trouble containing and modulating the fierce anger he harbors against all authorities. He has managed to do so but at considerable cost in terms of psychic energy expended. That is, he needs to be constantly vigilant against the possibility that he will flout authority in some inappropriate way, such as laughing at a general, or lashing out and even killing someone (as he felt he might do with Bill). One way he defends against the anxiety generated by this danger is by acting in an overly compliant manner with his perceived (and actual) attackers.

Jim not only has to struggle to contain his rage against authority but also to cover over and displace his sadness at not having received the nurturance and care he wished for. He does so by minimizing and rationalizing his own needs, and projecting his despair of having his dependency needs met onto others (e.g., the President, "who does not care for the people"). Another way in which he contains troubling feelings and impulses is by focusing on study and work areas that are "sensible, logical and orderly"; hence his interest in computers, where the messiness of feelings can be readily avoided. His effort is to keep in control at all costs. His drive/defense configurations are characteristic of an obsessive-compulsive personality, although they are not severe or pervasive enough to constitute a personality disorder.

Object-Related Functions. Jim tries to act with others as if everything is fine and to compliantly meet their expectations. He wants to look good and keep the peace, and this picture of a cooperative, helpful person constitutes his internal representation of self. His view of others is that they make demands to fulfill their own needs but not his or others, and that they take advantage of him (e.g., professors, who expect too much of their students; Bill and Audra, who had an affair at his expense; his parents, who mistreated him; the President, who "doesn't care about us," etc.). Thus, the internalized relationship between self and other can be characterized as that of giver to taker, or victim to victimizer.

Self-Related Functions. Jim's sense of self is coherent and fairly stable, but also quite negative and, in some ways, false. It is negative insofar as he is subject to strong feelings of shame about his work or his actions and to lowered self-regard. It is false in that he tries to be the perfect son, husband, Army man, and student but, in so doing, suppresses his own identity. Jim wants to be himself, speak up for himself, and take care of his own needs, but instead feels that he lives at the whims of his wife, the Army, and his professors. As such he is not a fully individuated person.

Dynamic Features of Personality

A central conflict for Jim, largely unconscious, is whether to obey authority slavishly or to flout it defiantly. Currently, Jim either complies with others' standards, which he assumes to be as unreasonable as his father's, or he rebels in a passive way by doing what he wants to on the sly. For example, he turns to pornography, thereby defying his wife's wishes and satisfying his own sexual needs. He shows up at the college exam but rebels against the "tough" professor by blanking out and refusing to comply with the professor's implied demands that he perform, and perform well. The symptom of cognitive confusion may be viewed as a compromise between a wish to go his own way by not even showing up at the exam (retreating to the hills), thereby defying the demand, and the contrary wish to be the good, obedient student who performs flawlessly. So he comes to take the exam but then doesn't perform.

Although Jim says he hates his father and never wants to see him again, he has internalized many of his father's standards and acknowledges still feeling some caring for him, which creates internal tension. He tends to see his mother in an overly positive light, failing to recognize her rejection of him and his siblings as a burden and her failure to intercede on his behalf with his brutalizing father. In other words, there are splits between the good and bad internalized images of both parents.

Developmental Antecedents

Regarding the symptom, there are oedipal elements that may be unconsciously interfering with exam taking. From both Jim's self-report and his recurrent dream, we can discern his strong wish as a child to have his mother to himself and his father out of the picture. That this is a sexualized wish may be hypothesized from the fact that, in the dream, his mother is dressed up as she would be to go out with his father and that, until the age of six, Jim would cuddle with his mother in bed until extruded by his father. (If Jim were to enter therapy, one would seek further evidence to support or refute this hypothesis.) In any case, one possible consequence is that his rageful and competitive feelings toward his father are getting displaced to other authorities, such as the professor, whom he unconsciously wants to defeat even if it means bringing the house down, Samson-like, on himself—that is, failing the exam.

The wish to have his mother to himself, however, may also represent early dependent longings and efforts to get the kind of nurturance he needed to blossom. (As was learned later in therapy, mother herself was like a needy child who looked to him to assume premature responsibility in the house and to meet her emotional needs. She would also kiss him in a way that made him very uncomfortable.)

Another motive for Jim's blocking in exam taking may be oedipal guilt which requires that he arrange to fail in order not to surpass his father. The closely related concept of survivor guilt (e.g., Weiss, 1993) may also be at play in his feeling that fate dealt harshly with his parents and that he ought not do better in life than they did, nor should do better than he "deserves." That is, there are several perspectives that can be brought to bear in an attempt to understand Jim's symptom/complaint. Not all will prove to be accurate or resonant for him, but more than one may well apply in accordance with the psychoanalytic concept of the multidetermination of symptoms.

Jim was emotionally abused as a child by a domineering, controlling father and a seductive, immature mother who did not protect him from his father's inappropriate demands. He hates them, yet longs for what he missed out on as a child. Because of Jim's abrupt withdrawal from his family during adolescence, he was never able to sort out his ambivalent feelings toward his parents. The sudden loss has left him with a barely acknowledged feeling of sadness, and there exists a lack of internal separation from them.

Adaptive Features: Assets and Strengths

Despite all these difficulties, Jim has considerable assets. He is very bright, has artistic talent in addition to his computer skills, and has gained recognition of these by others. He has always been able to find some contentment by escaping into art, music, and books. Even removing himself from a noxious environment in adolescence speaks to his self-preservative abilities. He has compassion for others, including his wife with whom he now has a reasonably good relationship. His defenses are flexible enough such that he can access feelings without becoming overwhelmed by them. He also seems able to trust the interviewer and to form the beginnings of a therapeutic relationship.

APPLICATION TO
PSYCHOTHERAPY TECHNIQUE

Within a psychoanalytic framework, one of the uses of a formulation is to determine suitability for an expressive, exploratory psychoanalytic therapy. In evaluating the patient for the latter, the following seven criteria are among those most important to consider: (1) willingness to share personal thoughts and feelings with the interviewer; (2) access to, and an ability to experience and tolerate, dysphoric feelings such as anxiety, guilt, and sadness; (3) motivation for change; (4) psychological-mindedness, or the capacity for introspection; (5) flexibility of defenses; (6) the degree and intensity of fixation at the oedipal versus preoedipal stages; (7) a positive response to interpretation such as demonstrable affect, new associations, increased reflectiveness, and fresh memories. The formulation can help determine suitability for a range of approaches including brief psychodynamic therapy (when a clear focus is discernible), supportive therapy (when defense strengthening is necessary), group therapy (to help alleviate interpersonal problems), behavior therapy (e.g., for stress reduction), and so forth.

Another major use of the formulation is to set out reasonable goals and outcomes for the therapy depending on the time and intensity of work possible. Here is a set of goals for Jim, based on the formulation, were he to enter an open-ended psychoanalytically oriented therapy:

1. *Autonomous ego functions: the symptom.* He will explore and come to understand the dynamics underlying his symptom of blanking out on tests and gain relief from it.

2. *Dynamic and self-related issues.* He will acquire a clearer sense of his own wishes and needs and be able to express more of who he is and what he wants, that is, allow a truer self to emerge. He will be less conflicted about complying versus rebelling and will have a greater sense of freedom in choosing to act in either direction. His self-esteem will increase and will be less subject to buffeting by others.

4. *Affects, drives, and defenses.* Jim will be more able to face and accept his many mixed feelings including anger, longing, deprivation, sadness, and guilt. He will have less need to escape to the hills or abroad, or to minimize, rationalize, and project feelings. He will be less inclined to act out violent feelings and will be somewhat more relaxed and at peace with himself. He will work at expressing anger in a modulated way.

5. *Object relations: general.* In his relationships with others, he will come to feel less compelled to acquiesce automatically to fulfill other's needs and will be able to ask appropriately to have his own needs met. That is, he will not allow himself to be victimized, nor need to view the world according to the sharp dichotomy of victimizer/victimized. In general, he will tend to be more open and comfortable with people.

6. *Object relations: parental introjects.* He will start to sort out his feelings about his parents and see them more realistically, with both their good and bad features. He will engage in a process of separating from them internally, while feeling freer to visit his family if he wishes.

7. *Object relations: marital interaction.* Jim will resolve his compulsion to view pornography, either by enjoying it without guilt or feeling less need for it, or both. The role it plays in his marital interaction will become clarified and at least partially resolved.

Broader aspects of a satisfactory therapeutic outcome are that the patient internalizes and comes to use the analyzing function initially supplied by the therapist and is able to arrive at a more integrated, self-accepting state. Although the formulation is not conveyed immediately or directly to the patient, its major elements would become clear as the therapy proceeds. The therapist's role is to act as a catalyst for the patient's self-exploration, using the case formulation as a road map for the journey. Thus, in addition to its role in prescribing the nature of the therapy and setting goals for it, the formulation serves like a ship's rudder, helping first the therapist and then the patient to steer a course that is most likely to result in reaching the desired shore.

In the case of Jim, the formulation served as a guide for the treatment, including setting the seven overlapping goals. The case was formulated primarily in accordance with concepts highlighted in contemporary Freudian and object relations theory. Jim's major conflict was seen in impulse/defense terms as one between his wish to defy authority and to submit to it. This conflict could be expected to express itself in the way that Jim would interact with the therapist, namely, in a defiant and/or overly compliant manner. Interpretations in the therapy would address these themes, and the patient's responses would help to elaborate the case formulation. It was also noted that Jim longs for what he missed out on as a child, that he does not feel sufficiently separate from his parents, and that there are splits between the good and bad internalized images of both parents. These aspects of the formulation lend themselves more readily to interpretations that stem from object relations theory, so that in this case concepts from different yet related analytic theories influence the therapist's interventions. For example, the formulation would lead us to expect that Jim will experience the therapist as someone whose nurturance he craves but from whom he expects to receive very little or by whom he expects to be mistreated. These enactments can turn out to be an obstacle to treatment or corrective emotional and interpersonal experiences.

Because there is a fair amount of self-selection of patients who seek psychodynamically oriented psychotherapy, they often have some familiarity with the general procedures and goals of this kind of treatment. Following the initial intake sessions, the patient and therapist talk about the central issues and problems on which they will focus as the treatment begins. It is understood that the more time-limited the therapy, the more that there will be a focus on the most pressing and accessible problems. However, even in brief psychodynamic therapy the exploration of thoughts and feelings has to have a certain open-ended quality if the underlying issues are to surface (Messer & Warren, 1995). Thus, the therapist and patient decide upon the goals of psychotherapy collaboratively in the context of a frank discussion of the conditions of the treatment.

As for conveying the case formulation to patients, therapists vary in how much and at what level they share their developing working model of the patient. Most therapists offer a tentative, general, jargon-free formulation that points to the repetitive, ego-alien issues already somewhat familiar to the patient. In most instances the formulation presented by the clinician is more descriptive than explanatory and does not include interpretation of unconscious content. In fact, most psychoanalytic clinicians strive to create a therapeutic atmosphere in which the therapist and patient are coinvestigators and coauthors of a series of formulations that will emerge in the moment-to-moment interactions of the two participants. (See Wolitzky, 1995, for a more detailed exposition of the theory and practice of psychoanalytic therapy.)

TRAINING

In order to train students to prepare a psychodynamic formulation, they need to have knowledge of developmental and adult psychopathology and various psychoanalytic theories. Obviously, they need to learn interviewing and psychotherapeutic skills and techniques so that they will be able to collect the data necessary to construct the formulation. Thus, supervised exposure to intake interview material, therapy transcripts, psychodiagnostic test data, and their own therapy cases will provide the clinical experience to complement the student's theoretical knowledge. Psychoanalytic training programs often consider the student's own psychoanalytic therapy to be a vital source of knowledge in developing the clinical acumen necessary to create a complex dynamic formulation of the patient.

With respect to training, our view is that it should attempt to illustrate concretely for the student the choice points for intervention as a function of the theory of pathology and change that one embraces. Thus, if one formulates that the patient suffers primarily from a disorder of the self stemming from failures in parental empathy and that the amelioration of self-defects requires the opportunity to form idealizing and mirror transferences to compensate for the failure of the parents to function as idealizing and mirroring selfobjects, then one will want to act in ways most likely to facilitate these kinds of transferences. The specifics, however, will derive from the formulation.

A Kohutian supervisor would encourage the student to allow these kinds of transferences to blossom and to be careful lest the patient experience a retraumatization at the hands of the therapist. A Freudian supervisor, on the other hand, would be more inclined to point to the defensive functions of these kinds of transferences and to advise the student to begin to offer interpretations of the wishes and conflicts that presumably underlie the manifest clinical material, as presented in the case formulation (Pulver, 1987). In fact, it has been shown (Fine & Fine, 1990) that analysts of different theoretical persuasions can be distinguished on the basis of the interpretations that they are prepared to offer the patient. It should be noted, however, that both for the experienced clinician and the novice, the relationship between theory and technique is sufficiently loose to allow for considerable variation among practitioners of the same psychoanalytic approach.

RESEARCH SUPPORT FOR THE APPROACH

There is the danger that, once made, a case formulation will become fixed in the clinician's mind, leaving him or her less open to other possibilities. For example, in a research project in which one of the authors participated several years ago (Dahl, 1983), eight analysts met as a group and read aloud the verbatim transcript of the early sessions of an audio-recorded analysis. When one of the participants came upon an observation that sparked a hypothesis, it was recorded. The group subsequently read a series of transcripts from later sessions. When a member thought that there was evidence, pro or con, bearing on any hypothesis previously generated, that person would indicate the lines in the transcript that he or she considered relevant to the hypothesis in question, and all members then rated the strength of the evidence.

Rarely did anyone find evidence that was judged to be negative with respect to the hypothesis under consideration. Furthermore, the person who called attention to the evidence consistently rated it as more positive than the average rating of the rest of the group, whether or not that person generated the hypothesis originally. This finding suggests that there is a tendency to overestimate the value of psychoanalytic evidence that one finds in clinical material. One implication is that clinicians need to be cautious about the degree of their investment in a particular formulation.

Involvement in the process of drawing inferences and making interpretations based on clinical material leads inevitably to a concern with the issues of reliability and validity. This topic is of vital importance with respect to the soundness of theory and the efficacy of treatment. Grünbaum (1984) has argued that data from the consulting room are "epistemologically contaminated." That is, the factor of suggestion carried in the therapist's interpretations, however inadvertent, prevents us from being in a position to validate core theoretical propositions within the context of the treatment situation. Grünbaum also argues that treatment outcome cannot be used to verify or disconfirm the accuracy of clinical interpretations. Others (e.g., Edelson, 1992), however, have taken issue with Grünbaum's conclusions.

To give one example of how the issue of reliability and validity can be framed and studied, Caston (1993, p. 493) has pointed out that psychoanalysis is as much endangered by overinflated agreement on stereotypical dynamic formulas as by lack of agreement. That is, even when there is good agreement among judges (and often there is not; see Seitz , 1966), it can be spurious if judges are using stereotypical inferences that are not particular to a given case. In a study designed to test this hypothesis, Caston and Martin (1993) used verbatim transcripts from the first five sessions of an audio-recorded psychotherapy. Their novel methodology included having some analysts make ratings *without benefit of reading the transcripts*. The authors demonstrated that, in most domains of behavior, analysts agreed well among themselves and to a greater degree than would be expected if they were basing their judgments on theoretical stereotypes. In other words, they were responsive to the particulars of a given case.

On the other hand, using a different method of study, Collins and Messer (1991) have shown to what extent case formulations can be dependent on one's theoretical viewpoint. They found that two different research groups, guided either by Weissian cognitive-dynamic theory or by object relations theory, endorsed very different formulations of the same cases. This raised the interesting and important question of whether adherence by the therapist to one or the other formulation had a differential effect on patient progress. To study this, Tishby and Messer (1995) compared the relationship between therapist interventions that were compatible with either a cognitive-dynamic or an object relations formulation, on the one hand, and patient progress, on the other. They found that therapist interventions compatible with the object relations formulation were the better predictor of in-session patient progress in the middle phases of brief psychodynamic therapy for the two patients studied, as well as in the early phase for one of them. More such studies are needed in which the same cases are formulated from different perspectives and the relationship of such formulations to patient progress and outcome studied. It is these and other formal methods described in the chapters of this book that will be an important testing ground for the value of psychoanalytic case formulation.

NOTES

1. It could be argued that the reference to three major models neglects Harry Stack Sullivan's interpersonal approach, the neo-Freudian schools such as those of Carl Jung, Karen Horney, and Alfred Adler, and the disciples of Melanie Klein (e.g., Schafer, 1994). Nor does this categorization give adequate consideration to theorists who have attempted to integrate two models such as Kernberg's (1980) effort to combine traditional Freudian and ego-psychological theory with object relations concepts. Nevertheless, the present classification is sufficient for our goal here of explicating the nature of, and the issues involved in, psychodynamic case formulation. Also note that for present purposes we will use the terms "psychoanalytic" and "psychodynamic" interchangeably.

2. The postmodern sensibility in contemporary culture is seen not only in literary criticism and in the humanities but has influenced psychoanalysis as well. As Leary (1994) notes, a key feature of postmodernism is that there is no "truly objective" knowledge of the "real order" of things. As applied to psychoanalytic discourse, this view suggests that meanings are generated or created in a dyadic context; they are a coauthored narrative based on the interaction of two subjectivities. That is, whereas in Freud's day there were meanings to be discovered, in the postmodern view there are no "essential meanings" to be unearthed. In keeping with Freud's archaeological metaphor, one could dig into deeper and deeper layers of the unconscious and find important pieces of the individual's past history that were living in the present. Even if the idea that recall of a traumatic event would cause the symptom to disappear had to be abandoned, one could fall back on the notion that interpretations that "tally with what is real" would alleviate symptoms. When it became evident that one could not reliably demonstrate any kind of cause-and-effect relationship between interpretations with specific content and symptom remission, the door was open to the theoretical pluralism that characterizes contemporary psychoanalytic thought.

ACKNOWLEDGMENTS

We appreciate the helpful suggestions of Nancy McWilliams, Kathryn Parkerton, and Jamie Walkup on an earlier draft of this chapter.

REFERENCES

Brenner, C. (1973). *An elementary textbook of psychoanalysis* (Rev. ed.). New York: International Universities Press.

Brenner, C. (1982). *The mind in conflict.* New York: International Universities Press.

Breuer, J., & Freud, S. (1955). Studies on hysteria. In J. Strachey (Ed. and Trans.), *Standard edition of the complete psychological works of Sigmund Freud* (Vol. 2, pp. 1–305). London: Hogarth Press. (Original work published 1893–1895)

Caston, J. (1993). Can analysts agree? The problems of consensus and the psychoanalytic mannequin: I. A proposed solution. *Journal of the American Psychoanalytic Association, 41,* 493–512.

Caston, J., & Martin, E. (1993). Can analysts agree? The problems of consensus and the psychoanalytic mannequin: II. Empirical tests. *Journal of the American Psychoanalytic Association, 41,* 513–548.

Collins, W. D., & Messer, S. B. (1991). Extending the Plan Formulation Method to an object relations perspective: Reliability, stability and adaptability. *Psychological Assessment: A Journal of Consulting and Clinical Psychology, 3,* 75–81.

Dahl, H. (1983). On the definition and measurement of wishes. In J. Masling (Ed.), *Empirical studies of psychoanalytic theories* (pp. 39–67). Hillsdale, NJ: Erlbaum.

Edelson, M. (1992). Telling and enacting stories in psychoanalysis. In J. Barron, M. Eagle, & D. L. Wolitzky (Eds.), *Interface of psychoanalysis and psychology* (pp. 99–124). Washington, DC: American Psychological Association.

Fairbairn, W. R. D. (1952). *Psychoanalytic studies of the personality.* London: Tavistock Publications and Routledge & Kegan Paul.

Fine, S., & Fine, E. (1990). Four psychoanalytic perspectives. A study of the differences in interpretive interventions. *Journal of the American Psychoanalytic Association, 38,* 1017–1048.

Freud, S. (1953). The interpretation of dreams. In J. Strachey (Ed. and Trans.), *Standard edition of the complete psychological works of Sigmund Freud* (Vols. 4 & 5). London: Hogarth Press. (Original work published 1900)

Friedman, R. S., & Lister, P. (1987). The current status of psychodynamic formulation. *Psychiatry, 50,* 126–141.

Greenberg, J., & Mitchell, S. A. (1983). *Object relations and psychoanalytic theory.* Cambridge, MA: Harvard University Press.

Grünbaum, A. (1984). *The foundations of psychoanalysis: A philosophical critique.* Berkeley: University of California Press.

Guntrip, H. (1971). *Psychoanalytic theory, therapy and the self.* New York: Basic Books.

Kernberg, O. (1980). *Internal world and external reality: Object relations theory applied.* New York: Aronson.

Klein, M. (1948). *Contributions to psychoanalysis, 1921–1945.* London: Hogarth Press.

Kohut, H. (1971). *The analysis of the self: A systematic approach to the psychoanalytic treatment of narcissistic personality disorders.* New York: International Universities Press.

Kohut, H. (1977). *The restoration of the self.* New York: International Universities Press.

Kohut, H. (1984). *How does analysis cure?* Chicago: University of Chicago Press.

Leary, K. (1994). Psychoanalytic "problems" and postmodern "solutions." *Psychoanalytic Quarterly, 63,* 433–465.

MacKinnon, R. A., & Michels, R. (1971). *The psychiatric interview in clinical practice.* Philadelphia: Saunders.

McWilliams, N. (1994). *Psychoanalytic diagnosis: Understanding personality structure in the clinical process.* New York: Guilford Press.

McWilliams, N. (in press). Relationship, subjectivity, and inference in diagnosis. In J. Barron (Ed.), *Making diagnosis meaningful: New psychological perspectives.* Washington, DC: American Psychological Association.

Messer, S. B., Sass, L. A., & Woolfolk, R. L. (Eds.). (1988). *Hermeneutics and psychological theory: Interpretive perspectives on personality, psychotherapy and psychopathology.* New Brunswick, NJ: Rutgers University Press.

Messer, S. B., & Warren, C. S. (1995). *Models of brief psychodynamic therapy: A comparative approach.* New York: Guilford Press.

Perry, S., Cooper, A. M., & Michels, R. (1987). The psychodynamic formulation: Its purpose, structure, and clinical application. *The American Journal of Psychiatry, 144,* 543–550.

Peterfreund, E. (1976). How does the analyst listen? On models and strategies in the psychoanalytic process. In D. P. Spence (Ed.), *Psychoanalysis and contemporary science* (Vol. 4, pp. 59–101). New York: International Universities Press.

Pine, F. (1990). *Drive, ego, object, and self: A synthesis for clinical work.* New York: Basic Books.

Prince, M. (1905). *The dissociation of a personality.* London: Longmans Green.

Pulver, S. (1987). How theory shapes technique: Epilogue. *Psychoanalytic Inquiry, 7,* 289–299.

Rapaport, D., & Gill, M. M. (1959). The points of view and assumptions of metapsychology. *International Journal of Psycho-Analysis, 40,* 153–162

Schafer, R. (1976). *A new language for psychoanalysis.* New Haven, CT: Yale University Press.

Schafer, R. (1992). *Retelling a life: Narration and dialogue in psychoanalysis.* New York: Basic Books.

Schafer, R. (1994). The contemporary Kleinians of London. *Psychoanalytic Quarterly, 63,* 409–432.

Seitz, P. F. D. (1966). The consensus problem in psychoanalytic research. In L. A. Gottschalk & A. H. Auerbach (Eds.), *Methods of research in psychotherapy* (pp. 209–225). New York: Appleton-Century-Crofts.

Silverman, D. K. (1986). A multi-model approach: Looking at clinical data from three theoretical perspectives. *Psychoanalytic Psychology, 3,* 121–132.

Sullivan, H. S. (1954). *The psychiatric interview.* New York: Norton.

Tishby, O., & Messer, S. B. (1995). The relationship between plan compatibility of therapist interventions and patient progress: A comparison of two plans. *Psychotherapy Research, 5,* 76–88.

Weisman, A. B. (1959). The psychodynamic formulation of conflict. *Archives of General Psychiatry, 1,* 288–309.

Weiss, J. (1993). *How psychotherapy works: Process and technique.* New York: Guilford Press.

Winnicott, D. W. (1965). *The maturational processes and the facilitating environment.* New York: International Universities Press.

Wolitzky, D. L. (1995). The theory and practice of traditional psychoanalytic psychotherapy. In A. S. Gurman & S. B. Messer (Eds.), *Essential psychotherapies: Theory and practice* (pp. 12–54). New York: Guilford Press.

3

The Core Conflictual Relationship Theme: A Basic Case Formulation Method

LESTER LUBORSKY

HISTORICAL BACKGROUND OF THE METHOD

An old goal of personality assessment—to devise a reliable measure of the central relationship pattern—began to be attained about 1974. An inkling of the new measure started to take shape during my self-imposed exercise of examining sessions for the ways in which they revealed this pattern. My first papers dealing with this idea (Luborsky, 1976, 1977) already had all of the essentials of the current Core Conflictual Relationship Theme (CCRT) method (Luborsky, in press-a, Chap. 2). Those essentials have led in recent years to the CCRT becoming recognized as an operational measure of what Freud (1912/1958a; 1912/1958b) conceived of as the "transference template"; the CCRT's qualities converge with most of Freud's observations about that "template" (Luborsky, 1998c). In the last few years the advances in CCRT scoring and research have required the old CCRT guide (Luborsky & Crits-Christoph, 1998) to be reshaped into a new edition (Luborsky & Crits-Christoph, 1998). The purpose of the present chapter is to provide a model for those who would use the CCRT for case formulation either clinically or for research.

CONCEPTUAL FRAMEWORK

The field now has in the CCRT a clinically and quantitatively sound measure of the concept of the central relationship pattern that is applicable to psychotherapy sessions and other interviews and is not limited to dynamic psycho-therapies. The CCRT method is based on the principle that redundancy across relationship narratives is a good basis for assessing the central relationship pattern. That pattern reflects an underlying relationship schema: it is each person's partly conscious and partly unconscious knowledge structure about how to conduct relationship interactions.

Starting during my personal scoring exercise with psychotherapy sessions in 1974, I traced the cues that led me to infer a central relationship pattern: (1) the information is provided by a special focus on the narratives about relationships with others and relationships with the self; (2) the three main components that need to be scored within the relationship episodes are wishes toward others and toward the self, the responses from others, and responses of the self; (3) the definition of the central relationship pattern that became known as the CCRT is the combination of *the most frequent of each type of the three components across the relationship episodes in each session*—this last point in italics is referred to as the *pervasiveness* of each component.

That the CCRT is the combination of each of the most frequent of the three types of components was decided upon because it forms part of a useful case formulation for assessing the benefits of psychotherapy. The second and third of these components, that is, the response of the other and the response of the self, are especially valuable in terms of measuring the benefits of psychotherapy or of other forms of psychological treatment. Some of the benefits of psychotherapy are shown in the following findings: (1) in changes in the CCRT during psychotherapy toward decreased pervasiveness (Crits-Christoph & Luborsky, in press-a); (2) in the correlation of pervasiveness with psychiatric severity (Cierpka et al., 1997); (3) in the correlation of accuracy of interpretation, defined as convergence of the interpretation with the CCRT, with the benefits the patient received in psychotherapy (Crits-Christoph, Cooper, & Luborsky, 1988); and (4) in the mastery of the central relationship patterns, because such mastery appears to correlate with the outcomes of psychotherapy (Grenyer & Luborsky, 1996).

In making clinical case formulations guided by the CCRT method, the following assumptions are basic:

1. The unit of text to be scored is the narrative told during sessions about relationship episodes with other people and with the self.
2. The CCRT can be reliably extracted from the relationship episodes.
3. The CCRT is based on pervasiveness: the frequency-across-relationship episodes is the numerator; the denominator is the number of relationship episodes examined.
4. The CCRT is a central pattern, for it underlies a variety of relationship interactions and is associated with the major conflicts in psychotherapy.

In all these assumptions the CCRT method fits within the field of "object relations" methods. The formulation of the CCRT includes both interpersonal and intrapersonal conflicts. The conflicts are of two main kinds. The first type is conflict between wishes; for example, in a phobia case (Luborsky & Luborsky, 1995) the wish for independence in the face of another person's potential control conflicts with another wish, which is for getting guidance from the other person and not displeasing that person. The second type of conflict is more interpersonal, although still from the patient's viewpoint: between the W (Wish) component and the RO (Responses from Others) component.

INCLUSION/EXCLUSION CRITERIA

All people, whether they have a psychiatric diagnosis or not, when they tell relationship episodes provide material for assessment of their CCRT. As Freud (1912/1958, p. 100) said, people have "one relationship template (or several such)." The experience with the method suggests that it can be applied to people across all levels of psychiatric severity and the CCRT pattern is unique for each person.

STEPS IN CASE FORMULATION CONSTRUCTION

There are two very different settings in which a CCRT is formulated: (1) *during the session*, when the patient tells narratives to a therapist and the therapist uses them in the session to make formulations; (2) *after the session*, when an evaluator or researcher reviews the narratives, usually when the session is in transcript form (rather than on tape or videotape), and scores the CCRT.

The CCRT can form the heart of a case formulation. The procedures for scoring the CCRT *during the ongoing session* are given later in the chapter under "Applications" and "The Therapist's During-the-Session CCRT Formulations," as well as in the clinical guide by Book (1998), which presents many helpful examples. The usual *after-the-session* CCRT procedures follow.

The After-the-Session CCRT from Relationship Episodes Told during Psychotherapy

As in the diagram of the method of CCRT formulation shown in Figure 3.1, the CCRT scoring is in two phases: phase A is for locating the relationship episodes, and phase B is for extracting the CCRT from the relationship episodes.

By far the most usual source of relationship episodes is psychotherapy sessions. These episodes are almost always spontaneously told. On the average about four relationship episodes are told per session. These episodes are defined as the part of a session in which there is an explicit narrative about relationships with others or at times with the self.

First, these relationship episodes are marked off on a transcript of the session by an experienced independent "prescoring judge." Second, these episodes are then scored by "CCRT judges" (see "Case Example," below, for details of scoring). The CCRT scoring is done with knowledge of the narra-

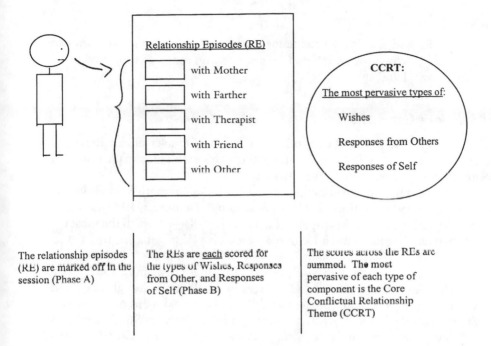

Relationship Episodes (RE)

with Mother

with Farther

with Therapist

with Friend

with Other

CCRT:

The most pervasive types of:

Wishes

Responses from Others

Responses of Self

The relationship episodes (RE) are marked off in the session (Phase A)

The REs are each scored for the types of Wishes, Responses from Other, and Responses of Self (Phase B)

The scores across the REs are summed. The most pervasive of each type of component is the Core Conflictual Relationship Theme (CCRT)

FIGURE 3.1. How to see the CCRT: A diagram of the CCRT procedure.

tives in the context of the session. This in-context-of-the-session scoring may be essential in guiding the scorer to the most accurate assessment.

Each relationship episode (RE) has a main other person with whom the patient interacts in the course of the narratives, and it is part of the prescoring judge's job to designate the main other person and the boundaries of the episodes. These episodes tend to be easy to recognize because they have a typical narrative structure, with a beginning, middle, and ending. Also, just before the patient begins to tell a narrative, the intention to tell it is often introduced by some usual signs, such as a pause followed by a direct statement introducing the narrative, such as "I met *Joe* today and we had a chance to talk it out" (the naming of another person with whom an event has occurred is a good sign of the beginning of a narrative), or "I have this problem and here's an example of what happened with Ruth" (Luborsky, Barber, & Diguer, 1992).

Scoring Methods (see also Appendix A)

Scoring Units

The prescoring judge also identifies the scorable components in each relationship episode by underlining or by slash marks before and after the scorable thought units and the component in the scorable thought unit, that is, a W, RO, or RS (see Appendix A).

Tailor-Made Categories

The CCRT judge first does the tailor-made categories. These categories are the types of components inferred by each clinical judge as expressed in the judge's own language.

Standard Categories

In contrast, the standard categories specify a uniform set of categories that are to be used by all judges. The judge translates each tailor-made statement into the best-fitting standard categories.

These standard categories come in at least four alternative sets: Edition 1 (Luborsky, 1986), Edition 2 (Crits-Christoph & Demorest, 1988), and Edition 3 (Barber, Crits-Christoph, & Luborsky, 1998)—of which the most recommended for ease of use is Edition 3, based on a cluster analysis that yielded eight Ws, eight ROs, and eight RSs—and a fourth set provided by the Structural Analysis of Social Behavior (SASB) categories (Benjamin, 1993, Chap. 3). The SASB categories have advantages in reliability, although one disadvantage is that their conceptual space is limited to two dimensions. (Two different central relationship pattern scoring methods rely on SASB categories: the one by Schacht, Binder, & Strupp, 1984, and the one by Crits-Christoph & Demorest, 1991.)

The Most Desirable Range of Inference for Proper Scoring

A range with two main levels of inference must be distinguished: (1) the manifest statements of the patient that directly fit each scorable category so that almost no inference (or very little) is required; (2) the moderate level of inference for a scorable category, to be noted by putting parentheses around the component, such as (W). For example, the *RE Thought Unit*: "So I don't even have unemployment coming in" is the *CCRT Scoring*: (W) wants to get money (Edition 2 standard categories: 13, 23). A third, higher level of inference should not be used because such categories tend not to be reliably scorable; examples of these are masochism and libido.

Positive and Negative Responses

Each scorable thought unit is also given either a positive or negative response score for both ROs and RSs (Luborsky, 1998a). Note that the score is a judgment *from the patient's point of view*. The positive and negative are further subdivided: a strong positive is PP, moderate positive is P, moderate negative is N, and a strong negative is NN (the P and N are illustrated in the REs in Appendix A). The idea for this type of scoring distinction follows Freud (1912/1958a), who designated transference patterns as either positive or negative.

The Intensity of Each Type of Component (Optional)

Intensity is rated on a 1–5 scale for each type of component, with 1 as "little or none" and 5 as "very much." Intensity in the thought unit refers to the degree to which the patient experiences, or is inferred to experience, affect. As an example on a 1–5 scale, the thought unit "that irritated me" would be rated 4; "I wish to assert this" would be rated 3.

Further studies of intensities reveal a moderate correlation between intensity of the type of component with the frequency of appearance of that type of component. If the correlation is high, the ratings of intensity may be redundant and so not worth doing; currently this rating is therefore optional.

Subdivision of ROs (Optional)

It may make a difference that patients sometimes distinguish ROs that are expected from ROs that have happened. Those that are expected should be scored as "RO-expected" so that we can check and see whether these have different significance from the ROs that have happened.

Time Required for Scoring the CCRT

A formulation of the CCRT during a psychotherapy session takes no extra time, for it is done in the session. The therapist who is familiar with the CCRT from time to time will organize what the patient says into the CCRT framework.

In scoring a transcript of a session, however, it takes about 3 hours to score 10 relationship episodes. That may seem to be a lot, but it can take a bit less time after practice. Generally, this time required is less than that for the other transference-related measures. Typically, this type of scoring is done for research purposes by an experienced CCRT judge.

Randomization of Narratives before Scoring

For some research purposes it may be of value to randomize the narratives so that the judge has no information about the set of narratives from which each narrative came, as in Crits-Christoph and Demorest (1991) and Crits-Christoph, Demorest, and Connolly (1990). But for the usual unrandomized method recommended here the judge has the advantage of knowing the other narratives told by the patient; this should help estimate the correct meaning of the components of the narrative. A study is needed comparing the usual method with the randomized method.

Additional CCRT Procedures

The Relationship Anecdote Paradigms Interview

This Relationship Anecdote Paradigms (RAP) interview method of obtaining narratives about relationships hugely broadens the sources for obtaining data for the CCRT (Luborsky, 1998d, Chap. 7). It does this by an interview that is specifically designed to have the patient tell relationship episodes, usually 10 of them in about 30 minutes. The estimated time happens to be the mean length of the interview after the patient is told at the outset to tell 10 narratives with *about* 3 minutes per narrative. From the information we have so far, these RAP narratives are scorable in ways that give somewhat similar results to the session narratives told in the course of psychotherapy (Barber, Luborsky, Crits-Christoph, & Diguer, 1995).

The CCRT Self-Report Questionnaire

A questionnaire form of the CCRT by Crits-Christoph (1986) was used in an early study by Crits-Christoph and Luborsky (1998b, Chap. 14). Likewise in Luborsky, Crits-Christoph, and Alexander (1990) the same questionnaire yielded interesting correlations between the CCRT categories from the CCRT questionnaire and repressive style measures.

There are high correlations of CCRT wishes with each other across methods: for example, "Wish: dominance" from the questionnaire correlated .85 ($p < .001$) with "Wish: to be competitive" from the self-interpretation of the narratives.

At least three versions of the CCRT questionnaire are now in varying states of completion, one by Barber (1989), another by Dahlbender et al. (1990), and yet another by Leichsenring and Seinfeldt (1996). However, the questionnaire method does not yet have a validity study that compares the CCRT questionnaire with the usual CCRT from psychotherapy sessions.

The Self-Interpretation of the CCRT

A self-interpretation procedure can be used to learn more about how much of their CCRT patients are aware of or can become aware of. The patient is given a transcript of the patient's narratives and asked to interpret them. The self-interpretation procedure (Luborsky, 1965) can be used for the narratives from the session or for the RAP narratives as illustrated by Crits-Christoph (1986). The perspective of the clinicians has some similarity to that of the patients (Crits-Christoph & Luborsky, 1998b).

A CCRT Scoring Method Based on the Sequence of Components

The usual CCRT method relies on the highest frequency of each type of CCRT component regardless of whether it is or is not presented in the relationship episode as part of a sequence of components. The sequence-of-components method is an alternative scoring method that focuses only on sequences of components in the relationship episode (Albani et al., 1990), as in this example from RE #1: W: "I went on appeal" → NRO: "And then the employers are denying me unemployment" → NRS: "I really don't know what move to take."

APPLICATION TO PSYCHOTHERAPY TECHNIQUE

Help in Formulating

In most forms of psychotherapy, and certainly in dynamic psychotherapy, the therapist continually tries and retries to make an accurate formulation of the patient's main conflicts (Luborsky, 1994). Accurate formulations will lead to accurate interpretations, as well as limit the countertransference expressed in the interpretations (Singer & Luborsky, 1977).

How to make accurate formulations and interpretations in supportive-expressive dynamic psychotherapy is explained for patients in general in Luborsky (1984); for depressed patients in Luborsky, Mark, Hole, Popp, et al. (1995); for opiate-addicted patients in Luborsky, Woody, Hole, and Velleco (1995); for cocaine-addicted patients in Mark and Luborsky (1991) and Mark and Faude (1995); and for marijuana-addicted patients in Grenyer, Luborsky, and Solowij (1995).

To formulate the CCRT during a session the therapist listens for the redundant components across the narratives that patients tell. The CCRT is formulated by keeping track of the most redundant Ws, ROs, and RSs.

Help with Shaping Interpretations

As a general principle, the shorter the time limit of the treatment, the more a consistent focus of interpretations on the CCRT is useful. The consistent focus on the CCRT provides more impetus for the patient's recognition of the CCRT pattern and gradually provides more stimulus to the patient's growth through mastering conflicts in the pattern.

Because the CCRT is a complex formulation, it is rarely appropriate to present the entire CCRT in one interpretation. Instead, these guidelines will help in deciding how to present the CCRT piecemeal so that the patient builds up a concept of a main pattern and attends to the mastery of the problems within it:

1. Begin with the aspects of the CCRT that the patient is able to deal with most readily.

2. Choose interpretations that especially involve the W and the RO components; there is more support for the use of these components in interpretations (Crits-Christoph, Cooper, & Luborsky, 1998).

3. Fashion some interpretations with CCRT components that contain the symptom. In this way the patient will form a concept of the context in which the symptom appears. As with Ms. Smyth (see Table 3.1 below in the "Case Example" section), "You want to be helped but are rejected and so become depressed."

4. Especially concentrate interpretations on the negative components, as Freud (1912/1958b) recommends.

5. Choose a style of interpretation that helps strengthen the alliance and does not provoke resistance, as Wachtel (1993) suggests. A blaming, confrontational, or putting-down manner of providing interpretations stimulates resistance.

6. Where needed, ask the patient for elaborations of some of the narratives so that they will be filled out more completely. It can be useful to ask the patient to describe more fully some parts of an event or an experience; such elaboration can be helpful to the patient as well as to the therapist. With one patient, for example, she felt on coming into the session "an experience of feeling little, almost fainting and having an adrenaline rush." The therapist asked her to tell more about that experience and finally was able to say, "So I hear you better now; you are feeling very little and helpless in relation to me and that scares you and depresses you."

Help with the Treatment Atmosphere

In short-term hospital settings the CCRT has a special value. When the initial evaluation team includes a CCRT and then uses it to set treatment goals, the atmosphere of the residential setting becomes more treatment and less custodially oriented (Luborsky, Van Ravenswaay, Ball, Steinman, et al., 1993).

CASE EXAMPLE

The patient for this main example is Ms. Sandy Smyth, who was treated in supportive–expressive (SE) dynamic psychotherapy for depression (Luborsky & Friedman, in press). The example illustrates (1) how a helping alliance is formed, (2) how to use the relationship episodes to derive a CCRT (Luborsky, 1998a, Chap. 2), and (3) how to use the CCRT as a focus of the interpretations (Luborsky, in press-b, Chap. 15; Luborsky, Popp, Luborsky, & Mark, 1994).

> Ms. Smyth was a 32-year-old single woman, a recovering alcoholic, who came for treatment for depression. On top of her long-term dysthymia (chronic depression) she had become severely depressed (major depression) when she flunked out of a training course. In fact, her DSM-III-R diagnosis based on the initial evaluation was "major depression with dysthymia."
>
> The therapy began inauspiciously when she showed up a half an hour late and then said she was unable to schedule the next appointment. The therapist felt filled with anger but contained the anger and used her own awareness of it to understand and to empathize with what the patient was doing in the interaction with her. When the patient said she was afraid of "sabotaging herself," the therapist replied that she thought the patient was correct to be afraid. Although the patient continued to have difficulty keeping appointments she nevertheless responded to the treatment remarkably

well, much to the surprise of the therapist, who noted in her final report that she "had not expected that someone with such severe depression and who already was making full use of self help via therapeutic groups, such as AA, could have resolved her depression without the use of psychopharmacology."

In the termination interview she said she was feeling good and "everything is a lot better." She was less pessimistic and more confident and hopeful. She felt she could take care of herself and no longer showed the disorganized quality she had shown at the time of the initial evaluation. She was working regularly in a clerical job, and she had set up a stable living arrangement with a female roommate.

At 6 months posttermination she had remained free of depression; her Beck Depression Inventory was 9. She had continued working full-time at the same job. She found she was pregnant by the man who she had been seeing for the last 5 months of the treatment. She plans to be married, but the man is uncertain. She is angry and anxious but feels she can handle whatever happens, and she will have the baby. She and the boyfriend have started weekly couples therapy and will continue it.

A helping relationship in psychotherapy appeared to come about (1) through the communication of the therapist's intention to be helpful and caring about the patient's best interests and concerns and (2) through the therapist's interpretative focus around the patient's having maintained self-hurting relationships with a boyfriend and others who were painfully the opposite of caring and helpful. The therapist was surprised at the patient's good response to the therapy, but it is a not uncommon response that a good alliance forms as a consequence of the therapist's helpful and accurate interpretive focus.

The Therapist's During-the-Session CCRT Formulation

An example is given in Table 3.1 derived from Ms. Smyth's session 3. It includes (1) four relationship episodes from that session, (2) the CCRT as the therapist formulated it while listening to the session's relationship episodes, and (3) two samples of accurate interpretations based on the CCRT. In formulating the CCRT through the steps diagrammed in Figure 3.1, the therapist had examined the relationship episodes with each of the main people who were the subject of the session's narratives. The therapist saw the CCRT's components within all four relationship episodes.

The use of the CCRT to help the patient to become aware of the relationship context in which depression appears is illustrated by two sample interpretations given at the bottom of Table 3.1. In each interpretation special prominence is given to the symptom by its inclusion in its context of relationship conflicts, for example, the therapist said, "I see you get depressed after you deal with people who won't give you what you need." This is an accurate interpretation, for it fits with the CCRT as derived by the therapist (as well as independently derived by researchers, as given below).

TABLE 3.1. A Therapist's Version of Ms. Smyth's CCRT within a Session: (1) Four Relationship Episodes (REs) from Session 3; (2) Formulation of the CCRT; (3) Sample of "Accurate" Interpretations

(1)
Four Relationship Episodes

The other person in the relationship episode	CCRT components in each episode		
	W: Wish	RO: Response from Other	RS: Response of Self
RE1: Therapist	W1: I want treatment	RO1: Will not give treatment without money	RS1: Unhappy, Depression
RE2: Ex-employer	W1: I want job and help	RO1: Discharges me	RS2: Helpless RS1: Depression, Discouragement
RE3: Brother	W1: I want care	RO1: Treats me badly	RS3: Get angry, Discouragement RS1: Depression
RE4: Boyfriend	W1: I want him to care	RO1: Gives no support	RS1: Crying, sad RS3: Anger

(2)
CCRT formulation by the therapist during the session

W1:   4REs: To get care and support
RO1: 4REs: Rejects
RS1: 4REs: Discouragement and depression
RS3: 2REs: Anger
RS2: 1RE: Helplessness

(3)
A sample of "accurate" interpretations based on the CCRT

Interpretation: "I see you get depressed after you deal with people who won't give you what you need"
Interpretation: "You could see me as one of those people"

Researcher's After-the-Session CCRT Formulation

A sample of four scored REs, also from Session 3, are given here so that they can serve as a much needed scoring model for researchers and other assessors (Appendix A). The summary of the scores from the REs are given in Table 3.2; it is a later edition of the one in Luborsky & Friedman, in press, Chap. 4).

These are the steps to be followed by researchers and other assessors in the current CCRT scoring procedures (as a supplement to Appendix B):

1. *Use only reasonably complete REs.* Only those REs in the transcript are included that have a rating of completeness of 2.5 or greater on the five-point completeness scale (Luborsky, 1998a, Chap. 2). These ratings are mostly easy to make; further anchors are noted in Luborsky and Crits-Christoph (1998, Chap. 2).

2. *Use only scorable thought units.* A prescoring judge divides the transcript for each RE into thought units marked off by double slashes. Then, only for the scorable thought units, that is, thought units that the prescoring judge

TABLE 3.2. A Researcher's CCRT Summary from Four REs in Session 3 (Ms. Sandy Smyth)

Judge: LL
Date: June 2, 1995

Tailor-made categories	RE #	Two top standard categories (Edition 2)	Summary: Most frequent categories and their REs	Frequency across different REs	Clusters (Edition 3)
Wishes			**Wishes**		
Wants money	1	(13, 23)	23[1, 3, 4][a]	3	#1
For help	1	(13, 34)	(to be independent)		
Wants job	2	(13?, 22)	13[1, 2][b]	2	#3
Get out of bad relationship	3	(28, 23)	(to be helped)		
Be in good relationship	3	(25?, 14?)			
Reject him	4	(18, 23)			
Not to feel isolated	4	(32, 24)			
Negative Responses from Other			**Negative Responses from Other**		
Stop me from money	1	(14, 4)	4[1, 2, 3, 4]	4	#5
Fired me	1	(4, 17)	(rejecting)		
Cut off help	1	(14, 4)	14[1, 2, 4]	3	#5
Rejected for job	2	(4, 14)	(Unhelpful)		
Rejecting	3	(6, 4)			
Negative person	3	(25, 10)			
Dishonest	3	(8, 15)			
Put me down	3	(4, 15)			
Rejecting	4	(4, 10?)			
Stop talking to me	4	(4, 10)			
Gave no support	4	(14, 4)			
Positive Response from Other					
Friends gave support	4	(13, 9)			
Negative Response of Self			**Negative Response of Self**		
Can't get money	1	(17, 20)	22[1, 2, 3, 4]	4	#7
Helpless	1	(17, 19)	(Depressed)		
Depressed	1	(22, 20)	20[1, 2, 4]	3	#7
Anger	2	(21, 20?)	(Disappointed)		
No job	2	(17, 20?)	21[2, 3, 4]	3	#7
			(Angry)		
Horrible state	2	(22, 20)	6[3, 4]	2	#2
			(Dislike others)		
Helpless	2	(19, 17)	17[1, 2]	2	#6
Discouraged	2	(22, 20)	(Helpless)		
Feel bad	3	(26, 22)			
Feel bad	3	(22?, 26?)			
Dislike others	3	(6, 21)			
Anger	4	(21, 6)			
Stop contact	4	(11, 21)			
Lonely, crying	4	(23, 22)			
Isolated	4	(23, 20)			
Positive Response of Self					
Stop bad relationship	4	(14, 15)			
Assertive	4	(15, 11)			

[a]Each of the top frequency standard categories and, in brackets, the RE number in which they appeared.
[b]The count is for the two top standard categories.

considers as Ws, ROs, or RSs, the judge notes the component to be scored just above the beginning of the thought unit.

3. *Score the same thought units by all CCRT judges.* All CCRT judges score the same transcript prepared by the prescoring judge that notes the thought unit to be scored (to save time the first CCRT judge can also serve as the prescoring judge). The CCRT judge writes the tailor-made statement on the left margin of the transcript. Then the judges score each thought unit in terms of standard categories. Two options are recommended: (1) choose the two best-fitting standard categories from Edition 2 (and translate into Edition 3), as in the example "Four REs from Ms. Sandy Smyth, Session 3" in Appendix A. (2) A useful alternative is to rate all of the standard categories in Edition 2 for each thought unit on the forms provided in Appendix B. The score for each category would be the highest mean ratings of the categories (as illustrated in Luborsky, Luborsky, Diguer, Schaffler, et al., 1995).

4. *Summarize the results by counting only one component per RE.* Only one type of CCRT component is counted *per RE* for the summary in Table 3.2. The rationale for this rule is that the CCRT is constructed to reflect redundancy *across Res*, not within REs. For example (see Table 3.2), Wish 13 appears several times *within* RE #1 but is only counted once. It is the second most frequent Wish *across* the four REs; it appears in two REs: RE #1 and RE #2. The summary in Table 3.2 contains this patient's CCRT: the Wish is, "I want to be independent" (present in three of the four REs); the Response from Other is "rejecting" (in four of the four REs); and the Response of Self is "gets depressed" (in four of the four REs) or "I get disappointed" (in three of the four REs).

5. *Compare judges' agreement by weighted Kappas.* Agreements between pairs of CCRT judges are computed according to Luborsky and Diguer's (1998) weighting system: 1.00 for perfect agreement; .66 for first-second or second-first; .33 for both second places. Cohen's weighted kappa is computed from these weights.

TRAINING

The training of therapists to use the method during psychotherapy sessions only requires that they learn the basics of the CCRT method. In contrast, training to use the method in research means knowing all of the basics plus the fine points (as in the "case example," above).

The beginning step in training is to read the usual descriptions of the CCRT method such as the one in Luborsky (1998a, Chap. 2). A further helpful exercise is to examine the illustrations of scoring of the three cases given in Luborsky and Friedman (in press). The text of the relationship episode is given on the right side of the page and its scoring on the left. To gain more skill in scoring, the reader should cover the scoring on the left and score the text on the right and then compare with the scoring on the left. Only score the parts of the text with thought units that begin with a notation of the component. Then, a few more practice cases may be scored followed by checking the scoring. To be useful in reliability studies, a candidate scorer should agree, perhaps as high as a correlation of .75, with other judges.

RESEARCH SUPPORT FOR THE APPROACH
Reliability of Scoring the CCRT

The reliability of the CCRT is generally good. A recent review (Luborsky & Diguer, in press) includes reliability of scoring for eight samples from six studies. The reliabilities across the studies are not markedly different from sample to sample or even from component to component: for W the weighted kappa is .60; for RO the weighted kappa is .68; and for RS the weighted kappa is .71. Because of the consistency in level of reliability across almost all studies, we expect that future studies will generally show at least this level of reliability. This level was obtained even though none of these samples used many of the recently developed currently recommended reliability procedures (see "Case Example," above).

The currently recommended scoring procedures include these improvements over past reliability procedures (Luborsky & Diguer, 1994):

1. An independent prescoring judge prepares the transcript for the CCRT judges to do their scoring. The prescoring judge identifies the thought units to be scored by the CCRT judges so that they all score the same units, and he or she identifies the type of component to be scored in each unit.
2. The CCRT judges score the two top-ranking categories or, even better, all of the types of categories to be scored.
3. The CCRT judges selected are ones who have been able, after practice, to reach a particular level of agreement with other judges (about .75).
4. The entire sample should be rated by the same judges rather than by each judge rating only part of the sample.
5. The similarity of scoring of each of the judges should be measured by the weighting system devised by Diguer and Luborsky (1998), which gives different weights to different degrees of similarity.

Validity

Comparisons of the CCRT with Other Measures of Central Relationship Patterns

Several of these studies have been done but none systematically. The other measures show impressively similar results to the CCRT. Examples of these studies include Horowitz, Luborsky, and Popp (1991), Luborsky and Barber (1994), Luborsky, Barber, Binder, Curtis, et al. (1993), and Luborsky, Popp, and Barber (1994).

Characteristics of the CCRT

The following are a sample of some of the correlates of the CCRT. A more extensive review along with discussion of the meaning of the findings for the understanding of the CCRT is reviewed in Luborsky, Kächele, Dahlbender, and Diguer (1997) and in *The CCRT Newsletter* (Luborsky, Kächele, & Dahl bender, 1991–1997, Chap. 18), and Luborsky (1998c).

1. *Narratives about relationship episodes are routinely told in psychotherapy sessions.* The average number of relationship episodes per session is 4.1, with a range from 1 to 7 (as reported in Luborsky, Barber, Schaffler, & Cacciola, in press, Chap. 8, and Luborsky, Barber, & Diguer, 1992).

2. *Similar CCRTs appear in different states of consciousness.* A similar CCRT appears in dreams as in waking narratives (Popp et al., 1996).

3. *The most usual types of CCRTs have been established.* In the Penn Psychotherapy Study (Luborsky & Crits-Christoph, 1990, Table 8–3) the most frequent Wish is to be close and accepting, the most frequent Response from Other is rejecting and opposing, and the most frequent Responses of Self are disappointed, depressed, and angry.

4. *Narratives told outside of sessions are similar to narratives told in sessions.* Significant similarity has been shown for the CCRT before psychotherapy (the RAP interview) versus the CCRT from the early psychotherapy sessions (Barber, Luborsky, Crits-Christoph, & Diguer, 1995).

5. *Over the period of treatment the CCRTs show some consistency.* The pervasiveness of the CCRT from beginning to end of psychotherapy shows moderate consistency, with the wish showing the greatest consistency (Crits-Christoph & Luborsky, 1998a).

6. *Differences in CCRTs for different diagnoses have not been established.* There are many such studies; for example, one of the earliest is for major depression by Eckert, Luborsky, Barber, and Crits-Christoph (1990, Chap. 16). However, comparisons with other diagnoses have not yet been attempted.

7. *Some consistency was found in CCRTs over the lifespan.* There are a few studies that show some signs of such consistency, for example, the CCRT of children at age three and the same children at age five (Luborsky, Luborsky, Diguer, Schaffler, et al., 1995) and a study in progress on changes during adolescence (Waldinger, Guastella, Diguer, Luborsky, & Hauser, 1997).

8. *Consistency of CCRTs within each person across different types of other people has been shown.* This consistency was expected on the basis of Freud's (1912/1958a) observation that the transference template tends to be a general pattern across relationships with other people, including parents and other close relationships. Similarly, in our experience a pattern appears across the different other people within each person's narratives. This has been demonstrated in a sample of 35 patients in the Penn Psychotherapy Study (Fried, Crits-Christoph, & Luborsky, 1992) showing that the CCRT for the therapist is significantly similar to the CCRT for other people.

9. *Associations of the CCRT with defenses have been shown.* Evidence has been accumulating for associations between the CCRT and some defenses. The first of these studies is that of Luborsky, Crits-Christoph, and Alexander (1990), where relationships were shown between the CCRT and measures of repression.

10. *Greater pervasiveness of CCRT components in narratives has been shown to be associated with greater psychiatric severity.* The recent study by Cierpka et al. (1997) has shown that greater pervasiveness of components across narratives is associated with greater psychiatric severity, a finding that would be expected but had not been shown before.

APPENDIX A

Symbols for CCRT Scoring

// //	Slashes mark the beginning and end of each thought unit.
W, RO, or RS	Abbreviations of Wish, Response from Other, or Response of Self components are placed in the text at the start of each *scorable* thought unit (by the prescoring judge); these are to be scored (by the CCRT judges) in the left margin at the beginning of the thought unit.
( )	Parentheses around a component mean that the score is inferential rather than manifest.
P or N	Placed before all ROs and RSs; stands for positive or negative (toward or against the satisfaction of the Wishes).
(20, 17)	Two numbers in parentheses after the tailor-made categories on the left margin are the standard category numbers. The first number is the best-fitting category; the second is the next-best fitting category. A line under a number means it is an exact fit to a category in the list; a question mark means a questionable fit.
- - -	Interrupted or broken-off speech.
xxx	Inaudible word.
xxx- - -	Inaudible text longer than one word.
. . .	Section of text omitted in this example.

Four REs from Ms. Sandy Smyth, Session 3

CCRT SCORING	RELATIONSHIP EPISODES from
	RE #1: Ex-Employers, completeness rating 2.5
NRS: Can't get money (17, 20)	P: //RS I cannot collect unemployment//RO because the
NRO: Stop me from money (14, 4)	ex-employers who put in a big stink, //W so I don't
(W) Wants help to get money (13, 23)	even have unemployment coming in.//
	T: xxx(inaudible)
NRO: Fired me (4, 17)	P: //RO The ex-employers who fired - - //W I went on

W: Asked for help (13, 34)

NRO: Cut off help (14, 4)

NRS: Helpless (17, 19)

NRS: Depressed (22, 20)

appeal // ^{RO}and then the employers (clears throat) are denying me unemployment,// ^{RS}I mean I really don't know - - what move to take. //^{RS}(pause)It's horrible.

RE #2: Ex-employers, completeness rating 4.0

NRO: Rejected for job (4, 14)

//^{RO}And then the other job was ah, they didn't even give me a chance. // I was supposed to work on this computer and the computer wasn't hooked up and they said, well you don't have to work it. // We're replacing you with somebody else. // So I was replaced with somebody else. //^{RS}It really pissed me

NRS: Anger (21, 20?)

NRS: Have no job, nothing (17, 20?)

NRS: Horrible state (22, 20)

W: I want job (help) (13?, 22)

off // ^{RS}(pause) cause I gave up another job to get this job and I ended up with nothing at all, no unemployment, no nothing. //^{RS}It's horrible. //^WI call 'em every day, // but they always say we don't have anything. // It's just terrible. //^{RS}Because I don't know

NRS: Helpless (19, 17)

what I'm going to do. //(Pause) ^{RS}It's really

NRS: Discouraged (22, 20)

discouraging. //It's so hard to get out and—get the door slammed in my face constantly. (pause)//

RE #3: Brother and sister-in-law, completeness rating 4.5

(W): To get out of bad relationship (28, 23)

NRO: Rejecting (6, 4)

//^WAnyway, I want to move out of Bob and Jane's (brother and sister-in-law) house as soon as possible.

//^{RO}Treated like a second rate citizen there. //^{RS}It's not

NRS: Feel bad about self (26, 22)

W: To be in good relationship (25?, 14?)

NRS: Feel bad (22?, 26?)

NRO: Negative (25,10)

NRO: Dishonest (8,15)

NRO: Put me down (4,15)

very good for my self-esteem. //Like they're both addicts and they have the personality of addicts. //(pause) ^WI guess —I, I much rather be around sober people. // . . . Yeah. The old tapes start running and it's just real bad. //^{RS}I mean I start thinking negatively as soon as I'm around them, //^{RO} cause they're both negative. //^{RO}They're dishonest.

//^{RO}They're acting like they're doing me a big favor,// but I'm paying half the rent there, for their apartment // and I have this tiny little room, no closet, and their junk's in the room and uh I have to work around

NRS: Dislikes others (6, 21)

their lives. //^{RS}(pause) So, I, ah just can't stand them.//

RE #4: *Boyfriend*, completeness rating 5.0

PRS: Stop a bad relationship (14,15)	[RS]Yeah, I've, and I've stopped speaking to that
NRO: Rejecting (4, 10?)	married guy //[RO]cause he got to be a real asshole.
PRS: Assertive against	about stopping, bad//[RS]I mean I'm not
negative relationships (15,11)	
	taking any shit from anybody this year - - for the rest
	of my life //[RO]and uh, he just sort of stopped
NRO: Stop talking to me (4, 10)	talking to me and uh, he didn't
	contact me, //he didn't even - - (ask?) where was I going to
NRS: Anger (21, 6)	move to this week. //He didn't contact me //[RS]so
NRS: I stop contact with him (11, 21)	screw him, // [RS]I'm not going to contact him not at all
	either . . . //it just makes me mad. //[W]I really don't
W: Reject other (18, 23)	want anything at all to do with him. //Never again
	will I - - [RS]Christmas eve I spent alone in church
NRS: Lonely, crying (23, 22)	crying my eyes out cause it was an intensely lonely
	feeling. //[W]and I said no way am I ever gonna feel
W: Not to feel isolated (32, 24)	that bad again. No way. // [RS]I'm isolated from my
NRS: Isolated (23, 20)	friends and family because of this guy I wanted - - this
	married guy. //It's just a conflict between honesty and
PRO: Friends gave support (<u>13</u>, 9)	dishonesty. // . . . I just ah, he pissed me off. //[RO]All
	my other friends gave me all kinds of moral support,
	even some financial support for this horrible dilemma
NRO: Gave no support (<u>14</u>, 4)	I'm in right now. //[RO]He didn't do shit . . . //He
	didn't buy me a Christmas present or a card, or a
	birthday - - //

APPENDIX B

Thought Unit (1–5 Scale) Ratings·

Standard CCRT Categories
WISHES
Date: _____
Rated by: _____
(Write in the Thought Unit →
and rate it and note P or N)

Edition 3 (clusters)	Edition 2																
1. to assert self and	21. to have self-control																
be independent	28. to be my own person																
	34. to assert myself																
	23. to be independent																
2. to oppose, hurt,	18. to oppose others																
and control others	16. to hurt others																
	19. to have control of others																
3. to be	15. to be hurt																
controlled,	20. to be controlled by others																
hurt, and not	29. to be *not* respon/obligated																
responsible	13. to be helped																
	27. to be liked by others																
4. to be distant and	17. to avoid conflicts																
avoid conflicts	14. to not be hurt																
	10. to be distant from others																
5. to be close and	4. to accept others																
accepting	5. to respect others																
	9. to be open																
	6. to have trust																
	8. to be opened up to																
	11. to be close to others																
6. to be loved and	33. to be loved																
understood	3. to be respected																
	1. to be understood																

	2. to be accepted																				
	7. to be liked																				
7. to feel good and comfortable	30. to have stability																				
	31. to feel comfortable																				
	32. to feel happy																				
	24. to feel good about self																				
8. to achieve and help others	22. to achieve																				
	25. to better myself																				
	12. to help others																				
	26. to be good																				

Thought Unit (1–5 Scale) Ratings

Standard CCRT Categories
RESPONSES FROM OTHER
Date: _____
Rated by: _____
(Write in the Thought Unit →
and rate it and note P or N)

Edition 3 (clusters)	Edition 2																	
1. strong	24. strong																	
	23. independent																	
	29. happy																	
2. controlling	26. strict																	
	20. controlling																	
3. upset	16. hurt																	
	22. dependent																	
	28. anxious																	
	27. angry																	
	19. out of control																	
4. bad	8. not trustworthy																	
	25. bad																	
5. rejecting and opposing	7. don't trust me																	
	6. don't respect me																	

		Thought Unit (1–5 Scale) Ratings
	2. are not understanding	
	4. rejecting	
	10. dislike me	
	12. distant	
	14. unhelpful	
	17. oppose me	
	15. hurt me	
6. helpful	13. are helpful	
	18. cooperative	
7. likes me	30. loves me	
	5. respects me	
	9. likes me	
	21. gives me independence	
8. understanding	11. open	
	1. understanding	
	3. accepting	

Thought Unit (1–5 Scale) Ratings

Standard CCRT Categories
RESPONSES OF SELF
Date: _____
Rated by: _____
(Write in the Thought Unit →
and Rate it and note P or N)

Edition 3 (clusters)	Edition 2	
1. helpful	7. am open	
	1. understand	
	9. am helpful	
2. unreceptive	2. don't understand	
	8. am not open	
	6. dislike others	
3. respected and	28. feel comfortable	
accepted	29. feel happy	

	30. feel loved																				
	4. feel respected																				
	3. feel accepted																				
	5. like others																				
4. oppose and hurt others	11. oppose others																				
	10. hurt others																				
5. self-controlled and self-confident	14. self-controlled																				
	15. independent																				
	18. self-confident																				
	12. controlling																				
6. helpless	13. out-of-control																				
	17. helpless																				
	19. uncertain																				
	16. dependent																				
7. disappointed and depressed	21. angry																				
	20. disappointed																				
	22. depressed																				
	23. unloved																				
	24. jealous																				
8. anxious and ashamed	27. anxious																				
	26. ashamed																				
	25. guilty																				

ACKNOWLEDGMENTS

This paper was supported in part by Research Scientist Award No. MH 40710-22; by NIDA Grant No. 5U18 DA07085 and NIDA Research Scientist Award No. 2KO5 DA00168-24 (to Lester Luborsky); and NIMH Clinical Research Center Grant No. MH 45178 (to Paul Crits-Christoph).

REFERENCES

Albani, C., Dahlbender, R., Pokorny, D., Kächele, H., Geyer, M., & Cierpka, M. (1990). *A sequence-of-components method for the CCRT.* Manuscript in preparation.
Barber, J. P. (1989). *The Central Relationship Questionnaire.* Manuscript in preparation.

Barber, J. P., Foltz, C., Mone, J. Q., & Weinryb, R. M. (1997). *Consistency of themes across interpersonal relationships.* Manuscript in preparation.

Barber, J. P., Crits-Christoph, P., & Luborsky, L. (1998). A guide to CCRT standard categories and their classification. In L. Luborsky & P. Crits-Christoph (Eds.), *Understanding transference: A guide to the CCRT—The Core Conflictual Relationship Theme method in research and practice* (Rev. ed.). Washington, DC: APA Books.

Barber, J. P., Luborsky, L., Crits-Christoph, P., & Diguer, L. (1995). A comparison of Core Conflictual Relationship Themes before psychotherapy and during early sessions. *Journal of Consulting and Clinical Psychology, 63,* 145–148.

Benjamin, L. S. (1993). *Interpersonal diagnosis and treatment of personality disorders.* New York: Guilford Press.

Book, H. (1998). *How to practice brief psychodynamic psychotherapy: The CCRT method.* Washington, DC: APA Books.

Cierpka, M., Strack, M., Benninghoven, D., Dahlbender, R., Pokorny, D., Frevert, G., Blaser, G., Kächele, H., Geyer, M., & Koerner, A. (1997). *Stereotypical relationship patterns and psychopathology.* Manuscript in preparation.

Crits-Christoph, P. (1986). *Assessing conscious and unconscious aspects of relationship themes from self-report and naturalistic data.* Paper presented at a MacArthur Workshop on Person Schemata, Palo Alto, CA.

Crits-Christoph, P., Cooper, A., & Luborsky, L. (1988). The accuracy of therapists' interpretations and the outcome of dynamic psychotherapy. *Journal of Consulting and Clinical Psychology, 56,* 490–495.

Crits-Christoph, P., Cooper, A., & Luborsky, L. (1998). The measurement of accuracy of interpretations. In L. Luborsky & P. Crits-Christoph (Eds.), *Understanding transference: A guide to the CCRT—The Core Conflictual Relationship Theme method in research and practice* (Rev. ed.). Washington, DC: APA Books.

Crits-Christoph, P., & Demorest, A. (1988). *A list of standard categories (Edition 2).* Unpublished manuscript, University of Pennsylvania.

Crits-Christoph, P., & Demorest, A. (1991). Quantitative assessment of relationship theme components. In M. J. Horowitz (Ed.), *Person schemas and maladaptive interpersonal patterns* (pp. 197–212). Chicago: University of Chicago Press.

Crits-Christoph, P., Demorest, A., & Connolly, M.B. (1990). Quantitative assessment of interpersonal themes over the course of psychotherapy. *Psychotherapy, 27,* 513–521.

Crits-Christoph, P., & Luborsky, L. (1998a). Changes in CCRT pervasiveness during psychotherapy. In L. Luborsky & P. Crits-Christoph (Eds.), *Understanding transference: A guide to the CCRT—The Core Conflictual Relationship Theme method in research and practice* (Rev. ed.). Washington, DC: APA Books.

Crits-Christoph, P., & Luborsky, L. (1998b). The perspective of patients versus clinicians in the assessment of relationship themes. In L. Luborsky & P. Crits-Christoph (Eds.), *Understanding transference: A guide to the CCRT—The Core Conflictual Relationship Theme method in research and practice* (Rev. ed.). Washington, DC: APA Books.

Dahlbender, R., Torres, L., Reichert, S., Stupner, S., Frevert, G., & Kächele, H. (1997). *A self-report central relationship pattern measure.* Manuscript in preparation.

Diguer, L., & Luborsky, L. (1998). The CCRT method—The scoring procedures and the main findings. *Psicologia.*

Eckert, R., Luborsky, L., Barber, J. P., & Crits-Christoph, P. (1990). The CCRT in patients with major depression. In L. Luborsky & P. Crits-Christoph (Eds.), *Understanding transference—The CCRT method* (pp. 222–234). New York: Basic Books.

Freud, S. (1958a). The dynamics of the transference. In J. Strachey (Ed. and Trans.), *The standard edition of the complete psychological works of Sigmund Freud* (Vol. 12, pp. 99–108). London: Hogarth Press. (Original work published 1912)

Freud, S. (1958b). Recommendations to physicians practicing psycho-analysis. In J. Srachey (Ed. and Trans.), *The standard edition of the complete psychological works of Sigmund Freud* (Vol. 12, pp. 111–120). London: Hogarth Press. (Original work published 1912)

Fried, D., Crits-Christoph, P., & Luborsky, L. (1992). The first empirical demonstration of transference in psychotherapy. *Journal of Nervous and Mental Disease, 180,* 326–331.

Grenyer, B. F. S., & Luborsky, L. (1996). Dynamic change in psychotherapy: Mastery of interpersonal conflict. *Journal of Consulting and Clinical Psychology, 64,* 411–416.

Grenyer, B. F. S., Luborsky, L., & Solowij, N. (1995). *Treatment manual for supportive-expressive psychotherapy: Special adaptation for treatment of cannabis (marijuana) dependence* (Technical Report 26). Sydney, Australia: Sydney National Drug and Alcohol Research Centre.

Horowitz, M., Luborsky, L., & Popp, C. (1991). A comparison of the Role Relationship Models Configuration and the Core Conflictual Relationship Theme. In M. Horowitz (Ed.), *Person schemas and maladaptive interpersonal behavior.* Chicago: University of Chicago Press.

Leichsenring, F., & Seinfeldt, B. (1997). *A self-report central relationship pattern measure.* Manuscript in preparation, University of Gottingen, Germany.

Luborsky, L. (1965). Clinical manual for the self-interpretation of the TAT. In M. Kornrich (Ed.), *Psychological test modifications* (pp. 242–265). Springfield, IL: Thomas.

Luborsky, L. (1976). Helping alliances in psychotherapy: The groundwork for a study of their relationship to its outcome. In J. L. Claghorn (Ed.), *Successful psychotherapy* (pp. 92–116). New York: Brunner/Mazel.

Luborsky, L. (1977). Measuring a pervasive psychic structure in psychotherapy: The core conflictual relationship theme. In N. Freedman & S. Grand (Eds.), *Communicative structures and psychic structures* (pp. 367–395). New York: Plenum Press.

Luborsky, L. (1984). *Principles of psychoanalytic psychotherapy: A manual for supportive–expressive (SE) treatment* (pp. 1–270). New York: Basic Books.

Luborsky, L. (1986). *A set of standard categories for the CCRT (Edition 1).* Unpublished manuscript, University of Pennsylvania, Philadelphia.

Luborsky, L. (1994). The benefits to the clinician of psychotherapy research: A clinician–researcher's view. In P. F. Talley, H. H. Strupp, & S. F. Butler (Eds.), *Psychotherapy research and practice: Bridging the gap.* New York: Basic Books.

Luborsky, L. (1998a). A guide to the CCRT method. (Chap. 2) In L. Luborsky & P. Crits-Christoph (Eds.), *Understanding transference: A guide to the CCRT — The Core Conflictual Relationship Theme method* (Rev. ed.). Washington, DC: APA Books.

Luborsky, L. (1998b). The everyday clinical uses of the CCRT. In L. Luborsky & P. Crits-Christoph (Eds.), *Understanding transference: A guide to the CCRT— The*

Core Conflictual Relationship Theme method in research and practice (Rev. ed.). Washington, DC: APA Books.

Luborsky, L. (1998c). The convergence of Freud's observations about transference with CCRT evidence. In L. Luborsky & P. Crits-Christoph (Eds.), *Understanding transference: A guide to the CCRT—The Core Conflictual Relationship Theme method in research and practice* (Rev. ed.). Washington, DC: APA Books.

Luborsky, L. (1998d). The Relationship Anecdotes Paradigms (RAP) interview as a versatile source of narratives. In L. Luborsky & P. Crits-Christoph (Eds.), *Understanding transference: A guide to the CCRT—The Core Conflictual Relationship Theme method in research and practice* (Rev. ed.). Washington, DC: APA Books.

Luborsky, L., & Barber, J. P. (1994). Perspectives on seven transference-related measures applied to the interview with Ms. Smithfield. *Psychotherapy Research, 4*, 152–154.

Luborsky, L., Barber, J. P., Binder, J., Curtis, J., Dahl, H., Horowitz, L. M., Horowitz, M., Perry, J. C., Schacht, T., Silberschatz, G., & Teller, V. (1993). Transference-related measures: A new therapy-based class. In N. Miller, L. Luborsky, J. P. Barber, & J. Docherty (Eds.), *Psychodynamic treatment research: A handbook for clinical practice* (pp. 326–341). New York: Basic Books.

Luborsky, L., Barber, J. P., & Diguer, L. (1992). The meanings of the narratives told during psychotherapy: The fruits of a new operational unit. *Psychotherapy Research, 2*, 277–290.

Luborsky, L., Barber, J. P., Schaffler, P., & Cacciola, J. (1998). The narratives told during psychotherapy and the different types of CCRTs within them. In L. Luborsky & P. Crits-Christoph (Eds.), *Understanding transference: A guide to CCRT—The Core Conflictual Relationship Theme method in research and practice* (Rev. ed.). Washington, DC: APA Books.

Luborsky, L., & Crits-Christoph, P. (1990). *Understanding transference: The CCRT method (the Core Conflictual Relationship Theme)* (pp. 1–313). New York: Basic Books.

Luborsky, L., & Crits-Christoph, P. (1998). *Understanding transference: The CCRT method* (Rev. ed.). Washington, DC: APA Books.

Luborsky, L., Crits-Christoph, P., & Alexander, K. (1990). Repressive style and relationship patterns: Three samples inspected. In J. Singer (Ed.), *Repression and dissociation: Implications for personality theory, psychopathology and health*. Chicago: University of Chicago Press.

Luborsky, L., & Diguer, L. (1994). *Advances in procedures for evaluating CCRT results*. Unpublished manuscript, University of Pennsylvania, Philadelphia.

Luborsky, L., & Diguer, L. (1998). The reliability of the CCRT. In L. Luborsky & P. Crits-Christoph (Eds.), *Understanding transference: A guide to the CCRT—The Core Conflictual Relationship Theme method in research and practice* (Rev. ed.). Washington, DC: APA Books.

Luborsky, L., Kächele, H., Dahlbender, R., & Diguer, L. (Eds.). (1991–1998). *The CCRT Newsletter*. Philadelphia: University of Pennsylvania.

Luborsky, L., Kächele, H., Dahlbender, R., & Diguer, L. (Eds.). (1997). *The CCRT method and its discoveries*. Manuscript in preparation.

Luborsky, L., & Luborsky, E. (1995). The era of measures of the transference: The CCRT and other measures. In T. Shapiro & R. Emde (Eds.), *Research in psy-

choanalysis: Process, development, outcome (pp. 329–351). Madison, CT: International Universities Press.

Luborsky, L., Luborsky, E. B., Diguer, L., Schaffler, P., Schmidt, K., Dengler, D., Faude, J., Morris, M., Buchsbaum, H., & Emde, R. (1995). Extending the Core Conflictual Relationship into childhood. In G. Noam & K. Fisher (Eds.), *Development and vulnerability in close relationships.* New York: Erlbaum.

Luborsky, L., Mark, D., Hole, A. V., Popp, C., Goldsmith, B., & Cacciola, J. (1995). Supportive–expressive (SE) dynamic psychotherapy of depression: A time-limited version. In J. P. Barber & P. Crits-Christoph (Eds.), *Psychodynamic psychotherapies for psychiatric disorders (Axis I).* New York: Basic Books.

Luborsky, L., Popp, C., & Barber, J. P. (1994). Common and special factors in different transference-related measures. *Psychotherapy Research, 4,* 277–286.

Luborsky, L., Popp, C., Luborsky, E., & Mark, D. (1994). The Core Conflictual Relationship Theme. In L. Luborsky, J. P. Barber, C. Popp, & D. Shapiro (Eds.), Seven transference-related measures: Each applied in an interview with Ms. Smithfield [Monograph]. *Psychotherapy Research, 4,* 172–183.

Luborsky, L., & Friedman, S. (in press). Illustrations of the CCRT scoring guide. In L. Luborsky & P. Crits-Christoph (Eds.), *Understanding transference: A guide to the CCRT—The Core Conflictual Relationship Theme method in research and practice* (Rev. ed.). Washington, DC: APA Books.

Luborsky, L., Van Ravenswaay, P., Ball, W., Steinman, D., Sprehn, G., & Bryan, C. (1993). Come centrare il trattamento in ambiente psichiatrico: Uso del metodo CCRT–FIT (trattamento ospedaliero centrato) [How to focus psychiatric hospital treatment: Use of the CCRT–FIT (Focused Inpatient Treatment) method]. *Prospettive Psicoanalitiche nel Lavoro Istituzionale, 11,* 9–16.

Luborsky, L., Woody, G., Hole, A. V., & Velleco, A. (1995). Supportive–expressive dynamic psychotherapy for treatment of opiate dependence. In J. P. Barber & P. Crits-Christoph (Eds.), *Psychodynamic psychotherapies for psychiatric disorders (Axis I).* New York: Basic Books.

Mark, D., & Faude, J. (1995). The dynamic focus. In H. Strupp & J. Binder (Eds.), *Psychotherapy in a new key: A guide to time-limited dynamic psychotherapy* (pp. 65–109). New York: Basic Books.

Mark, D., & Luborsky, L. (1991). *Manual for supportive–expressive psychotherapy for cocaine abuse.* Unpublished manuscript.

Popp, C., Diguer, L., Luborsky, L., Faude, J., Johnson, S., Morris, M., Schaffer, N., Schaffler, P., & Schmidt, K. A. (1996). Repetitive relationship themes in waking narratives and dreams. *Journal of Consulting and Clinical Psychology, 64,* 1073–1078.

Schacht, T. E., Binder, J. L., & Strupp, H. H. (1984). The dynamic focus. In H. Strupp & J. Binder (Eds.), *Psychotherapy in a new key: A guide to time-limited dynamic psychotherapy* (pp. 65–109). New York: Basic Books.

Singer, B., & Luborsky, L. (1977). Countertransference: The status of clinical vs. quantitative research. In A. Gurman & A. Razin (Eds.), *The therapist's handbook for effective psychotherapy: An empirical assessment* (pp. 431–448). New York: Pergamon Press.

Wachtel, P. L. (1993). *Therapeutic communication: Principles and effective practice.* New York: Guilford Press.

Waldinger, R., Guastella, F., Diguer, L., Luborsky, L., & Hauser, S. (1997). *Ego development and relationship themes in adolescence.* Manuscript in preparation.

4

Cyclical Maladaptive Patterns: Case Formulation in Time-Limited Dynamic Psychotherapy

HANNA LEVENSON
HANS H. STRUPP

HISTORICAL BACKGROUND OF THE APPROACH

Time-Limited Dynamic Psychotherapy (TLDP) is an interpersonal, time-sensitive approach for patients with chronic, pervasive, dysfunctional ways of relating to others. Its goal is to modify the way a person relates to him- or herself and others. The focus is not on the reduction of symptoms per se (although such improvements are expected to occur), but rather on changing ingrained patterns of interpersonal relatedness or personality style.

While the framework of TLDP is psychodynamic, it incorporates current developments in interpersonal, object relations, and self psychology theories, as well as cognitive-behavioral and system approaches. The type of formulation we discuss in this chapter—the cyclical maladaptive pattern—is structured to inform the therapist about the patient's present mode of relating, the goals for the work, and how to keep the therapy attuned to these goals.

TLDP makes use of the relationship that develops between the therapist and patient to kindle fundamental changes in the way a person interacts with others and him- or herself. Its premises and techniques are broadly applicable regardless of time limits. However, its method of formulating and intervening makes it particularly well suited for the so-called difficult patient seen in a brief or time-limited therapy. Its particular strengths include (1) applicability to the treatment of difficult patients (broad selection criteria), (2) relevance and accessibility for psychodynamically trained clinicians who want to work more effectively and more efficiently, (3) empirical scrutiny of the model, (4) a flexible framework that allows therapists to adapt it to their own unique therapeutic styles, and (5) avoidance of complex metatheoretical constructs by staying close to observable data where possible.

A treatment manual describing TLDP, *Psychotherapy in a New Key: A Guide to Time-Limited Dynamic Psychotherapy* (Strupp & Binder, 1984), was developed for research purposes and published in book form. A recently published clinical casebook, *Time-Limited Dynamic Psychotherapy: A Guide to Clinical Practice* (Levenson, 1995), translates TLDP principles and strategies into pragmatically useful ways of thinking and intervening for the practitioner.

Historically, TLDP is rooted in an object relations framework. It embraces an interpersonal perspective, as exemplified by the early work of Sullivan (1953), and is consistent with the views of modern interpersonal theorists (e.g., Anchin & Kiesler, 1982; Benjamin, 1993; Greenberg & Mitchell, 1983). As such, the search for and maintenance of human relatedness is considered to be a major motivating force within all human beings. This relational view is in sharp contrast to that of classical psychoanalysis, which emphasizes predetermined mental structures to deal with conflicts between gratification of instinctual impulses and societal constraints.

The relational view focuses on transactional patterns where the therapist is embedded in the therapeutic relationship as a participant observer; transference is considered not a distortion but (at least in part) the patient's plausible perceptions of the therapist's behavior and intent; and countertransference does not indicate a failure on the part of the therapist, but rather represents his or her natural reactions to the pushes and pulls from interacting with the patient.

In TLDP psychological symptoms and problems are seen as arising from interpersonal difficulties. Often when people enter therapy, the presenting complaint involves some symptom (e.g., anxiety, depression) that forms the basis for an Axis I diagnosis (DSM IV; American Psychiatric Association, 1994). Only after tracking the origin of such dysphoric feelings does it become apparent that its source is interpersonal. For example, a woman enters therapy saying that she's been depressed since the autumn "for no good reason"; upon inquiry, however, the therapist learns that her only child left for college at that time. While some patients may actually enter therapy complaining of their lifelong interpersonal difficulties, they often perceive that it is other people or circumstances that need to change (e.g., "If only my husband were more attentive, we would have a happy marriage"; "If I won the lottery, my problems would be over").

CONCEPTUAL FRAMEWORK

Assumptions

The TLDP model makes five basic assumptions:

1. *Maladaptive relationship patterns are learned in the past.* Disturbances in adult interpersonal relatedness usually stem from faulty relationships with early caregivers—usually in the parental home. Bowlby (1973) elaborated that early experiences with parental figures result in mental representations of these relationships or working models of one's interpersonal world. The child learns that in order to maintain connections with others and feel secure, he or she must behave in certain ways. These "certain ways" form the building blocks of what will become organized, encoded experiential, affective, and cognitive data (interpersonal schemas) informing one about the nature of human relatedness and what is generally necessary to sustain and maintain emotional connectedness to others.

2. *Such maladaptive patterns are maintained in the present.* This emphasis on early childhood experiences is consistent with the basis for much of psychoanalytic thinking. From a TLDP framework, however, the individual's personality is not seen as fixed at a certain point, but rather as continually changing as it interacts with others. While one's dysfunctional interactive style is learned early in life, this style must be supported in the person's present adult life for the interpersonal difficulties to continue. For example, if Bob learned as a child to be placating and deferential because he grew up in a home with authoritarian parents, he will unwittingly and inadvertently attempt to maintain this role as an adult by pushing and pulling others so they act harshly toward him. Thus, dysfunctional interactions tend to be sustained in the present, including that of the patient–therapist relationship. Accordingly, one can concentrate on the present to alter the patient's dysfunctional interactive style. Focusing in the present allows change to happen more quickly, since time is not spent working through childhood conflicts and discovering historical truths.

3. *Dysfunctional relationship patterns are reenacted in vivo in the therapy.* The patient interacts with the therapist in the same dysfunctional way that she or he interacts with significant others, trying to enlist the therapist in playing a complementary role. From an interpersonal therapy perspective this reenactment is an ideal situation, because it provides the therapist with the very situation that gets the patient into difficulties in the outside world.

4. *The therapeutic relationship has a dyadic quality.* The therapist by entering into the relationship, becomes a part of the reenactment of the dysfunctional interpersonal interaction. In Sullivan's terms (1953), the therapist becomes a *participant observer.* The therapist cannot help but react to the patient; that is, the therapist inevitably will be pushed and pulled by the patient's dysfunctional style and will respond accordingly. This transactional type of reciprocity and complementarity (interpersonal countertransference) does not

indicate a failure on the part of the therapist, but rather represents his or her "role responsiveness" (Sandler, 1976) or "interpersonal empathy" (Strupp & Binder, 1984). As the contemporary interpersonal theorist Donald J. Kiesler (1982, 1988) framed it, the therapist inevitably becomes "hooked" into acting out the corresponding response to the patient's inflexible, maladaptive pattern. To get unhooked, it is essential that the therapist realize how he or she is fostering a replication of the dysfunctional pattern. The therapist should then use this information to change the nature of the interaction in a more positive way and collaboratively invite the patient to look at what is happening between them. Importantly, too, the patient must come to appreciate how he or she manages to get the therapist involved in such a manipulative pattern.

5. *The TLDP focus is on the chief problematic relationship pattern.* While patients may have a repertoire of different interpersonal patterns depending upon their states of mind, who they are interacting with, etc. (see Horowitz, 1987), the emphasis in TLDP is on discerning what is a patient's most pervasive and problematic style of relating (which may need to incorporate several divergent views of self and other). This is not to say that other relationship patterns may not be important, but rather that focusing on the most frequently troublesome type of interaction should have ramifications for other less central interpersonal schemas and is pragmatically essential when time is of the essence.

Goals

The TLDP therapist seeks to provide a *new experience* and a *new understanding* for the patient.

New Experience[1]

The first and major goal in conducting TLDP is for the patient to have a new experience. "New" is meant in the sense of being different and more functional (i.e., healthier) than the maladaptive pattern to which the patient has become accustomed. And "experience" emphasizes the affective-action component of change—behaving differently and emotionally appreciating behaving differently. From a TLDP perspective, behaviors are encouraged that signify a new manner of interacting (e.g., more flexibly and independently) rather than specific content-based behaviors (e.g., being able to go to a movie alone).

The new experience is actually composed of a set of experiences throughout the therapy in which the patient has a different appreciation of him- or herself, of the therapist, and of their interaction. These new experiences provide the patient with experiential learning so that old patterns may be relinquished and new patterns may evolve.

The therapist determines the type of new experiences that are particularly helpful to a particular patient based on the therapist's formulation of the case (see below). The therapist identifies what he or she could say or do (within the therapeutic role) that would most likely subvert the patient's maladaptive interactive style. The therapist's behavior gives the patient the opportunity to disconfirm his or her interpersonal schemata. This *in vivo* learning is a critical component in the practice of TLDP. The patient has the opportunity actively to try out new behaviors in the therapy, to see how they feel, and to notice how the therapist responds. This information then informs the patient's interpersonal schemata of what can be expected from self and others.

These experiential forays into what for the patient has been frightening territory make for heightened affective learning. A tension is created when the familiar (though detrimental) responses to the patient's presentation are not provided. Out of this tension new learning takes place. Such an emotionally intense process is what "heats up" the therapeutic process and permits progress to be made more quickly than in therapies that depend solely upon more abstract learning (usually through interpretation and clarification). As Frieda Fromm-Reichmann is credited with saying, what the patient needs is an experience, not an explanation.

There are parallels between the goal of a new experience and procedures used in some behavioral techniques (e.g., exposure therapy) where clients are exposed to feared stimuli without negative consequences. Modern cognitive theorists voice analogous perspectives (e.g., Safran & Segal, 1990) when they talk about interpersonal processes that lead to *experiential disconfirmation*. Similarities can also be found in the Plan Formulation Method of Sampson and Weiss (1986; see also Weiss, 1993) in which change occurs when therapists pass their patients' "tests."

The concept of a *corrective emotional experience* described more than 50 years ago is also applicable (Alexander & French, 1946). In their classic book *Psychoanalytic Therapy: Principles and Applications,* Alexander and French challenged the then-prevalent assumption concerning the therapeutic importance of exposing repressed memories and providing a genetic reconstruction. Their concept of the corrective emotional experience has been criticized for promoting manipulation of the transference by suggesting that the therapist should respond in a way diametrically opposite to that expected by the patient. For example, if the child had been raised by an intrusive mother, then the therapist should maintain a more restrained stance.

The TLDP concept of the new experience does not involve a direct manipulation of the transference, nor is it solely accomplished by the offering of a good enough therapeutic relationship. Specifically, a therapist can help provide a new experience by selectively choosing from all of the helpful, mature, and respectful ways of being in a session those particular aspects that would most effectively undermine a specific patient's dysfunctional style.

With sufficient quality or quantity of these experiences, patients can develop different internalized working models of relationships. In this way TLDP promotes change by altering the basic infrastructure of the patient's transactional world, which then reverberates to influence the concept of self. This emphasis on *experiential learning* allows TLDP to benefit a wider range of patients (broader selection criteria) than many other types of psychodynamic brief therapies that emphasize understanding through interpretation.

New Understanding

The second goal of providing a new understanding focuses more specifically on cognitive changes than the first goal, just discussed, which emphasizes the affective-behavioral arena. The patient's new understanding usually involves an identification and comprehension of his or her dysfunctional patterns. To facilitate a new understanding, the TLDP therapist can point out repetitive patterns that have originated in experiences with past significant others, with present significant others, and in the here and now with the therapist. Therapists' disclosing their own reactions to the patients' behaviors can also be beneficial. Patients begin to recognize how they have similar relationship patterns with different people in their lives, and this new perspective enables them to examine their active role in perpetuating dysfunctional interactions.

Although the two foregoing TLDP goals have been presented as separate entities, in actuality the new experience and the new understanding are part of the same picture. Both perspectives are always available, but at any one time one becomes figure and the other ground. New experiences, if they are to be more than fleeting events, have elements of representations (understandings) of self and others. Similarly, new understandings, if they are to be more than mere intellectualizations, have experiential and affective components.

However, in teaching TLDP a conceptual division is made between the idea of a new experience and a new understanding for heuristic reasons; this helps the trainees attend to aspects of the change process that are helpful in formulating and intervening quickly. In addition, since psychodynamically trained therapists are so ready to intervene with an interpretation, placing the new experience in the foreground helps them grasp and focus on the "big picture"—how not to reenact a dysfunctional scenario with the patient.

Procedurally, a therapist encourages a different type of processing depending upon whether he or she seeks to promote a new understanding or a new experience at any particular point in the therapy. The emphasis on getting to underlying emotional material by challenging the patient's conceptual framework directly represents *top-down processing*; the approach of accessing the emotional experience directly through facilitating behavioral change or experiential awareness is a *bottom-up* approach (Safran & Greenberg, 1991). The goals outlined in this chapter encourage both bottom-up and top-down processing.

The Cyclical Maladaptive Pattern

In the past, in psychodynamic brief therapy clinicians used their intuition, insight, and clinical savvy to devise formulations of cases. While these methods may work wonderfully for the gifted or experienced clinician, they are impossible to teach explicitly. One remedy for this situation was the development of a procedure for deriving a dynamic, interpersonal focus—the Cyclical Maladaptive Pattern (CMP; Schacht, Binder, & Strupp, 1984).

Briefly, the CMP outlines the idiosyncratic "vicious cycle" of maladaptive interactions that a particular patient gets into when he or she relates to others. These cycles or patterns involve inflexible, self-perpetuating behaviors, self-defeating expectations, and negative self-appraisals, that lead to dysfunctional and maladaptive interactions with others (Butler & Binder, 1987; Butler, Strupp, & Binder, 1993). The CMP comprises four categories that are used to organize the interpersonal information about the patient:

1. *Acts of the self.* These include the thoughts, feelings, motives, perceptions, and behaviors of the patient of an interpersonal nature. For example, "When I meet strangers, I think they wouldn't want to have anything to do with me" (thought); "I am afraid to take the promotion" (feeling); "I wish I were the life of the party" (motive); "It seemed she was on my side" (perception); "I start crying when I get angry at my husband" (behavior). Sometimes these acts are conscious, like those above, and sometimes they are outside awareness, as in the case of the woman who does not realize how jealous she is of her sister's accomplishments.

2. *Expectations of others' reactions.* This category pertains to all the statements having to do with how the patient imagines others will react to him or her in response to some interpersonal behavior (Act of the Self). "My boss will fire me if I make a mistake." "If I go to the dance, no one will ask me to dance."

3. *Acts of others toward the self.* This third grouping consists of the actual behaviors of other people, as observed (or assumed) and interpreted by the patient. "When I made a mistake at work, my boss shunned me for the rest of the day." "When I went to the dance, guys asked me to dance, but only because they felt sorry for me."

4. *Acts of the self toward the self.* In this category belong all of the patient's behaviors or attitudes toward him- or herself—when the self is the object of the interpersonal pattern. How does the patient treat him- or herself? "When I made the mistake, I berated myself so much I had difficulty sleeping that night." "When no one asked me to dance, I told myself it's because I'm fat, ugly, and unlovable."

In addition to these four categories of the CMP, the therapist should also consider his or her reactions to the patient. How are you feeling while in the room with this patient? What are you being pulled to do or not do? The therapist's internal and external responses to the patient provide important sources of information for understanding the patient's lifelong dysfunctional interactive pattern. One's reactions to the patient should make sense given the patient's interpersonal pattern. Of course, each therapist has a unique personality that might contribute to the particular shading of the reaction elicited by the patient, but the first assumption from a TLDP perspective is that ideally the therapist's behavior is *predominantly* shaped by the patient's evoking patterns (i.e., the influence of the therapist's personal conflicts is not so paramount as to undermine the therapy).

The CMP provides an organizational framework that makes comprehensible a large mass of data and leads to fruitful hypotheses. A CMP should not be seen as an encapsulated version of Truth, but rather as a plausible narrative incorporating major components of a person's current and historical interactive world. It is a map of the territory—not the territory itself (Strupp & Binder, 1984). In addition, a successful TLDP formulation should provide a blueprint for the entire therapy. It describes the nature of the problem, leads to the delineation of the goals, serves as a guide for interventions, enables the therapist to anticipate reenactments within the context of the therapeutic interaction, and provides a way to assess whether the therapy is on the right track—in terms of outcome at termination as well as in-session mini-outcomes. Yet the CMP is a fluid working formulation that is meant to be refined as the therapy proceeds. The focus provided by the CMP permits the therapist to intervene in ways that have the greatest likelihood of being therapeutic. Thus the therapy can be briefer *and* more effective at the same time.

INCLUSION/EXCLUSION CRITERIA

TLDP is seen as most suitable for people who have lifelong dysfunctional interpersonal difficulties. The first session is presented to patients as an evaluation session—an assessment of the appropriateness of TLDP treatment for them. However, the evaluation actually begins with the very first contact with the patient, whether directly (e.g., by phone) or indirectly (e.g., through a referral). How a patient handles the first contact with the therapist can be very telling about the patient's hopes, expectations, fears, attitudes, and overall style. For example, the patient who responds in a deferential and obsequious manner to the first phone call from the therapist ("Oh, doctor, I so much appreciate your willingness to see me. I have heard what a marvelous therapist you are, and I am so much looking forward to meeting you and am so glad you will be able to see me although you are so busy with more important things.") is already affecting the therapist differently than the patient who replies in a challenging, argumentative way ("I can only come in for appointments on Thursday afternoons, and I cannot work with anyone who is going to be late. Are you late for sessions?"). And in the face-to-face meeting, much can be learned about dysfunctional patterns of relating to others by observing the nonverbal and paralingual behavior of patients right from the outset.

Five major selection criteria are used in determining a patient's appropriateness for TLDP:

First, patients must be in *emotional discomfort* so they are motivated to endure the often challenging and painful change process and to make sacrifices of time, effort, and money as required by therapy. Most therapists have confronted the enormous (and frequently insurmountable) problem of trying to treat people who are court referred or "dragged" into the consultation room by an exasperated family member.

Second, patients must *come for appointments and engage with the therapist*—or at least talk. Initially such an attitude may be fostered by hope or faith in a positive outcome. Later it might stem from actual experiences of the therapist as a helpful partner.

Third, patients must be *willing to consider how their relationships have contributed* to distressing symptoms, negative attitudes, and/or behavioral difficulties. The operative word here is "willing." Suitable patients do not actually have to walk in the door indicating that they have difficulties in relating to others. Rather, in the give-and-take of the therapeutic encounter, they must evidence signs of being willing to consider the possibility that they have problems relating to others.

Fourth, patients need to be *willing to examine feelings* that may hinder more successful relationships and may foster more dysfunctional ones. Also, Strupp and Binder (1984) elaborate that the patient needs to possess "sufficient capacity to emotionally distance from these feelings so that the patient and therapist can jointly examine them" (p.57).

And fifth, patients should be capable of having a *meaningful relationship* with the therapist. Again, it is not expected that the patient initially relates in a collaborative manner. But the potential for establishing such a relationship should exist. Patients cannot be out of touch with reality or so impaired that they have difficulty appreciating that their therapists are separate people. It would be impossible to conduct an interpersonal therapy if the patient did not know where he or she ended and the therapist began.

The exclusionary criteria for TLDP are very similar to criteria for red-flagging patients in other brief dynamic approaches (MacKenzie, 1988). Specifically, the TLDP exclusionary criteria are:

- Patient is not able to attend to the process of a verbal give-and-take with the therapist (e.g., patient has delirium, dementia, psychosis, or diminished intellectual status).
- Patient's problems can be treated more effectively by other means (e.g., patient has a specific phobia or manic–depressive illness).
- Patient cannot tolerate the active, interpretative, interactive therapy process, which often heightens anxiety (e.g., patient has impulse control problems, abuses alcohol and/or substances, or has a history of repeated suicide attempts).

STEPS IN CASE FORMULATION

Table 4.1 contains the steps in TLDP formulation and intervention. These "steps" should not be thought of as separate techniques applied in a linear, rigid fashion, but rather as guidelines for the therapist to be used in a fluid

TABLE 4.1. Steps in TLDP Formulation and Intervention

---

1. Let the patient tell his or her own story in his or her own words.
2. Explore the interpersonal context related to symptoms or problems.
3. Use the categories of the CMP to gather, categorize, and probe for information.
4. Listen for themes in the patient's content (about past and present relationships) and manner of interacting in session.
5. Be aware of reciprocal reactions (countertransferential pushes and pulls).
6. Be vigilant for reenactments of dysfunctional interactions in the therapeutic relationship.
7. Explore patient's reaction to the evolving relationship with the therapist.
8. Develop a CMP narrative (story) describing the patient's predominant dysfunctional interactive pattern.
9. From this CMP, outline the goals for treatment.
10. Facilitate a new experience of more adaptive relating within the therapeutic relationship consistent with the CMP (Goal 1).
11. Help the patient identify and understand his or her dysfunctional pattern as it occurs with the therapist and others in his or her life (Goal 2).
12. Assist the patient in appreciating the once adaptive function of his or her manner of interacting.
13. Revise and refine the CMP throughout the therapy.

---

and interactive manner. In the initial sessions, the therapist lets the patient tell his or her own story (Step 1), rather than relying on the traditional psychiatric interview, which structures the patient's responses into categories of information (e.g., developmental history, education). By listening to *how* the patient tells his or her story (e.g., deferentially, cautiously, dramatically) as well as to the content, the therapist can learn much about the patient's interpersonal style. The therapist then explores the interpersonal context of the patient's symptoms or problems (Step 2). When did the problems begin? What else was going on in the patient's life at that time, especially of an interpersonal nature? By using the four categories of the CMP and his or her own reactions (Step 3), the therapist begins to develop a picture of the patient's idiosyncratic, interpersonal world, including the patient's views of self and expectations of others' behavior. The therapist listens for themes in the emerging material by seeing commonalities in the patient's transactional patterns over person, time, and place (Step 4). As part of interacting with the patient, the therapist will be pulled into responding in a complementary fashion, recreating a dysfunctional dance with the patient. By examining the patterns of the here-and-now interaction and by using the Expectations of Others' Reactions and the Behavior of Others components of the CMP, the therapist becomes aware of his or her countertransferential reenactments (Steps 5 and 6). The therapist can then help the patient explore his or her reactions to the relationship that is forming with the therapist (Step 7). By incorporating all the historical and present interactive thematic information, the therapist can develop a narrative description of the patient's idiosyncratic primary CMP (Step 8).

From this formulation, the therapist then discerns the goals for treatment (Step 9). The first goal involves determining the nature of the new experience (Step 10). The therapist discerns what he or she could say or do (within the therapeutic role) that would most likely subvert or interrupt the cyclical dynamic nature of the patient's maladaptive interactive style. Consistent with this way of conceptualizing a new experience, Gill (1993) suggests that what is needed are *specific* mutative transference–countertransference interactions. The therapist–patient "interaction has to be about the right content—a content that we would call insight if it became explicit" (p. 115).

In TLDP the most potent intervention capable of providing a new understanding (Step 11) is thought to be the examination of the here-and-now interactions between therapist and patient. It is chiefly through the therapist's observations about the reenactment of the CMP in the sessions that patients begin to have an *in vivo* understanding of their behaviors and stimulus value. By ascertaining how the pattern has emerged in the therapeutic relationship, the patient has the opportunity, perhaps for the first time, to examine the nature of such behaviors in a safe environment.

It is usually helpful for the therapist to share his or her formulation with the patient *at whatever level the patient can comprehend it* and to collaborate with the patient to derive a mutual understanding of the dysfunctional nature of his or her interactions. However, the degree to which a patient can join the therapist in elaborating a new life narrative is limited by such factors as his or her intellectual ability, capacity for introspection, psychological-mindedness, and the quality of the therapeutic relationship. For example, for some concrete-thinking patients the most they can comprehend is a linear connection between their behavior and another's response. Others with more psychological sophistication can appreciate the nuances of their interactive patterns, can delineate how their patterns of relating began, and can discern the subtle manner that they manifest in the present.

The therapist can help depathologize (Step 12) the patient's current behavior and symptoms by helping him or her to understand their historical development. From the TLDP point of view, symptoms and dysfunctional behaviors are the individual's attempt to adapt to situations threatening interpersonal relatedness. For example, in therapy a passive, anxious client began to understand that as a child he had to be subservient and hypervigilant in order to avoid beatings. This learning enabled him to view his present interpersonal style from a different perspective and allowed him to have some empathy for his childhood plight.

The last step (13) in the formulation process involves the continuous refinement of the CMP throughout the therapy. In a brief therapy, the therapist cannot wait to have all the "facts" before formulating the case and intervening. As the therapy proceeds, new content and interactional data become available that might strengthen, modify, or negate the working formulation. For example, the therapist could be developing a CMP of a patient's lifelong passive, dependent style only to learn that the patient used to be a take-charge, successful business executive of a large firm prior to his retirement. Clearly, the revised CMP would need to take account of this dramatic shift in style.

APPLICATION TO PSYCHOTHERAPY TECHNIQUE

We consider the formulation to be essential in understanding the case. It is not necessarily shared with the patient but may well be, depending on the patient's abilities to deal with the material. Rather than presenting intellectual generalizations to the patient, the shared understanding of what is important to work on in the therapy is a collaboratively derived process. For some patients with minimal introspection and abstraction ability, the problematic interpersonal scenario may never be stated per se. Rather, the focus may stay very close to the content of the presenting problems and concerns of the patient (e.g., wanting to be accorded more respect at work). The therapist, however, is constantly using the CMP to inform him- or herself regarding how to facilitate a new experience of self and other in session (e.g., the patient's experiencing him- or herself as a respected and responsible partner in the therapeutic process). Other patients enter therapy with a fairly good understanding of their own self-defeating and self-perpetuating interpersonal patterns (e.g., "I have decided to come into therapy at this time because I can see I am going to get fired from this job, just like all the other jobs, if I don't stop antagonizing my boss"). In these cases, the therapist and patient can jointly articulate the parameters that foster such behavior, generalize to other situations where applicable, and readily recognize its occurrence in the therapy.

The CMP is critical for guiding the therapist in the direction of the most facilitative interventions. The following examples of two patients with seemingly similar behaviors but differing CMPs will illustrate. Marjorie's maladaptive interpersonal pattern suggested she had deeply ingrained beliefs that she could not be appreciated unless she were the entertaining, effervescent ingenue. When she attempted to joke throughout most of the fifth session, her therapist directed her attention to the contrast between her joking and her anxiously twisting her handkerchief. (New experience: The therapist invites the possibility that he can be interested in her even if she were anxious and not cheerful.)

Susan's lifelong dysfunctional pattern, on the other hand, revealed a meek stance fostered by repeated ridicule from her alcoholic father. She also attempted to joke in the fifth session, nervously twisting her handkerchief. Susan's therapist listened with engaged interest to the jokes and did not interrupt. (New experience: The therapist can appreciate her taking center stage and not humiliate her when she is so vulnerable.) In both cases the therapist's interventions (observing nonverbal behavior; listening) were well within the psychodynamic therapist's acceptable repertoire. There was no need to do anything feigned (e.g., laugh uproariously at Susan's joke), nor was there a demand to respond with a similar therapeutic stance to both presentations.

In these cases the therapists' behavior gave the patients the opportunity to disconfirm the patients' own interpersonal schemata. With sufficient quality and/or quantity of these experiences, patients can develop different internalized working models of relationships. In this way TLDP promotes change by altering the basic infrastructure of the patient's transactional world, which then reverberates to influence the concept of self.

CASE EXAMPLE

We are going to give a clinical illustration of CMP formulation by using the first 5 minutes of a first meeting between therapist and patient. We realize that in a real-life clinical situation the therapist would have much more than 5 minutes of clinical material from which to draw, but we will use this approach as a didactic device to demonstrate the TLDP formulation process.

Lydia Ludlow presented for therapy with multiple problems which she discussed in a tangential, unfocused manner. She was a 45-year-old married woman who was recently separated from her husband. Her numerous problems included compulsive eating, marital difficulties, financial problems, an alcoholic mother, and "I don't know what love is." Her previous therapist recently increased her fee to an amount which the patient felt she could not afford. She, therefore, came to the outpatient clinic of a large teaching hospital and was referred to the Brief Psychotherapy Program.

Her therapist, Dr. Margaret Ellison, at the time of this therapy, was a third-year psychiatry resident. She had just rotated off the inpatient unit. Not only was Ms. Ludlow her first brief psychotherapy patient, she was also her very first outpatient case. The segment below is a transcript of the first 5 minutes of the first session.

THERAPIST: Well, maybe you can tell me a little bit about what's going on for you in getting into this program.

PATIENT: Um. (*pause*) I've never been in with any kind of psychology until I was married. I used religion to try to get better. I didn't hate psychologists, but I just didn't turn to them. I've gone to StayWell, my HMO, and most recently to the Care Center. The lady's leaving the Care Center and their fees were going up. She said she'd keep me on, but she's caught in the middle.

THERAPIST: Where is this Care Center?

PATIENT: Downtown Funston.

THERAPIST: How long have you been working with her?

PATIENT: Not that long. There was a long waiting list. I did an intake at Mount Rushmore Clinic and the Care Center and they both said that's fine, but there was a long waiting list. And when I needed it the most, I've had to wait and wait. And I lost my HMO coverage, so I've been making do. But I've done a lot of reading. Alice Miller's book on child abuse and Scott Peck's *People of the Lie*. That's my parents. I can't get all the answers. Positive affirmations aren't enough. I need more.

THERAPIST: Can you say what's troubling you now and what brought you into therapy?

PATIENT: When I see what my parents did and what they taught me—I don't know what love is with my husband. I'd like to get back with him. It isn't manipulation. I'm a compulsive eater. If I'm on a strict diet, honest to God, my metabolism changes. It really does. I'm eating measured protein. I'm on the edge of answers. I watch Bradshaw on TV and they talk about compulsive behavior and manipulation. And I think I've almost got it.

THERAPIST: You said you don't know what love is with your husband. Can you say more about that?

PATIENT: Well, a real duck soup example is if I say "I love you," in the old days, he was supposed to say "I love you" right back. It called for it. And sometimes he would say "I know that." And it would drive me up the wall. And, of course, I can laugh about that now. But I really don't know what being together and being OK is. Because my parents are like this. (*Interlocks her fingers and pushes and pulls hands together in front of her.*) My mother's drinking; dad's pouring. I don't feel loved; I don't feel OK. I realized my parents weren't there for me. They're self-centered and holier-than-thou. They've concentrated on my problems all my life. My dad is a doctor; he specializes in weight control. My mother is a health fanatic and a size 4. They concentrated on my physical defects. I was beautiful. But then it was one damn thing after another. My lip curled so they made me massage it, and then they got me braces. And I was grateful for that. But it's one thing after another. They've been trying to fix me all my life.

THERAPIST: What was that like for you, when you were younger?

PATIENT: They were perfect. I didn't see them as human beings until a few years ago.

Following the steps in formulating the case, Dr. Ellison let the patient tell her story in her own way. She tried to discover what was troubling her and why she came to the clinic at this time. The patient readily revealed an interpersonal context for her problems. Table 4.2 contains the categorization of what the patient was saying according to the four components of the CMP. Under *Acts of the Self* are such patient behaviors as Ms. Ludlow's reading books

TABLE 4.2. Basic Data for Ms. Ludlow's CMP

Acts of the Self

Used religion, gone to an HMO, had to wait and wait, making do, done a lot of reading, need more, like to get back together with husband, compulsive eater, on the edge of answers, watch TV, don't feel loved, used to see my parents as perfect.

Expectations of Others' Reactions

Husband was supposed to say "I love you."

Acts of Others toward the Self

My therapist is leaving the mental health center, she's caught in the middle, there was a long waiting list at the clinic, my mother's drinking and dad's pouring, my parents weren't there for me, have concentrated on my problems all my life, been trying to fix me all my life, made me massage my lip, got me braces.

Acts of the Self toward the Self (Introject)

Don't feel OK, don't know what being together and OK is, was beautiful, compulsive eater, massaged my lip.

---

about psychological issues and watching educational "pop psychology" TV programs. Usually such activities as reading and watching TV are not thought to be interactional. But for Ms. Ludlow they have interpersonal meaning. It seems she wanted to learn about how others relate to her and their motivations so she could better understand what was going on in her interpersonal world. Ms. Ludlow seemed to convey by the tone and phrasing of her material that it was the others in her life who need the help. She was more the innocent bystander.

We know far less about Ms. Ludlow's *Expectations of Others' Reactions* than about her own thoughts, feelings, and behaviors. The CMP structure can be helpful in alerting the therapist to areas of scant information. The therapist can then follow up with questions designed specifically to elicit the relevant material. For example, "When you go home for a visit now, how do you expect your parents will treat you?"

Ms. Ludlow does allude to her unfulfilled desire to have her husband tell her that he loves her when she says, "I love you." One also gets a pervasive feeling that she believes that others will not come through for her or meet her needs. However, we give less emphasis to clinical inference in this initial attempt at developing a working formulation and prefer to stay close to the descriptive data. This does not mean that one cannot hold hypotheses (even some far-fetched guesses), but at the outset, when one's amount of information about a patient is so limited, it is wise not to fill in too many blanks.

Ms. Ludlow gives us much information about how she interprets the *Acts of Others toward the Self*. For example, she saw that her parents bought her braces (and she is grateful for that), but she viewed their attempts to fix her as designed to deflect attention from their own problems by highlighting her deformities. Ms. Ludlow considers her parents self-centered and holier than thou. They were not there for her. Similarly we hear how her previous therapist increased her fee and also was not there for her "when I needed it the most."

The fourth category, *Acts of the Self toward the Self (Introject)*, is usually the most difficult category about which to gather information. Patients often do not disclose how or why they treat themselves in certain ways until the treatment is well underway and a positive therapeutic alliance has been established. Butler and Binder (1987) make the point that the action component of the introject is critical for understanding the patient's active role in developing his or her CMP. For example, if a patient stated, "When she approached me, my self-esteem fell to zero," the therapist should try to clarify what *behaviors* (public or private) the patient engaged in that resulted in this deflation. (For example, the therapist could ask, "What do you say to yourself that made you feel so unworthy?") In this way, the therapist not only begins to understand the patient's automatic thoughts (Beck, Rush, Shaw, & Emery, 1979) that contribute to the dysfunctional dynamic but also conveys to the patient that the patient is *actively* doing something to promote or encourage the very feeling s/he finds intolerable.

In addition to using the content of what Ms. Ludlow says to understand her customary way of interacting with people, we can also use the *way* in which she presents her story to formulate her case. For example, while Ms. Ludlow has sought guidance from many sources, she otherwise has remained rather *passive* (waiting, making do). Others are seen as *actively* doing things to her (fixing her, concentrating on her problems). And Ms. Ludlow's manner of talking (high-pitched voice and pleading, whiny tone) and nonverbal behavior (slouched in the chair) contribute to the therapist's estimation of her presentation (e.g., that of a petulant little girl).

When initially formulating the CMP, some therapists become concerned about whether they have correctly placed what the patient is saying into the right category. There are simple guidelines, such as the patient's own behaviors toward others usually go under *Acts of the Self*, whereas behaviors directed toward the self usually go under *Acts of the Self toward the Self*. But sometimes the meaning of a particular behavior (whether it is directed at others or toward the self) is not so obvious. For example, does Ms. Ludlow eat compulsively to annoy her diet doctor father (Acts of the Self) or to soothe herself (Acts of the Self toward the Self), or both? Fortunately, one need not become obsessed with the correct placement because these categories are primarily designed to be of heuristic value—to help the therapist obtain, assess, and organize large amounts of incoming data; eventually all components will be combined into one narrative.

Dr. Ellison's reaction to the patient was that she felt quite overwhelmed, irritated, and frustrated by Ms. Ludlow's passive, subtly hostile presentation. In addition, she felt doomed to failure. In supervision she stated, "Everyone has tried to fix her and I am going to fall into the same situation. I feel a pressure to fix her and keep her on track, but I fear I'm going to be another in a long list of people who have let her down." Dr. Ellison was feeling helpless and hopeless about this case. After an entire session (of which the reader has only sampled a small portion), Dr. Ellison concluded, "This woman is very tangential, very circumstantial, very overwhelming, very unfocused, and perhaps prepsychotic." For these reasons Dr. Ellison thought that the patient might be inappropriate for a brief psychotherapy and requested another training case. Dr. Ellison's supervisor on this case, not convinced that Ms. Ludlow should be excluded from the brief therapy program, suggested that the therapist meet with the patient for a second evaluation session to gather more information relevant to the CMP.

The following is an excerpt from the beginning of the second session. The therapist has just explained to the patient that more information was needed in order to make a judgment about the appropriateness of brief therapy for her.

THERAPIST: What do you want to work on for yourself?

PATIENT: I thought we talked about that.

THERAPIST: Well, we're working on it. We're making progress.

PATIENT: Are we? It's frustrating.

THERAPIST: Do you feel like it's frustrating to, um, for yourself to try to reflect on what it is that you want to work on or change or find as a problem area?

PATIENT: No, I want to do all these things. Sometimes your questions, I can't believe you're that dumb. I know you are a smart lady. Would you ask me again?

THERAPIST: Um. What is there about my questions that seem dumb to you?

PATIENT: I just thought my problems were obvious.

THERAPIST: Do you . . . What makes you think that they are obvious to other people?

PATIENT: Well, I have already told you a lot. And I thought you would have figured some things out. I don't know.

THERAPIST: Do you think that happens with other people? Do you sometimes get, um, frustrated with them because you think they should know more about what's going on with you or have you figured out?

PATIENT: Oh, I suppose that's happened with my husband and also with my folks. They're off in left field. But, no. I'm finding out that most people are coming from their own inadequacy. Like in the office. If I use good manners and good cheer, and just try to communicate the work stuff, um, (*pause*) I just want to be sure that people know that I am not going to do them in or hang them or betray them. I just want to make my own way. I don't want to step on anybody while I'm doing it.

THERAPIST: Uh huh.

PATIENT: And I see people afraid. I have a coworker I am having trouble with. She's messed up and she's clearing her throat and discrediting me.

THERAPIST: Do you think she's afraid of you?

PATIENT: Yeah. She's cringing inside. But she's hurting me pretty bad. I am angry at her.

THERAPIST: Why would she be afraid of you?

PATIENT: Well, I'm good, but she's good, too. And if she doesn't know it, that's her problem. And I don't want to make her look bad, but I just want to do good myself. And, uh, she ridiculed me in front of a dozen people in one room. And she interrupts, and she just, I just don't like it and I don't need it.

THERAPIST: Do you think she does this intentionally to you?

PATIENT: Yeah. This goes back to the same experience I came through grade school with a girl who did this. She was conniving, grasping. She wanted the boys to like her. Her own daddy wasn't there for her. And our mothers were friends. I had to suffer this little bitch all the way through school. And I would just go cold inside. I would be talking to a boy. She would come up and butt in and get the guy's attention. And he would look at her. And I would just freeze up. And that's how it is. I lost. I just get cold. But on the work situation with this woman, I just don't want to be her friend.

THERAPIST: Do you think that it feels like people want to make you feel stupid or wrong in a way very similar to what your parents used to do?

PATIENT: (*nodding*) Sure.

THERAPIST: Do you get that sense with my questions that I have been asking you, that you somehow feel that I might be making you look stupid.

PATIENT: Yeah. (*giggling*) I feel like I'm something that just came from the moon and you never saw anything quite like this before. (*laughing*) And I think really that a lot of my challenges can be put in neat little slots.

THERAPIST: Your challenges?

PATIENT: My little problems. Yeah.

THERAPIST: 'Cause I'm just wondering why you would think—why you would expect me to sort of know all these things, the questions I have been asking trying to get information from you. Why would you expect me to know all these things and not have to ask?

PATIENT: Just, well, you kind of ask them another way. (*pause*) It's been done before to me, I mean.

THERAPIST: What is that—that's been done?

PATIENT: I went through a laborious intake procedure at Mount Rushmore Hospital, and then I didn't go through with it. And the guy asked questions the way you are. So . . .

THERAPIST: Was there something about the way he asked questions that made you uncomfortable?

PATIENT: I had so much happen to me, he just looked amazed. He looked a little like, my goodness, I'm a walking soap opera!

As part of the TLDP model we stated that in response to patients with entrenched, persistent, maladaptive modes of relating the therapist cannot help but act out the role in which the patient casts the him or her. The therapist gets drawn into a destructive "game" (Berne, 1964) with the patient in which the therapist is a participant and not merely an observer. "The patient unwittingly behaves in ways that tend to provoke others (including the therapist) to respond reciprocally. This has the effect of confirming the patient's expectations of how the kind of person he or she is evokes certain responses in others. In other words, the patient's behavior becomes a self-fulfilling prophecy. This unconscious and self-defeating conduct is the *action* component of the transference . . ." (Strupp & Binder, 1984, p. 142). Similarly, Dr. Ellison's almost rejecting the patient for treatment is the action component of her countertransference.

Ms. Ludlow's unfocused, demanding style engendered a negative reaction in her therapist. Dr. Ellison wanted to reject this patient. Not only had Ms. Ludlow's presentation made it difficult to assess if she met the selection criteria, but it had contributed to Dr. Ellison's wanting another (i.e., "easier") patient; one who might know how to ask for and utilize help. Dr. Ellison felt wary of trying to help Ms. Ludlow, because so many others had failed to be of assistance to this overwhelmingly needy person, who sounded more like a whiny child than a 45-year-old woman.

Dr. Ellison's supervisor also colluded with Dr. Ellison in acting out the countertransferential reaction, by suggesting that a second evaluation session was in order. In essence, they reenacted a significant portion of this patient's cyclical maladaptive pattern with others—rebuffing her because of her diffuse, critical, and needy presentation.

However, it should be remembered that Ms. Ludlow was Dr. Ellison's first outpatient case and that she might have felt overwhelmed by almost any patient. Clearly, Dr. Ellison's inexperience has nothing to do with Ms. Ludlow's presenting pathological style. If Dr. Ellison's reaction to Ms. Ludlow was based solely on her lack of training and experience, then it would not be of help to us in delineating the patient's CMP. Since Dr. Ellison's reaction to Ms. Ludlow seems rather understandable based on the dynamic formulation derived for the patient, we can proceed on the assumption (until proven otherwise) that Dr. Ellison had become ensnared in a dysfunctional scenario with the patient that was driven by engaging in the patient's style. In this case, the therapist almost acted out her countertransference in a major destructive manner (i.e., rejecting the patient for treatment).

It should be emphasized that from the TLDP point of view, the therapist's strong countertransferential reaction to this patient was not a "mistake." Rather it would have been a mistake not to use such internal data as a source of information about what it is like to interact with this patient. It would have been a mistake to deny that one was having such negative reactions in order to maintain a view of oneself as an all-accepting, empathic therapist. Also it would have been a mistake to think such reactions were idiosyncratic manifestations of neurotic conflicts that the therapist needed to work through in her own therapy or in consultation (in the absence of a compelling reason to come to this conclusion).

Thus, it appears that Dr. Ellison's telling the patient that a second evaluation session was needed is an example of how the therapist can be drawn into the patient's self-defeating style of getting others to reject her. Further, we saw how this "rejection" caused a series of angry responses in the patient. What emerged here in the second session illustrates how critical transference–countertransference patterns manifest very early in a therapy and can be worked with almost immediately.

In the second session, we hear about a repetitive interpersonal interaction—an emerging theme—in which Ms. Ludlow perceived others as rejecting and hurting her for no good reason, to which she reacted with anger and disappointment. We see a strikingly similar pattern unfolding with the therapist. Ms. Ludlow felt rejected by the therapist (i.e., not being accepted after the first session with the ultimate possibility of being found unsuitable altogether) and responded with hostility ("Sometimes your questions. I can't believe you're that dumb.") and disappointment ("Well, I have already told you a lot. And I thought you would have figured some things out.")

In fact, we can view the beginning of this second session as the patient's experience of being hurt and frustrated by the therapist unconsciously evoking memories of other similarly upsetting interpersonal interactions. Thus the patient's stories about the coworker and grade-school companion serve as allusions to what is happening in the transference (Gill, 1979).

From an object relations perspective, it is assumed that the patient's experience of the therapist is mirrored in what the patient says about transactions with others. Sometimes these parallels are obvious (as with the coworker and childhood companion examples); sometimes the similarities are more subtle. An example of a possible subtle allusion to the transference occurs when Ms. Ludlow refers to the coworker's "ridiculing her in front of a dozen people in one room." The patient had been informed by her therapist in the first session that videotaped segments of her therapy would be shown to the Brief

Psychotherapy Program (BPP) team, composed of other trainees and a supervisor. She did not know exactly how many people would be observing her via tape, but perhaps it is reasonable to think there might be a dozen such people in one room.

While such transferential allusions cannot be proven in the clinical situation, they provide useful hypotheses for the therapist to consider, providing invaluable glimpses into the unconscious or censored areas of the patient's schemata. Is the patient concerned that Dr. Ellison might be ridiculing her behind her back? Is she afraid that her therapist is trying to discredit her? Does she get cold inside when she does not get the attention she wants from Dr. Ellison? Does she see her therapist as afraid of her and therefore intentionally trying to hurt her?

Such connections between interactions with others and the therapist can be made explicit to further the patient's awareness and understanding of such patterns. Dr. Ellison made such an interpretation when she asked Ms. Ludlow if she saw people such as her coworker making her feel stupid in a way very similar to what her parents did (a connection between present significant others and past significant others). Dr. Ellison then went further and inquired if Ms. Ludlow had the sense that she (Dr. Ellison) might also be trying to make her look stupid (a reference to what is happening within the transference between therapist and patient).

By the end of the second session, Dr. Ellison could formulate a narrative CMP (see Table 4.3) and comprehend how this CMP had been reenacted in the therapeutic setting. Dr. Ellison's countertransference had not shifted significantly (i.e., she still would have preferred another patient), but she was beginning to understand how her feelings of being overwhelmed and frustrated by this patient were part of the pull of Ms. Ludlow's CMP. The patient was accepted for TLDP treatment.

Since the CMP is designed to provide a blueprint for the therapy, one uses the formulation to derive the goals of her therapy. If our conceptualization of Ms. Ludlow's CMP captures her chronic, problematic style, then what *new experience* and what *new understanding* would be helpful for her to have in the process of the brief therapy?

Dr. Ellison opined that the type of experiences (of self and other) that might facilitate change by derailing a repetitive pattern would include Ms. Ludlow's experience of her as trying to understand and collaborate without trying to fix her, and Ms. Ludlow's experience of herself as effective and not defective. Further, she set as a goal facilitation of Ms. Ludlow's understanding of how she pushes and pulls others to respond as demanding parents when she presents as a needy, frustrating child. A corollary new understanding is for Ms. Ludlow to see that she could have relationships that were not founded on her being defective.

In addition to delineating the goals, the CMP should also be helpful in anticipating the unfolding of the patient–therapist (transference–countertransference) interaction. A useful question for the therapist to ask him- or

TABLE 4.3. TLDP CMP

Acts of the Self

Ms. Ludlow sees herself as trying to "improve herself" and deal with her "problems," but she feels very needy and victimized by others. Her resentment about the way she has been treated by others keeps her waiting for someone who could give her what she needs.

Expectations of Others' Reactions

While Ms. Ludlow hopes that someone perfect will provide for her, she has come to expect that others will find fault with her and reject her at worst, and try to "fix" her at best. However, both of these approaches convey to her that she is defective and unacceptable as she is.

Acts of Others toward the Self

Others find Ms. Ludlow's passive–aggressive behavior, resentful neediness, and diffuse presentation irritating and overwhelming. If they try to help, Ms. Ludlow interprets their behavior as nonempathic attempts to humiliate her; if they leave her alone, she understands this as evidence that they see her as unlovable.

Acts of the Self toward the Self

Ms. Ludlow sees herself as a victim in a world of nonempathic people. Putting other people down in righteous indignation helps her to feel vindicated and "special," but her self-defeating behaviors (e.g., overeating) only serve to confirm her own fears that she is truly defective and unlovable and therefore in need of someone to fix her.

Therapist's Reaction to Patient

Overwhelmed, irritated, frustrated, doomed to failure, pressure to fix her, helpless, hopeless.

Goals

New Experience. Experience herself as effective, not defective. Experience therapist as trying to understand and collaborate with her, not trying to fix her.

New Understanding: Understand how her needy, helpless, but hostile behavior pulls for others to respond in a parental fashion: appreciate that she could have relationships not founded on being defective; have some understanding of the adaptive function of her past behavior.

herself is what potential difficulties could be expected in working with a particular patient based on that patient's idiosyncratic CMP. If one can use the CMP to anticipate the problematic nature of the unfolding therapeutic relationship, then truly the formulation can provide a blueprint of the entire therapy.

Trainees in the BPP who had seen clinical vignettes of Ms. Ludlow and Dr. Ellison on videotape have offered these various anticipated interactions:

- Ms. Ludlow will let Dr. Ellison know that she is not doing a good enough job. She will be expecting that Dr. Ellison will try to fix her. If Dr. Ellison falls for this trap, then Ms. Ludlow will feel betrayed.
- I would warn Dr. Ellison not to go with the pull to rescue, organize, and ultimately fix Ms. Ludlow because it will boomerang. The pull is for Dr. Ellison to outfit Ms. Ludlow with emotional braces and send her off all rehabilitated. But then Ms. Ludlow will feel victimized by someone who cannot accept her for who she is.
- There is the danger that Dr. Ellison will be pulled to abandon the field— if not in reality, then emotionally, as she becomes frustrated with Ms. Ludlow's passive resistance.
- The therapist could feel so attacked by Ms. Ludlow that she could be pulled to retaliate by saying some subtly hostile things back to the patient.
- I would advise Dr. Ellison to avoid plans, advice, and getting caught in "yes-buts." Dr. Ellison has to maintain her own sense of being worthwhile. Otherwise she will end up feeling helpless and incompetent.

Because this is a chapter on case formulation, there is not the space to indicate the strategies through which the therapist achieved the objectives. Suffice it to say, the goal is not content based, such as encouraging Ms. Ludlow to join Weight Watchers. Rather, the goals are process focused. The therapist is not constrained to imagine or define specifically how the new experience and new understanding might be accomplished. The precise form this might take in the actual therapeutic situation can rarely be predicted. The CMP facilitates the therapist's awareness and sensitivity to recognize and promote *anything* that transpires between patient and therapist that fosters movement in the desired direction.

TRAINING

Clinical Aspects of Training

For the reader who wants to learn more about TLDP case formulation and intervention, we recommend a multifaceted approach including reading, supervision (expert or peer), consultation, and workshops with instructional videotapes.[2] There are presently two TLDP manuals available: *Psychotherapy in a New Key: A Guide to Time-Limited Dynamic Psychotherapy* (Strupp & Binder, 1984) describes the basic principles and strategies of TLDP; *Time-Limited Dynamic Psychotherapy: A Guide to Clinical Practice* (Levenson, 1995) provides a practical and pragmatic casebook approach. Instructional videotapes are also commercially available.[3] After reading further about TLDP, we advise becoming familiar with the steps in TLDP formulation and intervention outlined in Table 4.1 and reviewing the Vanderbilt Therapeutic Strategies Scale (VTSS) and accompanying manual included in the appendixes of the Levenson (1995) book. Next, therapists can practice devising CMP formulations and TLDP goals for their problematic patients (e.g., those with poor therapeutic alliances). Going through this exercise even for ongoing patients in long-term therapies can be quite informative for therapists, helping them see more clearly where they might be unintentionally colluding with patients in some dysfunctional dynamic. For those therapists who wish to try out a TLDP therapy, we advise video- or audio-taping sessions, and then reviewing these sessions using the VTSS to assess adherence and deficient areas needing further attention and/or guidance. Peer (or, if possible, expert) consultation is invaluable in becoming aware of nuances in the therapeutic interchange that inform the CMP. In addition, workshops on TLDP occur nationally and regionally through service-oriented agencies and professional associations.

When teaching TLDP to clinicians (whether they be neophytes to the field or experienced professionals), we have preferred to use small-group supervision focusing on video- or audiotapes of therapy hours in combination with didactic sessions, also using videotapes to illustrate teaching points.

In the BPP at the U.S. Department of Veterans Affairs (VA) Medical Centers in San Francisco and Palo Alto, California, directed by one of us (HL) since 1979, clinical service is combined with a comprehensive structured training program for psychiatry residents, psychology interns, social work interns, and clinical staff. Training in the BPP consists of a 1-hour didactic seminar and a 2-hour group supervision per week for 3–5 trainees at a time over a 6-month training rotation. The didactic portion of the training covers in depth the theoretical and clinical aspects of TLDP. Videotapes of actual therapy sessions (by skilled and beginning therapists) are used to illustrate important basic principles and strategies and common therapeutic dilemmas. As they watch videotapes of these sessions in a stop-frame approach, the trainees are asked to say what is going on in the vignettes, to distinguish between relevant and irrelevant material, to propose interventions a therapist might use, to justify their choices, and to anticipate the moment-to-moment behavior of the patients. This learning approach is consistent with the teaching format of "anchored instruction," where knowledge to be learned is specifically tied to a particular problem using active involvement of the learner in a context that is highly similar to actual conditions (Binder, 1993; Bransford, Franks, Vye, & Sherwood, 1989; Schacht, 1991).

Each trainee is assigned to videotape one patient for an entire therapy (up to 20 sessions) using the TLDP model. The average number of actual sessions is approximately 14 (due to vacations, illnesses, holidays, and cancellations). Trainees write up their CMPs and goals at the beginning of the therapy and share these with the others in the class. In this way, the driving force of the therapy is made explicitly salient, and supervision focuses on how to devise strategies designed to further the goals consistent with the formulation.

Each trainee privately reviews his or her entire videotape of that week's session and selects portions to show in the group supervision. This format allows trainees to receive peer and supervisory comments on their technique as well as to observe the process of a brief therapy with other patient–therapist dyads. In this way, trainees learn how the model must be adapted to address the particular dynamics of each case and also what is generalizable about TLDP across patients. In addition, changes are made in the formulations as clinical knowledge grows, allowing trainees to observe the reciprocal process of formulation informing the direction of the therapy, which then informs the nature of the formulation.

In both instruction and supervision, we feel strongly that videotape is an essential part of TLDP training, since it provides a vivid account of what actually occurs in therapy, permitting an examination of the nuances of the therapeutic relationship, unlike a therapist's summary, which often glosses over critical details and portrays the therapy as more coherent and cogent than it ever was. In addition, the realistic context provided by videotape can be used to facilitate an active wrestling with relevant material, which counteracts the negative effects of inert knowledge (Schacht, 1991).

The reader who is particularly interested in TLDP training is referred to the book by Levenson (1995), since it contains actual transcripts of exchanges between supervisor and trainees as they deal with clinical and didactic material.

Research Studies of Training

Strupp and his research group undertook a direct investigation into the effects of training on therapist performance (Strupp, 1993; Henry, Schacht, Strupp, Butler, & Binder, 1993a; Henry, Strupp, Butler, Schacht, & Binder, 1993b). These studies (Vanderbilt II) explored the effects of manualized training in TLDP for 16 experienced therapists (8 psychiatrists and 8 psychologists) and 80 patients. In the first year of the study, each therapist was asked to treat two patients (one relatively "easy"; one relatively "difficult") in up to 25 weekly sessions as he or she ordinarily would. In the second year, the therapists were assigned to work with one patient each while they went through a TLDP training program (didactics, small-group supervision using audio- and videotapes of the training cases). In the third year, therapists again each treated two patients, this time with an emphasis on the tenets of TLDP. The main results indicate that the training program was successful in changing therapists' interventions congruent with TLDP strategies (Henry et al., 1993b) and that these changes held even with the more difficult patients (Henry et al., 1993a).

However, the Vanderbilt II findings also revealed some unintended and potentially untoward training effects. Although there were positive changes in therapists' skills following training, there were also indications of negative changes. For example, after training the activity level of the therapists increased, giving them more of an opportunity to make "mistakes." Following training, therapists appeared less approving and less supportive, and they delivered more disaffiliative and complex communications to patients. The investigators speculated that there may be a posttraining phase in which therapists' performance declines as they grapple with integrating new techniques into their existing therapeutic mode.

There are several problems with the Vanderbilt II studies, not the least of which is that the researchers recruited successful, local, private practitioners, who while they were motivated to participate in a prestigious study at Vanderbilt University, were probably less motivated to learn brief therapy strategies. One's attitude toward brief therapy can affect how well one learns and can competently implement new knowledge (Levenson & Butler, 1997). In addition, since these therapists were all experienced practitioners, they probably had much to "unlearn." Supportive of this view is the finding that those therapists who had *more* supervision in their own model before the training began were *less* likely to adhere to the new TLDP strategies (Henry et al., 1993a).

Among the more striking findings of Vanderbilt II were differences in training effects due to whether the therapist was in Trainer A's or Trainer B's group. Trainer A's therapists showed greater changes in adherence to TLDP. Inspection of differences between the two trainers' styles indicated that Trainer A's approach was more directive, specific, and challenging. This finding led the investigators to suggest how to maximize training effects:

- Choose competent but relatively less experienced therapists.
- Select therapists who are less vulnerable to negative training effects (e.g., less hostile and controlling).
- Assume that even experienced therapists are novices in the approach to be learned.
- Provide close, directive, and specific feedback to therapists, and focus on therapists' own thought processes.

Levenson and Bolter (1988) examined the values and attitudes of psychiatry residents and psychology interns before and after a 6-month seminar and group supervision in TLDP. To maximize training effects, the format was an active, specific approach consistent with that suggested above. They found that after training there were significant changes in the students' attitudes as measured by a questionnaire designed to highlight value differences between short-term and long-term therapists (Bolter, Levenson, & Alvarez, 1990). Specifically, posttraining participants were more willing to consider using brief therapy for other than minor disorders, more positive about patients' achieving significant insight, more expectant that the benefits would be long lasting, and less likely to think that an extended period of "working through" was necessary. Also they were more willing to be active, more likely to see that a time limit was helpful, and more prepared to believe that patients would change significantly after the therapy was over.

RESEARCH SUPPORT FOR THE APPROACH

The background for TLDP comes from a program of empirical research begun in the early 1950s. Strupp (1955a, 1955b, 1955c, 1957, 1958, 1960) asked practicing therapists to pretend they were responding to patients' statements that were presented in written form or on film. He was initially interested in the relationship between technique and therapist variables (e.g., theoretical orientation, level of experience) but was intrigued with results indicating that the therapists' interventions reflected their personal (positive or negative) attitude toward the patients. "On the basis of these data, I hypothesized that the therapist's initial attitude toward the patient might give rise to a self-fulfilling prophecy and that the therapists' communications embodied both technical and personal elements" (Strupp, 1993, p. 431).

The following decade of Strupp's research focused on how outcomes were affected by the relative contributions of so-called specific (technical) and nonspecific (interpersonal) factors. As part of a program of empirical studies at the Vanderbilt University Center for Psychotherapy Research, brief psychotherapies conducted by experienced psychotherapists were compared with those done by college professors who had no formal training in psychotherapy but who had a reputation for being warm and understanding individuals (Strupp & Hadley, 1979). Results focusing on good and poor outcome cases treated by the same therapist (Strupp, 1980a, 1980b, 1980c, 1980d) revealed that patients who were hostile, negativistic, inflexible, mistrusting, or otherwise highly resistant uniformly had poor outcomes, whether or not they were treated by therapists or professors. (It should be noted that the professional therapists had good outcomes with those patients who were able to form good working relationships by the third session.)

Strupp reasoned from the results of these studies (Vanderbilt I) that the difficult patients had characterological styles that made it very hard for them to negotiate good working relationships with their therapists. In such cases the therapists' skill in managing the interpersonal therapeutic climate was severely taxed. Since the therapies were brief, this inability to form a therapeutic alliance quickly had deleterious effects on the entire therapy.

The findings from Vanderbilt I revealed that therapists made little progress dealing with the negative transferences of the more difficult patients. Furthermore, these therapists appeared to get entrapped into reacting with negativity, hostility, and disrespect, and, in general, responded antitherapeutically to the patients' pervasive negativism and hostility. Such negative responses from their own therapists probably served to heighten the patients' helpless and hopeless stance and to solidify a negative view of self and others.

Henry, Schacht, and Strupp (1986) reexamined several cases from the Vanderbilt I project using the Structural Analysis of Social Behavior (SASB; Benjamin, 1974, 1982). The SASB employs a circumplex model (see Henry, Chapter 9, this volume) to discern and code patterns of transactions as distributed along the two axes of affiliation–disaffiliation and independence–

dependence. Findings indicate that in the cases with better outcomes, the therapists were significantly more "affirming and understanding," more "helpful and protecting," and less "belittling and blaming." Patients who had poorer outcomes were significantly less "disclosing and expressing," more "trusting and relying" (passively and deferentially so), and more "walling off and avoiding." Furthermore, multiple communications (e.g., simultaneously accepting and rejecting) by both the patients and therapists were related to poorer outcomes.

Johnson, Popp, Schacht, Mellow, and Strupp (1989), using a modification of the CMP coded by the SASB, found that for a single case, relationship themes were identified that were similar to themes derived using another psychodynamic relationship model (the Core Conflictual Relationship Theme method, CCRT; see Chapter 3, this volume).

Quintana and Meara (1990) found that patients' intrapsychic activity became similar to the way patients perceived their therapists treated them in short-term therapy. Harrist, Quintana, Strupp, and Henry (1994) went one step further. Using cases from the Vanderbilt II project and the SASB, they found that patients internalized both their own and their therapists' contribution to the therapeutic interaction and that these internalizations were associated with better outcomes.

The VA Short-Term Psychotherapy Research Project—the VAST Project—examined TLDP process and outcome with a personality-disordered population (Levenson & Bein, 1993). As part of that project, Overstreet (1993) found that approximately 60% of the 89 male patients achieved positive interpersonal or symptomatic outcomes following TLDP (average of 14 sessions). At termination, 71% of patients felt their problems had lessened. One-fifth of the patients moved into the normal range of scores on a measure of interpersonal problems.

In the VAST Project long-term follow-up study (Bein, Levenson, & Overstreet, 1994; Levenson & Bein, 1993), patients were reassessed a mean of 3 years after their TLDP therapies. The findings reveal that patient gains from treatment (measured by symptom and interpersonal inventories) were maintained and slightly bolstered. In addition, at the time of follow-up, 80% of the patients thought their therapies had helped them deal more effectively with their problems. Other analyses indicate that patients were more likely to value their therapies the more they perceived that sessions focused on TLDP-congruent strategies (i.e., trying to understand their typical patterns of relating to people, exploring childhood relationships, and trying to relate in a new and better way with their therapists). Interventions incongruent or at variance with TLDP (e.g., therapists' giving advice, focusing on symptoms, assigning homework) were unrelated to patients' judgments of benefit.

A recent study using the VAST Project data is relevant for the meaningfulness of TLDP case formulation in a real clinical situation (Hartman & Levenson, 1995). CMP case formulations written by the treating therapists (after the first one or two sessions with their patients) were read by five clinicians who did not know anything about the patients or their therapies. These raters were able to agree on the patients' interpersonal problems solely based on the information contained in the CMP narratives. There is also a statistically significant relationship between what interpersonal problems the raters felt *should* have been discussed in the therapy (based only on the patients' CMPs) and those topics the therapists said actually *were* discussed. Perhaps most meaningful is the finding that better outcomes were achieved the more these therapies stayed focused on topics relevant to the patients' CMPs. Thus, these preliminary findings indicate that the TLDP case formulations convey reliable interpersonal information to clinicians otherwise unfamiliar with the case, guide the issues that are discussed in the therapy, and lead to better outcomes the more therapists can adhere to them.

NOTES

1. The goal of a new experience presented here and elsewhere in more detail (Levenson, 1995) is somewhat of a modification of that originally presented by Strupp and Binder (1984).

2. A recent national survey of psychologists, psychiatrists, and social workers who reported they do some brief therapy (84% of the total sample) found that self-selected reading is the most common form of their brief therapy training. Supervision, however, was rated as the most helpful, followed closely by consultation and reading (Davidovitz & Levenson, 1995).

3. For instructional video tapes contact: Newbridge, P.O. Box 949, Hicksville, NY 11802; American Psychological Association, 750 First Street NE, Washington, DC 20002; Psychological and Educational Films, 3334 E. Coast Highway #252, Corona del Mar, CA 92625.

ACKNOWLEDGMENTS

Portions of this chapter are reprinted from *Time-Limited Dynamic Psychotherapy: A Guide to Clinical Practice* (copyright 1995 by Hanna Levenson) with permission of Basic Books, a division of HarperCollins Publishers.

REFERENCES

Alexander, F., & French, T. M. (1946). *Psychoanalytic therapy: Principles and applications.* New York: Ronald Press.

American Psychiatric Association. (1994). *Diagnostic and statistical manual of mental disorders* (4th ed.). Washington, DC: Author.

Anchin, J. C., & Kiesler, D. J. (Eds.). (1982). *Handbook of interpersonal psychotherapy.* New York: Pergamon Press.

Beck, A. T., Rush, A. J., Shaw, B. F., & Emery, G. (1979). *Cognitive therapy of depression.* New York: Guilford Press.

Bein, E., Levenson, H., & Overstreet, D. (1994, June). Outcome and follow-up data from the VAST project. In H. Levenson (Chair), *Outcome and follow-up data in brief dynamic therapy: Caveat emptor, caveat vendor.* Symposium conducted at the annual international meeting of the Society for Psychotherapy Research, York, England.

Benjamin, L. S. (1974). Structural analysis of social behavior. *Psychological Review, 81,* 392–425.

Benjamin, L. S. (1982). Use of Structural Analysis of Social Behavior (SASB) to guide intervention in psychotherapy. In J. C. Anchin & D. J. Kiesler (Eds.), *Handbook of interpersonal psychotherapy.* New York: Pergamon Press.

Benjamin, L. S. (1993). *Interpersonal diagnosis and treatment of personality disorders.* New York: Guilford Press.

Berne, E. (1964). *Games people play.* New York: Grove Press.

Binder, J. L. (1993). Is it time to improve psychotherapy training? *Clinical Psychology Review, 13,* 301–318.

Bolter, K., Levenson, H., & Alvarez, W. (1990). Differences in values between short-term and long-term therapists. *Professional Psychology: Research and Practice, 4,* 285–290.

Bowlby, J. (1973). *Attachment and loss: Vol. 2. Separation, anxiety, and anger.* New York: Basic Books.

Bransford, J. D., Franks, J. J., Vye, N. H., & Sherwood, R. D. (1989). New approaches to instruction: Because wisdom can't be told. In S. Vosniadou & A. Ortony (Eds.), *Similarity and analogical reasoning.* New York: Cambridge University Press.

Butler, S. F., & Binder, J. L. (1987). Cyclical psychodynamics and the triangle of insight: An integration. *Psychiatry, 50,* 218–231.

Butler, S. F., Strupp, H. H., & Binder, J. L. (1992). Time-Limited Dynamic Psychotherapy. In S. H. Budman, M. F. Hoyt, & S. Friedman (Eds.), *The first session in brief therapy.* New York: Guilford Press.

Davidovitz, D., & Levenson, H. (1995, August). *A national survey of training and practice in brief therapy.* Paper presented at the American Psychological Association Convention, New York.

Gill, M. M. (1979). The analysis of the transference. *Journal of the American Psychoanalytic Association, 27,* 263–288.

Gill, M. M. (1993). Interaction and interpretation. *Psychoanalytic Dialogues, 3,* 111–122.

Greenberg, J. R., & Mitchell, S. A. (1983). *Object relations in psychoanalytic theory.* Cambridge, MA: Harvard University Press.

Harrist, R. S., Quintana, S. M., Strupp, H. H., & Henry, W. P. (1994). Internalization of interpersonal process in Time-Limited Dynamic Psychotherapy. *Psychotherapy, 31,* 49–57.

Hartmann, K., & Levenson, H. (1995, June). *Case formulation in TLDP.* Paper presented at the annual international meeting of the Society for Psychotherapy Research meetings, Vancouver, British Columbia, Canada.

Henry, W. P., Schacht, T. E., & Strupp, H. H. (1986). Structural analysis of social behavior: Application to a study of interpersonal process in differential psychotherapeutic outcome. *Journal of Consulting and Clinical Psychology, 54,* 27–31.

Henry, W. P., Schacht, T. E., Strupp, H. H., Butler, S. F., & Binder, J. L. (1993a). Effects of training in Time-Limited Dynamic Psychotherapy: Mediators of therapists' responses to training. *Journal of Consulting and Clinical Psychology, 61,* 441–447.

Henry, W. P., Strupp, H. H., Butler, S. F., Schacht, T. E., & Binder, J. L. (1993b). Effects of training in Time-Limited Dynamic Psychotherapy: Changes in therapist behavior. *Journal of Counseling and Clinical Psychology, 61,* 434–440.

Horowitz, M. (1987). *States of mind: Analysis of change in psychotherapy* (2nd ed.). New York: Plenum Press.

Johnson, M. E., Popp, C., Schacht, T. E., Mellon, J., & Strupp, H. H. (1989). Converging evidence for identification of recurrent relationship themes: Comparison of two methods. *Psychiatry, 52,* 275–288.

Kiesler, D. J. (1982). Confronting the client–therapist relationship in psychotherapy. In J. C. Anchin & D. J. Kiesler (Eds.), *Handbook of interpersonal psychotherapy.* New York: Pergamon Press.

Kiesler, D. J. (1988). *Therapeutic metacommunication: Therapist impact disclosure as feedback in psychotherapy.* Palo Alto, CA: Consulting Psychologists Press.

Levenson, H. (1995). *Time-limited dynamic psychotherapy: A guide to clinical practice.* New York: Basic Books.

Levenson, H., & Bein, E. (1993, June). VA Short-Term Psychotherapy Research Project: Outcome. In D. A. Shapiro (Chair), *Long-term outcome of brief dynamic psychotherapy.* Symposium conducted at the annual international meeting of the Society for Psychotherapy Research, Pittsburgh, PA.

Levenson, H., & Bolter, K. (1988, August). Short-term psychotherapy values and attitudes: Changes with training. In H. Levenson (Chair), *Issues in training and teaching brief therapy.* Symposium conducted at the convention of the American Psychological Association, Atlanta, GA.

Levenson, H., & Butler, S. F. (1997). Brief dynamic individual psychotherapy. In R. E. Hales, S. C. Yudofsky, & J. A. Talbott (Eds.), *The American Psychiatric Press textbook of psychiatry* 3rd ed. Washington, DC: American Psychiatric Press.

MacKenzie, K. R. (1988). Recent developments in brief psychotherapy. *Hospital and Community Psychiatry, 39,* 742–752.

Overstreet, D. L. (1993). *Patient contribution to differential outcome in time-limited dynamic psychotherapy: An empirical analysis.* Unpublished doctoral dissertation, Wright Institute Graduate School of Psychology, Berkeley, CA.

Quintana, S. M., & Meara, N. M. (1990). Internalization of the therapeutic relationship in short-term psychotherapy. *Journal of Counseling Psychology, 37,* 123–130.

Safran, J. D., & Greenberg, L. S. (1991). Affective change processes: Synthesis and critical analysis. In J. D. Safran & L. S. Greenberg (Eds.), *Emotion, psychotherapy, and change.* New York: Guilford Press.

Safran, J. D., & Segal, Z. V. (1990). *Interpersonal process in cognitive therapy.* New York: Basic Books.

Sampson, H., & Weiss, J. (1986). Testing hypotheses: The approach of the Mount Zion Psychotherapy Research Group. In L. S. Greenberg & N. M. Pinsof (Eds.), *The psychotherapeutic process: A research handbook.* New York: Guilford Press.

Sandler, J. (1976). Countertransference and role-responsiveness. *International Review of Psycho-Analysis, 3,* 43–47.

Schacht, T. E. (1991). Can psychotherapy education advance psychotherapy integration? A view from the cognitive psychology of expertise. *Journal of Psychotherapy Integration, 1,* 305–319.

Schacht, T. E., Binder, J. L., & Strupp, H. H. (1984). The dynamic focus. In H. H. Strupp & J. L. Binder, *Psychotherapy in a new key: A guide to time-limited dynamic psychotherapy*. New York: Basic Books.

Schacht, T. E., & Henry, W. P. (1994). Modeling recurrent patterns of interpersonal relationship with structural analysis of social behavior: The SASB–CMP. *Psychotherapy Research, 4,* 208–221.

Strupp, H. H. (1955a). An objective comparison of Rogerian and psychoanalytic techniques. *Journal of Consulting Psychology, 19,* 1–7.

Strupp, H. H. (1955b). The effect of the psychotherapist's personal analysis upon his techniques. *Journal of Consulting Psychology, 19,* 197–204.

Strupp, H. H. (1955c). Psychotherapeutic technique, professional affiliation, and experience level. *Journal of Consulting Psychology, 19,* 97–102.

Strupp, H. H. (1957). A multidimensional system for analyzing psychotherapeutic techniques. *Psychiatry, 20,* 293–306.

Strupp, H. H. (1958). The psychotherapist's contribution to the treatment process: An experimental investigation. *Behavioral Science, 3,* 43–67.

Strupp, H. H. (1960). *Psychotherapists in action: Explorations of the therapist's contribution to the treatment process.* New York: Grune & Stratton.

Strupp, H. H. (1980a). Success and failure in Time-Limited Psychotherapy: A systematic comparison of two cases (Comparison 1). *Archives of General Psychiatry, 37,* 595–603.

Strupp, H. H. (1980b). Success and failure in Time-Limited Psychotherapy: A systematic comparison of two cases (Comparison 2). *Archives of General Psychiatry, 37,* 708–716.

Strupp, H. H. (1980c). Success and failure in Time-Limited Psychotherapy: With special reference to the performance of a lay counselor (Comparison 3). *Archives of General Psychiatry, 37,* 831–841.

Strupp, H. H. (1980d). Success and failure in Time-Limited Psychotherapy: Further evidence (Comparison 4). *Archives of General Psychiatry, 37,* 947–954.

Strupp, H. H. (1993). The Vanderbilt psychotherapy studies: Synopsis. *Journal of Consulting and Clinical Psychology, 61,* 431–433.

Strupp, H. H., & Binder, J. L. (1984). *Psychotherapy in a new key. A guide to time-limited dynamic psychotherapy.* New York: Basic Books.

Strupp, H. H., & Hadley, S. W. (1979). Specific versus nonspecific factors in psychotherapy: A controlled study of outcome. *Archives of General Psychiatry, 36,* 1125–1136.

Sullivan, H. S. (1953). *The interpersonal theory of psychiatry.* New York: Norton.

Weiss, J. (1993). *How psychotherapy works: Process and technique.* New York: Guilford Press.

5

The Plan Formulation Method

JOHN T. CURTIS
GEORGE SILBERSCHATZ

The Plan Formulation Method (PFM) was developed as a way of operational-izing the process that clinicians engage in when formulating a clinical case. The evolution of the PFM was spurred by the need to develop reliable com-prehensive formulations for clinical research, that is, formulations that not only identify a patient's manifest and latent problems but also the patient's stated and unstated goals for therapy, possible obstacles and resistances to achieving these goals, and how the patient is likely to work in therapy to solve the prob-lems. Prior to the development of the Plan Diagnosis Method (a precursor to the PFM; see below), comprehensive clinical formulations were not used in psychotherapy research because of problems in obtaining adequate interjudge reliability (DeWitt, Kaltreider, Weiss, & Horowitz, 1983; Seitz, 1966).

The PFM does not really constitute a new method for formulating a case. Indeed, the components of a plan formulation and the processes involved in developing it are common to most approaches to psychotherapy case formu-lation. The PFM requires that clinicians review and evaluate clinical material to determine what is relevant and necessary for understanding a particular case and developing a treatment plan. The PFM is unique because it allows clini-cians who share a common theoretical orientation to develop a *reliable* com-prehensive case formulation.

The clinical applications of the PFM are the same as those of any formu-lation: it identifies a patient's goals, the conflicts and inhibitions that inhibit or prevent the patient from pursuing or attaining these goals, the source(s) of these conflicts and inhibitions, information that might be helpful to the pa-tient in understanding and overcoming his or her conflicts, and behaviors or interventions on the part of the therapist that will be helpful. The PFM may differ from other approaches in one basic assumption—that an accurate formulation of an individual patient can often be developed quite early in the therapy. Indeed, for research purposes (e.g., predicting patient responses to interventions across the course of a therapy), plan formulations have been developed arbitrarily on as little as a single intake interview. In clinical use, the therapist is well served by trying to formulate a patient's plan as early in the therapy as possible. However, when used by a therapist, the plan formulation is not a static creation set in cement early in the therapy. Rather, it is a working hypothesis that is constantly evaluated and fine-tuned based upon such factors as the patient's responses to interventions and the emergence of new history.

HISTORICAL BACKGROUND OF THE APPROACH

For over 20 years, the San Francisco Psychotherapy Research Group (formerly known as the Mount Zion Psychotherapy Research Group) has conducted studies of psychoanalyses, psychodynamic psychotherapy, and time-limited psychotherapies. One primary focus of this enterprise has been to study the role of the analyst or therapist in the process of treatment. Specifically, the Group has tried to identify what it is that a therapist does that leads to patient improvement, stagnation, or deterioration in the course of treatment. In a variety of studies, the Group has tested the broad hypothesis that when a therapist responds in accord with a patient's goals for therapy, the patient will show immediate improvement in the process of the treatment and that this improvement will translate into an overall positive therapy outcome. Of course this hypothesis is deceptively simple, for how does one identify, operationalize, and respond appropriately to a patient's goals for therapy? In clinical practice, a case formulation is usually implicitly or explicitly developed by the therapist in order to understand the meaning of an individual patient's problems, to evaluate the appropriateness of therapeutic interventions, and to measure response to treatment (see Perry, Cooper, & Michels, 1987). To keep the research as clinically relevant as possible, the Group decided to employ individual case formulations in studies of the process and outcome of psychotherapy. However, as noted earlier, in order to employ clinical formulations, the Group had to address the problem of getting clinicians to agree among themselves, an issue that had bedeviled researchers for years. The groundbreaking work in this area was conducted by a member of the Group, Joe Caston (1977, 1986), who developed the Plan Diagnosis Method, the precursor to the PFM.

The Plan Diagnosis Method entails a team of clinicians (the formulation team) developing by consensus a case-specific dynamic formulation. To do so, the formulation team reviews transcripts of the early sessions of a psychotherapy and develops a narrative formulation. From this formulation are abstracted lists of items (e.g., goals, insights). The formulation team then adds to these lists "alternative" items that are thought to be plausible for the particular case but less pertinent than the other items. These lists, containing "real" and "alternative" items, are then given to a separate team of clinical judges (reliability judges), who independently review the same clinical material as the formulation team and then rate the relevance of each item to the case (see Curtis, Silberschatz, Sampson, Weiss, & Rosenberg, 1988, for a more complete description of the method). Excellent interjudge reliabilities have been reported for the Plan Diagnosis Method (Caston, 1986; Curtis et al., 1988; Rosenberg, Silberschatz, Curtis, Sampson, & Weiss, 1986).

Though the Plan Diagnosis Method has proven to be very reliable, there are several problems with it:

1. The development by consensus of the original formulation and alternative items does not ensure the equal participation or input of all group members and thus may not reflect the ideas of all the formulation team members.

2. There are no clear guidelines for how the formulation team should work (e.g., how to elicit the contribution of each team member or how to develop the final document); consequently, different formulation teams can employ very different procedures in developing formulations.

3. The formulation team creates a narrative formulation from which individual items (e.g., goals, insights) are abstracted and then combined with the alternative items and given to judges for rating. Thus the reliability judges never rate the actual narrative formulation, only individual items taken from it. The meaning of an item or idea in the context of a narrative can be different than when it is presented in isolation; consequently, agreeing on the ratings of individual items is not the same as agreeing on a narrative formulation.

4. Though a number of safeguards have been introduced to ensure that the alternate items are reasonable and not just "straw men" (see Curtis et al., 1988), the procedure is still vulnerable to such an accusation.

5. The second group of raters (the reliability team) is restricted to rating only those items developed by the formulation team. The reliability team members cannot add items they think important, and thus there is the possibility of not capturing an important element of a case that the reliability team might pick up.

In response to these concerns, a new procedure was developed, the PFM (Curtis & Silberschatz, 1991; Curtis, Silberschatz, Sampson, & Weiss, 1994). First, the procedures followed by the formulation team were changed. Rather than creating a consensus formulation, each of the formulation judges independently reviews the clinical material and develops lists of "real" and "alternative" items (goals, insights, etc.) for the case. The formulation team only develops lists of items; they do not attempt to create a consensus formulation. The second significant change involves using only one team of judges. After the formulation team members have created their lists of items, these lists are collected and compiled into master lists that are then returned to the judges, who independently rate all of the items for their relevance to the case (see "Steps in Case Formulation Construction," below, for a more thorough description of the PFM).

CONCEPTUAL FRAMEWORK

Both the Plan Diagnosis Method and the PFM were developed in order to study a cognitive psychoanalytic theory of therapy developed by Joseph Weiss (1986, 1993). The theory holds that psychopathology stems largely from pathogenic beliefs that, in turn, develop out of traumatic experiences usually occurring in childhood. Pathogenic beliefs suggest that the pursuit of certain goals will endanger oneself and/or someone else and thus are frightening and constricting. Consequently, an individual is highly motivated to change or disconfirm these beliefs in order to pursue his or her goals. Irrational beliefs in one's power to hurt others, excessive fears of retaliation, and exaggerated expectations of being overwhelmed by feelings such as anger and fear are all examples of beliefs that can act as obstructions to the pursuit or attainment of goals.

In therapy, the patient uses the relationship with the therapist to attempt to disconfirm pathogenic beliefs. The therapist's function is to help the patient understand the nature and ramifications of the pathogenic beliefs by interpretation and by allowing the patient to test these beliefs in the therapeutic relationship. The manner in which an individual will work in psychotherapy to disconfirm pathogenic beliefs, overcome problems, and achieve goals is called the patient's "plan." The plan is not a rigid scheme that the patient will invariably follow; rather, it comprises general areas that the patient will want to work on and how the patient is likely to carry out this work (see Weiss, 1986, 1993, for a thorough description of the theory; also see Curtis & Silberschatz, 1986, and Silberschatz & Curtis, 1986, for further discussion of the applications of the theory to clinical phenomena). Formulations developed according to Weiss's theory have five component parts: the patient *goals* for therapy; the *obstructions* (pathogenic beliefs) that inhibit the patient from pursuing or achieving these goals; the events and experiences (*traumas*) that lead to the development of the obstructions; the *insights* that will help the patient achieve therapy goals; and the manner in which the patient will work in therapy to overcome the obstacles and achieve the goals (*tests*).

INCLUSION/EXCLUSION CRITERIA

A plan formulation can be developed for all individuals suffering from psychogenic psychopathology. For research purposes, the PFM has been applied to children (Foreman, 1989; Gibbins, 1989), adolescents, and adults of all ages

(Curtis & Silberschatz, 1991), including geriatric cases (see Silberschatz & Curtis, 1991). The majority of cases we have formulated in our research program have received DSM-III-R Axis I diagnoses of dysthymia or generalized anxiety disorder, frequently accompanied by an Axis II Cluster C personality disorder (DSM-III-R; American Psychiatric Association, 1987). The cases have displayed mild to severe symptomatology, with moderate to catastrophic psychosocial stresses.

STEPS IN CASE FORMULATION CONSTRUCTION

As noted above, a plan formulation developed for clinical use may be characterized as a working hypothesis (or set of hypotheses) that is constantly being evaluated for its accuracy by the clinician. The clinician carefully monitors the patient's responses to interventions to determine whether they are in accord with what is predicted by the formulation. If not, the formulation should be modified accordingly. A formulation may also be altered or elaborated based upon new data (e.g., memories) that emerge in the course of therapy.

In contrast, plan formulations developed for research purposes are based solely on transcripts of early therapy hours, with no additional information (e.g., concerning the subsequent treatment or outcome) included. By restricting the data from which the plan formulations are developed, these formulations can then be used, for example, to predict a patient's response to a therapist's intervention in the later hours of the therapy (e.g., Silberschatz & Curtis, 1993; Silberschatz, Fretter, & Curtis, 1986). For a brief therapy, we ordinarily use an intake interview and the first 2 therapy hours of the case; for a psychoanalysis, we usually employ the intake and first 10 hours of treatment. However, we have reliably formulated cases based on as little as one interview (Curtis et al., 1994; Perry, Luborsky, Silberschatz, & Popp, 1989).

For our research, we typically use three or four clinical judges. The judges are all experienced with and adhere to Weiss's theory of psychotherapy. We have used judges with widely varying degrees of clinical experience and of experience applying the theory to therapy (Curtis & Silberschatz, 1991).

The PFM involves five steps:

1. Clinical judges independently review the transcripts of the early therapy hours, and each develops a formulation for the case. Each judge then creates lists of "real" and "alternative" goals, obstructions, traumas, insights, and tests for the case. The items are written in a standard format described in the instruction manual. This facilitates comparison between items and helps to disguise which judge created which item. The judges are instructed to include in their lists both items they believe are relevant to the case and any items they think reasonable for the case, but of lesser relevance (e.g., items of which they are unsure or items that they at one point thought were highly relevant but ultimately decided were of lesser relevance). These "alternative" items are not

"straw men" that can be readily discounted. Indeed, these items are some-times given high ratings by other judges.

2. The judges' lists are combined into master lists of goals, obstructions, traumas, insights, and tests. In the master lists, the authors of the items are not identified and the items developed by any given judge are randomly distributed within the appropriate list.

3. The master lists of goals, obstructions, trauma, insights, and tests are returned to the clinical judges, who independently rate the items on a 5-point Likert scale for their relevance to the case (0 = not relevant; 1 = slightly relevant; 2 = moderately relevant; 3 = highly relevant; 4 = very highly relevant).

4. Because different formulations are developed for each case, there tends to be relatively little overlap of items across cases. Consequently, reliability is measured for each of the five plan components (goals, obstructions, tests, insights, traumas) for each case by calculating an intraclass correlation (ICC) for pooled judges' ratings (Shrout & Fleiss, 1979). Two figures are calculated, the estimated reliability of the average judge ($r_{(1)}$, referred to by Shrout and Fleiss as ICC 3, 1) and coefficient alpha, the estimated reliability of K judges' ratings ($r_{(K)}$, referred to by Shrout and Fleiss as ICC 3, K).

5. After determining reliability, the development of the final formulation involves a two-step process. First, items rated as being of lesser relevance to the case are dropped from the list. This is done by taking the mean of judges' ratings per item, determining the median of the mean item ratings per category (goals, obstructions, etc.), and then dropping all items within each category that fall below the median rating for that category. In our experience, this is a conservative criterion; the final items usually have received mean ratings falling at or above the "highly relevant" range. The second step entails a separate team of judges individually reviewing the final items to identify redundancies. The judges then meet and decide by consensus which items are redundant and should be eliminated. The remaining items are included in the final formulation.

The plan formulation is cast in the following format: There is a description of the patient and of the patient's current life circumstances followed by a narrative of the patient's presenting complaints. Then the goals, obstructions, tests, insights, and traumas are listed for the patient. Depending upon the nature of the formulation and how it is to be used, a paragraph summarizing the main features of the individual items may be included under each of the rubrics. (A complete manual of the PFM is available from the authors.)

APPLICATION TO PSYCHOTHERAPY TECHNIQUE

A basic assumption behind the development of a plan formulation is that a clinician cannot and should not proceed to treat a patient without an understanding of that individual's true goals for therapy and the conflicts that have inhibited the patient from obtaining those goals. As with all formulations, the plan formulation contains the clinician's understanding of the causes and manifestations of the patient's symptoms and conflicts. According to Weiss's theory, the causes can be discerned from the traumas that the individual has experienced (Weiss, 1986, 1993). The identification of traumas can alert the therapist to potential issues in the therapy, in particular to what Weiss describes as pathogenic beliefs. These are beliefs that suggest that the attainment of goals will lead to danger to oneself and/or others. For instance, individuals who have experienced neglect and abandonment are likely to work on issues of basic trust and worthiness, as manifested in beliefs about their worth and/or the trustworthiness of others. Similarly, a patient who comes from a family in which members experienced significant losses or disabilities might have survival guilt stemming from pathogenic beliefs that personal success in life would hurt others. Thus, an awareness of the traumas experienced by a patient can alert the therapist to the obstructions, or pathogenic beliefs, that that individual will want to work on in therapy. A picture of the patient's pathogenic beliefs can often clarify the patient's true goals for therapy, as well as the meaning and origins of symptoms. Without a formulation, the therapist cannot determine whether the patient's stated goals represent true treatment goals or compromises (i.e., less ambitious goals) or even false goals (e.g., when patients feel guilty about their true goals and thus present with goals that may even be the opposite of their real aspirations; see Curtis & Silberschatz, 1986).

Identifying the traumas endured by a patient and the consequent pathogenic beliefs that developed can be essential to understanding the meaning of a patient's behaviors. Such an understanding enables the therapist to respond to these behaviors appropriately. A good illustration of this is when a patient is testing by turning passive into active, that is, when a patient who has been traumatized by the behaviors of others enacts similar behaviors with the therapist. For example, a patient who was repeatedly browbeaten by a parent may be critical and argumentative with the therapist (see Weiss, 1993, for a thorough explanation of testing). At such times, the patient may appear to be resisting or even sabotaging the treatment. However, a thorough understanding of the patient's pathogenic beliefs and of the manner in which these beliefs might be tested in the therapy can assist the therapist in seeing these behaviors for what they really are, the patient's active attempts to work on and master a problem by literally bringing it into the therapy. On a broader level, the case formulation can help the therapist to determine what degree of activity on the part of the therapist will be appropriate and helpful to the patient. For example, a patient who was traumatized by intrusive parents may be similarly traumatized—or, minimally, have important tests failed—by an active therapist. On the other hand, a patient who has experienced neglect or abandonment may be traumatized by a passive, "neutral" therapist.

Finally, a formulation is necessary to evaluate the progress of the therapy. Without clear-cut goals and a sense of what must transpire for the patient to achieve them, both therapist and therapy, and ultimately the patient, will be at sea. When the therapy is not going according to the formulation, it suggests either that the therapist is not using the formulation appropriately or that the formulation is wrong and needs to be revised. Patients do not change their basic plans. They may change how they go about trying to achieve their plans; for example, they may try new testing strategies if the therapist consistently fails certain types of tests, or they may work on different goals if the therapy does not help them progress in certain arenas (see Curtis & Silberschatz, 1986). However, these may be seen as shifts in focus, not a change in the patient's overall plan.

Should the therapist share the formulation with a patient? In a sense, the course of therapy may be seen as the unfolding and explication of a patient's plan. However, how and when this is done can be tricky. It may take time for the therapist to feel confident with a formulation, for the therapist is also, in a sense, testing the formulation in the course of the therapy. Certainly, sharing an inaccurate formulation with a patient would be problematic. Sharing an accurate formulation can also be troublesome if, for example, doing so discourages the patient's testing and/or identifies unconscious conflicts that the patient is not yet aware of or ready to consider. Thus, questions about when and how to share the formulation with a patient are best answered by considering what the formulation suggests about how the patient is likely to hear and respond to both the words and the therapist's actions.

CASE EXAMPLE

The following case is drawn from our ongoing research on the process and outcome of time-limited psychodynamic psychotherapy (Silberschatz, Curtis, Sampson, & Weiss, 1991). The patient, whom we shall call "Millie," was referred to the research project by an employment counselor because Millie's depression and despair were preventing her from making any progress in securing employment. The plan formulation for Millie presented below is not that of the therapist; rather, it was developed after the treatment by a team of four clinicians based upon written transcripts of an intake interview and the first 2 (of a total of 16) therapy hours. The formulating clinicians knew nothing about the case other than what was contained in the transcripts; that is, they knew nothing about what happened in the later hours of the case or about the outcome. They were also blind as to the identity of the therapist. Though not developed by the therapist, later conversations with the therapist confirmed that the formulation is consistent with his own formulation and can be used to explain much of the process and outcome of the treatment.

The formulation presented below differs slightly from the actual one developed for this case. Due to space limitations, only a few individual goals, obstructions, tests, and insights are included; the entire lists have been replaced by summary paragraphs. At the time the plan formulation for Millie was developed, our research group did not include key traumas in formulations; this was a later development. Therefore, in the "Traumas" subsection below, we have reported some events from Millie's history that we feel are representative of the experiences that led to the development of her pathogenic beliefs.

Plan Formulation for Millie

Presenting Complaints

Millie, a 54-year-old married female was born in Europe and lived in Israel for a short period after World War II before emigrating to the United States with her husband. She has two children: an older son, who is married and attends graduate school out of state, and a younger daughter, who attends college nearby and lives away from home. Recently, Millie's husband was placed in a nursing home. For the past 4 years he has suffered from a degenerative terminal neurological disorder that has rendered him bedridden, unable to speak, and incapable of self-care.

Millie's presenting complaints are that she feels depressed and paralyzed. She is unable to make up her mind about what she wants to do with her life and feels unable to cope. Because of the loss of income due to her husband's illness, she needs to find employment, but she feels incapable of holding a job and cannot decide what kind of work to pursue. She complains of problems in concentrating and feels that she cannot learn. She also feels lonely and alienated from her peers and, in particular, from her married friends.

Formulation

Traumas. Millie was the younger of two daughters born to a professional man and his wife. Millie described herself as being an active, curious child who was often accused by both of her parents of wanting too much, being too active, and not being satisfied. During Millie's childhood, her father had numerous, blatant affairs to which her mother responded passively or by returning to her parents' (Millie's grandparents') home. When Millie was 5 years of age, her mother left for good. A year later, she came for a visit and told Millie that she had left because Millie had been too much for her to handle. Millie was crushed by this accusation. In the following years, she and her sister lived with their father and his various mistresses. In her early teens, during World War II, she was held in a prison camp where she experienced extreme emotional challenges and physical deprivation. At the end of the war, she and her sister were released after 3 years of captivity. Their mother initially balked at seeing them, fearing that she would find their physical condition upsetting. When their father learned of their release, he spent most of his money on a vacation with his mistress, figuring that he would have little opportunity to travel after his children returned. As a result, when Millie and her sister moved in with their father, there were few resources to help with their recovery or education. Though neither had finished her education, which of course had been interrupted by their imprisonment, they were forced by their father to find work immediately and pay their own way. Millie eventually married a divorced man, 10 years her senior; and they later emigrated to the United States, where he worked and she stayed at home raising their two children. The marriage was unhappy. Millie's husband wanted little to do with her or the children. He dismissed her requests to engage in activities or to have a more active social life, complaining that work left him with little energy for anything else. Millie described raising the children more or less on her own.

Goals. Broadly stated, Millie's goals for therapy are to regain a sense of direction and purpose and to get on with her life. She wants to find employment and to expand and improve her social life. She would like to be less self-punitive and self-critical and to be comfortable acknowledging her capabilities and needs. In addition, she would like to feel comfortable giving herself more as well as receiving more from others. To do so, she will need to feel less responsible for others and thereby less guilty about attending to her own needs and aspirations. In particular, she would like to feel less responsible for her husband's condition and better able to attend to her own needs.

Examples of individual goals formulated for Millie:

To find employment
To be more active socially; develop new relationships and enjoy old ones
To feel less like a terrible, bad, unworthy person
To feel more deserving of help, satisfactions, and having a life of her own

Obstructions. A family of pathogenic beliefs obstruct Millie's pursuit and attainment of her goals. These beliefs suggest that she is bad and therefore undeserving of happiness, success, or love. She feels that she deserves the scorn and mistreatment of others. Millie appears to believe that as a child she was too much to handle, so overpowering that she hurt her mother and drove her away. She developed the belief that people are threatened and bothered by her abilities and needs and that she can overwhelm them by complaining or getting angry. Consequently, Millie believes that the pursuit of her own needs or goals is at the expense of others. Thus she feels she should give but not receive and that to take care of others she should devote herself entirely to them. Her omnipotent feelings of responsibility for her mother have generalized to other relationships such that, for example, she feels blameworthy for her husband's problems.

Examples of individual obstructions formulated for Millie:

She believes that she does not deserve to be admired and loved.
She believes that her awful behavior (wanting more, energy, assertiveness, noncompliance, intellectual abilities) overwhelmed her mother and drove her mother away.

She believes that if she gets or achieves something it is at someone else's expense.

She believes that if she pursues her interests and goals then she will be guilty of abandoning others (e.g., husband, mother) and ignoring their needs.

Tests. In therapy, Millie will work to disconfirm her pathogenic beliefs. For instance, she will test her belief that she is bad and undeserving by observing whether the therapist is critical of her or disapproving of her wishes and needs. She will display her abilities and may also act willful and assertive to see if the therapist is bothered or overwhelmed by her (as she has experienced others as being). Generally, she will monitor whether the therapist can tolerate (or possibly encourage) her strengths and abilities or whether he is critical of her and focuses on her problems or failings. Related to this, she will test whether the therapist is critical of her pursuing her goals and of her not devoting herself to others (e.g., her husband).

Millie may also test by turning passive into active, for example, by behaving in a weak, needy, or helpless fashion to see if the therapist feels unusually responsible for *her*. When testing in this fashion, she will also observe whether the therapist wants or needs for her to be weak and incapable.

Examples of individual tests formulated for Millie:

She will act helpless and incompetent to see if the therapist expects or needs her to be that way.

She will act whiny and complaining to see if the therapist is defeated or becomes rejecting.

She will hide actual progress and achievements (e.g., by putting them in an unfavorable light) to test whether the therapist wishes to focus instead on her failings.

She will criticize her husband and begin to be less attentive to him to see if the therapist will criticize her for it.

She will act willful, assertive, and inquisitive to see if the therapist puts her down or is bothered by this.

Insights. Millie will be assisted in achieving her goals for therapy by developing insight into the genetics and manifestations of her pathogenic beliefs. She would be helped by developing insight into how her relationships during childhood (especially with her mother) led her to believe that she is bad and that her needs and abilities are overwhelming. She may discover how these experiences have led to the development of an omnipotent sense of responsibility and to the belief that what she gets is at others' expense. Achieving insight into the manifestations of her pathogenic beliefs may allow her to see how she has been excessively self-critical and how she has inhibited herself to avoid threatening, depriving, or surpassing others. She might also be helped by understanding how her worry about and guilt over surpassing others has led her to comply and identify with them (e.g., she regards herself as being bad and feels paralyzed and helpless like her husband).

Examples of individual insights formulated for Millie:

To become aware that she always feels at fault when there is any problem in a relationship

To become aware that she believes that she should not be taken seriously and should not feel important

To become aware that she feels omnipotent responsibility for her husband and others

To become aware that she believes that anything she gets is at the expense of husband, children, or others

To become aware that she is uncomfortable about feeling satisfied with any achievement

To become aware that she has complied with the abuse of her parents and husband in order to protect them

While space does not allow for a thorough review of this case, it can be used to illustrate several important points about how the plan can guide the therapist in the course of the therapy. In the first place, while a plan formulation usually identifies a number of goals that a patient might want to work on in therapy; it is the patient, not the therapist, who actually determines the focus of the treatment. As will be noted, Millie's life was a mess, and there were many arenas in which she might have worked—her husband's illness and impending death, the changes in her financial and social circumstances, the changes in her relationships with her children, the impacts of a very traumatic childhood, and her feelings of depression and anxiety, to name a few. However, in the actual treatment, the therapist did not focus the process, but rather followed Millie's lead. Millie concentrated primarily on overcoming her fears and inhibitions about employment and finding work. In this vein, she addressed pathogenic beliefs concerning her ability and right to be successful, her survivor guilt, and other obstructions that impacted her pursuit of other goals. However, as she stated in a posttherapy follow-up interview, when she entered therapy her most pressing problems were financial and work related and thus that was where she focused her efforts. The broad point is that if the therapist had attempted to be more directive—either in the course of the work or, for example, by trying to contract with her at the beginning of the treatment—he might have misdirected her and/or interfered with some important areas in which she needed to test (e.g., tests addressing her right and ability to pursue her own goals and to be autonomous). As discussed in greater detail elsewhere (Curtis & Silberschatz, 1986; Weiss, 1993), a basic premise of the plan formulation and its application is that the formulation identifies the patient's plan in order to assist the therapist in helping the patient to enact that plan. In other words, it helps the therapist follow the patient, not lead the treatment.

The plan formulation also helps the therapist to understand the patient's symptoms and complaints. For instance, Millie's depression was certainly an understandable reaction to recent events and her circumstances; however, the overriding pessimism and sense of defeat that inhibited her from dealing with her circumstances could, from the plan formulation, be seen as this patient's identifications with her passive mother and her sick husband. Consequently, the therapist expressed little direct sympathy for Millie's plight; rather, he focused on her inhibitions about appropriately addressing her circumstances. This is illustrated in an interchange that occurred in Session 5: (The following clinical examples have been edited for length; ellipses indicate where text has been deleted.)

I'm not in very good shape. I just cry all the time. (*silence*) It all seems so pointless; I don't know. . . . It's been 4 years since my husband's illness and about 2 years now since my oldest moved out—more than 2 years I guess. Going on 3 years pretty soon. And, uhm, people used to say, "My God, you're so strong. You're a strong woman, how you manage, it's wonderful, and you always seem to be in good spirits and everything." And suddenly it's all gone. I just lost it. It seems as though everyone went away. (*crying*). . . . I was all right until now. I think it finally caught up with me. . . .

/You say it caught up to you now./

Mm-hmm. It's as though finally it's been waiting to pounce. And as long as my husband was so critically ill and the time he was at home and then in the hospital, I didn't have time to think. You know, the children were still at home. I was needed, I was rushing around. I was so busy 24 hours a day, and it gave me a lot of momentum. And I was angry, and that gave me a lot of energy. Not necessarily negative energy, but it produced—I was angry at what was happening, that we could not get a diagnosis. Uhm, I was fighting. And now I've stopped fighting, and I've stopped being angry. Instead I'm a blob. Not doing anything, not going anywhere. . . . There is the stress in going to the hospital and seeing what's going on there—not just with him but with some of the other people. They're DYING there all the time, and I should accept that as being good because they're old and they're certainly not without suffering, and one should say they've had enough of this. . . . And they're so terribly in need of warmth and loving and gentleness and softness. . . . They're not even fighting anymore; they're not even demanding anymore. I like it when they are demanding and obnoxious. Because then (*laugh*) I know they are still hanging in there. . . . When they stop that, that's when I get REALLY worried, because I know they're just giving up and are no longer willing to pitch in. . . . I can tell now, I've seen it so often. And there is no recourse from it. I can't go home (*pause*) to anything. I come home to an EMPTY house—such a still, still house. (*crying*) And I don't feel like doing anything.

/So are you drawing a parallel between the way that you're feeling and be-having and say, these people in the home, who are in some way giving up?/

I don't know. I never thought that through. I wanna reach out to them. I think the way I would like somebody to reach out to me. I think that's where the parallel is.

/You know, I think though, that it's more than that. I think that, for ex-ample in this home, you go and you see the people who are sick, who are dying, and for whom there is no recourse. And you are well, and healthy, and have a considerable amount of life before you. I suspect that you begin to feel uncomfortable about having all of that time before you./

Survivor guilt?

/That might be one word for it. And maybe begin to feel like a victim in order to keep from feeling like a victimizer. Is it okay for you now to go on with your life? Is it okay for you to have a good time? To get on with it./

The plan formulation also provides guidance for understanding and re-sponding to the process of the therapy and, in particular, to the patient's tests. This will be illustrated by examining a theme of Millie's treatment, her defeated and pessimistic attitude, which reflects both transference and passive-into-active testing. Especially in the early hours of the therapy, Millie was persistently pessimistic and downtrodden. She claimed to be inept, incompetent, and with-out skills. The therapist responded to this as a transference test of whether he could appreciate and encourage her skills and abilities and believed she was deserving of something more. Thus when she complained of being inept, he would generally respond by noting her abilities and, on occasion, interpret-ing the origins of her self-doubts. For example, in Session 8, the following interchange occurred:

And when I have to make a decision, should I do this? It's always as though, you know, my decisions were never good enough in the past — so why should they be good enough now? Now I'm suddenly supposed to be independent and make all these far-reaching decisions about my life and the future, and god-knows-what-else.

/What are you saying?/

That I'm not equipped to do it.

/Kind of like your mother?/

Touché. (*pause*) I suppose, in a way, I'm saying that I'm not equipped to do it; and so I'm running away from it. (*silence*) That's a very good point.

/Tell me your thoughts about it./

In a way I repeat my mother's pattern in this way. She failed with us. And I'm failing myself. (*pause*)

/But I suspect for different reasons. You're saying that your mother, for whatever reason, wasn't able to handle things, and she fled. And I think in a sense you're fleeing now because you're concerned about what it means if you do handle them, if you are strong, unlike her./

. . . (*silence*) Maybe it's the fear of falling flat on my face if I start something and I can't finish it. That used to be a big thing around our house. You know—"You started something, now finish it." And if somehow you failed . . . It's as though decisions were always so irrevocable. Even my husband. You know? Things were always so final.

/Then I think that's the real issue. That you're now in a position to make decisions and to be flexible, and to adjust things as necessary for what is best for you. And that the concern about failure is really secondary to the issue of feeling comfortable making these decisions./

Even in later hours of the therapy, when she had procured a job, Millie continued to enact tests of whether she was truly capable and deserving. In the following excerpt from Session 15, Millie is discussing her reactions to being offered a teaching job. She suggests that since she has never received formal training as a teacher that she should not have gotten the job, that she may have gotten it through some form of fraud, and that she will probably fail at it. The therapist, in countering her self-deprecation and in noting the origins of her concerns, passes the test of whether he, unlike others in Millie's past, believes that she is deserving and capable of more:

I feel I'm arrogant, really arrogant, in assuming that I can do something for which I have basically no training whatsoever. That I can do off the top of my head what other people go through lengthy studies for, to learn how to do . . .

/And that you can be a good teacher when your father couldn't?/

I never connected the two. (*pause*) I'm a more perceptive teacher than he. I think, that's just my personality. Uhm. (*pause*) Maybe that is so. Maybe I can be a better teacher than he was. But certainly, uhm, I could never rival his knowledge. You know—even get close. . . . I'm just terrified of failing. Just terrified of failing. And not being able to allow myself to fail, because if I do it will be such a loss of face. That I don't know whether I—you know, how I will deal with that. I'm afraid of having to deal with that.

/It's not clear to me whether you're as worried about failing as about the fact that you'll probably do a good job at this./

I think I should—I should be very happy to think that I will do a good job and I won't have to—but you see that never really occurs to me.

/Isn't that curious?/

And when I DO think about that, just in a little flash, "What if I did a really good job?"—then I think to myself, "Oh, come on Millie! Be realistic." You know? That's not gonna really happen; it CAN'T really happen. It's never happened before. You've never been really, really good at anything. . . . And that's what scares me, that, uhm, there are these people are paying me to do something which I purport to be able to do, but in reality haven't got the FAINTEST notion at this point how I will carry it off.

/So what you're telling me is that somehow, despite your miserable abilities, your uh—obvious incompetence, and uh—your overwhelming inadequacy, you've—/

(*laugh*) /—Once again managed to pull the wool over these people's eyes, for the large part by using massive deceit and dishonesty, to uh—squeeze yourself into another position in which you'll have to inevitably fail./

(*hearty laugh*) Sounds right! Yeah.

/I think the scenario is pretty uh—/

(*laugh, laugh*)

/Pretty firmly established./

So why? Why do I aspire to things? . . . I know people who work at five dollars an hour, but I'm not willing to do that. . . . So why am I so arrogant? Why do I have to prove to my friends that, "Look, I can get paid more?"

/I think you're feeling like you're being arrogant, just because you've gotten a job./

Millie's pessimism may also be seen as a passive-into-active enactment in which she discouraged the therapist in the same way her parents discouraged her. Certainly, Millie had good reason for pessimism: her home life was in a shambles, she was financially strapped, and she had few resources to fall back on. However, by recognizing the early traumas she had experienced and the pathogenic beliefs that she developed as a result of them, the therapist did not sympathize with her discouragement but rather, in a truly empathic way, challenged it. In so doing, he did not interpret her behavior as testing but rather focused on the inhibitions she had developed as a result of her parents' behavior. Consequently, when she criticized her children for not helping her enough (as she had been criticized by her father and mother) the therapist responded in the following way:

My daughter doesn't pull her weight around the house (*sniff*). She doesn't do anything, but she brings all her friends home, and everybody eats, and you know, makes themselves at home. . . . She hasn't gone to see her father in weeks, but she has time for everything else, after work, or in between work, or taking a day off work. But there is never time to go see dad. . . . She doesn't pull her weight. She doesn't do anything. She's being self-centered and flighty and superficial, and all she can think of right now is just you know, having a good time with her friends after work and stuff. . . . On the weekend she sleeps until eleven in the morning, and then she has other things to do—.

You know, but there is never time to help me with something around the house, a project or something that's too heavy or too complicated to do by myself. Uhm, there is just no feeling of teamwork at all. And I have that same feeling with [my son] Matthew. It's not their house, you know, anymore. They USE it. And in a sense I feel they're using me, and maybe that's what a parent is for. (*pause*) But I'm obviously unhappy with it, so something's wrong. I have nobody to turn to; I have nobody. (*sniff*) And . . . they all go away from the house in twos, in pairs. They're together. And I remain behind with the dirty dishes and the dirty laundry in the house alone. It is not right; something's wrong. And I'm sure it's me. How come I can't handle it? (*pause*) Where's my sense of humor gone? I don't understand that either, but it sure disappeared. I'm just gloomy all the time and melancholy.

/Are you saying that your kids are doing the sorts of things that you'd like to be doing?/

(*whisper, sniff*) Yes. In other words I'm jealous.

/Well I wonder if some of your criticism of your kids is really a criticism that you would be directing against yourself if you were to let yourself go ahead and do some of these things that you would enjoy. That you're not being— if you did you wouldn't be responsible, or you wouldn't be taking care of things. You wouldn't be visiting your husband—things of this nature./

(*sniff*) So where's the solution? If I went ahead, I could not bring myself to do it, although vicariously I (*pause*) you know, I sense it, I see it in them. (*sniff*) I can NOT be irresponsible that way, I just couldn't.

/Irresponsible what way?/

To shirk my responsibility in terms of the house, and my husband, and all of that. I can no more do that than change myself over completely uhm,—

/Are you saying that your going out and having fun and pursuing things that you would like to do necessarily means that you would also be shirking your responsibilities?/

In light of Millie's history, if the therapist had interpreted her discouragement and pessimism as a resistance, she might have experienced it as a reenactment of parental criticisms. By being aware of the early traumas Millie had experienced and of the pathogenic beliefs they engendered, her need to test these beliefs, and the possibility that these tests might occur in a passive-into-active manner, the therapist was able to see how Millie's behavior in fact represented efforts to resolve her conflicts and active involvement in her treatment.

TRAINING

As noted above, while the PFM was developed to study the theory of psychotherapy developed by Joseph Weiss, it has been applied by other researchers who adhere to a different theoretical stance (Collins & Messer, 1991) and to therapies conducted under widely varying theoretical orientations, both psychodynamic and nonpsychodynamic (Curtis & Silberschatz, 1991; Curtis et al., 1994; Persons, Curtis, & Silberschatz, 1991). Thus, for purposes of training in the PFM, the first consideration is that the clinicians share and be well versed in a common theoretical position. It should be noted that this is often easier said than done. One of the interesting findings from adapting the PFM for use by other researchers is that theories and their applications are often poorly operationalized, and clinicians who think they share a common perspective may find, after applying the PFM, that they differ widely in how they understand or apply that perspective (Collins & Messer, 1991; see also Seitz, 1966). We see this as a strength in the PFM; it does not allow for sloppy thinking. Once a group of clinicians share a common, well operationalized theoretical perspective, the PFM can be applied with good reliability (Collins & Messer, 1988; Curtis & Silberschatz, 1991). Even relatively inexperienced clinicians have been able to develop plan formulations with reliabilities approaching those of more seasoned veterans of the procedure (Curtis & Silberschatz, 1991).

RESEARCH SUPPORT FOR THE APPROACH

We have obtained excellent reliabilities applying the PFM to long- and short-term therapies from different settings (research programs, private practice, and hospital and university clinics), treated under differing theoretical models (including psychodynamic psychotherapy, psychoanalysis, interpersonal psychotherapy, and cognitive-behavioral therapy) (Curtis & Silberschatz, 1991; Curtis et al., 1994; see also Persons et al., 1991; Silberschatz, Curtis, Persons, & Safran, 1989). Across six cases reported elsewhere (Curtis & Silberschatz, 1991), coefficient alpha averaged: goals, .90; obstructions, .84; tests, .85; insights, .90.

The PFM has also been used by other investigators with good reliability. Collins and Messer (1988, 1991) employed the PFM and obtained good interjudge reliabilities among their judges, who were generally less clinically experienced than the typical judges used by our research group. We have found no significant differences between ratings of judges who have had previous experience with the PFM and those who have not, nor have we found level of clinical experience to be a barrier to learning this method (Curtis & Silberschatz, 1991).

The validity of the PFM has been tested in studies in which formulations have been used to measure the impact of therapist interventions (Fretter, 1984; Norville, 1989; Silberschatz, 1978, 1986; Silberschatz & Curtis, 1993; Silberschatz et al., 1986) and patient progress in psychotherapy (Nathans, 1988; Silberschatz, Curtis, & Nathans, 1989). For instance, in several studies we have demonstrated that the "accuracy" of therapist interventions (defined as the degree of adherence of the interpretation to the individual patient's plan formulation) predicts subsequent patient progress in therapy (Broitman, 1985; Fretter, 1984; Silberschatz, 1986; Silberschatz & Curtis, 1993; Silberschatz, Curtis, Fretter, & Kelly, 1988; Silberschatz, Curtis, & Nathans, 1989; Silberschatz et al., 1986; see also Bush & Gassner, 1986). In preliminary studies, we have also shown that Plan Attainment, a case-specific outcome measure that rates the degree to which a patient has achieved the goals and insights and has overcome the obstacles identified in his or her plan formulation, correlates highly with other standardized outcome measures and is a good predictor of patient functioning at posttherapy follow-up (Nathans, 1988; Silberschatz, Curtis, & Nathans, 1989). These studies support the hypothesis that the plan formulation identifies important factors that influence the nature and maintenance of a patient's psychopathology. The clinical relevance of these findings is reflected in the fact that when therapists respond in accord with a patient's plan the result is improvement both in the process and the outcome.

REFERENCES

American Psychiatric Association. (1987). *Diagnostic and statistical manual of mental disorders* (3rd ed., rev.). Washington, DC: Author.

Broitman, J. (1985). *Insight, the mind's eye: An exploration of three patients' processes of becoming insightful.* Unpublished doctoral dissertation, Wright Institute Graduate School of Psychology, Berkeley, CA.

Bush, M., & Gassner, S. (1986). The immediate effect of the analyst's termination interventions on the patient's resistance to termination. In J. Weiss, H. Sampson, & the Mount Zion Psychotherapy Research Group, *The psychoanalytic process: Theory, clinical observations, and empirical research* (pp. 299–320). New York: Guilford Press.

Caston, J. (1977). Manual on how to diagnose the plan. In J. Weiss, H. Sampson, J. Caston, & G. Silberschatz, *Research on the psychoanalytic process: I. A comparison of two theories about analytic neutrality* (Bulletin No. 3, pp. 15–21), San Francisco: The Psychotherapy Research Group, Department of Psychiatry, Mount Zion Hospital and Medical Center.

Caston, J. (1986). The reliability of the diagnosis of the patient's unconscious plan. In J. Weiss, H. Sampson, & the Mount Zion Psychotherapy Research Group, *The psychoanalytic process: Theory, clinical observations, and empirical research* (pp. 241–255). New York: Guilford Press.

Collins, W., & Messer, S. (1988, June). *Transporting the Plan Diagnosis Method to a different setting: Reliability, stability, and adaptability.* Paper presented at the Annual Conference of the Society for Psychotherapy Research, Santa Fe, NM.

Collins, W. D., & Messer, S. B. (1991). Extending the Plan Formulation Method to an Object Relations perspective: Reliability, stability, and adaptability. *Psychological Assessment, 3,* 75–81.

Curtis, J. T., & Silberschatz, G. (1986). Clinical implications of research on brief dynamic psychotherapy: I. Formulating the patient's problems and goals. *Psychoanalytic Psychology, 3,* 13–25.

Curtis, J. T., & Silberschatz, G. (1991). *The Plan Formulation Method: A reliable procedure for case formulation.* Unpublished manuscript.

Curtis, J. T., Silberschatz, G., Sampson, H., & Weiss, J. (1994). The Plan Formulation Method. *Psychotherapy Research, 4*, 197–207.

Curtis, J. T., Silberschatz, G., Sampson, H., Weiss, J., & Rosenberg, S. E. (1988). Developing reliable psychodynamic case formulations: An illustration of the Plan Diagnosis Method. *Psychotherapy, 25*, 256–265.

DeWitt, K. N., Kaltreider, N. B., Weiss, D. S., & Horowitz, M. J. (1983). Judging change in psychotherapy. *Archives of General Psychiatry, 40*, 1121–1128.

Foreman, S. (1989, June). *Overview of the method to study psychotherapy with children, based on the Mount Zion Method.* A paper presented at the Annual Conference of the Society for Psychotherapy Research, Toronto, Ontario, Canada.

Fretter, P. B. (1984). The immediate effects of transference interpretations on patients' progress in brief, psychodynamic psychotherapy. (Doctoral dissertation, University of San Francisco, 1984). *Dissertation Abstracts International, 46*(6). (University Microfilms No. 85–12, 112)

Gibbins, J. (1989, June). *The plan diagnosis of a child case.* A paper presented at the Annual Conference of the Society for Psychotherapy Research, Toronto, Ontario, Canada.

Nathans, S. (1988). *Plan Attainment: An individualized measure for assessing outcome in psychodynamic psychotherapy.* Unpublished doctoral dissertation, California School of Professional Psychology, Berkeley.

Norville, R. L. (1989). *The relationship between accurate interpretations and brief psychotherapy outcome.* Unpublished doctoral dissertation, Pacific Graduate School of Psychology, Menlo Park, CA.

Perry, S., Cooper, A. M., & Michels, R. (1987). The psychodynamic formulation: Its purpose, structure, and clinical application. *American Journal of Psychiatry, 144*, 543–550.

Perry, J. C., Luborsky, L., Silberschatz, G., & Popp, C. (1989). An examination of three methods of psychodynamic formulation based on the same videotaped interview. *Psychiatry, 52*, 302–323.

Persons, J. B., Curtis, J. T., & Silberschatz, G. (1991). Psychodynamic and cognitive-behavioral formulations of a single case. *Psychotherapy, 28*, 608–617.

Rosenberg, S. E., Silberschatz, G., Curtis, J. T., Sampson, H., & Weiss, J. (1986). A method for establishing the reliability of statements from psychodynamic case formulations. *American Journal of Psychiatry, 143*, 1454–1456.

Seitz, P. F. D. (1966). The consensus problem in psychoanalytic research. In L. Gottschalk & A. H. Auerbach (Eds.), *Methods of research in psychotherapy* (pp. 209–225). New York: Appleton-Century-Crofts.

Shrout, P. E., & Fleiss, J. L. (1979). Intraclass correlations: Uses in assessing rater reliability. *Psychological Bulletin, 86*, 420–428.

Silberschatz, G. (1978). Effects of the analyst's neutrality on the patient's feelings and behavior in the psychoanalytic situation. *Dissertation Abstracts International, 39*, 3007-B (University Microfilms No. 78-24, 277).

Silberschatz, G. (1986). Testing pathogenic beliefs. In J. Weiss, H. Sampson, & the Mount Zion Psychotherapy Research Group, *The psychoanalytic process: Theory, clinical observation, and empirical research* (pp. 256–266). New York: Guilford Press.

Silberschatz, G., & Curtis, J. T. (1986) Clinical implications of research on brief dynamic psychotherapy. II: How the therapist helps or hinders therapeutic progress. *Psychoanalytic Psychology, 3*, 27–37.

Silberschatz, G., & Curtis, J. T. (1991). Time-limited psychodynamic therapy with older adults. In W. A. Myers (Ed.), *New techniques in the psychotherapy of older patients* (pp. 95–108). Washington, DC: American Psychiatric Press.

Silberschatz, G., & Curtis, J. T. (1993). Measuring the therapist's impact on the patient's therapeutic progress. *Journal of Consulting and Clinical Psychology*, *61*, 403–411.

Silberschatz, G., Curtis, J. T., Fretter, P. B., & Kelly, T. J. (1988). Testing hypotheses of psychotherapeutic change processes. In H. Dahl, G. Kächele, & H. Thomä (Eds.), *Psychoanalytic process research strategies* (pp. 128–145). New York: Springer-Verlag.

Silberschatz, G., Curtis, J. T., & Nathans, S. (1989). Using the patient's plan to assess progress in psychotherapy. *Psychotherapy*, *26*, 40–46.

Silberschatz, G., Curtis, J. T., Persons, J. P., & Safran, J. (1989, June). *A comparison of psychodynamic and cognitive therapy case formulations.* A panel presented at the Annual Conference of the Society for Psychotherapy Research, Toronto, Ontario, Canada.

Silberschatz, G., Curtis, J. T., Sampson, H., & Weiss, J. (1991). Research on the process of change in psychotherapy: The approach of the Mount Zion Psychotherapy Research Group. In L. Beutler & M. Crago (Eds.), *Psychotherapy research: An international review of programmatic studies* (pp. 56–64). Washington, DC: American Psychological Association.

Silberschatz, G., Fretter, P. B., & Curtis, J. T. (1986). How do interpretations influence the process of psychotherapy? *Journal of Consulting and Clinical Psychology*, *54*, 646–652.

Weiss, J. (1986). Part I: Theory and clinical observations. In J. Weiss, H. Sampson, & the Mount Zion Psychotherapy Research Group, *The psychoanalytic process: Theory, clinical observations, and empirical research* (pp. 3–138). New York: Guilford Press.

Weiss, J. (1993). *How psychotherapy works: Process and technique.* New York: Guilford Press.

6

The Idiographic Conflict
Formulation Method

J. CHRISTOPHER PERRY

HISTORICAL BACKGROUND OF THE APPROACH

I began my training during the era in which psychoanalytic and psychodynamic approaches were widely taught in clinical work. Clinical treatment approaches were based more on the early science of discovery and hypothesis generation, combined with good clinical experience, rather than on a more mature scientific understanding gained by systematic validation. I enjoyed the controversies, for instance, about the dynamics and treatment of borderline personality disorder (BPD), but was distressed that the lack of scientific resolution of some of these questions lead to some real disasters. For instance, when therapists and hospital staff treated patients with BPD by different approaches, these differences were magnified by the patient's use of splitting and related defenses. The result was often traumatic for all parties, but especially for the patient. Understandably, some people believed that such patients were untreatable, but from my perspective the problem lay with a lack of scientific understanding of the patient's dynamics, which so quickly became entangled in those of the help-giver. A confluence of my own interests, in chronological order of their appearance, in the philosophy of science, psychiatric research, personality disorders, and psychodynamics has led me to participate in an exciting era of psychodynamic studies. The Idiographic Conflict Formulation (ICF) is one method that formulates an individual's psychological functioning from a psychodynamic perspective in ways that are experience-near for the clinician.

In 1980, I began a longitudinal study of the psychopathology and course of BPD in comparison to several near-neighbor disorders, antisocial personality and bipolar type II affective disorders. Prior to this, many articles had been written about the psychodynamics of borderline personality; however, systematic empirical research was largely absent. The field of psychodynamic assessment was left largely to clinical description because the necessity of using clinical inference presented considerable problems in obtaining acceptable measurement reliability and validity. While some of these problems had been confronted with partial success in measuring ego functioning (Bellak, Hurvich, & Gediman, 1973; Bellak & Goldsmith, 1984) and defense mechanisms (Vaillant, 1977; Perry & Cooper, 1987), the assessment of dynamic conflicts presented more obstacles. Reviews of the reliability problems with prior formulation methods have been presented elsewhere (Perry, Luborsky, Silberschatz, & Popp, 1989; Perry, 1989; Barber & Crits-Christoph, 1993).

In this context in 1980–1981, I devised the ICF method for describing an individual's unique dynamic conflicts. Several colleagues including Steven H. Cooper, Ph.D., Gerald L. Klerman, M.D., and Philip Holzman, Ph.D., offered useful suggestions on early versions of the method. I simultaneously developed the Psychodynamic Conflict Rating Scales (PCRS) to complement the idiographic description, thereby producing a standardized assessment of 14 specific conflicts (Perry & Cooper, 1986). These scales would facilitate comparisons both within subjects and among groups of subjects. Stephen H. Cooper, Ph.D., Philip Holzman, Ph.D., and Bennett Simon, M.D., offered valuable contributions and collaboration on this instrument as well. The ICF's rich individualized description of conflicting motives and their resultants can aid in focusing therapeutic intervention, while the PCRS supplies the quantitative scores necessary for research, categorization, and the assessment of change. With time, however, I have also modified the ICF method itself, by the introduction of standard categories, and the quantitative assessment of the motive components in rating transcripts. Together these additions improve the ability to detect dynamic improvement. Through all of this I benefited from collaborations with and advice from the aforementioned colleagues and, in recent years, like others in the dynamic community, from Lester Luborsky, Ph.D.

This chapter extends the description of the ICF method presented elsewhere (Perry, Augusto, & Cooper, 1989; Perry, Luborsky, Silberschatz, & Popp, 1989; Perry, 1994) with an update on work on standardization of several components of the ICF, providing some further helpful guidelines, and considering some of its research and clinical uses.

CONCEPTUAL FRAMEWORK

Motives

The ICF method starts with the dynamic assumption that behavior is motivated. These motives are both biologically and psychologically based to varying degrees and consist in their simplest forms as wishes and fears. These motives can operate consciously or even when partially or fully out of conscious awareness, thus including so-called unconscious motivation. Conflicts among motives are a common source of problems for individuals. When such conflicts are highly salient, frequent in their occurrence, and/or seemingly unresolvable to the individual, they may lead to resultant symptoms (e.g., dysthymia) or symptomatic behaviors (e.g., engaging in frequent arguments), as well as to constrictions in living that function to avoid triggering motives and their conflicts. In older psychoanalytic terminology these resultants are compromise formations. Sometimes these conflicts are triggered by the symbolic meaning of events unique to the subject, leaving those around the individual somewhat mystified by the sudden appearance of a symptom or otherwise inappropriate behavior. Motives also can remain overly important to an individual based on traumatic experiences or repetitive learning (fixation, in older terminology). These same situations also lead to repetitive use of certain defense mechanisms with generally less adaptiveness and flexibility than so-called mature defenses.

Putting motives and the resultants of conflicts among motives at the centerpiece of the ICF is consistent with an ego-psychological perspective. However, motives do not exist in isolation from the rest of the world, and many motive elements themselves refer to desired or feared roles for other individuals. For instance, the wish "to communicate my needs to others and have others respond to them" has a very clear interpersonal element, although at a very early developmental stage. Thus a so-called object relations perspective is brought in via the motive. It may also show up in how symptoms, symptomatic behaviors, and avoidant behaviors affect relationships. By contrast, some other methods, such as the Core Conflictual Relationship Theme (CCRT) approach, more explicitly follow an object relations perspective by introducing a specific component that describes the responses of others to the subject's motives. Finally, some of the motives involve self-esteem and its regulation, consistent with a so-called self-psychological view. While the ICF is avowedly psychodynamic, it is largely jargon free, does not violate any basic tenets of learning theory, and is largely free of the more problematic elements of earlier psychoanalytic theory. In that regard, my wish has been to take the best of the dynamic approach—which I believe are its basic assumptions and observational approach—adapt them for systematic empirical study, and leave many of the older theoretical debates behind. The result, I hope, is theoretically guided empiricism, not scholasticism.

Most human motives appear quite normal whenever viewed in isolation. Similarly some conflicts among motives are an inevitable part of development and thus quite normal. For instance, in the toddler, the wish to become independent inevitably conflicts with the wish to have some significant caretaker continually available. How this conflict is negotiated depends on one's temperament interacting with traumatic and nontraumatic life experiences, which in turn result in avoidant, insecure, or secure attachment patterns. Because of past traumatic experiences, some motives that are otherwise normal become highly salient in seemingly inappropriate situations. For example, the wish to survive or the fear of bodily harm operate frequently in seemingly innocuous situations for some individuals who have been physically abused as children or who, as adults, have developed posttraumatic stress disorder following life-threatening encounters. However, by the time the clinician is consulted, such conflict patterns may have been present for decades and very resistant to commonsense arguments against their appropriateness.

The purpose of the dynamic formulation then is to help the clinician discern the conflicting motives that underlie presenting complaints and symptoms. The clinician can help the patient become aware of important motives, their conflicts, and the effect on his or her life. The final therapeutic goals are to improve the handling of motives, thereby enhancing functioning and life experience. This requires learning to use more adaptive defense mechanisms, another area of my research interest (see Perry, 1993). The use of more adaptive defenses may diminish the effect of traumatically learned fears, facilitate the patient's learning of better ways to contain their effects, and improve the integration, prioritization, and pursut of his or her wishes.

A Developmental Framework

One assumption built into the ICF is that motives may themselves adapt or mature based on positive developmental experiences. Motives are explicitly arranged in a developmental sequence according to Erik H. Erikson's (1963, 1968) eight stages. This allows the clinician to track the developmental maturation of motives as well as improved adaptation to existing motives. For example, the wish (1) to communicate one's needs and have others respond to them (Wish 4) can develop into (2) the wish to find a good mentor who facilitates learning to do things for oneself (Wish 25), and later (3) to being a good mentor or parent or giving to one's community (Wish 36).

The choice of Erikson's developmental framework was added after the development of three-quarters of the Standardized Wish and Fear List. Through examining a series of ICFs, I and my assistants identified a hodge-podge of motives. I began to look for an organizing schema for them similar to the successful hierarchy of adaptiveness for defenses. I first tried organizing the motives into Sigmund Freud's phases of psychosexual development but found that the schema only worked well for the first two, preoedipal phases and offered poor guidance for categorization beyond that. Next I tried Erikson's eight-stage framework and immediately found good agreement for 90% of the motives, while the remaining motives required some reworking of definitions for a better fit. Beyond that, the heuristic value of this choice become obvious when the Eriksonian hierarchy pointed out topic areas where additional motives should be included, although I had not yet identified them in my limited sample. Thus the Eriksonian hierarchy helped in the search for motives much as the periodic table helped in the search for the basic elements in an earlier era of physics. In retrospect, given the conceptual grounding of the ICF in ego psychology, it is no surprise that Erikson offered a good organizing principle for the ICF.

I believe that this organization works well for motives but not for the Resultants as a rule. Thus I have somewhat resisted the urge to try organizing symptoms along the same principle. There already exists an organization for defenses which play an important role in the Resultant component. However, there are just too many routes to the same symptom, thus making a simple organizational structure unlikely. When there are some naturally occurring hierarchies of symptoms (e.g., dysthymia is often more impairing than panic disorder), it is probably because the defenses associated with the disorders are hierarchically different in their general adaptiveness. For example, Bloch, Shear, Markowitz, Leon, and Perry (1993) found that overall defensive functioning was at a lower level in dysthymia than in panic disorder.

Dynamics Complement Descriptive Diagnosis

Psychodynamic and descriptive psychiatry generally focus on different aspects of psychological distress. The former is theoretically grounded, emphasizes the central importance of human motives, and requires inference in the process of observation. The latter espouses atheoretical empiricism and largely leaves human motives aside along with other etiological issues in favor of focusing on surface symptoms and behaviors for diagnosis. Paradoxically, because of these differences the two approaches are not exclusive but actually complementary. One original complaint about the descriptive approach is that it offered little in the way of direction for patient management and treatment (Karasu & Skodol, 1980), with some degree of exception in the area of medication. Conversely, a good dynamic formulation should help guide the clinician as to where the problems are, helping to prioritize them in some way (saliency, frequency, etc.). By contrast, the dynamic formulation will not guide one as to the choice of medications, although it might be very helpful in guiding patient management around medication usage. Therefore, I suggest that a thorough DSM-type diagnostic assessment be conducted routinely in conjunction with composing the ICF. This provides a comprehensive list of symptoms to consider for the Resultants component of the ICF.

Comprehensive Formulations

A comprehensive understanding of an individual's psychodynamics requires an empirically justified assessment of the following, which are presented in order of the increasing degree of "depth" or inference required to assess them:

- Defenses commonly used (defense repertoire)
- Salient motives
- Recurrent conflicts between motives

- Maladaptive relationship patterns resulting from recurrent conflicts (object relations)
- Etiological factors
  Temperament
  Early experiences with important people
    Recurrent and/traumatic learning experiences
    How self-esteem was built from the esteem of others
- How all the above show up in current relationships and events, including those with the therapist (transference)

An adequate formulation serves as the basis for accurate interpretation. The ICF includes some elements of all of the above. However, the etiological elements are most likely to be underrepresented whenever an ICF is based only on a single or several assessment interviews.

Data Requirements for Justification

The ICF is applicable to dynamic interview data recorded from assessment interviews or psychotherapy. The method requires a minimum of one 50-minute dynamic assessment interview, although data from two or three interviews are more desirable. As originally devised as a research method, two experienced clinician raters view a videotaped interview of the subject, discuss it, and then formulate the subject's idiographic conflicts. The format is specified to ensure comprehensive coverage of all the components of the conflict patterns. Clinical inferences are necessary, but the rater-observers are required to support each assertion by listing the available evidence. Data from the whole interview are used, unlike what is done in the CCRT method of Luborsky (1984; see Crits-Christoph et al., 1988; also Chapter 3, this volume), which uses only data from relationship episodes reported in the interview. Guidelines are used to justify the clinical judgments offered and to protect against insupportable inference and mere speculation. The ICF is best construed as a collection of psychodynamic hypotheses rather than as a unitary hypothesis like Malan's (1976) method.

The written ICFs are generally four to eight pages in length, the bulk of which enumerates the supporting evidence for the first two components, Wishes and Fears. When the evidence is omitted, the ICF is generally about one to two pages in length.

The Observer and Clinical Inference

The ICF method is not a substitute for clinical acumen, training, or experience, since dynamic patterns require clinical inference. The formulator observes an interview and then articulates the raw data in it until able to infer how they fit together in a series of patterns relating to underlying dynamic motives, as well as conflicts among them. The ICF method offers guidelines on organizing dynamic phenomena and justifying inferred dynamic patterns to others. As a guided method, the results still reflect the level of clinical training of the raters; highly experienced raters should yield different results than those of untrained raters. This is also true for the interpretation of data from sonar, radar, or radiological procedures. All these methods and the ICF also share the feature that equally trained observers, while agreeing much of the time, can sometimes see different patterns or interpret the same patterns differently. When the observers have had less training and experience, the result is usually greater disagreement. In addition, the less adequate the database, the greater the likelihood of rater disagreement. Determining which patterns or interpretations are more valid then requires additional data, for instance, testing the predictive validity of the hypothesized patterns.

Are Treatment Goals Built In?

In its present development, the ICF does not incorporate treatment goals explicitly. However, the use of a developmental framework gives the therapist an aid for ordering and prioritizing competing motives when they arise in the therapy. In general, if two motives are equally present, the earlier developmental motive usually requires attention first whenever they conflict. For example, when an individual is blocked in pursuit of an achievement wish (stage IV) by an earlier developmental fear, such as the stage II fear of criticism, the earlier developmental fear will require attention before much success with the achievement wish is likely. At present, further research is needed to determine more about the heuristic value of this organization for aiding the clinician. Other aspects of prediction, both response to therapy and naturalistic outcome, also require further longitudinal research, so stay tuned in!

The ICF Format

The ICF format is as follows:

1. Wishes
2. Fears
3. Resultants
    a. Symptomatic Outcomes
    b. Avoidant Outcomes
4. Vulnerability to Specific Stressors
5. Best Available Level of Adaptation to Conflict

The first three components, Wishes, Fears, and Resultants, constitute the core of the dynamic formulation and are most congruent with how other methods construe intrapsychic conflict. The Wish and Fear components delineate the dynamic motives important to the individual who may be involved in conflict. The Resultant component describes the surface manifestations of conflicting motives as either Symptoms and Symptomatic Behaviors or Avoidance outcomes. The importance given to motives is what most clearly distinguishes dynamic from other systems of personality assessment. The fourth component identifies those specific stressors that often trigger the individual's conflicts. This serves as a list of likely triggering events or stressors that should be monitored in the course of therapy. When treatment is complete, the adaptation to this list of stressors should be sufficient to obviate distressing Resultants, such as Symptomatic Outcomes. The fifth component, Best Available Level of Adaptation to Conflict, serves as a benchmark of the individual's potential healthy functioning. During treatment, the clinician should recognize that these represent striving for healthy adaptation amid conflict and should be supported. They also should improve as dynamic change occurs.

INCLUSION/EXCLUSION CRITERIA

The ICF was originally applied to individuals with personality and affective disorders. I realized that such individuals had more than one or two conflicting dynamics and devised the ICF to be flexible throughout a wide range of psychopathology. A reasonably well-adapted individual with a focal problem might have one or two salient Wishes and Fears that conflict, whereas an individual with a highly traumatic background, such as many individuals with BPD, might have half a dozen or more of each. The ICF has been explicitly used on individuals with multifocal, confusing dynamics. However, in such cases the formulation cannot be more simple than the patients' dynamics, but the developmental organization of the motive elements helps bring order to the elements within each component.

At the present time, there is no apparent basis for excluding any individual capable of giving an interview as unsuitable for a formulation by the ICF. I do not recommend considering a formulation as complete whenever, at the time of an interview, the individual is intoxicated or in an unusual mood state, such as severe depression or hypomania. Nevertheless, assessing the salient dynamics during such states of mind can be very useful for guiding management of the acute states, such as during emergency or crisis intervention, but not necessarily for any subsequent psychotherapy.

STEPS IN CASE FORMULATION CONSTRUCTION

The original method employed only the clinicians' judgment in identifying the presence of individual wishes and fears. This was facilitated by the later (third) edition of the Standardized Wish and Fear List; an abbreviated form is shown in Table 6.1 (Perry, 1989, 1990, 1996a) for the motive components. Finally, for research purposes there are additional modifications in rating that take advantage of the possibility of quantifying motives whenever an interview transcript is available. The ICF components are listed above (in the "Conceptual Framework," final subsection) and described more fully below.

As noted earlier, I suggest that one make thorough descriptive diagnoses (currently DSM-IV Axes I through V, or an equivalent system) prior to composing the ICF. The review of symptom and medical data will also ensure thoroughness in constructing the Resultants component.

Wishes

The rater describes the subject's conscious and unconscious wishes that have a determining influence on his or her life and psychopathology. A dynamic wish differs from a simple desire or wish by playing a causal role in a variety of overtly different behaviors, fantasies, and experiences. For instance, the wish to gain self-esteem through achieving personally valued goals is dynamic because it may affect the subject in a wide variety of situations, whereas the wish to have a particular job is not a dynamic wish per se.

There may be some aspects of wishes or fears which are conscious to the subject. However, wishes and fears may operate outside of awareness, giving unconscious meaning to certain experiences, behaviors, and events.

Relevant data from the interview are listed following each wish. Most subjects have from two to four centrally important wishes, generally supported by three to five observations from the history or interview. In addition there may be other wishes and fears of lesser salience, or lower frequency by the quantitative method.

Fears

Fears are negative beliefs, expectations, or aversive experiences that the subject wishes to avoid. Dynamic fears differ from simple dislikes or phobias because they motivate a variety of behaviors or underlie a variety of experiences that may not appear similar on the surface. For instance, a fear of losing control of one's emotions is a dynamic fear, whereas a fear of public speaking is not dynamic per se but rather the symptomatic outcome of a conflict, for example, a conflict between the wish to compete and win and the fear of hurting others and incurring guilt.

The rater lists the countervailing fears that operate in opposition to the subject's wishes. Evidence is listed for each fear. The number of fears may differ from the number of wishes.

Fears often counter wishes, leading to an experience of conflict, but opposing wish–wish or fear–fear conflicts are also common. For instance, a wish to remain dependent and be taken care of may conflict with a wish for autonomy and independence as readily as with a fear of trusting others whom one needs.

TABLE 6.1. Abbreviated Standardized Wish and Fear List, Third Edition

Wishes	Fears
I. Trust vs. Mistrust	
1. Survive	1. Physical harm
2. Be protected from harm	2. Others won't tolerate
3. Have needs met	3. Abandonment
4. Communicate needs, elicit appropriate response	4. Being alone
	5. Unable to communicate
5. Be comforted, soothed	6. Dependent upon others
6. Find others trustworthy	7. Disappointment
7. Be near significant other	8. Deprivation
8. Have others contain me	9. Trusting others
	10. Distressing feelings
	11. Strangers, unfamiliar
II. Autonomy vs. Shame and Doubt	
9. Be independent, autonomous	12. Fragmented by feelings
10. Have one's privacy respected	13. Loss of self-control
11. Control one's feelings	14. Criticism, punishment
12. Retaliate, get revenge	15. Being dominated, controlled
13. Do whatever one wants	16. Being powerless, helpless
14. Control, dominate others	17. Loss of independence, freedom
15. Be spontaneous, carefree	
16. Be perfect, avoid shame	
III. Initiative vs. Guilt	
17. Assert oneself	
18. Relief from guilt feelings	18. Not being admired, accepted
19. Be admired, special	19. Losing in competition
20. Compete and win	20. Failure to achieve
21. Cooperate and be helpful	21. Hurting others, guilt
22. Fair treatment, reparation	22. Sexual wishes, acts
IV. Industry vs. Inferiority	
23. Succeed, achieve goals	23. Adult responsibilities
24. Gain esteem for actions	24. Being without friends
V. Identity vs. Identity Confusion	
25. Attention from opposite sex	25. Social/gender role failure
26. Relationships develop self	26. Identity Confusion
27. Mentor, role model	27. Aimless, no goals
28. Belong, fit in social group	28. No mentor, guide
29. Attract others, have friends	29. Accepting guidance, advice
30. Meaning, purpose	30. Being unattractive
31. Sexual gratification	
VI. Intimacy vs. Isolation	
32. Intimacy, love, be loved	31. Intimacy, closeness
33. Mutual satisfying relationship	32. Sexual relationships
	33. Not changing relationship patterns

(*continued*)

TABLE 6.1. *continued*

Wishes	Fears
VII. Generativity vs. Isolation	
34. To procreate	34. Being uncaring, bad parent
35. Be a good parent	35. Being poor model, provider
36. Be a good mentor, model	36. Lacking creativity, imagination
37. Create, innovate	37. Inability to procreate
38. Cope with moral dilemmas	
VIII. Integrity vs. Despair	
39. Self-assessment and change	38. Social disconnection with age
40. Accept personal limits	39. Selfishness, losing dignity
	40. Loss of hope, faith in ideals

Resultants

This section lists the results of the subject's conflicts in two areas. Each subcomponent describes resultants of a single type and hypothesizes their relationship to specific core Wish and Fear components. In completing each of these subcomponent sections, first list the symptoms and symptomatic behaviors evident from the interview, and then hypothesize how they result from conflicts among specific motives listed in the Wish and Fear components. Then proceed in similar fashion for the Avoidant Outcomes.

Symptoms and Symptomatic Behaviors

This subcomponent describes the relationship between specific psychiatric symptoms and symptomatic behaviors and the subject's conflicting wishes and fears. The DSM Axis I symptom disorders fit in this section insofar as one can justify a relationship between conflicting motives and the production of symptoms. The meaning and function of a symptom would be described in this section. Symptoms are construed broadly as subjective experiences that cause the individual distress. Common examples are Axis I disorders like depression or dysthymia, other mood states like irritability, or recurrent negative experiences like often feeling cheated in interactions. Pathological beliefs, negative schemas of self and others, and overreactions to events are also symptomatic outcomes. Symptomatic behaviors are behaviors that are associated with subjective distress and/or impairment. Binge eating, stealing, arguing, procrastination, difficulty in intimate relationships, and trouble holding a job are common examples of symptomatic behaviors. An example of a Symptomatic Outcome is as follows:

> The subject often feels resentful and jealous of others. This results from his fear of trusting others and being disappointed which conflicts with his wish to communicate his needs and elicit an appropriate response from others.

One simple and one more complicated example of Symptomatic Behaviors follow.

> The subject is commonly dysphoric. This results from the conflict between his wish to gain self-esteem through personal achievement and his fears of criticism and of incurring guilt for his independent actions which his parents see as selfish.

> The subject steals from his parents because of his disappointed wish to elicit an appropriate response from them as well as to seek revenge for this disappointment and a wish to do whatever he wants without being thwarted by others expectations. These conflict with his wish to feel special and be admired, so he feels like the "worst son" as a substitute for wanting to feel like the best in their eyes.

Avoidant Outcomes

This subcomponent describes the characteristic ways by which the subject avoids or mitigates the experience of his or her conflicts. Inferring Avoidant Outcomes requires noticing things that the subject does not do, particularly things that one would normally expect to be present. Character pathology that protects the subject from awareness of his or her conflicts would be described here. Raters can list specific defense mechanisms that the subject uses to avoid awareness of conflicts, as well as the resulting limitations in achievement, intimacy, handling of affect, and so on. The following are two examples of Avoidant Outcomes:

> The subject avoids intimate relationships by going out with a woman only a few times before moving on. This somewhat gratifies his wishes for admiration and for sex while avoiding his fears of criticism and being dominated by significant others.

> The subject's use of repression keeps him unaware of his anger when confronted by authority figures, thereby limiting his self-assertiveness and leaving him chronically unaware of what bothers him at work, for example.

Sometimes Resultants have both symptomatic and avoidant features because the outcome involves distress but also serves to avoid awareness of Wishes or Fears. In these cases, the same outcome should be listed under both subcomponents. The following exemplifies this:

> The subject chronically procrastinates finishing his course work. This results from his wish to be seen as a very promising student, which conflicts with both his wish to be dependent and his fear that anything he does will be criticized as inadequate. While the procrastination is distressing, it helps him preserve his image as *potentially* very successful.

Vulnerability to Specific Stressors

The rater defines the characteristics of specific stressors that activate or trigger the subject's conflicts. This component captures the specific meanings of those things that are subjectively most threatening. It facilitates later determination of whether the subject has successfully resolved or adapted to his or her conflicts, shown by more mature handling of these specific stressors. The following is an example of a specific stressor:

> The subject's fear of being dominated is triggered by disagreements, especially in collaborative work relationships and intimate relationships.

Best Available Level of Adaptation to Conflicts

This section contains a description of the subject's most successful ways of adapting to his or her conflicts. Delineating the subject's sublimations and best level of adaptation to existing conflicts provides a benchmark of potentially useful solutions currently available to the subject. The therapist should likely support these even if imperfect, as they are temporarily useful adaptations.

APPLICATION TO PSYCHOTHERAPY TECHNIQUE

An adequate formulation informs good therapeutic management and accurate interpretation. If the clinician does not formulate the patient's problems and test its validity in the therapy, then he or she is navigating without the tools of navigation. This may result in a long, roundabout journey—one which might have been concluded in less time and with less expense given adequate guides. Therefore the clinician is encouraged to begin the formulation close to the outset of the therapy.

At the Outset of Therapy

The timing for constructing a formulation depends on the manner in which the therapist takes a history.

In the first case, the therapist conducts a formal evaluation over the first several sessions, systematically taking a history from the patient. At completion, one has a fairly comprehensive set of information to serve as the basis for the formulation. Relying on the Standardized Wish and Fear List (Table 6.1), one should identify the prominent Wishes and Fears, grouping those in the same stage together and justifying each by reference to the history, interview behavior, problem patterns with previous treatments, etc. Then one lists the Resultants and their hypothesized relationship to the Wishes and Fears. Finally, noting the stressors will serve as warning signs for events that may cause especial distress as the therapy unfolds. The Best Available Level of Adaptation to Conflict also warns the therapist of areas of adaptation that should not be disturbed because they are reasonably adaptive compromises given the apparent conflicts. Having the ICF on computer allows one to modify it later, or append new observations as they occur, thus making the ICF an evolving rather than a static aid.

In the second case, common for different reasons among both experienced and slipshod therapists, there is little systematic, formal history taking in the early sessions. Rather, the therapist jumps right into the therapeutic task, taking history on the fly. This may work quite well with some therapists who have a good foundation of experience. They engage the patient at the outset, respond to the patient's concerns more quickly, and refine the therapy, while ensuring a fairly high alliance, as they go. They tend to formulate as they go, but still do a better job if they make a formal formulation early on and update it as experience requires. On the other hand, this does not work well in the hands of therapists with lesser training, experience, and or skill. The slipshod therapist, of whom there is no shortage, tends to take only enough history to be able to categorize the patient, and then therapy proceeds to treat the category more than the patient. The formulation tends to be a brief, overly broad, explanatory template (e.g., adolescent rebellion, authority problem, adjustment reaction) into which the patient is continually squeezed whether he or she truly fits or not. Alas, such therapists probably would not use the ICF or any other formulation method without supervisory input. Therefore I suggest to those supervising therapists in training that teaching them how to conduct an evaluation and to make and use a formulation is one of the best scientific gifts one can give each of these novice therapists. It is also primary prevention for slipshod therapy!

As Therapy Proceeds

There are many hypotheses about how a dynamic formulation, and the ICF in particular, may aid treatment, but tests of these are yet to be conducted. Some of the following may pertain to many dynamic formulations methods, while a few are more specific to the ICF, principally because of its hierarchical, developmental organization of the motive components. Given the recency of the method, I offer the following as psychotherapy "futures" to be redeemed as true or not after the coming generation of research.

Managing versus Exploring and Interpreting Motives

All therapists recall their early experiences discerning dynamic patterns and then interpreting them forthwith to their patients. The "ah-hah!" pleasure was often fleeting, however, as the reality of the patient's failure to agree, downright dismissal, or entrenching resistance appeared in response. In the best cases, this is followed by a lifetime of active learning about the appropriateness and timing of interpretations. In the worst cases, it is followed by some rationalized attempt to blame the patient.

1. Upon examining the patient's ICF, if most of the motives are stage VI (intimacy vs. isolation) and above, then one can probably make focal interpretations fairly early in the therapy process. Conversely, if most of the individualized motives are stages I and II (trust vs. mistrust, and autonomy vs. shame and doubt), then interpretation is probably going to lead to regression until the patient has established a trusting relationship with the therapist, feels safe, and has negotiated a sense of shared control of the sessions. In many borderline and other personality disorders, this may require several years. In these latter cases, managing rather than interpreting will provide support and build toward future sessions in which more active interpretation can be beneficial. If most of the motives are in stages III to V (initiative vs. guilt, industry vs. inferiority, and identity vs. identity diffusion), then the balance between management and deeper exploration will be somewhere in between them.

2. If, apart from the developmental levels, there are a large number of different motives, then the patient probably has global conflicts that pervade many areas of functioning. Such patients need more support, successful management of crises, and time in therapy to sort out which motives are the most frequent, salient, and interpretable. Conversely, those patients with a few distinct or focal motives are likely to be more amenable to an active interpretive treatment. These may be the patients for whom one makes almost the same one or two interpretations across each vignette or transference episode discussed, and of course they are the most suitable for shorter-term therapies as well.

When to Manage Motives by Gratifying Them

Part of offering a supportive therapy to individuals with predominantly lower-stage motives and more global conflicts is the need to occasionally manage a wish or fear that has become poignant by gratifying it. For instance, if a patient feels criticized (stage II, Fear 14) and responds with mistrust of the therapist (stage I, Fear 9) and a demand for reparation of the injury incurred (stage III, Wish 22), the therapist may need to gratify some of these motives to preserve the alliance. This may involve acknowledging the hurt (e.g., "I see my comment hurt you") and apologizing for the unintended affect (e.g., "I'm sorry that my comment hurt you. I didn't mean for that to happen"). Sometimes validation and reparation provide the needed support, mitigating the sense of suffering or victimization, which subsequently allows mutual exploration of the patient's reaction to the therapist's comments. Therapists who studiously avoid gratifying all motives of such patients will be experienced as unsupportive and likely to cause regressions. Paradoxically, therapists who gratify motives too readily will also cause a regression. This results from the failure to help teach tolerance of the early-stage motives, which, when continually stimulated, feel to the patient like a bottomless pit needing to be filled.

Conversely, patients with predominantly higher-stage motives will be more tolerant of the deprivation associated with not gratifying their wishes or responding supportively to their fears. Too much support can actually be counterproductive by forestalling the exploration and wish to understand and master one's conflicts.

Acknowledge When a Wish Is Disappointed, When a Fear Is Realized

Many so-called fixations on particular wishes or fears come from repeated experiences in having the wish disappointed or the fear realized. Thus, repetitions of these scenarios in therapy are particularly important learning experiences. In order not to repeat the trauma of disappointment and realization, and therefore reinforce the maladaptive learning around them, it is important to acknowledge whenever a salient wish is or has been disappointed. This is more a clarification of the state of disappointment, rather than an interpretation per se. Similarly, if an important fear has been experienced in some vignette, it is also important to acknowledge that. Acknowledgment is a form of validation. It legitimizes the patient's motive and brings it into the therapeutic dialogue. This is even more important whenever the therapist is the one who must disappoint a wish (e.g., patient: "Can I sit in your lap and have you hold me?") or actuate a fear (e.g., patient: "I hate it when you change appointment times. Can't you see how being unpredictable hurts me?"). Disappointing the patient sometimes is a necessary part of a good therapy, as it is of being a good parent. Acknowledging that one is doing so brings the experience into the therapeutic dialogue, rather than ignoring it and having it join the resistance.

Fears Often Need Different Treatment than Wishes

From the perspective of learning theory, avoidance conditioning is more resistant to extinction than classical or operant conditioning. This gives dynamic fears some different properties than those of wishes. Patients may have learned to avoid letting fears come up at all. If avoidance is complete, the therapist must explore and bring the fear up when it is probably relevant to a situation, for instance, an Avoidance Outcome resulting in constrictions in one's social life. The patient may resist this exploration, in which case the therapist must find the best way to approach it, using some sense of a hierarchy both of the developmental stage of the fears as well as their strength. Indeed, in highly traumatized cases early in treatment, the therapist must support the patient's sense of safety from salient fears by all means possible, including by avoidance. Then, after a sense of safety and partial mastery have been established, this strategy should give way to exploration, clarification, interpretation, and improving one's defensive responses (e.g., self-observation rather than repression, self-assertion rather than reaction formation, suppression rather than displacement). As therapy helps the patient move up the hierarchy of defensive functioning, the patient becomes his or her own learning theorist, able to cooperate in devising strategies of confronting and suppressing fears, and substituting ways of mastering them rather than avoiding them.

If the therapist has not been sufficiently supportive and has not enabled the patient to develop a sense of safety and partial mastery, then the therapist may find certain fears to be recalcitrant. By confronting the patient with salient fears prematurely, the therapist may well engage the following type of resistance. The patient may overtly comply with the therapist's direction but covertly resist. The telltale signs of such a situation are the defenses of passive aggression, help-rejecting complaining, rationalization, and repression. If this scenario develops, progress halts. In such a case, the therapist should retreat without shame to a more supportive and exploratory approach before taking on that particular fear more definitively. Perhaps the fear has some extensive meaning or is intertwined with an important wish that has been bypassed (e.g., Wish 13, to do whatever one wants without being thwarted). Attention to these may then unstick the fear, making it more amenable to subsequent exploration and more definitive treatment.

Understanding fears is one area where previous training in behavioral analysis, constructing hierarchies of fears or irrational beliefs, and doing both imaginal and *in vivo* desensitization will help one learn this process. However, one difference from the purely cognitive or behavioral approach is that dynamic therapy explores the meaning of the fear and looks for its relationships to and conflicts with other motives as well. Conflicts involving fears are thus a bit more complex than a straightforward desensitization of a hierarchy of feared situations, or the Socratic process of challenging a series of automatic "catastrophizing" thoughts.

Behind a Fear May Lie a Wish

Some patients appear stuck, repeating a litany of stories that exemplify particular fears. Whenever the therapist tries the usual methods of support and exploration, the patient's response may be a stereotyped repetition. In such cases, it may be that the therapist has overlooked a wish that lies behind the fear. For example, when a patient believes that a fear is a justified response to some traumatic incident, he or she may not be directly amenable to including it as a focus of treatment, until one recognizes such underlying wishes as the following: Wish 3, to have one's needs met without having to express them; Wish 12, to obtain revenge (i.e., using the story to blame others); Wish 22, to have reparation for past injuries. When the therapist enlarges the scope of the dialogue to address these unspoken wishes, the conflict over the fear becomes more workable.

Explore Resultants and Their Meanings to Find the Underlying Motives

The patient often expects the therapist to focus attention on the patient's symptoms. However, given that the symptom is theoretically more a result than a cause itself (except for distress), one should explore the symptom, keeping in mind that its meaning will likely lead back to the motives in conflict. A frustrated wish and a fear that something aversive will follow recognition or expression of this frustration are often found underlying the symptom that results from their conflict. Helping the patient learn more adaptive ways to handle both motives and their conflict should lead to the symptom becoming more responsive to treatment.

One hypothesis likely to be controversial regards the interaction between medication and attention to the patient's dynamics. I believe that adequate attention to the motives and conflicts related to a particular Axis I episode, such as major depression, will improve responsiveness to treatment. This includes the personal observation that lower dosages, say, of an antidepressant, may be required to obtain remission than might be necessary without a dynamic approach. Thus, I believe that there are some additive effects of dynamic treatment to medication, although I recognize that the effect size might be modest, say, at 4 or 8 weeks, making it nondetectable at the usual sample sizes. However, it should certainly be detectable over long-term drug maintenance treatment that includes dynamic therapy for the underlying psychological vulnerability. It should also be evident for so-called treatment-resistant cases over the long term.

Explore the Meaning and Historical Origins of a Wish or Fear When It Appears to Be Overly Important

In dynamic therapy, one continual goal is to seek understanding of the origins of repetitive patterns. This is particularly important when the patient is fixated on a particular wish or fear. Working with these motives in current vignettes does not have the same power as finding vignettes that played a formative role in earlier learning. Exploring the meaning of these formative experiences allows the patient to contemplate the meaning of current conflicts among these motives, rather than just to repeat the patterns.

Help Explore and Diminish a Conflicting Fear to Aid Gratification of a Wish

In the simple situation where a fear conflicts with a wish, one may need to work with the fear first. Diminishing its effect frees the wish up for further exploration and allows the patient to use higher-level defenses (e.g., self-observation rather than repression). The ultimate goal is to allow the patient either to find a way to gratify the wishes fully (e.g., using self-assertion) or partially (e.g., using displacement) or to aid their development into derivative wishes at higher Eriksonian stages (e.g., using altruism or sublimation).

Look for Important Wishes and Fears to Show Up in the Transference

Psychoanalysis and psychodynamic psychotherapy ascribe a central role to addressing the transference. When important motives appear in the transference, they provide a powerful opportunity for experiential exploration and insight. The transference is a microcosm of the same patterns occurring elsewhere. A skillful therapist can help crystalize change that occurs more slowly when just dealing with events outside the patient–therapist relationship. Understanding the motives in the transference fosters generalization of learning to other relationships more readily than is true for understanding derived from other types of vignettes.

There is a corollary of the above. Stereotyped complaining about Resultant symptoms, often expressed as suffering in excess of what might be expected, is a common sign of unrecognized wishes and fears in the transference. Two common examples are the following: Wish 5, to be comforted or soothed; Fear 10, fear of distressing feelings. The therapist needs to look for the motives behind the experience of suffering and bring them into the dialogue. Talking about the unmet wish, for example, helps legitimize the experience of deprivation, while the caring attention given helps satisfy the wish somewhat. This way excessive suffering is relieved, allowing a greater degree of mutual exploration.

CASE EXAMPLE

"Mr. Catullo" is named after Catullus, the first-century B.C. Roman poet who had a very turbulent relationship with his lover. In his early 30s, Mr. Catullo sought treatment after a failed suicide attempt and destruction of a room in his apartment during a rage for which he was amnestic. After initial evaluation he was diagnosed as having an episode of major depressive disorder superimposed on late onset dysthymia, a history of opiate dependence (he is now abstinent), and dissociative episodes. On Axis II he met criteria for borderline, dependent, and passive–aggressive personalty disorder types and had a history of childhood conduct disorder with some adult antisocial features.

The following ICF, based on a single hour-long videotaped dynamic interview prior to therapy, is the consensus of two raters. It was done for research purposes, so the evidence is included. The Standardized Wishes and Fears are used (Table 6.1), juxtaposed as the evidence suggests clinically. The supporting evidence then offers the context, which gives them a more individualized, clinical meaning. If the evidence were omitted, the ICF would be reduced in length some 30–50% on average. This ICF is longer than most because the subject has a number of global conflicts in the earlier developmental stages (principally stages I, II, and III).

Wishes

1. The subject has a strong Wish for dependency, specifically noted by Wishes (3) to be nurtured by both maternal and paternal figures, (5) to be soothed and comforted whenever upset, and (7) to be near or have someone significant continually available.

   a. He refers several times to getting upset, having his distress snowball, and using sleep as a means of comfort. This occurs primarily when he is alone.
   b. He states: "I remember wishing a lot for a father [after his parents divorced] and was jealous of kids who had fathers."
   c. In adolescence he could have had a relationship with his father, but eschewed it because he wanted his father to come to him without asking.
   d. He notes a pattern of intense involvements with girlfriends, usually having one. He states that after a breakup "any girlfriend eases the pain."
   e. He states that his mother was always there for him, was very loving, and he says, "I wish I lived closer to her now."
   f. He describes his drug use following graduating from high school as "I took anything I could take, valiums, uppers . . ." presumably to deal with a very stressful transition to adulthood.

2. The subject has a strong Wish (6) to find others trustworthy and predictable.

   a. In his relationship with his recent ex-girlfriend he says he felt very secure and thought she was going to be his mate for life. His wish for permanence was so strong it blinded him to problems leading to her leaving.
   b. He states that he had few friends growing up because "I really had to trust somebody to be a friend; otherwise I avoid them . . . both boys and girls."
   c. Because of his father's abandonment of the family he states, "I'd never cheat on my wife; I'd never abandon my kids." This underlines his disappointed wish to trust his own father, who did both.

3. The subject has a Wish (12) for revenge for perceived injuries.

   a. He states that he hates his father because of the infidelity and abandonment of the family. He won't ever talk to him, plans to change his last name, and says, "I wouldn't even go to his funeral."

b. "If someone dated 'L.' [his ex-girlfriend], I'd try to kill him. I would premeditate it." This is said in defiance but without intent or a specific victim in mind.

c. "I used to be vicious toward all my mother's boyfriends."

4. The subject has a Wish to construct (or reconstruct) a happy family life specifically by (21) being helpful and cooperative in response to others, (32) to love and be loved in an intimate relationship, and (35) to be a good parent.

a. He talks about taking pride in having been such a good mother's helper in taking care of his younger sister and being "the man of the house" from age 14 on. Immediately after that he says, "I want to have a wife and kids and bring them up right."

b. He says several times how important it is for him to bring up kids and have a happy family, rather than live alone.

c. When he first met his ex-girlfriend "L." he noted that she was a bad hypochondriac and saw a therapist. He said, "I wanted to just be there for her."

d. Contrary to his mistrust, he states, "I generally try to get along with anybody."

5. He has a minor Wish to take action to better his life by (17) asserting himself to get his needs met and (24) gaining other's esteem through his actions.

a. He was very proud that he kicked opiates on his own without help and later sought help for his alcohol and cocaine habit. He is currently abstinent, which he feels proud about.

b. He talks about looking for work on a day shift because he has realized that the night shift is bad for him.

Fears

1. He has a powerful Fear that his actions will lead to (2) others not tolerating his feelings, that (3) he will be abandoned by those he is close to, and (4) that he will be consigned to a dismal life of aloneness.

a. He blames himself for "being a drag" and states that he doesn't blame his ex-girlfriend "L." for leaving him.

b. He was very upset at himself when he slept through his ex-girlfriend's knocking on the door Christmas Eve. When he awoke in the middle of the night, realizing what happened, he wrecked part of the apartment.

c. He has a powerful Fear of dying alone without a wife and children. This is mentioned at several points.

    d. When talking about his breakup he states he is not mad at his ex-girlfriend over not being there for him at his time of need, although "I think I probably should be mad."

    e. At one point he states, "I can picture myself being institutionalized, people thinking I'm crazy and not believing me, not responding to my requests."

2. He has a Fear of certain feelings that (10) when distressed he cannot be soothed or comforted and (13) he will lose control of his feelings and get sicker.

    a. He reports several instances of losing control and wrecking his apartment when he is upset, primarily about his ex-girlfriend and when mad at himself.

    b. "I wrecked the bathroom and immediately checked my roommate. I couldn't live with myself if I hurt him."

    c. He talks about desperately trying to fall asleep when upset because otherwise he'll become violent or suicidal.

    d. He is frightened about how angry he gets. Noting that he had a relative who died in a mental hospital, he notes having a fantasy that he will be incarcerated and crazy.

    e. At the beginning and the end of their interview, he talks about how difficult therapy and the interview are. He says that talking about things makes him feel worse and, crying, says, "I can't just make myself feel happy."

    f. He has a Fear that his depression will snowball and he'll end up killing himself.

3. He has a Fear (9) of trusting and being betrayed by others.

    a. He is very angry that his father abandoned the family.

    b. Concerning his mother's boyfriends, he says, "I was vicious toward them, I assumed they'd all be like my dad. I remember wishing I had a father, but not my father, I didn't trust him."

    c. Talking about friends: "I really have to trust them or I avoid them. . . . [Concerning a girl currently interested in him] I avoid her because I just don't trust her."

4. He has a Fear of doing the wrong thing, specifically (14) being criticized and blamed, (19) feeling ashamed at his failures to achieve, and especially (20) hurting or being a burden to others and incurring guilt.

    a. "I wrecked the bathroom and immediately checked my roommate. I couldn't live with myself if I hurt him."

b. Describing the events leading to his recent breakup with his girlfriend: "I can't blame her, I blame myself (*cries*). . . . This stupid depression will ruin my life if I don't do something about it."
c. After talking about how his father hurt him and his mother, he states, "I would never cheat on my wife or abandon my kids."
d. While talking about why he can't play his saxophone when upset, he states that playing it makes him feel worse because it isn't very good and "I'm not proud of it . . . otherwise I really enjoy it."

Resultants

1. Symptomatic Outcomes

a. He has a history of drug use to escape his disappointed wishes and rage and to soothe himself (acting out).
b. He has violent outbursts in which he expresses his rage over disappointment and perceived rejection and betrayal by others (acting out). The outbursts occur in a dissociated state (dissociation), which preserves the illusion of his not really being responsible for feelings and impulses that otherwise stimulate fears of criticism and abandonment. The trade-off is that after the outbursts he is even more afraid of losing control and getting sicker (help-rejecting complaining).
c. He has a striking inability to sense and address problems that prevent him from sustaining a close relationship. His avoidance mechanisms leave him largely unaware of problems as they evolve (repression); hence he cannot deal with interpersonal conflict.
d. He is prone to moments of despair and self hatred, which occur when he blames himself for severe disappointments, much as he blamed his father for his family's travails growing up (splitting of self-images, passive-aggression). These can lead to his feeling suicidal and self-destructive, and may eventuate in suicidal actions (acting out).

2. Avoidant Outcomes

a. Repression of instances when he is out of control serves to keep him unaware of some of his powerful angry feelings.
b. Dissociation leading to episodes of violence serve to keep him from feeling responsible for his violent and revengeful feelings. He uses reaction formation against violent feelings toward those upon whom he is dependent in reality or fantasy (e.g., his ex-girlfriend) while expressing these through splitting of others' images (i.e., the all-bad image of his father, or a potential suitor of his ex-girlfriend).
c. Not communicating in his close relationships keeps the illusion that all is happy (repression, reaction formation), yet this prevents him from working on relationship issues as needed.

Vulnerability to Specific Stressors

1. Threats of or actual loss of an intimate relationship with a woman trigger his dependency wishes and related fears.

2. Feeling guilty that he has really (or in fantasy) hurt someone close to him, who may then blame or abandon him, stimulates his fears.

3. Betrayal by someone with whom he is close stimulates his mistrust and weakens his ability to control his dependent wishes and desire for revenge.

Best Level of Adaptation to Conflict

1. He has been able to stop his drug and alcohol abuse because he perceived it as escapist rather than adaptive coping.

2. He sought help after his recent breakup with his girlfriend rather than make a suicide attempt or let things get worse.

3. On some occasions, when upset, he is able to soothe himself by going to sleep, thereby breaking up an otherwise vicious self-critical cycle.

4. His wish to construct a happy family life may eventually serve him well, but only after he has learned to be aware of his feelings and cope more directly with them.

TRAINING

To date the ICF has been used primarily in dynamic research and secondarily for clinical purposes. Training consists of three phases: (1) reading appropriate introductory materials; (2) formulating preselected case(s) and discussing agreements and disagreements from an expert consensus formulation on the case; and (3) formulating two to four other cases, followed by having a consensus discussion.

Reading the present chapter and or the following introductory materials orients one to the ICF method: Perry (1994); Perry, Augusto, and Cooper (1989). This should also include the Standardized Wish and Fear List, third edition (see Table 6.1; Perry, 1996a), which lists the 40 Wishes and 40 Fears and their related synonyms. The accompanying *Manual for the Wish and Fear List* (Perry, 1996b) presents real examples of the interplay of motives in interview and psychotherapy texts, along with justification for their identification.

Formulating one's first case is difficult, and therefore it is best to have a preformulated case to check oneself against. One is available in Perry (1994; see the interview presented in that same issue). Graduate students and others who train with me also have other unpublished cases with which to train, but matters of informed consent prevent these from being made generally available. Ideally one should have the opportunity to formulate several preselected cases to include individuals with highly focal conflicts as well as those with global and multifocal conflicts. Several may be available from myself by the time this is published.

In the case where one is learning the ICF as a research tool, this second step has an important modification to it. Instead of the qualitative identification of motives, one uses a quantitative approach. In the qualitative method, after conducting, viewing, or reading the interview, the formulator tries to identify the presence of the main Wishes and Fears that are salient in the case. The judgment "present and salient" is all that is required. In the quantitative method, one identifies each Wish and Fear as it occurs in a transcript of the interview material, allowing one to count the number of occurrences of each. This yields a quantitative score for each Wish and Fear, typically ranging from 0 to 10, but occasionally higher. The ICF then proceeds based on the most frequent Wishes and Fears. The "stragglers" (motives with only 1 or 2 occurrences each) may serve as potential motives that the subject might switch to as therapy proceeds.

The third part of training is to gain experience on several other cases with the addition of a consensus process with another formulator (or several, if in a seminar setting). This forces one to use the justification procedure, which elevates the consensus process above the usual competitive fray of the case conference to a more scientific level. The consensus process improves one's skills at articulating the raw data of the interview into justifiable patterns that others can agree upon. It also helps teach the conceptual boundaries of each motive as well as how to discriminate between lower- and higher-level motives that bear something in common (e.g., Wish 4, to communicate my needs and elicit a response from others, vs. Wish 17, to assert myself to meet an individual need). A by-product of the consensus process is to appreciate how much more can be gained by further experience with dynamic formulation. Practice makes (more) perfect.

After formal training, it is important to utilize the ICF on new cases. As learning a foreign language is not complete at the end of classwork, so the formulation process will not settle in as a permanent skill unless one uses and adapts it to one's own cases. A pleasant reward for such usage will occur on those occasions when one shares a formulation with a colleague who then comments on how helpful it is compared to what he or she is used to seeing. Enjoy this when it happens.

RESEARCH

Reliability of the Nonstandardized ICF Method

The reliability of the ICF was tested using two independent formulations of 20 cases, comparing the similarities of correctly matched versus mismatched pairs of formulations (Perry, Augusto, & Cooper, 1989). Two pairs of clinician raters independently and blindly derived an ICF on each of the 20 cases from videotaped dynamic interviews. The original nonstandardized method was employed. Sixty comparisons were then made by a third team of three raters kept blind to the identity of each ICF. A Type A comparison involved comparing the two ICFs correctly matched for each case. A Type B comparison involved comparing two mismatched ICFs but both from cases with the same gender and diagnosis ($n = 20$). A Type C comparison also involved 20 mismatched comparisons from cases with different diagnoses but still matched as to gender.

The similarity team rated each pair of ICFs using a 7-point scale ranging from 1 (no areas of overlap) to 7 (essential overlap with no appreciable disagreements). The mean similarity of correctly matched pairs of formulations (4.41) was significantly higher ($p < .0001$) than mismatched formulation pairs either with the same diagnoses (3.05) or with different diagnoses (2.91). This denotes that, on average, the correctly matched pairs of formulations were rated somewhere between 4.0, "equal amounts of overlap and nonoverlap," and 5.0, "definite overlap with some distinct disagreements or differences in description." By contrast the mismatched pairs were rated near 3.0, "definite non-overlap with some distinct areas of agreement or similarity of description." The overall finding held for each of the five major ICF components (i.e., Wish, Fear, etc.) assessed individually.

This study offers significant support for the reliability or reproducibility of the ICF method of psychodynamic formulation. Astonishingly, these findings are almost identical to those obtained on a similar test of the reliability of the CCRT in which the mean similarities were 4.54 for correctly matched CCRTs and 2.89 for mismatched CCRTs (Crits-Christoph et al., 1988). As noted elsewhere (Perry, 1989), this method for comparing idiographic data has the disadvantage of not providing an estimate of the shared variance between ratings of the same subject. Such comparisons require standardized categories rather than purely idiographic descriptions.

Reliability of the Standardized ICF Method

We conducted a study of the interrater reliability of the ICF Wish and Fear components using the Standardized Wish and Fear List (Perry, 1990). Two raters independently read existing ICFs from 35 subjects devised in the original nonstandardized way. They then rated these Wishes and Fears according to the standardized list. The weighted kappa statistic was used to examine the chance-corrected agreement for the Wishes and Fears rated by independent raters. Rater disagreements of Wishes and Fears within the same Eriksonian stage (near misses) were weighted by "1," while disagreements from different stages (not near misses) were weighted by "2," thereby penalizing a "far miss" more than a "near miss." Among those Wishes and Fears endorsed in at least 5% of cases, the median weighted κ for individual Wishes was .64, while the median for individual Fears was .46. A consensus rating was made by the two raters subsequent to determination of the interrater reliability and is used for more substantive data analyses. Although we have not tested the reliability of the consensus ratings, extrapolating from work with defenses (Perry & Cooper, 1989) we calculate that consensus ratings should increase reliability by 15–25%. The consensus justification process inherently improves reliability and validity.

Although the ICF was designed to be applicable without the availability of transcripts, a reliability study currently under way is examining whether quantitative assessment of each standardized motive leads to improved reliability. The addition of a manual of examples to aid rater training and calibration should further enhance reliability.

Concurrent Validity: Comparison to Other Formulation Methods

One case study examined the degree of agreement among three dynamic formulation methods in identifying a subject's Wishes, the one component shared by all three methods (Perry, Luborsky, Silberschatz, & Popp, 1989). A single case was rated independently by each method. Blind raters then judged the similarity of each Wish identified by each method, comparing two Wishes at a time from different methods. The ICF Wishes were significantly similar to Wishes identified by both the CCRT and Plan Diagnosis methods. This can be viewed as evidence of concurrent validity for the Wish component of the ICF, CCRT, and Plan Diagnosis.

This comparison was subsequently enlarged to include other methods, and a more complex comparison of the degree of similarity of the methods was carried out (Luborsky, Popp, & Barber, 1994). The ICF was less similar to the CCRT than several other methods. This finding is consistent with differences of the more ego-psychological perspective of the ICF as opposed to the more interpersonal or "object relations" perspectives of the CCRT and some other methods.

The Heuristic Value of the Developmental Hierarchy

A study near completion examined the Wishes and Fears in a sample with personality disorders (PDs), and particularly a subgroup with BPD. In the total sample, about half of the total Wishes and Fears rated from dynamic interviews were in Erikson's stages I and II (trust vs. mistrust, and autonomy vs. shame and doubt), synonymous with so-called preoedipal developmental issues. In addition BPD subjects had a mean developmental level lower than the other nonborderline subjects with PDs. While I generally eschew such terms as "primitive" or "higher-level" personality disorders, these findings are compatible with others' views about where BPD fits in such a schema. More useful, however, is the finding that there are specific motives in these two earliest developmental stages that BPD subjects are concerned with. The next step will be to quantify these motives in a larger sample, examining their etiological correlates and their relationship to treatment response. The results can inform us as we revise our treatments accordingly. This highlights the heuristic value of the developmental ordering of Wishes and Fears and suggests that the ICF is an important scientific approach to dynamics.

REFERENCES

Barber, J., & Crits-Christoph, P. (1993). Advances in measures of psychodynamic formulations. *Journal of Clinical and Consulting Psychology, 61,* 574–585.

Bellak, L., & Goldsmith, L. A. (Eds.). (1984). *The broad scope of ego function assessment.* New York: Wiley.

Bellak, L., Hurvich, M., & Gediman, H. (1973). *Ego functions in schizophrenics, neurotics and normals.* New York: Wiley.

Bloch, A. L., Shear, M. K., Markowitz, J. C., Leon, A. C., & Perry, J. C. (1993). An empirical study of defense mechanisms in dysthymia. *American Journal of Psychiatry, 150,* 1194–1198.

Crits-Christoph, P., Luborsky, L., Dahl, L., Popp, C., Mellon, J., & Mark, D. (1988). Clinicians can agree in assessing relationship patterns in psychotherapy: The Core Conflictual Relationship Theme method. *Archives of General Psychiatry, 45,* 1001–1004.

Erikson, E. H. (1963). *Childhood and society* (2nd ed.). New York: Norton.

Erikson, E. H. (1968). *Identity, youth and crisis.* New York: Norton.

Karasu, T. B., & Skodol, A. (1980). VIth Axis for DSM-III: Psychodynamic evaluation. *American Journal of Psychiatry, 137,* 607–610.

Luborsky, L. (1984). *Principles of psychoanalytic psychotherapy: A manual for supportive–expressive treatment.* New York: Basic Books.

Luborsky, L., Popp, C., & Barber, J. (1994). Common and special factors in difference transference-related measures. *Journal of Psychotherapy Research, 4,* 277–286.

Malan, D. H. (1976). The current position of research in psychotherapy. In D. H. Malan (Ed.), *Toward the validation of dynamic psychotherapy: A replication.* New York: Plenum Press.

Perry, J. C. (1989). Scientific progress in psychodynamic formulation. *Psychiatry, 52,* 245–249.

Perry, J. C. (1990). *Wishes and Fears: A standardized list for assessing dynamic motives.* Cambridge MA: Author.

Perry, J. C. (1993). The study of defense mechanisms and their effects. In N. Miller, L. Luborsky, J. Barber, & J. Docherty (Eds.), *Psychodynamic treatment research: A handbook for clinical practice* (pp. 276–308). New York: Basic Books.

Perry, J. C. (1994). Assessing psychodynamic patterns using the Idiographic Conflict Formulation (ICF) method. *Journal of Psychotherapy Practice and Research, 4*(2), 238–251.

Perry, J. C. (1996a). *Wishes and Fears: A standardized list for assessing dynamic motives, third edition.* Copyright J. C. Perry, M.D., Stockbridge, MA: Author.

Perry, J. C. (1996b). *A manual for the Wish and Fear List.* Stockbridge, MA: Author.

Perry, J. C., Augusto, F., & Cooper, S. H. (1989). Assessing psychodynamic conflicts: I. Reliability of the Idiographic Conflict Formulation method. *Psychiatry, 52,* 289–301.

Perry, J. C., & Cooper, S. H. (1986). A preliminary report on defenses and conflicts associated with borderline personality disorder. *Journal of the American Psychoanalytic Association, 34,* 863–893.

Perry, J. C., & Cooper, S. H. (1987). Empirical studies of psychological defense mechanisms. In J. O. Cavenar & R. Michels (Eds.), *Psychiatry* (pp. 1–19). New York: Lippincott.

Perry, J. C., Luborsky, L., Silberschatz, G., & Popp, C. (1989). An examination of three methods of psychodynamic formulation based on the same videotaped interview. *Psychiatry, 52,* 302–323.

Vaillant, G. E. (1977). *Adaptation to life.* Boston: Little, Brown.

7

Configurational Analysis: States of Mind, Person Schemas, and the Control of Ideas and Affect

MARDI J. HOROWITZ
TRACY D. EELLS

Configurational Analysis (CA) is an approach to psychotherapy case formulation that focuses on organizing a patient's history and relevant signs and symptoms into low-level inferences about that patient's clinically salient states of mind, concepts of self and other, and habitual ways of managing emotional information. It is a flexible tool that can be applied to difficult patients presenting with mixed-symptom disorders and personality problems, as well as with less complex patients or those with well-circumscribed problems for which a brief psychotherapy is indicated. CA was originally introduced by Horowitz in 1979 (see second edition, 1987) and has recently been updated as a system of formulation for planning psychotherapy treatment (Horowitz, 1997).

HISTORICAL BACKGROUND OF THE APPROACH

CA is an integrative approach to case formulation in the sense of attempting a theoretical synthesis (Norcross & Newman, 1992) of psychodynamic and cognitive-behavioral concepts into a new theory, which we call "person schemas theory" (Horowitz, 1987, 1988, 1989, 1991, 1997; Horowitz, Merluzzi, et al., 1991). CA is rooted in psychodynamic theory, especially its emphases on conflict in intrapsychic and interpersonal relationships. It organizes personal meanings according to wish–fear–compromise configurations. These configurations focus on multiple schemas of self and of others, and on the control of associational linkages among schemas in order to manage stress and conflict.

Horowitz's (1986) work on individuals with posttraumatic stress disorder provided him with insights as to how these individuals adaptively and maladaptively attempt to process the memories and fantasies associated with the traumatic events. CA is also influenced by cognitive science, primarily information processing models of mind–brain activities. The influence of information processing on CA is seen in the assumption of CA that mental representations mediate thought, feeling, and behavior. Our focus on these mental representations, or schemas, is consistent with demonstrations by cognitive psychopathologists that schemas appear to mediate major depressive disorder and anxiety disorders (e.g., Hope, Rapee, Heimberg, & Dornberg, 1990; Segal, Truchon, Horowitz, Gemar, & Guiguis, 1995; Williams, Mathews, & MacLeod, 1996). Our use of the schema concept reaches beyond what has been reliably demonstrated in research. We feel justified in doing so, however, due to the heuristic and practical value of our concepts and because we recognize that CA is only an initial step toward bridging gaps between theoretical and empirical findings emerging from cognitive science laboratories and the practical demands of busy day-to-day clinical work.

Eric Berne's (1961) transactional analysis has also played a role in its emphasis on multiple self-states and transactions among them. Berne's is an attractive and deceptively simple theory about how individuals engage in social maneuvers ("games") and play out unconscious life plans ("scripts") that often deprive them of longed for self-esteem and intimacy. Berne proposed a triad of ego states—Parent, Adult, and Child—that compete for dominance in personality. For example, the "parental" role is often harshly judgmental and offers only conditional affection. In CA, this may correspond to a schema of an internal critic, or introject, as a "harsh and critical parent."

CA has also been influenced by circumplex-based interpersonal theories (see Henry, Chapter 9, this volume), which permit quantitative assessments of maladaptive interpersonal patterns (Anchin & Kiesler, 1980), and by Luborsky's Core Conflictual Relationship Theme (CCRT; Luborsky & Crits-Christoph, 1990; see Chapter 3, this volume), particularly its focus on wish–wish and wish–fear conflicts.

CONCEPTUAL FRAMEWORK

There are four classes of information that are formulated in CA: significant clinical phenomena; states of mind; schemas of self, other, and relationships; and the control of ideas and affect. The CA formulation process moves stepwise from attending to observations about a patient to making inferences about the patient's personal meaning system.

Clinical Phenomena

These include the patient's presenting symptoms and list of problems, as well as any other observable or near-surface events occurring in the consultation room or reported by the patient as occurring elsewhere. Phenomena might include unusual gestures, facial expressions, manner of speech, topics discussed, and style of managing emotion. The clinician tries to pay close attention to the patient without his or her observations being overly influenced by a priori theoretical considerations or by where the patient may try to direct the clinician's attention. These phenomena provide the material to be explained by the remaining classes of information in CA.

States of Mind

States of mind are recurrent, coherent complexes of affect, thought, experience, and behavior. They are assumed to limit the accessibility of certain ideas and affect. To illustrate, Jill, who entered treatment after the death of her father, seemed to alternate between *depressed and helpless* and *excitedly working* states of mind. When in the *depressed and helpless* state, Jill felt unable to generate the energy, interpersonal skills, or positive self-concept that accompanied the *excitedly working* state of mind. It was as if the latter state never existed. Similarly, when in the *excitedly working* state, she avoided any thoughts of her father as if thinking of him would precipitate the onset of her *depressed and helpless* state and its accompanying tears and fear of loss of control. The concept of a state of mind is similar to that of mood but is more inclusive because mood usually refers only to an emotion that is sustained through time and does not directly reference accompanying cognition, behaviors, gestures, expressions, and the like.

In addition to describing states in adjectival terms, as just illustrated, the clinician can classify them into one of the four broad categories shown in Table 7.1. As indicated there, undermodulated states are those in which intense and poorly controlled emotions are expressed; in well-modulated states, the individual readily accesses and integrates a variety of emotional and ideational expressions; overmodulated states involve excessive control of behavior; and shimmering states are those in which the individual appears to fluctuate rapidly between two states of mind or to experience them simultaneously. Table 7.2 shows how a variety of states of mind can fit into these broad categories.

Schemas of Self, Others, and Relationships

At the heart of CA lies the assumption that individuals possess a repertoire of person schemas. Schemas are relatively stable knowledge structures that help organize an individual's self-concept, concept of others, and dominant self-with-other relationship patterns (Singer & Salovey, 1991). They result from overlearned and generalized interpersonal experiences—as well as from constitutional, genetic, and intrapersonal sources—that become ingrained into an

TABLE 7.1. Major States of Mind and How They Are Experienced by the Patient and Observers

State of mind	Definition	Experience of patient	Experience of observers
Undermodulated	Dysregulation of emotional expression.	Intense sobbing, impulsive outbursts of anger; impulsivity; feeling out of control. Sharp increases in the intensity of verbal expressions may appear as the patient experiences emotional surges or pangs.	Empathic emotional surges; an urge to intervene to help the patient regain control. "Freezing" in response to attacking outbursts of anger.
Well-modulated	A relatively smooth flow of ideas and affective expression.	Affective displays are experienced as genuine, and thoughts as freely flowing and spontaneous. The individual feels a sense of poise, regardless of the intensity of affective or ideational expression.	Subjective interest and empathy; feels connected to an individual engaged in an organized communication process without major discords between verbal and nonverbal modes of expression.
Overmodulated	Excessive control of expressive behavior.	Constricted, stiff, enclosed, anxious, or walled off. There is a narrowing of experience to verbal expression; affect seems forced or feigned; the person feels false.	A feeling of disconnection, boredom, or difficulty paying attention. The observer appraises the individual as distant.
Shimmering	Rapid shifting between, or simultaneous experience of, under- and overcontrolled states of mind.	Excited, distracted; drawn toward and away from a topic; alternately undercontrolled and overcontrolled.	Puzzlement, confusion, caught up in patient's excitement.

individual's psychological makeup. Schemas are not consciously experienced, but they influence conscious experiences. They can increase the efficiency of information processing by focusing attention on particular elements of one's intrapersonal and interpersonal world and by enabling one to readily anticipate their meaning. Social cognition researchers have also posited multiple selves as a possible cognitive model of personality and social functioning (e.g., Kihlstrom & Cantor, 1984; Kihlstrom et al., 1988; Markus, 1990; Markus & Nurius, 1986).

Role Relationship Models

Role Relationship Models (RRMs) are diagrams that organize core interaction patterns, or relationship schemas. As shown in Figure 7.1, an RRM has three components: a self schema, schema of other, and a relationship script. The script includes the following: (1) an anticipated action, emotion, wish, or motivation

TABLE 7.2. Dictionary of States of Mind Organized by Degree of Modulation and Emotional Coloration

Emotional coloration	Degree of modulation		
	Undermodulated	Well-modulated	Overmodulated
Sadness	Distraught Out-of-control crying Demoralized and deflated Desperately overwhelmed	Quietly needy Crying Struggle against crying Poignantly empathic Unhappily vulnerable	As if sad Phony poignancy As if remorseful
Fear/anxiety	Bodily panic Panicky emptiness Frightened vulnerability Panicky helplessness	Fearful worry Apprehensive vigilance Mixed rage/fear Nervously irritable	As if anxious Numbing from fear
Self-disgust/ shame/guilt	Shameful mortification Revolted self-disgust Intrusive guilt Panicky guilt	Ashamed disgrace Bashfully shy Remorseful Angry self-disgust	As if self-disgust Sham guilt
Anger	Explosive fury Panicky rage Self-righteous rage Grandiose bellicosity Tantrum Defiance Shame/rage/fear	Angry Bitter Resentful Annoyed, skeptical Sniping Whining	As if angry Blustering Cutely angry
Tension	Excitedly disorganized Confused Overwhelmed and pained Hypervigilant Anxious and withdrawn Distracted	Tentative engagement Struggle with Vulnerability	As if strained
Dullness	Foggy withdrawal Listless apathy Fugue or coma Hurt and unengaged	Bored Meandering	Coldly remote
Communication	Pressured confusion Pressured dumping Frenzied activity	Assured, productive Compassionate Composed, authentic Earnest activity	Rigid reporting Technical display As if bold Pontification Controlled Documentarian
Engagement	Giddy engagement Foolishly excited	Composed, authentic Earnest activity Elated and poised Shining (smiling, beaming)	As if bold Pontification Social chitchat Snide sociability As if lighthearted
Affection	Foolishly enthralled Overawed	Tender Assured compassion	As if illuminated
Creative excitement	Excited hyperactivity Frenzied creativity Shining (smiling, beaming)	Oceanic Illuminated Creative flow	As if illuminated

(*continued*)

TABLE 7.2. (*continued*)

Emotional coloration	Degree of modulation		
	Undermodulated	Well-modulated	Overmodulated
Joy	Foolishly enthralled Foolishly excited, histrionic	Cheerful Sharing	As if lighthearted
Sexual excitement	Enthralled love Flooded with eroticism Sexually titillated	Flirtatious pleasure Eroticized sensuality	As if eroticized

of the self; (2) the expected response of the other; (3) the reaction of the self to the response of the other; (4) a self-appraisal of these reactions; and (5) the expected other's appraisal of these reactions. The first three often suffice.

As shown in Figure 7.2, mental working models combine an individual's perception of an actual situation with a priori person schemas. The largest box in Figure 7.2 symbolizes the social transactions between self and other. The large circle to the left represents the self and its contents, symbolizing mental processes of perceiving, thinking, emotion, schematizing, and action planning. The working model of the relationship between self and other is partially organized through perceptual activity directed into the interpersonal world and partially by information from enduring schemas about how transactions unfold. From this repertoire of organized meaning structures, one schema may dominate the template of the working model, as shown by the heavy arrow. Enduring schemas of a type may also have layers of more progressive or regressive forms.

Enduring schemas may not accord with the real properties of self and other in the transaction situation. Nonetheless, they may so affect the inner working

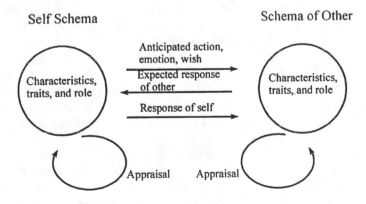

FIGURE 7.1. Format for a Role Relationship Model (RRM).

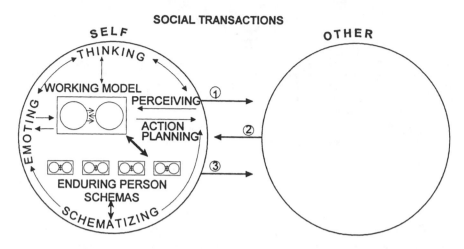

FIGURE 7.2. RRMs as working models, and enduring person schemas, of current social transactions. The circled numbers indicate a sequence of actual interpersonal expressions.

model of that situation that transference reactions occur. That is, the person repeats an earlier schematized pattern that is currently "erroneous" in some way.

Role Relationship Model Configurations

Role Relationship Model Configurations (RRMCs) are organizations of RRMs into a wish–fear–compromise format. As shown in Figure 7.3, the bottom half of an RRMC comprises desired and dreaded RRMs. The desired RRM organizes states of satisfaction. The dreaded RRM organizes states of intense suffering and loss of control. The top half of the RRMC comprises the compromise RRMs, which organize states of greater control. Compromise RRMs are divided into more and less adaptive versions.

As shown in Figure 7.3, self schemas are arrayed within a circle at the center of the RRMC format. These multiple self schemas may or may not be forged into the supraordinate self-organization suggested by this circle. The reader may also note that schemas with negative emotional potential are to the left of an RRMC and those with positive emotional potential to the right. Several RRMCs can be constructed for complex cases, classifying RRMs into sets according to type of relationship or type of self schemas. See Horowitz (1997), Horowitz, Merluzzi, et al. (1991) for further details on constructing RRMCs and clinical examples.

A filled-in RRMC for the case example discussed later in this chapter is shown in Figure 7.4. Although patients may initially offer information that would be placed in a problematic compromise RRM, we have found that for narrative purposes RRMCs are best read beginning at the desired quadrant, moving to the dreaded quadrant, then to the adaptive compromise, and finally to the problematic compromise. Figure 7.4 can be summarized narratively as follows:

Desired quadrant. This patient wishes to be an adoring daughter who admires her idealized father and is supported and admired by him.

Dreaded quadrant. This wish for mutual admiration is obstructed, however, by a view of herself as an overly trusting girl in relationship to a cold and selfish father figure who tricks her; she responds by remaining loyal but is then scorned and suppresses her rage rather than display out-of-control emotions as her mother did. This scenario leaves her feeling ashamed and guilty.

Adaptive compromise quadrant. To escape this wish–fear conflict and as a consequence of it, the patient feels worthless and dissociates herself from important male figures; she is uncommunicative, but when encouraged she has the capacity to restore a concept of self as worthwhile and to guardedly engage in productive work with men.

Problematic compromise. Alternatively, the patient may respond to her wish–fear conflict by viewing herself as worthless and degraded by critical others; she withdraws but still feels attacked, so she develops a "counter-identity" as a compensation for feelings of worthlessness and to avoid feeling too depressed.

As this example illustrates, the information in an RRMC is quite condensed. For this reason, we have found the RRMC to be a helpful format for efficiently

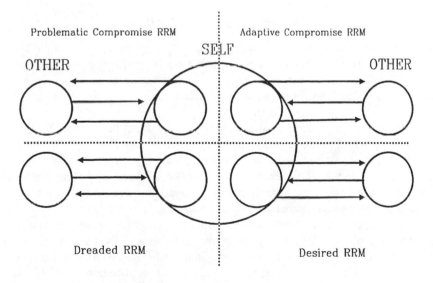

Problematic Compromise RRM   Adaptive Compromise RRM

SELF

OTHER   OTHER

Dreaded RRM   Desired RRM

FIGURE 7.3. Format for configurations of RRM.

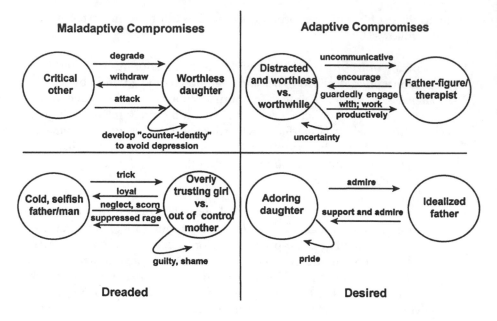

FIGURE 7.4. RRMC of Connie.

and succinctly conveying a large amount of information; nevertheless, the clinician may elect instead to summarize the same information in a narrative format, as we have just done.

Control of Ideas and Affect

The concept of defense mechanisms remains a controversial one in psychology (Singer, 1990). Although consensus has not been reached about the existence of defense mechanisms (Holmes, 1990), the concept is one of the most resilient in clinical psychology and has probably been one of the most useful for those who practice psychotherapy.

Although many mechanisms of defense have been proposed, all rest on the assumption that three preconditions of mental functioning must be met for defensive operations to occur (Horowitz, Markman, Stinson, Fridhandler, & Ghannam, 1990). The first precondition is the presence of a motivational force aimed at conscious representation or action. Second is a capacity to process the motives into forms accessible to conscious representation. Third is the capacity to anticipate the consequences of conscious representation or action. The third precondition is problematic, however, because it leaves open the question of how it is possible to anticipate (and then ward off) the consequences of a conscious representation without that representation itself existing in consciousness.

Information-processing theory suggests two possible answers. First, the consequences of conscious representation might be anticipated in unconscious information processing without any conscious representation. Horowitz et al. (1990) suggest that memory traces of past associations and sensitizations might operate entirely in unconscious information processing. A second possibility is that small amounts or periods of conscious representation could occur, but with feedforward inhibitions as a result of assessing these episodes. Both of these possibilities assume a "smart" unconscious (Loftus & Klinger, 1992), that is, one capable of assessing threats and selecting control operations likely to reduce the threat. Regardless of which "answer" one prefers, it is useful to think of the regulation of thought and affect in terms of three categories: purposes, outcomes, and processes (Horowitz, 1988; Wallerstein, 1983).

Control Purposes

The concept of a *control purpose* provides a motivational component to CA. Control purposes include a person's wishes, goals, hopes, and intentions; they do not assume conscious awareness of these purposes. Purposes may be categorized broadly as adaptive or maladaptive. Adaptive purposes are those that facilitate personal growth and development, the satisfaction of emotional needs, interpersonal relationships, and the like. Maladaptive purposes are those that inhibit growth and development, narrow the individual's life and range of experience, fail to meet emotional needs, and inhibit the development of healthy interpersonal relationships.

Readers might note that the concepts "defense mechanism" and "coping style" are similar in that both are marshaled to manage threatening ideas and feelings. Although some theorists characterize defenses as maladaptive and coping mechanisms as adaptive, we agree with Vaillant (1992) that there are conceptual advantages to viewing certain defensive outcomes as adaptive and others as maladaptive. Furthermore, we believe that both coping and defensive mechanisms can involve unconscious regulatory processes (Horowitz & Stinson, 1995; Horowitz, Znoj, & Stinson, 1996).

Control Outcomes

Outcomes are the resultants of the regulatory purposes and processes involved in managing conflictual ideas and affect that aim at conscious representation. They reflect varying degrees of deflections from awareness of these ideas and affect. Thus, instead of thinking, "I hate my deceased spouse," a person may deflect this idea into "I idealize my deceased spouse" (reaction formation), "He had his reasons for being hateful" (rationalization), or "My feelings about my deceased spouse are unimportant" (minimization). A standard list of defense mechanisms, such as that found in the appendices of DSM-IV (American Psychiatric Association, 1994), can serve as a list of control outcomes.

Control Processes

Processes lie between purposes and outcomes. They are analogous to the various paths that individuals might follow to a given destination. There are many routes to the same destination, but the route can affect the meaning of arriving at a destination. For example, a grieving person might rationalize the thought "I hate my deceased spouse" into "My feelings about my spouse don't matter" by any of the following processes or combinations of them: (1) switching topics; (2) decreasing arousal level; or (3) shifting from a multimodal representational set (i.e., the ability to access information in the form of images, words, smells, and tactile memories) to a unimodal set (e.g., only words).

For present purposes we will refer to a control process as any of a variety of ways in which incipient thoughts and feelings might be inhibited, facilitated, or otherwise regulated. We distinguish three categories of control processes. These are the regulation of *mental set, schemas,* and *topic selection and flow*. We briefly summarize these categories below. Readers wishing a more elaborated discussion of them are referred to Horowitz and Stinson (1995), Horowitz (1997), and Horowitz et al. (1996); see also Table 7.3.

Control of Mental Set. Mental set is the most basic level of a control process. It is a "state of preparedness for processing a constellation of ideas and emotions" and includes "a determination of the next theme for conscious representation and how this theme will be processed" (Horowitz et al., 1990, p. 66). Mental set refers to an individual's present capacity to contemplate and adaptively manage a theme once it enters consciousness, as well as one's readiness to permit entry of a stressful theme into consciousness. Some of the parameters that are determined by the notion of a mental set are the following: (1) the setting of an "intentional hierarchy," reflecting one's capacity to select one from among a set of themes for contemplation; (2) "temporal set," or the expanse of time one is able to take into account when processing a theme (short-term vs. long-term); (3) "sequential set," which address one's problem-solving style, for example, systematic and orderly, through reverie, or chaotically and randomly; (4) "representational set," or the mode in which ideas and feelings take form, including words, images, and behavior, either in isolation or in concert; (5) locus of attention (either toward thought or action); and (6) level of arousal.

Control of Schemas. These controls regulate processes associated with an individual's sense of identity and self, as well as how she or he thinks, feels, and acts in relationships. As shown in Table 7.3, one might control the flow of ideas and affect into consciousness by altering self schemas, schemas of others, and relationship schemas.

Control of Topic Selection and Flow. This category of controls includes those governing how individuals select topics for contemplation and how these topics are organized, consciously represented, and presented to others. Individuals might control the flow of representations either by facilitating or inhibiting associations. The sequencing of ideas might be described by seeking information or by topic switching. Other controls in this category are altering meanings, the hierarchical complexity or simplicity of information, revision of working models, and enacting new modes of thinking and feeling. Table 7.3 presents adaptive and maladaptive outcomes for each of these processes.

These thoughts about the control of conflictual ideas and affect provides a language close to signs observed during psychotherapy. Our clinical experience tells us that these control purposes, processes, and outcomes are often habitual patterns adopted by patients, operating largely outside of awareness.

INCLUSION/EXCLUSION CRITERIA

CA is appropriate for any individual undergoing a course of psychotherapy in which interpersonal relationships and concepts of self and others play an important role, or where one of the goals of therapy is to alter the patient's system of interpersonal meanings. CA is not restricted to any psychotherapy modality but is applicable to therapies as diverse as psychodynamic, cognitive, interpersonal, experiential, or behavioral. A CA formulation may offer an especially fresh perspective to therapists practicing in nondynamic modalities who may not accept the entire theory from which CA grew. Control process theory, for example, may illuminate obstacles to treatment success based on cognitive-behavioral principles. As noted above, however, CA is particularly appropriate in the treatment of individuals with DSM-IV Axis II diagnosis or those seeking to change long-standing interpersonal problems.

STEPS IN CASE FORMULATION CONSTRUCTION

There are four basic steps in CA case formulation. The goal of these steps is to proceed systematically from readily observable material exhibited by a patient to a set of inferences that the therapist can use to better understand and treat the patient. Each step moves toward a greater level of inference and builds on what is learned in the previous steps. The four steps are as follows: (1) describing clinically relevant phenomena; (2) identifying the patient's repertoire of states of mind; (3) identifying and organizing the patient's central relationship schemas and schemas of self and other; and (4) labeling unresolved emotional themes and defensive control processes. Table 7.4 summarizes these steps. Materials to use are intake assessments, process or progress notes, and the clinician's recall of therapy sessions. In research, we use audiovideo recordings or transcripts of therapy sessions. Readers interested in more details are referred to book length treatments by Horowitz (1987, 1997).

TABLE 7.3. Control Purposes, Processes, and Outcomes in Configurational Analysis

Control process	Control outcome/Control purpose	
	Adaptive	Maladaptive
Control of mental set		
Intentional hierarchy	Dosing	"Forgetting"
Temporal set	Telescoping to gain perspective, close examination to gain understanding	Continual focus on crises, denial or avoiding examination of episodic memories
Sequential set	Planning, generation of positive imagery	Chaotic, haphazard
Representational set	Verbal dominant, other modes accessible via dosing	Numbing, denial, intrusion of images, acting out
Locus of attention	Toward thought, toward action	Easily distractible, dissociated
Level of arousal	Alert, attentive	Suppression, somnolence
Control of schemas		
Altering self schemas	Flexible adaptation	Reaction formation, turning against the self, regression
Altering schemas of others	Flexible adaptation	Projection, passive aggression
Altering relationship schemas	Sublimation, succorance, nurturance, altruism	Role reversal, projective identification, devaluation, splitting, excessive idealization
Control of topic selection and flow		
Control of representations by:		
Facilitation of associations	Working through	"As if" working, intellectualization, rumination
Inhibition of associations	Dosing to adaptive modulation	Denial, repression, suppression, disavowal, undoing, minimization, somatization
Sequencing ideas by:		
Seeking information	Working through, understanding, learning	Intellectualization, displacement

(*continued*)

TABLE 7.3. (*continued*)

Control process	Control outcome/Control purpose	
	Adaptive	Maladaptive
Switching concepts	Facilitative associations, smooth transitions, affect and thought concordance	Isolation of affect, rationalization, undoing, reaction formation
Altering meanings	Humor, wisdom, appreciation of irony	Narcissistic devaluation, exaggeration, lying, omnipotent control
Hierarchical arrangement of ideas	Purposeful discourse, self-control	Paranoia, suspiciousness, rigidity
Revision of working models	Empathy, compassion for the self, self-control	Projection, externalization, blaming
Practicing new modes of thinking and acting	Self-efficacy	Regression, acting out

Note. Adapted from Horowitz (1988).

Step 1: Describe Clinically Relevant Phenomena

In this first step, the clinician simply makes a list of significant signs and symptoms observed in therapy or reported by the patient to occur outside of therapy. In day-to-day clinical practice, this step can take place in the context of usual preliminary evaluations and updated as new information emerges.

There is no effort at inference in Step 1. Instead, the clinician notes what any observant and interested individual would see. Information the clinician might list includes presenting symptoms and problems, posture, affective style, unusual verbalizations or gestures, any idiosyncratic mannerisms, salient traits, the style in which information is organized and presented, topics discussed, and the patient's pattern of shifting topics or of avoiding some topics altogether. The therapist should also be alert to what the patient is *not* saying. If a patient talks for several minutes about her mother, then shifts to siblings, then to work problems with a male supervisor, the therapist might wonder why the patient did not mention her father.

"Behavioral leakage" is particularly important to note at this stage of the formulation process. Behavioral leakages are signs exhibited by a patient that may suggest unexpressed affect or significant themes. Examples are perspiration that is out of context to the current topic, a reddening of the eyes that appears and then disappears as if the patient were about to cry but then suppressed the tears, fidgetiness, or a change in the patient's usual style of eye contact.

TABLE 7.4. Steps in Configuration Analysis Case Formulation and Their Application to Treatment Planning

Phenomena
>Select and describe symptoms, problem list, and noteworthy signs.

States of mind
>Describe states in which the selected phenomena occur and do not occur. Describe patterns of state cycles. Refer to Tables 7.1 and 7.2 to select state descriptors.

Schemas of self and other
>Describe the roles, beliefs, and scripts of expression and action that organize each state. Describe wish–fear dilemmas in relation to desired and dreaded RRMs. Infer how control processes and compromise RRMs may ward off such dangers. Identify dysfunctional attitudes and how these are involved in maladaptive state cycles.

Control of ideas and emotion
>Describe themes of concern during problematic states. Describe how expressions of ideas and emotions are obscured. Infer how avoidant states may function to ward-off dreaded, undermodulated states. (Use Table 7.3 and Appendix X of DSM-IV; American Psychiatric Association, 1994.)

Therapy technique planning
>Consider the interactions of phenomena, states, controls, and RRMs. Plan how to stabilize working states by support, how to counteract defensive avoidances by direction of attention, and how to alter dysfunctional attitudes by interpretation, trials of new behavior, and repetitions; integrate psychological plan with biological and social plans, when indicated.

Note. Adapted from Horowitz (1997). Each step can also include social and biological levels as well as past developmental contributors to the current situation.

The therapist should also be alert to his or her reaction to the patient. One assumption of CA is that patients unwittingly cast therapists into roles that conform to interpersonal expectations, goals, and fears based on previous experiences with important others. Therefore, the therapist should also note his or her own behaviors, thoughts, and feelings—in particular those that deviate from the usual.

At the completion of Step 1, the clinician should have a list of observations, some of which may be clinically significant, some of which may not be. The goals of the following steps is to select those that might be significant, then test them in the psychotherapy.

Step 2: Identify Patient's Repertoire of States of Mind

The clinician begins to label states of mind by grouping the phenomena observed in Step 1 into sensible patterns. If a patient becomes *angry* when discussing his being passed over for a promotion, says, *"Nothing ever works out for me,"* then *goes silent,* the therapist might label these phenomena (indicated in italics) as an "angry powerlessness" state of mind. (The clinician may be helped in choosing state names by consulting Table 7.2.) Terminology from Benjamin's (1993) Structural Analysis of Social Behavior (SASB) is also useful in labeling states of mind.

The following suggestions are offered to assist therapists further in identifying states of mind:

1. Common indications of states include changes in facial expression, speech intonation and inflection, the content of verbal reports, degree of self-reflective awareness, overall level of awareness, and experienced capacity for empathy.

2. Be alert to the degree of control associated with a state. Assessing the level of control prepares the way for inferring control maneuvers used to avoid undermodulated states.

3. States can also be labeled as positive or negative. Positive states of mind are those that the patient probably experiences as more pleasurable than displeasurable. Conversely, negative states of mind are those that are experience with displeasure or which include negative appraisals. In Step 3, this labeling will be used to classify self, other, and relationship schemas.

4. Notice the sequence in state shifts. Is there a pattern of moving from one state to another? For example, a patient may enter a state in which she challenges the therapist to do more for her, then shift to a self-deprecating state, and subsequently become remote and seemingly indifferent to the therapist. The therapist should also be attentive to any external events that trigger a state shift, such as the telephone ringing, a seemingly innocuous comment, starting a session late, or seeing another patient in the waiting room.

At the end of Step 2 the therapist has a list of states, each tentatively labeled as positive or negative, and as undermodulated, overmodulated, or well-modulated. These states may not initially seem to cohere well. The list may be long or short, although the usual range is from three to seven.

Step 3: Identify Self, Other, and Relationship Schemas

The third step in CA case formulation is to use the list of states of mind to identify a patient's recurrent views of self and other. The following guidelines are helpful:

1. Note expressions such as "I am the sort of person who . . . ," "I always . . . ," and "My husband (friend, parent) is a very . . . person."

2. Be particularly attentive to narratives told by patients. The clinician can keep an RRM format in mind to aid in inquiry. For example, if a patient says, "I felt stupid when the professor called on me" (self schema), the therapist may ask, "What do you imagine was going through the professor's mind when she called on you?" in an effort to elicit a schema of other.

3. If a patient repeatedly describes himself as shy with friends, or relates stories that indicate this, one might include "shy friend" as a role of the self. Similarly, if the patient describes friends as better than she or he is, "superior friend" may be included as a role of the other.

4. Action sequences, which include communications about intentions, judgments, and emotions, are listed in an RRM as transaction scripts. These can be noted in verb–adverb pairs, as in "approach tentatively," "feels disparaged," "withdraws." A dictionary of RRM scripts published elsewhere may also be helpful (Horowitz, Merluzzi, et al., 1991).

5. Organize self and other schemas into RRMs, as shown in Figures 7.1 through 7.4.

6. Include memories and fantasies about the past to show how the patient's current schematic and motivational structure developed.

7. Tentatively label schemas as desired, dreaded, adaptive compromises, or maladaptive compromises. Arrange them into RRMs and RRMCs, as shown in Figures 7.1 and 7.2.

Step 4: Identify Control Purposes, Processes, and Outcomes

Because several controls might operate in a single session, we recommend focusing on one part of a session at a time, perhaps a narrative told by the patient. After a section has been identified, first note the patient's "mental set." Consider the following questions: Do ideas flow easily and naturally or in a constricted manner? Do multiple ideas compete for expression, or does the patient have difficulty finding ideas? Can the patient shift from generalizations to episodic memories and vice versa? What structure does the patient impose on his or her narratives? Are these narratives relatively coherent or disorganized? How complete are they? Is the patient alert and attentive or sleepy, distant, and distracted? Do thoughts and feelings appear concordant or discordant?

Using the above information to estimate the patient's mental set, consider next how concepts of self and other are presented. Notice different roles into which the self and others are cast. Observations of this type help the therapist determine the extent to which the patient alters schemas of self and other to avoid potentially painful information. To what extent are these roles consistent or inconsistent across narratives? Does the patient describe others in a stereotypical way or in a way that permits the therapist to formulate an image of a unique human being? How are themes of power and affiliation portrayed in narratives? Are distinct roles assigned to self and other, or do these roles tend to blend into each other?

Finally, a detailed consideration of topic selection and flow can aid in identifying control processes. Focusing again on specific narratives, consider whether the patient engages in genuine, focused self-examination that aims at increasing self-understanding or whether there is an "as if" quality or an intellectualized tone to the patient's expressions. Does the patient make assertions, then qualify, retract, or otherwise deflect meaning away from the original content? Does the patient downplay the significance of clearly important life events? It is also helpful to contrast how a range of topics are communicated. Ideas, states, and emotions associated with some topics may be "welcomed" into awareness, whereas those associated with other topics may be experienced only with difficulty.

Once the therapist has completed these steps, the formulation can be transposed into a narrative or can remain as an RRMC and a worksheet with formulation components completed.

APPLICATION TO
PSYCHOTHERAPY TECHNIQUE

We do not typically share the entire formulation with the patient in one intervention. Doing so would inevitably produce an unwieldy intervention and might also overwhelm the patient. Instead, parts of the formulation are tested with the patient in parts, through simple and to-the-point interventions. The therapist also attempts to maximize the therapeutic impact of a formulation-based intervention by timing it appropriately, as relevant topics and themes arise.

Each of the four steps listed above generates information that can contribute to psychotherapy process and content, as well as to the evaluation of treatment success. Identifying noteworthy phenomena can help increase a patient's self-awareness, capacity for self-observation, and sense of control and self-mastery. For example, an overcontrolled and emotionally constricted patient seen by one of the present authors (TE) struggled for months to change a destructive interpersonal pattern in which he demeaned family members, then felt guilty for his aggressive behavior. A turning point seemed to be reached after the therapist pointed out how sad it was that the patient was perpetuating a pattern with his own children that was inflicted upon him as a child. The patient's face reddened, signifying behavioral leakage. When attention was called to his flushed face, the patient initially indicated a lack of awareness, but then began to feel sad and tears welled in his eyes for the first time in therapy.

It is also useful therapeutically to label major states of mind or to help the patient to do so. This activity helps patients realize the impermanent nature of these states, which in itself can aid the goals of therapy. In addition, pointing out patterns of state shifts helps a patient avert entry into undermodulated states or into self-impairing repetitive patterns and interpersonal relationships.

The self and other schemas depicted in RRMs and RRMCs also provide a practical way to help the patient understand contradictions within identity, and the different, sometimes competing patterns that may come up in different states within relationships.

Finally, a greater awareness of control processes can help a patient more fully recognize patterns of avoiding important ideas and feelings.

CASE EXAMPLE

Death of a Parent

"Connie" was a 28-year-old single Caucasian woman with a college degree who, when entering therapy, was supporting herself on unemployment assistance while retraining for a more fulfilling career. She had recently broken off a live-in relationship with a man and moved in with other friends. Connie came self-referred with complaints of crying spells and depression that began after the death of her father 5 weeks earlier.

Step 1: Clinically Significant Phenomena

Connie complained of intrusive crying spells, which she criticized and attempted to suppress. During conversations with others, she was unable to follow the thread of meaning and instead became dazed. After the death of her father, her creative work stopped. She was frightened by these symptoms because they seemed to lead into states where she had less and less control over herself. She was preoccupied with thoughts of death, experienced sudden outbursts of sadness, and felt that her life lacked purpose and direction.

Connie's problems in living included frequent disruptive love affairs. She selected men she saw as cold and remote, and vainly tried to teach them about love. Connie was also unable to achieve an adult understanding of her relationship with her father, an issue exacerbated by his death.

Problematic topics included Connie's inability to understand the meaning of various episodes in which her father had rejected her. She was unable to experience any resentment toward him for rejecting her, without having to distort the meaning of the good relationship that she remembered. This led to feelings of confusion about who she was, who he was, and how she should respond to his death appropriately. This problem was intensified by Connie's inability to know where she stood with her mother, except for a relatively imperative need to be different from her. Connie, her father, and her siblings all shared a view of the mother as a person who gave way to messy, out-of-control episodes of rage and depression.

Step 2: States of Mind

The most upsetting problematic state was characterized by *uncontrolled and intrusive crying*. There were other states used to avoid painful crying, primarily increased *sleeping* and feeling *dazed and distracted*. Connie also experienced a high-pressured state in which she felt *as if she was going crazy*.

Step 3: Self and Relationship Schemas

Connie was vulnerable to concepts of herself as defective, especially regarding her vocational identity. Like her father, she earned a college degree in business and found work in banking. Connie felt that her career was at a dead end, however, and her lack of more advanced skills left her feeling worthless. She quit her job in order to reorient her values and develop new skills. She was in the midst of this development when her father died. His death meant the interruption of her plan in which he would come to see that she was a worthwhile person, revise a rejection she had felt for the past 5 years, and so restore an early adolescent relationship of mutual admiration. Five years earlier, her father divorced her mother, and Connie sided with him. Soon after the divorce, however, she experienced her father as remote and rejecting. During this time, he married a woman much younger than himself and they had a baby, which Connie also experienced as rejection.

Her father's rejection of her perplexed and troubled Connie even before his death. When she last saw him, Connie had tried to regain the positive attachment of her earlier adolescence or at least to find out the reasons for his neglect and remoteness. At times, she saw her father as a cold, selfish man who had tricked and used her in his eventual divorce from her mother, then neglected and no longer needed her when he remarried. She experienced scorn and then felt herself to be either defective or unfairly rejected. Connie interpreted her father's death as a final rejection because it meant the impossibility of his ever reendorsing her worth. She also felt that his death might be his way of punishing himself for rejecting her. That is, the early and unexpected stroke was seen as a psychosomatic response to his recognition that he had destroyed a meaningful attachment.

Connie was unable to identify with her mother, although she had lost some of the basis for her identification with her father and her projections of what she ought to be. Her father wanted the divorce supposedly because of her mother's episodic, out-of-control rages and crying spells. Connie feared that by expressing reactive anger, fear, and sadness after his death, she would appear to be too much like her mother. These concepts of self and other are depicted in an RRMC format in Figure 7.4.

Step 4: Control of Ideas and Affect

The death of Connie's father set in motion a train of thought that would ideally lead to a greater understanding of her past relationship with him. Achieving this understanding appeared to be obstructed, however, by Connie's unwillingness to experience resentment, anger, and hurt toward her father. When these impulses arose, she inhibited them for fear of losing control or feeling too guilty or ashamed. If her efforts at suppression were not entirely successful, she was prone toward entering the previously mentioned distracted and dazed state of mind. Another significant control was idealization of her father, which also served to inhibit a view of him as cold and rejecting.

Formulation of Therapy Processes

Connie underwent a 12-session psychotherapy that aimed at relieving her symptomatology, at increasing feelings of self-efficacy, and at enhancing her understanding of her relationship with her father, thus laying a foundation for greater satisfaction in future intimate relationships.

States of Mind

Connie experienced *intrusive crying* with an evaluation interviewer but suppressed crying while talking with the therapist. The therapist detected her inhibition and blinking back of beginning tears. He told her that he would not feel critical of her if she did cry. She gradually became able to engage in *open crying*. As she worked through themes of mourning and of resentment toward her father, she was increasingly able to engage in a *working* state, expressing her emotions with fear of losing control.

Because the therapist was helpful and concerned, she could see him as an ideal father reestablishing the lost ideal relationship. During some episodes, she exhibited a *shining* state, which was like one previously referred to as mutual admiration with her father.

Although most of the time in therapy was spent by both persons working productively together, there were early episodes in which Connie began the interview in a *distracted* state, not knowing what to say.

Self and Relationship Schemas

A therapeutic alliance was established quickly, facilitated by Connie's intense need, and her symptoms decreased rapidly over the first few sessions. Subsequently, however, Connie appeared skeptical and challenged the therapist, as if testing whether he would reject her, whether he could tolerate her resentment, and whether meaningful communication could take place.

A critical emerging issue was whether the therapist would see Connie as worthwhile or worthless because some of her attitudes might run counter to his presumed cultural stance of conformity and conservatism. These counterculture attitudes were also revealed to be "counterfather" attitudes. As she found that the therapist did not refute or degrade her values, she herself tended to feel them as more authentic and an increase in self-esteem resulted. As self-esteem increased, she was more willing to accept the challenge of further exploration of her ideas and feelings.

Control of Ideas and Affect

The main theme explored during therapy was the need to understand the meaning of her father's rejection of her. It appeared that Connie deflected feelings of resentment and hurt toward her father through self-distraction, suppression of crying, and idealization. As the therapist labeled these controls, Connie was gradually able to get in touch with feelings of resentment, weakness, and degradation in connection with her father. Immersion in early experiences with her parents, especially with her father, during the first few sessions led to an increased focus on her current life. One of the important themes interpreted by the therapist was Connie's tendency to repeat the relationship with her father in her selection of men whom she could idealize but who were older, cold, and remote. It seemed that the death of her father also created a pivotal point at which she might reject men altogether as persons who were incapable of returning love and care. Another version of this theme was the need to rescue men and some remorse that she had failed to rescue her father from what she saw as a psychosomatic illness.

Formulation of Outcome

States of Mind

Three months after the termination of therapy, Connie no longer had episodes of *intrusive crying*. She was less depressed and felt generally more purposeful and able to have long periods in which she was in a *working* state.

Self and Relationship Schemas

Connie felt an increased self-worth, which she viewed as a return to how she felt before her father's death rather than a new development. At the follow-up, she was engaged in reviewing the meaning of her father's death and accepting the mourning process without fear or blocking. She was considering new relationships and had embarked on one that she felt might be potentially long lasting.

Control of Ideas and Affect

The major change in the status of ideas was the development of a concept of the development and meaning of her relationship with her father. She integrated various self-images and relationship models so that she now had a central view of him not as cold and rejecting but as presenting multiple self-images: as needing her while standing aloof and expressing an absence of need, and as telling her to be independent while covertly telling her to be tied to his views and person. She was able to differentiate her fear of weakness, sadness at loss, resentment at scorn, and remoteness from "messy emotions," and also to develop a more complex, less stereotyped view of her mother. The premise that she could not feel angry with her father for being neurotically conflicted was altered so that she believed it acceptable to express anger with him and with related male figures. Because of these changes, she could allow herself to progress through waves of grief work characteristic of mourning. She was aware in part of her inhibitory operations, but little if any alteration of this habitual style occurred.

TRAINING

Because it is a relatively complex method of psychotherapy case formulation, CA requires a commitment of time and effort to learn. Those familiar with psychodynamic concepts, particularly object relations theory and self psychology, will probably find CA easier to learn than those working in other modalities. A first step is to become familiar with concepts and terminology such as states of mind, multiple schemas, and control processes. After working with these terms for a while, they will become second nature. A second step, one that can be taken concurrently with the first, is simply to try out the method on a patient—new or not new—and see for oneself whether one has gained a better understanding of the patient. Third, it may be helpful to read more published case studies of individuals formulated with CA and compare one's own formulation with those of the authors.

RESEARCH SUPPORT FOR THE APPROACH

Two studies have been completed assessing the reliability of the person schemas components of CA (Horowitz & Eells, 1993; Eells, Horowitz, et al., 1995). Horowitz and Eells (1993) demonstrated that trained clinical judges could correctly match RRMCs to videotapes of psychotherapy session of patients for whom the RRMCs had been constructed. Eells, Horowitz, et al. (1995) showed that two groups of clinicians were able to construct similar RRMCs when working from the same set of psychotherapy transcripts.

Reliability of state descriptions has also been established (Horowitz, Ewert, Milbrath, & Sonneborn, 1994.) Preliminary data on the reliability of control purposes, processes, and outcomes is promising (Horowitz et al., 1996), especially because many researchers have had difficulty measuring defenses reliably (Vaillant, 1992).

The validity of a case formulation method can be established in different ways. In a study by Horowitz, Luborsky, and Popp (1991), convergent validity of the RRMC was measured by qualitatively comparing it with the CCRT method of case formulation (Luborsky & Crits-Christoph, 1990; see Chapter 3, this volume). The results were that the methods identified similar core emotional and interpersonal conflicts, that the CCRT was easier to perform, but that the RRMC yielded more information about defense processes. In another study (Horowitz, Eells, Singer, & Salovey, 1995), RRMCs constructed early in a long-term therapy were compared with psychotherapy transcripts in the second and third thirds of the psychotherapy. Findings were that key interpersonal, emotional, and defensive themes identified early in therapy were still the focus of attention at later points in the therapy. This might be considered a form of predictive validity.

Other approaches showing validity have compared the RRMC approach to those from multidimensional scaling using repertory grid-type ratings of adjectives as applied to self and significant others. These are reported in detail elsewhere (Tunis, Fridhandler, & Horowitz, 1990; Eells, 1995; Eells, Fridhandler, & Horowitz, 1995; Hart, Stinson, Field, Ewert, & Horowitz, 1995; Merluzzi, 1991).

CONCLUSION

CA is a systematic approach to case formulation. It has a good level of complexity: it permits one to examine multiple states of mind in terms of multiple self and other concepts that may organize emotional themes differently. In addition, CA facilitates an examination of how a patient copes with external stressors and attempts to control potentially disturbing feelings and thoughts. The advantage of the "good level of complexity" is that it avoids static, unitary, oversimplified inferences that fit the patient only some of the time.

CA proceeds from surface to depth. It cannot be completed in a single interview, but a good start can be made and followed up by additions and revisions. The levels can be done sequentially: phenomena, states, person schemas, and controls. But one can also make inferences from any level, then move back and forth to see if these inferences illuminate other facets of one's formulation. Sometimes really clear self-concepts are revealed as irrational aspects of a patient's identity, and these then clarify how to label a state of mind or infer a defensive distortion.

CA also points to technique: What phenomena are key problems to address first? What therapist interventions might increase well modulated states and protect the patient from dreaded out-of-control states? Which dysfunctional attitudes about self and others can be changed at this point in treatment? What countermeasures are available to modify maladaptive control processes yet help the patient to tolerate strong emotions in more realistic ways? Individualized answers to such questions may emerge as the formulation is clarified.

REFERENCES

American Psychiatric Association. (1994). *Diagnostic and statistical manual of mental disorders* (4th ed.). Washington, DC: Author.

Anchin, J. C., & Kiesler, D. J. (Eds.). (1980). *Handbook of interpersonal psychotherapy.* New York: Pergamon Press.

Benjamin, L. S. (1993). *Interpersonal diagnosis and treatment of personality disorders.* New York: Guilford Press.

Berne, E. (1961). *Transactional analysis in psychotherapy*. New York: Ballantine Books.

Eells, T. D. (1995). Role reversal: A convergence of clinical and quantitative evidence. *Psychotherapy Research, 4,* 297–312.

Eells, T. D., Fridhandler, B., & Horowitz, M. J. (1995). Self schemas and spousal bereavement: Comparing quantitative and clinical evidence. *Psychotherapy, 32,* 270–282.

Eells, T. D., Horowitz, M. J., Singer, J., Salovey, P., Daigle, D., & Turvey, C. (1995). The Role-Relationship Models method: A comparison of independently derived case formulation. *Psychotherapy Research, 5,* 154–168.

Hart, D., Stinson, C., Field, N., Ewert, M., & Horowitz, M. (1995). A semantic space approach to representations of self and other in pathological grief: A case study. *Psychological Science, 6,* 96–100.

Holmes, D. S. (1990). The evidence of repression: An examination of sixty years of research. In J. L. Singer (Ed.), *Repression and dissociation: Implications for personality, psychopathology, and health* (pp. 85–102). Chicago: University of Chicago Press.

Hope, D. A., Rapee, R. M., Heimberg, R. G., & Dombeck, M. J. (1990). Representations of the self in social phobia: Vulnerability to social threat. *Cognitive Therapy and Research, 14,* 177–189.

Horowitz, M. J. (1986). *Stress response syndromes* (2nd ed.). Northvale, NJ: Aronson.

Horowitz, M. J. (1987). *States of mind: Configurational analysis of individual psychology* (2nd ed.). New York: Plenum Press.

Horowitz, M. J. (1988). *Introduction to psychodynamics: A new synthesis*. New York: Basic Books.

Horowitz, M. J. (1989). Relationship schema formulation: Role-Relationship Models and intrapsychic conflict. *Psychiatry, 52,* 260–274.

Horowitz, M. J. (1991). *Person schemas and maladaptive interpersonal patterns*. Chicago: University of Chicago Press.

Horowitz, M. J. (1997). *Formulation for psychotherapy*. Washington, DC: American Psychiatric Press.

Horowitz, M. J., & Eells, T. D. (1993). Role-Relationship Model Configurations: A method for psychotherapy case formulation. *Psychotherapy Research, 3,* 57–68.

Horowitz, M. J., Eells, T. D., Singer, J., & Salovey, P. (1995). Role Relationship Models for case formulation. *Archives of General Psychiatry, 52,* 625–632.

Horowitz, M. J., Ewert, M., Milbrath, C., & Sonneborn, D. (1994). *American Journal of Psychotherapy, 151,* 1767–1770.

Horowitz, M. J., Luborsky, L., & Popp, C. (1991). A comparison of the Role-Relationship Models Configuration and the Core Conflictual Relationship Theme. In M. J. Horowitz (Ed.), *Person schemas and maladaptive interpersonal patterns* (pp. 213–220). Chicago: University of Chicago Press.

Horowitz, M. J., Markman, H. C., Stinson, C. H., Fridhandler, B., & Ghannam, J. H. (1990). A classification theory of defense. In J. L. Singer (Ed.), *Repression and dissociation* (pp. 61–84). Chicago: University of Chicago Press.

Horowitz, M. J., Merluzzi, T. V., Ewert, M., Ghannam, J. H., Hartley, D., & Stinson, C. H. (1991). Role-Relationship Models Configuration. In M. J. Horowitz (Ed.), *Person schemas and maladaptive interpersonal patterns* (pp. 115–154). Chicago: University of Chicago Press.

Horowitz, M. J., & Stinson, C. H. (1995). Consciousness and processes of control. *Psychotherapy Research, 4,* 123–139.

Horowitz, M. J., Znoj, H., & Stinson, C. (1996). Defensive control processes: Use of theory in research, formulation, and therapy of stress response syndromes. In M. Zeidner & N. Endler (Eds.), *Handbook of coping* (pp. 532–553). New York: Wiley.

Kihlstrom, J. F., & Cantor, N. (1984). Mental representations of the self. *Advances in Experimental Social Psychology, 17,* 1–47.

Kihlstrom, J. F., Cantor, N., Albright, J. S., Chew, B. R., Klein, S. B., & Niedenthal, P. M. (1988). Information processing and the study of the self. *Advances in Experimental Social Psychology, 21,* 145–178.

Loftus, E., & Klinger, M. R. (1992). Is the unconscious smart of dumb? *American Psychologist, 47,* 761–765.

Luborsky, L., & Crits-Christoph, P. (1990). *Understanding transference: The Core Conflictual Relationship Theme method.* New York: Basic Books.

Markus, H. (1990). Unresolved issues of self-representation. *Cognitive Therapy and Research, 14,* 241–253.

Markus, H., & Nurius, P. (1986). Possible selves. *American Psychologist, 41,* 954–969.

Merluzzi, T. V. (1991). Representation of information about self and other: A multidimensional scaling analysis. In M. J. Horowitz (Ed.), *Person schemas and maladaptive interpersonal patterns* (pp. 155–166). Chicago: University of Chicago Press.

Norcross, J. C., & Newman, C. F. (1992). Psychotherapy integration: Setting the context. In J. C. Norcross & M. R. Goldfried (Eds.), *Handbook of psychotherapy integration* (pp. 3–45). New York: Basic Books.

Segal, Z. V., Truchon, C., Horowitz, L. M., Gemar, M., & Guirguis, M. (1995). A priming methodology for studying self-representation in major depressive disorder. *Journal of Abnormal Psychology, 104,* 205–241.

Singer, J. L. (Ed.). (1990). *Repression and dissociation: Implications for personality theory, psychopathology, and health.* Chicago: University of Chicago Press.

Singer, J. L., & Salovey, P. (1991). Organized knowledge structures and personality. In M. J. Horowitz (Ed.), *Person schemas and maladaptive interpersonal patterns* (pp. 33–79). Chicago: University of Chicago Press.

Tunis, S., Fridhandler, B., & Horowitz, M. J. (1990). Identifying schematized views of self with significant others: Convergence of quantitative and clinical methods. *Journal of Personality and Social Psychology, 59,* 1279–1286.

Vaillant, G. E. (Ed.). (1992). *Ego mechanisms of defense: A guide for clinicians and researchers.* Washington, DC: American Psychiatric Press.

Wallerstein, R. (1983). Defenses, defense mechanisms, and the structure of the mind. *Journal of the American Psychoanalytic Association, 31,* 201–225.

Williams, J. M. G., Mathews, A., & MacLeod, C. (1996). The emotional Stroop task and psychopathology. *Psychological Bulletin, 120,* 3–24.

8

Case Formulation in Interpersonal Psychotherapy of Depression

JOHN C. MARKOWITZ
HOLLY A. SWARTZ

Interpersonal psychotherapy (IPT) is a simple, practical, and proven time-limited approach for the treatment of outpatients with major depression. Its success in a series of randomized clinical trials (Klerman, Weissman, Rounsaville, & Chevron, 1984; Elkin et al., 1989) has led to its expansion to treat a variety of depressive subtypes and other psychiatric syndromes (Klerman & Weissman, 1993; E. Frank et al., 1990). In this chapter, we shall focus on IPT as a treatment for major depressive disorder. Until recently IPT was practiced almost exclusively by researchers, but its research achievements have encouraged interest among clinicians, and training programs are now underway for non-research psychotherapists in New York and elsewhere.

The late Gerald L. Klerman, M.D., who with Myrna M. Weissman, Ph.D., developed IPT, believed that process research should await proof of the efficacy of an intervention. Hence research on IPT has focused on outcome rather than process. Most studies of IPT have examined whether it effectively treats depression, rather than the nature of the sessions. Case formulation, an important aspect of the treatment process, is central to the IPT approach, but it has received little specific study to date.

In this chapter, we shall describe the elements of IPT case formulation and discuss its function in clinical context. The reader should note, however, that *case formulation in IPT exists primarily as a treatment tool rather than as a theoretical construct* (see Table 8.1). It serves not only to help the therapist

TABLE 8.1. Features of the IPT Case Formulation

1. Simple
2. Employs a "medical model" of psychiatric illness
3. Based on linkage of—
   a. Medical diagnosis of psychiatric illness (depression) with
   b. Patient's interpersonal circumstances
4. Focuses on one of four interpersonal problem areas:
   a. Grief (complicated bereavement)
   b. Role dispute
   c. Role transition
   d. Interpersonal deficits
5. Explicitly delivered to patient
6. Determines the focus of time-limited treatment
7. Therapist and patient must agree on formulation for treatment to proceed
8. Generally well accepted by patient as affectively meaningful

understand the patient but also as a powerful tool to focus and advance this brief (12 to 16-session) treatment.

The crux of IPT is the empirically demonstrated link between mood and life events (Klerman et al., 1984). IPT therapists help patients identify specific life events and interpersonal issues that appear temporally and thematically related to the onset and maintenance of their depressions, using this information to help them understand the connection between their mood and current life situation. Patients learn that by altering their interpersonal environment they can improve their mood and alleviate their mood disorder. The IPT case formulation is the initial means by which this crucial information, the focus of all further therapy sessions, is conveyed to the patient.

An IPT case formulation must be coherent, convincing to both therapist and patient, well grounded in the patient's interpersonal experiences, and clearly tied to the onset and persistence of the mood disorder. Within this framework, the case formulation encapsulates both the guiding principles of IPT and the individual patient's particular issues, that is, those that make him or her unique from others with similar interpersonal issues or diagnosis. That the case formulation lead logically into the treatment plan is a sine qua non of IPT.

The ability to rapidly develop and deliver such a formulation is for many therapists among the more difficult but also most valuable aspects of learning a time-limited, focused psychotherapy like IPT.

HISTORICAL BACKGROUND OF THE APPROACH

IPT was developed in the 1970s by the late Gerald L. Klerman, M.D., Myrna M. Weissman, Ph.D., and colleagues as a simple, reproducible, and testable psychotherapy for outpatients with major depression (Klerman et al., 1984).

They based the therapy both on the ideas of the interpersonal school (Sullivan, 1953) and on research demonstrating the effect on mood of life events and stressors (Klerman et al., 1984). Adolf Meyer, Harry Stack Sullivan, Frieda Fromm-Reichmann, and other interpersonal psychotherapists of the late 1940s and the 1950s had stressed the importance of environmental events as a counterbalance to the strictly intrapsychic approach that had previously dominated psychoanalysis. Research had subsequently corroborated theory in demonstrating that depressive episodes frequently arise following the loss of a loved one (i.e., complicated bereavement), in the setting of chronic marital strife (what IPT calls a "role dispute"), or in the absence of social supports ("interpersonal deficits") (Klerman et al., 1984). By contrast, the presence of social supports protects against depression (Klerman et al., 1984; Brown & Harris, 1978; Kendler et al., 1995).

Guided by these data, Klerman, Weissman, and their colleagues honed and codified the basic principles of the interpersonal school in a treatment manual outlining a time-limited approach to psychotherapy of outpatients with major depression. IPT met a need for a psychotherapeutic treatment that could be tested in outcome studies and in which therapists could be reliably trained. Its approach is sufficiently simple that it can be reproduced by therapists, is comprehensible to patients, and yet is not so mechanical that following the IPT manual reduces therapy to a "cookbook" formula.

CONCEPTUAL FRAMEWORK

IPT focuses on the intuitively reasonable concept that events in one's psychosocial environment affect one's mood, and vice versa. When painful events occur, mood worsens and depression may result. Conversely, depressed mood compromises one's ability to handle one's social role, generally leading to negative events. This simple yet powerful concept forms the core of IPT and its case formulation. IPT therapists use the connection between mood, environment, and social role to help patients understand their depressions within an interpersonal context, and to teach them to handle their social role and environment so as to both solve their interpersonal problems and relieve their depressive syndrome.

The reader should understand that IPT does not espouse a causal theory: life events, when found, are not necessarily the cause of a depressive episode, which is probably multidetermined. It may often be that unhappy events follow the onset of depression as the mood disorder impairs social functioning. Regardless of the etiology of the depression, the human mind seeks meaning from life and willingly connects life events to their apparent consequences. The key goal is to establish a connection that is credible to the patient, with the intent of providing a context for the depressive episode and, more importantly, an escape from it. The case formulation provides the vehicle for communicating this rationale to the patient.

It may help at this juncture to compare IPT and psychodynamic case formulations. Of the manualized psychotherapies for depression that have been tested in time-limited trials, IPT is probably closest to the kind of psychodynamic psychotherapy most therapists practice. Both focus on the patient's feelings and relationships. On the other hand, an IPT case formulation differs markedly from the psychodynamic formulation described by Perry, Cooper, and Michels (1987). The IPT formulation concentrates on the patient's relationship to the surrounding world and on the patient's depressive symptoms rather than on internal processes or conflicts. The IPT formulation elaborates on current, rather than past, interpersonal issues. The IPT therapist concedes that aspects of relationships may repeat patterns from and have roots in the past but emphasizes that an intervention made in the present—without addressing past conflicts—can improve the current interpersonal environment and alleviate the patient's depression.

Unlike a psychodynamic approach, IPT does not consider the patient's intrapsychic issues germane to the case formulation or the thrust of treatment. Transference, dreams, and fantasies are not interpreted. More subliminally, however, a knowledge of psychodynamics may usefully inform the therapist's approach to a given patient: for example, influencing how the therapist interacts with a histrionic, paranoid, or dependent patient.

The stance of the IPT therapist in delivering a formulation also differs from that of most psychodynamic clinicians. The IPT therapist is generally active and vocal in sessions. The structure and time limit of IPT require that the formulation be explicitly presented to the patient by the end of the third session. The delivery of the case formulation is, indeed, the culmination of the opening phase of IPT. This differs from a strict psychoanalytic approach in which a neutral, seemingly withholding analyst conserves the case formulation—at least initially—as a private construct.

The IPT formulation focuses on the "here and now" and the potential for future growth rather than reconciliation with the past. No assumptions are made about personality structure (since this "trait" is often confounded by the "state" of depression; see Hirschfeld et al., 1983), self-concept, or intrapsychic conflict. Rather, the IPT therapist uses a medical model, defining depression as a *medical* illness independent of the patient's personality or character.

In IPT, the therapist defines depression for the patient as a medical illness with biological underpinnings that interact with environmental life events. The formulation offers the patient a hopeful, optimistic, empowering, and forward-looking approach by identifying a treatable illness and by encouraging the patient to seek happiness while offering strategies to achieve that goal.

As part of the case formulation, the patient is explicitly assigned the "sick role," which excuses the self-blaming depressed patient of responsibility for having gotten ill but charges him or her to work toward getting better (Parsons, 1951). This encourages the patient to separate the depression from his or her sense of self and to participate actively in the treatment. It also allows the therapist to provide psychoeducation about depression, another important part of the formulation and treatment.

The case formulation is formally conceptualized and stated within the first one to three sessions. This constitutes the first of the three phases of an acute IPT treatment. In this beginning phase the tasks of the therapist include diagnosing depression as a medical disorder, determining the nature of and changes in key relationships in the patient's "interpersonal inventory," and presenting the patient with an interpersonal formulation (i.e., case formulation) that links the onset of the patient's mood disorder to one of four interpersonal problem areas (see Tables 8.1 and 8.2).

Although IPT uses little jargon, the IPT "interpersonal problem area" is labeled and explicitly included in the case formulation. In a sense, the term *becomes* the case formulation. The four IPT problem areas are (1) *grief* (complicated bereavement), (2) *role dispute*, (3) *role transition*, and (4) *interpersonal deficits*. Grief refers to depressive symptoms that extend beyond a normal mourning period following the death of a significant person in the patient's life. A role dispute is a disagreement (or series of disagreements) with a spouse, boss, parent, friend, or other significant person. Role transition encompasses all major life events such as graduation, retirement, moving, changing jobs, being diagnosed with a severe illness, divorce, etc. Conceptual "losses"—say, loss of a dream or an ideal—that do not involve the death of a significant other are categorized as role transitions rather than grief. The last category, interpersonal deficits, is the least well developed and probably carries the worst prognosis. It defines a long-standing pattern of impoverished interpersonal relationships.

The case formulation explicitly assigns the patient a problem area:

"Your move from California to New York has been very difficult for you. This *role transition* has meant coming to a strange new city while losing touch with friends and giving up an apartment that you loved. We'll be talking about how this *role transition* is related to your depression and exploring how you can make this transition more manageable for you."

TABLE 8.2. Tasks of the Opening Phase of IPT

Usually the first 1–3 sessions. Goals include:

1. Diagnosing the depression ("medical model")
2. Eliciting the interpersonal inventory
3. Establishing the interpersonal problem area
4. Giving the sick role
5. Developing a treatment plan
6. Making the interpersonal formulation
7. Obtaining patient's agreement to the formulation
8. Establishing the therapeutic alliance
9. Beginning psychoeducation
10. Instilling hope

The patient must agree upon the salience of the problem area proposed in the case formulation and agree to work on it in treatment before IPT proceeds to its second phase. Although patients may fit into several or all of the four IPT problem areas, the need for a sharply delineated focus dictates limiting the choice to one, or at most two, problem areas, lest the treatment become diffused and lose coherence for both therapist and patient.

Thus case formulation is a necessary component of the early phase of IPT. The therapist's formulation includes a diagnosis of depression, the provision of reassurance and hope, the assignment of the sick role, and, most importantly, the identification of one (or at most two) interpersonal problem areas that set the agenda for the remainder of the treatment.

How does one know the "right" formulation? Sometimes, of course, one problem demands attention and the course appears clear. The patient may present material leading in the direction of only one of the four problem areas. Even here, there is the danger that a covert role dispute or other interpersonal problem area may be significant, so the therapist must search for all possibilities.

It may be difficult to ascertain a single neat formulation for a given patient. Because IPT is a time-limited treatment, however, it is imperative to clearly define a focus and thereby hone the treatment goals. Case formulation serves to explicitly define this focus. In selecting a problem area, the clinician can assume that the right answer is probably the one that makes most sense to, and carries most affective weight for, the patient. This area of IPT process deserves but as yet has not received systematic study.

IPT after the Formulation

The second phase of IPT, comprising most of the 12 to 16 sessions of a typical treatment for depression, focuses on the interpersonal problem area selected in the case formulation. Each of the four interpersonal problem areas has a particular treatment strategy. It is the coherence of these strategies, rather than particular elements of what is an avowedly eclectic approach, that make IPT a focused and distinct treatment. The nature of the IPT formulation determines the direction and mechanics of the treatment that follows.

In treating complicated bereavement, the therapist's goal is to help the patient to mourn, and then gradually to explore new activities and relationships to replace the one that has been lost. Patients are encouraged to recount the good and bad aspects of their relationship with the lost other, to describe the things they did together or never had a chance to do, and to describe the details of the death of the significant other and their relation to that situation. Patients are encouraged to look at mementos and picture albums, to visit the grave site, and in other ways to evoke the lost person so as to facilitate catharsis. Once the mourning process begins in earnest, the therapist often spends much of sessions empathically listening. As the therapy proceeds, the therapist helps the patient explore new areas of interest, new activities, and new relationships.

In the instance of a role dispute, the therapist helps the patient to examine the dispute and to seek its resolution. Sometimes depressed patients imagine a relationship has reached an impasse, yet a simple clarification or discussion with the significant other resolves the dispute. When there is a serious dispute, the therapist helps the patient explore what he or she wants from the relationship and what options exist to achieve those desired goals. The skills that depressed patients often need in self-assertion, expression of anger, or social risk taking can be developed in role playing during sessions, with the implicit goal that the patient will attempt these behaviors during the week to come. Finally, if all the patients' efforts fail to resolve a true impasse in the role dispute, the therapist may help the patient dissolve the relationship, mourn its loss, and seek better alternatives.

A depressed patient in a role transition feels his or her life is out of control. In formulating the case, the therapist redefines and explicitly labels this seeming chaos as a role transition involving the loss of a familiar old role and the potential assumption of a new one. The goal of the therapy is to help the patient navigate this transition as smoothly as possible and to fullest advantage. The patient is encouraged (1) to see both the good and bad aspects of the old role and the benefits and liabilities of the new one; and (2) to mourn the loss of the past and accept the possibilities of the present and future.

Interpersonal deficits is a default category: the patient has suffered neither a complicated bereavement, a role dispute, nor a role transition. Such patients tend in fact not to have much happening in their lives and to have only a few relationships; they tend to be isolated and to have trouble in either making or sustaining relationships. In short, these are more difficult patients to treat in any psychotherapy, and perhaps more so in IPT because of their global deficits in the area where IPT works (Elkin et al., 1989). The goal is to help the patients recognize the link between mood and their social difficulties, to help the patients expand their social skills and to gain social comfort. This is often akin to attempting to modify aspects of personality in a brief intervention—a difficult but not impossible task.

By the final phase of IPT, the last few sessions of the treatment, the patient has usually improved. The therapist notes the approaching end to therapy, now that the initial goals of relieving depression and solving the interpersonal problem area have been achieved. The therapist acknowledges that it is sad to break up a good team, as both therapist and patient tend to be pleased with their collaboration and are tempted to continue indefinitely. They review the patient's accomplishments during the brief therapy—which are often considerable—in solving the interpersonal problem area and in reducing symptoms. They also review the symptoms of depression, the potential for relapse, and the interpersonal issues that might be likely to trigger such a relapse for the patient.

Not all patients improve, of course, but few leave empty-handed: most at least make progress in their interpersonal problem area. In such cases, the therapist can point out that it is not the patient that has failed but the treatment, which promised to concomitantly relieve depression as the interpersonal problem was solved. It is important that such still-symptomatic patients leave not feeling guilty about their role in the therapy if they have worked at it and that they leave IPT aware of alternative treatments for their depression.

INCLUSION/EXCLUSION CRITERIA

Inclusion and exclusion criteria depend upon the syndrome under treatment. IPT has been used successfully to treat acute major depressive disorder; various subpopulations of depressed patients including adolescent, geriatric, HIV-positive, and dysthymic patients; other psychiatric syndromes such as bulimia (Klerman & Weissman, 1993; Fairburn, Jones, Peveler, Hope, & O'Connor, 1993; Weissman & Markowitz, 1994); and, less successfully, substance abuse (Klerman & Weissman, 1993; Rounsaville, Glazer, Wilber, Weissman, & Kleber, 1983; Carroll, Rounsaville, & Gawin, 1991). For each of these studies, a syndromal diagnosis based on contemporary diagnostic criteria was an inclusion criterion. Further applications of IPT include primary treatment of depressed pregnant and postpartum women (Stuart & O'Hara, 1995), social phobics, and adjunctive therapy for lithium treated patients with bipolar disorder. Hence the modal IPT patient was suffering from a significant mood disorder or other Axis I diagnosis.

IPT has been most frequently used to treat moderately depressed outpatients, individuals whose illness is not severe enough to warrant hospitalization. Concurrent administration of pharmacotherapy does not exclude a patient from IPT (unless so specified by a research protocol). Although combination treatment has not been extensively studied, it is a reasonable clinical strategy: because of its emphasis on a medical model, IPT is easily compatible with antidepressant medication. Severe depressive symptoms, particularly overwhelming neurovegetative symptoms or active suicidal ideation, should suggest consideration of pharmacotherapy instead of or in addition to IPT. Although it has been difficult to show greater efficacy for combined therapy than monotherapy, combined therapy does no worse in treating depressive samples (Manning, Markowitz, & Frances, 1992). Many individuals may benefit from the combination of pharmacotherapeutic symptom relief with psychosocial support, skill building, and change in outlook.

Typical exclusion criteria for IPT research studies include psychosis, severe suicidal or homicidal risk, and (save in the studies addressing these disorders) active substance abuse. It is reasonable to apply similar criteria to nonresearch patients. Another group that may do poorly in IPT is individuals with severe interpersonal deficits. Reexamination of data from a large study comparing IPT with other psychotherapies suggested that patients with severe interpersonal deficits might do better in a cognitive behavioral treatment rather than IPT (Sotsky et al., 1991). This counterintuitive finding suggests that patients may need, a priori, a modicum of interpersonal skills in order to benefit maximally from IPT.

As IPT spreads from clinical trials into general practice, its primary focus will likely remain on specific diagnostic indications—a boast few other psychotherapies can make. As noted, the targeting of a specific medicalized diagnosis is part of the treatment formula. Yet the principles of IPT are in essence universally applicable: almost all people can find a relationship between their mood and interpersonal situation.[1] How diagnostically "dilute" IPT may become in clinical practice remains to be seen.

STEPS IN CASE FORMULATION

IPT case formulation usually requires between one and three sessions of a 12- to 16-week treatment. Its length depends on the complexity of the patient's presenting history and the proficiency of the therapist. In order to formulate the case, the tasks of the therapist include (1) diagnosing depression, (2) evaluating interpersonal relationships or taking an *interpersonal inventory*, (3) establishing an *interpersonal problem area*, and (4) making initial therapeutic interventions.

Diagnosing Depression

The therapist takes a formal psychiatric approach, diagnosing psychopathology based on current diagnostic criteria, that is, DSM-IV (American Psychiatric Association, 1994). Therapists rely on a standard psychiatric interview to carefully review the nature, duration, and severity of symptoms. Because diagnosing depression is a vital piece of the case formulation, the therapist must accurately assess all relevant criteria.

Therapists frequently use measures like the Hamilton Depression Rating Scale (Hamilton, 1960) both to ensure a thorough review of symptoms and to educate the patient about them. Using a standardized instrument emphasizes that the patient is not (as he or she often feels) idiosyncratically lazy, willful, bad, or mysteriously overwhelmed, but rather suffering from a common, discrete, understandable, and treatable disorder that is not the patient's fault. Assessment measures can usefully be repeated over time to demonstrate the patient's progress in therapy. The therapist must collect enough data in the initial interview to be able to incorporate into the case formulation a statement about the nature and severity of the patient's illness. In the context of diagnosing a depressive episode, the patient is also assigned the sick role, as discussed above (p. 195).

Evaluating Interpersonal Relationships
(Taking the Interpersonal Inventory)

In the initial interviews, the therapist also develops the "interpersonal inventory," a catalogue of important relationships in the patient's life. The interpersonal inventory is not a formal instrument, but rather refers to a thorough anamnesis in which the therapist inquires about the important people in the patient's life, particularly his or her current life: relationships with spouse, children, parents, boss, friends, and others. The therapist attempts to establish a temporal relationship between the onset of the depression and changes in the patient's interpersonal relationships, using both open- and closed-ended questions.

It is important to ask about omissions in the interpersonal inventory as well as the relationships the patient more easily discusses. For instance, if a patient describes in detail his or her relationships with friends and bosses but skips romantic interests and family, the therapist should probe for information about those categories omitted by the patient.

The therapist cares not only about the relationships themselves but also their patterns, qualities, and level of intimacy, as well as any nonreciprocal wishes and intentions that the patient and significant others may have. Generally, this requires that a therapist elicit enough detail to form a clear conception of the nature of these relationships. For instance, if a patient said, "The most important person in my life is my wife and we get along wonderfully," the therapist would inquire, "Tell me more about the two of you." If an open-ended question failed to yield the degree of detail required, the therapist would follow with more structured questions, such as the following:

> How long have you been married?
> Does your wife know how badly you've been feeling?
> Is she someone you can easily tell your feelings? (If not, whom do you tell?)
> What exactly have you said to her?
> How do you divide household responsibilities?
> How are your finances?
> What about your sexual relationship?
> Do you argue a lot? How do those disagreements start? How do they end?
> Has anything changed between the two of you in the past few months?

As in all good clinical practice, the therapist's stance is inquiring, empathic, and respectful.

Although the past importantly determines these patterns and their chronicity, the therapist focuses on current relationships and on recent changes in relationships that may provide the interpersonal focus in the middle phase of IPT. As such, the therapist asks about the patient's childhood relationships with family members and friends but does not explore these past relationships in the same depth as current significant relationships. Information about the patient's psychosocial development is useful background material, but it is not incorporated into the case formulation except in passing. For example, part of a case formulation might include the following statement about the patient's past relationship with her father. Notice, however, that the patient's attention is drawn to the present:

"Your difficulties with your husband sound a lot like a pattern, similar to problems you had with your father, with your camp counselor, and with a number of boyfriends in the past. You seem to put up with what the men in your life want, and then to silently resent it. That seems to be part of your role dispute with your husband and to be contributing to your depression. There may be other ways of handling these situations: you are in a position to expect, to insist on, better treatment from your husband. Does that make sense to you? . . . Let's talk about how you might be able to improve the way you handle things with your husband."

In exploring the interpersonal inventory, the therapist needs to ensure insofar as possible that he or she comprehends the patient's interpersonal situation and so can confidently formulate a focus for treatment. To determine the wrong focus might lead to therapy addressing an interpersonal situation that is not the nidus of the patient's affective distress. Thus if a patient blandly reports that his work situation is "fine," the therapist nonetheless should seek corroborating themes and incidents from relationships with coworkers to forestall the possibility of a covert role dispute arising later in treatment.

Establishing an Interpersonal Problem Area

Having completed an interpersonal inventory, the therapist must decide into which of the four IPT problem areas the patient's problem falls (i.e., grief, role dispute, role transition, or interpersonal deficits). At Cornell University Medical College in New York City, therapists use a checklist called the Interpersonal Problem Area Rating Scale (IPARS; see the Appendix). The IPARS merely ensures that the therapist has considered all of the relevant possibilities in choosing among the four interpersonal problem areas. Therapists learning IPT may find the IPARS a useful reminder of the range of possible formulations for this therapy. Audio- or videotaping of treatment sessions may also be helpful, enabling therapists to review material as they seek to construct interpersonal problem areas for patients.

In choosing a problem area, the therapist should focus on salient interpersonal events in the patient's life that are temporally proximate to the onset (or exacerbation) of the disorder. Indeed, such events are usually available to the therapist. Either a loved one has died, suggesting complicated bereavement; or the patient is involved in a role dispute with a significant other at home, in his or her family or circle of friends, or at work; or else the patient is undergoing a role transition, navigating a major life change less than smoothly.

Occasionally the history and interpersonal inventory are bare. Such a patient typically has an impoverished social life with few meaningful relationships, none of which may have changed. Such patients often have schizoid or other personality disorders, which makes treatment more difficult but not impossible. These patients fall into the default category of "interpersonal deficits." Disadvantages for the therapist are that these are inherently more difficult patients, that they have a glaring weakness in the area on which IPT needs to build (Sotsky et al., 1991), and that rather than working on an acute precipitant, the therapist and patient must face a usually long-standing adjustment in the patient's lifestyle. The therapist typically describes the problem to the patient as "a difficulty in making or sustaining relationships." The goal of therapy then becomes finding a better, more comfortable social adjustment.

The elements of a patient's situation will vary, and it is important to subsume the patient's specific issues under a more general problem area. By labeling the problem (much as one labels the depression), the patient begins to find meaning and order in an experience that has previously felt random and out of control. This immediately reduces anxiety and gives the patient and therapist a common language in which to discuss issues as the treatment unfolds.

Making Initial Therapeutic Interventions

From the start the therapist offers hope, an alternative optimistic viewpoint to the patient's depressed outlook, namely, the conviction that depression is a treatable disorder. Many patients experience an initial improvement in symptoms just from beginning therapy in this newly hopeful atmosphere. This provides momentum for the treatment. (Of course, if the therapist then fails to deliver the goods, these initial gains may evanesce.) Providing a sympathetic, understanding listener, a setting, a ritual, and an explanation for the patient's woes are of course not unique to IPT but part of the nonspecific armamentarium of most psychotherapies (J. Frank, 1971). Nonetheless they are explicit ingredients of the treatment. The provision of a simple, clear, intuitively reasonable case formulation, grounded in the patient's recent interpersonal life experience and carrying affective meaning, probably has a therapeutic benefit over and above its functions as an explanation and technical frame for the treatment.

Deciding upon the Interpersonal Formulation

The anamnesis of the psychiatric history and elaboration of the interpersonal inventory may require one or more sessions. In any event, before the end of the third session the therapist should have gathered sufficient information about the patient's symptoms and interpersonal life to develop an interpersonal formulation.

Before offering the case formulation to the patient, the therapist must also decide whether IPT is an appropriate option for the patient. Does the patient have a disorder for which IPT has demonstrated efficacy (i.e., major depressive disorder)? Does the patient seem interested in treatment and able to engage with the therapist? Would the patient be better suited to another treatment modality such as cognitive-behavioral therapy or pharmacotherapy? (See the section above on "Inclusion/Exclusion Criteria" for a fuller discussion of these issues.)

Presenting these therapeutic options to the patient should follow from and complete the case formulation. Differential therapeutics should indeed determine *which* kind of case formulation the therapist gives the patient. If it were apparent that IPT would not be the treatment of choice, the therapist should abandon the IPT case formulation and instead present an alternative psychotherapeutic or psychopharmacological alternative.

Making the Interpersonal Formulation

Although further sessions generally flesh out the nature of the interpersonal problem area, the first one to three sessions should provide its solid skeleton. Once comfortable with his or her case formulation, and having decided that IPT is an appropriate option, the therapist then presents it to the patient directly. In IPT, the formulation is stated explicitly and marks the end of the beginning phase of treatment.

The patient must agree with this formulation before the therapy can proceed into the middle phase of IPT. This agreement is more than symbolic acquiescence. It underscores the patient's expected active role in the treatment, and it affirms the therapeutic alliance. Perhaps most importantly, agreement signals to both patient and therapist that they share an understanding of the patient's situation and can try to jointly address it. Without such agreement, the therapy might trail off vaguely and inconclusively rather than focusing on the area of greatest affective valence to the patient.

Should the patient disagree with the therapist's formulation, which is rare in our experience, therapist and patient would further explore the patient's interpersonal environment and situation. Based on this added information, the therapist might then propose a new formulation for the patient to consider.

A depressed woman who had refused to speak to her mother for the preceding 6 months because of a perceived slight was initially presented with a case formulation that linked her depressive symptoms to a role dispute with her mother. The therapist suggested that her mother had provided important support for the patient and that their "feud" had significantly contributed to the patient's despair and isolation. The patient contested this view, arguing that she and her mother had had frequent difficulties, that her mother was often absent from her life from long stretches of time, and that she experienced this episode "like all the other times." On the other hand, she felt that the change in her relationship with a coworker, which had deteriorated over the same period of time, was more meaningful to her because "it affects me every day." Seemingly to prove this to the therapist, the patient contacted the mother between sessions and made plans to see her—but denied any connection to her depression because this did not alleviate her symptoms.

The therapist collected further information about the patient's work difficulties, learning that work had functioned as a refuge for the patient from her difficult family situation but now had become fraught with conflict. The formulation was reframed as a role dispute with the patient's coworker. Although the therapist felt that the dispute with the mother was also important, the patient's affective investment in her struggle with her coworker was impressive. Despite feeling that either role dispute could function as a treatment focus, the therapist selected the one that meant the most to the patient, who accepted the reformulation and proceeded with IPT.

APPLICATION TO PSYCHOTHERAPY TECHNIQUE

Case Formulation in the Initial Phase of Treatment

In the beginning phase (Sessions 1–3) of IPT the clinician must define the nature of the therapy to follow. Patients who have previously experienced psychodynamic or other forms of psychotherapy may need reorientation for IPT. The therapist explains the time limit, the limited goal of treating the interpersonal problem area and mood disorder (rather than personality traits or other aims), the nature of the sick role, and the therapist's expectations of the patient in the treatment. These expectations are that the patient become expert in the nature and treatment of depression, learn the connection between mood and interpersonal issues, and use this knowledge to confront his or her interpersonal problem area.

Case formulation, like most other aspects of IPT, is straightforward. The simplicity of IPT is presumably one of its strengths: the narrative developed for the patient is generally accepted as intuitively reasonable, based as it is on recent events in the patient's life (rather than on unconscious processes, e.g.). Successful therapies generally provide a coherent explanatory framework for patients (Sotsky et al., 1991), but IPT's is simpler than most,[2] and can be easily tied to life events. This simple, clear, and direct approach probably explains, at least in part, why IPT is so well accepted by most patients. The delivery of the case formulation is in keeping with the generally supportive, anxiety-reducing approach of IPT.

Case Formulation in the Middle and End Phases of Treatment

In the middle and end phases of therapy (from Sessions 4 to 12 or 16), the case formulation receives frequent mention. It is useful to repeat at least a compressed version of the formulation for two reasons: it corrects the tendency of depressed patients to lapse into self-blame, and it maintains the focus of treatment. During sessions, the therapist repeatedly raises the interpersonal problem area at the core of the formulation: "complicated bereavement"; "your role dispute with your husband"; "the role transition you're going through." Although this terminology may seem cumbersome at first, terms like "role dispute" and "role transition" reify as *external* the problems and issues that the depressed patient has previously internalized and blamed him- or herself for. The formulation thus serves both as a reminder of the therapeutic focus and a reassurance that the problem is not idiosyncratic to the patient but a common interpersonal problem, attached to a psychiatric syndrome, which has a technical name.

The approach to patients with interpersonal deficits differs somewhat. To say a patient has "interpersonal deficits" may sound critical and is probably unhelpful, so the therapist refers instead to "your discomfort in getting close to people," or something akin, rather than using the formal label of the problem area.

The therapist spends the bulk of each session on the issues raised in the case formulation. He or she begins each session with the question "How have you been since we last met?" in order to immediately focus the patient on contemporary interpersonal issues. In the event that the patient deviates from the focus (e.g., recalls a dream, discusses an unrelated problem), the therapist listens empathetically but then guides the patient back to the original focus by invoking the case formulation. For instance, the therapist may say, "It sounds like your children have been really difficult for you to manage this week. Because depressed individuals often feel frustrated and overwhelmed, it's not surprising that child care may be difficult for you at this time. But let's get back to what has been happening with your husband. As we discussed before, that role dispute seems to be connected to your depression; if we can work through that problem, your depression will lift and you will probably find it easier to cope with your children." Alternatively, the therapist might seize on the question of parental division of child care responsibilities to lead back to the marital role dispute.

One would only abandon the case formulation in unusual circumstances. For instance, if the patient suddenly developed new, life-threatening symptoms such as active suicidal ideation or frank psychosis, the case formulation would be abandoned in order to attend to patient safety. Alternately, if the patient experienced an unexpected important life event in midtreatment (e.g., the death of an important person, significant changes in socioeconomic status), it would be reasonable to suspend the treatment focus in order to attend to the patient's pressing needs. One would hope to return to the focus as soon as possible, but alternatively one could consider altering the focus or abandoning the IPT treatment approach.

The brevity of the treatment leaves little room for error in formulating the IPT case. The therapist must use the initial treatment sessions to aggressively pursue all potential interpersonal problem areas and to determine a treatment focus prior to embarking on the middle phase of treatment. It is unlikely for a diligent therapist to discover, midway through treatment, that he or she has seriously misjudged the salience of a chosen problem area. If a covert and imposing interpersonal problem area should arise in the middle phase, however, the therapist would have to renegotiate the treatment contract to address it.

Other Applications of the IPT Case Formulation

To put depression (or other psychiatric disorders) in an interpersonal and social context may also be a useful technique for non-IPT therapists. Depressed patients in particular tend to look inward and to blame themselves as weak, lazy, impotent, and bad, forgetting the usually intuitive connection that events affect our moods, and vice versa. Patients receiving antidepressant medication with supportive clinical management, for example, might be relieved to be reminded of the effect environmental stressors might have on their lives and to be told that medication may soon give them greater energy and initiative to deal with these stressors.

CASE EXAMPLES

Case Example 1

The first case is an example of the "formula" used to share the case formulation with the patient during the beginning phase of treatment. The tone of voice should be serious, empathic, yet relaxed and conversational:

> "You have an illness called major depression, as we discussed when we did the Hamilton Depression Rating Scale. Again, it's not your fault, not something to blame yourself for, but we do need to treat it. Your job over the next several weeks will be to be a patient with the medical illness called depression. You should focus on your treatment and not worry too much if you don't yet feel like your usual self. The good news is that depression is very treatable, and I expect that you'll be feeling much better in a matter of a few weeks.
>
> "From what you've told me, I think your depression has something to do with what's been going on in your life—namely, [the role transition you've been going through in your career / things haven't been the same since your husband died, and you've had trouble really grieving his death / the role dispute you're having with your wife / what hasn't been going on in your life: the difficulties you have in making or keeping relationships]. If you solve that problem, not only will you be better off for having solved it, but your depression should also clear up. Does that make sense to you?
>
> "There are a number of proven ways to treat depression. One way is with interpersonal psychotherapy, which is a brief antidepressant treatment that focuses on the connection between your mood disorder and what's going on in your life. Understanding that connection and using that understanding should allow you to choose the best options to deal with your situation and should help you to feel better. If you're willing, and this makes sense to you, what I'd suggest is that we spend the next 12 weeks working on this. IPT has been carefully tested in research studies and shown to be effective in treating the kind of depression you have. So we have a good chance of doing *two things* in the next 12 weeks: help-

ing you solve your [interpersonal problem: role dispute, etc.] and, at the same time, getting you out of this horrible episode of depressive illness."

Case Example 2

This case is an example of a role dispute. It illustrates the processes necessary to elucidate a case formulation from clinical material. It also shows how long-standing behavior patterns are acknowledged but not directly addressed in IPT.

Ms. A., a 31-year-old recently married Catholic businesswoman, presented with her first episode of major depression, which had endured for 11 months. She had begun to feel pressured by her husband of a year, to whom she had been engaged for 3 years prior to their wedding. Mr. A., although "for equal rights for women," had begun subtly, and then not so subtly, to encourage her to leave work in order to have children. She loved her husband and welcomed eventual motherhood, but had long defined herself through her work, had recently been promoted, and was reluctant to give up her job. Around this time she noted the onset of sleep disturbance, loss of energy, appetite, and libido. She felt guilty about her unexpressed but conscious anger toward her husband, feeling that if they had such troubles so early in marriage, their future was doomed. She began seeing a therapist but dropped out after 8 months because she felt she was making no progress. What precipitated her second search for treatment was a late menstrual period that made her fear that she was pregnant.

Her Hamilton Depression Rating Scale score was 28 (i.e., significantly elevated), and she easily met DSM-IV criteria for major depression. There was no history of substance abuse, dysthymia, or other psychiatric disorder; her mother, however, had been treated for depression. When her father had died 3 years previously, she was able to grieve, feeling sad but not depressed. The elder of two sisters, Ms. A. described a reasonably happy childhood with overly strict and demanding, but loving, parents. Her role in the house had been to achieve high grades and other school honors for her parents' approval, and to serve at times as a surrogate mother to her sibling. She had had two significant sexual relationships, lasting several years each, prior to meeting her husband. She was appreciated at her job for her hard work, and described good relations with her boss and coworkers. Ms. A. described herself as generally being an "up person," one who made the best of things, handled disappointments stoically, and did not like to get angry. She and her husband had had few disagreements before the issue of her job came up, as she generally deferred to his wishes. He, although increasingly worried by her deteriorating state, seemed not to grasp the importance of her work to her, nor the effects of his own wishes: her worsening depression was to him just another reason for her to stop working.

At this point the reader may want to stop and take stock. Which interpersonal problem areas appear likely prospects as a focus for therapy? There is little suggestion here of complicated bereavement, given Ms. A's reported ability to grieve and the lack of temporal connection between her father's death—admittedly a significant interpersonal stressor—and the onset of her mood disorder. Nor is there evidence of a role dispute in her workplace. At home, however, we find an obvious role dispute with her husband, which Ms. A. seems bewildered about how to handle. Her marriage and job promotion might each constitute role transitions (as would be pregnancy): indeed, they appear to pull from opposing directions on her sense of identity and life trajectory. Her good relationships and marriage argue against interpersonal deficits; given the presence of alternative problem areas, we would in any case avoid using interpersonal deficits. Hence the choice lies between a role dispute and a role transition.

Ms. A.'s therapist decided to frame the formulation as a role dispute, feeling that the struggle with her husband was a more central issue than the role transitions. (A role transition focusing on the marriage would have differed mainly in semantics.) She said:

> "We've diagnosed the problem as a major depression—although you feel guilty about your situation, that's just a symptom of your illness, called depression. It's not your fault. Your Hamilton score is quite high: 28. But don't worry, within a few weeks we'll try to have you down below 7, in the normal range. And, you know, your depression seems to have started with your husband's pressure on you to stop the work that's been, and still is, so important to you. You don't seem to know how to handle that situation, and I think that's contributing to your depression. We call this a role dispute.
>
> "There are a number of treatments for depression, including antidepressant medication, which you've said you don't want. We can talk about the reasons for and against medicine. Another approach is called interpersonal psychotherapy, or IPT. IPT works by helping you understand the connection between what's going on in your life and how that might affect your mood; once you understand that, you can figure out how to handle your life situations. As you solve those interpersonal issues—for you, the role dispute with your husband—you're very likely to feel better. IPT has been tested in research studies and found to be a highly effective treatment for depression like yours. It works in a matter of weeks, too: we should be able to treat your depression meeting weekly for 12 weeks. Does that sound okay to you?"

It did. Although she at that point saw little prospect of extricating herself from the "mess" of her life, Ms. A. was relieved by the formulation and agreed to IPT. She returned the next week feeling considerably better, happy to discover that she was not pregnant. Therapy focused on her learning to assert her needs to her husband, first role playing with her therapist, and on seeing anger as a sometimes useful response to her social environment that could be expressed without guilt.

After 4 weeks the Hamilton score had fallen to 9, by 8 weeks to 4, and at termination it was 3. Ms. A. used the weeks of therapy to open a more balanced dialogue with her husband, who began to recognize the importance of his wife's work role, was delighted by her symptomatic improvement (if somewhat taken aback by her new assertiveness), and agreed to postpone parenthood for a couple of years.

The therapist had acknowledged that many of Ms. A.'s patterns were longstanding, but focused sessions on her current relationships outside the office rather than on her childhood. In midtherapy Ms. A. spontaneously reported that she had had a long and helpful talk with her mother about women's rights and the role of the wife in marriage. They had agreed that Ms. A. would do well not to repeat her mother's too submissive stance. In the final sessions Ms. A. dealt with the issues of termination smoothly. Some 6 and 12 months later, the therapist received letters from Ms. A. reporting continuing euthymia. Several years later, she received a baby announcement in a letter explaining that Mr. and Ms. A. had now happily agreed on parenthood. Ms. A., who had received another promotion, planned to continue working part-time after her maternity leave.

Case Example 3

This case is an example of a role transition. It illustrates the point that IPT can be combined with medication.

> Mr. B., a 50-year-old separated Jewish businessman, presented with a 3-month history of major depression. Although he denied any precipitants, it soon became apparent that he had recently been passed over for a job promotion. Having just turned 50, he saw that he would never reach the pinnacle of the company in which he had worked for 25 years. His social supports were limited, as he had typically given precedence to work rather than his family. His wife of 27 years had asked him to move out the year before, and his children were away in college. His circle of friends were business colleagues whom he was ashamed to tell of his debacle. His symptoms included passive suicidal ideation, a hopeless feeling that his life was over and might as well be ended. Sleep disturbance and poor concentration impeded his ability to work. His Hamilton score was 23. A previous episode of depression, at age 30, had concerned a lesser setback at work and had been successfully treated with antidepressant medication by his internist.

What interpersonal problem area would you choose? We've heard nothing about death, so complicated bereavement might be discounted. There is a possibility of a role dispute with boss or coworkers: it was in fact difficult to determine from Mr. B. the reasons for his not being promoted. There is also the suggestion of a role dispute with the wife from whom he is separated.

The therapist also weighed the benefits of various treatment modalities. Unlike Ms. A., who had no history of pharmacotherapy, Mr. B. had a history of medication response. Yet it seemed clear that, even if medication again relieved his symptoms, Mr. B. would need psychotherapy to resolve this major life crisis.

Having ruled out role disputes as the central problem, the therapist told

Mr. B. that he had a major depression and linked it to a role transition, namely, the realization that he would never achieve the high title he had long coveted. The therapist acknowledged that this was painful but insisted the situation was not hopeless: Mr. B. had options that would be worth exploring. Although Mr. B. proved a more difficult patient to work with than Ms. A., he did work effectively in IPT. His symptoms responded to IPT combined with a serotonin-reuptake inhibitor. He mourned his lost dream of success, but also explored alternative job situations while trying to renegotiate his position at his own company. In the meantime, his therapist encouraged him to talk to friends and family. They were for the most part far more sympathetic than he had anticipated; he was relieved to find that they did not see him as weak or a failure. Mr. B. eventually got an offer of a high-ranking position at another company, but in the meantime he had come to terms with his own company's superiors. Although he never got the promotion he craved, he was given a face-saving raise and decided to stay. His Hamilton score was in the normal range, 5, long before the 16 weeks of IPT concluded. He remained euthymic on medication during a 2-year follow-up.

Case Example 4

This case is an example of a patient with two illnesses: depression and HIV. It is also an example of complicated bereavement. IPT has demonstrated efficacy in the treatment of depressed HIV-positive patients (Markowitz et al., 1995).

> Mr. C., a 38-year-old gay photographer, had suspected for many years that he was HIV-positive but had been tested only 2 years before, when his lover of 12 years, Mr. D., developed symptoms of AIDS. Mr. C., too, was positive. He took a leave of absence from his newspaper job to nurse his lover through a wasting terminal illness, which began 14 months and ended 5 months before he sought help. He had managed to bring him home from the hospital to die, as both had wanted, but was unfortunately out of the house running an errand at the moment Mr. D. died, surrounded by other friends. Mr. C. felt he had been able to mourn the death to a degree but that his last minute "mistake" was irretrievable. His mourning was further complicated by a numbness he associated with having already lost many other friends to AIDS. His sleep gradually worsened, he lost weight, appetite, and libido. His Hamilton Depression score was a markedly elevated 32.
>
> Following Mr. D.'s death, Mr. C. left his job and withdrew from what had been a large social circle. Never having told his distant parents about his homosexuality, he did not even consider telling them about his HIV infection. Nor did he feel comfortable telling the one sister he had been close to, from whom he now retreated. He spent his days in bed, curled up, waiting to die. Although his physical health was otherwise unremarkable and his doctor advised him that his T cell count was too high to consider taking AZT, he felt that these physical symptoms were due to HIV.

Mr. C.'s case illustrates the plethora of psychosocial stressors that tend to accompany HIV infection: people living within communities hardest hit by the epidemic tend to have suffered multiple losses and hence to be at risk for complicated bereavement. They are also liable to role disputes, either caused by avoiding disclosure of HIV to significant others—as with the sister in this case—or by the strains HIV infection can put on sexual and other close relationships. And the very discovery of HIV infection represents a role transition, in this case compounded by the loss of a job and live-in relationship.

Although a number of formulations were possible, the most salient one seemed to be complicated bereavement, with difficulty in mourning the loss of his longtime companion. The therapist explained:

"You have *two* medical problems: a major depression and HIV infection. Your job over the next few months will be to understand these illnesses and do all that you can to get better; you should become an expert about both of these problems. You already know a lot about HIV because of your experiences with Mr. D., but you seem surprised to hear me call depression an illness. Well, many of the things that you've been feeling can be attributed to the depression. The Hamilton score, which was a very high 32, indicates that your depression is quite severe. The good news is that IPT has been shown to effectively treat depression, so we can expect your Hamilton scores to drop into the normal range over the next few months.

"You've been through an awful lot, but it seems to me that your depression started when Mr. D died. The numbness that you've been feeling and the guilt that you feel about being on an errand the moment that he died have made it very difficult for you to mourn his passing. Your wish to "crawl into a hole" seems related to your difficulty imagining life without Mr. D. We call this complicated bereavement or a grief problem. Although he can never be replaced, there may be things that you still want to do now that Mr. D. is gone, such as going back to work or building up your social network. I suggest we spend the next few weeks talking about your relationship with Mr. D. and your life right now; I bet we'll find out that although you've lost a tremendous amount that there is still a lot to live for."

Mr. C. agreed with the formulation. In therapy, he was able to address his guilt, mourn appropriately, and begin to reestablish contacts and career directions. This was accomplished by reviewing his relationship with Mr. D., allowing him to express the positive and negative feelings about their life together. Together, Mr. C. and the therapist meticulously discussed the details of the day of Mr. D.'s death, allowing Mr. C. to express his regret that he had not been present for the final moments, but also to recollect a few private moments earlier in the day when Mr. C. had sung a favorite song to Mr. D. and had detected a faint smile of recognition. Mr. C. was encouraged to visit Mr. D.'s grave, go through his personal effects, and speak with mutual friends about fond—and not so fond—memories.

Mr. C. was also encouraged to make future-oriented changes in his life. When Mr. C. spontaneously decided to redecorate the apartment he had shared with Mr. D., his therapist suggested that he gather some friends together for a "post-decorating" party. Slowly, Mr. C. became less withdrawn and depressed. He ended a 16-week course of IPT sad but euthymic (his Hamilton Depression score was 5), and proud of the devotion he had shown during his lover's final years.

Case Example 5

This final case is an example of a patient with interpersonal deficits. As is typical for this type of patient, IPT produced significant gains, including some new awareness of and changes in interpersonal behaviors, but her underlying personality style was not altered in 16 weeks. The patient required a referral for additional treatment at the end of the course of IPT.

Ms. E., a 42-year-old divorced paralegal, was referred by her internist after a workup for a series of medical complaints was unrevealing. Ms. E. reported feeling sad and hopeless for many months. She had multiple somatic concerns including recurrent headaches, stomach pains, backaches, and bloating. She was satisfied with her internist's thorough workup but stated, "I still don't feel right." Her Hamilton Depression score was 16, reflecting a high level of somatic complaints.

There were no clear recent stressors. Ms. E. had worked in the same legal offices for 12 years. She was proud of her work and was known around the office as someone who could "always come through in a pinch." Despite her good reputation and obvious pleasure in her work, Ms. E. had little contact with her coworkers. She generally worked alone in a cubicle and spent her lunches at a local restaurant reading novels.

Ms. E. lived alone. She had one friend, Ms. F., with whom she spoke daily by telephone but rarely met. She enjoyed reading and sewing. An avid participant in folk dancing, she attended group dancing sessions twice a week. She interacted with other group members there but did not form relationships outside of the scheduled activities.

She had no current romantic relationships but had been married briefly in her early 30s. She had met a man at a folk-dancing weekend retreat and had become intimately involved. They spent several nights together over a 2-month period before Ms. E. learned that she had become pregnant. Against the man's wishes, Ms. E. terminated the pregnancy. Paradoxically, she felt so guilty about the abortion that she later agreed to marry him when he pressed her. The marriage ended less than a year later. Ms. E. was estranged from her family, who lived in another part of the country.

At this point, the therapist had reviewed all interpersonal arenas and found a paucity of relationships. Ms. E. nevertheless met criteria for major depressive disorder and wanted help. The therapist was left with the interpersonal deficits *category by default and agreed to treat the patient. The data about the marriage, which emerged as a surprise given her presentation as socially isolated, show the importance of taking a careful history and seeking levels of higher functioning.*

"It seems to me that your many physical problems may be related to a mood disorder. According to this Hamilton score and my clinical impression, you have a major depressive disorder. This will often cause or worsen the physical problems that you describe. It also makes it difficult for you to feel motivated to go out and spend time with people. You have talked a bit about how much you enjoy socializing during folk dancing but find that you interact very little with people at other times. You've said that you'd like to see more of Ms. F. and perhaps get involved in another romantic relationship. I feel that your depression is related to your difficulty meeting and being with people. We could think about ways for you to develop more satisfying interpersonal relationships and at the same time help to relieve your depressive symptoms."

Ms. E. was surprisingly enthusiastic about this formulation and agreed to treatment. Initially, the therapist asked Ms. E. to consider changes she would like to make in her one existing relationship. Ms. E. thought she would enjoy spending more time with Ms. F. in person, rather than over the phone, but feared Ms. F. would "not be interested." The therapist encouraged her to think about options for raising this possibility with Ms. F. Encouraged by role playing in the therapy sessions, Ms. E. decided she would risk asking Ms. F. to join her for a movie. To her astonishment, not only did Ms. E. enjoy the outing, but Ms. F. asked her to come to dinner the following week.

Pleased by these successes, Ms. E. began to consider trying to widen her social contacts. Although Ms. E. stated that she would like to spend time with more people, she lacked the social skills necessary to initiate contact. Taking a social skills training approach, the therapist suggested that she consider striking up a conversation with a fellow folk dancer, Ms. G., whom she felt she would like to get to know. They again used role playing to test out the situation in a "safe" environment before the patient tried it out of the office.

As you can see, the therapist must be quite active with these patients, encouraging them to take interpersonal risks and to deviate from their routine. Because these patients lack interpersonal skills, direct suggestion, role playing, and communication analysis become particularly important interventions. It is also important not to push such socially anxious patients too far too fast, but to build slowly on initial successes.

Ms. E. successfully engaged Ms. G. in conversation at the next folk-dancing session and was surprised when Ms G. asked Ms. E. to join her and two male companions for a drink after the dance. Reflexively, Ms. E. declined the invitation. When the events were reviewed in therapy, Ms. E. admitted that she was frightened of repeating the events that led up to her marriage and felt that a drink with men would inevitable lead to "sex and complications." The therapist encouraged Ms. E. to find a more neutral activity, and Ms. E. finally agreed to suggest to Ms. G. that they go out for frozen yogurt (rather than a drink) after the next class.

With much coaxing and practice, Ms. E. began to spend time regularly with Ms. F. and Ms. G. At the end of 16 sessions, she was socializing on a weekly basis but was still far from her stated goal of a new romantic relationship. Her physical symptoms had abated somewhat, and her mood was much brighter. Her Hamilton score of 10 remained in the mildly depressed range.

Ms. E. was congratulated on the strides that she had made in therapy. She was told that because she had made progress already she was a good candidate for ongoing psychotherapy to continue to work on her goals. She was referred for continued supportive psychotherapy with another clinician.

TRAINING

IPT training is available to therapists of all mental health disciplines. The only prerequisites are several years' experience as a psychotherapist, and clinical experience with the disorder to be treated (e.g., major depression). To obtain specific IPT training, interested therapists should read the IPT manual (Klerman et al., 1984) and attend a workshop offered at a national professional conference (e.g., the American Psychiatric Association annual meeting). Alternatively, the reader could seek out a specialized IPT training program, such as at the Cornell Psychotherapy Center in New York City. Because of growing demand for time-limited, diagnostically specific therapies of demonstrated potency, like IPT, more and more workshops are being held for experienced therapists, and psychiatric residents are learning IPT in at least a few, forward-looking training programs (Markowitz, 1995).

A review of Klerman and colleagues' text (1984) and a training workshop are important first steps to learning IPT. This will usually suffice for experienced clinicians to gain a general appreciation of the technique, which they can then try to apply to their practices. In order to master the technique, however, therapists must videotape or audiotape three training cases that are closely reviewed, session by session, with a trained IPT supervisor. Successful completion of three supervised cases makes a therapist "officially" trained in IPT. At present, there are no specific credentials offered to the therapist with IPT expertise.

RESEARCH SUPPORT FOR THE APPROACH

In developing IPT, Klerman and Weissman placed outcome as a goal ahead of process research. This was contrary to the prevailing approach to psychotherapy research in the 1970s but not entirely irrational. Their feeling was that process was of limited interest if the treatment itself could not be proven to have efficacy. Now that the efficacy of IPT has been well demonstrated (Klerman et al., 1984; Elkin et al., 1989; Klerman & Weissman, 1993; Frank et al., 1990), process research appears indicated. To date little has been done however.[3]

At Cornell, we have a few preliminary data to support the reliability of the IPT case formulations. As part of a larger study, we tested rater agreement on the existence of the four IPT problem areas in cases of depression. The four IPT problem areas may be seen as rough equivalents of "case formulation." Two Masters-level psychologists rated audiotapes of brief psychotherapy sessions of depressed HIV-positive patients from early in their treatment with one of four modalities: IPT, cognitive behavioral therapy, supportive therapy alone, or supportive therapy plus the antidepressant medication imipramine. The psychologists were not therapists in the randomized clinical trial from which the patients were drawn, nor were they trained in any of the psychotherapies.

In reviewing five tapes, the two raters agreed on the presence or absence of the four IPT problem areas in 16 of 20 instances (80% of the time) and were concordant each time in choosing the primary IPT problem area (grief, $n = 1$; role transition, $n = 4$). As neither rater was trained in IPT, agreement among actual IPT therapists might be expected to be higher. These data, while hardly conclusive, indicate the feasibility of a more rigorous reliability study and suggest preliminary reliability for an approach to classification that has, after all, straightforward face validity.

Research from the University of Pittsburgh provides indirect evidence for reliability and validity of case formulation in IPT. E. Frank and colleagues (1990) found that patients in a 3-year study using monthly, maintenance IPT had better outcomes when their maintenance sessions focused on a clear interpersonal theme. Patients whose sessions had high interpersonal specificity survived a mean 2 years before developing depression, whereas those with a low interpersonal focus gained only 5 months of protection before relapse. In fact, however, this study allowed maintenance therapy sessions to focus on *any* interpersonal theme, which hence may have been far removed and divergent from the original, acute case formulation (E. Frank, Kupfer, Wagner, McEachran, & Cornes, 1991).

Perhaps surprisingly, little research has addressed whether IPT case formulation and treatment lead to changes in the targeted interpersonal problem area. That is, we know that IPT efficaciously reduces depressive symptoms, but not whether it changes the problem area that has been the focus of the formulation and treatment. The only trial to really address this was small; it did find that individual and particularly conjoint IPT did improve the marriages of depressed women (Weissman & Klerman, 1993). To assess whether IPT formulations and the treatment foci they yield have an interpersonal effect, we are currently employing an IPT Outcome Scale in a study of dysthymic patients (see Appendix).

CONCLUSION

Case formulation is a relatively unstudied but important facet of the initial phase of IPT. Now that the efficacy of IPT has been demonstrated for several mood and nonaffective disorders, research on the ingredients of IPT, including case formulation, deserves greater attention. Readers of this chapter who are not trained in IPT may nonetheless experiment with using the principles inherent in formulating IPT cases in the evaluation and treatment of patients with depression and other psychiatric disorders.

APPENDIX
IPT Problem Area Rating Scale

Rater: _____ Date:_____

Tape #: _____

Mark whether each problem area is present or absent, and check ALL appropriate explanatory items. At the end you will be asked to choose a primary focus for IPT with this subject based on the information available from the tape.

A. Interpersonal Problem Areas

1. Grief   present _____   absent _____
        uncomplicated _____   complicated _____

   If grief is present, identify:
      a. deceased _____
      b. relationship to subject _____
      c. date of death _____
      d. number of months between death and onset of depression _____

2. Interpersonal Dispute   present _____   absent _____

   If present, identify:
      a. significant other _____
      b. does an impasse exist? Yes _____   No _____
      c. predominant theme of dispute:
         i. authority/dominance _____
         ii. dependence _____
         iii. sexual issue _____
         iv. child-rearing _____
         v. getting married/separation _____
         vi. transgression _____
      d. Which theme checked in c is primary? _____
   Approximate duration of dispute in months _____

3. Role transition   present _____ absent _____

   If present, identify:
       a. geographic move _____
       b. marriage/cohabitation _____
       c. separation/divorce _____
       d. graduation/new job _____
       e. loss of job/retirement _____
       f. health issue _____
       g. other (specify): _____

   If more than one checked, which predominates? _____
   Number of months between event and onset of depression _____

4. Interpersonal deficit   present _____ absent _____

   If present, specify characteristics:
       a. avoidant _____
       b. dependent _____
       c. masochistic _____
       d. borderline _____
       e. schizoid _____
       f. paranoid _____
       g. lacks social skills _____
       h. other (specify) _____
   If more than one checked, which predominates? _____

B. Formulation of Therapeutic Task

1. Rank interpersonal problem areas marked as "present" in order of their apparent impact on the subject's mood (1 = most important; 2 = secondary importance; 3= less important):

       Grief _____ Dispute _____ Transition _____ Deficit _____

2. Which problem areas would you use to formulate a treatment contract with the subject? (List up to two, ranking 1 = most important)
       Grief _____ Dispute _____ Transition _____ Deficit _____

3. What is the rationale for your answer to question 2?

4. Did the interviewer on the videotape bias your response by indicating his/her opinion of problem areas? (circle) Yes   No

5. Did the videotape provide information adequate to formulate a problem area diagnosis? Yes   No

6. Other comments _____

****

For scoring only:

Interpersonal Psychotherapy Outcome Scale—Therapist Version

Therapist _____ Patient _____ # _____

Date _____ Treatment phase completed: ____ Acute ____ Continuation

To be completed at the end of the treatment phase:

1. The primary focus of the this treatment was (check one):

    ____ grief (complicated bereavement) ____ role transition
    ____ role dispute ____ interpersonal deficits

2. Secondary foci of treatment (check all addressed):

    ____ grief (complicated bereavement) ____ role transition
    ____ role dispute ____ interpersonal deficits

3. Regardless of the outcome of depressive *symptoms*, how much did the interpersonal problem area(s) change during the course of the treatment phase? Circle one number for each relevant treated problem area:

	worsened significantly	worsened slightly	no change	improved slightly	improved greatly
grief	1	2	3	4	5
role dispute	1	2	3	4	5
role transition	1	2	3	4	5
interpersonal deficits	1	2	3	4	5

Describe changes: _____
_____
_____
_____

version 1.0, 1/97

Interpersonal Psychotherapy Outcome Scale—Patient Version

Name _____ Therapist _____

Date _____

1. Was there a *clear focus* to the treatment you just received, a theme that you and your therapist came back to again and again? (Check one:)

    ____ grief (complicated bereavement) ____ role transition

    ____ role dispute ____ interpersonal deficits

    ____ no particular focus

    If there was *no* focus to your treatment, you need not answer the following questions.

2. Was there also *another* area you focused on? If so, please check:

    ____ grief (complicated bereavement) ____ role transition

    ____ role dispute ____ interpersonal deficits

3. How much were you able to change the interpersonal problem area(s) during the course of your treatment? Please circle a number for each of the relevant areas:

	worsened significantly	worsened slightly	no change	improved slightly	improved greatly
grief	1	2	3	4	5
role dispute	1	2	3	4	5
role transition	1	2	3	4	5
interpersonal deficits	1	2	3	4	5

Comments: _____

_____

version 1.0, 1/97

NOTES

   1. This approach was implicit in the development and application of interpersonal counseling (IPC) for medical clinic patients (see Klerman et al., 1987).

   2. The reader is invited to compare the simplicity and clarity of the IPT formulation to the others in this volume.

   3. One nice exception shows that more difficult, "help-rejecting" patients drive therapists out of a pure IPT paradigm, whereas initial symptom severity does not affect therapist performance (Foley, O'Malley, Rounsaville, Prusoff, & Weissman, 1987). This paper does not, however, address the issue of case formulation.

ACKNOWLEDGMENTS

Work on this chapter was supported in part by grants nos. MH-46250, MH-37103, and MH-49635 from the National Institute of Mental Health, and by a fund established in The New York Community Trust by DeWitt-Wallace.

REFERENCES

American Psychiatric Association. (1994). *Diagnostic and statistical manual of mental disorders* (4th ed.). Washington, DC: Author.

Brown, G. W., & Harris, T. (1978). *Social origins of depression: A study of psychiatric disorder in women.* New York: Free Press.

Carroll, K. M., Rounsaville, B. J., & Gawin, F. H. (1991). A comparative trial of psychotherapies for ambulatory cocaine abusers: Relapse prevention and interpersonal psychotherapy. *American Journal of Drug and Alcohol Abuse, 17*(3), 229–247.

Elkin, I., Shea, M. T., Watkins, J. T., Imber, S. D., Sotsky, S. M., Collins, J. F., Glass, D. R., Pilkonis, P. A., Leber, W. R., Docherty, J. P., Fiester, S. J., & Parloff, M. B. (1989). National Institute of Mental Health treatment of depression collaborative research program: General effectiveness of treatments. *Archives of General Psychiatry, 46,* 971–982.

Fairburn, C. G., Jones, R., Peveler, R. C., Hope, R. A., & O'Connor, M. (1993). Psychotherapy and bulimia nervosa: Longer-term effects of interpersonal psychotherapy, behavior therapy, and cognitive behavior therapy. *Archives of General Psychiatry, 50,* 419–428.

Foley, S. H., O'Malley, S., Rounsaville, B., Prusoff, B. A., & Weissman, M. M. (1987). The relationship of patient difficulty to therapist performance in interpersonal therapy of depression. *Journal of Affective Disorders, 12,* 207–217.

Frank, E., Kupfer, D. J., Perel, J. M., Cornes, C., Jarrett, D. B., Mallinger, A. G., Thase, M. E., McEachran, A. B., & Grochocinski, V. J. (1990). Three-year outcomes for maintenance therapies in recurrent depression. *Archives of General Psychiatry, 47,* 1093–1099.

Frank, E., Kupfer, D. J., Wagner, E. F., McEachran, A. B., & Cornes, C. (1991). Efficacy of interpersonal psychotherapy as a maintenance treatment of recurrent depression. *Archives of General Psychiatry, 48,* 1053–1059.

Frank, J. (1971). Therapeutic factors in psychotherapy. *American Journal of Psychotherapy, 25,* 350–361.

Hamilton, M. (1960). A rating scale for depression. *Journal of Neurology, Neurosurgery, and Psychiatry, 25,* 56–62.

Hirschfeld, R. M. A., Klerman, G. L., Clayton, P. J., Keller, M. B., McDonald-Scott, P., & Larkin, B. H. (1983). Assessing personality: Effects of the depressive state on trait measurement. *American Journal of Psychiatry, 140,* 695–699.

Kendler, K. S., Kessler, R. C., Walters, E. E., MacLean, C., Neale, M. C., Heath, A. C., & Eaves, L. J. (1995). Stressful life events, genetic liability, and onset of an episode of major depression in women. *American Journal of Psychiatry, 152,* 833–842.

Klerman, G. L., Budman, S., Berwick, D., Weissman, M. M., Damico-White, J., Demby, A., & Feldstein, M. (1987). Efficacy of a brief psychosocial intervention for symptoms of stress and distress among patients in primary care. *Medical Care, 25,* 1078–1088.

Klerman, G. L., & Weissman, M. M. (Eds.). (1993). *New applications of interpersonal therapy.* Washington, DC: American Psychiatric Press.

Klerman, G. L., Weissman, M. M., Rounsaville, B. J., & Chevron, E. S. (1984). *Interpersonal psychotherapy of depression.* New York: Basic Books.

Manning, D. W., Markowitz, J. C., & Frances, A. J. (1992). A review of combined psychotherapy and pharmacotherapy in the treatment of depression. *Journal of Psychotherapy Practice and Research, 1,* 103–116.

Markowitz, J. C. (1995). Teaching interpersonal psychotherapy to psychiatric residents. *Academic Psychiatry, 19,* 167–173.

Markowitz, J. C., Klerman, G. L., Spielman, L. A., Jacobsberg, L. B., Fishman, B., Frances, A. J., Kocsis, J. H., & Perry, S. W. (1995). Individual psychotherapies for depressed HIV-positive patients. *American Journal of Psychiatry, 152,* 1504–1509.

Parsons, T. (1951). Illness and the role of the physician: A sociological perspective. *American Journal of Orthopsychiatry, 21,* 452–460.

Perry, S., Cooper, A. M., & Michels, R. (1987). The psychodynamic formulation: Its purpose, structure, and clinical application. *American Journal of Psychiatry, 144,* 543–550.

Rounsaville, B. J., Glazer, W., Wilber, C. H., Weissman, M. M., & Kleber, H. D. (1983). Short-term interpersonal psychotherapy in methadone-maintained opiate addicts. *Archives of General Psychiatry, 40,* 629–636.

Sotsky, S. M., Glass, D. R., Shea, M. T., Pilkonis, P. A., Collins, J. F., Elkin, I., Watkins, J. T., Imber, S. D., Leber, W. R., Moyer, J., & Oliveri, M. E. (1991). Patient predictors of response to psychotherapy and pharmacotherapy: Findings in the NIMH treatment of depression collaborative research program. *American Journal of Psychiatry, 148,* 997–1008.

Stuart, S., & O'Hara, M. W. (1995). Interpersonal psychotherapy for postpartum depression: A treatment program. *Journal of Psychotherapy Practice and Research, 4,* 18–29.

Sullivan, H. S. (1953). *The interpersonal theory of psychiatry.* New York: Norton.

Weissman, M. M., & Klerman, G. L. (1993). Conjoint interpersonal psychotherapy for depressed patients with marital disputes. In G. L. Klerman & M. M. Weissman (Eds.), *New applications of interpersonal psychotherapy* (pp. 103–127). Washington, DC: American Psychiatric Press.

Weissman, M. M., & Markowitz, J. C. (1994). Interpersonal psychotherapy: Current status. *Archives of General Psychiatry, 51,* 599–606.

9

Interpersonal Case Formulation: Describing and Explaining Interpersonal Patterns Using the Structural Analysis of Social Behavior

WILLIAM P. HENRY

Just as the twig is bent, the tree's inclined.
—ALEXANDER POPE

Lay "psychologists" have long observed the lasting effects of early interpersonal experiences. From Pope's poetic statement above to general folk wisdom ("The apple doesn't fall far from the tree") to vernacular speech ("He's a chip off the old block") we see the same idea repeated—namely, that children often develop into adults that closely resemble the important caretakers from their youth or represent a clear reaction to these same early figures. While it may seem self-evident that we are strongly influenced by our early interpersonal environment, there remains the scientific task of explaining more precisely *why* this is the case and *how* this process unfolds. The how and why may be seen along biological, psychological, or sociocultural lines. In this chapter I will focus on the psychological theories that attempt to link early interpersonal experience to adult personality and problem states. This linkage provides the framework for interpersonal case formulation (ICF), that is, the structured understanding of an individual for the purpose of guiding therapeutic interventions designed to ameliorate the suffering caused by repetitive and maladaptive interpersonal patterns that have their basis in early learning. My approach to interpersonal formulation represents a synthesis of the ideas of many other writers and clinicians to whom I owe an intellectual debt (most notably to Harry Stack Sullivan, John Bowlby, and Lorna Smith Benjamin). My goal in this chapter is to take the consensual ideas of interpersonal theory, organize them using the conceptual and measurement framework provided by the Structural Analysis of Social Behavior (SASB; Benjamin, 1974), and present a concrete, reliable set of procedures for arriving at a case formulation. This formulation may in turn be applied to a number of intervention techniques representing a variety of therapeutic orientations.

HISTORICAL BACKGROUND OF THE APPROACH

The term "interpersonal theory" is most typically linked to the writings of Sullivan (1953), who emphasized the process of introjection. This is the idea that we come to treat ourselves as we have been treated by our parents, or as Sullivan succinctly put it, "The self is comprised of the reflective appraisals of others." When the historical evolution of psychoanalytic thinking is traced from Freud's original drive model to later ego, self, and object psychologies (Pine, 1990), there is a clear trend across the twentieth century. Overall, theorists have moved away from seeing behavior as the product of internalized inborn drive states and their related conflicts toward seeing behavior as the product of emergent interpersonal *transactions*. Put another way, the centrality of social learning has come to dominate more hard-wired or deterministic philosophies. Clearly Sullivan represented a major, perhaps *the* major, force in this trend. However, just as there is no single "object relations theory," there is no single or unified "interpersonal theory" per se. To truly represent and understand the scope, importance, and potential of ICF, I feel that it is important to go beyond the usual recounting of the analytic Sullivanian tradition. We should also consider the contributions of a variety of theorists, many of whom are often placed in opposition to one another in clinical textbooks. Behind the competing schools and labels, however, lies a startling convergence of basic ideas that provide a shared historical foundation for contemporary interpersonal case formulation.

Strange Bedfellows: From Horney to Rogers to Perls

Any number of theorists across orientations and time periods have based their approaches on the same fundamental underlying principle: as children develop they have a natural desire or need to be accepted, loved, and protected. The child's early interpersonal environment may or may not provide some or all of these conditions. Through the process of social learning, children come to understand the local familial "rules" and in turn form self-concepts and alter their behavior in ways designed to maximize the chances that they will indeed be accepted, loved, and protected.

The analyst Karen Horney (1945) hypothesized that if these basic needs are not met, children may employ three strategies to make their lives safer, more predictable, and more satisfying. These interpersonal possibilities include the following: (1) moving *toward* others by being compliant and self-effacing, and suppressing expressions of hostility and needs for separateness; (2) denying normative needs for loving intimacy (and the security it provides) and instead moving *against* others through anger and rebelliousness in an attempt to gain respect and a sense of power or mastery; and (3) moving *away* from others, relying on a perceived sense of self-sufficiency to reduce anxiety. According to Horney, a child may try all of these approaches, eventually settling into a given style because it is the most rewarded or tolerated and produces the greatest sense of safety or lowered anxiety. However, these compromise interpersonal solutions are purchased at the price of denying basic needs for a balance of dependency, intimacy, and separateness.

While Horney had a strong interpersonal emphasis, she is considered squarely within the analytic domain. The broadly defined existential, humanistic, and Rogerian traditions that developed later were seen as a distinct reaction to and break from this analytic tradition. Despite some obvious differences, however, the same basic interpersonal ideas emerged in these supposedly reactionary approaches. Psychopathology was again seen as the result of early interpersonal or social learning that produced maladaptive patterns for seeking love, approval, and the like. For example, Carl R. Rogers (1961) stated that all people have one basic drive or motivation—*actualization*, the inherent, positive tendency of an organism to develop all of its capacities through personal growth and the movement from external to internal controls. However, Rogers hypothesized that as self-consciousness emerges, we also have an inborn, universal need for the *positive regard* of others. Eliciting this positive regard from others is so compelling that it supersedes the inborn "valuing process" that leads to self-actualization. When individuals begin to act in accordance with the internalized values of others they are attached to in order to receive positive regard, they have acquired the *conditions of worth* (i.e., the local familial rules) and can no longer regard themselves positively unless they meet these conditions of worth imposed by others.

Anyone who has ever seen films of Fritz Perls and Carl Rogers working with patients could hardly confuse the two stylistically. It would also seem that the bedrock of their respective theories differ radically. While Rogers proposed a fundamentally psychological motivation (self-actualization), Perls stated that humans are organisms whose primary daily end goals are really based on biological needs such as hunger and sex (Perls, 1969). However, the same fundamental interpersonal ideas of Horney, Rogers, and others become central to Perls as well when he goes on to state that *social roles* are the means by which we meet these end goals. The idea once again emerges that early social learning and interpersonal pressures may transform normal needs into maladaptive behavior designed to win approval and love. According to Perls, we begin to identify with and put all of our energy into playing roles, thus becoming stuck and fearing the repercussions of deviating from these expectations. In sum, all of these theorists (as well as Sullivan himself) place their central emphasis on anxiety—how it is created when interpersonal conditions do not allow for normal developmental processes, and how ultimately maladaptive interpersonal adjustments or compromises are employed to lower this anxiety.

Interpersonal Principles Broadly Defined

In summary, there are a number of main points drawn from a generic interpersonal tradition as exemplified by the theorists described above, as well as many others not mentioned (such as W. Reich, J. Bowlby, H. Kohut, D. Kiesler, R. Carson, L. S. Benjamin, and W. P. Henry). Clearly, the basic idea is that early interpersonal transactions with significant others shape the self-concept through a variety of processes that form internalized representations of self and others in interaction. Instinctual motivations—the universal interpersonal drives to achieve acceptance, love, protection, a sense of self-worth, and such— are seen as positive. When these goals are not met due to early shortcomings in parenting the result is anxiety, and the child attempts to reduce the anxiety by altering his or her interpersonal behavior. That is, the child attempts to achieve the best possible compromise between true needs and the realities of the environment. Unfortunately, these compensatory strategies invariably create imbalances—behavioral deficits and excesses—and a tendency toward more rigid perception, action, and reaction to others. These imbalances help to promote repetitive, cyclic, and problematic interpersonal patterns that tend to occur across relationships.

Of prime importance to ICF is the proposition that these behavioral patterns, while forged in the past, doggedly persist because they are actively maintained in the present. The tendency toward rigid actions, reactions, and perceptions *re-create* and hence reinforce the old patterns through ongoing interactions with important others. Traditional psychiatric symptoms such as depression, anxiety, suicidality, substance abuse, and somatization are often embedded in these interpersonal patterns (L. M. Horowitz & Vitkus, 1985). That is, the interpersonal patterns help both to create and maintain the symptoms, which in turn help to maintain the behavioral patterns. In therapy, how the therapist behaves interpersonally toward the patient thus becomes an important change mechanism in and of itself because it represents the chance for new interpersonal experiential learning (see Henry & Strupp, 1994).

Structure and Measurement of Interpersonal Concepts: The Circumplex Tradition

Historically, the most common type of system used to conceptualize and measure interpersonal styles and behavior has been the circumplex. A circumplex system is simply a mathematical structure based on two underlying orthogonal (independent) X and Y axes. Each point on the circle surrounding the two axes represents a unique combination of differing "amounts" of the two variables. The interpersonal circumplex can be traced conceptually to Henry Murray (1938), who developed a list of basic human needs drawn from psychoanalytic drive theory, and to Harry Stack Sullivan (1953), who proposed that interpersonal behavior rather than traditional psychiatric symptoms should serve as the basis of diagnosis. Timothy Leary and colleagues (1957), influenced by both Murray and Sullivan, took Murray's original list of needs, reduced them to a smaller set of categories, and arranged them in circular form. This original interpersonal circumplex (IPC) was based on the fundamental axes of affiliation (love–hate) and control (dominance–submission). Several years later, Earl Schafer (1965) developed a circumplex model of parenting behavior that was similar to the IPC but differed in one important regard. While the IPC model conceptualized dominance and submission as opposite poles on the control axes, Schafer's model did not. Rather, Schafer stated that the opposite of dominance or control was autonomy granting or differentiation. Benjamin (1974) combined the ideas of Leary and Schafer, constructing a new circumplex system, the Structural Analysis of Social Behavior (SASB), the most complex and comprehensive interpersonal circumplex system to date.

CONCEPTUAL FRAMEWORK

Structural Analysis of Social Behavior

Benjamin (1974) made two crucial refinements in the original IPC. First, she defined her interpersonal control dimension to represent *enmeshment* at one pole and *differentiation* at the other. In an enmeshed interpersonal state, one party is controlling and the other submitting. At the differentiated pole, one party is autonomy granting and the other autonomy taking. This refinement reflects Benjamin's agreement with Schafer that the dominance–submission continuum represented only one type of interpersonal control phenomenon. Second, Benjamin added an "introject" circumplex to measure how actions by others toward the self become part of the self-concept.

An adequate account of these three interpersonal constructs—enmeshment, differentiation, and introjection—required expanding the traditional single IPC into a system of three interrelated circumplex surfaces. As shown in Figure 9.1, Benjamin labeled them "Focus on Other," "Focus on Self," and "Introject"; each has a horizontal *affiliation axis* and a vertical *interdependence axis*. Surface 1, called *Focus on Other*, reflects transitive actions by one person toward another (see Figure 9.1). The horizontal axis runs from extreme disaffiliation, hatred, or attack on the left to extreme affiliation, approach, or love on the right (the meaning of the horizontal axis is identical across all three surfaces). The vertical or interdependence axis of surface one ranges from extremely controlling behavior at the bottom to freeing or autonomy grant-

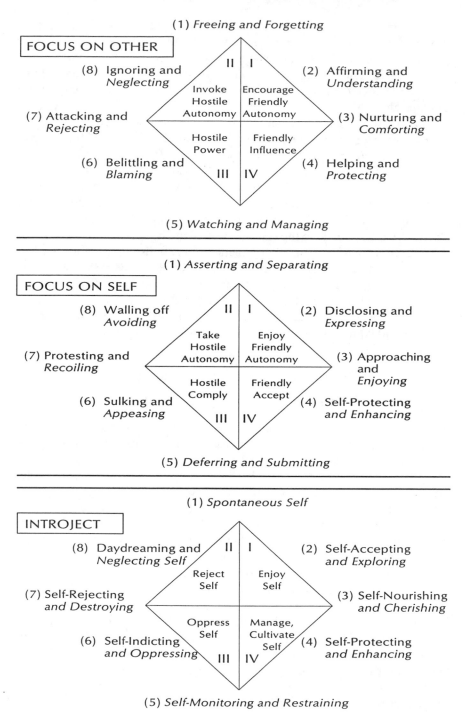

FIGURE 9.1. The SASB circumplex system (from Benjamin, 1974). Copyright 1974 by the American Psychological Association. Reprinted by permission.

ing at the top. Surface 2, called *Focus on Self*, charts intransitive interpersonal actions, that is, the *reactions* of one person to another. Actions involving surface 2 are self-focused actions in which the individual is not trying to directly do something to or toward the other person. The vertical interdependence axis on surface 2 runs from submission at the bottom to autonomy taking or separation at the top. While surfaces 1 and 2 measure the interpersonal or *transactional* behaviors between two or more people, surface 3 is labeled the *Introject* and taps intrapsychic phenomena, that is, how a person acts toward him- or herself. Are they self-accepting, self-critical, or self-ignoring? Theoretically the introject is formed by the actions of important others toward the self (i.e., surface 1 actions), which become the way a person acts toward him- or herself. Thus the vertical dimension of the introject mirrors that of surface 1, running from self-control at the bottom to self-freeing at the top.

The full SASB model contains 36 points around each of the three circumplexes, with each point representing a unique blend of differing amounts of the underlying basic axes—affiliation and interdependence. The most widely used version of SASB is the cluster model in which these 36 points are collapsed into eight clusters around each surface. The simplest way to use SASB is to refer only to the four quadrants in each surface (e.g., hostile control, friendly submission, friendly self-autonomy, etc.). In this chapter, I will frequently refer to cluster codes such as "1-4." The first number always refers to surface, while the second number refers to one of the eight clusters on that surface. With practice, using these numeric codes becomes second nature.

SASB may be used either to describe the ongoing interpersonal *process* between individuals (regardless of content) or to code the interpersonal *content* of the verbal dialogue. For example, a therapist might ask in an open-ended fashion, "Tell me a bit more about your mother." The therapist's process is affiliative, inviting a continuation of autonomous self-disclosure by the patient. The process code for the therapist's statement would be 1-2, representing Focus on Other (surface 1), cluster 2 (friendly autonomy granting or affirming). Perhaps the patient responds, "Well, to tell you the truth, I hate my mother because she is responsible for all of my problems." The process of this utterance in relation to the therapist would likely receive a code of 2-2, representing Focus on Self (surface 2), cluster 2 (friendly autonomy taking or self-disclosure). However, the interpersonal *content* of the patient's statement would be quite different. The content code would likely be a 1-6, reflecting the Focus on Other (mother; surface 1), cluster 6 (hostile control, or blame). The interpersonal process between interactants can always be coded, but the content is not necessarily codable all of the time because the content of the statement may not be in the form of an interpersonal transaction. For example, there is no interpersonal content to be coded for statements such as "I feel depressed" or "I missed work today." Understanding the difference between interpersonal process and content is crucial to using SASB for ICF. Some people find the distinction difficult at first, but they rather quickly grasp the concept when specific examples are given.

As a measurement system SASB may be used in one of two general ways. First, it may be employed by independent raters to code the ongoing interpersonal process or content of a dyad or group. This coding may be done from either audiotape or preferably videotape (the use of transcript-only ratings for process coding is highly discouraged because of the loss of vital cues such as posture, facial expression, and tone of voice, but it may be appropriate for content coding). "Coding" may also be done in real time by a clinician as he or she tracks the emergent process and content of a session or interview. Secondly, a written self-report version, the Intrex questionnaire (Benjamin, 1995), permits individuals to describe various relationships in the SASB metric. The Intrex is flexible in that any relationship may be rated, the ratings may reflect any time period (past or present), and the ratings may reflect specific *states* (such as "Rate your relationship with your husband when it is at its best or worst"). The standard Intrex battery includes ratings of the introject in best and worst states, a significant other relationship in best and worst states, the rater's relationship with mother and father (separately) when aged 5–10 years, and the observed relationship between mother and father. Each rated relationship actually involves four distinct sets of ratings: how the other acts toward the ratee, how the other reacts to the ratee, how the ratee acts toward the other, and how the ratee reacts to the other.

Interpersonal Principles of Development and Social Learning

The SASB three-surface structure provides a heuristic framework for understanding in a systematic manner how early experiences become manifest as adult interpersonal and intrapsychic problems. The mechanisms which theoretically form the bridge between early experience and adult behavior have been called "copy processes" (Benjamin, 1996; Henry, 1994). There are posited to be three basic copy processes crucial to ICF—identification, internalization, and introjection—and these three processes may be seen to relate to the three SASB surfaces. *Identification* is the process of acting like another through imitation. Typically, SASB surface 1 actions toward others would provide the basis of identification and hence may drive an individual's actions toward other people. *Internalization* is the process by which an abstract representation of significant others' typical actions serves as a basis for interpersonal expectancies. These internalized representations are hypothesized to shape a person's reactions to others as measured on SASB surface 2. *Introjection,* the process by which the child comes to act toward themselves as they have been treated by others is measured on SASB surface 3.

The Transactional Interpersonal Process: Maintaining the Past

These developmental processes help us understand how self-concept or personality comes into being and is made manifest as interpersonal behavior. Now we turn briefly to several theoretically important principles about how these interpersonal behaviors "pull for" certain behaviors in others and how these behaviors by others maintain an individual's self-concept. In short, these are the interpersonal principles that guide behavioral maintenance and/or change in the present—complementarity, contemporary introjection, and antithetical behavior.

Complementarity is the idea that interpersonal behaviors tend to evoke a specific response in others. More specifically, friendliness pulls for friendliness, hostility for hostility, control for submission (and vice versa), and autonomy granting for autonomy taking (mutual differentiation—whether friendly or hostile). In the SASB system, a given behavior represented by a point on surface 1 or 2 tends to evoke the same point on the other surface. For example, hostile control (SASB cluster 1-6) pulls for hostile submission (SASB cluster 2-6). *Contemporary introjection* occurs when ongoing behaviors directed at us by important others are turned inward or introjected, just as they were in childhood. Early learning creates a set of expectancies that shape our reactions to others (often in maladaptive distorted fashion), thus evoking complementary actions in current others that are similar to early experiences. Hence the negative introject structures are confirmed and entrenched via contemporary introjection. However, if important others act and react to us with *antithetical behaviors* (the opposite of the complement—e.g., 1-2 instead of 1-6), this produces the conditions over time for new complementary patterns of behavior that may result in ameliorative, not self-confirming, contemporary introjection.[1]

These principles provide a descriptive account of the centrality of early interpersonal experience—namely, how such experiences mold a person's expectations and perception, behavior with others, and self-concept, and how these variables unfold in everyday life to maintain rigid, self-defeating, and self-maintaining problem cycles.

What Are the Basic Elements of Case Formulation?

Since interpersonal thinking primarily traces its roots to analytic and object relations theory, it is useful to review briefly some of the current psychodynamic formulation methods. Henry, Strupp, Schacht, and Gaston (1994) reviewed a number of well-developed methods that propose a variety of elements that a formulation should contain: (a) interpersonal wishes, fears, or intentions and their imagined consequences (Core Conflictual Relationship Theme, CCRT; Luborsky, 1977; see also Chapter 3, this volume); (b) conscious and unconscious goals for therapy, the pathogenic beliefs that interfere with reaching goals, and specific patient in-therapy tests of these beliefs (Plan Diagnosis; Weiss et al., 1986); (c) wishes, fears, symptomatic and avoidant resultants of the wishes and fears, vulnerability to specific stressors, and best available level of adaptation to conflicts (Idiographic Conflict Formulation Method; Perry, Augusto, & Cooper, 1989; see also Chapter 6, this volume); (d) recurrent patterns of linked experience, affect and behavior (states of mind) that are ephemeral and clustered into the categories of desired states, dreaded states, problematic compromises, and adaptive compromise states. Embedded in these states are prototypic interpersonal role-relational models involving imagined transactional sequences and information processing patterns (Configurational Analysis; M. J. Horowitz, 1991; see Chapter 7, this volume); and (e) acts of self (including cognitions, affects, and behaviors as they relate to others), acts of others, expectations of others and resultant actions toward self (Cyclical Maladaptive Pattern, CMP; Schacht, Binder, & Strupp, 1984; Schacht & Henry, 1995; see also Levenson and Strupp, Chapter 4, this volume).

Despite the different language, labels, and contexts, there is much in common across these methods. They are strikingly interpersonal or transactional in nature (as opposed to older drive theories) and share the following common themes: the bedrock of formulation is the patient's internalized world of imagined prototypic interpersonal transactions that often take the form of fantasized "if-then" sequences (i.e., expectancies); problem states are organized around conflicting wishes and fears that are interpersonal in nature; the problems for which people seek therapy are part of a *patterned, repetitive sequence*; these sequences involve a linked set of co-occurring cognitions, affects, and behaviors; and patients are not passive sufferers but are trying to actively cope as best they can using compromise solutions that are ultimately maladaptive or unsatisfactory.

In the broadest sense then, ICF should describe central, repetitive patterns of interpersonal transaction. It should explain these patterns with reference to an individual's motivation to achieve certain wishes and avoid certain fears. Finally, pattern maintenance should be linked to rigid perceptions and expectations fueled by the prototypical mental images of self and others in interaction. The building blocks of a complete ICF thus include a *behavioral description of the interpersonal transactions*, the *transactional principles* that maintain the repetitive cycle (i.e., complementarity and introjection), the *linked copy processes* thought to account for the behaviors, the *motivation* of behavior in terms of interpersonal wishes and fears, and the *belief system of interpersonal expectancies and perceptions* that explain why the individual's wish–fear motivations are translated into the specific observed behavioral transactions. This completes the loop leading from surface interpersonal behavior through various developmental, motivational, and cognitive processes back to the problem behaviors again.

Levels of Understanding in Case Formulation

ICF as an outgrowth of more traditional psychodynamic formulation seeks ideally to integrate three levels of understanding: (1) concrete conscious problems that can be quickly articulated, (2) recurrent patterns of problems, and (3) the more unconscious core ordering or guiding processes responsible for pattern maintenance (Henry et al., 1994; cf. Mahoney, 1991). A comprehensive ICF would address all of these levels. However, since individual therapists and theorists may disagree about whether or not a complete integration of the three potential levels of understanding is necessary for the purpose of successful treatment, the context of interpersonal thinking is flexible in this regard. In a later section, I shall describe six possible levels of complexity specific to SASB-based ICF. Some type of behavioral pattern is always identified, but the complexity of the pattern and the extent to which core ordering processes are integrated may vary. Formulations of varying depth may then be applied to a variety of specific technical interventions ranging from behavioral to cognitive to psychodynamic as well as to different modalities from individual to family therapies.

General Components of Interpersonal Case Formulation

ICF rests on first uncovering and describing problem patterns in terms of *specific interpersonal behaviors* and sequences of observable behavior. Second comes the understanding of *how the three copy processes link the developmental history and the presenting problems* for any given individual. That is, how a person's actions, reactions, perceptions, expectations, and self-concept relate to early social learning. For example, perhaps Ken, a patient, has identified with and acts like his father but expects others to treat him the way his mother has (thus perceiving and reacting as if he is interacting with his mother); thus he has introjected both parents, resulting in a mixture of acts toward the self that can be differentially traced to his father or mother.

The third step is to understand *how these contemporary actions toward and reactions to others (and the related perceptions and expectancies) work to maintain problem patterns in the present*. While the individual is "set up" or "programmed" by these copy processes, the two interpersonal principles that are thought to account for the rigid contemporary persistence of maladaptive behavioral cycles—complementarity and current introjection—must now be integrated.

Finally, *the specific behavioral patterns described in the first step, the problematic copy processes described in the second step, and the contemporary interpersonal mechanics that maintain CMPs described in the third step are integrated within the context of understanding the deep motivations for the pattern (wishes and fears designed to achieve normative interpersonal goals).* This completes the formulation that guides therapy.

INCLUSION/EXCLUSION CRITERIA

The range of patients and problems for which the ICF method is suitable is quite broad, potentially encompassing *any* candidate for psychotherapy. My belief is that maladaptive interpersonal expectations, perceptions, and behavioral patterns contribute to the presenting symptoms of most psychotherapy patients, regardless of their DSM-IV diagnosis or the chronicity or severity of their problems. It is important to separate the issue of suitability for ICF per se from the question of whether any given patient is suitable or not for a specific therapeutic approach that might utilize information derived from ICF. For example, it is quite possible to formulate a comprehensive ICF for a patient that would not meet selection criteria for some contemporary short-term approaches to dynamic/interpersonal therapy designed to work on a central interpersonal pattern (such as Time-Limited Dynamic Psychotherapy, TLDP). For the purposes of ICF in and of itself, it is necessary only that the patient and/or collateral sources be able to provide at least minimal interpersonal information to construct a beginning ICF (see the specific steps in the next section). Except for the occasional specific research use, however, it would seem fruitless to construct an ICF for a patient for whom some interpersonally targeted interventions (regardless of the theoretical approach or modality) were not intended. In summary, ICF is potentially appropriate for any patient in short-term or open-ended therapy of any modality for any problem, as long as (a) the patient's difficulties are embedded in identifiable interpersonal phenomena and (b) these interpersonal phenomena can be at least minimally articulated.

STEPS IN CASE FORMULATION CONSTRUCTION
Sources of Information

The ICF model does not directly specify necessary or sufficient sources, types, or amount of interpersonal information to be obtained. Interpersonal data may be extracted from interview or session transcripts, self-report measures, collateral interviews with others, clinical records, or direct observation of the patient during the interview or in other settings. Interview and self-report data may come from existing materials or may come from procedures designed specifically for the purpose of ICF. Clearly the more information the better, and the ICF interview procedures and self-report measures described below will likely result in a more complete, structured, and replicable database for clinical and research use.

Conducting a Clinical Interview for Interpersonal Case Formulation

In most cases, clinicians will construct an ICF based on one or more initial interviews. For a comprehensive ICF, the clinical interview must yield information sufficient to allow the clinician to form a working hypothesis that combines the following: (1) the specific central figure(s) from childhood that have been "copied"; (2) the copy process(es) related to each central figure identified; (3) how these copy processes are manifested in current behavior and self-concept; and (4) the interpersonal processes by which these contemporary behaviors pull for specific actions and reactions from others, reinforcing the self-concept or introject, and maintaining a cycle. Obtaining this level of understanding in a single interview session may be a tall order in some cases. The clinician must maintain an active focus on interpersonal phenomenon. In the next subsection, I list five principles that should help maximize the amount of useful information obtained for ICF.

Five Principles That Guide the Interview

There are five main keys to interviewing patients for the purpose of ICF that may be summarized by the words *transaction, organization, sequence, process,* and *therapist stance*. This subsection is designed to instruct the clinician in the general principles prescribing how to conduct an interview and organize the resulting information into an interpersonal formulation.

1. *Soliciting transactional language.* The first main principle is to elicit information, whenever possible, in the form of interpersonal transactional behavior. For example, a man might say that he is seeking therapy for marital problems. Further inquiry might reveal that he is angry at his wife for not paying enough attention to him. In order to construct an interpersonal narrative, it is also important that we find out what the man and his wife actually *do* in these situations and to uncover this information in a complete enough fashion to allow the behaviors to be SASB-coded for affiliation and interdependence. In this case for instance, it may be that the wife criticizes her husbands interests (SASB cluster 1-6) or changes the subject when he brings up important topics (SASB cluster 2-8 or 1-8).

2. *Organizing interpersonal information.* The second principle involves the importance of mentally categorizing the interpersonal information obtained *as the interview progresses,* to ensure that the interview will yield sufficient material for a complete formulation. Often some patients spontaneously provide only certain types of interpersonal information that are most compelling to them at the time (such as how others act toward them or how they treat themselves). The simplest organizational scheme for ICF is based on the "dynamic focus" procedure first developed for guiding TLDP (Schacht et al., 1984; see also Levenson & Strupp, Chapter 4, this volume) and later renamed CMP (Butler & Binder, 1987). Levenson (1995, p. 49) in her updated guide to TLDP describes the *four basic categories* into which the interpersonal information obtained during the interview may be placed. It is important that the interviewer solicit interpersonal material in each of these categories:

a. *Acts of Self.* These include the patient's thoughts, feelings, wishes, and behaviors of an interpersonal nature. For example, "When I meet strangers, I can't help thinking they wouldn't want to have anything to do with me" (thought); "I am afraid to take the promotion" (feeling); "I wish I were the life of the party" (wish); "I yell and scream at my kids when they get in my way" (behavior). Sometimes these acts are conscious, like those just mentioned, and sometimes they are outside of awareness, as in the case of the woman who does not realize how jealous she is of her sister's accomplishments.

b. *Expectations of Others' Reactions.*[2] This category pertains to all the statements having to do with how the patient imagines others will react to him or her in response to some interpersonal behavior (act of self). "My boss will fire me if I make a mistake." "If I go to the dance, no one will ask me to dance."

c. *Acts of Others Toward the Self.* This third grouping consists of the actual behaviors of other people, as observed (or assumed) and interpreted by the patient. "When I made a mistake at work, my boss shunned me for the rest of the day." "When I went to the dance, guys asked me to dance, but only because they felt sorry for me."

d. *Acts of Self Toward the Self (Introject).* In this category belongs all of the patient's behaviors or attitudes toward her- or himself—when the self is the object of the interpersonal dynamic. How does the patient treat her- or himself? "When I made the mistake, I berated myself so much I had difficulty sleeping that night." "When no one asked me to dance, I told myself it's because I'm fat, ugly, and unlovable."

A more complex organizational form that fully incorporates the SASB three-surface structure—the *SASB–CMP*—has been presented by Schacht and Henry (1995). As depicted in Table 9.1, the general categories of Acts of Self and Acts of Others are further subdivided according to interpersonal focus, resulting in four distinct types of transactional behavior: actions by others toward the patient, reactions by others to the patient, the patient's actions toward others, and the patient's reactions to others. Additionally, the category of introject is expanded to include the introjective acts of others in relation to the patient, and actual interpersonal behaviors are more clearly separated from the patient's expectations, wishes, and fears.

3. *Sequencing the organized information.* In addition to simply obtaining examples of behaviors, thoughts, and feelings in each of the CMP or SASB–CMP categories, it is important for the interviewer to understand and confirm prototypic *sequences* of the specific acts of self, expectancies, and the actions and reactions of others that result in self-perpetuating and maladaptive interpersonal reactions, self-concepts, and actions toward the self. Toward this end, it is helpful if the interviewer regularly verbalizes his or her emergent understanding of the pattern (at whatever level of completeness) in order to (a) correct any misunderstanding, (b) display empathic connection that might further disclosure, (c) highlight the areas in which more information is needed, and (d) ensure that the potentially vast amount of interpersonally relevant information being obtained is organized correctly into the appropriate cyclic

TABLE 9.1. Structural Domains of the SASB–CMP

Interpersonal Acts (SASB surfaces 1 and 2)
  1. Interpersonal acts by the patient
      a. Acts by the patient toward others in patient's best and worst state (surface 1)
      b. Reactions of the patient to others in patient's best and worst state (surface 2)
  2. Interpersonal acts by others
      a. How others act toward the patient in their best and worst state (surface 1)
      b. How others react to the patient in their best and worst state (surface 2)

Introjective Acts (SASB surface 3)
  1. By the patient: how the patient treats him- or herself in transactions with others
  2. By others: how others treat themselves in transactions with the patient

Expectancies: Predictions, Wishes, and Fears (all SASB surfaces)
  1. Predictions
      a. Patient's predictions about how others will act toward them and react to them
      b. Patient's beliefs about how they will act toward others and react to them
  2. Wishes: patient's desired transactions involving self, others, and introject
  3. Fears: transaction involving the self, others, and introject that the patient dreads and avoids if possible.

---

patterns. For example, the interviewer might say something like, "It seems that you want your wife to greet you lovingly when you come home, but you expect her to ignore you. When you do come home and she doesn't say much you feel she's angry at you for some reason, even though you have no idea why. You then feel angry, as if her silence is an effort to control you—to make you do or be something different. Does this sound right?" If the patient agrees, the interviewer might inquire further, "What do you do at those times?" (seeking acts of self), "How is the silence broken?" (seeking an act of self or other), or "How does all this leave you feeling about yourself?" (seeking an introjective state).

   4. *Observing the interview process.* The clinical interview is not simply an intellectual fact-finding mission, it is also a sample of the patient's behavior. In addition to the interpersonal content of the patient's story, there is also the important dimension of *how* the story is told, giving the clinician another potential source of information for ICF. Does the patient present her or his "story" in a very dramatic and pressured fashion, extremely deferentially (as if apologizing for asking for help), or perhaps cautiously (always gauging the interviewer's response before going on)? How does the observed style fit with the narrative interpersonal information being obtained?

   An important related source of information is the interviewer's personal reactions to the patient's process or style. It is likely that in more cases than not the interviewer's reaction to the patient is similar to that of others in the patient's environment, and as such becomes more information for ICF. Does the interviewer feel a pull to rescue the patient? Does he or she feel irritated (and if so why)? Does the interviewer feel really disconnected with the patient, as if they are each talking past the other? Does the patient make the interviewer feel incompetent and defensive? It is important that the interviewer make brief ongoing notes on his or her own reactions for further reference.

5. *Maintaining an optimal stance.* I have found that as a general strategy it is better to start with a relatively nondirective approach, letting the patient tell his or her story with relatively little interruption. Some minimal direction may be important to keep the interview interpersonally focused (such as "Tell me about your parents and how you got along with them when you were younger," or "Could you tell me something about the people who are most important to you now?" This less directive approach allows the clinician to observe more of the natural process or behavior of the client. It also permits the clinician to recognize *omissions* in a patient's interpersonal narratives, which may indicate "blind spots" that will become important for therapeutic work. After a period of relative nondirectiveness, it may be necessary for the clinician to become more structured by asking follow-up questions needed to complete the cyclic patterns.

Semistructured Interview Format

There are no required interview formats for ICF. The following sequence is designed to provide examples of the types of questions that will facilitate the ICF interview:

1. If several problems are spontaneously mentioned, ask the patient to select a "main problem" to look at more closely, and ask why it was chosen.
2. If the patient does not spontaneously mention interpersonal aspects of the problem, and remains focused on such things as affect (i.e., depression, anxiety, anger, etc.) search for the interpersonal context of the problem. For example, the interviewer might say, "How does your depression affect others? Who are they? How do their actions affect your depression? How do you act with others when you are depressed? How is this different from when you are not depressed? What do other people think of your problem? What do they do or say to you?"
3. If the patient has marked difficulties shifting to an interpersonal focus, get very directive and concrete (testing the patient's capacity to represent and describe in this domain), asking questions such as "Tell me about a relationship in which you felt loved or accepted," "Tell me about times you feel in charge," or "Tell me about a relationship that hurt you and why."

4. Keep in mind the basic CMP categories (Acts of Self, Acts of Others, etc.), perhaps even having a blank template into which brief notes can be made in each category. By gently guiding the patient's narrative, help them begin to tell stories in the form of "What do you do? How do you expect (wish, fear) that they might react? How do they respond? How do you feel about (or treat) yourself afterwards? When you feel that way, what do you do then?" The key is to always emphasize *concrete interpersonal actions and reactions*—what people *do*.

5. If the patient is able to articulate a reasonably clear pattern to serve as the basis for formulation, the interviewer might then go on, keeping the SASB circumplex in mind, to explore how each of the following might relate to the presenting problem cycle: anger/assertiveness, intimacy/affection sexuality, passivity/dependence, autonomy, tolerance of separation, and dominance/control/authority.

6. Inquire about the patient's parents, siblings, and any other significant early caretakers or relationships, including the nature of those relationships in the past and present. Be particularly sensitive to ongoing efforts to please, win the love and acceptance of, avoid the censure of, or be like these important early figures. What are the "conditions of worth" according to these significant others?

7. The interviewer should conclude by stating, insofar as possible, his or her understanding of the sequence of the chosen problem pattern (i.e., articulate the CMP or SASB–CMP sequence) to give the patient a chance to confirm or provide corrective feedback. Tentative hypotheses about the links between this pattern and descriptions of significant caretakers and developmental history might also be made.

8. Finally, solicit information about how the interview has been for the patient. Did he or she feel interpersonally comfortable or not, and why? How did it feel to talk about these things? What are the fantasies about what the interviewer thinks of the patient or his or her problems?

A Potential Problem in the Interview

In ICF, problems are crafted in interpersonal terms. The definition of a problem, however, may be less straightforward than it seems, and patients often do not present us with a list of problems per se—we must help construct and define them. A problem is *not* necessarily a complaint or a symptom, the typical types of information first presented in a clinical interview. Rather, *a problem is a discrepancy between a perceived and a desired state of affairs.* For example, the statement "I am depressed" is a symptom, while "I want to be more active playing with my children, but I just seem to sit there all day and do nothing" is a problem.

Defining problems is particularly germane to ICF. By its very nature, ICF is most applicable to individuals presenting with Axis II personality disorders, or Axis I symptom states that have clear interpersonal components. Many people with chronic interpersonal difficulties have problems that affect *others,* secondarily creating problems in their own lives. However, they often see nothing problematic with their own behavior. Examples might include the grandiose behavior of the narcissist, the attention seeking and shallow emotionality of the histrionic, the rigid perfectionism of the obsessive–compulsive, or the pervasive suspicion of the paranoid. With these patients it may be necessary to define problems initially in terms of discrepancies between the actual and desired behaviors of others, not the self. In these cases it is important to elicit a description of the specific behaviors of *others* that the patient finds problematic so that the IFC may help clarify how the patient evokes these behaviors in others, helping to create his or her own problems.

The Use of Self-Report Measures for the Interpersonal Case Formulation

Any number of potentially relevant self-report measures exist. For example, Horowitz's Inventory of Interpersonal Problems (IIP; L. M. Horowitz, Rosenberg, Baer, Ureno, & Villasenor, 1988) and the Interpersonal Check List (ICL; LaForge & Suczek, 1955) provide interpersonal information that can be viewed in circumplex form. It may even be possible to construct a hypothetical ICF solely from self-report data. There are three main ways to use self-report data: (a) as the only source of data for ICF (while this may be the least satisfactory method in many ways, it does also provide for maximum reliability or standardization across clinicians or research groups); (b) as an additional source of data to be considered after the interview (to expand upon, confirm, or contradict the interview-based interpersonal information); or (c) as a guide to the interview itself, pointing out promising avenues of exploration (when the self-reports are administered before the interview and available to the interviewing clinician).

There are currently five self-report instruments based on SASB, with all items written to correspond to specific interpersonal and/or intrapsychic cluster codes. Two of these, the Intrex battery (Benjamin, 1995) described earlier and the Wisconsin Personality Inventory (WISPI; Klein et al., 1993), a measure of Axis II personality disorders, are already well normed and widely used. Three remaining instruments, the SASB–Interpersonal Locus of Control Scale (SILCS; Henry & Cheuvront, 1995; Schacht & Henry, 1984), the Early Experiences Questionnaire (EEQ; Henry, 1996b), and the Attitudes about Significant Relationships (ASR; Henry, 1996b) have been developed and are currently undergoing psychometric validation procedures (see Henry, 1996a, for complete descriptions of these three new instruments). The principles for using these instruments mirror the procedures found in the following subsections that describe the construction of an ICF from interview data. The difference is that instead of extracting and then applying SASB codes to transcript passages, the clinician or researcher would use data that was already directly in the form of SASB coded items. For an example of how to use Intrex scores to directly construct an ICF, see Henry (1996a).

Steps in Constructing the Interpersonal Formulation

Establishing the Level of Complexity

As I have previously discussed, ICF as a form of psychodynamic formulation may integrate three levels of understanding—concrete problems, problem patterns, and underlying core ordering processes. Starting with some simple pattern as a minimum base, it is possible to construct an ICF at varying levels of complexity based on these three general categories. The level chosen may be predetermined for clinical or empirical reasons, or may be emergent based on the amount of available information for any given case. The following is a general guide to possible levels of complexity:

Level 1. The most basic formulation would list specific interpersonal and introjective behaviors, in sequence, based on the four-category CMP model.

Level 2. A more differentiated but still basic formulation of the problem pattern per se would employ the more differentiated SASB–CMP categories, which incorporate the concept of interpersonal focus.

Level 3. The next step up is to form a *cyclic hypothesis* explaining how the pattern is maintained in the present. The simplest form of this hypothesis involves applying only transactional principles—complementarity and introjection.

Level 4. A more complete cyclic hypothesis would integrate the underlying motivational elements. That is, how do the patient's perceptions and expectancies of others interact with central wishes and fears to result in manifest interpersonal behavior?

Level 5. Forming a hypothesis about the historical or developmental etiology of the problem pattern adds still more richness to the formulation. While the cyclic hypothesis involves transactional behavioral principles, the *etiological hypothesis* is based on specifying how the observed behaviors of the patient may be accounted for via the three copy processes—identification, internalization, and early introjection.

Level 6. A final level of complexity (which will not be discussed in depth in this chapter) would involve the complete integration of the cyclic and etiological hypotheses with a number of other phenomena or "maintaining conditions" such as prototypic defense mechanisms, interpersonal locus of control, typical power tactics, archaic needs to please the internalized images of significant figures (see Benjamin, 1993a), perceived conditions of worth, and perhaps even variables related to biological temperament.

Extracting, Categorizing, and Summarizing Interpersonal Information

For the clinician who does not have the luxury of typed transcripts, audiotapes, or videotapes, it is quite possible to construct an ICF from interview notes alone. It is helpful if the notes have been organized into the CMP categories, but this is not essential as a precondition. As a general rule, the more information the better. Notes might add information about a therapist's countertransference reactions, transcripts permit verbatim extraction of patients' interpersonally relevant statements, and videotape will enhance the ability to use the process of the interview as a source of information. However, it is quite possible to arrive at an ICF from transcripts alone, and it is this procedure I will discuss here.[3]

To learn the basics of SASB-based ICF, I recommend initially using a "four-pass" approach. The first step is for the rater(s) to read the transcript, highlighting or underlining every statement that contains an interpersonal transaction, introjective statement, or a patient's feelings about an interpersonal relationship. The next step is to place each of these statements into one of the four basic CMP categories. The material placed into these categories should at this step be all inclusive; that is, *all* interpersonal/introjective content should be recorded. It may have to be paraphrased a bit at times to make the interpersonal meaning clear—though a low level of inference should be maintained. The third step is to further differentiate the categorization of these statements into the SASB–CMP structure of *Interpersonal Acts* (patient acts on others, patient reacts to others, others act on patient, others react to patient), *Introjective Acts* (by patient or others), and *Expectancies: Predictions, Wishes, and Fears* (predictions/expectancies regarding others, predictions/expectancies regarding the self, interpersonal/introjective wishes, interpersonal/introjective fears). Some summarization occurs at this stage, when one is translating from the raw statements as organized by the four basic CMP categories into the SASB–CMP structure. That is, raw statements that are very similar and involve the same interpersonal process with the same person may be listed only once (perhaps in paraphrased, summary form). Finally, where applicable, interpersonal information stemming from the interview process itself is added to the appropriate categories.

The Application of SASB Codes

At this point, the raters' notes should contain a list of summary statements each nested under the proper SASB–CMP category. The next step is to assign a SASB surface and cluster code to each statement. For instance, the information "Patient's husband constantly criticizes her" would be an act of other toward the patient and receive the code 1-6 (active blame). The SASB codes should be listed in column form beside each statement.

Final Data Summary

The exact procedures at this stage may differ depending upon whether a single or multiple patterns are to be formulated. Looking at the SASB codes listed by each category will often result in a clear-cut preponderance of a single code. If the summary in the preceding step has been done correctly, these codes will represent the occurrence of identical (or very similar) interpersonal processes across a number of different relationships and contexts (as opposed to simply reflecting a series of similar complaints about the same person). In this step, one, two, or at most three SASB codes are selected to represent each category based on their frequency (i.e., prototypicality).[4] Clinical judgment is obviously called for at this point, and the single versus multiple pattern decision will also play a role.

Placing Codes into the Interpersonal Model
of Cyclic Psychopathology

Figure 9.2 represents a graphic depiction of the processes contained in the cyclic and etiological hypotheses. In other words, it is an organized flowchart combining a patient's history, the three copy processes, and the ongoing mechanisms of complementarity and introjection. The different types of arrows differentiate among hypothesized copy processes (dashed arrows), in-

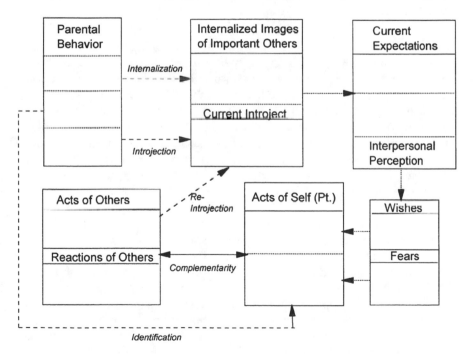

FIGURE 9.2. Interpersonal model of cyclic psychopathology.

ternalized cognitive operations (dotted arrows), and interpersonal transactions (solid arrows). In short, the chart traces the history of contemporary behavior back to its roots in early experience and suggests how problem cycles are maintained intrapsychically (rigid expectancies, wishes, and fears), maintained behaviorally (interpersonal complementarity), or changed via re-introjection (introjecting current more ameliorative interpersonal process directed by others toward the self). The summary SASB codes generated in the previous step are now placed into their appropriate places in this graphic template.

Using the Cyclic Model to Generate Causal Hypotheses

The graphic depiction of the central interpersonal codes in proper sequential and theoretical relationship to one another is used to generate one or more causal hypotheses. These causal hypotheses incorporate the four general components of ICF discussed earlier. That is, the formulation incorporates (1) the specific sequence of interpersonal and introjective behaviors, (2) how the three copy processes link the developmental history and these problem behaviors, (3) the process of how the contemporary actions and reactions of the patient and others work to maintain the problem, and (4) the underlying motivations for the pattern (wishes and fears designed to achieve normative interpersonal goals).

Producing a Final Case Narrative

Writing a final case narrative is simply a matter of stating the causal hypotheses in a clear and organized way. If two or more patterns have been developed, they should be presented as separate narrative sequences, with the context for each pattern clearly stated. For example, "With older female friends, Ms. X tends to . . ."; "However, when she is around men her own age who appear interested in her romantically, she feels. . . ." If the patterns are linked in any way, for instance if one sequence tends to provoke another, this too should be mentioned in the final narrative. The narrative typically is presented in natural, non-jargon-laden language, but it is possible to also parenthetically insert SASB codes and/or dimensions for the purpose of training, research, greater clarity, etc. For example, "Mr. Y initially trusts others (cluster 2-4, friendly moderate submission) and feels they will like him (cluster 1-3/2-3, active/reactive love). However, the minute someone else is preoccupied with his or her own thoughts (cluster 2-1, neutral differentiation), he expects he is about to be abandoned (cluster 1-8, active hostile differentiation) and withdraws in a huff himself (cluster 2-8, reactive separation). After he has done this several times, people do indeed begin to neglect and ignore him (cluster 1-8) and Mr. Y berates himself (cluster 3-6, hostile self-control or self-blame) for once again having been stupid enough to believe anyone would ever take care of him (cluster 1-4, active friendly control or nurturance)."

APPLICATION TO
PSYCHOTHERAPY TECHNIQUE

Therapeutic Targets

The therapist may choose to confront any of the formulation elements, depending on what understanding or new experiences the patient appears to need most at the time. As an example, the therapist may focus on the internalized image of a parent, on rigid interpersonal expectations, or on central fears. Figure 9.2 provides an organizing scheme to help the therapist think about the different parts of the problem cycle. Rather than attempt to focus on all of these elements simultaneously, the therapist more typically focuses on one or two links in the formulation, such as how the internalization of a parent has led to specific, rigid expectancies of others. In general, the therapist is usually confronting patterns that lead to unhealthy overenmeshment or a maladaptive degree of separateness or differentiation.

Therapeutic Techniques

Employing ICF as a guide for therapeutic interventions implies an acceptance of some basic underlying principles, such as the importance of early social learning, and mechanisms, such as identification, introjection, and complementarity. However, there are many possible theoretical frameworks within which to conceptualize the effects of early social learning, and the mechanisms that have been proposed to sustain problematic patterns of interpersonal behavior and its sequelae. Therapeutic approaches that are particularly well suited for ICF include TLDP (Strupp & Binder, 1984), brief SASB-directed reconstructive learning therapy (Benjamin, 1993b), and my own (Henry & Strupp, 1994) proposed reformulation of Orlinsky and Howard's (1986) generic process model. Other approaches for which ICF can be useful include behavioral, cognitive-behavioral, experiential, and family systems therapies. In each of these approaches, the therapist may choose to emphasize different parts of the ICF formulation (e.g., surface behaviors, cognitions, wishes and fears, reinforcement, secondary gain.) For example, a behavioral therapist might directly teach new behaviors that should theoretically change the complementary reactions of others. The cognitive therapist might use collaborative empiricism and homework assignments to attack core expectancies and perceptions that drive a patient's typical reaction to others. The experiential therapist might deliberately encourage in-session affect arousal to access "hot cognitions" such as previously unrecognized core interpersonal wishes and fears. The family systems therapist might choose to alter actions by others toward the patient, resulting in a chance for direct reintrojection.

ICF combines a variety of elements including problematic interpersonal *behaviors, cognitions* in the form of prototypic expectancies and perceptions of others, and *experiential affects* about central wishes and fears that form a motivational base. From the standpoint of ICF it is ultimately the *pattern* that is the problem: expectancies, perceptions, actions, and reactions of self and others, the resulting introjective acts, and dysphoric emotions are all connected. The outcome of *any* successful therapy, whether psychodynamic/interpersonal or not, likely involves changes in observable behavior (SASB surfaces 1 and 2) and changes in self-concept (such as an increased sense of self-efficacy) and self-treatment (SASB surface 3). Theoretically, to intervene at any point in the cycle should cause changes in other parts of the cycle, for example, through changed patterns of complementarity, re-introjection of more ameliorative behaviors, changed cognitive expectancies, or abandonment of archaic wishes and fears. I propose that *all* effective therapies combine some blend of common processes that can be measured and understood through the framework of the SASB circumplex, the related interpersonal theory of behavior, and the use of ICF to structure these elements.

It is also important to emphasize that ICF does not dictate specific therapeutic *techniques*, and does not impose any particular sequence of issues to be addressed. Once an ICF is constructed, specific therapeutic techniques can be chosen to fit a given patient's circumstances, strengths, and weaknesses, as well as to fit the therapist's preferred manner of intervention. In fact, one potential strength of ICF is that it may serve as a common formulation scheme applicable to many types of intervention. *This approach of disengaging formulation from technique differs dramatically from the traditional status quo, in which case formulation and intervention are viewed as theoretically bound together.* The exciting potential of ICF is that while it provides a tight theoretical link between formulation and intervention in one sense, it does not *limit* the range of possible interventions and may thus serve as one possible foundation for the often discussed but elusive drive toward integrative therapy.

CASE EXAMPLE

The following case example is based on the first 20–30 minutes of an interview specifically conducted for the purposes of ICF by a novice to the approach (though not a novice as a clinician).[5] The patient was a single 37-year-old female, diagnosed with schizophrenia, who had more than a 10-year history of inpatient and outpatient care. At the time of the interview she was on an inpatient unit due to psychotic symptoms (recurrent hallucinations),[6] but she had been stabilized on neuroleptic medication.

Initial Extraction and Categorization of Interpersonal Information

In this first section I will include several verbatim transcript passages (clinician statements are denoted by "C," with "P" indicating patient comments). The interpersonal information that was extracted is printed in italics, followed by a number that corresponds to the summary statements contained in Table 9.2, below, in the next subsection (some irrelevant information has been deleted from the transcript).

Transcript Passages

C: Which friends do you have, who do you see . . . ?

P: . . . I have been moving so much I have not been able to keep contact . . .

C: You have been moving a lot?

P: Yes, and *people have withdrawn because I went ill* (1)

P: . . . I live alone now [in an apartment-type halfway house]

C: . . . do you have any contact with the others [there]?

P: . . . not very much, *most of them stick to themselves* (2)

C: . . . I see, what about you?

P: . . . *I somewhat miss being more together with somebody you see* (3)

C: . . . So you would like it if you all saw each other more?

P: . . . Yes, it is also unlucky because it is all men.

C: . . . It is more difficult for you when it is only men?

P: . . . Yes, *when you are the only woman, you can't exchange femininities together.* (4).

P: . . . *I have not found any girls to talk with in a really good way. I have found some here* [in the hospital], *but it does not last . . . the friendship doesn't last. You can sit here and say to each other "Yes, we will see each other when we get out" and such, then you call maybe once, and then it stops . . . you can't count on that kind of friendship that you make inside here . . .* (5) *everybody suddenly has something to do or take care of* (6) . . .

C: . . . But it sounds as if you have tried to get some girlfriends.

P: . . . *Yes I have* (7). *Then they promise to call and then they don't do it* (8). *. . . I always ask them to call me, because I want to give them a chance to say, "Well this was it," you see* (9).

C: . . . Do you think that it is because they don't want to see you after all that they don't call?

P: . . . *Yes* (10). *. . . . or then they call me and then you are feeling too bad* [ill] *to be able to start any kind of friendship you see* (11)

C: . . . but you in fact had a friendship with a man

P: . . . that is *because he was much older than me, and there is no danger really* (12)

C: . . . so this danger, of what kind is that?

P: . . . *That is that they want something sexually from me, you see* (13)

C: . . . mmm . . . so that is what keeps you away?

P: . . . *Yes, I am tired of it . . . that is not what I'm looking for* (14)

C: . . . so you have had bad experiences with that?

P: . . . yes, . . . *some of my own age . . . I don't want to experience that* (15) . . . *also the way men talk to each other . . . I am submitted to this . . . that is irritating* (16) . . . the way they talk about women and the way they behave you see. *Then it is, "Oh mom, come here," you see* . . .

C: . . . They either want something sexually from you, or you have to be a mother to them.

P: . . . *Yes* (17). . . . *I would rather be alone* (18)

Examples of Categorized, Summarized Transcript-Derived Statements

In this stage, the verbatim patient statements are categorized into the four basic CMP categories. No statements are omitted, but some generalization of the language may occur. For example, the exact statement "I somewhat miss being more together with somebody you see" might become "Misses being with other people." A complete list of the summarized and categorized transcript passages quoted above is displayed in Table 9.2.

Completed, SASB-Coded Statements in Final SASB–CMP Form

As noted earlier, another level of summarization and further differentiation is now applied to the type of information contained in Table 9.2. Similar interpersonal processes involving the same person or context are listed only once, and salient process data from the interview itself may be included. Then, each statement is given a SASB surface–cluster code (or complex code). The completed list for this case is found in Table 9.3.

Summarized Central SASB Codes

This section lists the codes extracted from Table 9.3 that were deemed to be the most central, reoccurring aspects of the patient's interpersonal pattern. They have also been inserted into their appropriate categories in Figure 9.3.

Wishes: The patient wants more friends (1-3 from others), nurturance (1-4 from others), and wishes she could trust others more easily (2-4 from self).

TABLE 9.2. Examples of Interpersonal Information Placed into Basic Four-Category CMP Format

Acts of Self: Actions by self toward others and reactions to others (including thoughts, feelings, and behaviors of an interpersonal nature)

   3. Misses being with other people
   4. Misses female companions who can talk about feminine things[a]
   7. Tries to befriend females
   9. Asks others to call her
 11. Often can't respond to overtures of friendship from others, because when they call she is "too ill"
 14. Not interested in a sexual relationship
 16. Irritated by the way men talk to each other in her presence
 18. Prefers to be alone rather than to provide sex or mothering to men her age

Expectations of Others: How the patient imagines others will act toward or react to him or her in response to some interpersonal behavior (act of self by the patient)

   4. Men can't or won't talk about "feminine things"
   5. Hospital friendships won't last; you can't count on female friends from hospital to follow through with plans to call
   6. Hospital friends will be too busy with their own lives after discharge to call
 10. Others don't call because they don't really want to see her
 12. Older men are safe because they don't want sex
 13. Young men are only interested in having sex
 17. Men her age either want sex or to be mothered

Acts of Others: Actual observed or reported interpersonal behaviors of others in relationship to the patient

   1. Others withdraw because she is mentally ill
   2. Other people don't interact with her, they stick to themselves
   8. Others promise to call but don't
 15. Men her own age approach her for sex

Introject: Acts of Self Toward the Self

   9. Tries to protect self by asking others to call her [instead of calling them] to ensure that only people who are truly interested will contact her.

---

[a]It is possible to paraphrase a statement in different ways, placing it in several different categories. In this case, this statement is also placed under "Expectations of Others." Care should be taken, however to avoid undue levels of inference. Stay very close to the clinical material.

   Fears: The patient seems to primarily fear disaffiliative separation or autonomy. That is, she fears others will ignore her needs and withdraw from her (1-8 and 2-8 from others). Consistent with this, she fears introjective autonomy (3-1), which may lead to a variety of undesired outcomes such as the inability to adequately care for herself (i.e., no 3-4 or 3-5) or her own attack on others (1-6). She also seems to secondarily fear hostile control and ignoring of her needs from men her own age (typically a complex 1-6/1-8).

   Acts of Self: She describes her actions toward others as a benign mixture of pure approach and nurturance (1-3 and 1-4). Her reactions to others, however, are almost exclusively self-focused, disaffiliative separation or hostile autonomy taking (2-1 and 2-8). The only exceptions to this pattern seem to

TABLE 9.3. Final Summary Information for ICF in SASB–CMP Format

Formulation category	Formulation component inferred	SASB cluster code	Source
	Interpersonal Acts		
Acts of Self: Patient acts toward others	Invites John (older male friend) for visits	1-3	*
	Asks girlfriends (other patients) to call her after discharge	1-4	9, 7
Acts of Self: Patient reacts to others	Avoids men her own age because of sexual pressure	2-8	13, 14, 18, *
	Uses humor to avoid showing her feelings	2-8	*
	Remains mostly alone; is distant with others	2-1	*
	Declines social invitations when [psychiatrically] ill	2-1	11
	Speaks impulsively	2-1	*
	Feels shared togetherness and support from John	2-3 and 2-4	*
	At times, submits and exposes herself to men she finds irritating just for contact	2-6	16,*
Acts of Others: Others act toward patient	Others can often tell when she feels bad and approach her so she can talk	1-2	*
	Parents and John sometimes phone asking to visit	1-3	*
	John helps her with her poetry and in understanding her medication	1-4	*
	"Grown-ups" help her by "sorting things out" for her	1-4	*
	Nurses help her when she asks; they don't reject her	1-4	*
	Feels her mother rejects her and pushes her away	1-7 and 1-8	*
	Others promise to call but don't	1-8	8
Acts of Others: Others react to patient	Mother never took time for patient as a child or now—too busy with her own life	2-8	*
	People withdraw because she is mentally ill	2-8	1
	Others don't call when invited to	2-8	8,*
	Others where she lives stick to themselves	2-1	2
	Others are too busy for her	2-1	*
	John doesn't visit when he is "ill"	2-1	*
	Introjective Acts		
By Patient	Recognizes when she is ill and admits herself to the hospital	3-4	*
	Speaks to herself; tries to analyze her own reactions because she knows she sometimes confuses perceptions of others with expectations her parents had of her	3-4	
	Tells herself she needs contact with others, so denies feminine identity to spend some time with men (complex introject—denies self to nurture self)	3-4/3-8 complex	*
	Takes care of herself; lets herself "breathe" by being her spontaneous self	3-4/3-1 complex	*

(continued)

TABLE 9.3. (*continued*)

Formulation category	Formulation component inferred	SASB cluster code	Source
	Struggles hard with herself to overcome her fears of rejection and ask for what she needs from nurses (3-5 in order to 2-4)	3-5	*
	Claims she doesn't know what she needs	3-8	*
By Others	None inferred		

Expectancies: Predictions, Wishes, and Fears

Predictions about Others	Others won't call because they don't want to see her	2-8	10,*
	Hospital friend will be too busy with their own lives to see her after discharge	2-1	5,6
	Others can't be her friends because of her mental illness or theirs	2-1	11,*
	Nurses won't have time for her if she needs something	2-1 or 2-8	*
	Others will reject her	1-7	*
	Men her age want sex or to be mothered[a]	1-8	13,15, 17
	Older men are safe because they don't want sex	No 1-6 or 1-8	12
Predictions about Self	Will sometimes impulsively say what is on her mind	2-1	*
	Won't be able to talk personally with other patients	No 2-2	*
	She will not be able to directly state her needs without great struggle because she finds it hard to trust others	No 2-4	*
Wishes	Others will call her, check up on her	1-3 and 1-4	*
	Wants female friends	1-3 and 2-3	4,*
	Wants more friendly contact with people in general	1-3 and 2-3	3
	Wishes she could more easily talk to and trust "grown-ups" for help	2-4	*
Fears	Others will have no time for her if she seeks contact	1-8	5, 6
	Men just want sex	1-8	13
	Men will pressure her for sex, which is "dangerous"	1-6 or 1-3/1-6	13,17,*
	If she spontaneously says what is on her mind, she will hurt a close male friend	2-1/1-6 complex	*
	If she can't express herself freely, she won't be able to handle her problems	No 2-1 and 3-1 leads to no 3-4 and 3-5	*

Note. An asterisk (*) indicates that the information needed for the statement and the SASB code is contained in parts of the transcript that were omitted due to space limitations.
[a]The acts of sex and mothering would be coded as men's desires for 1-3 and 1-4. However, since she seems to make it clear she does not desire to do either, their continued insistence becomes a 1-8 because it ignores and neglects her true needs and stated desires.

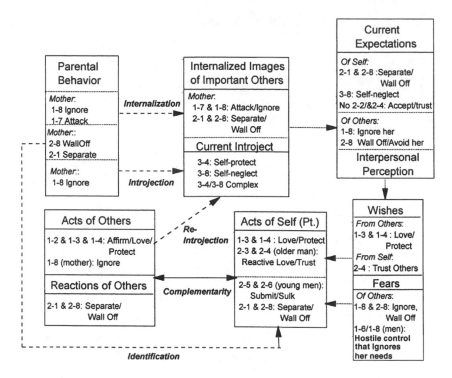

FIGURE 9.3. SASB interpersonal case formulation. Dashed arrows denote copy processes; dotted arrows denote internal cognitive processes; solid arrows denote transactional interpersonal processes.

be her capacity for shared "togetherness and support" (2-3 and 2-4) with one older man, and occasional hostile submission (2-6) to men her own age, just for the sake of some interpersonal contact she thinks she needs (3-4).

Expectations of Others. Again, her expectations of others are quite uniform and fall in the SASB space of hostile differentiation (1-8 and 2-8). She expect that others will ignore her, abandon her, and withdraw from her either because she is mentally ill, they don't like her, they have their own lives that don't leave time for her, or that's just the way they are (in the case of most men).

Expectation of Self. Her self-expectations are by and large complementary with her expectations of others—she expects to withdraw not only from others (2-8) but also from herself at times (3-8). What she does not expect is equally important. She states directly that she does not expect to be able to talk directly with others about herself (2-2) or trust others (2-4).

Acts of Others. While the patient expects *active* abandonment by others (1-8), the bulk of what she describes actually involve others understanding when she needs to talk (1-2), approaching her for visits (1-3) and helping her (1-4). She does feel actively rejected by her mother (1-8). It is in her descriptions of others' *reactions* to her that we see the exclusive emphasis on dis-afilliative separation by others (2-1 and 2-8).

Introject: The patient's introjective statements show a struggle between self-nurturance and self-control (3-4 and 3-5), on the one hand, versus self-abandonment (3-8), on the other. Several introjective behaviors are a complex combination of both (3-4/3-8). The number of attempts at self-protection and enhancement, however, should not go underestimated clinically as they seem to be predominant (suggesting the presence of benign sources of intro-jection either historically or currently, or both).

Final Narrative Summary

This is a patient who wishes she could trust others to provide the love and protection she desperately wants. However, she is unable to reach these goals. She expects others will abandon and separate from her because she (or at times they) are mentally ill or others will simply be too involved in their own lives to make time for her. Additionally, she expects that younger men will try to control her with hostility by sexualizing the relationship in a way that ignores her true desires. At times she submits to being around men who ignore her interests simply to have some human contact she feels she needs. She has been able to establish at least one positive relationship with an older man who is "safe" because he is not interested in sex. Her expectations that others will actively abandon her seem to be true only for her mother (at the present time that is even questionable). Despite her expectancies, she describes others' actions toward her as basically benign—a combination of attachment group behaviors of acceptance, approach, and nurturance. However, she does describe others as reacting to her with neutral or hostile separation.

On the basis of what is known from this brief interview, we can speculate about the dynamics that caused and perpetuate her difficulties. Her mother appears to have acted toward her with hostile differentiation (abandonment) and neutral to hostile reactive separation. The internalization of these experi-ences likely resulted in her expectancies and fears that others will do the same toward her, as well as accounting for the self-abandoning portion of her ac-tions toward herself via introjection. The patient's own tendency to separate and wall off from others could be accounted for via both identification with the mother as well as being the complement of the abandonment she expects from others. Her most fixed wish seems to be for friendly enmeshment—se-quences of trust and protection—the opposite of what she experienced as a child.

In terms of her interpersonal patterns, there seems to be both a major negative pattern and a minor but positive one. Her expectation that others will abandon her and separate from her (likely based on early treatment by her mother) causes her to act and react in complementary ways. In other words, her expectation of active abandonment leads her to be aloof and separate from others, who may perceive her as ignoring them, so they separate via complementarity which does seem to pull for the abandonment–separation she fears. This entrenches her tendency to separate as well as reinforcing the self-abandoning part of her introject.

TRAINING

There are no set procedures or protocol for ICF training at this time. Much depends on an individual's preexisting knowledge and experience. In order to construct an ICF, one must have a basic working knowledge of SASB, the copy and maintenance principles discussed, and a general grasp of the model of psychopathology based on the normative drives of bonding (enmeshment) and exploration (differentiation). If the Intrex battery is used as part of the ICF procedure, a working familiarity with the interpretation of computer-scored Intrex indices is required. Finally, skill is required to conduct a thorough interpersonally based interview that helps reveal specific transactional patterns in behavioral terms and sheds light on the patient's internalized object images and expectations, wishes, and fears related to important others. For someone who is adept at interpersonally based interviewing and already familiar with the SASB system, learning ICF is a fairly simple matter of applying these skills to the organization of information and the application of the process principles. For novices, however, training might involve teaching those skills necessary to conduct an ICF interview, the ability to identify and extract interpersonal material for coding, and the skills necessary to construct the ICF from the raw data.

For beginners, training should always begin with training in the SASB system itself. The first step is to understand the meaning of the underlying axes (affiliation and interdependence) and surface structure (interpersonal/intrapsychic focus). Next, the trainee should become at least moderately proficient at using SASB to code interpersonal process and content. Coding manuals and other instructional materials for SASB as well as the Intrex battery are available from the Department of Psychology, University of Utah, Salt Lake City. Additionally, Benjamin's (1993) book on the interpersonal diagnosis and treatment of Axis II disorders is an excellent general source for acquainting trainees more completely with how various clinical phenomena "translate" into SASB (not to mention being a treasure trove of rare clinical insight and wisdom that may be applied therapeutically after deriving an ICF). Finally, the original sources that describe the interpersonal model of psychopathology (Henry, 1994; Benjamin, 1993b), the interpersonal process model of therapy (Henry & Strupp, 1994), the SASB–CMP (Schacht & Henry, 1995), and the integrated SASB-based research program of the present author (Henry, 1996a) may be used for training.

Before training is complete, two or more trainees should be able to demonstrate acceptable interrater reliability. Because an ICF may be constructed at differing levels of complexity, there is no automatic procedure for demonstrating reliability. I suggest that reliability should be achieved at the final level used (four-category CMP, SASB–CMP, etc.), and calculated with a weighted kappa for SASB cluster assignment. This procedure is similar to that found in the SASB coder training manual for judging the interrater reliability of coders. For the purpose of training, it may also be useful to initially calculate reliability (either formally or informally) for earlier steps in the ICF generation process (such as the reliability of extracting initial interpersonal information from transcripts) if it seems necessary.

RESEARCH SUPPORT FOR THE APPROACH

To date, there have been no reliability studies of the entire ICF procedure per se. However, there are sufficient data on most of the specific steps to be able to reasonably infer the probable reliability of ICF, although ultimately formal reliability testing should and will be performed. It is my experience that with minimal exposure to SASB, raters are able to extract the interpersonally relevant passages to be coded with high reliability. Similarly, the categorization of the extracted material into the four basic CMP categories is highly reliable with minimal or even no training.[7] Informal experience suggests that differentiating the general interpersonal categories of acts of self and others into the more refined SASB–CMP format, which subdivides this general information on the basis of focus, is more difficult. To construct an ICF at this level of complexity requires an adequate familiarity with the concept of interpersonal focus, and it may be wise to calculate reliability at this step during training. Applying SASB cluster codes to the categorized material is identical to SASB content coding for which good levels of reliability have been consistently demonstrated, even with raters who are not clinically trained (weighted kappas of .70 and above are common). Additionally, the psychometric properties, reliability, and validity of the Intrex battery have been formally demonstrated with these self-report data (see the *Intrex User's Manual* by Benjamin, 1995, for details). ICF as presented in this chapter is based on time-tested SASB-based procedures, but the actual formalized steps, including the use of the graphic process template, are relatively new. Therefore, I feel that it is important to formally demonstrate that agreement can be reached on the central codes to be placed into the template, as well as demonstrating the reliability of the final written case formulation. The latter could be accomplished simply by SASB coding the content of the formulation and judging interrater reliability with a weighted kappa based on cluster assignment for each of the formulation categories (i.e. acts of self, wishes, expectations, etc.).

I have reported data on the use of the Intrex-derived CMP as a change measure following short-term (approximately 25 sessions) psychodynamic therapy (Henry, 1990). Three primary conclusions emerged based on a sample of 80 patients: (a) the Intrex-derived CMP is a sensitive measure of change over relatively brief periods (4–6 months); (b) changes appear to follow a fairly predictable and theoretically consistent pattern or sequence (at least at the level of group data)—the introject appears to change first, followed by reactions of the patient, and finally changes in the actions of significant others (which often appear only at 1-year follow-up); and (c) changes observed in the "best state" appear more enduring than changes in the "worst state," although the ratings of worst state do not typically return to pretherapy levels.

CONCLUSIONS

The SASB-based procedures for ICF just outlined have enormous potential. First, SASB permits operational, standardized measurement of many important psychodynamic, interpersonal, and object relational constructs that have previously been resistant to traditional empirical, replicable study. Unlike many previous attempts to operationally measure dynamic constructs, SASB translates clinical phenomena in a manner that maintains the richness and complexity of human experience without unduly sacrificing the empirical, psychometric rigor that permits cumulative knowledge across different studies and research groups. Secondly, SASB enjoys a unique strength as a system in that a patient's problems, the etiology of these problems, the treatment processes, and the clinical outcomes may all be measured within the same metric (see Henry, 1996a). Finally, the ICF procedures I have outlined are based on actual observed and reported behavioral patterns and cognitive expectancies that are accessible. While a behavior therapist or a cognitive therapist may find ideas such as the three copy processes, wishes and fears, and the desire to please internalized images of important others as unnecessary baggage, I do not believe that these concepts are actually antithetical to their theories. In fact, these constructs at the level of interpersonal transaction are quite easy to construe in the traditional language of reinforcement contingencies and cognitive distortions. In short, ICF may provide a valuable case formulation method for cross-theoretical integrative research, particularly since ICF does not dictate specific therapeutic techniques. Indeed, it is quite easy to imagine a number of behavioral, cognitive, experiential, and psychodynamic interventions that might help change the problematic patterns we are charged with ameliorating. As therapists and researchers it is primarily interpersonal phenomena with which we deal. A common language and procedure for at least framing these problems will at last give us the basic conditions for scientific progress—a shared phenomenon to study from all of our different perspectives.

NOTES

1. This principle helps provide a theoretical basis for understanding the curative workings of the therapeutic alliance in all therapies (for a complete explanation of these principles, see Henry and Strupp, 1994).

2. The language describing this category in the original CMP model (Strupp and Binder, 1984) used the term "Reactions of Others" in a general sense. In the SASB–CMP reformulation, "Reactions" are found only on surface 2, and this category is differentiated into the separate distinctions—Acts and Reactions of Others.

3. A transcript is not absolutely necessary. Raters may look at a videotape, pausing when needed, and extract the same information that is contained in the transcript. The procedure for utilizing this information is the same as if a transcript was used. In the same vein, interview notes alone may be used as the source of raw data. In this example, I will construct a fairly complete, or level 5, formulation.

4. It is sometimes the case that a single set of codes across categories will be very different from the predominant pattern. Most typically this will be a benign exception to a more toxic overall pattern. While this information would not be included in a case formulation designed to describe CMPs, it is useful to take note of clinically.

5. I would like to thank my Danish colleague Susanne Harder and the anonymous patient for permission to use this clinical material.

6. I deliberately chose this case for two reasons. First, the interviewer was a good clinician but had no previous experience conducting ICF interviews per se. Nonetheless, within less than half an hour she had uncovered enough information for a good beginning ICF. The second reason I chose this case is that the patient was considered psychotic, possibly schizophrenic (although it is unclear to me whether or not this was an appropriate diagnosis). I feel that far too often the formulation of interpersonal dynamics contributing to the symptom presentation is ignored with such patients in today's clinical environment (at least in the United States). They are too often written off as "chemically imbalanced," and the fact that they are unique individuals with a personality, interpersonal patterns, and the like is not considered in treatment planning. However, I do not mean this case formulation to be considered as any sort of "prototypical" case formulation for a Schizophrenic patient. Additionally some interpersonally relevant information that might have lead to a more complex ICF was deliberately omitted from this example due to space constraints.

7. The only relatively difficult distinction for some raters is the distinction between Acts of Others and Expectations of Others. Acts of Others should be recorded only when it is clear that a specific, actual incident is being referred to, rather than a general statement (e.g., "Men can't be trusted").

REFERENCES

Benjamin, L. S. (1974). Structural Analysis of Social Behavior. *Psychological Review*, *81*, 392–425.

Benjamin, L. S. (1993a). Every psychopathology is a gift of love. *Psychotherapy Research*, *4*, 1–24.

Benjamin, L. S. (1993b). *Interpersonal diagnosis and treatment of personality disorders.* New York: Guilford Press.

Benjamin, L. S. (1995). *Intrex user's manual.* Salt Lake City: University of Utah.

Benjamin, L. S. (1996). An interpersonal theory of personality disorders. In J. Clarkin & M. Lenzenweger (Eds.), *Major theories of personality disorder*. New York: Guilford Press.

Bowlby, J. (1988). *A secure base: Parent–child attachment and healthy human development.* New York: Basic Books.

Butler, S. F., & Binder, J. L. (1987). Cyclical psychodynamics and the triangle of insight: An integration. *Psychiatry, 50,* 218–231.

Henry, W. P. (1990, June). *The use of the SASB Intrex questionnaire to measure change in cyclical maladaptive interpersonal patterns.* Paper presented at the Annual Convention of the Society for Psychotherapy Research, Wintergreen, VA.

Henry, W. P. (1994). Differentiating normal and abnormal personality: An interpersonal approach based on the Structural Analysis of Social Behavior. In S. Strack & M. Lorr (Eds.), *Differentiating normal and abnormal personality.* New York: Springer-Verlag.

Henry, W. P. (1996a). Structural Analysis of Social Behavior as a common metric for programmatic psychopathology and psychotherapy research. *Journal of Consulting and Clinical Psychology, 64*(6), 1263–1275.

Henry, W. P. (1996b, June). *New assessment instruments and training procedures based on the Structural Analysis of Social Behavior (SASB): Expanding the interpersonal tradition.* Paper presented at the annual convention of the Society for Psychotherapy Research, Amelia Island, GA.

Henry, W. P., & Cheuvront, C. (1995, June). *The measurement of interpersonal control.* Paper presented at the annual convention of the Society for Psychotherapy Research, Vancouver, CA.

Henry, W. P., & Strupp, H. H. (1994). The therapeutic alliance as interpersonal process. In A. O. Horvath & L. S. Greenberg (Eds.), *The working alliance: Theory, research and practice.* New York: Wiley.

Henry, W. P., Strupp, H. H.; Schacht, T. E., & Gaston, L. (1994). Psychodynamic approaches. In A. E. Bergin & S. L. Garfield (Eds.), *Handbook of psychotherapy and behavior change* (4th ed.). New York: Wiley.

Horney, K. (1945). *Our inner conflicts.* New York: Norton.

Horowitz, L. M., Rosenberg, S. E., Baer, B. A., Ureno, G., & Villasenor, V. S. (1988). Inventory of Interpersonal Problems: Psychometric properties and clinical applications. *Journal of Consulting and Clinical Psychology, 56,* 885–892.

Horowitz, L. M., & Vitkus, J. (1985). The interpersonal basis of psychiatric symptoms. *Clinical Psychology Review, 6,* 443–469.

Horowitz, M. J. (Ed.). (1991). *Person schemas and maladaptive interpersonal patterns.* Chicago: University of Chicago Press.

Klein, M. H., Benjamin, L. S., Rosenfeld, R., Treece, C., Husted, J., & Greist, J. H. (1993). The Wisconsin Personality Disorders Inventory: Development, reliability and validity. *Journal of Personality Disorders, 7,* 285–303.

LaForge, R., & Suczek, R. F. (1955). The interpersonal dimensions of personality: III. An interpersonal check list. *Journal of Personality, 24,* 94–112.

Leary, T. (1957). *Interpersonal diagnosis of personality: A functional theory and methodology for personality evaluation.* New York: Ronald Press.

Levenson, H. (1995). *Time-Limited Dynamic Psychotherapy: A guide to clinical practice.* New York: Basic Books.

Luborsky, L. (1977). Measuring a pervasive psychic structure in psychotherapy: The core conflictual relationship theme. In N. Freedman & S. Grand (Eds.), *Communication structures and psychic structures.* New York: Plenum Press.

Mahoney, M. (1991). *Human change processes.* New York: Basic Books.

Murray, H. (1938). *Explorations in personality.* New York: Oxford University Press.

Orlinsky, D. E., & Howard, K. I. (1986). Process and outcome in psychotherapy. In S. L. Garfield & A. E. Bergin (Eds.), *Handbook of psychotherapy and behavior change* (3rd ed.). New York: Wiley.

Perls, F. (1969). *Gestalt therapy verbatim*. Lafayette, CA: Real People Press.

Perry, J. C., Augusto, F., & Cooper, S. H. (1989). Assessing psychodynamic conflicts: I. Reliability of the Idiographic Conflict Formulation Method. *Psychiatry, 52*, 289–301.

Pine, F. (1990). *Drive, ego, object and self*. New York: Basic Books.

Rogers, C. R. (1961). *On becoming a person*. Boston: Houghton Mifflin.

Schacht, T. E., Binder, J. L., & Strupp, H. H. (1984). The dynamic focus. In H. H. Strupp & J. L. Binder (Eds.), *Psychotherapy in a new key*. New York: Basic Books.

Schacht, T. E., & Henry, W. P. (1984). *The Vanderbilt Interpersonal Locus of Control Scale*. Unpublished manuscript, Vanderbilt University, Nashville, TN.

Schacht, T. E., & Henry, W. P. (1995). Modeling recurrent relationship patterns with structural analysis of social behavior: The SASB–CMP. *Psychotherapy Research, 4*, 208–221.

Shafer, E. (1965). Configurational analysis of children's reports of parental behavior. *Journal of Consulting Psychology, 29*, 552–557.

Strupp, H. H., & Binder, J. L. (1984). *Psychotherapy in a new key*. New York: Basic Books.

Sullivan, H. S. (1953). *The interpersonal theory of psychiatry*. New York: Norton.

Weiss, J., Sampson, H., & the Mount Zion Psychotherapy Research Group. (1986). *The psychoanalytic process: Theory, clinical observations, and empirical research*. New York: Guilford Press.

10

Plan Analysis

FRANZ CASPAR

Plan Analysis serves as a basis for clinical case conceptualizations and therapy planning. Clinically relevant information about an individual's behavior and experience is gathered through careful observation and synthesized into a meaningful whole. The fundamental question that guides Plan Analysis is as follows: Which purpose, conscious or unconscious, underlies an individual's behaviors and experiences? The focus of Plan Analysis is instrumental, that is, on how patients' behaviors serve their basic goals.

"Plans" are an individual's hierarchically organized conscious and unconscious goals and the means serving these goals. They refer not only to a patient's stated goals for therapy but to the whole of that patient's interpersonal and intrapsychic strategies to satisfy the most important needs. Individuals are assumed to have multiple, independent Plans, some of which may be mutually harmonious and others disharmonious. In these respects and others the concept of "Plan" in Plan Analysis differs from the Mount Zion "Plan Formulation" concept (Curtis & Silberschatz, Chapter 5, this volume; Curtis, Silberschatz, Sampson, & Weiss, 1994). Plan Analysis attempts to achieve a balance in focusing on motivations as well as behaviors. Emotions are also an important focus in Plan Analysis but are subsumed within the method's overall instrumental orientation. Plan Analysis can be viewed as a set of heuristic rules that guide the clinical analysis of an individual's interpersonal behavior, thoughts, and other behaviors. The method does not claim to be a comprehensive psychological theory, but rather is a pragmatic approach combined with a concrete methodology.

HISTORICAL BACKGROUND OF THE APPROACH

In its original form, Plan Analysis was called "*Vertical* Behavior Analysis." It was developed around 1976 by Klaus Grawe and Hartmut Dziewas as an aid to improving their understanding of the interactional behavior of patients in behavioral group therapy. Traditional functional behavior analyses were seen as providing an insufficient basis for dealing with difficult therapeutic relationships. It became clear that a less reductionistic and more interactionally focused revision of the method was needed. Drawing largely from information-processing theory and the schema concept, the method was expanded over the next several years (Caspar, 1984, 1995; Grawe, 1980, 1986, 1992) to encompass therapy planning, therapeutic change, interpersonal relationships, and the analysis of a patient's emotions.

Plan Analysis incorporates concepts from a broad array of sources in psychology. These include the following: Miller, Galanter, and Pribram's (1960) conceptualization of human behavior as hierarchically organized and goal oriented; the interactionist views of Mischel (1973) and Bandura (1977); interpersonal theory (Argyle, 1969; Beier, 1966; Kiesler, 1973; Leary, 1957; Sullivan, 1953); systemic and communications theory (Selvini-Palazzoli, Boscolo, Cecchin, & Prata, 1987; Watzlawick, Beavin, & Jackson, 1967); cognitive conceptualizations of problem solving (Simon & Newell, 1970); cognitive therapy (Ellis, 1962; Beck, Rush, Shaw, & Emery, 1979; Mahoney, 1974; Meichenbaum, 1974; Persons, 1989); behavior therapy (Kanfer & Grimm, 1980; Kanfer, Reinecker, & Schmelzer, 1991; Urban & Ford, 1971— among others); theories about human change processes and self-organization (Mahoney, 1991; Piaget, 1977; Prigogine, 1976); states-of-mind theory (Horowitz, 1979); theories about emotions (Bandura, 1977; Greenberg & Safran, 1987; Lazarus, 1966; Lazarus, Kanner, & Folkman, 1972; Leventhal, 1980; Mandler, 1975; Ortony, Clore, & Foss, 1987); and modern theories of cognitive-emotional functioning (connectionism; Caspar, Rothenfluh, & Segal, 1992). The compatibility of Plan Analysis with these sources reflects the belief that valid case conceptualizations should be consistent with the current state of scientific knowledge within psychology in general.

With respect to conceptualization of particular problems, Plan Analysis draws from a broad spectrum of etiological concepts. For example, the understanding of a patient's depression can be furthered by Lewinsohn's (1974) loss of reinforcement theory, Seligman's (1975) learned helplessness approach, Beck and colleagues' (1979) concept of dysfunctional thinking, and Weissman and Klerman's (1990) interpersonal approach, as well as by psychodynamic concepts of avoiding overt aggression and by systemic concepts (Coyne, Downey, & Boergers, 1992; Feldman, 1976). Typically the individual case determines how much of any one of these concepts contributes to the formulation, and usually it is by combining concepts, often complemented by ideas developed for a specific patient, that a satisfactory understanding is gained.

In sum, Plan Analysis draws from many well-established concepts in psychology; it has developed over 20 years and is thereby enriched by ample experience. One effect of the maturing of this approach is its limitation to delivering a current picture of a patient from an instrumental perspective. We resist the temptation to increase the approach's power by adding more and more elements. The payoff is robustness and compatibility with other complementary approaches.

CONCEPTUAL FRAMEWORK

The Importance of Case Conceptualizations

Therapists' actions are based on theories, but these theories, of course, do not primarily have an impact in their original elaborate form. Rather, they have shaped each therapist's strategies and belief system in the past and therefore have an ongoing implicit impact (Caspar, 1994). In the present they are used explicitly only in a simpler form. Overall, therapy-guiding theories determine the therapist's thinking and behavior both consciously and unconsciously, explicitly and implicitly.

Somehow, theoretical concepts need to be related to the individual patient. In the view of Plan Analysis, a main task of individual case conceptualizations is to connect the individual patient to the general body of professional knowledge. Case conceptualizations in Plan Analysis insure that, in spite of utilization of existing theoretical concepts, there is a strong inductive component and that assumptions about the patient are made as explicit as is feasible in therapy practice. Ideally, a case conceptualization is a balanced combination of theoretical and experiential knowledge, on the one hand, and concrete observations of a particular patient, on the other.

Inherent to Plan Analysis is the belief that therapy manuals can be of great help (Beutler & Clarkin, 1990). Manualized procedures that are not based on a thorough understanding of the individual patient, however, are of limited use when the patient suffers from a rare problem, when there is a dynamic combination of problems, or when the focus of therapy is on the patient as a whole, beyond his or her "presenting" problem. In these cases, which in our practice constitute the majority, therapists need to construct an individualized procedure (Caspar, 1995); to do so in a reasonable way, they need a comprehensive case conceptualization that goes beyond a narrow focus on the problem.

The Elements of Plan Analysis

Plans

The components of a Plan Analysis formulation are interrelated and hierarchically organized Plans, each of which has a goal and an "operations" component. The goal is a statement of the patient's intention, hope, wish, or some other "end state" that the individual consciously or unconsciously strives to achieve. The operations element indicates the means to reach this goal. For example, I may invest a lot of preparative work (operation) to get a contract (goal; see Figure 10.1).

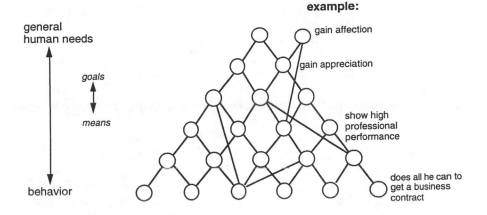

FIGURE 10.1. Schematic Plan structure. Goals or purposes (superordinate elements) are higher in the vertical dimension than the means that serve them (subordinate elements). The lines relate Plans that are in a direct instrumental relation with each other. Elements at the level of behaviors are formulated in the indicative form; Plans, in the imperative form. From Caspar (1995). Copyright 1995 by Hogrefe and Huber. Reprinted by permission.

In addition, one Plan can instrumentally serve another Plan, placing it in a hierarchically subordinate relationship to the Plan it serves. In such cases, the goal element of the subordinate Plan is the operations component of the superordinate Plan. For example, the getting of a contract (which is the goal of investing a lot of work) could serve a superordinate Plan of being professionally successful. The same Plan can thus be superordinate (to hierarchically lower Plans) and at the same time subordinate (to hierarchically higher Plans). For simplicity and ease of understanding, a Plan Analysis formulation is usually depicted diagrammatically, as shown in Figures 10.1 and 10.3 (the latter figure will be presented and explained further in the "Case Example" section).

In a Plan Analysis formulation, it is typical for important superordinate goals to have multiple operational elements. That is, a person may use several means simultaneously or sequentially to achieve a goal. For example, to be successful with a contract, I may not only do paperwork but also try to get some personal information about those involved, or I may do relaxation exercises before the negotiations take place. Such "redundancy" increases the chances that a goal will be achieved. Having several alternative strategies for important goals may be considered an index of psychological health.

It is also typical for means each to serve several goals. For example, pursuing professional success may serve the goals of enhancing a person's self-esteem, winning the admiration and affection of others, and guaranteeing a good income. In Plan Analysis we use the term "multiple determination" if behaviors or Subplans serve several superordinate Plans simultaneously.

The last two considerations are depicted in a Plan diagram by multiple lines going from one Plan to others. For example, in Figure 10.3, the Plan of resisting tasks in therapy is related to the means (operations) of "cannot do imagination exercise" and "forgets homework assignment," and it serves simultaneously the purposes of resisting control and of maintaining anxiety as an excuse.

The Plans depicted in a Plan Analysis formulation may address a variety of aspects of a person's intrapsychic and interpersonal functioning. For example, the formulation can include positive Plans (those serving adaptive needs of a person or that capitalize on the person's psychological resources), avoidance Plans (those that typically obstruct the achievement of adaptive ends), Plans regarding the self-concept, Plans associated with the generation of positive and negative emotions, Plans related to coping, and Plans regarding the therapeutic relationship. These are illustrated in the "Case Example" below. The formulation should also depict conflict between Plans, how effectively the Plans serve the individual's most hierarchically superordinate goals, and patients' constructions of their problems and what perpetuates them.

Relating Emotions to Plans

As noted earlier, emotions play a central role in Plan Analysis, but they are conceptualized from an instrumental point of view. For example, the idea (cognition) "I need to be perfect" can be embedded in a person's functioning in many ways: it may represent a desperate wish to win others' attention and appreciation, possibly based on the assumption that a perfect being simply deserves this; it may represent resistance of a depressed patient against letting him- or herself into behavioral trials that could lead to new disappointment; and so forth. The appropriate treatment of the idea "I need to be perfect" and whether it should be treated at all depend, of course, on a valid view of the deeper meaning of the idea.

Although the instrumental relation of emotions to Plans is emphasized, there is no assumption in Plan Analysis that emotions serve only instrumental purposes. Four considerations are central with respect to how emotions are related to Plans: (1) which Plans are threatened when negative emotions arise; (2) which Plans shape emotions; (3) which Plans are used to cope with emotions; and (4) does the emotion itself have an instrumental function? Each of these questions is discussed below.

Blocked Plans

In Plan Analysis it is assumed that negative emotions, such as fear, anger, shame, and sadness, usually arise when important Plans are threatened or blocked. As long as a person is able to act according to his or her most important Plans, there is no significant arousal. If a threat causes strong emotions, however, one may assume that important Plans are blocked or threatened and that adequate alternatives or coping Plans are lacking or cannot be developed easily.

For example, sudden illness before an exam brings about stronger emotions when a success on the exam represents important Plans (such as finishing one's studies, getting a well-paid job, or satisfying one's father's expectations). The availability of alternatives will also influence one's emotional response to this situation. These may include the opportunity to take the exam at a later date or other possibilities of pursuing an attractive life course.

A Plan may also be blocked by life changes such as geographic relocation, aging, physical disability, or bereavement. A threat can also stem from conflicts between Plans. More concretely, a behavior serving one Plan may negatively affect another. All actions, after all, have positive and negative side effects beyond the primarily intended effect. A threat may be linked to a concrete situation, or it may be diffuse and of a long-term nature. An example of the latter would be when a basic need, such as for companionship, is neglected over a long period of time due to a "workaholic" lifestyle a person may have chosen.

A threat need not exist objectively. Rather, it is the subjective experience of threat that matters. For example, a single situational cue can trigger a sense of threat in a situation that, objectively speaking, is not at all threatening. Furthermore, the appraisal of threat need not be conscious. In many cases, a Plan Analysis can help therapists and patients understand which specific Plans were threatened when an emotion occurs.

There are two reasons why the concept of threat or blockage is of special significance within the context of therapy. First, patients come to therapy when they are at an impasse, that is, when they are confronted with a blockage. Such situations are often accompanied by strong negative emotions. In therapy one wants to understand these emotions and relate them to the blocking situation. Second, therapy necessarily involves the therapist acting in a way that disturbs the patient because the patient cannot integrate easily what happens without adapting his or her structures (Caspar & Grawe, 1981). Drawing from Piaget's (1977) assimilation–accommodation concept, Grawe (1986) views this focused disturbing function as a major change factor in therapy. In accord with this perspective, some negative emotions arising during therapy are viewed as unavoidable and potentially therapeutic.

Plans Shaping the Emotion

In addition to the presence of threats to Plans, the rise of emotion may also depend upon further Plans. For example, if a situation would normatively give rise to aggressive emotions (e.g., a patient's mother-in-law restricts the patient's rights in a domineering manner), such emotions may be prevented by aggression-avoiding Plans. This conflict between avoiding Plans and the emotion increases the likelihood of other negative emotions, such as anxiety. If all conscious emotion is prevented by suppressive Plans, there may also be an increased risk of tensions being expressed as psychosomatic symptoms. At times the type of threat suggests a specific emotional reaction. Usually, however, a range of emotional reactions is possible, and it is not the originally threatened Plans, but additional Plans permitting or not permitting particular emotions, that codetermine the resulting emotional reaction.

Coping Plans

Another aspect of the relation between Plans and emotions is the tendency to avoid negative emotions and seek positive ones. If a negative emotion exists or is anticipated, a person usually activates Plans aimed at removing or preventing the emotion. These coping strategies may aim at the source of the disturbance. Examples include completing work that has caused sleepless nights, and seeking new friends when one is depressed due to a loss. Or, if the threat has arisen internally due to conflicts between Plans, one can try to develop an understanding of one's conflicts through therapy. Frequently, skills and abilities must be acquired and anxieties decreased in therapy before adequate coping activities become possible.

Unfortunately, it is not always possible to remove the disturbance at its source. For example, the threat of losing one's job during an economic depression, or terminal illness, or technical and natural disasters cannot simply be averted by the individual. In such cases, palliative coping behavior aimed at dealing with the negative emotions themselves may be necessary. Depending on the situation, it may be more efficient to face the emotion directly or to limit one's awareness of the emotion, up to and including the extreme of complete repression.

Plans for Which an Emotion Has an Instrumental Function

Finally, emotions themselves may have an instrumental function within the Plan structure of an individual. To begin with, they may function to support behavior. It is difficult to withdraw from a source of conflict if one is full of energy, but it is much easier if one feels powerless, anxious, or depressed. It is difficult to approach other people if one is not in an appropriate mood or able to bring oneself into such a mood. For example, some socially anxious patients can only assert themselves after they enter a state of rage. This example shows how emotions can serve the general function of integrating cognitive processes and action. A direct instrumental function of emotions is so common that it is only given explicit consideration in a Plan Analysis when it helps to explain a specific observation.

Another frequently observed function of emotions is the *interactional* impact they may have when they are expressed. The attention agoraphobics often get as a result of their anxiety is a classic example of the instrumental reinforcement of a particular disorder. A depressed mood can have a similar impact, depending on the interactional system. Showing hostile nervousness can cause another person to back off and maintain greater distance after having come too close.

Concerning the aspects of emotion presented above, in our experience it is usually possible to achieve an adequate understanding of such emotions relevant to therapy using Plan Analysis. The analysis of emotion has been emphasized here because, first, understanding and dealing with emotions is a cornerstone in every psychotherapy and, secondly, the issue exemplifies how Plan Analysis in spite of its emphasis on instrumental relations is not limited to the analysis of overt instrumental behavior.

Plans and Psychological Disorders

In the view of Plan Analysis, psychological disorders may have a direct instrumental function. That is, they may have been developed and/or may be maintained by an intrapsychic or interpersonal advantage they have in the functioning of a person. Such an advantage is usually unconscious and often is hidden by the obvious disadvantages and the patient's subjective suffering. Common examples include agoraphobias obliging a partner to stay home, psychosomatic disorders providing an acceptable reason to withdraw from an overdemanding job, and the role of compulsive behavior in limiting diffuse anxiety. Whereas such hypotheses can easily be applied to a patient without conducting a Plan Analysis, more probing questions such as "Under what conditions will a patient be able to give up using this problem as part of a strategy?" require more diligent analysis. For example, Caspar (1987) described a case where agoraphobic anxiety and depression did not serve to bind a partner, but rather served to paralyze the patient's strong but subjectively threatening wish for a divorce from her violent husband.

Psychological problems can sometimes be viewed as having an instrumental function themselves, one which often develops later in a pathogenic process. If psychological problems do not have an instrumental function, they are nevertheless related to an individual's instrumental strategies in various ways. Often they are *side effects* of instrumental strategies. For example, social withdrawal may serve the goal of avoiding subjectively threatening situations, but it may produce, as a side effect, a loss of active behaviors and positive experiences. Such a pattern is typical for depressive disorders. The depression may or may not have an instrumental function in itself; mainly it must be seen as a consequence or side effect of instrumental withdrawal.

Rigid and avoidant Plan structures bear a high risk of bringing about endless negative side effects, and not many situations and domains remain in which the person can have positive experiences. It should be noted, however, that Plan Analysis suggests that problems always be viewed as an interaction of individual structures and situations that need to be mastered. There may be structures enabling an individual to master a broad range of difficult situations or tasks coming up in a lifespan, but there is not such a thing as a "perfect structure." This is illustrated by posttraumatic stress disorders: although some individuals seem to enter traumatic situations with structures allowing them to overcome even extreme traumata, there are probably traumatic impacts that would be too severe for even the most healthy structure.

Overall, the disorder concept of Plan Analysis is very open and individual. The primary reason for a disorder may be in the past or in the present; it may be intrapsychic or interpersonal. Typically, in Plan Analysis one does not one-sidedly focus on *the* cause; rather, one considers different causal factors operating at different points. It is normally the interaction of these factors that brings about and maintains a problem. The *price* for this approach is that complex case conceptualizations may result. The *payoff* is that usually it also yields several points at which therapeutic change can be brought about; it gives a therapist a broader range of possibilities in comparison to most approaches of which we are aware (Grawe, Caspar, & Ambühl, 1990).

INCLUSION/EXCLUSION CRITERIA

It seems fair to state that Plan Analysis is applicable wherever interpersonal and intrapsychic conscious and unconscious strategies need to be understood, given that the instrumental aspect is always a central if not the most central key to an understanding of such strategies. Instrumental strategies play a role in an emotionally healthy person, in "neurotically disturbed" patients, in psychotic patients, and in people with a state strongly determined by a physical handicap, be it in the genes, the brain, or other parts of the body.

Some disorders that are presently among the more difficult ones for psychotherapy, such as personality disorders, clearly have a strong interpersonal component, and although we have limited experience with this type of disorder, we see a great potential for the use of Plan Analysis in this domain. Plan Analysis has been most broadly used in the therapy of anxiety, depression, and psychosomatic disorders, and to some extent in obsessive–compulsive disorders and addictions. Colleagues have used it in other domains, such as work with children (Schonauer, 1992). Because the approach is so general and compatible with many specific approaches, it is hard to see a limitation on its use. If there are limitations, they come from a utility perspective, that is, the question of whether it is actually necessary to do a detailed individual analysis of every new case of agoraphobia, for example. It is true that many insights can be transferred from the "typical" agoraphobic to a new agoraphobic patient. But it is also true that if one takes a closer look, a "standard" agoraphobic often has some surprising peculiarities that are crucial for successful therapy, particularly if therapy is not limited to alleviating the main complaint but is also aimed at making the patient happier.

Exclusion criteria pertain to therapists rather than to patients. Although good Plan Analyses require sound clinical intuition in many parts of the procedure, the method also requires some rational-analytic thinking. Even when the approach is combined with a great deal of creativity, some therapists are not keen on disciplined reasoning, and a few seem to be unable to handle complexity mentally. An additional difficulty for therapists who like simple truths, as provided by the more dogmatic schools of psychotherapy, seems to be in accepting a constructivist perspective. On the other hand, therapists who are tired of dogmatic or simplistic approaches will find rich and rewarding possibilities of working toward an individualized understanding of their patients, even the difficult aspects of their functioning.

STEPS IN CASE FORMULATION CONSTRUCTION
General Comments

Plan Analysis is a highly individualized and flexible approach. The advantages of such a heuristic approach become obvious very quickly. Experiences from past analyses can be used in subsequent ones, and psychotherapists become increasingly efficient. Unlike other case formulation methods, the use of standard components is discouraged due to the risk of jeopardizing the fit of the formulation to the patient and, by extension, the usefulness of the formulation (Caspar, 1988). Although the richness of available technical advice for flexibly and individually inferring Plans is a distinguishing property of the approach, providing a step-by-step algorithmic description of how to construct a Plan Analysis formulation runs counter to the nature of the approach. For didactic purposes, however, I will describe general procedures for constructing a Plan Analysis formulation.

All of the following *sources of information* can be used in inferring Plans: the therapist's observations inside and outside of therapy; patient's self-reports about behaviors and experiences inside and outside of therapy; patient's introspective reports, including thoughts, experiences, fantasies, and daydreams; how the patient affects others, particularly the therapist, a spouse, other patients (in the case of group therapy); standardized questionnaires; and reports of others, for example, relatives, friends, nurses, or fellow group therapy members. Plan Analysis pays particularly close attention to directly observable information, especially instrumental and reactive nonverbal behavior. For example, a patient may covertly try to discourage a therapist from insisting on a particular theme by showing subtle signs of tension, which would be instrumentally interpreted.

Because we are all limited in our ability to introspect accurately, a patient's self-reports need to be evaluated carefully and should not automatically be taken at face value. Often, however, a statement can be revealing in a way the patient may not intend. For example, a patient who states, "I believe I am attractive to this woman because I am a reliable person" may reveal a Plan "Make yourself attractive". The statement might also refer to the therapy alliance and be inferred to mean, "Let the therapist know you are reliable." The statement could also refer to the patient's self-concept: "Sticks to his view of being reliable" serves the Plan, "Maintain the self-concept of being an attractive person." Those factors that plausibly can determine patients' behavior and experiences (the "regulating self"; Grawe, 1992) may or may not be represented in their self-concept. As Plan Analysis relies heavily on observation, it is useful for detecting factors that participate in such self-regulation without being represented in the self-concept.

A central task in Plan Analysis is to find a *common denominator* or denominators of the available data or parts of it, with a dominating instrumental and constructivist perspective, as described above. Typical formulations would be of the form, "Patient *X* behaves and feels as if he has an important Plan *A*." Normally, a Plan hypothesis is based on several observations. For example, "The misbehavior of this child could serve the Plan of getting his mother's attention. The behaviors are frequent when she is busy with other things, and the child gets upset when his Plan is blocked by his mother's continued attention to competing tasks." The therapist should then look for confirming, disconfirming, or differentiating information about a Plan. In the above case, one could ask, "Does the child show the same misbehavior with others as he does with his mother?" or "In what situations, if any, does he act differently with his mother?"

When inferring a Plan, therapists can ask themselves the following questions: What emotions and impressions does the patient trigger in me? How does the patient want me and others to be? What would the patient like me and others to do? What self-image does the patient try to attain or maintain? What self-image does the patient try to convey to me? What behaviors of mine does the patient try to prevent?

In general, there are five ways to infer plans:

- From one behavior one infers a Plan directly and subsequently examines whether other observed behaviors confirm this hypothesis or whether one must search for such confirming (or differentiating) behavior.
- One looks for a common denominator in several behaviors, infers a Plan, and then looks for further substantiating behaviors.
- One infers a Plan from the patient's impact upon an interaction partner, looks for the means by which the patient causes this impact, and then seeks further substantiating behavior.
- Plans are inferred from the traces they leave in a patient's reactions, for example, in emotions when a Plan is blocked.
- Plans are inferred from top down, in contrast to the bottom-up procedure in the other four ways of inferring Plans. One asks oneself, for example, "How does this patient satisfy his or her need for such and such?" This search direction complements the common bottom-up search and is especially useful for finding deficit domains in a patient's Plan structure.

It is important to include aspects that represent strengths and resources of a patient, and to pay attention to how the individual structure is interlocked with the functioning of a patient's environment. Plan Analysis is an especially good means of showing how problematic parts can be viewed as related to well-functioning parts and how even problematic parts enclose positive elements that can be used and furthered. As far as the functioning of an individual in his or her environment is concerned, the compatibility of the approach with systemic approaches due to the shared instrumental view is a special advantage.

The Formulation of Plans and the Plan Diagram

Plans should be formulated as idiographically as possible. Idiosyncratic terms used by the patient can help to develop a distinctive structure. We recommend formulating the label of behaviors in the indicative form (e.g., "Tells others about his initiative for the homeless"), and Plans in the form of an imperative directed toward oneself (e.g., "Gain other people's appreciation"). The former indicates that at present one does not intend to break down the respective behavior into components (Subplans); the latter helps avoid inadvertently including noninstrumental elements. For example, "anxiety" in this form would not be a proper element of a Plan structure, because it is in neither an indicative nor an imperative form and it is unclear what aspect of anxiety is seen as instrumental. It should be formulated so that its position in the structure becomes more obvious, for example, "Maintain anxiety" (serving the Plan "Keep the husband at home") or "Cope with anxiety" (with the means of "Drinks excessively"). The imperative form is not meant to suggest conscious awareness for the relevant part of one's functioning.

Plans are usually drawn in a diagram as elements related by links representing instrumental relations. Normally, one just starts with a behavior or Plan that seems central and then adds to it element by element and link by link. The only strict rule is that of two Plans one always needs to be graphically higher than the other, indicating that it is the superordinate Plan, and vice versa. The knowledge of where to put an element to develop a structure that is maximally clear from a graphic point of view develops with experience. For drawing, we recommend the use of technical devices, which facilitate making changes and adaptations later. These devices include a blackboard with or without self-sticking papers for the Plan labels, or general-purpose drawing programs on the computer, which help keep a structure attractive for reading even after series of changes.

Because the graphic representation of instrumental Plan structures are such a characteristic part of Plan Analysis, it may be necessary to emphasize that such a diagram is only an intermediate step: the crucial product is a case conceptualization that is *based* on an analysis of Plans but could be formulated without using the term "Plan." The typical elements of such a case conceptualization are described below in the "Case Example" section.

The process of inferring Plans extends over the entire course of therapy and is never really completed. Interventions are always based on a provisional understanding. Nevertheless, the first few minutes in therapy are often particularly informative because patients try to shape the interactional situation in line with their dominant interactional needs. After a well-conducted intake interview, it is usually possible to infer the Plans that are most important for the interactional therapy planning. Experienced therapists can do this "on line" as the interview proceeds. Interactional therapy planning has the greatest priority in the beginning of a therapy, and it is pivotal because many therapies that stall in the initial phase do so as a result of a poor therapeutic relationship.

The detail and complexity of analysis can be flexibly adapted in different parts of the patient's functioning. For example, if "perfectionism" is conspicuous but not considered very important by the analyzer, it may be represented in only one Plan without consuming further space and attention; when considered important, however, it may be addressed in several Plans. Often an issue is first represented in a simple way, then differentiated in more detail later on, as its importance becomes more evident or if the range of validity of a Plan needs to be specified.

Concepts from various sources (from common sense to traditional learning theories, psychodynamic ideas, etc.) can provide ideas for how the individual elements of an person's functioning may be interrelated. Some psychodynamic concepts, which were not the point of departure of Plan Analysis, are compatible with it in many respects (Horowitz, 1979; Luborsky, 1990; Strupp & Binder, 1984; Thomä & Kächele, 1988; Weiss et al., 1986; Willi, 1982). In any case, theoretical concepts should be used in such a way that a given idea makes immediate sense in the individual case conceptualization.

The process of analyzing Plans may appear predominantly rational-analytic, especially when one is describing explicit practical rules. It is desirable that as great a part of the process as possible be rational and explicit. On the other hand, when one endeavors to process raw information and fit it together in such a way that a meaningful model of an individual patient develops as a basis for a therapy that goes beyond the surface, intuitive processes unavoidably come into play. Intuition is especially important when one is "framing" the raw information, creatively speculating about possible instrumental functions, and judging whether an elaborated case conceptualization actually captures the essence of a case. Rational-analytic and intuitive processing should be combined in such a way that they complement and control each other.

The search and collection of data and the inference of Plans are never neutral but are determined by the therapist's hypotheses, selective attention, and processing style. If one follows the rules of always supplying several concrete pieces of evidence for each hypothesis, of remaining curious about the unexpected, and of paying attention to possible biases and honestly engaging in openness, severe distortions can usually be avoided; early explicit hypotheses tend to reveal rather than hide what is not in agreement with them. Plan Analysis, like all comparable approaches, always moves between the Scylla of being overinterpretive and inappropriately projecting concepts onto a patient and the Charybdis of not taking clinically important factors into account out of a reluctance to engage in deeper interpretations. There is no way of minimizing the risk of one type of error without increasing the risk of the other.

APPLICATION TO PSYCHOTHERAPY TECHNIQUE

Plan Analysis is designed to provide a picture of the present functioning of a patient, including insights into how a Plan structure developed and what the potential for change might be. Based on such a case conceptualization the therapist determines where changes are needed in order for the patient's problems to be solved, eventually leading to a more satisfactory life overall. Based on a case conceptualization, the therapist could emphasize the need for greater insight into the patient's functioning in order to increase the individual's freedom from old patterns: one could emphasize the acquisition of skills to help a patient master a difficult situation; or one could emphasize the need to work through particular emotions to decrease the need of avoiding such emotions in the future.

The same desired *main effect* in therapy can normally be achieved in various ways. A Plan Analysis case conceptualization should also answer the question as to what positive and negative *side effects* can be expected for different techniques. It can serve as a basis for a strictly functional view of therapy methods and for using them as prototypes for an individualized therapeutic procedure in which main and side effects are optimized. This kind of therapy planning is done partly outside the therapy session and partly during it.

Case conceptualizations are present in therapists' minds, although in a simplified form, whenever they see their patients or think about them. The conceptualizations serve as a basis for quick interpretations, predictions, and decisions. For example, when a patient brings up a completely unexpected topic, the therapist must decide quickly whether to pursue what was originally planned for the session (say, because the new topic is interpreted as an indicator of resistance), or to completely switch to the new topic, or to utilize the new material for the old goal. Typically, therapists using the Plan concept seem to be flexible in a strategic sense (Thommen, Ammann, & von Cranach, 1988). They stick to important therapeutic Plans, but in a flexible way as far as the means are concerned, and they are able to take advantage of the possibilities offered by a concrete situation. In most therapies there are times when the therapist plays a very active, structuring role, and other times when processes develop well without much overt therapist action and so the therapist only monitors them with a high amount of mental presence, always ready to intervene when needed.

A case conceptualization is always used for the analysis of the *patient's problem(s)* as well as the requirements and possibilities in the *therapeutic relationship*. The problem and the therapeutic relationship can be interlocked in many ways. In many therapeutic relationships that are interactionally less complicated, an intuitive understanding is sufficient to prevent severe mistakes and to allow a solid therapeutic bond to develop. Elaborated analyses, however, generally reveal more precise points where the therapist can intervene. The more flexibility therapists show on the technical level, the lower the risk of stressing the relationship unnecessarily. In addition, a comprehensive case conceptualization should include the information needed to construct an individualized offer of a complementary relationship. Complementary therapist behavior does not simply mean reacting in the way that the patient seems to suggest by his or her problematic behavior. Learning theory might even lead one to expect that such contingent behavior would have a reinforcing effect, and this is not without validity. From a Plan Analysis point of view, however, a therapist should not react on the behavioral level but actively develop a strategy that is complementary on the level of superordinate Plans, which themselves are unproblematic.

For example, as shown in Figure 10.2, a patient may spend a lot of time in therapy complaining, guided by hypothetical Plans like "Show the therapist that you are not well at all," which serves a Plan of causing the therapist to treat the patient carefully or a Plan of causing the therapist to take the problems seriously and to fully engage in therapy. With such a patient, the therapist should not react with reluctant pity. Depending on the individual analysis, the better strategy would be to show that one is fully engaged in therapy, that one has understood how bad things are, and that one will not be overdemanding.

The basic idea is rather to neutralize the patient's use of problematic instrumental behavior by providing what the patient seems to want on a higher level. The therapist actively appeases and even oversatiates these wants. Although long-standing problematic behavior is often very persistent, frequently a patient's behavior changes dramatically when the therapist finds the right complementary behavior and does precisely that. Time and attention that were absorbed by the patient's attempts to bring the therapist into the desired interactional position are now suddenly freed for real work on the problem(s).

To develop complementary therapist behavior, the patient's Plans, in particular interactional behavior causing problems in the therapeutic relationship, need to be analyzed for superordinate Plans. The analysis goes up the instrumental hierarchy step by step until a point is reached where the goals—in contrast to the strategies used to reach them—are no longer problematic. A basic assumption of Plan Analysis is that Plans highest in the instrumental hierarchy are not "bad" by definition, because they stand for generally acceptable human needs.

Once these higher Plans are recognized, a therapist can develop therapist Plans complementary to the patient Plans. They circumvent the patient's problematic strategies and give the therapist some freedom, because he or she is no longer *re*active but active based on a deeper understanding of the situation. Complementary therapist Plans are used to construct therapist behavior that has the main purpose of creating a complementary therapeutic alliance.

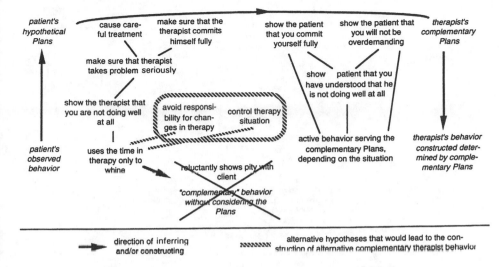

FIGURE 10.2. Complementary therapist behavior. For an explanation, see the text. From Caspar (1995). Copyright 1995 by Hogrefe and Huber. Reprinted by permission.

Secondly, they are used to construct a "technical" procedure serving the solution of the patient's problems in such a way that the requirements of a complementary therapeutic relationship are met. Thus no "technical" intervention should take place without cross-checking it for complementarity. This does not exclude confronting patients with some aspects of their functioning by behaving in a noncomplementary way, but a confrontation should be an intervention in the foreground, with a safe background of a generally complementary relationship.

A final issue in using Plan Analysis in therapy is *communication with patients* about "their Plans." Plan Analysis primarily gives the therapist a means of developing a clear view of a patient. As increasing insight is an important goal in most therapies, therapists will usually communicate with their patients at least about parts of their view, but preferably in terms of an essential or derived insight, not necessarily in terms of Plans. If parts of a Plan structure are discussed explicitly, this should be restricted to a limited number of Plans and relations. Anything else would be too demanding for most patients, and patients who do well with complex kinds of analysis are often the ones whose tendency to rationalize is precisely what the therapist does *not* wish to further.

CASE EXAMPLE

The following case was selected to illustrate the typical application of Plan Analysis in clinical practice. It was not selected for demonstrating how crucial aspects can be discovered exclusively by Plan Analysis. Figure 10.3, which shows the graphic Plan diagram, was developed after four sessions. To readers unfa-

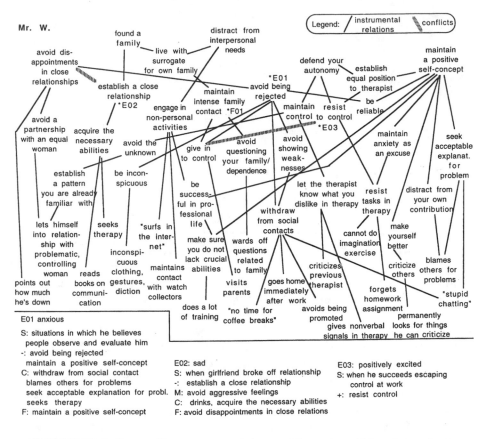

FIGURE 10.3. Drawn Plan structure of the case illustration. Abbreviations in the structure (*F01, *E01, . . . , *E03) point to additional not instrumentally related information (F = "general" frame with unspecified information, open to whatever additional information has to be stored explicitly; E = emotion frame with information related to emotions following the concept explained above; S = situation; – = blocked Plans; M = Plans shaping the emotion (*manifestation*); C = coping Plans; F = Plans for which the emotion has an instrumental function). For a further explanation, see the text.

miliar with such figures, a word of encouragement is warranted. Although the diagram looks complicated, the accompanying text should make it intelligible and digestible. With experience, such structures are readily interpretable.

The following is a sample case conceptualization based on a list of "topics" as normally used in Plan Analysis. The first two topics are descriptive and noninterpretive; the impact of Plan Analysis becomes apparent in topics 3 through 11. *Explanations that would not normally be included in a case conceptualization are printed in italics.*

1. The Patient's Present Life Situation
(*Summary without Deeper Analysis*)

Mr. W., a single man, 37 years old, works in an administrative position. He likes his work and feels competent at it. He earns more than he needs for his modest lifestyle. Originally, he had no higher education. However, when he got older, he obtained additional training with an admirable investment of energy, as it was accomplished in addition to his regular workload. He is relatively small, a little overweight, and average in appearance. He dresses inconspicuously and in his nonverbal behavior does not attract attention. In his leisure time he attends night classes, most of them related to his work, and collects and repairs old watches.

He is still heavily entangled with his parents. They live in a village in the neighborhood, and he visits them several times a week, often for dinner. In addition, his mother calls several times a week, which he experiences as controlling. To the second interview (to which we usually invite at least one person close to the patient) he brought his parents, who indeed seemed very interested in him in the helpless controlling manner already described by him. But they were not very understanding of the psychological dimension of his problems. In their view he was well off; one day he would have a family, sure, but there was no hurry. The therapist was addressed like a physician able to help in some way, but actually not important because there was no real problem. The parents were rather silent and did not interact with each other. The mother controlled the patient by subtle, often nonverbal cues.

The patient does not have many experiences with women due to his shy nature, but recently he had a closer relationship with a woman who had mental problems and was dependent, yet exploitative and controlling to such an extent that he finally ended the relationship.

Mr W.'s difficulties are in the domain of private contacts; he suffers from social phobia. He is anxious and avoidant mainly with women, but also with men, for example, at work when the issue of a conversation is not professional or related to his watches. However, he has managed to get into a position where at work he does not suffer too much from his impairment. The reasons for seeking therapy are that he still feels involved with his past relationship and that he feels he would have difficulties establishing a stable and intense relationship with a woman, although his ideal would be to have a good family including children. He saw another therapist for four sessions for the same reason, but then ended the therapy because in his view the therapist imposed too many of his own concepts on him and pressured him to do things, yet did not support him enough when he needed it. Mr. W. has no significant medical, financial, or other problems.

2. Biography (*Summary without Deeper Analysis*)

The patient grew up in a village near a fairly large city. He describes his parents as good parents, who, however, never showed much affection or personal interest in him. It sounds as though they were reliable but rather unromantic partners to each other. He is the only child.

He passed school without problems but also without a lot of excitement. He had intense contacts with neither girls nor boys, and it sounds as if he has lived in a world of (passive) sports and building aircraft models.

When he was about 3 years old, his parents founded a little factory for manufacturing underwear, which consumed all their energy and time. Owing to difficult economic conditions, they had to give it up when he was 15. The patient believes that they lacked the abilities needed to convince banks to provide the loans needed to survive that difficult period. The episode ended without significant financial gain or loss. Now his father works as an employee in the same field, and both parents have excessive time to devote to the patient.

Originally his parents came from farmer families. Apart from a mysterious early death of his maternal grandmother nothing conspicuous is known about the family, and the patient seems not very interested in this topic.

(Normally, a section with results from an assessment battery answered by the patient himself and a person close to him would follow here, but it is omitted to save space and because it is not specific to the Plan Analysis approach. A diagnosis—social phobia and possibly dependent personality, in this case—would also be included.)

3. The Patient's Most Important Positive Plans and Resources

The description given here refers to the drawn structure in Figure 10.3. Positive Plans, in contrast to avoidance Plans, are Plans serving positive needs of a person. Usually they can be recognized as "positive" by their labels. Often superordinate avoidance Plans also contain subordinate positive Plans, and vice versa; the distinction is thus not a distinctive classification but serves to give the description some structure. Whenever the text says that the patient "has" a Plan, that is to be understood as a hypothesis in a constructivist sense. The description of Plans in topics 3 and 4 is more detailed than in most cases; most often only the most important Plans would be highlighted for readers already familiar with the concept.

There are several relevant positive Plans. One of the most superordinate Plans, as indicated by its location at the top of Figure 10.3, is to start a family and establish a close relationship. This Plan is not supported by a sufficient repertoire of strategies, which is mainly why the patient is seeking therapy. His remaining in close contact with his parents can be viewed, in part, as a substitute for having his own family. The Plan of establishing a close relationship was so important that it blinded him enough so that he engaged in a relationship that was problematic from the outset. *(In a more detailed Plan Structure, one would relate the distortions in his perception of this woman to the dominant Plan of establishing a close relationship.)*

The Plan of maintaining a positive self-concept, which is more salient for him than for many others, also determines a broad range of behaviors. Positive parts of this Plan include his striving for professional success, which includes efforts to obtain additional educational training. His being very reliable is also an important resource, along with an obvious strong will and intellectual abilities that were not fully used because his parents did not care much about education and were not good models in this respect. Mr. W's striving for autonomy and for an equal position with the therapist are at the same time positive and avoidance Plans (see below). In spite of his need to maintain control, and his difficulties in more personal communication, he has good conversational skills when dealing with nonpersonal topics.

4. The Patient's Most Important Avoidance Plans

The patient has many avoidance Plans. Most prominent is a Plan to avoid rejection. As part of this Plan, he uses many avoidance strategies typical of social phobics. These include not exposing himself to situations in which weaknesses could be revealed and withdrawal from social situations. An exception is any situation in which a nonpersonal topic such as his hobby or work provides structure. He pretends to have no time for conversation after work or during coffee breaks, describing such talk as "stupid chatting." He avoids being promoted into a position where greater social skills would be required. These avoidance Plans have also led to a lack of skills and experience related to such situations, which increases the risk of failure and thus the tendency to avoid any such risks. He avoids drawing attention to himself, for example, by dressing inconspicuously and using inconspicuous gestures and diction. A specific Subplan of avoiding rejection is his giving in to being controlled by his parents. His maintaining intense contacts with his parents and his engagement in nonpersonal contacts, apart from having a positive function, also distract him from unfulfilled interpersonal needs with which he would otherwise be fully confronted. He protects the relationship with his parents and at the same time his self-concept, with which dependence would be incompatible, by avoiding a debate about the relationship.

Another superordinate Plan is the avoidance of disappointments in close relationships. Because he desperately wants a close relationship and has no experience in constructively coping with disappointment, he sees the need to avoid further disappointment absolutely. His pointing out how much he is "down" after the last negative experience, and also his social anxiety, may have the function of preventing him from engaging in a new relationship.

His making sure that he does not lack crucial abilities certainly has a positive function, as mentioned above, but also serves to avoid repeating his parents' negative experiences with the lack of abilities.

Plans serving the maintenance of autonomy and control can be understood as resulting from the need to defend himself from his parents' attempts to control him. He maintains control actively, by verbally and nonverbally indicating what he expects the therapist to do or not to do. He also shows signs of passive resistance, for example, by not engaging in imagination exercises (which would require giving up some control) and by forgetting therapy homework assignments.

Mr. W.'s problems are a threat to his self-esteem. He copes with this threat by blaming others and circumstances for failures; he seeks acceptable situational and somatic explanations. Not focusing on his own contribution may also be interpreted as an attempt at maintaining his anxiety, which is embarrassing yet protects him from letting himself get into potentially even more embarrassing situations. Another subordinate Plan is to make himself (relatively) better by criticizing others; at times he appears to monitor his environment with the goal of finding something he can criticize. His previous therapist reported a similar impression.

In sum, his avoidance Plans make it difficult for him to use situations that would allow him to have positive experiences in line with his positive Plans.

5. Conflicts between Plans

Mr. W.'s structure is characterized by a number of conflicts between Plans, resulting in ambivalent behaviors and problematic compromises.

A central conflict is between establishing a close relationship and avoiding disappointments or being rejected. His avoidance Plans made it difficult to develop abilities and seek situations that would increase his chances of finding a good relationship. The fact that he has been engaged in a relationship with a dependent, unequal woman who seems unlikely to reject him can be viewed as a compromise between these two Plans.

Achievement Plans are also in conflict with withdrawal and avoidance Plans. The compromise is to involve himself in nonpersonal activities in which personal contacts are limited.

His control Plans are in conflict with his Plan of maintaining intense family contact and the Plan of improving his situation by therapy, because they are related to accepting strong control by his mother and potentially giving at least some control to the therapist. His compromises are to avoid awareness of his dependence on his parents and occasional weak attempts at escaping the control, and in therapy persistent attempts at controlling the therapist.

6. The Patient's Self-Concept

(*This includes the most important means of maintaining the patient's self-concept for her- or himself and the means of conveying it to others. Also included is information about which parts of her or his functioning the patient is apparently unaware of.*)

Mr. W. sees himself as a reliable, competent person with good qualities as a potential family man. He wants to be equal to the therapist. Based on neglect by his parents, he may be secretly afraid of being unlovable and therefore tries to repress or justify weaknesses. The degree to which his behavior and experience is determined by avoidance Plans and dependency upon his parents is not represented in his awareness.

7. The Most Important Stressors and the Most Important Positive Situations for the Patient: Strong Positive and Negative Emotions

The most stressful situations are clearly those in which Mr. W. would expose himself to scrutiny and rejection, in particular by women. Usually he can avoid these situations; if not, he experiences anxiety. The loss of his close relationship, even if it was not a good one, was painful to him. When he experiences the conflict between escaping from his parents' control and being rejected for such attempts, he feels stressed and annoyed, although he is not as aware of his dependency as are observers.

Positive situations are experiences of success in his job and leisure activities, for example, when receiving compliments for his collection of watches and his skill in repairing them. He also experiences positive excitement when he can escape control at his workplace, which he achieves by playing games.

(*Some of the experienced emotions are explicitly mentioned and related to the Plan structure [Figure 10.3] by the types of relations described in the text earlier [blocked Plans, Plans shaping the emotion, coping Plans, Plans for which the emotion has an instrumental function]. Establishing such explicit relations often gives additional information and is a test as to what degree the patient has already been understood. The most explicit way of relating emotions to Plans is the use of "emotion frames," labeled by "E" plus a number, each containing the information relevant to an emotion, and relating it to the Plan structure.*)

8. Relation between the Problems and the Plan Structure: Where Did the Patient (Partially) Succeed in Solving Problems?

His social phobia is the result of the patient's Plans of avoiding rejection and maintaining a positive self-concept being threatened by exposure and achievement situations and by conflictual positive Plans. The resulting concrete avoidance preoccupies him and restricts positive experiences. In particular, in contact with women he has not developed appropriate interpersonal skills and experience, which leads to a vicious circle. Plans of avoiding rejection by his parents keep him in an environment that additionally inhibits a development appropriate to his age.

That the patient has succeeded in acquiring good training and good employment is positive. The work- and hobby-related contacts and the contact with his parents prevent complete isolation, but the latter is obviously a dead end.

9. The Patient's View of His or Her Problems and Why the Patient Got into an Impasse

In general, the patient has a view of his problems that corresponds to topic 8, with the exception of a tendency to blame others, to use his being "down" and his anxiety as excuses against change, and to deny his dependency on his parents. The impasse developed as a consequence of lacking encouragement from his parents or others, which prevented him from developing skills and experiences appropriate to his age and necessary to achieve a situation corresponding to his wishes. A vicious circle developed with avoidance and increasing lack of self-efficacy expectation.

10. The Therapeutic Relationship

The patient is handicapped by his strong Plans of maintaining control, by his conflictual wish that the therapist structure the therapy and take responsibility for it, and by the persistent criticism of others. The fear of rejection and of threats to his positive self-concept also need to be considered. The fear of disappointment in close relationships may lead the patient to test the therapist before he lets himself enter into a closer therapeutic relationship.

Consistent with the goal of achieving a complementary relationship, the therapist should encourage the patient to maintain control and should ask for permission when he wants to restrict the patient's control. The therapist should actively and positively enhance the patient's self-esteem, emphasizing the patient's equal position. The therapist should acknowledge the patient's abilities whenever he can, mentioning the patient's expertise in his work; and openly and assertively admit his or her (the therapist's) insecurity when it occurs. The general strategy is to make the patient's problematic control and defense strategies superfluous as far as possible, to obviate their use rather than react to them contingently later on.

11. General Outline of What in the Therapy Could Help the Patient to Develop in a Desirable Direction

The therapeutic relationship is a major concern in this therapy and should be treated as described above.

In line with what the patient expects from the therapy, his social phobia and ability to achieve and maintain a close relationship should be treated with high priority. Goals to be achieved are a reduction in dysfunctional thoughts ("To be rejected would kill me," "One is either loved or rejected completely," etc.), working through emotions related to scrutiny and rejection (including experiences he had in the past), building up concrete skills needed in interpersonal interaction (above all with women), and skills needed for coping with failures and anxiety. It is crucial that he have positive experiences with previously avoided situations to enhance his self-efficacy expectation. Much could be gained if he would satisfy part of his interpersonal needs in other relationships, so that not everything would be loaded onto that one close relationship he wants so badly.

Means to reach these goals would, for example, be the following:

- Debating his assumptions and interpretations (as in cognitive therapy)
- Activating previously avoided emotions, for example, by using Gestalt therapy techniques (although one would need to pay a lot of attention to not threaten his need for control), and, above all, by well-prepared exposure
- Enhancing his skills by role playing and assignments for his real world, as well as building up self-instructions in the sense of Meichenbaum (1974)
- Concrete discussions and assignments related to establishing several personal relationships
- Including his parents occasionally in an attempt to gain their support for the processes their son needs to go through, or at least to neutralize any possible undermining of these processes on their part.

The procedure would partly be planned, partly take advantage of chances provided by situations occurring in the patient's life and of fluctuations in Plan activations and motivations in his life.

TRAINING

Plan Analysis should be seen as a set of heuristic concepts, rules, and strategies. Although developing good Plan Analysis case conceptualizations requires having at one's disposal most of this set, the use of Plan Analysis is not an all-or-nothing issue. Some of the elements required for Plan Analysis (such as diligently observing nonverbal behavior, and knowledge of heuristic etiological concepts of the development of depressive states) are generally useful in psychotherapy practice and not specific to Plan Analysis. The extent to which a therapist or trainee has such elements available determines largely what remains to be trained and at what level of proficiency the approach can be used after the training. Based on generally useful concepts and skills, some additional special elements need to be conveyed to most therapists interested in Plan Analysis.

A basic body of conceptual and technical knowledge can be acquired by reading. Literature is available describing the handling of many details and proposing exercises that can be done by individuals or small groups without a human trainer (Caspar, 1995). The ideal is to obtain a basic working knowledge of Plan Analysis through reading, then practicing one's skills in a workshop setting where participants engage in therapy role plays, which are analyzed in terms of possible Plan Analysis formulations. One needs to run into practical difficulties in order to learn how to master them. Trainees learn not only a technique but also about themselves by comparing their performance and their conclusions with those of others: they see blind spots in their perception, for example, tendencies to overinterpret, or the opposite, missing clinically important points by remaining too restrained in their interpretations, and so forth.

Because the first few analyses include many necessary discussions and clarifications, they are much more time consuming than are later analyses, but they represent necessary learning steps in achieving expertise. Whereas a trainee may need a day or more for a first comprehensive case conceptualization, an expert in his or her regular practice needs an hour or even less to work out the crucial points for a case of average difficulty. In our experience, students generally familiar with psychotherapy need about 2 weeks of guidance to develop the proficiency needed to produce reliable, comprehensive research analyses; but for most therapists a 2- or 3-day workshop, ideally with some time to practice on their own, enables them to develop reasonably good and clinically useful case conceptualizations.

RESEARCH SUPPORT FOR THE APPROACH

It is obvious that attempts at determining the "reliability" of complex Plan structures and case conceptualizations in the same way as it would be done for quantitative values from, say, personality scales, would be inappropriate. We have argued in greater detail elsewhere (Caspar, 1995) that simple coefficients of agreement hide rather than reveal the factors determining the actual accuracy of case conceptualizations. Comparisons reported in that publication show that on average the clinically significant agreement is reasonably good, but varies just as is the case for similar approaches, depending on, among other factors, the homogeneity of the analyzers' background and particulars of the patients.

It may at first glance be amazing that authors such as myself and Klaus Grawe, who came originally from a client-centered and behavioral tradition and who are strictly empirically oriented, put—relatively speaking—less emphasis on reliability coefficients than do authors coming from the psychodynamic tradition, who might be expected to have fewer reservations about individual speculative interpretations. The actual state of affairs may be explained by the greater reservations we have against traditional measures of agreement and by the greater importance we give to strictly empirical proof of the *utility* as opposed to the *veridicality* of case conceptualizations.

In several studies typical Plan structures have been worked out, for example, in comparing structures of patients with social phobia to patients with psychosomatic disorders. Such studies are summarized in Caspar (1995). In a series of studies, Plan Analysis has been used to analyze the resistance of patients; it was found to be useful in understanding and predicting resistance phenomena.

Effects of using Plan Analysis case conceptualizations have been investigated in several studies. A study done by independent social psychologists (Thommen et al., 1988) revealed striking differences in the ways of constructing and controlling therapeutic action between client-centered therapists and broad-spectrum behavior therapists using Plan Analysis. The latter were much more flexible in utilizing the situation while pursuing their central strategies.

Grawe et al. (1990) found that in a comparison of client-centered therapists and of broad-spectrum behavior therapists using traditional functional behavior analysis versus Plan Analysis, on average all forms of therapy produced good results. The latter therapists, however, had better achievements related to individually important patient goals, and they had, above all, strikingly better therapeutic relationships, along with lower dropout rates. Our fear turned out not to be justified that patients might feel that their therapists often only say part of what they really think, that they speak in an overly complicated way, or that they pay too little attention to patient feelings. Overall, therapies based on Plan Analysis are somewhat better in important *outcome measures* and, above all, make a much better impression in a broad spectrum of *process measures*. An aspect of high importance is that therapists were, just like their patients, much more satisfied with what they did. Another surprising result was the degree to which the therapeutic procedure in Plan-Analysis-based therapies was richer in terms of the types of techniques used.

There are interesting applications of Plan Analysis in other fields. One especially worth mentioning is the analysis of politician's self-presentation in TV discussions by Schütz (1992). The study shows that parts of the clinical Plan Analysis approach can be creatively utilized in fields that appear very different on the surface but have some similarities, such as using interactional strategies in order to make others feel and behave in a way that is favorable to oneself.

ACKNOWLEDGMENTS

I would like to thank Sarah Wright and Tracy D. Eells for their help in putting the manuscript into proper English.

REFERENCES

Argyle, M. (1969). *Social interaction*. London: Methuen.

Bandura, A. (1977). Self-efficacy: Toward a unifying theory of behavior change. *Psychological Review, 84*, 191–215.

Beck, A. T., Rush, J. A., Shaw, B. F., & Emery, G. (1979). *Cognitive therapy of depression*. New York: Guilford Press.

Beier, E. G. (1966). *The silent language of psychotherapy*. Chicago: Aldine.

Beutler, L., & Clarkin, J. (1990). *Systematic treatment selection*. New York: Brunner/ Mazel.

Caspar, F. (1984). *Analyse interaktioneller Pläne.* Unpublished dissertation, University of Bern.

Caspar, F. (1987). Anxiety: A complex problem calling for flexible therapy planning. In J. P. Dauwalder, M. Perrez, & V. Hobi (Eds.), *Controversial issues in behavior modification* (pp. 139–147). Amsterdam: Swets & Zeitlinger.

Caspar, F. (1988, June). *The dangers of standardizing the elements of dynamic formulations.* Paper presented at the annual meeting of the Society for Psychotherapy Research, Santa Fe, NM.

Caspar, F. (1994). Die Bedeutung von Theorie für die psychotherapeutische Praxis. *Verhaltensmodifikation und Verhaltensmedizin, 15,* 54–67.

Caspar, F. (1995). *Plan Analysis: Towards optimizing psychotherapy.* Seattle, WA: Hogrefe & Huber.

Caspar, F., & Grawe, K. (1981). Widerstand in der Verhaltenstherapie. In H. Petzold (Ed.), *Der Widerstand: Ein strittiges Konzept in der Psychotherapie* (pp. 349–384). Paderborn, Germany: Junfermann.

Caspar, F., Rothenfluh, T., & Segal, Z. V. (1992). The appeal of connectionism for clinical psychology. *Clinical Psychology Review, 12,* 719–762.

Coyne, J. C., Downey, G., & Boergers, J. (1992). Depression in families: A systems perspective. In D. Cicchetti & S. L. Toth (Eds.), *Developmental perspectives on depression* (pp. 211–249). Rochester, NY: University of Rochester Press.

Curtis, J. T., Silberschatz, G., Sampson, H., & Weiss, J. (1994). The plan formulation method. *Psychotherapy Research, 46,* 197–207.

Ellis, A. (1962). *Reason and emotion in psychotherapy.* New York: Stuart.

Feldman, L. B. (1976). Depression and marital interaction. *Family Process, 15,* 398–395.

Grawe, K. (1980). Die diagnostisch-therapeutische Funktion der Gruppeninteraktion in verhaltenstherapeutischen Gruppen. In K. Grawe (Ed.), *Verhaltenstherapie in Gruppen* (pp. 88–223). Munich: Urban & Schwarzenberg.

Grawe, K. (1986). *Schema-Theorie und interaktionelle Psychotherapie* (Report 1-86). Bern: Psychological Institute, University of Bern.

Grawe, K. (1992). *Schema theory and heuristic psychotherapy* (Forschungsberichte No. 1-1992). Bern: Psychological Institute, University of Bern.

Grawe, K., Caspar, F., & Ambühl, H. R. (1990). Differentielle Psychotherapieforschung: Vier Therapieformen im Vergleich—Die Berner Therapievergleichsstudie. *Zeitschrift für Klinische Psychologie, 19,* 294–376.

Grawe, K., Donati, R., & Bernauer, F. (in press). *Psychotherapy in transition.* Seattle, WA: Hogrefe & Huber.

Greenberg, L. S., & Safran, J. D. (1987). *Emotion in psychotherapy: Affect, cognition, and the process of change.* New York: Guilford Press.

Horowitz, M. J. (1979). *States of mind: Analysis of change in psychotherapy.* New York: Plenum Press.

Kanfer, F. H., & Grimm, L. G. (1980). Managing clinical change: A process model of therapy. *Behavior Modification, 4,* 419–444.

Kanfer, F. [H.], Reinecker, H., & Schmelzer, D. (1991). *Selbstmanagement-Therapie.* Berlin: Springer-Verlag.

Kiesler, D. J. (1973). *The process of psychotherapy: Empirical foundations and systems of analysis.* Chicago: Aldine.

Lazarus, R. S. (1966). *Psychological stress and the coping process.* New York: McGraw-Hill.

Lazarus, R. S., Kanner, A., & Folkman, S. (1972). Emotions: A cognitive-phenomenological analysis. In R. Plutchik & H. Kellermann (Eds.), *Theories of emotion* (pp. 189–217). New York: Academic Press.

Leary, T. (1957). *Interpersonal diagnosis of personality.* New York: Ronald Press

Leventhal, H. (1980). Toward a comprehensive theory of emotion. In L. Berkowitz (Ed.), *Advances in experimental social psychology* (pp. 140–207). New York: Academic Press.

Lewinsohn, P. H. (1974). A behavioral approach to depression. In R. J. Friedman & M. M. Katz (Eds.), *The psychology of depression: Contemporary theory and research* (pp. 157–185). Washington, DC: Winston Wiley.

Luborsky, L. (1990). Theory and technique in dynamic psychotherapy: Curative factors and training therapists to maximize them. *Psychotherapy and Psychosomatics, 53,* 50–57.

Mahoney, M. J. (1974). *Cognition and behavior modification.* Cambridge, MA: Ballinger.

Mahoney, M. [J.] (1991). *Human change processes.* New York: Basic Books.

Mandler, G. (1975). *Mind and emotion.* New York: Wiley.

Meichenbaum, D. (1974). *Cognitive behavior modification.* Morristown, NJ: General Learning Press.

Miller, G. A., Galanter, E., & Pribram, K. H. (1960). *Plans and the structure of behavior.* New York: Holt.

Mischel, W. (1973). Toward a cognitive learning reconceptualization of personality. *Psychological Review, 80,* 252–283.

Ortony, A., Clore, G. L., & Foss, M. A. (1987). The referential structure of the affective lexicon. *Cognitive Science, 11,* 341–364.

Persons, J. B. (1989). *Cognitive therapy in practice: A case formulation approach.* New York: Norton.

Piaget, J. (1977). *The development of thought: Equilibration of cognitive structures.* New York: Viking Press.

Prigogine, I. (1976). Order through fluctuation: Self-organization and social system. In E. Jantsch & C. H. Waddington (Eds.), *Evolution and consciousness* (pp. 93–133). Cambridge, MA: Addison-Wesley.

Schonauer, F. (1992). Gestern traf ich Huckleberry Finn. In Herrmann-Josef-Haus Urft (Ed.), *Leben formt Leben* (pp. 157–188). Kall-Urft: Hermann-Josef Haus.

Schütz, A. (1992). *Selbstdarstellung von Politikern: Analyse von Wahlkampfauftritten* [*Self-presentation of politicians: An analysis of election campaigns*]. Weinheim: Deutscher Studienverlag.

Seligman, M. E. P. (1975). *Learned helplessness.* San Francisco: Freeman.

Selvini-Palazzoli, M., Boscolo, L., Cecchin, G., & Prata, G. (1987). *Paradox and counterparadox.* New York: Aronson.

Simon, H. A., & Newell, A. (1970). Human problem solving. *American Psychologist, 25,* 48–59.

Strupp, H. H., & Binder, J. L. (1984). *Psychotherapy in a new key.* New York: Basic Books.

Sullivan, H. S. (1953). *The interpersonal theory of psychiatry.* New York: Norton.

Thomä, H., & Kächele, H. (1988). *Lehrbuch der psychoanalytischen Therapie: Vol. 2. Praxis.* Berlin: Springer-Verlag.

Thommen, B., Ammann, R., & von Cranach, M. (1988). *Handlungsorganisation durch soziale Repräsentationen.* Bern: Huber.

Urban, H. B., & Ford, D. H. (1971). Some historical and conceptual perspectives on psychotherapy and behavior change. In A. E. Bergin & S. L. Garfield (Eds.), *Handbook of psychotherapy and behavior change* (pp. 3–35). New York: Wiley.

Watzlawick, P., Beavin, J. H., & Jackson, D. D. (1967). *Pragmatics of human communication: A study of interactional patterns, pathologies, and paradoxes.* New York: Norton.

Weiss, J., Sampson, H., & the Mount Zion Psychotherapy Research Group. (1986). *The psychoanalytic process: Theory, clinical observations, and empirical research.* New York: Guilford Press.

Weissman, M. M., & Klerman, G. L. (1990). Interpersonal psychotherapy for depression. In B. B. Wolman & G. Stricker (Eds.), *Depressive disorders: Facts, theories, and treatment methods* (pp. 379–395). New York: Wiley.

Willi, J. (1982). *Couples in collusion.* New York: Aronson.

Zajonc, R. B. (1980). Feeling and thinking: Preferences need no inferences. *American Psychologist, 35,* 151–175.

11

Case Formulation in Cognitive Analytic Therapy

ANTHONY RYLE
DAWN BENNETT

HISTORICAL BACKGROUND OF THE APPROACH[1]

The origins of Cognitive Analytic Therapy (CAT) can be traced back to my (A. R.) involvement in outcome research into dynamic psychotherapy and the way in which this confronted me with the inadequacies of psychoanalytic case formulation. Even if the goals of dynamic therapy may be less precise than those of behavior therapy (including, e.g., the exploration of hitherto unrecognized issues), in practice most dynamic psychotherapy is focused on beliefs, behaviors, and experiences that the patient can describe and wishes to change. My attempt to identify and describe these was one source of CAT.

A second influence on the development of CAT was George A. Kelly (1955) and my extensive use of his repertory grid technique. My experience of treating patients in dynamic psychotherapy while researching the process with this essentially cognitive method (Ryle, 1975) led me to recognize the need for a common language for the psychotherapies and to associate myself with the emerging move toward psychotherapy integration (Ryle, 1978, 1987). My use of repertory grids led to new ways of conceptualizing dynamic issues that patients found accessible and useful.

A third influence was my review of a series of completed psychotherapies with the aim of identifying the issues that had been addressed. This suggested that the nonrevision of problematic ways of acting could be attributed to three patterns, which I labeled *dilemmas*, *traps*, and *snags* (Ryle, 1979a).

Dilemmas represent the narrowing of options for actions or roles to two polarized alternatives. Individuals who continue to exhibit damaging ways of acting or relating often do so because they perceive the only alternative to be equally or more damaging. Dilemmas can be described as "either–or," as in "*Either* I am in total control *or* in unmanageable chaos," or "*Either* I am controllingly caretaking *or* submissively dependent." They can also be expressed in terms of "if–then," as in "*If* I am feminine *then* I must be passive" or "*If* I am affectionate *then* I am weak."

Traps are circular sequences in which a negative belief or assumption generates ways of acting or relating that produces consequences appearing to confirm the negative belief. An example would be "Feeling that I am worthless I seek to avoid rejection by doing what others seem to want. The result is that I get used or abused, which confirms my feeling worthless."

Snags represent that abandonment or spoiling of appropriate acts or roles on the (true or false) prediction that others will react negatively, or because of (not necessarily conscious) responses from aspects of the self. For example, "In my life I seem to continually avoid or dismantle success as if these were not allowed. This may stem from feeling guilty when I did better than my handicapped sister."

While this identification of patterns was originally developed in order to provide a basis for measuring dynamic change, it quickly became apparent that the joint work with patients involved in arriving at the descriptions was itself therapeutically effective. At this point, therefore, my practice was modified and in place of conventional dynamic psychotherapy I began to evolve the particular approach that became CAT.

The defining features of CAT continue to be (1) the early recruitment of patients to the task of describing these processes and (2) the development by the therapist, over the first four sessions, of a draft "reformulation," to be discussed, modified if necessary, and finalized by the fifth session. This written reformulation combines Bruner's (1986) "narrative" and "paradigmatic" modes (Ryle, 1994a). The former consists of a letter written by the therapist that retells the patient's life story in a way seeking to link past and present, to name directly what appear to be distorted or denied feelings and meanings, and to allocate responsibility more equably. The letter ends in paradigmatic mode by listing, in the form of dilemmas, traps, and snags, the dominant negative patterns that therapy will seek to revise. In recent practice this is normally supplemented by a diagrammatic representation of the self-maintaining patterns.

These descriptive tools came to play a dominant role in therapy. They are used by the patient in a new form of self-monitoring through which the recurrence of the negative patterns in daily life can be first recognized and then blocked or replaced, and they provide the therapist with a way of avoiding collusion and of using in-session manifestations of the negative patterns to aid recognition and explore alternatives.

CONCEPTUAL FRAMEWORK

The full descriptions of dilemmas, traps, and snags involved identifying sequences of environmental, mental, and behavioral events, and such sequences, normally capable of revision, were seen to underlie all intentional action. The Procedural Sequence Model (PSM) (Ryle, 1982) explains intentional action in terms of (a) Mental Processes (perception, appraisal, the formation of an aim, the consideration of alternative means, or subprocedures, and the selection of one; (b) Behavior, Roles, or Acts; (c) Judging the Consequences; and (d) confirming or revising the aim or procedure.

This linking of intrapsychic, behavioral, and environmental factors offers explanations of how neurosis persists and provides a way of understanding how very different therapeutic processes, addressing different points in the sequence and different levels in the procedural hierarchy, may generate similar changes (Ryle, 1984). The relation of CAT to psychoanalytic ides was discussed in Ryle (1990, 1995a). The further development of the CAT model involved the fuller incorporation of ideas from object relations theories.

A key concept in this elaboration of what became the Procedural Sequence Object Relations Model (PSORM) was the *reciprocal role procedure* (RRP). Procedures are circular processes involving the prediction of the consequences and the matching of these against the actual consequences. In a role procedure involving action, affect, and communication, these consequences are the reciprocation offered by, or elicited from, the other. In the course of development an individual builds up a more or less stable *repertoire of RRPs* and relationships will be organized within this repertoire. These patterns are normally stable because of the way in which others can be chosen or induced to reciprocate in terms of the procedure, an understanding that is close to Wachtel's "circular psychodynamics" (see Gold & Wachtel, 1993). RRPs are elaborated on the basis of those acquired in the infant and child's interactions with parents, other caretakers, and siblings. They are derived from what Stern (1985) described as RIGS (Representations of Interactions that have been Generalized) and imply a formative role for parents and their procedures. This receives support from recent work in the attachment theory field (e.g., Fonagy, Steele, Steele, Higgitt, & Target, 1994). Following Ogden (1983), each early interaction is seen to allow the child to learn and play *two* roles, one initially his or her own, the other the reciprocating role initially played by the other (Ryle, 1985). Roles associated with unmanageable feelings may be replaced by defensive or symptomatic procedures, or they may be induced in others, an understanding of projective identification that is elaborated in Ryle (1994b). Transference and countertransference are understood similarly as the meshing of reciprocal roles or the attempt to induce such meshing.

While this model was being developed, a new technique was being introduced into the process of reformulation—that of Sequential Diagrammatic Reformulation (SDR). This was influenced by M. J. Horowitz's (1979) "configurational analysis" of therapy transcripts (see Chapter 7, this volume). In CAT the SDR is constructed during the early joint reformulation process and thereafter forms a basic "tool" of the therapeutic work.

The circularity and self-reinforcement of procedures are usually more accessibly presented through diagrammatic representations of patient's "systems" than through prose descriptions. Such diagrams developed from relatively simple sequences (Beard, Marlowe, & Ryle, 1990; Ryle, 1990) to a model based upon the generation of role, self-management, and symptomatic procedures from a central "core." This core lists, as a heuristic device, the repertoire of reciprocal roles that represents the individual's "rule book" for conducting relationships and self-management. Work with borderline patients led to a model of two or more alternating "self-states," more or less dissociated, each of which was described in terms of its core reciprocal role pattern. Shifts between self-states could be provoked by external events or could be the consequences of particular procedures. Each self-state has typical associated symptoms and patterns of emotional expression or control. The work involved in tracing these states and their connections proved of great benefit, resulting in the early involvement of borderline patients in therapy, and in many cases in the rapid development of a more continuous capacity for self-reflection leading to personality integration.

The most recent developments in CAT have involved the introduction of ideas from the work of Vygotsky (1962, 1978), Voloshinov (1973), and Bakhtin (1984). Vygotsky had in fact been an early influence, mediated by the work of Bruner, whose description of the "scaffolding" role of the teacher in providing ideas, pacing tasks and handing over responsibility (described in Wood, Bruner, & Ross, 1976) offered a model for the work of therapy. All higher learning is seen to involve the internalization of concepts derived from mediated interpersonal activity: in Vygotsky's words, "what the child does with an adult today she will do on her own tomorrow." Parallel with this work Voloshinov was developing and criticizing the ideas of Ferdinand de Saussure by insisting that language could only be understood when its existence as essentially *between* people was recognized. In this view the individual psyche was understood to be the product of the signs acquired interpersonally and culturally. Individual speech is a small corner of the ongoing conversation of humankind (Harré, 1987), and thought is essentially dialogic, an understanding explored in Bakhtin's literary and philosophical writings, to which Holquist (1990) has contributed a valuable commentary.

The relation of "activity theory" (which developed Vygotsky's approach) to object relations theory was discussed in Ryle (1991), as was their possible synthesis in the procedural model of CAT. The implications of the concept of *sign mediation* for human psychology are being actively developed by Leiman (1992, 1994, 1995). Sign mediation serves to indicate the specifically human aspects of development, whereby we inhabit, from an early age, a world mediated by the meanings conveyed to us in the signs we derive from those around us. In terms of abnormal development this suggests that both the experience of the child, for example, of deprivation or abuse, and the meaning accorded to it, from which the individual's sense of self and reality and capacity for self-reflection are derived, contribute to pathology.

In its emphasis on dialogue, with others and with the self, this model offers a general understanding of inner conflict or debate in which intrapsychic and interpersonal "voices" are involved; the dynamic unconscious (considered to be but one of many forms of unconsciousness) represents a "silenced voice" that makes itself known by acts, omissions, or more direct hints such as dreams.

The introduction of these ideas, and the fact that they seem to be consistent with recent observational studies of early development (e.g., Stern, 1985; Westen, 1990; Hobson, 1993), distinguishes CAT theory from both its cognitive and psychoanalytic roots. The richness of individual consciousness is the product of the culture. That what is transmitted may also be limiting or distorting is also evidently true and of particular concern to psychotherapists. Through language, however, we have the capacity to reflect consciously on both the biological and social "givens" of our early experience and can, to that extent, achieve some independence from them.

The Basic Concepts and Vocabulary of CAT

The main features of CAT may be summarized as follows:

The joint elaboration of high-level descriptions of patients' problematic processes is central to CAT practice. The chosen unit of description is the *procedure* or *procedural sequence* involving mental processes, action, and environmental events and consequences. Common patterns preventing the revision of problematic procedures are identified as *dilemmas, traps,* and *snags,* and these are located in a model of aim directed activity, the PSM.

The PSORM focuses on RRPs and points to the origin of an individual's *repertoire of reciprocal roles* in early interaction with caretakers. An individual's repertoire of reciprocal roles will be manifest (a) in the way relationships with others are conducted, in which either pole may be enacted with the reciprocal role being elicited (b) in relation to the *self-management procedures* (SMPs). In addition, (c) feared or disavowed roles may be replaced by *symptomatic or defensive procedures*; these involve patterns of relationship as well as the avoidance of affects or memories.

Problem procedures may be described verbally but are often best expressed diagrammatically through SDR. In this a core repertoire of reciprocal roles is listed and the manifestations of the different roles in relationship, self-management, symptomatic, or defensive procedures are drawn as *procedural loops.* Problematic procedures, often in the form of dilemmas, traps, or snags, will be self-reinforcing or will lead in some other way to the maintenance of the core repertoire.

Personality in this model is understood to be *dialogic,* in the sense that it originates in relation to others and insofar as internal division and debate is a central characteristic. All acts and communications seek a response. Severe personality disturbance can be usefully understood in terms of the existence and alternate dominance of two or more *self-states*, each with a characteristic repertoire of reciprocal roles. In such cases environmental events or enacting certain procedures may provoke *state switches*.

INCLUSION/EXCLUSION CRITERIA

CAT is a time-limited approach, usually given over 8–24 sessions. It is considered a safe and effective first intervention for the full range of neurotic and personality disordered patients encountered in outpatient practice. This confidence is based on my (A. R.) having run a psychotherapy department in an inner-city area for 10 years with a maximum of 1.5 trained psychotherapy staff available to supervise trainee therapists. Under these circumstances I felt bound to offer the minimum sufficient intervention to all 130 referrals assessed each year, and this meant that patients taken on received either CAT or group therapy, or a combination of the two.

Referrals came for general medical practitioners, from psychiatric colleagues, and from community centers of various kinds. Patients were of varying age, but mostly in the 25–50 range. There was the usual preponderance of women. The area was multiethnic; some groups, notably those from the Indian subcontinent, were seldom referred, and the proportion of graduates seen was above the average for the area; nonetheless, the majority of the patients were from traditional working-class homes and many were from first-generation immigrant families.

About 15% of referred patients were considered more suitable for cognitive behavioral interventions or other interventions such as detoxification. A very small number requested and could afford the time and money for longer-term individual therapy. The remainder were accepted for treatment, with the following exceptions: (1) major untreated depression—these cases, and bipolar affective disorders, would be treated once medication was established; (2) schizophrenia; and (3) ongoing heavy abuse of drugs or alcohol (but some intermittent abusers were accepted). Patients who were not "psychologically minded" were not excluded, it being considered the task of therapy to generate a capacity for self-reflection. Patients with powerful suicidal ideas or with a history of episodes of violence were not excluded, this seeming possible in a hospital setting, with inpatient support being available; patients were also recruited after episodes of deliberate self-harm (Cowmeadow, 1994, 1995). Patients using prescribed or illegal drugs or alcohol were required to keep diaries of their use, to decrease consumption, and to come free of the substance to therapy. Despite these broad entry criteria, the suicide rate during therapy and the follow up period was low: four cases in more than a thousand treated patients, all the patients being inpatients at the time, suffering from severe personality disorders, and in three of these cases from bipolar affective disorders.

Within such a comprehensive service, CAT can offer an economical first intervention, and an adequate one for about two-thirds of referrals. If further treatment is needed, CAT provides an introduction to therapy on the basis of which further appropriate interventions may be planned. In poorly resourced services, the indications for more intensive or extensive treatment need to be exacting, for two years of twice weekly dynamic therapy absorbs as much therapist time as do 12 CAT treatments.

STEPS IN CASE REFORMULATION CONSTRUCTION

The first four sessions of CAT are explicitly devoted to the reformulation of the patient's presenting problems into a form designed to convey an understanding of the life history and the conclusions drawn from it. The aim is to describe the continuing constructive or destructive procedures manifest in the patient's management of self and of relationships with others in a way that conveys understanding of the history and that identifies how revision of destructive or restrictive procedures has not been possible. Recasting the story in this way involves both the patient and the therapist in a great deal of work outside the therapy hour and requires, but also generates, a good working relationship.

The final form of this reformulation will be recorded in writing and a diagram; these will have been derived from preliminary descriptions and discussions during the first sessions, and will be honed until they are fully acceptable to the patient. The accuracy of this will depend upon the therapist's skill in balancing the formal tasks with the provision of time and an atmosphere that allows the patient to convey, directly and indirectly, the meanings he or she has derived from past experience. The aim is for the therapist to know the patient accurately in respect of those attributes that therapy must aim to modify. It is a formidable task, and accuracy in selecting and defining the issues is essential in a therapy that, in a 30-year-old patient, will occupy no more than 0.006% of the patient's lifetime.

Much of the time spent together in these first 3 sessions can be relatively unstructured, allowing patients to present whatever they see as relevant. In addition patients are given the Psychotherapy File (Ryle, 1990, 1995a) in the first session. This has three parts. The first describes the rationale of the patient's self-monitoring of moods and symptoms. Specific monitoring of the individual's unstable moods or variable symptoms is suggested. The second part offers a brief description of how problems may be maintained by the patterns labeled as dilemmas, traps, and snags, and provides a range of brief descriptions of common examples under each heading. The third part has screening questions designed to detect the state shifts common in borderline personalities.

The Psychotherapy File is not a questionnaire yielding scores; rather, it is a basis for joint discussion, a description of how one may think about problems, and an invitation to participate in the work of therapy. In the majority of cases patients find it useful, and discussing the items they have identified as applying to them usually shows they have been able to match their own procedures with the descriptions thoughtfully. In more inhibited patients, or with more uncertain therapists, the marked items on the file can indicate key issues. In patients who are disinhibited or histrionic, on the other hand, the file can be of help in encouraging detailed description rather than global emotional discharges. In other cases, the file may be left on the bus or serve as an agenda for a family meeting, or may be contemptuously dismissed as too simplistic; as with every enactment in therapy, the procedural understanding of what these acts express will need to be explored.

The self-monitoring of moods and symptoms will focus on triggering events and accompanying thoughts, as in cognitive therapy. Symptoms and moods are understood as alternatives to feared or disallowed procedures, most commonly in the areas of assertion, and the aim will be to transfer the patient's attention to the procedure that has been replaced rather than to the symptom. This view follows the Freudian concept of primary gain; secondary gain would be understood in CAT as a description of the interpersonal or intrapersonal function of the symptomatic procedure.

The following description of the reformulation task is abridged from Ryle (1995a):

Sessions 1–3: Gathering Data and the Preliminary Reformulation

The aim, in these early sessions, is to gain as extensive an understanding of the patient's experience as possible and to give the patient some experience of the kind of offer the therapist is making in order to recruit him or her to the work. The difficulties stem from the need to gather a full range of historical and diagnostic data, which encourages active questioning, while leaving choice of topic and theme as far as possible to the patient. In addition, the problem procedures of some patients are likely to limit their capacity or willingness to reveal much about themselves. At the first session it is best to say briefly what one has already gathered from the referral letter and invite the patient to expand on that. What patients say and how they say it, supplemented by prompts to speak of particular phases or themes in their life or to talk about particular people, is usually enough to convey a fairly comprehensive view of the nature of the problem. It is always a good idea to rehearse the main themes at the end of the session to confirm that one has understood the story correctly; if possible it is also helpful to identify some underlying assumptions or recurrent procedural patterns. At the end of this session the Psychotherapy File will be introduced, and self-monitoring and other work that may contribute to reformulation may also be asked for. Where no previous psychological/psychiatric assessment has taken place, the gaps in the history and symptom profile gathered at this session should be noted and a small part of the next session should be devoted to covering the ground. Symptom questionnaires that may have been issued before the patient was seen should be inspected, and evidence of symptoms not discussed in the session should be explored.

Over the ensuing two sessions the history will be amplified, the Psychotherapy File discussed, and increasingly the pattern of the therapeutic relationship will begin to emerge. This will usually combine a developing working relationship with the manifestation of the patient's problem procedures in most cases. Overcompliance and placation engendered by the hope for help may be useful in the short run but need to be named and later resistance anticipated. Failure to complete agreed tasks or evasiveness or silence in the room must, obviously, be addressed, but in the form of a procedural description, which can usually be linked with the presenting difficulties, rather than of a disciplinary admonition. Less overt aspects of the interaction may indicate problem-related feelings and attitudes and may evoke corresponding countertransference feelings in the therapist, contributing to the understanding to be recorded in the reformulation.

To a large extent conflict between the "cognitive" and "analytic" components of CAT is minimal, as all that takes place is aimed at the accurate understanding of the patient and the initiation of the therapeutic work. The cognitive component may become intrusive only if by "analytic" is implied an unyielding transference-centered interpretative mode. However, as far as possible, the introduction and discussion of cognitive tasks should be timed in such a way that it does not overstructure the session and block exploration. Conversely, in the more open-ended and exploratory aspects of the meetings, the need is to link the material not just to immediate associations but to the wider, overarching understandings of the emerging reformulation.

The Reformulation Session

This session (usually Session 4) will have been described in advance as being of a special nature. Even though most of the issues will have been discussed to some degree, it requires considerable preparation. The draft of the reformulation, in writing, should be read out in the session, and the patient's comments and responses to this should be carefully noted. Reactions are often intense and serve to confirm the understandings and the sense of a felt working alliance, but placatory responses must be distinguished from acceptance, and rejection of parts as inaccurate and needing correction must be distinguished from responses that are expressions of a dismissive or envious procedure. The finalized written version, prepared after this meeting, will take note of these responses. Any parts deemed important but not accepted by the patient should either be omitted or included but noted as not agreed upon.

The reformulation process, devoted to the formation of the central tool of the therapy, is at the same time a lived example of collaborative, respecting, and thoughtful relationship. Good CAT involves recruiting the patient to the task by (1) clearly describing its joint nature; (2) encouraging full discussion of homework tasks; (3) timing interventions, leaving gaps, etc. in order to elicit the patients' views; (4) making all suggestions in ways inviting comment and possible dissent; and (5) inviting patients to answer questions for themselves, before replying. The work orientation of CAT should not be misapplied; pauses and silences and tact provide the spaces into which the patient pours the material from which the understandings of the reformulation are built.

The Reformulation Letter

Most of the elements of the reformulation will have been discussed during the first three sessions, but re-presenting the story in a letter is an emotionally powerful moment, serving to cement the therapeutic alliance in most cases.

The letter should do the following:

1. Describe the patient's past experiences and name simply and directly the difficulties and pains of the life; this serves to validate experiences that have often been partially denied and can clarify what the patient was and was not responsible for.
2. Describe the procedures used by the patient to cope; the word "defence" is often felt to be critical, and it is better to talk in terms of ways of coping or strategies.
3. List current problems and problem procedures and note how these may affect therapy.

The problems listed should include those the patient complains of, for example, depression, fear of open spaces, or difficult relationships, but we need also to list the problems that patients manifest but do not name, perhaps because they have come to see their distress as normal or their negative beliefs as true. Thus problems such as "never really enjoying anything" or "being overcritical of myself" may be discussed.

Descriptions of problem procedures, normally in the form of dilemmas, traps, and snags, should trace the sequence of mental processes, action, and external events and consequences. An abbreviated version will be transferred to the rating sheet.

Sequential Diagrammatic Reformulation

The SDR offers the most complete representation of how problem procedures are generated and maintained. The core (or cores in multiple self-states) contains a list of the main reciprocal role procedures. These generate (1) relationship procedures, (2) self-management procedures, and (3) symptomatic or defensive procedures that have replaced the enactment of the feared or forbidden or unmanageable feelings and roles listed in the core.

In constructing the core repertoire therapists draw on all the data at their disposal—namely, the patient's history and current life, the patient's demeanor, the results of homework tasks, and the countertransference feelings elicited. The core patterns are derived from the rules and expectations learned in childhood and may include quite extreme versions of negative and positive roles. Procedural loops describing enacted procedures should be traced from the appropriate core role; they will usually include a "coping mode" such as placation, avoiding closeness, or perfectionism, a relationship pattern such as powerful caregiving to submissive needy others, self-management procedures such as striving in relation to internal demands, and defensive or symptomatic procedures.

APPLICATION TO PSYCHOTHERAPY TECHNIQUE

The reformulation process demands from the therapist both empathy and conceptual clarity. The participation of the patient in this process is a safeguard against including descriptions that are seen by the patient as meaningless or wrong. Once reformulation is complete, the patient and therapist will each hold a written copy of the letter, a list of problems and problem procedures, and a sequential diagram. Whatever is brought into therapy in the form of narratives (see Luborsky, Barber & Diguer, 1992) and whatever evolves in the therapy relationship will be considered in relation to these.

The "three R's" of CAT are reformulation, recognition, and revision, and much of Sessions 5–16 will be concerned with the second of these. Recognition will be achieved through specific, focused homework tasks, such as keeping diaries recording particular procedures (e.g., a placation diary) or by keeping a diary of personally significant events or experiences that is subsequently linked by the patient to the reformulation. Some patients can achieve change simply through this kind of work, but many, notably the more disturbed and fragmented personality disordered ones, will need the therapist to recognize the problem procedures as they occur in the room, when they can be named and where collusion with them can be avoided or quickly corrected. Collusion can lead to missed sessions and premature termination.

Descriptions of problem procedures and the SDR are used to develop recognition of the procedures in daily life and in the sessions. A rating sheet is completed weekly, recording the recognition and changes in intensity of the problem procedures; this serves to maintain the focus of the work as well as to record changes. A range of techniques directed toward modifying identified aspects of the patient's procedures and self-states can be employed, but enhancing the patient's self-reflective capacity through the reformulatory tools is the central aim. The therapist links, and later invites the patient to link, reported narratives of outside events to the SDR. The SDR is also valuable to therapists in aiding the prediction of transference and the recognition or avoidance of countertransference reactions, hence assisting in a noncollusive therapeutic relationship. We share the view of Wachtel (1991) that it is not possible to completely avoid falling into complementary behavior patterns but that the therapist needs to acknowledge and specifically describe this when it occurs. Accurate self-observation in combination with the experience of a noncollusive relationship with the therapist is thought to allow the tools and the therapist to be internalized.

A large proportion of what patients bring to the session in the form of memories, stories, or dreams will turn out to be illustrations of their main procedures. In addition, sooner or later most of their problem procedures will be manifest in the therapy relationship, either in behaviors such as lateness, disarming chat, direct anger or criticism, discounting what has been done and failures to do agreed homework, or in covert mood shifts, conveyed indirectly and nonverbally. These may affect a whole session or set of sessions or they may emerge as a "state shift" in the course of the session. The recognition of these transference manifestations may not be instantly possible, and sometimes the pattern is only apparent in retrospect at the end of the session or after the session (or in supervision).

Transference is conceptualized as an enactment of a procedure representing one pole of the patient's reciprocal role repertoire in the therapeutic relationship; pressure imposed on the therapist to reciprocate induces countertransference. The model hypothesizes five stages through which enactments can be used therapeutically. In the first, *Acknowledgment,* the therapist makes explicit his or her recognition of an in-session event and/or acknowledges the patient's feelings or expression directed at them. In the second stage, *Exploration,* the patient and therapist express and clarify their understandings of the in-session event. They negotiate and settle on a description of what is occurring between them. In the third stage, *Linking and Explanation,* the therapist begins to link, or invites the patient to link, the in-session experience to the SDR and to other in-session events, current relationships, and the past. Through the negotiation and adjustment of misunderstandings and disagreements they reach an understanding—in the fourth stage, *Negotiation*—that includes a consideration of their respective roles and responsibilities for the occurrence of the event. *Consensus,* the fifth stage, involves the explicit understanding of the parallels between in-session and outside-session experiences. The SDR is seen as a central tool in facilitating this task of procedural enactment recognition.

Termination and the Goodbye Letter

At the penultimate session the therapist and patient exchange "goodbye letters."

The goodbye letter from the therapist is a means of offering a realistic estimation of the changes achieved and of the work remaining; it should be accurate, should be linked with specific evidence, and should name or predict the element of disappointment, sadness, or anger, while "permitting" the patient to take away a realistic memory of the therapist and a clear account of the understandings reached. In brief therapy the patient must continue to be a therapist to him- or herself, and an ongoing internal conversation with the therapist should be encouraged. Patients are also encouraged to write a good-bye letter. The period between termination and follow-up is an important one in which it becomes clear how far the understandings have been taken on board; decisions about the need for further follow-up, more CAT, or other treatments are best left until this time, usually after 3 months. In cases evoking particular anxiety, a shorter interval or spaced sessions may be helpful without depriving the patient of the experience of termination.

CASE EXAMPLE

Nick is a 32-year-old clerical worker complaining of depression and reporting out-of-control anger. His partner of 5 years' standing had left him following physical violence. He is the eldest offspring of an immigrant Greek family. His childhood was marked by poverty and his father's physical brutality. When he was in his early 20s his marriage broke up and his father died, just as a better relationship was developing with him. One year later Nick overdosed and had 3 months of inpatient psychiatric care. Since that time he had been regularly abusing cannabis and alcohol. On the basis of the history and the Personality Assessment Schedule (PAS, Tyrer, 1988), Nick met the DSM-III-R (American Psychiatric Association, 1988) criteria for borderline, histrionic, and antisocial personality disorders.

Nick received 18 sessions of CAT and follow-up sessions at 1, 2, 3, and 6 months. In the first of three assessment ("reformulatory") sessions, Nick was encouraged to tell his own story. He described his current difficulties and significant relationships. Nick described feeling let down by his father, ex-wife, and current girlfriend (Jane) and feared that the same would happen with his daughter:

PATIENT: Say my daughter said she didn't want to see me any more, then I'd have to accept that and give her up.

THERAPIST: What's the feeling behind that, when you say you'll have to do that?

PATIENT: I feel betrayed because I mean, in my eyes, like with Jane. I've done so much for Jane and I know she's betrayed me once, let me down. She cheated on me. . . .

THERAPIST: . . . in relationships you feel very let down and I asked you the feeling and you said betrayed.

PATIENT: . . . I did everything, I gave all my love and care. I gave 100% and in return they've just shit on me . . . and that's the worst thing that I can't handle. Say, if I kept all my appointments and I was OK and you just said, "I don't want to see you any more," then I would feel let down by you and I wouldn't know why and that's sort of been happening to me.

This was explored in relation to the therapeutic relationship and developed over the course of the session into a target problem procedure (TPP) linking his target problem (TP) of anger and physical violence:

PATIENT: I feel a lot of people take advantage of my good nature, use me against me.

THERAPIST: Others use you against you.

PATIENT: Yes, I think so, and I just shut myself off from them, I switch off.

THERAPIST: How do you switch off?

PATIENT: I just avoid them. Occasionally there is a confrontation, but I don't like to confront because I've got a bad temper and I can be violent. I'm scared of what I might do to somebody.

Toward the end of the session the therapist encouraged Nick to describe his early history and it was made clear that this would be returned to. Nick offered the therapist the Psychotherapy File, which he had completed before the session. He was enthusiastic about it, but he reported responding differently to it on different occasions. This was noted as reflecting state shifts. The therapist explored his reactions to it, and they worked collaboratively to link it to the discoveries of the session, notably in respect of placation: Nick said, "Trying to please has been the story of my life." He was asked to complete a life chart for the next session.

In Session 2 the therapist used Nick's life chart and a developed family tree to discuss key life experiences and relationships. Nick's predominant memories were of being beaten by his father while his mother was helpless and beaten for trying to defend him. He felt protective toward his mother, and his perception of her as trapped was explored. Later he had felt cheated by his father's death. Nick had felt put down by his father, who called him a "nobody," and he had wanted to prove that he could be "someone" and make his father proud. He had also wanted to get to know his father "when he couldn't really hit me any more." This led to discussion of his own violence, notably a recent example with his girlfriend. Following this, a behavioral technique of issuing "warnings" to himself as signs of increasing anger was developed, using the red and yellow cards of football refereeing; the elaboration of this, along with self-monitoring of anger, was set as a homework task. The therapist summarized the theme of annoyance at feeling abused, and Nick offered an example of placating that was followed by being taken advantage of in work. The therapist offered the following procedural description, which Nick felt was accurate:

THERAPIST: Looking at that and what we talked of in the file last time, I just thought I'd feed back one way in which you and I recognize how you get from one state to another . . . to see how you feel about it; it gives a sort of résumé of where we are. It is "You give 100% of yourself, striving and pleasing others but you feel you are taken advantage of, so you feel let down and betrayed and disillusioned, which leaves you confused and angry at these contemptible people, and your mistrust is reinforced."

The therapist also introduced a diagram of this procedure, later developed into the SDR (Figure 11.1) and explained it in relation to two core states, one derived from his past experience in which the role pattern was "abusing in relation to abused" and one describing ideal closeness. The procedure (loop 1) that emerges from the first is an attempt to escape from the enduring sadness by searching for care in the second, which Nick called "Cloud Cuckoo Land."

Nick had completed all his homework for Session 3 and had made his own copy of the diagram from Session 2. The therapist discussed this and a "placating" event with a work colleague that led to anger, then moved to focus on their relationship and made a link to the diagram which Nick agreed with:

THERAPIST: Although at the moment you feel that we're working together and it's being a help, this is the "goody-goody" bit. It could also be that I do something that brings us down. Then, in your diagram, it will be seen that I'm actually being nasty or vicious and that will make you nasty in return, as one of the things you feel is "fire for fire."

The therapist presented a diagram including the early stages of loop 2, explaining the need to be aware that, once involved or cared for, Nick feels engulfed and trapped.

THERAPIST: You could also feel trapped and anxious if you feel I am coming on too strong. You put it very accurately last time, that your space is invaded with Jane, but that's something that you may also feel with me. Rather than feel it and stay away, let us be aware that exists here and we must be here to work it through.

Loop 2 was elaborated with reference to intimate relationships, tracing how feeling engulfed is followed by dismissing others, and then to being abusive and contemptuous or lonely and lost, resulting in feeling empty and a return to the abusing–abused state.

The therapist added a third loop to the SDR to represent Nick's mistrust and naming a central theme that he had brought to therapy, the theme of "wanting a better life but feeling cheated by life, which makes me feel envious and wary of others and angry at myself and others." Loop 3 describes the use of drugs and alcohol as a means of "blanking off" the pain of this.

Nick felt the diagram put his confusion into clarity and that he might, with help, be able to use it to help himself find alternative ways of acting. He illustrated this by reference to his work colleague:

PATIENT: When I came to here (points to loop 1) and I felt taken advantage of by her, what I could have done, instead of going up here, I could have gone back and said . . . but instead I let it go on. That's what happened, it went all the way up here and I could have stopped it.

A homework task of monitoring placation and anger was agreed upon. The therapist prepared Nick for the written reformulation in Session 4: "What I'm going to do next week is present you with the story of why and how these developed, how it is that you feel cheated."

The following is an extract from the reformulation:

. . . England gave a freedom and choice and variety of life you would not have discovered in Greece. But the "Better Life" seemed out of your grasp, for your mother whom you loved wished you to hold on to cultural values and your father appeared to develop your hate by violent pressure, anger, and abuse against your childish naughtiness, your career choices and through his insistence on work and marriage. You resisted, then gave in, each time feeling more cheated and hurt and becoming increasingly angry with yourself and others and envious of others. You developed a wary and defensive way of life and living—"Be Prepared" and "Fire for Fire" became your guidelines. This was based on the assumption that the world is a dangerous place. Inevitably, your mistrust of life and relationships grew. From time to time you took breaks from this—"Blanking Out" self-destructively on drugs, cigarettes, alcohol, or overdoses. . . . In real everyday life the "Cheating" seemed to leave you with nothing (Emptiness)—the close family you longed for was broken and disintegrated, your career, marriage, and daughter were lost to you. It seemed the Real Life gave you nothing (Emptiness). You began to seek refuge in the Ideal—the ideal togetherness, in life and relationships. The ideal was difficult to find and hold. You assumed if it was not ideal it was of no value. It seems you have downgraded, become contemptuous of the real, but nonperfect, life and relationships which you have and had. This has made you feel contemptuous of others, but Empty and contemptible (down-graded and small) in yourself. . . .

It seems reminiscent of the contemptuous abuse that your father meted out on you, leaving you in a state of contempt (smallness), abuse, powerlessness, unworthiness, and emptiness. This was and is a very painful state—to be avoided in any relationship. Thus it is as if you learnt to strive and please (100%) in all your relationships or you imagined an idealized closeness in a relationship and became engulfed (mother, wife, daughter, Jane). If you strove and pleased, you felt taken advantage of until you "clicked" into violence, anger, and confusion. If you felt taken advantage of over a long term you felt let down, betrayed, disillusioned—Hurt. On the other hand, if you idealized and engulfed yourself, you quickly began to feel anxious, trapped, and invaded, so you abusively and suddenly "froze" others out—betraying them, but you too were left—lonely and lost. Hopping from one pattern to another only brought Instability to your relationships. Gradually you made the assumption that "relationships are without trust." Worse still, you felt stuck and, so far, unable to change. . . .

The reformulation letter included a summary of the TPs and TPPs agreed upon in Sessions 1–3:

1. *Assumption:* The world is dangerous—MISTRUST.

   I want a "Better Life" but I feel cheated by life (Hurt), which makes me envious and wary of others and angry at myself and others.

2. *Assumption:* Relationships are without trust—INSTABILITY.

   In relationships it is as if there are two patterns: real and striving OR ideal and engulfed: EITHER I strive and please (100%), but am taken advantage of until I "click" into angry violence and confusion—if ongoing, I become disillusioned, mistrustful, let down and betrayed, which renders me SAD and DEPRESSED—OR I idealize a relationship, am engulfed by it and feel my space is invaded and I am anxiously trapped, causing me to abusively freeze others out, betraying them, and I am left LONELY and LOST.

Nick was moved by the prose reformulation, felt understood and that it was an accurate description. The subsequent sessions involved patient work in the application of the prose and diagrammatic descriptions to narratives of outside events brought by Nick and to the therapeutic relationship. For example, in Session 5 Nick described how he showed the reformulation to a friend whom he trusts; this relationship was explored in terms of "ideal closeness," and the therapist asked Nick to reflect how that may relate to the therapy. He demonstrated understanding:

PATIENT: Maybe I'm being more realistic now, since you've opened my eyes. I shouldn't be looking for the ideal. . . . Instead of coming in here and hoping, as I have a habit of, that everything is rosy and all up here (points to the SDR) . . . in reality I must keep my feet on the ground and accept that sometimes our sessions will go a bit wrong. . . . I [need to] think instead of act, think first, keep an open mind in the sessions, [not] keep up here in my "Cloud Cuckoo Land." I've learnt that's not reality. . . .

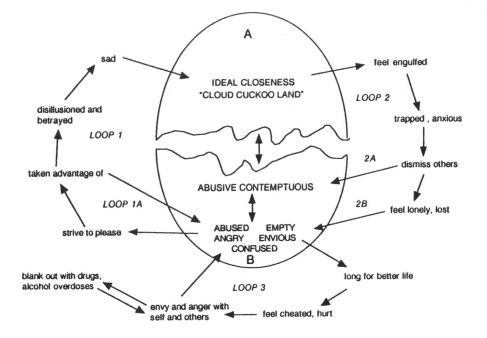

FIGURE 11.1. Nick. Sequential diagrammatic reformulation. From Ryle (1995b). Copyright 1995 by the British Psychological Society. Reprinted by permission.

The therapist then engaged Nick in exploring an "exit" from this and they agreed on self-observation, and Nick drew the eyes between the states in the SDR to represent his understanding of the need to be aware of all parts of himself.

In Sessions 5 and 6 the therapist used the SDR to comment on Nick's striving in the therapy:

THERAPIST: It's something you are doing now with the way you've gone in detail through your story. You're really striving hard to make sure you've got it all right, telling me how I've got it right. You've gone through each part of it, spent a lot of time through the week.

She then explored how he would feel if the therapist "didn't come up trumps." Expecting a lot of himself was also apparent in his evaluation of his efforts at recognition of procedures using the rating sheets. Acknowledging this accessed his fear of letting the therapist down and his expectation that she would be critical (the reciprocal roles of state B). This was linked to its origins in the relationship with his father. He was aware he was enacting loop 1 in the therapy but could imagine no other way, although he was committed to working at change. The use of "exits" to find places to break the procedures was settled on.

Two factors may have added to Nick's tendency to strive: first, CAT as a time-limited therapy requires active participation; secondly, this therapist through her directive style contributed to the establishment of "teacher" and "good pupil" roles. In supervision, the need was indicated for the therapist to be alert to these "reciprocal roles" and to the potential of the "benign teacher" being experienced as the "abusive father," in case the "striving pupil" should rebel and leave therapy.

In Session 10 the final contract of a further eight sessions was agreed upon, and Nick felt "a bit anxious, a little bit engulfed" and then realized that, in being truthful, he risked the therapist withdrawing the offer:

PATIENT: You could turn round and say, "Oh you want a bit less, Nick," and I'd have gone "Oh damn" because I wanted the sessions.

These experiences were located on the SDR (loop 2) and Nick's trust in conveying his feelings explored. He was depressed, confused, and anxious in Session 11 and dismissive of the therapist:

PATIENT: I'm seeing a doctor later. . . . That's it really, there's nothing else to say. . . . If you want to carry on normally with the session you can; I'm all right.

The therapist attempted to engage Nick in exploring his present state, locating their interaction on the SDR and saying:

THERAPIST: I feel sort of frozen out, what do you think of that?

Nick was initially dismissive but patient work by the therapist, exploring his feelings, identified that he felt both engulfed by the offer of eight more sessions but also overwhelmed by all there was to do and angry and "cheated" by the ending. This understanding was elaborated over Sessions 11–13, with clear and explanatory links made to the SDR. He was aware of enactments in the relationship with the therapist: "I got anxious; I thought, 'Come on [therapist], what else are you going to show me that's new? Are we just going to keep going around in circles?'" The therapist named Nick's experience of feeling abused and of him feeling she wasn't working hard enough and therefore being abusive. The SDR was linked to the origins in his history, and there was work on his difficulty in acknowledging anger and his fear of being abusive, eventually resolved through appropriate expression of anger.

In the course of therapy, Nick also wrote a moving letter to his dead father, expressing both deep anger and love, and was able to complete the mourning process. At termination and at follow-up at 1, 2, 3, and 6 months

Nick reported no episodes of violence, a greatly reduced use of "blanking out" (loop 3), and a new sense of control and self-understanding. A repeat PAS interview toward the end of this period indicated that the criteria for personality disorder were no longer met. The procedures and splitting described in the SDR had all been manifest in the therapy relationship, but the understanding offered by the use of the diagram and by the therapist's noncollusion had enabled Nick to control his long-standing destructiveness.

[At the follow-up assessment at 6 months, Nick's scores on the Beck Depression Inventory (Beck, Ward, Mendelson, Mock, & Erbargh, 1961) had fallen from 43 to 15 and on the Inventory of Interpersonal Problems (IIP; L. Horowitz, Rosenberg, Baer, Ureno, & Villasenor, 1988) from 2.17 to 1.38. At postal follow-up a year later he reported further progress, and these scores had fallen to 7 (Beck) and 0.81 (IIP), respectively. An account of transference and countertransference during Nick's therapy will be found in Ryle (1995b), from which Figure 11.1 is reproduced.]

TRAINING

CAT trainees are drawn from many backgrounds, notably from social work, occupational therapy, nursing, psychology, counseling, and medicine. These professions all provide some experience in basic interview skills, but to very different standards. Ideally, different inductions should be provided according to background, but in practice these issues are discussed in supervision.

The basic 2-year training involves an essentially skills-based program, allowing practitioners to graft on to the existing training the methods of CAT. A 3-year training course in which wider theoretical issues are addressed and more elaborated skills are taught is now offered. This leads to qualification as a psychotherapist.

Advanced trainees are required to be in a form of (non-time-limited) personal CAT during the training; this will use the model, among other things, to focus on issues of professional development. It is recommended that first-level trainees have a personal CAT; the majority will already have had, in addition, therapy in some dynamic mode.

The problem of working in the model differs for trainees from different backgrounds: those with dynamic training find the "cognitive" elements hard, whereas those from cognitive-behavioral backgrounds find transference–countertransference issues more problematic. Overall, it is probably more difficult to teach the cognitive behavioral skills to dynamic therapists than vice versa. In a small-scale audit of the audiotapes of first-year trainees, Denman (1993) found that those with little pre-CAT training used transference–countertransference issues more effectively than did those with either dynamic or cognitive backgrounds.

Training aims to help therapists get the balance and rhythm of "cognitive" and "dynamic" components right: "cognitive" preoccupations can serve to exclude emotional communication, whereas "dynamic sensitivity" can be an alibi for not getting on with thinking. These issues are the core of supervision. The use of written materials and diagrams serves as a good focus for the conceptual work, and in many ways the working out of letters and diagrams in the supervision group is a crucial learning experience for all the members. At the same time, differing individual reactions to the presented material and individual aberrations in responding to particular patients offer the opportunity to examine countertransference. The fact that the sequential diagram of a patient indicates so clearly the likely pressures or invitations the therapist is likely to be exposed to is very helpful in developing the "educated countertransference" that therapists need if collusion is to be avoided.

RESEARCH SUPPORT FOR THE APPROACH

CAT, as a therapy model, is unusual in that many of its features reflect psychotherapy research findings and in the fact that many of its features were developed in the course of outcome research. It developed over the same period as did the current widespread interest in process research and reflected a similar recognition of the fact that therapy tends to be concerned with a limited number of core themes. Despite this clear research link, the volume of both outcome and process research into CAT falls far short of what would be desirable. A review of past and present research is provided in Ryle (1995a); what follows here is a condensation of that work.

Early studies using repertory grids that contributed to the integration of cognitive and psychoanalytic ideas are reported in Ryle (1975). The use of grid measures to assess change and the relation of such change to patient's ratings of revision of target problems and procedures are reported in Ryle (1979). Brockman, Poynton, Ryle, and Watson (1987) reported in a controlled trial comparing 12-session CAT with 12 sessions using Mann's (1973) model; This study showed that CAT produced more change in three grid-derived measures, with effect sizes between 0.38 and 0.53.

Two other controlled trials are reported in Ryle (1995a): a comparison of intensive nurse education with CAT in the treatment of insulin-dependent diabetic subjects whose self-care was seriously deficient showed a significantly greater effect for CAT (see Fosbury, Bosley, Souksen, & Lowry, 1994), and a similar study in patients with asthma also showed that CAT was effective (Bosley, Fosbury, Cochrane, 1996).

A number of uncontrolled trials in various patient groups have been reported. Garyfallos et al. (1993) used the Minnesota Multiphasic Personality Inventory (MMPI) to assess change in patients attending a Greek community health center. Cowmeadow (1994) described the use of CAT in patients with deliberate self-harm. Clarke and Llewelyn (1994) reported the use of CAT in a sample of women who had been sexually abused. Pollock and Kear-Colwell (1994) described the treatment of two women who had stabbed their partners, demonstrating how diagrams were effective in enabling these "guilty abusers" to also acknowledge their own past victim status. Pollock (1996) has treated a further sample of seven such women, confirming the modification of the sense of guilt. He reports (personal communication) impressive reductions in the patients' scores on a dissociation questionnaire and on self-ratings of target problem procedures. Duignan and Mitzman (1994) report outcome in a time-limited CAT group. Current research includes an accumulating series of patients meeting standard criteria for the diagnosis of borderline personality disorder. Outcome is assessed by repeating the standard diagnostic interview, through a semistructured interview covering the individual problem procedures and by repeat psychometry. Long-term follow-up is planned. The evidence so far collected shows that, at the posttherapy assessment, about half the sample no longer meet borderline diagnostic criteria and show major changes in psychometric scores and interview ratings. This patient sample is also the base for various process studies reported in Ryle and Marlowe (1995) and Ryle (1995b). The accuracy with which SDRs reflect the themes of early sessions has been investigated by comparing them with analyses using the CCRT method (Luborsky & Crits-Christoph, 1990) and the SASB–CMP (Schacht & Henry, 1994) and high concordance has been demonstrated (Bennett & Parry, in press). Bennett is currently investigating how well therapists use the diagrams to identify and demonstrate the occasions on which patients' transference behaviors are a manifestation of identified self-states or problem procedures, and the task analysis paradigm (Greenberg, 1984, 1992) is being used to study how therapists respond to transference events, with the aim of developing and refining a model of ideal practice.

In summary, a variety of research studies into both outcome and process suggest that time-limited CAT is a relatively powerful intervention over a wide range of patient groups. More systematic and larger-scale studies would have been desirable, but the constraints imposed by working in an underfunded service, the paucity of research money in the United Kingdom over the past decade, the absence of accessible "business as usual" or contrasting treatment approaches for controls, and the very rapid growth in the training, with its demands on the small group of workers involved in the early development of CAT, have all conspired to prevent more extensive studies. It is to be hoped that the existing projects and the qualification of the first generation of CAT therapists, all of whom have had some research experience as trainees, may generate more extensive studies in the future and may begin to establish in greater detail the limits and achievements of the method and the ways in which it is effective.

NOTE

1. This section was written by Anthony Ryle.

REFERENCES

American Psychiatric Association. (1988). *Diagnostic and statistical manual of mental disorders* (3rd ed., rev.). Washington DC: Author.

Bakhtin, M. (1984). *Problems of Dostoevsky's poetics.* Manchester: Manchester University Press.

Beard, H., Marlowe, M., & Ryle, A. (1990). The management and treatment of personality-disordered patients: The use of sequential diagrammatic reformulation. *British Journal of Psychiatry, 156,* 541–545.

Beck, A. T., Ward, C. H., Mendelson, M., Mock, J. E., & Erbargh, J. K. (1961). An inventory for measuring depression. *Archives of General Psychiatry, 4,* 561–571.

Bennett, D., & Parry, G. (in press). The accuracy of reformulation in Cognitive Analytic Therapy: A comparison of two methods. *Psychotherapy Research.*

Bosley, C. M., Fosbury, J. A., & Cochrane, G. M. (1997). *The psychological problems associated with poor compliance with treatment of asthma.* Manuscript submitted for publication.

Brockman, D., Poynton, A., Ryle, A., & Watson, J. P. (1987). Effectiveness of time limited therapy carried out by trainees: Comparison of two methods. *British Journal of Psychiatry, 151,* 602–609.

Bruner, J. (1986). *Actual minds, possible worlds.* Cambridge, MA: Harvard University Press.

Clarke, S., & Llewelyn, S. (1994). Personal constructs of survivors of child sexual abuse receiving CAT. *British Journal of Medical Psychology, 676,* 273–289.

Cowmeadow, P. (1994). Deliberate self-harm and Cognitive Analytic Therapy. *International Journal of Short-Term Psychotherapy, 9,* 135–160.

Cowmeadow, P. (1995). Very brief interventions with deliberate self-harmers. In A. Ryle (Ed.), *Cognitive Analytic Therapy: Developments in theory and practice.* Chichester: Wiley.

Denman, F. (1993). Quality in a psychotherapy service: A review of audiotaped sessions. *Psychiatric Bulletin, 18*(2), 80–82.

Duignan, I., & Mitzman, S. (1994). Measuring individual change in patients receiving time-limited Cognitive Analytic Therapy. *International Journal of Short-Term Psychotherapy, 9*(2/3), 151–160.

Fonagy, P., Steele, M., Steele, H., Higgitt, A., & Target, M. (1994). The theory and practice of resilience. *Journal of Child Psychology and Psychiatry, 35*(2), 231–257.

Fosbury, J. A., Bosley, C. M., Sönksen, P. H., & Lowry, C. (1994). Cognitive Analytic Therapy with poorly controlled type 1 diabetic patients. *Diabetologia, 37*(1).

Garyfalos, G., Adamopoulou, M., Saitis, M., Sotiriou, M., Zlantanos, D., & Alektoridis, P. (1993). Evaluation of Cognitive Analytic Therapy outcome. *Neurologia et Psychiatria, 12*(3), 121–125.

Gold, J. R., & Wachtel, P. (1993). Cyclical psychodynamcs. In G. Stricker & J. R. Gold (Eds.), *Comprehensive handbook of psychotherapy integration.* London & New York: Plenum Press.

Greenberg, L. S. (1984). Task analysis: The general approach. In L. N. Rice & L. S. Greenberg (Eds.), *Patterns of change: Intensive analysis of psychotherapy process.* New York: Guilford Press.

Greenberg, L. S. (1992). Task analysis: Identifying components of intrapsychic conflict resolution. In S. G. Toukmanian & D. L. Rennie (Eds.), *Psychotherapy process research: Paradigmatic and narrative approaches.* Newbury Park, CA: Sage.

Harre, R. (1987). The social construction of selves. In K. Yardley & T. Honess (Eds.), *Self and identity: Psychosocial perspectives.* Chichester: Wiley.

Hobson, R. P. (1993). *Autism and the development of mind.* Hillsdale, NJ: Erlbaum.

Holquist, M. (1990). *Dialogism: Bakhtin and his world.* London & New York: Routledge.

Horowitz, L., Rosenburg, S., Baer, B., Ureno, G., & Villasenor, V. S. (1988). Inventory of Interpersonal Problems: Psychometric properties and clinical applications. *Journal of Consulting and Clinical Psychology, 56,* 885–892.

Horowitz, M. J. (1979). *States of mind: Analysis of change in psychotherapy.* New York: Plenum Press.

Kelly, G. A. (1955). *The psychology of personal constructs.* New York: Norton.

Leiman, M. (1992). The concept of sign in the work of Vygotsky, Winnicott and Bakhtin: Further integration of object relations theory and activity theory. *British Journal of Medical Psychology, 65,* 209–221.

Leiman, M. (1994). Projective identification as early joint action sequences: A Vygotskian addendum to the Procedural Sequence Object Relations Model. *British Journal of Medical Psychology, 67,* 97–106.

Leiman, M. (1995). Early development. In A. Ryle (Ed.), *Cognitive Analytic Therapy: Developments in theory and practice.* Chichester: Wiley.

Luborsky, L., & Crits-Christoph, P. (1990). *Understanding transference: The CCRT method.* New York: Basic Books.

Luborsky, L., Barber, J. P., & Diguer, L. (Eds.). (1992). The meanings of narratives told during psychotherapy: The fruits of a new observational unit. *Psychotherapy Research, 2*(4), 227–290.

Mann, J. (1973). *Time-limited psychotherapy.* Cambridge, MA: Harvard University Press.

Ogden, T. H. (1983). The concept of internal object relations. *International Journal of Psycho-Analysis, 64,* 227–241.

Pollock, P. H. (1996). Clinical issues in the cognitive analytic therapy of sexually abused women who commit violent offences against their partners. *British Journal of Medical Psychology, 69*(2), 117–128.

Pollock, P. H., & Kear-Colwell, J. J. (1994). Women who stab: A personal construct analysis of sexual victimisation and offending behaviour. *British Journal of Medical Psychology, 67,* 13–22.

Ryle, A. (1975). *Frames and cages.* London: Sussex University Press.

Ryle, A. (1978). A common language for the psychotherapies? *British Journal of Psychiatry, 132,* 585–594.

Ryle, A. (1979a). The focus in brief interpretive psychotherapy: Dilemmas, traps and snags as target problems. *British Journal of Psychiatry, 134,* 46–54.

Ryle, A. (1979b). Defining goals and assessing change in brief psychotherapy. *British Journal of Medical Psychology, 52,* 223–233.

Ryle, A. (1980). Some measures of goal attainment in focused integrated active psychotherapy: A study of 15 cases. *British Journal of Psychiatry, 137,* 475–486.

Ryle, A. (1982). *Psychotherapy: A cognitive integration of theory and practice.* London: Academic Press.

Ryle, A. (1984). How can we compare the different psychotherapies? Why are they all effective? *British Journal of Medical Psychology, 57,* 261–264.

Ryle, A. (1985). Cognitive theory, object relations and the self. *British Journal of Medical Psychology, 58,* 1–7.

Ryle, A. (1987). Cognitive psychology as a common language for psychotherapy. *Journal of Integrative and Eclectic Psychotherapy, 6*(2), 168–172.

Ryle, A. (1990). *Cognitive-Analytic Therapy: Active participation in change.* Chichester: Wiley.

Ryle, A. (1991). Object relations theory and activity theory: A proposed link by way of the Procedural Sequence Model. *British Journal of Medical Psychology, 64,* 307–316.

Ryle, A. (1994a). Persuasion or education? The role of reformulation in CAT. *International Journal of Short Term Psychotherapy, 9*(2/3), 111–118.

Ryle, A. (1994b). Projective identification: A particular form of reciprocal role procedure. *British Journal of Medical Psychology, 67,* 107–114.

Ryle, A. (1995a). *Cognitive Analytic Therapy: New developments in theory and practice.* Chichester: Wiley.

Ryle, A. (1995b). Transference and countertransference variations in the course of the CAT of two borderline patients: Relation to the diagrammatic reformulation of self-states. *British Journal of Medical Psychology, 68,* 109–124.

Ryle, A., & Marlowe, M. (1995). Cognitive Analytic Therapy of borderline personality disorder: Theory and practice and the clinical and research uses of the self-states sequential diagram. *International Journal of Short-Term Psychotherapy, 10*(1), 21–34.

Schacht, T. E., & Henry, W. P. (1994). Modelling recurrent relationship patterns with Structural Analysis of Social Behavior: The SASBY-co *Psychotherapy Research, 4*(3 and 4), 208–221.

Stern, D. N. (1985). *The interpersonal world of the infant.* New York: Basic Books.

Tyrer, J. (1988). *Personality disorders: Diagnosis, management and course.* London: Wright.

Voloshinov, V. N. (1986). *Marxism and the philosophy of language.* Cambridge, MA: Harvard University Press.

Vygotsky, L. S. (1962). *Thought and language.* Cambridge, MA: MIT Press.

Vygotsky, L. S. (1978). *Mind in society.* Cambridge, MA: Harvard University Press.

Wachtel, P. (1991). Transference schema and assimilation: The relevance of Piaget to the psychoanalytic theory of transference. *Annual of Psychoanalysis, 8,* 59–67.

Westen, D. (1990). Towards a revised theory of borderline object relations: Implications of observational research. *International Journal of Psycho-Analysis, 71,* 661–693.

Wood, D., Bruner, J. E., & Ross, G. (1976). The role of tutoring in problem-solving. *Journal of Child Psychology and Psychiatry, 17,* 89–100.

12

Cognitive-Behavioral
Case Formulation

JACQUELINE B. PERSONS
MICHAEL A. TOMPKINS

Cognitive-Behavioral (CB) Case Formulation, described in this chapter, is an elaboration of the method described by Persons (1989, 1993). Others who have presented methods for cognitive case conceptualization include Judith S. Beck (1995), Arthur Freeman (1992), and J. Christopher Muran and Zindel V. Segal (1992). Contributors to the field of behavioral case conceptualization are too numerous to mention; for overviews of this field, see Bellack and Hersen (1988) and Nelson and Hayes (1986a); for good clinical examples, see Haynes and O'Brien (1990) and Turkat (1985).

HISTORICAL BACKGROUND OF THE APPROACH

CB Case Formulation has its origins in cognitive therapy and theories and in functional analysis. It incorporates aspects of both *structural* assessment, which focuses on the topography and underlying causal mechanisms of behavior, and *functional* assessment, which focuses on the functions of behavior (Nelson & Hayes, 1986b).

Cognitive Therapy and Theories

CB Case Formulation draws heavily on cognitive diathesis–stress theories of depression, particularly A. T. Beck's (1976) cognitive theory of psychopathology. Beck's theory states that psychopathological symptoms and problems result from the activation of core cognitions (variously termed schemas, dysfunctional attitudes, and core beliefs) by stressful life events.

The links between CB Case Formulation and Beck's cognitive theory can be seen in the fact that three components of the CB Case Formulation match the three key components of Becks' model: the patient's symptoms and problems, the core beliefs underpinning the symptoms or problems, and the life events that activate the core beliefs. (We use the term "core beliefs" because it is easier to communicate to patients than the terms "schemas" or "dysfunctional attitudes.") Beck's model also proposes that schemas are learned via early childhood experiences, and the CB Case Formulation method includes a description of the origins of the patient's core beliefs.

Functional Analysis

Functional analysis has been defined by Haynes and O'Brien (1990) as "the identification of important, controllable, causal functional relationships applicable to a specified set of target behaviors for an individual client" (p. 654). The links between CB Case Formulation and functional analysis can be seen in three characteristics of the CB Case Formulation method: its emphasis on identification and measurement of overt problems, its specification of functional hypotheses, and in the fact that the quality of the CB Formulation is a function of its contribution to treatment outcome.

In emphasizing the specification and measurement of overt problems, the CB Case Formulation model borrows heavily from behavior therapy; indeed, a hallmark of functional analysis and of behavior therapy is its emphasis on identification of overt, concrete problems and the objective measurement of them so that treatment progress can be monitored.

The CB Case Formulation method allows for specification of a functional hypothesis in the Working Hypothesis component of the formulation. Not all CB Case Formulations involve functional hypotheses, but many do. For example, a CB Case Formulation of a depressed patient might include notions from Lewinsohn, Hoberman, and Hautzinger's (1985) proposal that depression in some individuals stems from reductions in interpersonal or other positive reinforcers.

CB Case Formulation adopts a functional approach to assessing the quality of the formulation (cf. Hayes, Nelson, & Jarrett, 1987). That is, the quality of the formulation is seen as a function of its contribution to treatment outcome. If the formulation does not have "treatment utility"—does not improve treatment outcome—then it is a poor CB Case Formulation no matter how much information it provides (Hayes et al., 1987).

In this functional model, the Working Hypothesis component of the CB Case Formulation serves as a hypothesis about the structural and functional mechanisms underpinning and maintaining problematic behaviors. The therapist (with the patient) uses the hypothesis to develop a treatment plan designed to alleviate or solve the symptoms and problems. The outcome of treatment based on the hypothesis serves as a test of its treatment utility. If the outcome is poor, we recommend that the therapist work to revise the formulation and the treatment plan based on it. This view of treatment as a single-case empirical study, in which case formulation, treatment planning, monitoring of outcome, and revision of the formulation are parts of an iterative process, is a hallmark of behavioral case conceptualization (cf. Barlow, Hayes, & Nelson, 1984; Kanfer, 1985).

CONCEPTUAL FRAMEWORK

Why Is Cognitive-Behavioral Case Formulation Necessary?

Individualized case conceptualization and cognitive-behavior therapy might, to some readers, seem odd bedfellows. One of the strengths of cognitive-behavioral therapy (CBT) is the body of outcome data supporting its efficacy (cf. Giles, 1993). However, the CB therapists in controlled outcome studies do not generally develop a comprehensive case formulation and use it to make an individualized treatment plan. Instead, they follow a standardized treatment protocol. If CBT has been shown to be effective in outcome studies in which therapists do not develop an individualized case formulation, why is CB Case Formulation necessary? We offer several answers to this question.

First, it is not strictly correct to say that therapists in controlled outcome studies do not conceptualize. Although a formal conceptualization is not usually done, certainly the therapist individualizes treatment by focusing on the individual patient's particular distorted cognitions, not on distorted cognitions typical of the average depressed patient. In addition, evaluators in the NIMH (National Institute of Mental Health) Treatment of Depression Collaborative Research Program (Elkin et al., 1989) developed individualized lists of each patient's presenting problems and treatment goals (however, it is not clear that this information was used to guide treatment). Linehan's (1993) protocol for treating parasuicidal behavior in women with borderline personality disorder is unusual in that it includes individualized behavioral analysis as a central aspect of treatment. For example, when a patient commits a parasuicidal act, the protocol stipulates that the therapist conduct a detailed behavioral analysis of the act, specifying, in gory detail, the chain of behaviors and circumstances leading up to and following the parasuicidal behavior.

Second, a limitation of standardized protocols in their application to routine clinical practice is that such protocols (at least those written to date) address single disorders, for example, clinical depression (Beck et al., 1979), social phobia (Heimberg, in press), or alcohol abuse (Sobell & Sobell, 1993). In contrast, most patients have multiple disorders and problems, and for many of these a treatment protocol is not yet available. To treat these cases, the therapist can use the CB Case Formulation model, using the cognitive-behavioral theories that underpin the currently available treatment protocols to develop an individualized formulation and treatment plan for his or her patient.

In cases where all of the patient's problems *are* described in standardized protocols, it might be possible for the therapist to use the protocols, one at a time, in sequence, until all of the problems are addressed. However, the sequential-protocol strategy is often inefficient because many protocols have overlapping components (e.g., relaxation strategies, cognitive restructuring). In addition, the sequential-protocol strategy does not provide any guidance to the clinician about the order in which to implement the protocols. Therefore, we believe that the strategy of using the CB model to develop a single, comprehensive treatment plan for each patient provides a conceptually more elegant and pragmatically more efficient approach to patient care.

Third, the CB Case Formulation is useful in helping the clinician understand and work therapeutically with the patient–therapist relationship and in planning homework assignments and handling homework noncompliance, as illustrated later in this chapter. A well-articulated, individualized formulation that is shared with the patient can strengthen patient–therapist collaboration and reduce treatment noncompliance.

Finally, a CB Case Formulation is particularly helpful to the therapist when his or her initial intervention efforts fail or when, after an apparently successful outcome, the patient relapses. In cases like this, the therapist working without a formulation may be reduced to seeking randomly for another intervention strategy. In contrast, the therapist who is carrying out a formulation-driven treatment has an algorithm to follow. If the treatment fails, this suggests that the working hypothesis (formulation) upon which the treatment plan was based may need revision. With this assumption in mind, the therapist reformulates the case and devises a new treatment plan based on the reformulation.

Two Levels of Formulation

CB Case Formulation occurs at two levels: the "case" level and the "situation" level. At the case level, the formulation describes all of the patient's presenting problems, their interrelationships, and the mechanisms underpinning and explaining them. At the situation level, the therapist examines a particular problematic situation (e.g., a parasuicidal act or a bout of depressed mood) and develops a hypothesis about the mechanisms underpinning or explaining that situation.

This chapter focuses primarily on formulation at the case level. However, we also discuss formulation at the situation level, as this level of formulation guides much of the work in therapy sessions and situation-level formulations are a key source of hypotheses about case-level formulation.

The CB Case Formulation Method

The CB Case Formulation has seven components: the Problem List; Core Beliefs; Precipitants and Activating Situations; the Working Hypothesis; Origins; the Treatment Plan; and Predicted Obstacles to Treatment (see Table 12.1). We describe each in turn.

The Problem List

The Problem List is an exhaustive list of the patient's difficulties, stated in simple, descriptive, concrete terms. It is useful to make a comprehensive Problem List, including even problems that do not at first seem to be psychological in origin, problems that are not likely to be a focus of treatment, and even those that the patient does not consider to be problems (e.g., substance abuse) (Nezu & Nezu, 1993; Turkat & Maisto, 1985). An all-inclusive Problem List ensures that important problems are not overlooked, and it can be helpful in the process of generating ideas about Core Beliefs and developing a Working Hypothesis.

TABLE 12.1. Cognitive-Behavioral Case Formulation

Identifying Information

Problem List
1.
2.
3.
4.
5.
6.
7.
8.

Core Beliefs

Precipitants and Activating Situations

Working Hypothesis

Origins

Treatment Plan
   Goals
   Interventions

Predicted Obstacles to Treatment

A typical Problem List for an outpatient has 5–8 items; we suggest a maximum of about 10 items—otherwise the list is unwieldy. We suggest that the format of each problem consist of a one- or two-word description of the problem, followed by a short description of the problem in terms of typical behavioral, cognitive, and mood components of the problem—for example, "Work difficulties; frequent lateness and procrastination, accompanied by thoughts like 'I hate my boss' and feelings of anger and frustration."

It is important to quantify problems so that evaluations of progress can be made. This can be done by noting the frequency, intensity, and/or duration of the patient's panic attacks, the score on an inventory like the Beck Depression Inventory (Beck et al., 1979), or by developing a hierarchy of feared driving situations.

Core Beliefs

In this section, the therapist offers hypotheses about the patient's views of self, others, and the world that appear to cause or maintain the patient's problems. For example, A. T. Beck, Emery, and Greenberg (1985) proposed that anxious patients view themselves as weak, helpless, and vulnerable and the world as dangerous and threatening. The therapist can also propose conditional (if–then) beliefs (cf. A. T. Beck et al., 1990) that appear to contribute to a patient's symptoms. For example, a common conditional belief held by unassertive individuals is, "If I speak up for myself, others will be upset."

Certainly the specification of core beliefs underpinning patients' problems does not exclude the roles that other factors, including biological, can play in causing problems. However, the CB Case Formulation method does give cognitions a central role in the formulation.

Precipitants and Activating Situations

Here the therapist specifies external events and situations that activate core beliefs to produce symptoms and problems or that serve as stimuli or reinforcers in a functional analysis. The term "precipitants" refers to activating events at the "case" level, and the term "activating situations" refers to the "situation" level. For example, a business executive might report that he is experiencing increased distress since taking a new job that requires extensive public speaking (precipitant) and that the public speaking situations themselves, particularly large ones with unfamiliar audiences (activating situations), produce anxiety, fears of negative evaluation, and urges to flee.

Working Hypothesis

This component is the heart of the formulation, and in fact sometimes when we use the term "formulation" we are referring to the Working Hypothesis. In the Working Hypothesis, the clinician "tells a story" that ties together the problems on the Problem List, the core beliefs, and the activating events and situations. The story attempts to account for all of the problems on the problem list. The Working Hypothesis can be an explanatory hypothesis that describes core beliefs activated by life events, it can be a functional hypothesis, or it may include both types of explanation. Biological factors can also be included in the Working Hypothesis.

Origins

In this section, the clinician briefly describes one or a few incidents or circumstances of the patient's early history—particularly episodes involving parents or other caretakers—that explain how the patient might have learned the core beliefs listed above. Origins can also include modeling experiences, or failures to learn important skills and behaviors, as in the case of a patient one of us treated who had significant social skills deficits because he had grown up in a family in which both parents also had marked social skills deficits.

Treatment Plan

In one sense, the Treatment Plan is not *part* of the formulation—it stems from and is based on the formulation (Working Hypothesis). We include it in the CB Case Formulation, however, to stress the point that the Treatment Plan is based directly on the Working Hypothesis. For example, if the therapist hypothesizes that the patient's social anxiety is due in part to social skills deficits, the treatment plan will include social skills training. If, instead, the social anxiety appears to result from core beliefs like "If I speak up for myself, others will get angry and attack me" and from avoidance of social situations, the treatment plan will include teaching the formulation, cognitive restructuring and behavioral experiments to test out the core beliefs, and exposure to feared social situations.

Before intervention strategies are described, it is important to state clear goals for treatment. Unless goals are specified, it is difficult to plan treatment to accomplish them. Thus, the Treatment Plan component of the formulation has two subheadings: *Goals* and *Interventions*.

Predicted Obstacles to Treatment

In this component of the formulation the therapist uses the formulation, and particularly the Problem List, Core Beliefs, and Working Hypothesis, to make predictions about difficulties that might arise in the therapeutic relationship or other aspects of the treatment. An early awareness of potential difficulties can avert an early termination, an unproductive power struggle, or other types of impasses. For example, a patient who believes, "If I speak up for myself, others will get angry and attack me," may be more likely to terminate treatment prematurely than to discuss her discomfort about any aspect of the treatment with the therapist.

INCLUSION/EXCLUSION CRITERIA

We cannot think of a case in which a CB Case Formulation is not helpful. We have found CB Case Formulation to be particularly helpful in the treatment of patients who have multiple problems and in the treatment of patients who do not make smooth progress in therapy.

Therapists, particularly inexperienced ones, often feel overwhelmed by complex, multiple-problem patients (and these patients are frequently treated by inexperienced therapists). The therapist wonders which problem to tackle first, how to track progress in the therapy, and how to intervene appropriately. The CB Case Formulation method is particularly helpful when one is working with these patients because of the method's emphasis on a comprehensive Problem List. The simple process of making a Problem List for a patient who has many problems can be helpful—to both the therapist and the patient. In addition, the CB Case Formulation method provides a framework for understanding how problems are related to each other and how they are related to core beliefs, allowing the therapist to intervene in several problem domains (e.g., financial, interpersonal, personal safety) and still see the therapy as having a central theme.

A CB Case Formulation is especially helpful when the therapy is not going well. For example, John, a computer programmer, came to therapy because he was depressed—feeling overwhelmed by new responsibilities at work—and was constantly arguing with his girlfriend because she felt ready for marriage but he did not. His therapy progressed in fits and starts. He was often late for appointments or canceled at the last minute. When John did arrive for his session, he frequently brought prepared notes, lists of questions or articles to discuss that did not seem relevant to any of his treatment goals. John often diverted his therapist's attempts to set an agenda for the session by chatting about current events or irrelevant matters.

Upon reviewing the formulation, the therapist hypothesized that John's core belief, namely, "The only person I can depend on is myself" and "Others are undependable," might be contributing to the therapeutic impasse. The therapist introduced this idea to the patient, suggesting that perhaps John's therapy had stalled because he was becoming uncomfortable with his feelings of dependence on the therapist. John agreed with this assessment, particularly after the therapist helped him see that his relationship with his girlfriend may have stalled for similar reasons.

To address this issue, the therapist first suggested that John examine the advantages and disadvantages of believing "I must not depend on my therapist." Next, John agreed to a plan whereby he rated his feelings of dependence on the therapist before and after a therapy session in which he engaged with the therapist in productive work, focusing on a suitable problem from his problem list. Using this strategy, John was surprised to learn that he tended to exaggerate the degree to which the discussion of a relevant problem fostered his dependence on the therapist. Thereafter, John made good progress toward resolving several problems on his problem list—including setting a date to ask his girlfriend to marry him.

STEPS IN CASE FORMULATION CONSTRUCTION

The final product of a CB Case Formulation takes the form of a written formulation using the format provided earlier in Table 12.1. In this section we focus on the "how to" of completing that form.

Generally, we try to write a case formulation within three to four sessions. We recommend that therapists begin to formulate immediately, developing hypotheses based on their very first interactions with the patient. This recommendation is supported by evidence collected by Elstein, Shulman, and Sprafka (1978), who, in studies of medical problem solving by physicians, found that "competent physicians begin generating hypotheses in the earliest moments of their encounter with patients" (p. ix).

Whenever possible, the process of formulation is a collaborative one, with patient and therapist working together to make a Problem List, propose some core beliefs, set goals for treatment, choose interventions, and monitor progress.

We do not use a formal structured interview in the formulation process. Some of the questions we use to obtain information about each component of the formulation are described below. We frequently use self-report inventories, like the Beck Depression and Anxiety inventories, to provide an objective assessment of treatment progress.

Although the items in the CB Case Formulation always appear in the same order, the therapist may obtain information about the various components of the formulation in a different order. For example, the patient may be so accommodating when scheduling the initial appointment that even before the therapist has much information about the patient's problems, he or she can speculate that the patient's core beliefs might include ideas like "My needs don't count; others are more important than me" or "I must defer to others; if I speak up for myself, something bad will happen." This said, the first step in constructing the CB Case Formulation is to obtain a comprehensive Problem List.

Making a Problem List

The process of creating a Problem List begins with the patient's chief complaint. Usually, the patient comes to the initial session with one or two problems she or he wants to describe in detail. When the patient has finished that description of the chief complaint, the therapist can ask if there are any other problems or areas of difficulty. If the patient is receptive to this line of questioning, the therapist can continue to probe in this manner until the patient offers no more problems. We recommend that the therapist probe all of the following domains: psychological/psychiatric, interpersonal, occupational, medical, financial, housing, legal, and leisure. Of course, two or three or even more sessions may be required to obtain information about all of these domains, particularly if the patient is in acute distress and needs some immediate interventions.

Common items on a Problem List include depressive symptoms, anxiety, panic, phobias, situations that are avoided (e.g., inability to drive on a freeway or over a bridge), overspending, overeating, unemployment, financial difficulties, marital conflict, medical problems, social isolation, and alcohol or drug abuse. Since behaviors, moods, and cognitions are the fundamental building blocks of a CB Case Formulation, we suggest that problems be described in these terms whenever possible. For example, through careful questioning the problem "My job performance is slipping" can become any of the following: "I'm not returning phone calls" (behavior); "I don't enjoy my job so at times I don't show up for work at all" (mood and behavior); or "I feel guilty because I know my coworkers think I'm a real flake" (mood and cognition).

Not all patients are forthcoming about all of their problems, sometimes because they are not aware of how the problem is a problem for them or because they are ashamed or afraid to admit to certain problems, including financial, drug, and alcohol problems, as well as past suicidal behavior and job and relationship failures. The therapist can sometimes uncover such problems with a thorough evaluation interview. A family and social history that reveals a series of unhappy marriages or relationships suggests interpersonal problems. A family history of alcohol or drug abuse may mean that the patient shares similar addictions. Not uncommonly, patients reserve information about particularly upsetting problems until later in the treatment, when they feel more able to trust the therapist with this information.

The patient's behavior with the therapist may also suggest problems that the patient has not reported. Bounced checks to the therapist or last minute cancellations or requests to reschedule appointments may point to financial problems or a chaotic lifestyle. A patient who is overly agreeable and compliant to the therapist's requests may act similarly with others.

When the therapist observes problems of which the patient is unaware, the therapist might or might not wish to immediately point these out. To decide whether and when to do this, the therapist relies in part on the case formulation. For example, patients who believe "If I have problems, I am worthless" may not be receptive to placing a new item on the problem list until they have developed a strong and trusting relationship with the therapist.

Proposing Some Core Beliefs

Sometimes the therapist can make a guess as to the core beliefs that may be operating by asking him- or herself, "What core beliefs might account for the problems on this person's Problem List?" Sometimes the psychiatric diagnosis can suggest some hypotheses about core beliefs; for example, patients with social phobia nearly always feel inadequate and view others as critical and rejecting.

A Thought Record (Persons, 1989; see Figure 12.1) is particularly helpful in generating a series of cognitions about a particular situation that may be related to the core beliefs. In order to unearth core beliefs that may be operating in a specific situation, Greenberger and Padesky (1995) suggest the therapist ask the patient these questions: "What was going through your mind just before you started to feel this way? What does this say about you? What does this mean about you, . . . your life, . . . your future? What are you afraid might happen? What is the worst thing that could happen if this were true? What does this mean about how the other person(s) feel(s)/think(s) about you? What does this mean about the other person(s) or people in general? Do you have images or memories in this situation? If so, what are they?"

It is not necessary to find one central dysfunctional attitude or core belief to explain all problems on the Problem List. Several core beliefs may be operating at once (self, others, world) and in different situations. For example, one of us recently treated a patient who had two prominent views of others, one apparently based on experiences with her mother (passive/weak/helpless) and one based on experiences with her father (angry/critical/attacking).

Precipitants and Activating Situations

To obtain information about precipitants and activating situations, the therapist can ask the patient to describe the sequence of events leading up to the presenting problems or the problematic situation. For example, the therapist can ask about major events in the patient's life immediately preceding the onset of the patient's recent bout of panic attacks, or the events immediately preceding the most recent panic attack. A Thought Record can formalize the inquiry about problematic situations by centering the interview around a specific situation that appears to activate maladaptive cognitions and cause distressing emotions and/or maladaptive behavior. The therapist can assist the patient in this process by asking questions that direct the patient to attend to specific and, when possible, recent events or situations during which she or he experienced a negative mood state (e.g., anxiety, anger, depression). For example, we suggest questions like these: "Can you think of a recent situation when you have felt this way? Can you think of another time when you felt this way? What were you doing or saying when you had this feeling?" More general questions like "Who?," "What?," "When?," and "Where?" are also helpful in defining the activating situation.

Working Hypothesis

The Working Hypothesis summarizes the relationships among the patient's problems, core beliefs, and activating events and situations. For example, a Working Hypothesis for a patient, Emmie, who sought treatment for anxiety and panic read:

THOUGHT RECORD

DATE	SITUATION (Event, memory, attempt to do something, etc.)	BEHAVIOR(S)	EMOTIONS	THOUGHTS	RESPONSES

FIGURE 12.1. Thought Record.

Emmie's beliefs—"I am responsible for everything" and "Others are unreliable, unhelpful"—cause her to feel anxious/panicky when confronted with the stresses of childbirth, gall bladder surgery, a demanding job situation, and a husband who travels frequently. These beliefs also lead to unassertiveness, further exacerbating her distress and fueling the belief, "The world is demanding and burdensome." Biological factors in pregnancy and childbirth may have contributed to the onset of her panic. When Emmie's anxiety/stress level gets high enough, she does sometimes ask others for help. However, because some of the people closest to her (her parents) are unreliable, they frequently let her down, and this increases her stress and strengthens her belief that others are unreliable. Because she doesn't expect others, most importantly her husband, to respond, she often handles requests for help in such a way as to let him know she doesn't really expect him to come through for her—with the result that he does not, creating some marital difficulties and again strengthening her belief that others are unreliable.

It is important to remember that the Working Hypothesis is just that—a "best guess" as to the way core beliefs and contingencies maintain problematic behaviors. Decisions as to whether to amend or discard a Working Hypothesis are based on whether the interventions derived from the Working Hypothesis seem to help the patient achieve her or his treatment goals.

Origins

To obtain information about the origins of core beliefs, we have found certain questions helpful, including: "How do you imagine you developed that idea? Where did that belief come from? What role do you think your parents played in forming that belief for you? Who else in your family believes this, and how do you think that person developed that idea?"

To obtain information about the origins of learned behavioral patterns, perhaps learned via modeling or reinforcement, we have found it helpful to ask: "Was there anyone else in your family who behaved like that?" "How did you learn to behave like that?" "What happened when you behaved like that as a child?" "How did your parents (or teachers or siblings or other significant others) respond?"

Treatment Plan

The first step in making a Treatment Plan is to set Goals for the therapy. The Problem List provides some guidance about things the patient wants to work on in therapy. However, most patients do not want to work on all of their problems. Generally they have one or two or a few problems they really want to work on, and these can be translated into goals for the therapy. Thus, although a Problem List gives a good start toward the task of setting goals, it is not a list of treatment goals.

A Problem List that defines problems concretely in terms of behaviors, cognitions, and moods helps the patient and therapist set clear treatment goals. It is far easier to design interventions focused on treatment goals like "Increase James's ability to be assertive with others" or "Decrease James's anxiety in social situations" than it is to "Decrease James's chronic anxiety." Clearly stated treatment goals help the therapist know how to intervene and are vital in the process of monitoring the progress of the treatment.

We have found the following questions to be useful in defining clear treatment goals: "How will you know when you have solved this problem? What will you be doing or saying differently when this is no longer a problem for you? How would your family or friends know you have solved this problem— how would you be relating to them differently? How would your life be different if you no longer had this problem?" Methods devised by Kiresuk and Sherman (1968) can also be useful in the process of setting and monitoring goals.

Predicted Treatment Obstacles

In this section of the formulation, the therapist offers one or two ideas about potential obstacles to progress in therapy. Ideas about items for this list come from the other components of the formulation, particularly the Problem List and the Core Beliefs. For example, if one problem on the patient's list is a tendency to fail to complete things, the therapist might want to be alert for the possibility that the patient will fail to complete the tasks he begins in therapy. Similarly, if the patient believes, "My needs don't count," she may feel that therapy is self-indulgent or unnecessary and she may wish to terminate treatment prematurely.

APPLICATION TO
PSYCHOTHERAPY TECHNIQUE

The formulation is used in every session of therapy. The case-level formulation guides the therapist's work at the situation level, and the situation-level formulation feeds back to the case-level hypothesis. The case level version of the Working Hypothesis appears in Table 12.1; this is a hypothesis that links all of the patient's problems, proposing core beliefs and functional relationships that explain as many of those problems as possible. The situation-level formulation is a hypothesis about the mechanisms explaining or underpinning a specific momentary situation, such as an evening of emotional turmoil following a poor evaluation at work, or an episode of wrist slashing following a rejection.

Sessions of CBT tend to focus on recent situations, often using a Thought Record (see Figure 12.1) to guide the work. The Thought Record provides an excellent format for a situation-level formulation. For example, Jane came to the session complaining of difficulty sleeping. Before her therapist can intervene, he needs a formulation of this situation—a hypothesis about the mechanisms explaining or underpinning this episode of insomnia. If the therapist has developed a case-level formulation, it may yield an initial hypothesis about the general sorts of mechanisms likely to be driving the current episode. In Jane's case, a review of the events preceding a recent sleepless night showed that she worked frantically on demanding tasks related to her job until 11 p.m. She then went to bed and when she did not fall asleep right away she thought, "What's wrong with me, I can't even sleep!" This internal dialogue increased her anxiety, which made it even more difficult to sleep, fueling a vicious cycle of anxiety, sleeplessness, and self-berating. This formulation suggested several intervention strategies and contributed to the case-level formulation as well, as Jane's concerns about her competence played a role in many of her problems.

The process of formulating the problem and working to solve it is highly collaborative; the term "guided discovery" captures the nature of this work. The goal here is for the patient to discover the answers she needs, guided by the therapist. As the process unfolds, the therapist checks repeatedly with the patient to be certain that the two agree on the formulation of the problem and that the proposed interventions based on the formulation make sense to the patient and seem worth trying. If at any point the patient does not accept the formulation or the proposed intervention plan, the therapist pauses to address the lack of collaboration and to attempt to regain it before proceeding.

Thus, we try to share the formulation with the patient whenever possible. If a patient understands the formulation, often she or he can see potential solutions that make sense for her or him that the therapist might not have thought of. In general, we find it easiest to educate patients about the formulation by laying out the formulation at the situation level and then showing the patient how this same set of core beliefs occurs (when it does) in other domains of the patient's life. Some patients ask for and benefit from reviewing the case-level formulation, and in these cases the therapist might even review the formulation outlined in Table 12.1 with the patient.

CASE EXAMPLE

This example illustrates four aspects of therapy in which the CB Case Formulation is helpful: choice of intervention points, choice of intervention strategies, choice of homework assignments, and management of therapy-interfering behaviors. The CB Case Formulation for this case is provided in Table 12.2.

Peter is a 24-year-old first-year law student who sought treatment complaining of anxiety, a recent panic attack, and "out-of-control drinking." He reported that he had always been troubled by anxiety and that transitions were particularly difficult for him. His anxiety had escalated upon entering law school, and he was now experiencing nausea, diarrhea, difficulty concentrating, tearfulness, and agitation. Peter was terrified that he was losing control and would fail his upcoming exams. He found social situations difficult and drank excessively "to relax." He had difficulty declining a second or third drink when his friends urged him on.

Peter's parents divorced when he was 10 years old. During the fourth and fifth grades Peter lived with his father, but then he moved to his mother's home, although he feared that his father was angry with him for choosing to live with his mother. Peter is on good terms with both his parents now and speaks to his mother daily. He often calls her to "run my decisions by her" but finds that he is generally more anxious after speaking with her. Peter describes his mother as an "I told you so-er."

Choice of Intervention Points

The CB Case Formulation guides the therapist through the many possible intervention points presented in an ongoing therapy. Intervention point, here, refers to the timing of an intervention, the order problems are to be addressed, and which maladaptive thoughts are to be taken up in therapy at any time. For example, Peter, who holds the belief, "I can't make good decisions," and who avoids making important decisions for himself, choosing instead to defer to others or wait for fate to intervene, comes to a therapy session discussing his annoyance with his mother but not mentioning the status of a recent interview for a highly coveted summer internship for which he had applied. The therapist, attending to the formulation, knows that he must ask Peter about the status of his application and, if Peter was successful, to spend time discussing this successful outcome. And the therapist knows that if he failed to get the appointment, Peter's explanations for this may warrant some restructuring. In the absence of a formulation, the therapist might miss an important therapeutic opportunity.

Choice of Intervention Strategies

Near the end of the therapy, Peter reported that he thought he had done well on a particularly brutal set of exams but was upset that he had become so anxious. He began his therapy session with the statement, "I guess I'm not as far along as I thought. I know we had talked about stopping therapy, but I decided I'm not ready. I'm still pretty screwed up. I need to work with you another six months at least." Without the CB Case Formulation, the therapist might agree with Peter that he would do well to continue his therapy. However, the formulation (particularly the belief "I must be perfect or I'm a failure") suggests that a better strategy would be to help Peter see that his anxiety was appropriate and his ability to handle it good given the brutal nature of the exams. In this way, the therapist avoids reinforcing Peter's belief that he must perform perfectly or he is a failure.

Peter often used his therapy to ask the therapist for advice. Many CB therapists are not shy about giving advice, but a look at Peter's formulation

TABLE 12.2. Cognitive-Behavioral Case Formulation for Peter

Identifying Information

Peter is a 24-year-old first-year law student who lives with his girlfriend.

Problem List

1. Panic attacks—one in the last 3 months. Fears of subsequent panic attacks.
2. "Out-of-control" drinking in social situations; unable to say "No" when offered a drink by a friend, accompanied by the thoughts, "If I say 'No,' they won't want to be around me anymore," and feelings of anxiety and uncertainty. Drinking three to four drinks in social situations about once a week when Peter would prefer to be drinking only one drink or none at all.
3. Chronic anxiety, particularly in social situations, prior to exams, when asked to speak in class.
4. Difficulties with girlfriend; unhappy with some of her habits but unable to let her know, accompanied by the thoughts, "It's not that important. Why can't I just accept her the way she is?" and feelings of anger and frustration.
5. Difficulties with friends; unable to tell friends what he really thinks about issues, unable to refuse unreasonable requests, due to thoughts like "They won't like me" and feelings of anxiety, resentment, and frustration.
6. Difficulties in relationship with mother; telephones her about once a week to ask for help with decision making due to automatic thoughts, "I can't make this decision on my own," with feelings of increased anxiety following his conversations with his mother.

Core Beliefs

"I can't make good decisions."
"I must be perfect or I'm a failure."
"I must be completely in control or I'm out of control."
"No one likes a failure."

Precipitants and Activating Situations

Transitions are difficult for Peter. His anxiety increased when he left home for college and when he began law school. Activating situations include: any social situation in which he feels "out of his element" or with peers whose friendship or association he values; circumstances that call attention to himself (e.g., entering a class late, leaving a class to go to the restroom); occasions when he must make a decision or when his judgment is questioned.

Working Hypothesis

Peter's beliefs—"I can't make good decisions," "I must be perfect or I'm a failure," "I must be completely in control or I'm out of control," and "No one likes a failure"—caused him to feel anxious during personal and professional transitions and in social settings. These beliefs also led to unassertiveness, which caused him to make decisions that stalled or compromised his personal and professional life, increasing his anxiety and further confirming the belief that he "can't make good decisions." At times, Peter was able to overcome his anxiety and make an important decision for himself. However, he would then seek reassurance from his parents, who, quite anxious themselves, questioned him to the point that he began to doubt himself. When Peter made a decision that resulted in a poor

(continued)

TABLE 12.2. (*continued*)

outcome, his mother's response was "I told you so," further strengthening his belief that he "can't make good decisions." Because he feared that his friends and family would desert him if he made the wrong decision, Peter seldom offered his opinion and generally "went along for the ride," with the result that he found himself with friends who were less motivated or resourceful than he was, again strengthening his belief that he must be a failure given the company he keeps.

Origins

Both Peter's parents appear to be anxious themselves and throughout their lives expressed their concerns and worries to Peter. His mother made many of Peter's decisions for him, even as a young adult, hoping to protect him from failure and hardship.

Treatment Plan

Goals

1. Eliminate panic attacks and anxiety about panic attacks.
2. Monitor and limit drinking to no more than two drinks per social occasion.
3. Reduce anxiety in certain situations (e.g., prior to exams, when asked to speak in class, and at parties or other social settings).
4. Increase assertiveness (e.g., Peter will tell his girlfriend at least once a week what he has liked and enjoyed and what he would like to see change in their relationship; Peter will express his opinion at least once each day; say "No" to his friends' unreasonable requests).

Interventions

1. Set goals for drinking and monitor use.
2. Relaxation training (breathing and progressive muscle relaxation) in session and at home.
3. Cognitive restructuring of the core beliefs (with the use of Thought Records in session and with out-of-session self-monitoring).
4. Hierarchy of feared social situations and role play and *in vivo* homework exposures to items on the hierarchy.
5. Assertiveness training (with role plays and practice in session and with out of-session experiments).

Predicted Obstacles to Treatment

1. Peter may be reluctant to be assertive in the therapy session, particularly if he disagrees with the treatment plan. As a result, he may not be motivated to comply with his homework or to participate fully in the therapy. If his progress falters, Peter may feel he has failed.
2. Peter may feel uncomfortable with the collaborative stance of the therapist, particularly when the therapist looks to Peter to make decisions about his therapy. At these times, Peter may become anxious and look to the therapist for reassurance and to set the agenda even if it is an agenda with which Peter disagrees.
3. Peter may be reluctant to bring up slips or missteps when executing his homework for fear that the therapist may think he is a failure.

suggested that this might not be a good strategy in his case. Instead, the therapist worked with Peter to develop his own decision and test out his fears that he would fail at doing this. At times, Peter left his therapy session more anxious than when he entered. But the case formulation helped reassure the therapist that this strategy was more therapeutic than telling Peter what the therapist believed would be a good decision. Over time, Peter became less anxious about the decisions he faced and stopped bringing them into therapy, choosing instead to solve them himself.

Choice of Homework Assignments

A CB Case Formulation helps the therapist make appropriate homework assignments. For example, Peter's belief, "I must be perfect or I'm a failure," prevented him from asking his professors to include him in activities that interested him because he feared he would fail at these new challenges. As a result, Peter watched as his friends were invited to conferences and asked to participate in writing projects. Peter's exclusion from these functions reinforced his belief, "I'm a failure."

The CB Case Formulation suggested that useful homework assignments would help Peter develop a more realistic appreciation of the probabilities of his success and failure. To that end, Peter was asked to predict the No-to-Yes ratio that would result if he asked 100 people over the next 7 days for something he wanted, and then to test out his prediction by making requests of others. Peter returned the next week pleased to report that he had greatly overestimated the number of times he would hear "No" to his requests—in fact, he had not yet heard "No" and had started to make bold and audacious requests that he would never have dreamed of making previously.

When asked to explain this turn of events, Peter stated, "I guess I never reached their limit." Without the assistance of a case formulation, the therapist might have ignored this statement. Instead, the therapist asked Peter to explain. A useful discussion followed in which Peter was able to see that it might not be accurate to assume that he had heard "Yes" more than "No" because he had failed to push people to their limit. Peter was able to generate some alternative explanations that did not minimize his accomplishment or undermine his sense of self-efficacy.

In another session Peter reported that he was tormented by the requests of friends who took advantage of his generosity and good nature. Although Peter felt that these fellows were selfish and boring, he was reluctant to say "No" to their requests because he considered them close friends. The case formulation suggested that Peter's association with these fellows was counterproductive, serving only to reinforce the belief that he must be a failure given the company he keeps. With Peter's permission, the therapist raised the issue of whether these fellows were really such good friends as Peter felt they were. To examine this idea, Peter was asked to complete a homework assignment in which he drew an interpersonal map of his friends and family, placing himself at the center of the paper and drawing concentric rings around himself, with the distance of the individual from the center corresponding to his emotional attachment to that person. Peter carried out this exercise and returned to the next session having realized that these classmates were not as dear and close as he had thought. With this new information, Peter was able to begin to say "No" to his friends requests because, as he put it, "I have less to lose."

Management of Therapy-Interfering Behaviors

Linehan (1993) coined the term "therapy-interfering behaviors" to describe any behavior that compromises or threatens the collaboration between therapist and patient. In order to intervene appropriately to address therapy-interfering behavior, Linehan believes that the therapist must understand the function the interfering behavior serves for the patient—that is, the therapist must have a formulation.

After about 4 months of therapy, Peter came to his session one day anxious and quiet. When the therapist suggested reviewing the homework from the previous week, Peter stated, "I've been thinking that perhaps I've solved my problems and I don't need to come here so often." Peter's therapist took a moment to review the CB Case Formulation and hypothesized that Peter's belief that "No one likes a failure" might make him exquisitely sensitive regarding his progress in therapy. He would likely become anxious and panicky if he sensed that he wasn't performing to the therapist's expectations. This formulation suggested to the therapist that it would be more profitable to return to a review of the previous week's homework. Without the case formulation, the therapist might tend to agree with Peter's assessment and move to a discussion of termination.

Upon reviewing the homework, the therapist discovered that Peter had to study for three exams and hadn't had time to do his homework. A Thought Record focused on Peter's decision not to do his therapy homework included these thoughts: "If I don't do the homework, my therapist will fire me"; "He'll think I don't care"; and "I've let him down." Peter was able to see that his belief that "No one likes a failure" might have prevented him from continuing his therapy and getting the help he wanted.

TRAINING

In our experience, training in CB Case Formulation happens best in a small group where therapists can work together to formulate their own and each others' cases. We have found that certain typical difficulties arise and that trainees can help one another overcome them.

Trainees often have difficulty making a Problem List. They have difficulty obtaining an exhaustive list, frequently omitting medical or "nonpsychological" problems (e.g., financial or legal problems). We encourage trainees to search for problems systematically by considering the domains outlined above. Trainees sometimes describe problems in psychological jargon (e.g., "codependency") rather than in terms of mood, cognitions, and behavior. Trainees' Problem Lists are sometimes vague, so that the trainee does not understand why the problem is a problem for the patient. The best remedy for this is to emphasize the importance of describing the mood, cognitive, and behavioral aspects of problems. Another useful strategy is to ask the trainee to think about why the problem of Jim, a patient, for example, depressed mood, is a problem for him. In response, the therapist may learn that Jim is no longer seeing his friends, is about to lose his job because of absenteeism, and has increased his alcohol intake. Surprisingly, sometimes trainees can sit with a patient who has obvious problems of self-care and not think to ask about exercise, sleep, diet, or grooming. The Problem List, then, is a good place to begin any discussion of a new case or review of an ongoing case.

Because the formulation is developed through collaboration between the patient and the therapist, what does or does not make its way to the patient's list of problems or core beliefs reflects aspects of both patient and therapist. Just as patients sometimes do not report important problems, therapists sometimes ignore significant issues, viewing them as trivial or beyond the scope of therapeutic intervention. When this happens, the trainee's own problems or core beliefs may be getting in the way.

Sometimes trainees do not recognize problems that belong on the Problem List because the patient appears to have solved them. In this case, it can be helpful for the trainee to learn that some solutions are problems themselves, as in the case of Linda, a patient who solves her problems by avoiding them. A trainee presented a short list of problems for Linda, who had been troubled by a series of panic attacks beginning 15 years earlier. The patient identified no other problems. However, when the trainee was asked, "What problems do you know of that the patient has already solved herself?" the Problem List expanded to include a number of long-standing avoidant solutions that had resulted in the loss of Linda's job and the dissolution of her marriage.

We have found that trainees are often reluctant to offer hypotheses unless they are confident that they are correct. As a result, they offer too few hypotheses. A limited set of hypotheses makes each one special, making it difficult for the trainee to dispense with a hypothesis that isn't useful. Therefore, we recommend that each CB Case Formulation begin with a period of brainstorming in which trainees are encouraged to offer as many ideas as possible, refraining from judging or editing any hypothesis offered by the group no matter how silly it may appear. Once a lengthy list of hypotheses is generated, the editing process can begin. Even then, it is helpful to keep several hypotheses on the table for a particular case and generate interventions based on each hypothesis. In this way, trainees are reminded that the goal is not to find the "correct" formulation but to become skilled at generating hypotheses and using them to formulate intervention strategies.

RESEARCH SUPPORT FOR THE APPROACH

Two studies provide some information about the reliability of the CB Case Formulation method. Persons, Mooney, and Padesky (1995) studied 46 clinicians who listened to audiotape recordings of part or all of initial interviews of two patients. The clinicians' ability to identify three problems for case 1 and five for case 2 was assessed. For case 1, the percentages of clinicians reporting the three problems were 97.8%, 82.6%, and 13.0%, respectively. This patient's third problem was mentioned only briefly and in passing, and therefore we are not troubled that most clinicians did not identify it. For case 2, the percentages of clinicians reporting each of the five problems were 100%, 95.7%, 67.4%, 93.4%, and 71.7%, respectively. Results of a second study (Persons & Bertagnolli, 1995) were similar. Thus, clinicians' ability to identify problems is good but not outstanding.

Persons, Mooney, and Padesky (1995) found that clinicians agreed fairly well with other clinicians' ratings of patients' schemas, or core beliefs, when clinicians' ratings were averaged over a group of five clinicians (interrater reliability coefficients averaged .76), but poor for single judges, averaging >.46 in that Persons et al. (1995) study, for example. A similar study with two more samples of clinicians reported similar results (Persons & Bertagnolli, 1995).

What do the low interrater reliabilities for judgments of core beliefs by single judges mean? How important is it that clinicians agree on initial judgments about core beliefs? Kanfer (1985) argues that it is *not* important that clinicians agree with one another about their initial formulations of a case. Instead, he argues that what *is* important is that clinicians use a hypothesis-testing approach to formulation and treatment, an approach in which the clinician develops a formulation, uses it to design an intervention, assesses the outcome of the intervention, and uses this information to reformulate as needed, in an iterative process. Kanfer (1985, p. 17) points out that "competent clinicians take different paths through the entire procedure," and he would not find this troubling. What is important, in Kanfer's view, is that clinicians follow this hypothesis-testing process, not that they begin with the same initial formulation. Thus, he argues that it is not important to demonstrate interrater reliability of behavioral formulations, particularly of initial formulations. Certainly this point of view is consistent with our model (and with our findings!).

Is the CB Case Formulation method valid? Our view of validity emphasizes the treatment utility of the method. That is, does treatment that is guided by a CB Case Formulation lead to a better outcome than treatment not guided by a formulation? This question has not yet been studied directly; however, the efficacy of treatment conducted using CB Case Formulation has been examined in a naturalistic study, and some comparative studies of other approaches to cognitive-behavioral case formulation are available.

Persons, Bostrom, and Bertagnolli (1995) reported that 45 depressed patients treated by the first author in individualized CBT guided by a CB Case

Formulation had outcomes similar to patients treated with standardized CBT in the NIMH Treatment of Depression Collaborative Research Program (TDCRP; Elkin et al., 1989). Most of the patients treated in this naturalistic study had comorbidities (e.g., coexisting panic disorder, substance abuse, or major medical problems) that would have precluded their participation in the TDCRP.

Jacobson et al. (1989) compared the treatment efficacy of individualized, "clinically flexible" vs. standardized marital therapy, using their own approach to case conceptualization. The individualized and clinically flexible treatment was constructed from the same elements as the standardized treatment (behavior exchange, companionship enhancement, communication training, problem-solving training, sexual enrichment, and generalization and maintenance). The difference between the two treatments was that therapists using the clinically flexible treatment used only the modules a couple needed (as determined by a case conceptualization discussed in a group supervision meeting), whereas therapists using the standardized treatment used all modules. Both treatments produced statistically significant improvements, and the treatments did not differ in efficacy at posttreatment. However, couples treated with clinically flexible treatment were more likely to have maintained their gains 6 months after treatment ended than couples treated with standardized treatment.

Mixed evidence of the superiority of individualized treatment over standardized treatment was provided by Schneider and Byrne (1987) in a study of 35 children with behavior disorders. Children were randomly assigned to individualized social skills training or nonindividualized social skills training. Posttreatment assessments showed that children who received individualized treatment showed more cooperative play but that the two groups did not differ in aggression.

Two studies provide evidence *disconfirming* the hypothesis that use of an individualized case formulation leads to improved outcome. Emmelkamp, Bouman, and Blaauw (1994) and Schulte, Kunzel, Pepping, and Schulte-Bahrenberg (1992) compared standardized and individualized treatment for patients with anxiety disorders and found no superiority for the individualized treatment. In both studies, patients who received standardized protocol treatment received exposure treatment. How can the failure to show an advantage to individualized over standardized treatment be accounted for? We offer two suggestions:

First, in the Schulte et al. (1992) study, the authors found that adherence to the treatment manual was poor, particularly for therapists in the standardized group. Thus, the difference between the standardized and individualized treatment conditions was less than had been intended, and this may account in part for the failure to find differences between the conditions. Second, in both studies, subjects were selected to meet criteria for certain anxiety disorders but to have few or no other psychiatric disorders; thus, patients had low levels of psychiatric comorbidity. We believe that case conceptualization is more important in the treatment of complex cases of patients with multiple comorbidities than in the treatment of simple cases. This hypothesis, however, has not yet been subjected to empirical test.

SUMMARY, CONCLUSIONS, AND FUTURE DIRECTIONS

We have presented a CB Case Formulation method that we find clinically useful, particularly for complex cases. Evidence of the efficacy of treatment based on CB Case Formulation is urgently needed, and we urge readers to collect data from their own cases. We encourage clinicians to collect these data as part of their day-to-day clinical work and to communicate with us about publishing them collaboratively. Also needed are outcome studies comparing efficacy, effectiveness, dropout, and relapse rates of standardized and individualized CB treatments (Persons, 1991). To address the apparent conflict between researchers' needs for standardized protocols and clinicians' needs for flexibility, we are working to develop a flexible standardized protocol for treating depressed multiple-problem patients. Another intriguing notion is the suggestion that protocol treatment and individualized treatment might be combined by using standardized components as the building blocks of individualized treatments (Eifert, 1995; Emmelkamp, 1995; Schulte, 1995). Future directions for developing the model include adding components that identify patients' adaptive beliefs and their strengths and resources (cf. Evans, 1993; also Surber, 1994), and including a greater consideration of the effects of biology and of cultural background in the case conceptualization (cf. Levine & Sandeen, 1985).

REFERENCES

Barlow, D. H., Hayes, S. C., & Nelson, R. O. (1984). *The scientist–practitioner: Research and accountability in clinical and educational settings.* New York: Pergamon Press.

Beck, A. T. (1976). *Cognitive therapy and the emotional disorders.* New York: International Universities Press.

Beck, A. T., Emery, G., & Greenberg, R. (1985). *Anxiety disorders and phobias: A cognitive perspective.* New York: Basic Books.

Beck, A. T., Freeman, A., & Associates. (1990). *Cognitive therapy of personality disorders.* New York: Guilford Press.

Beck, A. T., Rush, A. J., Shaw, B. F., & Emery, G. (1979). *Cognitive therapy of depression.* New York: Guilford Press.

Beck, J. S. (1995). *Cognitive therapy: Basics and beyond.* New York: Guilford Press.

Bellack, A. S., & Hersen, M. (1988). *Behavioral assessment: A practical handbook.* New York: Pergamon Press.

Eifert, G. H. (1995, July). *Why we need to match treatments to clients and not to labels— at least some of the time.* Paper presented at the World Congress of Behavioural and Cognitive Therapies, Copenhagen, Denmark.

Elkin, I., Shea, M. T., Watkins, J. T., Imber, S. D., Sotsky, S. M., Collins, J. F., Glass, D. R., Pilkonis, P. A., Leber, W. R., Docherty, J. P., Fiester, S. J., & Parloff, M. B. (1989). NIMH Treatment of Depression Collaborative Research Program: General effectiveness of treatments. *Archives of General Psychiatry, 46,* 971–982.

Elstein, A. S., Shulman, L. S., & Sprafka, S. A. (1978). *Medical problem solving: An analysis of clinical reasoning.* Cambridge, MA: Harvard University Press.

Emmelkamp, P. M. G. (1995, July). *Standardized versus individualized behavior therapy: A critical evaluation.* Paper presented at the World Congress of Behavioural and Cognitive Therapies, Copenhagen, Denmark.

Emmelkamp, P. M. G., Bouman, T. K., & Blaauw, E. (1994). Individualized versus standardized therapy: A comparative evaluation with obsessive–compulsive patients. *Clinical Psychology and Psychotherapy, 1,* 95–100.

Evans, I. M. (1993). Constructional perspectives in clinical assessment. *Psychological Assessment, 5,* 264–272.

Freeman, A. (1992). Developing treatment conceptualizations in cognitive therapy. In A. Freeman & F. Dattilio (Eds.), *Casebook of cognitive-behavior therapy.* (pp. 13–23). New York: Plenum Press.

Giles, T. R. (Ed.). (1993). *Handbook of effective psychotherapy.* New York: Plenum Press.

Greenberger, D., & Padesky, C. A. (1995). *Mind over mood: A cognitive therapy treatment manual for clients.* New York: Guilford Press.

Hayes, S. C., Nelson, R. O., & Jarrett, R. B. (1987). The treatment utility of assessment: A functional approach to evaluating assessment quality. *American Psychologist, 42,* 963–974.

Haynes, S. N., & O'Brien, W. H. (1990). Functional analysis in behavior therapy. *Clinical Psychology Review, 10,* 649–668.

Heimberg, R. G. (in press). *Treatment of social fears and phobias.* New York: Guilford Press.

Jacobson, N. S., Schmaling, K. B., Holtzworth-Munroe, A., Katt, J. L., Wood, L. F., & Follette, V. M. (1989). Research-structured vs. clinically flexible versions of social learning–based marital therapy. *Behaviour Research and Therapy, 27,* 173–180.

Kanfer, F. H. (1985). Target selection for clinical change programs. *Behavioral Assessment, 7,* 7–20.

Kiresuk, T. J., & Sherman, R. E. (1968). Goal Attainment Scaling: A general method for evaluating comprehensive community mental health programs. *Community Mental Health Journal, 4,* 443–453.

Levine, F. M., & Sandeen, E. (1985). *Conceptualization in psychotherapy: The models approach.* Hillsdale, NJ: Erlbaum.

Lewinsohn, P. M., Hoberman, T., & Hautzinger, M. (1985). An integrative theory of depression. In S. Reiss & R. Bootzin (Eds.), *Theoretical issues in behavior therapy.* New York: Academic Press.

Linehan, M. M. (1993). *Cognitive-behavioral treatment of borderline personality disorder.* New York: Guilford Press.

Muran, J. C., & Segal, Z. V. (1992). The development of an idiographic measure of self-schemas: An illustration of the construction and use of self-scenarios. *Psychotherapy, 29,* 524–535.

Nelson, R. O., & Hayes, S. C. (Eds.). (1986a). *Conceptual foundations of behavioral assessment.* New York: Guilford Press.

Nelson, R. O., & Hayes, S. C. (1986b). The nature of behavioral assessment. In R. O. Nelson & S. C. Hayes (Eds.), *Conceptual foundations of behavioral assessment* (pp. 3–41). New York: Guilford Press.

Nezu, A. M., & Nezu, C. M. (1993). Identifying and selecting target problems for clinical interventions: A problem-solving model. *Psychological Assessment, 5,* 254–263.

Persons, J. B. (1989). *Cognitive therapy in practice: A case formulation approach.* New York: Norton.

Persons, J. B. (1991). Psychotherapy outcome studies do not accurately represent current models of psychotherapy: A proposed remedy. *American Psychologist, 46,* 99–106.

Persons, J. B. (1993). Case conceptualization in cognitive-behavior therapy. In K. T. Kuehlwein & H. Rosen (Eds.), *Cognitive therapy in action: Evolving innovative practice* (pp. 33–53). San Francisco: Jossey-Bass.

Persons, J. B., & Bertagnolli, A. (1995). *Inter-rater reliability of cognitive behavioral case formulations of depression.* Manuscript in preparation.

Persons, J. B., Bostrom, A., & Bertagnolli, A. (1995, June). *Clinically-significant change in patients treated with cognitive-behavior therapy for depression in a private practice setting.* Paper presented at the Society for Psychotherapy Research, Vancouver, British Columbia, Canada.

Persons, J. B., Mooney, K. A., & Padesky, C. A. (1995). Inter-rater reliability of cognitive-behavioral case formulations. *Cognitive Therapy and Research, 19,* 21–34.

Schneider, B. H., & Byrne, B. M. (1987). Individualizing social skills training for behavior-disordered children. *Journal of Consulting and Clinical Psychology, 55,* 444–445.

Schulte, D. (1995, July). *Tailor-made versus standardized therapy of phobic patients: Empirical findings and a decision model.* Paper presented at the World Congress of Behavioural and Cognitive Therapies, Copenhagen, Denmark.

Schulte, D., Kunzel, R., Pepping, G., & Schulte-Bahrenberg, T. (1992). Tailor-made versus standardized therapy of phobic patients. *Advances in Behaviour Research and Therapy, 14,* 67–92.

Sobell, M. B., & Sobell, L. C. (1993). *Problem drinkers: Guided self-change treatment.* New York: Guilford Press.

Surber, R. W. (Ed.). (1994). *Clinical case management: A guide to comprehensive treatment of serious mental illness.* Thousand Oaks, CA: Sage.

Turkat, I. D. (Ed.). (1985). *Behavioral case formulation.* New York: Plenum Press.

Turkat, I. D., & Maisto, S. A. (1985). Personality disorders: Application of the experimental method to the formulation and modification of personality disorders. In D. H. Barlow (Ed.), *Clinical handbook of psychological disorders: A step-by-step treatment manual* (pp. 502–570). New York: Guilford Press.

13

Case Formulation in Dialectical Behavior Therapy for Borderline Personality Disorder

KELLY KOERNER
MARSHA M. LINEHAN

Dialectical Behavior Therapy (DBT; Linehan, 1993a, 1993b) is a cognitive-behavioral treatment for clients diagnosed with borderline personality disorder (BPD). Case formulation is essential to efficient, effective DBT. Skillful DBT intervention is guided by a stage theory of treatment, biosocial theory of the etiology and maintenance of BPD, behavioral principles, and ideas about common patterns that interfere with treatment. This chapter introduces the concepts and method of case formulation in DBT.

HISTORICAL BACKGROUND OF THE APPROACH

We begin with a brief description of DBT to orient readers unfamiliar with this approach. Marsha Linehan and her colleagues at the Suicidal Behaviors Research Clinic at University of Washington developed DBT as a treatment for women with a history of parasuicide who met criteria for BPD. (Parasuicide is any intentional self-injurious behavior including but not limited to suicide attempts.) By watching videotapes of Linehan's therapy sessions, she and her research team identified aspects of her style and her modifications of cognitive-behavioral techniques that seemed effective. The treatment was then standardized in treatment manuals (Linehan, 1993a, 1993b), demonstrated in empirical trials to be more effective than treatment as usually offered in the community

(Linehan, Armstrong, Suarez, Allmon, & Heard, 1991; Linehan, Heard, & Armstrong, 1993; Linehan, Tutek, Heard, & Armstrong, 1994), and now has been adapted for use in various settings in the United States and abroad (e.g., Barley et al., 1993; Miller, Eisner, & Allport, 1994; Swenson, Sanderson, & Linehan, 1996).

DBT is a complex treatment that blends cognitive-behavioral interventions with Eastern meditation practices and shares elements in common with psychodynamic, client-centered, Gestalt, paradoxical, and strategic approaches (cf. Heard & Linehan,1994). Dialectical philosophy influences every aspect of DBT from the rapid juxtaposition of change and acceptance techniques to the therapist's use of both irreverent and warmly responsive communication styles. Nevertheless, its guiding principle is simple. DBT is based on the theory that most "borderline" behavior regulates dysregulated emotions or is a consequence of failed emotion regulation. This emotion dysregulation both interferes with problem solving and creates problems in its own right. Maladaptive behaviors, including extreme behaviors such as parasuicide, function to solve problems. In particular, amelioration of unendurable emotional pain is always suspected as a consequence that reinforces dysfunctional behavior. Although such extreme responses are understandable given the chronic chaos and suffering experienced by many individuals with BPD, the consistent refrain in DBT is that a better solution can be found. The best alternative to suicide is to build a life that is worth living. DBT decreases maladaptive problem solving while working to enhance the capabilities and motivation needed to improve the client's quality of life.

Comprehensive treatment (1) enhances capabilities, (2) improves motivation to change, (3) ensures that new capabilities generalize to the natural environment, (4) enhances therapist capabilities and motivation to treat clients effectively, and (5) structures the environment in the ways essential to support client and therapist capabilities (Linehan, 1996). In the standard form of DBT, these functions are divided among modes of service delivery. For example, clients enhance capabilities by learning skills to regulate emotions, to tolerate emotional distress when change is slow or unlikely, to be more effective in interpersonal conflicts, and to control attention in order to skillfully participate in the moment. They may also enhance capabilities through pharmacotherapy. The client and therapist collaborate in individual therapy to motivate change by identifying patterns associated with problematic behavior and by addressing inhibitions, cognition, and reinforcement contingencies that interfere with solving problems in a more effective manner. To generalize new behaviors across situations in daily life, the individual therapist uses phone consultation and *in vivo* therapy (i.e., therapy outside the office). A weekly consultation meeting provides therapists with technical help and emotional support to remain able and motivated to treat clients effectively. Structuring the environment for both clients and therapists is done as needed by the clinic director or administration, and for the client through case management. In adapting DBT, the particular distribution of functions to modes of service delivery depends on the resources of a given setting—what is essential is that each function be in place. Typically, one primary therapist ensures that a given client has each function by providing it or acting as a services broker. Often the individual therapist has primary responsibility for crisis management and treatment planning. Case formulation influences each of these functions but is particularly relevant for the primary therapist conducting individual psychotherapy.

CONCEPTUAL FRAMEWORK

Theory-driven case formulation is the cornerstone of DBT. Individuals with BPD typically have multiple problems. The sheer number of serious (at times life-threatening) problems that therapy must address makes it difficult for therapists to establish and maintain a treatment focus. For example, it is difficult to decide what to treat first when the client has numerous problems (panics, is depressed, drinks too much, returns repeatedly to an abusive relationship, becomes mute during treatment interactions, and is chronically suicidal). Following the concern most pressing to the client can result in a different crisis management focus each week. Therapy can feel like a car veering out of control, barely averting disaster, with a sense of forward motion but not meaningful progress. With clients who have multiple serious problems, crisis management and stopgap reduction of acute problems can dominate the therapy to the extent that efficient, effective treatment becomes unlikely.

Treatment decisions are further complicated because clients with BPD often act in ways that distress their therapists. For example, despite experience or training, it can be a struggle to manage one's emotional reactions when a client is recurrently suicidal and both rejects help that is offered and demands help that one cannot give. Even when therapy is on the right track, progress can be slow and sporadic. All of these factors can induce the therapist to make errors, including premature changes to the treatment plan. In DBT, a partial solution to this problem is to use a theory-driven case formulation to guide treatment decisions.

At an introductory level, five sets of theoretical concepts are important in DBT case formulation: (1) stage theory of treatment; (2) biosocial theory of the etiology and maintenance of BPD; (3) learning principles and ideas from behavior therapy; (4) common behavioral patterns of BPD, and dilemmas created by the dialectical nature of these patterns, which interfere with efforts to change; and (5) dialectical orientation to change. These five sets of concepts can be considered the "lenses" through which any problematic behavior will be viewed. Just as one might inspect the same object through reading glasses, infrared goggles, a jeweler's eyeglass, a high-power microscope, and an orbiting satellite, these five conceptual lenses make apparent different facets of problematic behavior. The DBT therapist looks for opportunity to foster change with each lens. Theory-driven case formulation resolves confusing variability into specific hypotheses that guide assessment and intervention.

Stages of Treatment: Behaviors to Target in DBT

The first conceptual lens is stages of treatment. This is the commonsense notion that the current extent of disordered behavior determines what treatment tasks are relevant and feasible. DBT's stage model of treatment (Linehan, 1993a, 1996) prioritizes the problems that must be addressed at a particular point in therapy according to the threat they pose to a reasonable quality of life. The relevance of problem behaviors is determined both by the severity and complexity of the client's disordered behavior at the moment as well as the progress of therapy. The first stage of treatment with all DBT clients is pretreatment, followed by one to four subsequent stages. The number of subsequent stages depends on the extent of behavioral disorder when the client begins treatment.

In the pretreatment stage, the primary behaviors to target are therapist and client agreement as to treatment goals and mutual commitment to treatment. Before beginning formal treatment, DBT requires that all parties agree on the essential goals and the basic format of the treatment being offered and make a verbal commitment to them. Because DBT requires voluntary rather than coerced consent, both the client and the therapist must have the choice of committing to DBT over some other non-DBT option. So, for example, in a forensic unit or when a client is legally mandated to treatment, he or she is not considered to have entered DBT until a considered verbal commitment is obtained. In pretreatment, once the therapist commits to the client, the priority is to obtain engagement in therapy.

Stage 1 of therapy targets behaviors needed to achieve reasonable life expectancy, control of action, and sufficient connection to treatment and behavioral capabilities to achieve these ends. Treatment time is distributed to give priority to targets in the following order of importance: (1) suicidal/homicidal or other imminently life-threatening behavior; (2) therapy-interfering behavior of the therapist or client; (3) behavior that severely compromises the client's quality of life; and (4) deficits in behavioral capabilities needed to make life changes.

Stage 2 targets posttraumatic stress responses and traumatizing emotional experiences. Its goal is to get the client out of unremitting emotional desperation.

Stage 3 synthesizes what has been learned, increases self-respect and an abiding sense of connection, and works toward resolving problems in living.

Stage 4 (Linehan, 1996) focuses on the sense of incompleteness that many individuals experience, even after problems in living are essentially resolved. The goal is to achieve the capacity for sustained joy. The task is to integrate the past with the present and future, the self with others, and to accept reality as it is.

Although the stages of therapy are presented linearly, progress is often not linear and the stages overlap. It is not uncommon to hit a snag in stage 1 that requires a momentary return to pretreatment tasks. Indeed, with some clients this occurs repeatedly throughout therapy. The transition from stage 1 to stage 2 is usually fraught with difficulty, and it is not unusual to move back and forth between the two stages for quite some time. Stage 3 not only overlaps with stage 2 but is, at times, a review of the same issues from a different vantage point. Stage 4 is often a lifelong endeavor that requires acknowledgment and acceptance rather than completion. At termination or before significant breaks from treatment, especially if ill prepared, the client may revert briefly to stage 1 behaviors. The infrequency of stage 1 behaviors as well as the speed of reregulation (rather than the presence of any one instance of behavior) define the differences between stages.

The controlled treatment trials of DBT to date have been with clients entering treatment at stage 1. Across each stage of therapy, case formulation is organized by the extent of disordered behavior that determines the relevance and feasibility of treatment tasks. Although the principles of case formulation are consistent throughout all stages of DBT, the focus of case formulation does vary with the stage of therapy. The remainder of this chapter is about case formulation for stage 1 of DBT.

Biosocial Theory: The Central Role of Emotion Dysregulation

The second perspective guiding DBT case formulation is a biosocial theory of the etiology and maintenance of BPD. Linehan theorizes that the transaction of a biological vulnerability to emotion dysregulation with an invalidating environment, over time, creates and maintains borderline behavioral patterns. On the biological side, individuals with BPD are thought to be predisposed (perhaps due to high genetic loading for emotionality) to have (1) high sensitivity to emotional stimuli (i.e., immediate reactions and a low threshold for onset of emotional reaction); (2) high reactivity (i.e., intense experience and expression of emotion and cognitive dysregulation that goes along with high arousal); and (3) a slow return to baseline arousal (i.e., long-lasting reactions that contribute to high sensitivity to the next emotional stimulus). This biological vulnerability contributes to difficulty regulating emotion. Expanding Gottman and Katz's (1989) definition, emotion regulation requires the ability to (1) decrease (or increase) physiological arousal associated with emotion, (2) reorient attention, (3) inhibit mood-dependent action, (4) experience emotions without escalating or blunting, and (5) organize behavior in the service of external, nonmood-dependent goals.

Transaction with a particular social environment, termed the invalidating environment, can create or exacerbate this biological vulnerability. In an optimally validating environment, a person is treated in a manner that strengthens those responses that are well-grounded or justifiable in terms of the empirical facts, correct inference, or accepted authority, and those that are effective for reaching the individual's ultimate goals. The optimal environment treats the individual as relevant and meaningful, validates the individual's valid responses, and invalidates the invalid.

The invalidating environment, however, fails to confirm, corroborate, or verify the individual's experience and fails to teach the individual what responses are or are not likely to be effective for reaching the individual's goals. Invalidating environments communicate that the individual's characteristic responses to events (particularly emotional responses) are incorrect, inaccurate, inappropriate, pathological, or not to be taken seriously. By oversimplifying the ease of solving problems, the environment fails to teach the individual to tolerate distress or form realistic goals and expectations. By punishing communication of negative experiences and only responding to negative emotional displays when they are escalated, the environment teaches the individual to oscillate between emotional inhibition and extreme emotional communication.

Eventually, individuals learn to invalidate their own experiences and search the immediate social environment for cues about how to feel and think. The primary consequence of the invalidating environment is to punish (or fail to adequately strengthen) *self-generated behavior*. Self-generated behaviors are an individual's unique, uncensored responses that are not primarily under the control of immediate aversive social consequences or immediate external or arbitrary reinforcement. That is to say, self-generated behavior is "intrinsically motivated" or "free operant."

Childhood sexual abuse may be the prototypic invalidating environment related to BPD, given the correlation observed among BPD, suicidal behavior, and reports of childhood sexual abuse (Wagner & Linehan, 1997). However, because not all individuals who meet BPD criteria report histories of sexual abuse nor do all victims of childhood sexual abuse develop BPD, it remains unclear as to how to best account for individual differences in etiology. Linehan's theory argues that it is the invalidating aspect of childhood sexual abuse that is most crucial to development of BPD (Wagner & Linehan, 1997).

The transactional nature of this model implies that individuals may reach BPD patterns of behavior via very different routes: despite only moderate vulnerability to emotion dysregulation, a sufficiently invalidating environment may produce BPD patterns. Similarly, even a "normal" level of invalidation may be sufficient to create BPD patterns for those who are highly vulnerable to emotion dysregulation. The transactional result is a disruption of the organizing and communicative functions of emotion.

The stage of treatment and the biosocial theory suggest general hypotheses, that is, determine "what" is to be assessed as one formulates a DBT case. In particular, the running hypothesis for any targeted problematic behavior is that it is a consequence of emotion dysregulation, an attempt to modulate emotion, or both. Behavioral principles translate these general ideas into specific hypotheses about a given individual.

Theory of Change: Learning Principles and Behavior Therapy

The third perspective used in DBT case formulation is a behavioral theory of change. In general, persistent disordered behavior is viewed as a result of deficits in capabilities as well as problems of motivation. Principles of learning and ideas from behavior therapy specify methods to analyze behavior and influence behavior change. To understand a specific problematic behavior, DBT case formulation relies on functional analysis or behavioral chain analysis. This is where the "rubber meets the road," where general hypotheses regarding problematic behavior guide the analysis of specific antecedents and consequences that maintain (motivate) current problematic behavior. Each individual is likely to have a unique pattern of variables controlling problematic behavior, and these variables may differ from one set of circumstances to another.

Careful analysis of antecedents and consequences is particularly important due to the central role of emotion dysregulation in BPD. The hallmark of emotion dysregulation is instability. Therefore, capabilities disrupted by emotion dysregulation (e.g., an abiding sense of self, resolution of interpersonal conflict, goal-oriented action) are also likely to be unstable across settings and over time. When therapists mistakenly assume that behaviors covary, they may expect consistency beyond what the client produces. Similarly, by assuming that an observed dyssynchrony is traitlike, the therapist may treat the client as overly fragile. It is useful to distinguish between capabilities in a particular context (whether a person can do something under the best possible circumstances), performance difficulty in specific contexts (ease with which a person can perform a certain response), and traits (typical or average behavior across diverse contexts) (see Paulhus & Martin, 1987, for a similar distinction). Keeping these distinctions in mind helps the therapist assess whether the client lacks an ability or has the ability but is inhibited from skilled responding.

A behavioral chain analysis is an in-depth analysis of events and situational factors before and after a particular instance (or set of instances) of the targeted behavior. The goal is to provide an accurate and reasonably complete account of behavioral and environmental events associated with the problem behavior. Close attention is paid to reciprocal interactions between environmental events and the client's emotional, cognitive, and overt responses.

A chain analysis begins with a clear definition of the problem behavior. Next, the therapist and client identify both general vulnerability factors (those factors that are the context in which precipitating events have more influence, e.g., physical illness, sleep deprivation, or other conditions that influence emotional reactivity) and specific precipitating events that began the chain of events that led to the problem behavior. Therapist and client then identify each link between the precipitating event and the problematic behavior to yield a detailed account of each thought, feeling, and action that moved the client from point *A* to point *B*. Finally, therapist and client identify the immediate and delayed reactions of the client and others that followed the problem behavior. This detailed assessment allows the therapist to identify each juncture where an alternative client response might have produced positive change and averted conditions that lead to problem behavior. When dysfunctional links occur (behaviors that interfere with achieving the client's long-term goals), the therapist assesses what alternative behavior would have been more adaptive and skillful and why that more skillful alternative did not happen.

The absence of skilled performance is due to one of the following four factors, linked to behavior therapy change procedures:

First, the client may not have the necessary skills in his or her repertoire; that is, the client has a capability deficit. DBT views specific skills deficits as particularly relevant to BPD, and therefore the therapist assesses whether clients can (a) regulate emotions; (b) tolerate distress; (c) respond skillfully to interpersonal conflict; (d) observe, describe, and participate without judging, with awareness, and focusing on effectiveness; and (e) manage their own behavior with strategies other than self-punishment. When clients lack these skills, skills training is appropriate.

However, if assessment revealed that the client does at times behave more effectively in similar situations, then the therapist assesses which of the three other factors interfered with more skillful behavior. The second possible reason for the lack of skilled performance is that circumstances reinforce dysfunctional behavior or fail to reinforce more functional behavior. Problem behavior may lead to positive or preferred outcomes, or give the opportunity for other preferred behaviors or emotional states. Effective behaviors may be followed by neutral or punishing outcomes, or rewarding outcomes may be delayed. If problematic contingencies are identified, then contingency management interventions are appropriate.

The third possibility is that conditioned emotional responses block more skillful responding. Effective behaviors may be inhibited or disorganized by unwarranted fears, shame, guilt, or intense or out-of-control emotions. The person may be "emotion-phobic." She or he may have patterns of avoidance or escape behaviors. If this is the case, then some version of exposure-based treatment is indicated.

The fourth possibility is that effective behaviors are inhibited by faulty beliefs and assumptions. Faulty beliefs and assumptions may reliably precede ineffective behaviors. The person may be unaware of the contingencies or rules operating in the environment or in therapy. If problems are identified here, then cognitive modification strategies are appropriate.

BPD Behavioral Patterns and Dialectical Dilemmas

Change in primary targets (decreases in behaviors that threaten life, therapy, and quality of life, and increases in behavioral skills) is the main focus of stage 1 DBT. In order to successfully treat primary targets, however, other (secondary) behaviors or behavioral patterns may also need to be targeted. From clinical observation of the problems that prevent (and wreak havoc on) treatment and clinical progress, Linehan (1993a) distilled patterns organized into dialectical poles. Each pattern describes an aspect of the transaction between the experience of emotion dysregulation and a history of social consequences incurred as a consequence of emotion dysregulation. As the word "dialectical" implies, BPD individuals frequently jump from a behavioral pattern that underregulates to another that overregulates emotion, the discomfort of each extreme triggering oscillation between response patterns. These patterns perpetuate themselves and create new problems. These secondary targets are often common across behavioral chains and common across stages of treatment.

This fourth perspective orients the therapist to behavioral patterns that may destroy treatment if not directly treated. Each pattern highlights the dilemmas faced by both the client and the therapist whenever therapeutic change is initiated. DBT's aim is to help the client arrive at a synthesis or more effective balance of opposing behavioral tendencies.

Emotion Vulnerability and Self-Invalidation

Emotion vulnerability refers to the intense suffering that accompanies the experience of emotion dysregulation. By analogy, individuals with BPD can be considered the emotional equivalent of burn victims where the slightest movement is automatic extreme pain. Because the individual cannot control the onset and offset of internal or external events that influence emotional responses, the experience itself is a nightmare of intense emotional pain and the struggle to reregulate. This unpredictability foils personal and interpersonal expectations because the person can often meet expectations in one emotional state but not another, leading to frequent frustration and disillusionment in both the client and others. Even dysregulation of positive emotions creates pain. For example, a client reported, "I got so happy and excited when I went home for the holidays, I couldn't stand it. I laughed too loud, talked too much, everything I did was too big for them!" These individuals despair that vulnerability to uncontrollable emotion will ever lessen and suicide may seem the only way to prevent further suffering. Suicide can also be a final communication to an unsympathetic public. Emotional vulnerability is an important link to parasuicide and therefore becomes a target in itself.

The suffering associated with inability to regulate emotion creates numerous obstacles in therapy. Nearly any therapeutic movement evokes some emotional pain, much as debriding does in the treatment of serious burns. Sensitivity to criticism makes it painful to receive needed feedback; in-session dysregulation (dissociation, panic, intense anger) interrupts therapeutic tasks; generalization and follow-through on in-session changes and plans goes awry. Therapy itself may be traumatic. An understanding of emotion vulnerability means the therapist must understand and reckon with the intense pain involved in living without "emotional skin." The DBT therapist is empathic, coaches and soothes, and most importantly treats the emotion dysregulation in session. For example, in response to intense emotional reactions during therapeutic tasks (e.g., talking about an event from the week), the therapist validates the uncontrollable, helpless experience of emotional arousal, and teaches the individual to modulate emotion in session.

Self-invalidation occurs when the client responds to his or her own behavior (or the absence of needed self-generated behavior such as emotion control) as invalid, taking on the characteristics of the invalidating environment. Self-invalidation takes at least two forms. On the one hand, clients may judge themselves harshly for their vulnerability ("I should not be this way"), act in self-punitive ways, and feel self-hatred. The experience is of oneself as the agent of one's own demise. In this case parasuicide may function as punishment for transgression. On the other hand, clients may deny and ignore their vulnerability ("I am NOT this way") and hold unrealistically high or perfectionistic expectations. In doing so, the client minimizes the difficulty of solving life problems. By ignoring or blocking emotional experience, the person not only loses information needed to solve problems but disrupts the organizing and communicative functions of emotion. Self-invalidation is often a crucial link in the behavioral chain to parasuicide. Increasing self-validation and decreasing self-invalidation become essential secondary targets. The explicit focus on the necessity of appropriate self-validation is a hallmark of DBT.

The intense discomfort of either extreme results in an oscillation between experiencing vulnerability and invalidation of that experience. The dilemma for "June," a client, becomes who should be blamed for this predicament. She is either able to control behavior (as others believe she can) but won't, and therefore is "manipulative," or she *is* as unable to control emotions as she experiences herself to be, which means she will always be this way and dooms her to a never-ending nightmare of dyscontrol. June can try to fulfill expectations that are out of line with her capabilities and fail, feel ashamed, and decide she deserves to be punished or to be dead. Or she can see her vulnerability and adjust her standards. But if others do not also change their expectations of her, she can become angry that no one offers needed help and become convinced that suicidal behavior is the only means to communicate that she cannot do what is expected.

The dilemma in therapy is that focusing on accepting vulnerability and limitations may lead June to despair that she will always have the problems she has; focusing on change, however, may lead her to panic because she knows there is no way to consistently meet expectations. Further, if she changes her problematic behavior, she may feel ashamed that she could have done what was expected all along but did not because she was "lazy" or "manipulative." To negotiate this dilemma, the DBT therapist flexibly combines, moment to moment, the use of supportive acceptance and confrontive change strategies. The therapist communicates, in word and deed, that June is doing her best yet must do better.

Active-Passivity and Apparent Competence

The second set of opposing behavioral tendencies is active-passivity and apparent competence. Active-passivity is the tendency to respond to problems passively and to regulate oneself, if one tries at all, by regulating the relevant aspects of the environment. Regulating oneself by regulating the environment is not a problem per se—the problem is that the individual with BPD is not skillful *enough* at regulating his or her environment.

For example, "Paula," a client, returns from a psychiatric hospitalization and her roommate asks her to move out. Instead of searching for a new place to live, Paula spends the day in bed and is silent during therapy despite all efforts by the therapist to encourage active problem solving. Paula experiences herself as, and actually is, unable to do what is necessary without more help. If she had just been discharged with a broken leg, help might be forthcoming. However, without observable deficits, she may get feedback that it is socially unacceptable to need "too much" help or reassurance or to be "too" dependent. Thus, she either avoids getting necessary help or attempts to get it in a way that is experienced as demanding by others. That is, regulation of her environment to solve her problem is deficient or unskillful and ineffective. As the situation worsens, the therapist becomes frustrated that Paula creates a crisis that could easily be solved if she would cope actively (get the newspaper, find another place). Her experience, however, is that the situation is hopeless no matter what she does. This style of problem solving—acting extremely inadequate and passive in the face of insufficient help and at times magnifying problems if they are not taken seriously—is often overlearned from repeated failure despite one's best efforts in an environment where difficulties are minimized. Remaining passive in a manner that activates others confirms that, in fact, the problems could not have been solved without help, that in effect things are as bad as claimed. While regulating in this way can be effective, overreliance on this behavioral pattern often means problems are not solved and life gets worse. This pattern can contribute to parasuicide in many ways, including increasing life stress as problems go unsolved, alienating helpers, and making suicide one of the few means of communicating that more help is needed.

Therapeutic changes stay under the control of the therapy relationship rather than adequately generalizing to the client's natural environment unless this pattern is addressed directly. Consequently, in DBT it is as important to teach the client to solve problems as it is to get the problems solved. As one DBT therapist said to a client with activity-passivity (in spades), "I can see you are working hard in therapy, but you're not working smart. You've got to be learning to create your own therapy, not just following orders." The secondary targets here are to decrease active-passivity behaviors and increase active problem solving, especially skills to more effectively manage oneself and one's environment.

Apparent competence is the sum total of behavioral responses that influence observers to overestimate and overgeneralize response capabilities. Apparent competence takes one of two forms. First, observers are likely to overgeneralize when verbal and nonverbal expressions of emotion are incongruous. Often clients verbalize extreme negative emotions but convey little, if any, distress nonverbally. Observers are likely in these instances to believe nonverbal over verbal expression when, in fact, it is the verbal channel that is the more accurate expression. Second, observers overgeneralize when they ignore the critical context needed for skilled behavior. For example, in the context of either a positive mood or positive relationship, many behaviors are more easily performed. To the extent that Paula is a relational person and has little control of her emotional state (to be expected when the core problem is emotion dysregulation), then she has little control over her behavioral capabilities. Variable and conditional competence across settings and over time may be due to behavioral capabilities that are overly mood or context dependent. Nevertheless, the absence of expected competence is interpreted as manipulation and decreases others' willingness to help. The further implication here is that others have difficulty knowing when the person needs help, thereby creating the invalidating environment. Here the goal is to increase accurate expression of emotion and competencies and to decrease behavior that is overly dependent on mood and context.

The dilemma in therapy is that active-passivity and apparent competence make it difficult for the therapist to determine the level of help that should be offered with what Paula can do for herself. At times and for a variety of reasons, she may need more help than those in her environment are willing or able to provide. Apparent competence leads others (including the therapist) to expect more than can be delivered. The appearance of competence also desensitizes the therapist and others to low level communication of distress. "Doing for" the client when the client is passive but does have the capability to help herself reinforces the problematic learned helplessness and blocks her from learning active problem solving. But abandoning Paula to her own means without sufficient help prevents appropriate skill training, increases panic, and increases the probability of further dysfunctional behavior. The DBT therapist negotiates this dilemma by responding to low-level communication of distress with active help and coaching of more effective behavior while insisting that the client actively solve her own problems.

Unrelenting Crisis and Inhibited Grieving

Unrelenting crisis refers to a self-perpetuating behavioral pattern in which the person with BPD both creates and is controlled by incessant aversive events. Emotional vulnerability and impulsivity combine to make an initial precipitant quickly snowball into worse problems, as when a person impulsively acts to decrease distress and inadvertently increases problems. For example, yelling in anger at a case worker and impulsively ending an interview needed to complete a housing application can result in being unable to reschedule with another worker before being evicted and homeless. Incomprehensible overreactions make more sense when viewed against a backdrop of repeated experiences of helplessness. The inability to recover fully from any one crisis before the next one hits leads to a "weakening of spirit" (Berent, 1981) associated with parasuicide and other emergency behaviors. This crisis-of-the-week pattern interferes with follow-through on any behavioral treatment plan and has led DBT to separate crisis management (psychotherapy) from skills training (psychoeducation). The secondary targets are to decrease crisis-generating behavior and to increase realistic decision making and good judgment.

Inhibited grieving is an involuntary, automatic avoidance response of painful emotional experiences, an inhibition of the natural unfolding of emotional responding. The individual does not fully experience, integrate, or resolve reactions to painful events but, instead, inadvertently increases sensitization to emotion cues and reactions by avoidance and escape. Borderline individuals are constantly exposed to the experience of loss, start the mourning process, automatically inhibit the process by avoiding or distracting from relevant cues, reenter the process, and so on. The grief inhibited may be associated with childhood trauma or revictimization as an adult, or it may be evoked by the many losses that are the current consequence of maladaptive coping. Inhibited grieving is the primary target of stage 2 of DBT, but it is targeted in stage 1 when it is linked to the primary targets. The goal is to decrease inhibited grieving and increase emotional experiencing.

The dilemma in therapy is that unrelenting crisis and inhibited grieving interfere with crucial therapy tasks. Systematic behavioral interventions, particularly exposure-based therapy dealing with trauma, are not feasible when these patterns are prevalent. It is difficult to engage in "uncovering" work and, simultaneously, to inhibit grief reactions and to avoid exposure to cues that evoke memory of past loss and trauma, particularly when one is in perpetual crisis. Avoidance and escape from painful feelings with maladaptive behaviors that generate a crisis inadvertently increases exposure to crisis-induced losses, which in turn increases avoidance of cues through further maladaptive behavior, and so on. In part, this pattern differentiates a stage 1 client from one in stage 2. The DBT therapist expects oscillating expressions of extreme distress and complete inhibition of affect and teaches the client skills needed to tolerate emotional experience without engaging in behavior that worsens the situation while decreasing the behaviors that lead to further loss of relationships and other things she or he values.

Dialectics of Change: Philosophical Guiding Principles

Dialectics has been referred to as the logic of process and as a coherent system of exploring and understanding the world (Basseches, 1984; Kaminstein, 1987; Levins & Lewontin, 1985; Riegel, 1975; Wells, 1972). Within DBT (cf. Linehan & Schmidt, 1995), dialectics provides an overriding context for case conceptualization. In contrast to the four lenses reviewed so far, dialectics shifts attention from the client alone to the *context* within which the client interacts. The "case" that is formulated, from a dialectical perspective, is not the individual per se but rather the relationships among the client, the client's community, the therapist, and the therapist's community. Factors impinging on the therapist become as important as those impinging on the client.

As a worldview, there are several essential tenets of dialectics. First, it is assumed that a "whole" is a relation of heterogeneous "parts" in polarity ("thesis" and "antithesis") out of whose "synthesis" evolves a new set of "parts" and, thereby, a new "whole." The parts, which hold no intrinsic or previous significance in and of themselves, are important only in relation to one another and in relation to the whole that they define. Considering phenomena to be heterogeneously composed has important implications for case formulation. The fact that parts are not merely diverse but also are in contradiction or opposition to one another focuses the observer not on a taxonomic identification of the parts but rather on the relationship or interaction of the parts as they move toward resolution.

A second tenet of dialectics states that parts acquire properties only as components of a particular whole. The same part may have different qualities when viewed as an aspect of different wholes. Parts of different wholes will embody different contradictions and dialectical syntheses. The importance of this point for case conceptualization is that no clinical phenomenon can be understood in isolation from the context in which it occurs. Because the system itself is dynamic, the ever-changing relationship between clinical phenomena and their contexts must also be a focus of assessment, conceptualization, and change.

A third tenet is that parts and wholes are interrelations, not a mere collision of objects with fixed properties and immutable boundaries. As such, the parts cannot participate in creating the whole without simultaneously being affected themselves by the whole. An important implication of this view is that it is impossible for clients not to alter the therapy system within which they interact (and which would not exist without them), even as they are simultaneously affected by the system. Attention to the "parts" other than the client, therefore, is as important as attention to the client.

Fourth, as already mentioned, dialectics recognizes change to be an aspect of all systems, and to be present at all levels of a system. Stability is the rare occurrence, not the idealized goal. Dialectics is neither the careful balance of opposing forces nor the melding of two open currents, but instead is the complex interplay of opposing forces. Equilibrium among forces, when found, is discovered at a higher level of observation, namely, by looking at the overall process of affirming, negating, and forming a new, more inclusive synthesis (Basseches, 1984, pp. 57–59).

Examination of the root metaphors of dialectics (dialectical materialism vs. dialectical idealism) suggests how dialectics relates to DBT case conceptualization. In dialectical materialism, the "energy" or force that ultimately drives the creation and synthesis of opposites is the efforts of humans to compel change in their world. In contrast, in dialectical idealism this process is energized by the Universal Truth (i.e., the universe itself drives the process). DBT case formulation moves back and forth between the two views, employing human activity as the motivator in some instances (e.g., pointing out the contradiction between the ideals created and upheld in a culture and actual body types of individuals) and larger, natural contradictions in others (e.g., the interplay of chance and skill in the outcome of human interventions). While the philosophy of dialectical materialism relevant to DBT (corresponding to behavioral theory as a foundation of DBT) views humans as imposing an order on an uncaring world, dialectical idealism (corresponding to the roots of DBT in Zen psychology) believes that we can recognize and experience a unity and pattern inherent in the organization of the universe. Dialectical materialism focuses the therapy and the therapist on the application of change procedures, and the case formulation identifies both what needs to change as well as what procedures would be most effective. Dialectical idealism focuses the therapy and the therapist on radical acceptance of the whole—beginning, middle, and end.

To summarize the conceptual framework of DBT case formulation, the stage of treatment influences what problem behaviors are targeted in therapy as well as the goals one is working toward. The biosocial theory frames the key hypothesis about what variables are central to development and mainte- nance of the problem behaviors. Learning principles suggest both methods of behavioral analyses and change. BPD behavioral patterns and dialectical di- lemmas suggest secondary behavioral patterns functionally linked to both problem behavior per se and to difficulties changing these patterns. The dia- lectic between change and acceptance, between dialectical materialism and dialectical idealism, is the central dialectic of DBT and informs case conceptuali- zation at every level of treatment.

INCLUSION/EXCLUSION CRITERIA

Although DBT is currently being adapted for non-BPD client populations, there is empirical evidence only for its effectiveness with chronically parasuicidal female clients with BPD. Consequently, we focus on the issues encountered when working with clients who have severely disordered behavior. It is im- portant to note that the diagnostic criteria for BPD are considered as samples of behavior and appropriate targets of intervention in themselves, rather than as signs of an underlying phenomenon that is "manifested" or "indicated" by behavior.

STEPS IN CASE FORMULATION CONSTRUCTION

There are three steps to formulating a DBT case: (1) gathering information about treatment targets; (2) organizing information into a useful format; and (3) revising the formulation as needed.

Step 1: Gather Information about Treatment Targets

Problem Definition and History

This is the essential task of DBT case formulation: in the initial sessions one must assess the range of client problems to determine the appropriate stage of treatment. A client is in stage 1 if he or she is at least minimally committed to treatment and has life-threatening and/or parasuicidal behavior, behavior that interferes with therapy, and/or behaviors that severely compromise the client's quality of life. When the client enters therapy at stage 1, collaboratively identify and obtain a history of these primary target areas.

The first target area includes five types of behavior (in descending order of priority): suicide crisis behaviors; parasuicidal acts; suicidal ideation and communications; suicide-related expectancies and beliefs; and suicide-related affect. Either before treatment or early in treatment, the therapist should obtain a thorough parasuicide history. In the University of Washington research protocol, the Parasuicide History Interview is used to get this history (PHI-2; Linehan, Heard, & Wagner, 1995). The PHI asks for all details regarding parasuicide for the past year, including exactly what was done, the intent of the action, and whether medical attention was required. This history is essential to assess suicide risk accurately, to begin to identify situations that evoke parasuicide and suicide ideation, and to manage suicidal crises. In particular, one must identify the conditions associated with near-lethal suicide attempts, parasuicide acts with high intent to die, and other medically serious parasuicidal behavior.

The second target area, treatment-interfering behaviors, includes behavior of either the client or the therapist that negatively affects the therapeutic relationship or compromises the effectiveness of treatment. For clients this may include missing sessions, excessive psychiatric hospitalization, inability or refusal to work in therapy, and excessive demands on the therapist. For therapists this may include forgetting appointments or being late to them, failing to return phone calls, being inattentive, arbitrarily changing policies, and feeling unmotivated or demoralized about therapy. Information about these targets should be obtained from prior treatment history and prior supervision history.

The third target area, behaviors that severely compromise the client's quality of life, includes behaviors that disrupt stability or functioning and thereby curtail treatment effects. A diagnostic evaluation may help to assess the range of problems a client experiences. Structured diagnostic interviews such as the Personality Disorder Examination (Loranger, 1988) and the Structured Clinical Interview for DSM-III-R—patient version (SCID-P; Spitzer, Williams, Gibbon, & First, 1988; American Psychiatric Association, 1987) are useful. Mood and anxiety disorders, substance abuse, eating disorders, psychotic and dissociative phenomena, as well as inability to maintain stable housing and inattention to medical problems, impair the client's quality of life and may also influence parasuicidal behavior and interfere with therapy.

This history will allow an operational definition of the specific target behaviors. Frequency, duration, and past and present severity of the problem should be noted—for example, "Client cuts arms with a razor, 2–3 times per month, in the past requiring up to 20 stitches, but in the last year requiring no medical attention"; or "Client misses one out of every four sessions and then calls in a crisis, demanding help on the phone."

Chain Analysis

The next step is to specify the controlling variables for each targeted behavior. Returning to the metaphor of viewing behavior through the lenses of stage theory of treatment, biosocial theory, behavioral principles, behavioral patterns/dialectical dilemmas, and dialectics, it is as if the therapist were a quality-control inspector examining lengths of chain for problems with individual links. Clients monitor target behaviors using a diary card that is reviewed at the beginning of each DBT session. As the therapist reviews the card, asks about the week, and observes both him- or herself and the client in-session, he or she picks up those lengths of the behavior chain that end with parasuicide, therapy-interfering behavior, or behavior interfering with the client's quality of life.

Repeated chain analyses identify the precipitants, vulnerability factors, links, and consequences associated with each primary target. Each link (in-session or out) is considered in light of whether the client's response is functional or dysfunctional, that is, whether it moves the client toward or away from long-term goals. This sorting process is guided by hypotheses about controlling variables suggested by biosocial theory, behavioral principles, and the behavioral patterns/dialectical dilemmas. The biosocial theory suggests that the core problem is one of emotion dysregulation; it suggests further that the conditions that have created emotion dysregulation have led to other predictable skills deficits. Common dysfunctional links might include dysregulation of specific emotions, distress intolerance, punishment and perfectionistic self-regulation strategies, nondialectical thinking, crisis-generating behaviors, active–passivity, apparent competence, self-invalidation, and inhibited grieving. The behavioral principles and ideas from behavior therapy suggest searching for controlling variables in the current environment and examining ways that skills deficits, emotional responses, cognition, and contingencies interfere with more skillful responding. For example, Don, a client, may experience immediate relief from intense anxiety when he cuts his wrists and have no other reliable means for reducing anxiety. In addition, sporadically, his estranged parents take care of him after particularly serious parasuicide incidents. It is important to note that although increased care and attention follow parasuicide, this may or may not have been an intended consequence and may or may not increase the probability of suicide or parasuicide. Particularly when assessing the contingencies maintaining parasuicide, the therapist should assess (rather than assume) the functional relationship between consequences and parasuicide.

The behavioral patterns/dialectical dilemmas also suggest problematic patterns that may occur across chains and prevent therapeutic change. Maintaining a dialectical perspective reminds one to ask, "What is being left out?," thereby expanding analyses to include the effect the client has on the therapist and the influence of the therapist's own community and context on the process of therapy. As one gains information about the chain of events that leads to problematic behaviors and difficulties with change from each of these perspectives, patterns emerge.

At times a minimal intervention may replace a weak link (e.g., suggesting a solution that the client hadn't considered). More frequently, a problematic link will need a fair amount of work before it is replaced by more functional behavior. Then, the assessment task becomes to determine what specific functional behavior should replace dysfunctional links and what change procedure will best replace the target behavior.

Task Analysis

Identifying replacement behaviors for each target behavior and most usual dysfunctional links requires a task analysis. This means a step-by-step behavioral sequence for the particular set of circumstances needed to bypass the dysfunctional links and get to the desired behavior. The necessity of situation-specific solutions can be an incredible challenge—for example, how does one, in the midst of extreme emotional arousal, inhibit the associated action urge and do what is effective for that moment? Step by step, what is needed? There are three pools to draw ideas from. First, one should consider replacing dysfunctional links with DBT skills. Staying mindful of the balance between acceptance and change, one should consider interpersonal skills to change or leave the environment, emotion regulation (emotion observing, emotion describing, emotion experiencing, attention control, self-soothing, etc.), distress tolerance (including radical acceptance), mindfulness, self-management skills, active problem-solving behaviors, congruent emotional-expressive behaviors, self-validating behaviors (acting so as to increase self-respect instead of active–passivity and apparent competence patterns). Second, one should look to psychological literature on treatment and normal psychology for replacement behaviors. And, finally, one should consider personal experience. In similar situations, how exactly did one solve the problem?

From the situation-specific solutions of task analysis comes an understanding of the more general obstacles that interfere with replacing dysfunctional behavior. In other words, across situations, clients experience recurring problems when trying to adopt more functional behavior. Here, again, ideas from behavior therapy suggest one of four classes of problems. The client may lack the needed skills (behavioral deficits that preclude engaging in the desired behaviors), may have emotional reactions that interfere with skillful behavior or beliefs that are incompatible with being effective, or something about the situation may derail him or her (inappropriate stimulus control that elicits interfering behaviors or inhibits goal-directed behavior).

These standard steps of behavioral assessment are used to determine controlling variables and appropriate behavioral change strategies. One further step is needed, however, with many BPD clients. The question is what interferes with a straightforward use of change strategies? Here, secondary targets should be considered, and in particular the dialectical dilemmas of emotion vulnerability/self-invalidation, apparent competence/active-passivity, and unrelenting crisis/inhibited grieving. Also, attention should be paid to the transactional relationship of the individuals with the entire system—intra-organismic, within therapy, and among the individual's therapist(s) and the environment.

Step 2: Organize Information in a Useful Manner

Within the first 2 months of treatment, one should organize information on each target area into a written format. The purpose here is to create a format that helps identify areas that need further assessment, prioritize the areas that need change, and systematically consider the appropriate avenues of intervention. The content of the formulation will represent a synthesis of the five perspectives (stage of treatment, biosocial theory, behavioral theory of change, dialectical dilemmas that interfere with change, and dialectics per se) into a single statement of the problem, its controlling variables, and the behaviors required to get from problematic behavior to preferred behavior.

The written formulation should be in a format that is useful to those who will use it. A written format is particularly important with suicidal clients. The pressures and complexity of work with chronically suicidal, multiproblem clients increase the odds that a therapist will overlook, forget, or in some way miss important connections that a written format will bring to focus. For some a narrative would be most useful, whereas for others a flowchart would be best. The essential feature is that information on each target behavior be organized to guide further assessment and to keep a clear priority of targets to be treated. A flowchart is used in the "Case Example" section below.

Step 3: Revise the Formulation

DBT formulations are under constant revision as more is learned about the factors influencing problematic behavior or interfering with preferred behavior. These revisions tend to be refinements of original hypotheses, but at times significant revisions may be needed. It is difficult to decide, however, whether one is working from a mistaken formulation or whether one is in the midst of slow, sporadic progress expectable with this client population. A more fundamental reassessment of the formulation, the treatment plan, or both, is warranted when there is stagnation or impasse in the therapy. In DBT the emphasis is on changing the formulation or the treatment plan based on evidence from further assessment rather than based on the therapist's emotional responses to this often difficult work. The DBT therapist's first assumption is that lack of collaboration or progress is a failure in dialectical assessment—that is, something was missed in conceptualizing the case and the treatment. The therapist's job is to figure out a reformulation that will get the client moving toward agreed-upon goals.

The therapist looks for any information about the client that might be left out, and in a matter-of-fact manner raises questions regarding the formulation with the client. The therapist reviews case notes, particularly written chain analyses, and consults with other members of the treatment team to search for relevant patterns that were not noticed.

Impasses in DBT can also be caused by failure to balance technique (e.g., by too much emphasis on change or on acceptance); the therapist uses the consultation team and supervision to decide on the best means of regaining balance (Fruzzetti, Waltz, & Linehan, in press). Where other approaches might view lack of change as resistance or lack of motivation, DBT views patterns in light of environmental determinants. In particular, the DBT therapist considers how he or she may be contributing to therapeutic impasse. Transactions between the client and therapist must be examined as well as the larger context within which the therapist is working. The transaction between a client with BPD and a therapist can lead to therapeutic impasse or actually be iatrogenic even with therapists who are very effective with other clients. Clients with BPD frequently have interpersonal behaviors that interfere with the therapist's abilities to deliver treatment. Deficient abilities to self-regulate emotions and emotion-related actions are a common source of difficulty. This is not specific to clients with BPD. Across types of treatment, "client difficulty" rather than symptom severity may be a more important influence on therapist's ability to competently deliver therapy (e.g., O'Malley, Foley, Rounsaville, & Watkins, 1988). Hostility and help rejection can be extremely difficult for therapists to respond to, and clients with BPD have more than their fair share of difficult interpersonal behaviors. As Linehan has noted, such clients often seem to reinforce iatrogenic therapist behaviors and punish effective behaviors. In addition, quite independent of the client per se, factors unique to the particular therapist, such as therapy skills deficits, stressful work or home conditions, or difficult interactions with other therapists treating the client, may make conducting effective treatment extremely difficult. Limited skills, narrow personal limits, and conflicts with other staff members affecting the therapist–client interaction must all be assessed and their role in the treatment considered in the case conceptualization.

APPLICATION TO
PSYCHOTHERAPY TECHNIQUE

The case formulation guides each intervention. Usually there is no shortage of problematic behavior among chronically suicidal borderline clients, and the struggle is to choose where to intervene and how to sustain intervention in the face of slow change and extreme distress. Choosing well in stage 1 of DBT means to "pick up the correct length of chain" that leads to primary treatment targets (parasuicide, therapy-interfering behavior, and behavior interfering with the client's quality of life) and to work on change wherever the client happens to be on that chain. In the metaphor of inspecting lengths of chain for problematic links, our quality-control inspector faces an urgent task. He or she is to inspect chain that will be used as a rescue rope—in fact, the chain is already in use! For example, when a client is at imminent risk for suicide, the links that most need inspection and correction are those associated with immediate danger. In essence the inspector goes over the edge, tool kit in hand, and fixes each link within reach during the therapy hour, preferably in a manner that teaches the client to fix links for the rest of the week between sessions. When the client is further from the edge, then the therapist can "inspect and repair" those links that occur earlier in the chain. An important point in DBT is that the therapist always moves for in-session change whenever the opportunity presents itself. The following case example illustrates how DBT case formulation guides intervention.

CASE EXAMPLE

Step 1

Our composite client, "Mary," is a 27-year-old white female who has a history of parasuicide including two near-lethal suicide attempts. From the PHI, the therapist learned that Mary has injured herself by head banging and ingesting harmful substances since age 10. Currently she uses a razor to cut her arms and legs, and overdoses using prescribed medications. Due to physical abuse and neglect she was removed from the custody of her biological parents by Child Protective Services at age 10. Through various foster care placements, she hoped that she could return to live with her family, where she hoped to receive the care and assistance she felt she needed to get her life on track. At 16 she attempted suicide after a phone call in which her mother said that she never wanted Mary to return home and would prefer that Mary stop calling. Mary cut both wrists and only by chance was found by a friend before she died. This led to the first of many subsequent psychiatric hospitalizations.

Mary was referred to the DBT program after her second near-lethal attempt. After a 6-month period of high functioning (job, romantic relationship, successful outpatient treatment for alcohol dependence), she was laid off from work. For financial reasons she moved in with her romantic partner. Mary became depressed, failed to find work, and as her unemployment compensation dwindled, argued violently with her partner until in a state of intense anger she stormed out. She then had a panic attack, drove to a secluded spot, and overdosed on prescribed medications (which she always carried in her purse) with the intent to die.

Mary had past diagnoses of eating disorder (not otherwise specified), major depression with psychotic features, and alcohol dependence. When she started DBT, she met criteria for BPD and dysthymia, had panic attacks but did not meet criteria for panic disorder, and was socially avoidant but met criteria for neither avoidant personality disorder nor social phobia.

By Session 3, Mary and her therapist had reached agreement that their top priorities for a year would be to stop her cutting behavior and suicide attempts (parasuicide, primary target stage 1), reduce the use of psychiatric hospitalizations (both therapy-interfering and quality-of-life–interfering behavior), and reduce the frequency of panic attacks (quality-of-life–interfering behavior and also on the chain to parasuicide), and to replace these with more skillful coping. After 4 months in the DBT program of individual therapy and group skills training, Mary and her individual therapist had identified the most typical sequence of events that led to both cutting and increased suicidal ideation. A chain analysis of suicidal crisis behavior gathered about 2 months into therapy is representative. In the late evening, Mary called her therapist (who had just arrived back from vacation that night), sobbing, "It's over," and stating she wanted to die and it was all she could do not to slash her throat. As the therapist began to assess imminent suicide risk, Mary had a call on the other line. She returned to the therapist to say it had been her partner, crying, saying she was sorry they fought. Mary said she would be able to make it through the night and agreed to a session early the next morning.

In the behavioral chain analysis during the next session, they identified the vulnerability factors (difficulties at work) and immediate precipitating event (an argument with her partner about whether Mary should or should not quit her new part-time job). At work Mary was asked to take on a project that had been clearly stated in her job description but which she had no idea how to do. Rather than ask for help or ask that the task be modified, she set unrealistic standards for her performance (self-invalidation). As the week of orientation continued, she began to fail at the task but never communicated effectively that she was having difficulty (apparent competence). She left work early Thursday with a migraine and called in sick on Friday. Over the weekend, she lay on the couch fighting a migraine, ruminating about work. During a conversation with her partner about her work problems, Mary said she was thinking about quitting and her partner said, "I hope you're not thinking I'm going to support you. I can't take you quitting anymore." Panic at the thought of being on her own to handle a problem she experienced as overwhelming and out of her control ensued but within seconds changed to fury at her partner for withdrawing help and pressuring her not to quit. As the argument and anger escalated, Mary began to have vivid images of cutting her wrists and of blood pouring out. In-session she was unable to label the emotion other than to say she felt "incredibly tense, wound up," desperately wanted someone to help her, and thought, "You don't understand. I can't stand this." The argument ended with her partner's parting comment, "This is not going to work out." Mary then sat alone in their dark apartment. She began invalidating her disappointment in her partner and her legitimate work difficulties, planning to kill herself by cutting her wrists, imagined the process of dying, of being met by her nurturing grandmother who had died 2 years ago, and kept repeating to herself that she had failed again, things would never get better, and being dead would stop the pain. As this continued, the anger decreased and tearfulness, sadness, emptiness, and apathy increased. As she got out the razors, she thought of her therapist and called the answering service.

Step 2

A more general summary of the events leading to Mary's parasuicidal behavior is shown in the flowchart (Figure 13.1).

First, her vulnerability to emotion dysregulation was heightened by recurrent migraines. Second, she had a variety of problems that resulted from not keeping a job. Most work problems originated from not being appropriately assertive and from an appearance of competence, both of which kept her from obtaining needed help. Third, unstructured time alone regularly resulted in ruminative thoughts about past failures and a downward mood spiral that culminated in overwhelming shame, anxiety and limited-symptom panic attacks. Finally, when the situation was further complicated by conflict with a partner, she had panic, anger, and intense urges to cut herself and to escape. The best predictor of a chain ending with increased suicidal ideation or a suicide attempt was her interpretation of the likelihood of reconciliation with her partner versus being alone forever.

Even a brief task analysis suggests many possibilities of what could change to reduce Mary's suicide crisis behavior. Adequate pain management of migraines would lower her vulnerability to emotion dysregulation. The skills deficits that contribute to problems at work (a lack of appropriate assertiveness and apparent competence) would be remedied by skills group attendance and systematic work in individual therapy to apply these new skills to the work setting. Further, the individual therapist could watch for Mary's tendency to minimize problems and discrepancy between emotional experience and expression in-session and encourage change whenever these behaviors occurred. Another dysfunctional link to parasuicide is the pattern of rumination about past failures. The therapist could use a variety of strategies, from activity scheduling during the weekends to exposure and cognitive restructuring to modify the overwhelming shame evoked by thoughts of past failures. In addition to the emotion regulation and distress tolerance skills taught in the group sessions, the therapist also might teach basic panic management techniques. Practical measures such as removing razors and not keeping a lethal dose of any medications in the house would decrease her risk of impulsive parasuicide (self-management skills and contingency management). A final area for further assessment highlighted by this behavioral analysis is to identify exactly what it is about the loss of a love relationship that leads to suicide attempts. For example, Mary had the belief that if she makes someone who loved her reject her, she deserved to be dead; a belief that if she were dead the other person would regret leaving her; an unwillingness to exist unless she was loved in-

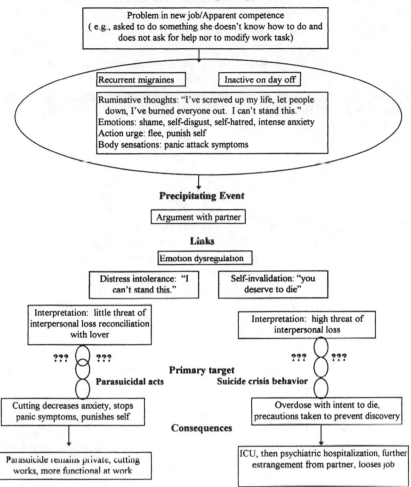

Antecedents to Precipitating Event

Problem in new job/Apparent competence
(e.g., asked to do something she doesn't know how to do and
does not ask for help nor to modify work task)

Recurrent migraines   Inactive on day off

Ruminative thoughts: "I've screwed up my life, let people
down, I've burned everyone out. I can't stand this."
Emotions: shame, self-disgust, self-hatred, intense anxiety
Action urge: flee, punish self
Body sensations: panic attack symptoms

Precipitating Event

Argument with partner

Links

Emotion dysregulation

Distress intolerance: "I
can't stand this."

Self-invalidation: "you
deserve to die"

Interpretation: little threat of
interpersonal loss reconciliation
with lover

Interpretation: high threat of
interpersonal loss

???   ???   ???   ???

Primary target

Parasuicidal acts   Suicide crisis behavior

Cutting decreases anxiety, stops
panic symptoms, punishes self

Overdose with intent to die,
precautions taken to prevent discovery

Consequences

Parasuicide remains private, cutting
works, more functional at work

ICU, then psychiatric hospitalization, further
estrangement from partner, looses job

FIGURE 13.1. Example of flowchart describing determinants of parasuicidal behavior.

tensely; and a belief that she was incapable of making it on her own. Again, there are many potential strategies to break the link between the threat of interpersonal loss and suicidal behavior, including cognitive modification of beliefs that maintain suicide as an effective solution, strengthening distress tolerance and reality acceptance skills, strengthening the therapeutic relationship to provide another source of love and regard, increasing other sources of social support, and increasing skills (and recognition of those skills) for coping with everyday problems in living.

The written formulation helps the therapist select, from all of these potential areas of change, those most likely to reduce parasuicide. Because Mary's suicide attempts had been so nearly lethal, the therapist's foremost goal was to break the link between threat of interpersonal loss and suicidal behavior. This included increasing Mary's skills at maintaining good relationships, couples work, practical agreements about not keeping lethal means available, and active use of distress tolerance skills during relationship conflicts. The other target selected as central was to stop rumination about past failures and to increase Mary's ability to self-validate and regulate shame reactions. While the therapist watched for opportunities for change in each of the areas in the task analysis, these two areas of change became the primary focus of the first stage of therapy.

Step 3

As therapy proceeded, it became clear that part of Mary's social avoidance was due to worries that if she increased her interactions with others, she would lose her temper and become physically violent. She reduced that possibility by limiting social interactions, placing few demands on the environment to avoid frustration and anger, and limiting her emotional expressiveness in general. Given her history of physical aggression toward others, these worries were realistic. Consequently, anger management techniques were added as a central intervention. The consultation team also helped the therapist see that she was responding to Mary's hostile statements and suicide threats by decreasing demands on the client, inadvertently reinforcing these behaviors and increasing their frequency over time. Analyses indicated that the therapist was experiencing a hostile work environment as well, which decreased her tolerance for client hostility and stress. The therapist was also unskilled in how to assess for and treat credible suicide threats. By problem solving with the therapist about her own work environment and its effects on the treatment, as well as by providing support, encouragement, and skills training (regarding response to suicidal behaviors), the team helped the therapist to decrease the rate of therapist reinforcement of hostile and suicidal behavior and to tolerate the resulting "behavioral burst" that occurred before the behavior decreased.

TRAINING AND RESEARCH

Training in DBT case conceptualization can be a complex task, depending on the previous training and experience of the therapist to be trained. Because DBT integrates behavior therapy with an Eastern psychological approach drawn from Zen, the therapist must think like a behaviorist and experience like a Zen student. In addition, the empirical-minded, hypotheses-generating and -verifying frame that DBT case conceptualization sits within requires a flexible mind and skill at logical and scientific testing of hypotheses. The necessity of using one's reactions to the client but not letting one's own emotional reactions control the case formulation requires therapists who are able to think clearly under stress and regulate emotions in situations where almost anyone would have a reasonable level of emotional arousal. The emphasis in the treatment on use of basic psychological principles as well as behavior therapy procedures suggests that DBT training should begin after an individual is already reasonably well trained in behavior therapy. To date, our primary method of training research therapists has been to combine the following into an ongoing training/supervision program: an intensive formal didactic seminar (approximately 100 hours), individual case supervision (1 hour weekly), ongoing didactic training in principles of DBT case conceptualization, observing and discussing videos of expert treatment, group outlining of case conceptualization of various training cases (1 hour weekly), DBT peer team consultation (1 hour weekly), and various readings via e-mail communications and journal articles. As yet, we have done no research on whether the adequacy of case conceptualization actually affects treatment outcomes. Obviously, this is an important area for future research.

SUMMARY AND CONCLUSIONS

In this chapter we have introduced the basic concepts and method of case formulation used in DBT individual therapy for stage 1. DBT is guided by the etiological theory that "borderline" behavior is a function of emotion dysregulation. In attempts to regain emotional equilibrium, clients oscillate between extreme behavioral patterns that are self-perpetuating and present significant obstacles to change. Stage 1 of DBT seeks to decrease parasuicide and behaviors that interfere with therapy and the client's quality of life. Repeated and detailed review of particular instances of problematic behavior identifies the unique antecedents and consequences that maintain the chain of environmental and experiential events leading to the problematic behavior. Through this process, the therapist identifies skills deficits, cognition, emotional responses, and contingencies that interfere with more functional behavior. The therapist uses this information to select the appropriate change strategies (skill training, cognitive modification, exposure therapy, and contingency management). Noncollaboration and therapeutic impasse are to be expected and should occasion further review of how both parties contribute to problems in therapy. The formulation is a "work in progress," under constant revision, yet maintaining coherence with respect to targeted behaviors and the conceptual framework within which they are analyzed.

Case formulation is a crucial element of effective, efficient DBT. Despite the time it takes, case formulation should be a standard of care with multiproblem interpersonally difficult clients. With these clients, therapist skill and motivation are often under siege. Case formulation helps direct focused activity, even when the therapist is under duress, and serves as a reference point for thoughtful changes in the treatment plan.

ACKNOWLEDGMENTS

The writing of this chapter was supported by Grant Nos. MH34486 and DA08674 from the National Institute of Mental Health and National Institute for Drug Abuse, Bethesda, Maryland (to Dr. M. M. Linehan).

REFERENCES

American Psychiatric Association. (1987). *Diagnostic and statistical manual of mental disorders* (3rd ed., rev.). Washington, DC: Author.

American Psychiatric Association. (1994). *Diagnostic and statistical manual of mental disorders* (4th ed.) Washington, DC: Author.

Barley, W., Buie, S., Peterson, E., Hollingsworth, A., Griva, M., Hickerson, S., Lawson, J., & Bailey, B. (1993). Development of an inpatient cognitive-behavioral treatment program for borderline personality disorder. *Journal of Personality Disorders, 7,* 232–240.

Basseches, M. (1984). *Dialectical thinking and adult development.* Norwood, NJ: Ablex.

Berent, I. (1981). *The algebra of suicide.* New York: Human Sciences Press.

Fruzzetti, A. E., Waltz, J. A., & Linehan, M. M. (in press). Supervision in dialectical behavior therapy. In C. Watkins (Ed.), *Handbook of psychotherapy supervision.* New York: Wiley.

Gottman, J. M., & Katz, L. F. (1989). Effects of marital discord on young children's peer interaction and health. *Developmental Psychology, 25*(3), 373–381.

Heard, H. L., & Linehan, M. M. (1994). Dialectical behavior therapy: An integrative approach to the treatment of borderline personality disorder. *Journal of Psychotherapy Integration, 4,* 55–82.

Kamigstein, D. S. (1987). Toward a dialectical metatheory for psychotherapy. *Journal of Contemporary Psychotherapy, 17,* 87–101.

Kohlenberg, R. J., & Tsai, M. (1995). I speak therefore I am: A behavioral approach to understanding problems of the self. *Behavior Therapist, 18,* 113–116.

Levins, R., & Lewontin, R. (1985). *The dialectical biologist.* Cambridge, MA: Harvard University Press.

Linehan, M. M. (1993a). *Cognitive-behavioral treatment of borderline personality disorder.* New York: Guilford Press.

Linehan, M. M. (1993b). *Skills training manual for treating borderline personality disorder.* New York: Guilford Press.

Linehan, M. M. (1996, August). *Treatment development, validation and dissemination.* Invited address at the Conference on Drug Abuse, American Psychological Association Meeting, Toronto, Ontario, Canada.

Linehan, M. M., Armstrong, H. E., Suarez, A., Allmon, D., & Heard, H. (1991). Cognitive-behavioral treatment of chronically parasuicidal borderline patients. *Archives of General Psychiatry, 48,* 1060–1064.

Linehan, M. M., Heard, H. L., & Armstrong, H. E. (1993). Naturalistic follow-up of a behavioral treatment for chronically parasuicidal borderline patients. *Archives of General Psychiatry, 50,* 971–974.

Linehan, M. M., Heard, H., & Wagner, A. (1995). *Parasuicide History Interview: Development, reliability and validity.* Unpublished manuscript (used in articles by Linehan et al., 1991, 1993; see above).

Linehan, M. M., & Schmidt, H., III (1995). The dialectics of effective treatment of borderline personality disorder. In W. O. O'Donohue & L. Krasner (Eds.), *Theories in behavior therapy: Exploring behavior change.* Washington, DC: American Psychological Association.

Linehan, M. M., Tutek, D. A., Heard, H. L., & Armstrong, H. E. (1994). Interpersonal outcome of cognitive behavioral treatment for chronically suicidal borderline patients. *American Journal of Psychiatry, 151,* 1771–1776.

Loranger, A. W. (1988). *Personality Disorder Examination (PDE) manual.* Yonkers, NY: DV Communications.

Miller, C. R., Eisner, W., & Allport, C. (1994). Creative coping: A cognitive-behavioral group for borderline personality disorder. *Archives of Psychiatric Nursing, 8,* 280–285.

O'Malley, S. S., Foley, S. H., Rounsaville, B. J., & Watkins, J. T. (1988). Therapist competence and patient outcome in interpersonal psychotherapy of depression. *Journal of Consulting and Clinical Psychology, 56,* 496–501.

Paulhus, D. L., & Martin, C. L. (1987). The structure of personality capabilities. *Journal of Personality and Social Psychology, 52,* 354–365.

Riegel, K. R. (1975). Toward a dialectical theory of development. *Human Development, 18,* 50–64.

Spitzer, R., Williams, J., Gibbon, M., & First, M. (1988). *Structured Clinical Interview for DSM-III-R: Patient version (SCID-P).* New York: Biometrics Research Department, New York State Psychiatric Institute.

Swenson, C., Sanderson, C., & Linehan, M. (1996). *Applying dialectical behavior therapy on inpatient units.* Unpublished paper, University of Washington, Seattle.

Turkat, I. D. (1988). Issues in the relationship between assessment and treatment. *Journal of Psychopathology and Behavioral Assessment, 10,* 185–197.

Wagner, A. W., & Linehan, M. M. (1997). A biosocial perspective on the relationship of childhood sexual abuse, suicidal behavior, and borderline personality disorder. In M. Zanarini (Ed.), *The role of sexual abuse in the etiology of borderline personality disorder.* Washington, DC: American Psychiatric Association.

Wells, H. K. (1972). Alienation and dialectical logic. *Kansas Journal of Sociology, 3,* 7–32.

14

Case Formulation in Behavior
Therapy: Problem-Solving and
Functional Analytic Strategies

ARTHUR M. NEZU
CHRISTINE MAGUTH NEZU
STEPHANIE H. FRIEDMAN
STEPHEN N. HAYNES

HISTORICAL BACKGROUND OF THE APPROACH

Behavior therapy is an empirical approach to clinical case formulation, intervention, and evaluation. It is a conceptual framework geared to understand, based on scientific findings, both "normal" and abnormal aspects of human behavior, as well as to articulate, based on this understanding, a set of empirically based guidelines by which such behavior can be changed. During its birth and adolescence, behavior therapy was defined as the application of "modern laws of learning" (Hersen, Eisler, & Miller, 1975) and was represented by clinical interventions based on operant (e.g., token economies) or classical (e.g., systematic desensitization) conditioning paradigms. However, during the past 20 years, the domain, concepts, and methods of behavior therapy have continued to expand greatly (O'Donohue & Krasner, 1995).

Our approach to behavior therapy falls within an experimental–clinical framework and incorporates a broad definition of behavior that includes overt actions, internal cognitive phenomena, and the experience of affect or emotions. These components range in complexity from molecular (i.e., lower-level) events (e.g., smoking a cigarette, hyperventilation, a critical comment in dyadic interaction) to molar (i.e., higher-level) pluralistic and multidimensional constructs (e.g., complex social skills, solving a difficult calculus problem, major depressive disorder). Our conceptual framework is closely associated with social learning theory (e.g., Bandura, 1977) as an overarching theory of personality or individual differences. We also adopt a biopsychosocial perspective regarding the factors that play an etiopathogenic role for behavior problems and disorders (Haynes, 1992; Nezu & Nezu, 1989).

There are four major stages of clinical judgment in behavior therapy (Nezu & Nezu, 1989): (1) screening and problem identification (e.g., *Can I help this person or should she or he be referred to someone else?*) ; (2) problem analysis and selection of focal target problems (e.g., *What is this person's problem and what are reasonable and meaningful treatment goals?*); (3) treatment design (e.g., *What treatment strategies or clinical interventions should be implemented to achieve treatment goals?*); and (4) evaluation of treatment effects (e.g., *What are the effects of this intervention?*). Within each of these stages, the behavior therapist must make a plethora of clinical decisions and judgments, ranging from "Should I treat this patient?" to "What measures should I use to evaluate the effects of therapy?" The validity of the decisions made at one stage can greatly affect the judgments made at other treatment stages and, ultimately, the effectiveness of treatment. For example, the accuracy of the therapist's problem analysis is hypothesized to have a large impact on the success of treatment. This chapter addresses the second stage—problem analysis, or behavioral case formulation.

A behavioral case formulation involves conducting a *functional analysis*, which is the clinician's assessment-derived integration of all of the important functional relationships among variables. It is a meta-judgment and a synthesis of several judgments about a client's problems and goals, their effects, related causal and mediating variables, and the functional relationships among such variables (Haynes & O'Brien, 1990). In generating a functional analysis, we advocate the use of a systematic problem-solving model of clinical decision making. In brief, this model represents "the clinician as problem solver" (Nezu & Nezu, 1989, 1993, 1995). According to this approach, each time a behavioral clinician makes an initial appointment with a prospective client, she or he is faced with a supraordinate "problem." This problem entails providing an optimally effective treatment to a given individual, who is characterized by a unique constellation of complaints, symptoms, life circumstances, developmental history, and biological makeup. In behavior therapy, this problem is addressed by undertaking the aforementioned four major clinical judgment tasks. For example, through a series of judgments, the behavioral clinician develops a case formulation specific to a given individual. Based on this formulation, the therapist then attempts to identify and implement an effective intervention. Successful completion of these clinical tasks, in essence, "solves the problem."

Historically, the preponderance of empirical efforts extended by behavioral therapists was aimed at developing, improving, and validating assessment and treatment protocols rather than at the process of clinical judgment invoked when designing and applying such protocols to a particular client (Haynes, 1994; Nezu & Nezu, 1989, 1993). For example, a multitude of efficacious intervention approaches have been developed by cognitive-behavioral clinicians for the treatment of a wide range of psychological disorders (e.g., Bellack & Hersen, 1993). Behaviorally oriented theorists have also participated greatly in the advancement of empirically based assessment protocols for such disorders (e.g., Hersen & Bellack, 1996). However, few studies and scholarly attempts have addressed the translation of assessment data into treatment design recommendations. Unlike the omnibus treatment guidelines associated with other theoretical orientations, behavior therapy endorses the concept that treatment be applied idiographically, focusing on the unique characteristics of a given case across a plethora of patient and environmental variables. However, unless significant attention is paid to this decision-making process, a particular case formulation and the treatment plan based on it can be erroneous.

Although several authors have underscored the lack of attention paid to clinical decision making in behavior therapy (e.g., Barlow, 1980; Barrios & Hartmann, 1986), it is only recently that conceptual models have been developed that offer overarching guidelines for behavioral clinicians to follow (e.g., Persons, 1989). The need for systematic approaches to clinical decision making in behavior therapy becomes especially important given the body of literature documenting the vulnerability that professional decision makers have toward making ubiquitous human reasoning errors (Arkes, 1981; Kanfer & Schefft, 1988). Tversky and Kahnemann's (1974) research concerning the negative impact that various judgmental heuristics have on the reliability and validity of prediction, decision making, and reasoning has been cited, for example, as underscoring the need for such models (Nezu & Nezu, 1989). Recently, Haynes (1992) and Nezu and Nezu (1989, 1995) have independently developed models of behavioral case formulation that attempt to minimize such errors as well as to facilitate the empirical flavor of this process. The remainder of the present chapter will describe these approaches.

CONCEPTUAL FRAMEWORK

Case formulation begins with those clinical tasks whereby the behavior therapist translates a client's complaints of distress into a meaningful set of target problems and treatment goals. Such complaints of distress can be viewed as an initial, albeit global, articulation of a patient's objectives or reasons for seeking psychotherapy. For example, the client stating that she or he is feeling "upset, agitated, and panicky" is likely coming to treatment in hopes of overcoming anxiety. Reductions in anxiety would likely be viewed universally as an appropriate goal for intervention. Therapy goals can involve reducing aversive symptoms or increasing positive states; such goals are usually client determined and generally considered valid by the therapist. Other examples of client-articulated goals include reducing depression, decreasing feelings of loneliness, improving one's marriage, and decreasing a child's behavior problems in school.

Rosen and Proctor (1981) and Mash and Hunsley (1993) defined these types of goals as *ultimate outcomes*. They are outcomes "for which treatment is undertaken and reflect the objectives toward which treatment efforts are to be directed" (Rosen & Proctor, 1981, p. 419). *Instrumental outcomes* (termed "immediate or intermediate outcomes" by Mash and Hunsley, 1993) are those changes or effects that "serve as the instruments for the attainment of other outcomes" (Rosen & Proctor, 1981, p. 419). Instrumental outcomes may have an impact on ultimate outcomes (e.g., increasing one's self-esteem can reduce the severity of depressive behaviors) or on other instrumental outcomes within a causal chain (e.g., improving a client's coping ability can increase his or her self-esteem, which in turn may decrease depressive severity).

Clinically, instrumental outcomes reflect the therapist's hypotheses concerning those variables that are believed to be pathogenically related to (i.e., causal variables that affect) the ultimate outcome(s). Experimentally, instrumental outcomes can be viewed as *independent* variables, whereas ultimate outcomes represent dependent variables. As such, many of these instrumental outcome variables serve as mediating variables and, as such, denote potential targets for interventions. *Mediating* variables are those that strengthen or weaken the relationship between two other variables (Haynes, 1992). A mediating variable may also have direct causal effects. For example, Nezu and his colleagues (Nezu, Nezu, Saraydarian, Kalmar, & Ronay, 1986; Nezu & Ronan, 1985) have shown social problem-solving skills to moderate the relationship between negative life stress and depression, as well as having a direct effect on depression per se. However, given the bidirectional causal relationships operating for many clients, the designation of variables as "dependent" or "independent" is often arbitrary in a functional analysis.

In general, the underlying assumption of our approach is that attaining the various instrumental outcomes will, either directly or indirectly, lead to achieving the ultimate outcomes. For example, Social Problem-Solving Therapy has been found to be an effective treatment intervention for major depression (Nezu, Nezu, & Perri, 1989). However, there are often several causal hypotheses regarding instrumental outcome–ultimate outcome relationships for a given clinical disorder. For example, in addition to this problem-solving formulation (Nezu, 1987), several additional cognitive-behavioral theories exist regarding the etiopathogenesis of major depressive disorder. These theories differ in the degree to which they emphasize potential instrumental outcome variables, such as *cognitive distortions* (e.g., Beck, Rush, Shaw, & Emery, 1979), *decreased levels of positive social experiences* (e.g., Hoberman & Lewinsohn, 1985), or *deficient social skills* (e.g., Hersen, Bellack, & Himmelhoch, 1980). Although these particular instrumental outcome–ultimate outcome relationships are all supported by research, studies have demonstrated individual differences in causal factors—that is, no independent variable is important for all depressed individuals.

Further, most behavior problems and goals can be affected by multiple and interacting causal factors (Haynes, 1992). Consequently, achieving a given instrumental outcome does not always lead to attaining the ultimate outcome (Nezu, 1987). Such findings suggest that for any ultimate outcome the behavior therapist can target a wide range of possible instrumental outcomes. In the absence of systematic guidelines, behavioral case formulation can be a formidable undertaking.

For example, Haynes (1992; also Haynes, Spain, & Oliveira, 1993) suggested that a functional analysis entails several clinical judgments, including (1) identification and specification of a client's problems and goals, (2) estimation of the relative importance of each problem and goal, (3) estimation of the form and strength of the relationships among a client's multiple problems and goals, (4) estimation of the sequelae of a client's problems and goals, (5) identification of the causal variables affecting a client's problems and goals, (6) estimation of the strength and form of the causal relationships, and (7) estimation of the modifiability of these causal variables. In order to best make these judgments, we suggest that the behavior therapist adopt a problem-solving framework, using similar principles as those underlying problem-solving training (D'Zurilla & Nezu, 1982; Nezu & Nezu, 1991).

Therapy as Problem Solving

In viewing the clinician as problem solver, we define (using problem-solving terminology) the "therapist's problem" as one where she or he is presented with a set of complaints by an individual seeking help to reduce or minimize such complaints. In addition, the therapist's problem can also involve helping the patient attain positive goals, such as developing a new career, becoming more assertive, or obtaining a promotion. This situation is considered a problem because the client's current state represents a discrepancy from the individual's desired state, whereby a variety of impediments (i.e., obstacles or conflicts) prevent or make it difficult for the client to reach his or her goals without a therapist's aid. Such impediments may include characteristics of the patient (e.g., behavioral, cognitive, and/or affective excesses or deficits) and/or the environment (e.g., lack of physical and/or social resources). Treatment is the clinician's attempt to identify and solve this problem (Nezu & Nezu, 1989).

Within this paradigm, the clinician's solution is represented by those treatment strategies that assist the client to achieve his or her goals. Identifying the most efficacious treatment plan for a given client who is experiencing a particular disorder, given his or her unique history and current life circumstances, by a certain therapist, becomes the overarching goal of therapy. Constructing a functional analysis for a client is an important component of the clinician's solution. To help achieve these goals, we advocate adoption of the problem-solving model of clinical decision making (Nezu & Nezu, 1993; Nezu, Nezu, & Houts, 1993).

The Problem-Solving Process

Our model of problem solving comprises a series of specific tasks and operations rather than a unitary ability. There are two general components of problem solving: (1) problem orientation; and (2) problem-solving skills (D'Zurilla & Nezu, 1982; Nezu et al., 1989). *Problem orientation* involves a set of orienting responses one engages in when attempting to understand and react to problems in general. These responses include a group of beliefs, assumptions, appraisals, values, and expectations concerning problems in general. Problem-solving skills entail those specific operations that are involved in the resolution of a problem and include the following: (1) *problem definition and formulation* (i.e., clarifying the nature of a given problem regarding obstacles to goal attainment, delineating realistic goals, identification of important functional relationships); (2) *generation of alternatives* (i.e., brainstorming a comprehensive list of alternative solutions); (3) *decision making* (i.e., conducting a cost-benefit analysis regarding potential consequences of each alternative and developing a solution plan)[1]; and (4) *solution implementation and verification* (i.e., carrying out a solution, monitoring its effects, and troubleshooting if the problem is not solved). In essence, we recommend that the behavioral clinician engage in each of the problem-solving operations when addressing the various clinical tasks and decisions encountered during the case formulation process, as well as the other three major stages of therapy.

Problem Orientation

What often differentiates various theoretical orientations from each other is their particular *worldview*. Worldviews are cohesive philosophical frameworks by which people attempt to understand how the world works (Pepper, 1942). From this perspective, one component of the worldview of a clinician, the psychological assessment paradigm within which she or he operates, provides a structured metaphor by which she or he can understand, predict, and explain human behavior.[2] This type of worldview, then, encompasses several underlying assumptions regarding cause–effect (or instrumental outcome–ultimate outcome) statements related to psychopathology and its treatment.

With regard to case formulation, this perspective implies that the focus and methods of clinical assessment depend heavily on the clinician's preconceptions about the proper content and methods of this process. Our problem orientation component of behavioral case formulation underscores the importance of three major themes: (1) planned critical multiplism; (2) general systems; and (3) generalizability.

Planned critical multiplism involves a methodological perspective that advocates the use of multiple operationalism in the conduct of scientific endeavors. With regard to case formulation, this entails a multiple causality frame-work, suggesting that a particular symptom can result from many permutations of multiple causal factors and multiple causal paths (Kazdin & Kagan, 1994). A variety of biological (e.g., genetic, neurochemical), psychological (e.g., affective, cognitive, behavioral), and social (e.g., social and physical environmental) variables can function to act, combine, and/or interact as causal or maintaining factors for a particular behavior problem or disorder. Such causal variables can act proximally (e.g., immediate antecedent or consequent stimulus) and/or distally (e.g., developmental history).

Continuing with depression as a clinical example, incorporating a critical multiplism approach to case formulation would involve conducting a search for confirming and disconfirming evidence regarding a variety of depression-related variables for a specific client (e.g., cognitive distortions, medical-related difficulties, poor self-control skills, low rate of reinforcement). The *boundaries* of the search for instrumental outcome variables should be largely defined by existing empirically based nomothetic findings. The applicability of such findings is later evaluated using evidence from pretreatment behavioral assessment and the effectiveness of consequent treatments.

Within the functional analysis, we emphasize the reciprocity and multiple connections often characteristic of the relationships among the instrumental outcome–ultimate outcome variables within a general systems model. From a multiple causality perspective, it is not only important to understand the relationship of a variety of causal variables to a client's problems, but it is also imperative to assess the manner in which these variables interact both proximally and distally (Haynes, 1992; Nezu & Nezu, 1989). For example, social learning theory argues that person-related factors and environmental factors operate as interlocking determinants of each other, whereby the relative influences exerted by these interdependent factors can differ in various settings for different behaviors (Bandura, 1977).

A *general systems approach* helps the behavioral clinician to evaluate how such biological, psychological, and social variables continuously relate to each other in reciprocal ways (Evans, 1985; Kanfer, 1985; Ollendick & Hersen, 1993). Moreover, such an approach allows the behavior therapist to identify variables that hold a key position in a given client's system and to later identify such areas as important treatment targets (Nelson, 1988). For example, the divorce of a child's parents may indirectly affect the child's performance in school by operating as an element in a chain of causal variables. Perhaps the child's fear of being separated from one parent and losing that parent's attention may distract the child; or the child may do poorly in school as an "attention-getting" behavior; or the parents may be preoccupied by their relationship difficulties and attend to or deliver contingencies for completion of schoolwork in a less consistent fashion. Exploring the noncontiguous and extended systems-level variables can provide important information for the case formulation. Unless the therapist uses a systemic, empirically guided approach to case formulation, important causal relationships may be overlooked. Further, in delineating the various components encompassing the network-like system, the behavioral clinician is also able to articulate multiple goals simultaneously as a means of increasing the probability of eventual and long-lasting success.

Following Kanfer's (1985) lead, we also advocate the desirability of identifying those instrumental outcomes that may facilitate the *generalization* of client goal attainment and positive treatment effects over time and across situations. This perspective goes beyond the view that espouses only the removal or change of hypothesized causative factors. For example, we have argued elsewhere that even if assessment reveals that a depressed client is not characterized by deficient social problem-solving skills, including such training in an overall treatment plan is likely to enhance adaptive functioning (Nezu et al., 1989). However, such approaches should only be used if they are empirically determined to facilitate temporal or situational generalization. This perspective is consistent with a constructionalist framework that advocates increasing a client's flexibility (e.g., Evans, 1993). It is with this orientation and by using the four problem-solving tasks (problem definition, generation of alternatives, decision making, solution verification) that we suggest the behavioral clinician attempt to conduct a case formulation that ultimately provides for treatment suggestions.

INCLUSION/EXCLUSION CRITERIA

One strength of both the behavioral construct system and our case formulation model is the potential widespread applicability across populations, behavior problems and disorders, assessment settings, and ages. The major constraints are imposed only by the lack of empirical data that exists for a given patient-related variable. Further, because it emphasizes a scientific approach to understanding human behavior, the problem-solving model of case formulation is especially useful at such times when little is available in the literature to guide the therapist's decision making (see also Kanfer & Busemeyer, 1982). Therefore, our model is appropriate for all types and ranges of client problems and for all types of patient populations. Last, this approach is particularly helpful with complex or complicated cases, as such cases are composed of a multitude of possible causal variables and intervention targets.

It is important to note that case formulations can be dynamic—the functional analysis and other elements of the case formulation can change over time. For example, the importance or severity of a client's problems, the sequelae to those problems, the modifiability of causal variables, and the strength of causal relationships can all change over time and across situations (Haynes, Blaine, & Meyer, 1993). The case formulation may particularly be unstable during the course of treatment. For example, patient "John B." might learn new social skills that would reduce the severity of his inappropriate sexual behaviors and lessen the frequency of his depressive episodes. Consequently, the comprehensiveness and validity of a case formulation *specific to Mr. B.* should be presumed to be transient and frequently tested and revised.

In addition, a given case formulation may be valid only within limited domains. It may be valid for a limited time, for certain situations and contexts but not others, and for some client "states" (e.g., alcoholic intoxication). For example, a certain case formulation for "Lisa," a client with developmental disabilities, might only be valid as long as she continues to live in a certain group home, with its unique social network and reinforcement system. Clinically meaningful changes in causal relationships and behavior problems can occur, for example, if she moves in with family members.

STEPS IN CASE FORMULATION CONSTRUCTION

In order to conduct the case formulation according to our model, the behavior therapist, using the tenets of the specific problem orientation previously described, engages in the following four major problem-solving steps: (1) problem definition and formulation; (2) generation of alternatives; (3) treatment decision making; and (4) solution implementation and verification.

Problem Definition and Formulation

During this initial problem-solving step, the behavior therapist attempts to gather all relevant information about the client's problem(s), separate facts from assumptions, and identify relevant instrumental outcome variables. In addition, she or he is encouraged to use unambiguous language in describing this information as a means of minimizing potential bias or misinterpretation. In attempting to better define and understand the nature of a client's problems, the behavior therapist asks the following general question: *In essence, which areas of this patient's life should be assessed?* To facilitate a comprehensive assessment and to minimize the use of biased search strategies, we recommend the use of a "funnel approach" to assessment (Hawkins, 1986; Mash & Hunsley, 1990). According to this approach the initial assessment activity involves a broad-bandwidth investigation of possible difficulties that a client is currently experiencing across a wide range of life areas, such as interpersonal relationships (e.g., marital, family, parent–child, friends), career, job, finances, sex, physical health, education, leisure, religion, and personal goal attainment.

As accumulating evidence indicates that no problems exist for a given client in a given problem area, the focus of the assessment process narrows. Further, for each problem area, the behavioral clinician's task next entails a more microanalytic approach, in which she or he begins to focus in greater detail on the characteristics of the client's problems. To guide this process, we recommend the use of a multidimensional model of assessment (Nezu & Nezu, 1989; see Figure 14.1). The first assessment dimension of this model

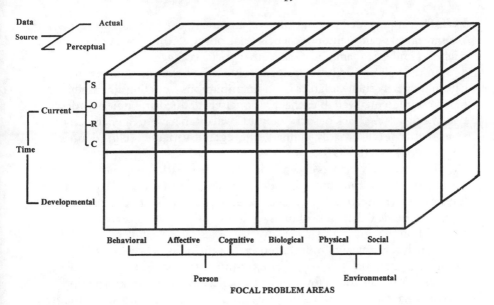

FIGURE 14.1. Multidimensional framework for clinical assessment and target problem selection. Adapted from Nezu and Nezu (1989). Copyright 1989 by A. M. Nezu and C. M. Nezu. Adapted by permission.

involves the client and his or her environment. Specifically, the clinician should inquire into six overall areas: four that are client specific (i.e., behavior, affect, cognition, biology), and two that are environmental in nature (i.e., physical environment, social environment).

For the purposes of the case formulation, problem *behaviors* can be globally categorized as either behavioral deficits or excesses (see Kanfer & Schefft, 1988). Behavioral *deficits* might include poor social skills, deficits in daily living skills, or lack of knowledge regarding self-control. Behavioral *excesses* might include compulsive behavior, avoidance of anxiety-provoking stimuli, frequent negative self-evaluation, or aggressive actions. *Affect* involves the wide array of emotions and mood states, such as anxiety, depression, hopelessness, fear, anger, and hostility. With regard to psychopathology-related *cognitive* factors, it is useful to distinguish between cognitive *deficiencies* and cognitive *distortions* (Kendall, 1985). Cognitive deficiencies are absences in one's thinking process (e.g., failure to contemplate the consequences of one's actions). Cognitive distortions refer to errors in cognitive processing (e.g., misinterpretations of certain events based on dichotomous thinking). *Biological* variables include the wide range of physiological, medical, and physical factors that may be functionally related to (i.e., covariates of, causal variables for, or sequelae of) a client's problems or goals. These can include such factors as a medical illness, physical limitation or disability, side effect of medication, or biological vulnerability to heightened arousal under stress. *Physical environmental variables* can include housing, climate, and living conditions. *Social environmental factors* can include a client's relationships to his or her network of friends, family, acquaintances, and other social contacts.

In the role as scientific problem solver, the behavior therapist needs to carefully specify such variables in an unambiguous but clinically useful manner. Less inferential variables that are concisely defined and uniquely descriptive of a client (e.g., lack of social support) will often have greater clinical utility than higher-level, broadly defined, aggregated variables (e.g., depression; Haynes & O'Brien, 1990).

The levels of variables chosen for a case formulation depend on the purpose of the case formulation. Lower-level variables often have greater utility for the design of treatment programs for an individual client because they point to more specific behavior problems, causal variables, and intervention strategies. Although higher- and lower-level variables can be valid and useful, functional analyses of clients more often err by including excessively high-level variables. Functional analyses for case formulations should be very individualized; therefore, the use of lower-level variables, which are more descriptive of the particular patient's difficulties, are particularly useful because it minimizes biased clinical judgments.

Linearly combining lower-order variables into higher-order variables is often efficient and essential to developing a valid case formulation. Highly correlated variables, such as lack of compatible coworkers, lack of social relationships, and minimal contact with family, may be represented by the higher-order variable "paucity of social support." Linear combinations of variables are valid and useful to the extent that the variables covary. A frequent error in clinical decision making is to invoke higher-order variables, such as "depression," in which the component variables exhibit low levels of covariation. In such a case, judgment errors may occur because variance in the higher-level variable may not be indicative of variance in their lower-level composites.

The therapist's goal in operationally defining the relevant variables is to account for the greatest amount of variance with the smallest number of explanatory variables. An "overspecified" model (i.e., too many variables) may confront the assessor with a case formulation that accounts for much of the variance in the problem but does not facilitate treatment decisions because the model includes too many variables. On the other hand, an "underspecified" model (i.e., too few variables) may confront the assessor with a formulation that fails to adequately explain the disorder.

A *temporal dimension* is the second major assessment factor and cuts across each of the aforementioned six areas. Specifically, information on both the client's current and past functioning can contribute to a case formulation. For example, information should be gathered about how clients currently think about their interpersonal relationships, but also how they thought about previous interpersonal relationships and whether any major shifts have occurred recently in their thoughts about these relationships. Variables that are temporally distant from the focal problems often contribute to the understanding of a client's difficulties. Identifying these noncontiguous variables provides another opportunity to investigate the causal mechanisms that may contribute to the patient's major problems. Note that inclusion of these distal variables is different than other theoretical construct systems that focus exclusively on past events.

The third dimension underscores the importance of attending to the source of the data. Data sources can be separated into two general categories: (1) *actual data* (i.e., data that are more factual in nature and generally supported by well-validated sources, such as inventories, psychological assessment procedures, and behavioral avoidance tests), and (2) *perceptual data* (i.e., data that are based exclusively on the client's verbal self-report and his or her appraisal of the nature of these variables). Identifying differences between the data sources can highlight potential discrepancies involving either the client's or the clinician's judgment. Although this difference may be only a matter of degree, a striking discrepancy between data sources can point to the possibility of distortions in a client's belief systems. An example may be comparison of the perceptual view that "No one likes me!" to actual data indicating that the client in fact has frequent dates.

Another clinically significant discrepancy may be the result of a clinician's biased appraisal of a client. For example, a clinician who identifies a behavior problem (e.g., excessive fear) for patient "Clara" on the basis of information presented during an initial assessment session may later find, based on a home visit, that the client's behavior was adaptive given her unique environment (e.g., a high-crime neighborhood).

The fourth and most important assessment dimension emphasizes the relationship between each of these variables and the identified problem area. Across the six targeted problem areas within the client's current state of functioning, each variable can be recognized as a *stimulus* (S), *organismic mediator* (O), *response* (R), or *consequence* (C). Organismic variables represent the biological, emotional, and/or cognitive state of an individual that can mediate the S–R–C relationship. Although each response may serve as a discriminative stimulus for the next S–R–C unit within the chain, can have bidirectional relationships with antecedent and consequent events, and can covary with other responses, presenting the targeted problem as the response can be useful for the purpose of case formulation. Identifying the client's ultimate outcome (e.g., depression, agoraphobia, drug addiction) as the response allows important variables that precede the behavior (e.g., cognitions) to be analyzed as antecedents, with results of the problematic behavior considered as consequences that maintain the targeted problem.[3]

Further, these variables can interact in reciprocal ways. For example, a particular consequence may not only increase the probability that a behavior will recur in the future (through a positive reinforcement paradigm) but may also increase the likelihood that a particular stimulus will be elicited. Optimal treatment gains can thus be obtained at a later time if the therapist addresses all such aspects within the chain.

To illustrate this SORC chaining, consider the case of "Paul," a patient who came into treatment because he has been feeling "really down during the past several months." A potential case formulation, following a multisource and a multimethod assessment procedure of Paul's "depression problem," can be as follows: Paul experiences depressed mood (R) when he is alone (e.g., in his bedroom at night; alone and inactive in the evenings), feels tired and thinks about his past failures and recent breakup with his girlfriend, which trigger thoughts of self-blame and hopelessness (S). His depressive reaction usually involves a sad mood, increased fatigue, thoughts of loneliness, hopelessness, and despair, and slight sensations of anxiety (topography of the overall response). When Paul begins to feel depressed, it becomes difficult for him to get out of bed and attempt to counteract the depressive mood (C). Often, when friends call to cheer him up, he tends to focus on his internal state and generally refuses to socialize with them. This behavior usually irritates his friends, who then cease to call him (social consequence), which in turn reinforces his feelings of rejection and isolation. Note that this is only one causal chain associated with Paul's depressed mood; there are probably multiple causal chains operating concurrently.

Intervention strategies can be identified to address each of the variables within this causal chain. For instance, (1) the amount of time Paul spends in isolation can be decreased (focus on the stimulus); (2) Paul can be trained in self-control and self-monitoring skills in order to redirect his attention toward positive events and skills (focus on the "organism"); (3) Paul can be taught relaxation skills to counteract feelings of depression when he is alone (focus on the response); (4) Paul can be taught problem-solving skills to increase or facilitate his ability to identify alternative ways to react in response to depressive feelings, such as developing new social relationships (focus on the consequence); and (5) Paul can be helped to develop new pleasurable activities (focus on the stimulus). Note that this example underscores the integral relationship among pretreatment assessment strategies, case formulation, and treatment design.

Guides for Directing the Search for Relevant Instrumental Outcomes

The collection of broadly focused, systems-level information from multiple sources and multiple methods, in combination with the client's reported reason for seeking treatment, helps the behavioral clinician to generate hypotheses regarding the best treatment focus for a particular patient. Therapists can use two general guides for identifying the causal (i.e., instrumental) variables for a patient: (1) a *theory-driven* strategy and (2) a *diagnosis-driven* strategy.

In a theory-driven strategy, the clinician's assessment strategies and case formulation are guided by empirically based literature relevant to the client's desired ultimate treatment outcome. The literature regarding nomothetic findings can provide various paths of exploration; however, it is crucial to remember that each individual is unique. From the multicausal perspective noted earlier, nomothetically based instrumental outcome–ultimate outcome relationships must be applied idiographically. Nomothetic information serves as the relevant "universe" of possible etiopathogenically related variables; some relationships will be, but others will not be, extant for a given client.

An excellent example of an empirically validated model that can provide for an assessment road map is J. E. Lochman's social-cognitive theory of aggression in children. According to this model (Lochman, White, & Wayland, 1991, pp. 29–30):

> [T]he child encounters a potentially anger-arousing stimulus event, but the emotional and physiological reaction is mediated by the child's perception and appraisal of the event. . . . These perceptions and appraisals can be accurate or inaccurate and are derived from prior expectations that filter the event, and from the child's selective attention to specific aspects, or cues, in the stimulus event. If the child has interpreted the event to be threatening, provocative or frustrating, he or she can then experience physiological arousal, and also will become engaged in another set of cognitive activities directed at deciding upon an appropriate behavioral response to the event. . . . [T]hree sets of internal activities, (1) perception and appraisal, (2) arousal, and (3) social problem solving, contribute to the child's behavioral response and to the resulting consequences the child receives from peers and adults and experiences internally as self-consequences. These consequent reactions from others can then become stimulus events, which feed back into the model, becoming recurrent, connected behavioral units.

This type of model provides a specific framework by which to identify treatment strategies geared to change the various causal factors (e.g., selective attention to threatening cues, distorted perceptions, inaccurate appraisals, deficient social problem-solving skills) associated with aggressive behavior. Diagnostic guidelines, such as DSM-IV (American Psychiatric Association, 1994), can also be useful in understanding response constellations and response covariations (Haynes, 1986; Kazdin, 1985). Clusters of symptoms that often covary and that have been categorized under universally understood labels can guide the clinician's search for information.

However, it is important not to rely solely on any taxonomy or theory-driven strategy, but rather to consider each strategy as one of many possible routes to identify functionally related constructs. Limiting one's assessment and treatment approach to only one theory increases the likelihood of judgment errors. Labeling and classifying patients often implies erroneously that individuals with the same label exhibit the same behavior problems and that their behavior problems are a result of the same causal variables, a concept antithetical to a multiple and idiosyncratic causality model (Nezu & Nezu, 1989). Psychiatric diagnosis can narrow the array of potential causal factors but will often be insufficient for a functional analysis (Haynes & O'Brien, 1988; Hersen, 1988).

Generation of Alternatives

To continue the process of case formulation, the behavioral clinician next generates alternatives. Note that she or he is continuing to *identify* those instrumental outcomes that may be causally related to a client's problems, not yet attempting to make final decisions about which variables to include in the functional analysis. This helps to prevent biased search strategies and to minimize the likelihood that the clinician overlooks vital information. The purpose of this problem-solving step is to identify as many ideas as possible and to maximize the probability that the best will be among them. To achieve this objective, the problem solver uses the brainstorming method of idea production, which is based on two general principles: (1) the *quantity principle* (i.e., the more ideas that are generated, the more likely that the potentially best ones are produced), and (2) the *deferment-of-judgment principle* (i.e., more high-quality ideas are produced if immediate evaluation is suspended until after a comprehensive list of possible solutions have been compiled).

Another guide to enhance idea production involves looking at differing *functional response classes*, which include behaviors that may appear very different in form but actually have a similar function (Haynes, 1992, 1996b). For example, there are many ways that a person can obtain money—investing in stocks or real estate, working for a paycheck, begging, stealing, selling possessions, prostituting, or borrowing money from a bank. These behaviors are all topographically different, yet the effects of these behaviors may be similar—all lead to obtaining money. Functional response classes are particularly important for treatment planning because they can point to alternative behaviors that serve the same function as, but possibly are more desirable than, behaviors identified as problematic. For example, increasing prosocial or adaptive behaviors that result in achieving the individual's desired goal will tend to decrease the rate of the undesirable responses that serve the same function. An individual who seeks out a paying job and applies for a loan at the bank may not have to sell meaningful possessions or resort to robbery.

Using these brainstorming principles within the context of the multimatrix model of assessment, the therapist continues to generate a list of possible variables to include within a given patient's unique case formulation. Under a social learning umbrella, empirically supported instrumental outcomes for a depressed client include the following: increased pleasant activities; decreased unpleasant activities; improved future expectations of positive outcomes; improved coping skills; increased tolerance of negative memories; changed negative attributions; decreased self-blame; changed irrational beliefs; changed cognitive distortions; increased perspective-taking skills; decreased self-punishment; increased self-reinforcement; reduced unrealistic expectations about attainable goals; decreased concomitant feelings of anxiety; decreased negative ruminations; decreased negative self-evaluations; decreased negative automatic thoughts; improved interpersonal relationships; an improved marital relationship; increased communication skills; increased assertive behavior; and improved social problem-solving skills (Nezu & Nezu, 1989).

As can be seen, a large pool of potentially relevant depression-related causal factors exist when one is considering the disorder of depression but which may or may not be particularly relevant to the client at hand. Developing a client-specific case formulation and functional analysis, therefore, requires the therapist to make decisions about which of these multiple causal factors demonstrate the greatest magnitude of shared variance with the client's depressive symptoms. To facilitate this decision-making process, we advocate the use of visual representations, such as a Clinical Pathogenesis Map or a Functional Analytic Causal Model (discussed next).

The Clinical Pathogenesis Map

Nezu and Nezu (1989, 1993) have previously suggested that a useful guide in developing a case formulation involves the depiction of client information in a visual format they term the Clinical Pathogenesis Map (CPM). The CPM pictorially delineates the various major elements hypothetically contributing to the initiation and maintenance of the patient's problems. This CPM can be likened to a visual depiction of a path analysis model or causal modeling statistical approach. For example, Figure 14.2 is a CPM based on Paul's depression prob-

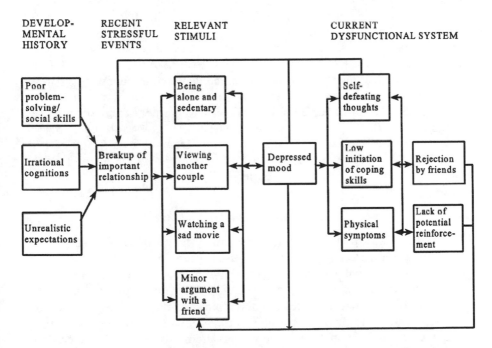

FIGURE 14.2. Example of a CPM of Paul. Adapted from Nezu and Nezu (1989). Copyright 1989 by A. M. Nezu and C. M. Nezu. Adapted by permission.

lem previously described. Note that it highlights various instrumental outcome–instrumental outcome chains, as well as several instrumental outcome–ultimate outcome relationships. Included are those variables previously identified using the multidimensional assessment matrix. Such factors are included under headings involving developmental history, recent triggers, and the current "dysfunctional system" serving to elicit and maintain the problem behavior(s).

The CPM serves as a working idiographic model of a patient's difficulties and a framework upon which new data can be added. As the therapist begins to learn more about the patient, the CPM may need to be revised or even replaced with a new CPM. Changes are likely during the actual course of treatment due to the nature of exigencies of the therapy process. In general, the CPM is a concrete statement of the clinician's hypotheses against which alternative hypotheses can be continuously tested.

The Functional Analytic Causal Model

Haynes and O'Brien (see Haynes, 1994; Haynes et al., 1993; O'Brien & Haynes, 1995) have also developed a model, similar to the CPM, that uses vector diagrams to help clarify causal and noncausal functional relationships among variables in a functional analysis, namely, the Functional Analytic Causal Model (FACM). The FACM helps to organize and symbolize important functional relationships relevant to a particular client. The FACM is a visual model of the behavior therapist's hypotheses about a client's behavior problems and goals, as well as those variables that affect such problems and goals. Moreover, because this approach borrows from traditional causal modeling and vector geometry, the FACM provides a means by which to estimate the strength of relationships among the hypothesized antecedents, consequents, covariates, mediating variables, and maintaining factors relevant to a client's behavior problem. Such information allows the clinician to better evaluate the relative magnitude of effect that would be expected from intervening with any hypothesized causal variable for the client's behavior problems or goals.[4] Figure 14.3 presents a FACM of an outpatient client who complained of frequent depressive episodes and unsatisfactory interpersonal relationships.

Treatment Decision Making

Up to this point, the behavior therapist, using the problem-solving model, has primarily focused on identifying those instrumental outcomes that are potentially functionally related to a client's ultimate outcomes. Having such a comprehensive model now allows the clinician to begin the process of selecting the most important variables and developing the most clinically useful case formulation for the client. According to the problem-solving approach, this entails a cost–benefit analysis of the various alternatives under consideration and the selection of the one(s) rated as most effective for potential implementation. This problem-solving activity is geared toward helping the therapist se-

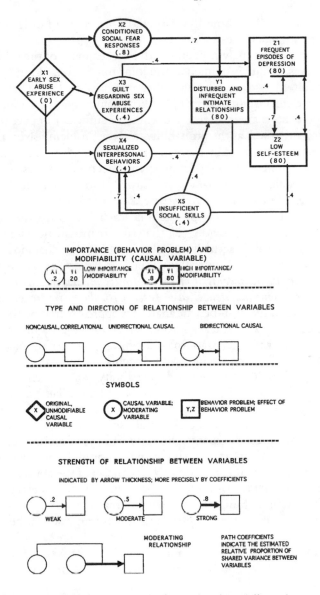

FIGURE 14.3. A hypothesized FACM of an isolated, socially anxious, and avoidant adolescent who complained of disturbed interpersonal relationships and depression. The figure and accompanying text illustrate unidirectional and bidirectional causal relationships, differences in the estimated strength of causal relationships, the estimated modifiability of causal variables (rectangles with X's), the importance of designated behavior problems ($Y1$), and the effects of and relationships between behavior problems (Y's and Z's). From Haynes, Uchigakiuchi, et al. (1993). Calculation of magnitude of effect estimates are discussed in Haynes (1994).

lect those variables that should be targeted for change in order to facilitate maximum treatment success.

The cost–benefit analysis begins with an assessment of the utility of various alternatives. Utility is defined as the joint function of (1) the probability that a given alternative actually achieves a particular goal and (2) the value of the alternative. Probability estimates of goal achievement take into account the likelihood that a given alternative will have sufficient impact to facilitate goal attainment, as well as the probability that the problem solver (in this case the therapist) will be able to implement such an alternative in its optimal form. Applying such principles to target-problem selection involves assessing the following probabilities: (1) that a given target problem is amenable to treatment (i.e., *On the basis of the literature, can this instrumental outcome be achieved?*); (2) that this target problem is amenable to treatment that this particular therapist can provide; (3) that the treatment necessary to effect change for this person is actually available; and (4) that changing this problem will achieve the client's overall goal (i.e., *Will reaching this instrumental outcome lead to the achievement of the ultimate outcome or at least another instrumental outcome more closely associated with the ultimate outcome?*).

In the FACM, the cost–benefit analysis is approximated by the estimated magnitude of effect, which takes into consideration the modifiability of the instrumental outcomes (1, 2, 3, above) and the importance of the behavior problem or goal, as well as the strength and direction of functional relationships.

With regard to the first issue, the amenability of a problem to treatment, it is important for the therapist to differentiate unmodifiable causal variables from their sequelae, which are often modifiable. For example, a therapist cannot eradicate a client's history of early sex abuse. However, this early developmental factor may affect the client's thoughts or ways of social interaction that may, in turn, serve as important causal variables for his or her marital difficulties. Moreover, it is possible to modify the sequelae of the abuse, such as conditioned fears, avoidance of interpersonal intimacy, or other interpersonal difficulties that actually function more as contemporaneous or proximal causal variables for the client's marital problems. Such sequelae can be defined as intervening variables for the marital difficulties and can easily be described within the SORC model. As such, it is especially these types of functionally-related variables that should be contained in the CPM or FACM (see Figure 14.3).

The second two considerations (i.e., the probability that the therapist can implement those strategies necessary to effect change and the probability that such treatment protocols are available) are less important in terms of a case formulation, but they are of extreme importance when making treatment planning decisions. In other words, although a particular clinical intervention can be highly efficacious for a given problem, if a therapist has not been well trained in its use, the expected treatment effectiveness will be reduced.

The fourth consideration, the likelihood that changing the target problem will help achieve the client's ultimate goal, involves an assessment of both the importance of the problem in question and the strength of the causal relationship between that particular instrumental outcome and ultimate outcome. The importance or severity of the target problem should be taken into consideration when one is later rank ordering or prioritizing which goals should be addressed earlier on. For example, in terms of a depressed client, if she or he also displays strong concomitant suicidal behaviors, it is likely that such behaviors are given a higher priority. In addition, certain treatment strategies may be effective for certain milder forms of a disorder, whereas more severe cases necessitate additional and/or different treatment protocols.

Further, if the strength of the association between instrumental outcome variable X, for example, and the ultimate outcome variable is stronger than that with a different instrumental outcome variable Y, then it is likely that variable X is targeted first. Estimates of the strength of such relationships can sometimes be obtained from the nomothetic literature. For example, research has strongly underscored the causal role of cognitive distortions for the maintenance (but not the onset) of depression symptoms (e.g., Barnett & Gotlib, 1988) As such, the therapist, using the multidimensional matrix should assess (through structured interviews or standardized inventories such as the Dysfunctional Attitude Scale; Weissman, 1978) the presence and form of cognitive distortions. If such distortions exist and they are hypothesized to have a causal role, then they should become part of the CPM/FACM for *that* patient. If not present, then this cognitive variable should not automatically become a clinical target for that patient regardless of the documented efficacy of cognitive therapy. Further, the importance of cognitive distortions as treatment targets would be related to their severity and hypothesized magnitude of effect on depressive behaviors.

Judgments regarding the *value* of an alternative are affected by assessments of four specific areas concerning the therapist, client, and significant others: (1) *personal consequences* (e.g., How much time, effort, and other resources are required to reach this instrumental outcome? What is the emotional cost or gain associated with achieving this outcome? Is the outcome consistent with one's values and ethics? Are there any physical or life-threatening effects of changing this target problem? What are the effects of changing this target problem on other problem areas?); (2) *social consequences* (e.g., What is the effect on other people, such as a spouse, family, or friends?); (3) *short-term effects* (e.g., What is the immediate impact on the client's other problem areas if this problem is changed?); and (4) *long-term effects* (e.g., What are the long-range consequences of changing this problem on future psychological functioning?).

Using these criteria as guidelines, the therapist evaluates the overall cost–benefit profile for each problem contained on the list previously generated. Those that are rated highly (i.e., those clinical targets or instrumental outcome variables that have been evaluated as having a high positive-to-negative ratio of effects and probabilities) are then selected as initial targets. Typically, several targets are selected as a means of enhancing maximal goal attainment. These variables are then noted in the client's CPM/FACM.

Solution Implementation and Verification

The final problem-solving task within the general model, solution implementation and verification, encompasses (1) implementing the solution plan, (2) monitoring the consequences of this plan, and (3) evaluating the match between one's predicted effects and the actual effects of this plan.

Construction of a client's CPM/FACM guides the implementation component of this problem-solving operation. During implementation, the behavior therapist continues to monitor the effects of case formulation decisions to compare predicted "consequences" with the outcome. Continuing multivariate, time-series assessment during the course of treatment is a basic tenet of the behavioral assessment paradigm (Haynes, 1996a, 1996b). Three levels of assessment can help guide this evaluation process:

First, the client can provide feedback about the validity of the CPM/FACM. Although client–therapist discussions concerning the client's case should be continuously occurring, a formal presentation of the CPM/FACM should be made in order to elicit feedback from the client and to ensure informed consent from the client regarding the therapy goals and strategies. Although a patient's perceptions may be biased and the resulting feedback inconclusive, without mutual agreement between therapist and client successful treatment is unlikely.

Second, predictions about current and future behavior can be made on the basis of a case formulation. For example, if an initial CPM/FACM analysis suggests that a patient's major presenting problem involves social anxiety, the patient would be expected to have high scores on self-report measures of social avoidance and distress and to display visible signs of anxiety and distress during a structured role play that involves meeting new people. Ongoing (i.e., time-series) broad-spectrum, multisource, multimethod assessment is the best approach to developing, testing, and refining the predictions of the original case formulation. As noted earlier, time-series assessment is particularly important in view of the dynamic nature of causal relationships in a CPM/FACM.

A third level of monitoring involves assessing the effects of treatment strategies implemented on the basis of the CPM/FACM. This particular form of validation provides a powerful source of feedback about the validity of the CPM/FACM. If the hypothesized CPM/FACM is valid, modification of important causal variables identified in the model should be associated with predicted changes in the associated behavior problems and goal attainment. If successful intervention with instrumental variables is not associated with expected effects, the content validity of the CPM/FACM becomes questionable. Important causal and mediating variables may have been omitted, the strength of causal relationships may have been over- or underestimated, or causal relationships may have changed.

If these three methods of evaluation indicate problems with the CPM/FACM, the problem-solving process is reinitiated to determine the source of the discrepancy (e.g., Were insufficient target problems generated?

Was insufficient data collected regarding the client's social relationships? Was the cost–benefit analysis inconclusive? Was the strength of causal relationships miscalculated?). If the evaluation supports the validity of the CPM/FACM, the behavior therapist then proceeds to the next stage of therapy—that of designing an idiographic treatment program based on the case formulation.[5]

APPLICATION TO PSYCHOTHERAPY TECHNIQUE

Case formulation and intervention strategies in behavior therapy are specific to each client (Cone, 1986). There is not a generic form of treatment or "cookbook" to follow based on the outcome of the therapist's hypotheses. Rather, the individuality of the functional analysis leads to goals and potential routes to reach those goals that are specific to each client. That is, behavior therapy is predicated on the idiographic application of nomothetic principles; it is not an omnibus "one size fits all" therapeutic approach. Therefore, the behavioral case formulation is integrally attached to the treatment plan. In essence, the CPM or FACM provides a treatment map that facilitates overall goal attainment.

The CPM/FACM is often shared with the client in order to obtain initial feedback about its veracity. Further, it is used collaboratively by the therapist and client as a means of identifying the specific goals of therapy and the impediments to the attainment of those goals. However, not all clients will benefit from the presentation of the functional analysis. The therapist may choose to share his or her hypotheses and ideas about treatment subgoals and obstacles in a less formal manner. Each client will have different desires, expectations, and cognitive abilities that may affect the therapist's decision about how much or how little should be directly shared. On the one hand, sharing the functional analysis with the patient may be useful as a means of education and motivation enhancement. When this formulation is shared, the patient can become more motivated to "work hard in therapy" as she or he is able to concretely understand what is going on. Alternatively, the number and severity of behavioral difficulties that have been identified as obstacles to goal attainment might be too discouraging for certain patients. Sometimes, it is advisable to omit variables (e.g., "ideas of reference") and to use commonsense language when presenting CPM/FACMs to patients.

CASE EXAMPLE

To illustrate the application of the problem-solving model of behavioral case formulation, we briefly present the following case example concerning an adult male sex offender.

Background Information

"D.J.," a 27-year-old, slightly overweight but husky white male, was referred for a psychological evaluation, behavioral risk assessment, and treatment recommendations. This client had a history of sexually aggressive behavior that included beating women and an attempted rape of a 12-year-old female neighbor.

D.J. recently moved back to a boarding home sponsored by a private agency following an extended period of hospitalization. He had been hospitalized approximately 4 months prior to this assessment following several incidents of assaultive behavior toward a female social worker, as well as "suicidal gestures." A review of D.J.'s records indicated that he maintained a long history of behavioral difficulties dating back to injuries sustained when he was the victim of a hit-and-run auto accident. He attended special education classes due to "emotional disturbance" and "neurological impairment" difficulties, was thought to be "borderline retarded," and was frequently hospitalized. He was originally removed from his mother's care as a function of her negligence and was placed in several foster homes between hospitalizations. His conviction of attempted rape and assault of a female neighbor occurred when he was 18 years old and residing in a foster placement. For this offense, he received a sentence of 10 years of probation. Because of a significant history of suicidal behavior and sexual aggression, he was considered a risk to the community and his continued residence in the boarding home was contingent upon his entering treatment.

This client's most recent clinical history indicated frequent exacerbations of problem behaviors and psychiatric symptoms over several months preceding the most recent hospitalization. These included social withdrawal, agitation, suicidal gestures, self-destructive behavior, and sexually assaultive behavior (e.g., attempting to choke a female social worker). Hospital notes during this time indicated continued fluctuations, with no clear stabilization of symptoms despite many different medication trials. He was currently prescribed carbamazepine for the treatment of a seizure disorder.

Assessment Plan

The overall plan for evaluation was based upon the multimatrix, empirical assessment model outlined previously. In brief, the objectives of this assessment were as follows: (1) to identify internal and external conditions affecting the probability of D.J.'s behavior problems; (2) to identify the behavioral, cognitive, and affective topographical components of the client's presenting problems; (3) to identify various client-specific biological, developmental, social learning, and environmental variables that may have been functionally related to his current difficulties; and (4) to develop clinical hypotheses and a CPM of the functional relationships among these variables. To accomplish these goals, the relevant literature, in addition to the therapist's previous experience with such clients, formed the basis upon which potential focal areas of assessment were initially identified. Next, an assessment protocol was developed to gain information about these areas from multiple sources (i.e., the client and knowledgeable residential staff). More specifically, D.J. underwent a testing protocol that included a semistructured interview, the Wechsler Adult Intelligence Scale—Revised (WAIS-R; Wechsler, 1981), the Multimodal Life History Questionnaire (Lazarus, 1980), the Social Problem-Solving Inventory (SPSI; D'Zurilla & Nezu, 1990), the Assertiveness Skills and Heterosexual Skills Role-Play Test (De Maso, Eiraldi, Nezu, & Nezu, 1993), the Cognition Scale (Abel et al., 1989), and the Role-Play Test of Anger-Arousing Situations (Benson, Rice, & Miranti, 1986). In addition, behavioral observation data included recordings of the antecedent and consequent events surrounding the problem behaviors, as well as their frequency, intensity, and topography and were collected by group-home staff and the therapist during milieu visits.

Assessment Results

The WAIS-R was administered in order to obtain a current and valid assessment of D.J.'s intellectual and cognitive abilities, as certain deficits were apparent during previous interviews. In addition, group-home staff repeatedly referred to him as "borderline retarded." His Full Scale IQ score was found to fall within the range of low average intellectual functioning. His verbal IQ also fell within the low average range, with no significant differences found regarding vocabulary, language comprehension, recall of information, or short-term memory. When his average scores were compared across all areas assessed, language comprehension represented a relative strength area for him, whereas deficits in abstract reasoning represented an area of particular weakness.

The Multimodal Life History Questionnaire was administered in order to assess biological, affective, sensory, imagery/fantasy, cognitive, interpersonal, and developmental areas of D.J.'s life. Feelings of inadequacy, hopelessness, and loneliness were prevalent throughout his responses to this inventory. He also showed many symptoms of fear, hypersensitivity, and hostility toward others, particularly women. Although feelings of sadness and depression were also reported, anxiety was his most frequent and troublesome symptom. Areas of inquiry regarding his first sexual experience and current sexual activity were not answered. For example, in response to such questions, D.J. responded, "I don't want to talk about stuff like that." He reluctantly admitted to having some fantasies concerning same-aged women.

The SPSI was administered in order to evaluate D.J.'s general approach to solving real-life problems. His responses indicated significant deficits in general, with particular difficulties regarding (1) an inability to identify those factors that make a situation a problem, (2) an appreciation and assessment of the consequences of his actions, (3) a strong tendency to engage in avoidance coping, and (4) an inability to inhibit his acting impulsively when reacting to stressful situations. The Assertiveness Skills and Heterosexual Skills Role-Play Test includes five role-play vignettes involving social–sexual situations that require appropriately assertive (as compared to aggressive) responses. D.J.'s participation in this role-play test revealed significantly inappropriate responses to four out of the five vignettes. His responses were generally aggressive and sexually inappropriate. The appropriate responses to one role-play situation indicated that he did have some knowledge of socially assertive behavior. This would indicate that aspects of D.J.'s social behavior were more related to deviant emotional arousal than to simple lack of knowledge. With regard to that part of the test that measures one's heterosexual social skills, D.J. continued to display many inappropriate responses, including aggressive statements and sexually inappropriate jokes.

The Cognition Scale is designed to assess the presence of cognitive distortions frequently associated with child molesters. The client's responses to this measure indicated that several of the distortions common to this population, such as "A child who does not resist an adult wants to have sex," were endorsed, suggesting certain cognitive distortions. D.J. also completed the Role-Play Test of Anger-Arousing Situations. This instrument measures one's behavior in situations that are potentially anger arousing. D.J.'s performance during the role-plays was consistent with his response style on the test of social–sexual assertiveness skills. Particularly with regard to situations in which he was challenged or criticized, his verbal responses were usually loud and aggressive.

Behavioral observation data obtained at his residence indicated frequent antecedents to D.J.'s aggressive incidents involving his misinterpretation of others' behavior. The trigger was often an innocuous comment made by another resident, whereupon D.J., who interpreted the comment in a concrete and distorted manner, reacted emotionally in a way that was grossly disproportionate to the situation. For example, when another resident in the home jokingly referred to D.J. as a "burger bandit" because he seemed to be enjoying this particular food, he responded with intense anger, stating that he was not a thief and perseveratively related stories attesting to his honesty. When the housemate attempted to tell him that she did not mean to imply that he was a thief, D.J. insisted that she was now calling him a liar and threatened her physically.

Consequences following such incidents varied across staff members and included threats of further hospitalizations, attempts to calm D.J. down by talking to him, leaving him alone, and threats of loss of residential placement. Although D.J. demonstrated some assertive skills and knowledge of socially appropriate responses during the role-play assessments, he appeared to have minimal skills for self-control of aggressive or suicidal behavior in real situations. The observed frequency of behavioral incidents occurred at a rate of 8 times per week over a 2-week period, and included the following behaviors: (1) *verbal aggression*, defined as threatening physical harm to others; (2) *physical aggression*, defined as hitting, pushing, kicking, choking, or threatening staff with a raised fist or a weapon; and (3) *suicidal statements*, defined as any talk concerned with harming self.

From the data, it appeared that his suicidal statements were most commonly triggered by perceived loss, rejection, and/or failed attempts to change the subject when confronted with any reference to his difficulties. One example included suicidal statements that were observed when a coworker did not make a promised visit to D.J.'s home and his social worker attempted to offer constructive criticism regarding his hostile and threatening comments about the friend.

Case Formulation

Based on the above data, the following case formulation was developed. D.J.'s intellectual functioning, as assessed by the WAIS-R, was in the low average range. He did reveal certain cognitive deficits in areas such as concrete thinking, impulsivity, and lack of adaptive self-control skills. These difficulties further appeared to represent significant obstacles for coping effectively with various emotional triggers, such as threats to his self-esteem. Consistent with a diagnosis of Personality Disorder, D.J.'s behavioral difficulties appeared to be functionally related to a combination of organic processing deficits, emotional dysregulation, and an often idiosyncratic and cross-situational way of misinterpreting environmental events.

D.J. also revealed symptoms of affective instability, aggressive outbursts, perserverative thinking, suspiciousness, and paranoid ideation involving misinterpretation of others' intentions that were grossly disproportionate to precipitating events. This is consistent with processing difficulties associated with brain impairment. Unfortunately, several caregivers in his environment had historically reacted to his distortion of events in argumentative or verbally combative ways. This had served as antecedents to escalations of aggressive behavior. In addition, there had been consistent and reinforcing consequences to D.J.'s excessive reactions, in that people in his environment often became frightened by such episodes and tended to increase social attention by attempting to calm him down. Regarding his sexually aggressive behavior, D.J. revealed deficits concerning social problem solving, including impulsivity, avoidance, and difficulty in evaluating the consequences of his actions. He seemed to have coped with his difficulty controlling sexual impulses by becoming increasingly focused on his job and simply denying that any problems existed. Although this had reduced the number of negative interpersonal situations, there appeared to be two predictable situations in which the client was likely to be at risk for engaging in sexually aggressive behavior: (1) if he was criticized at work, and (2) if he became attracted to, but was rejected by, any new woman in his life, although he continued to state that he has "no interest in sex." D.J.'s list of complaints also appeared to periodically meet criteria for a diagnosis of major depression. This seemed to reflect an excessive affective reaction to real or perceived loss, including suicidal gestures and threats, and was subject to rapid fluctuations. His lack of response to trials of antidepressant medication and lithium, as well as the presence of known triggers regarding depressive episodes, provided some validation for this hypothesis.

The Clinical Pathogenesis Map

D.J.'s initial CPM is presented in Figure 14.4.

Treatment Recommendations

Based on D.J.'s CPM, the following initial treatment recommendations were offered. He would likely benefit from a structured clinical intervention geared to improve his emotional regulation and problem-solving abilities. Because of D.J.'s hypersensitivity and proclivity to misinterpretation of various events, his therapist would need to be especially careful not to become involved in power struggles or arguments when the client made statements that appeared paranoid or hypersensitive. An empathic response such as, "It must be frightening to have such thoughts," plus redirection, would probably decrease the likelihood of escalations in agitation.

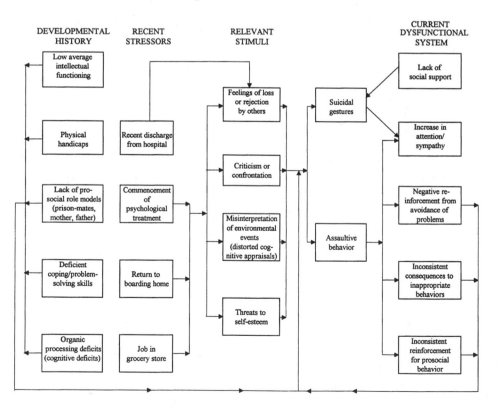

FIGURE 14.4. Example of a CPM of D.J.

At the time of this formulation, it would be difficult to predict the extent to which D.J. would be able to learn to change his interpretation of environmental events. His social information processing may not be remediable due to the unknown extent of his nonspecific brain injury. If, for example, specific testing proved this to be valid, then an initial goal of therapy could be the reduction of his aggressive verbal responses in reaction to emotionalizing triggers (e.g., perceived insults or rejection). Concurrently, more adaptive means of expressing or coping with distressing emotions such as fear, anger, and sadness could be taught to the client and differentially reinforced.

Both group and individual therapy should be focused on enhancing D.J.'s ability to tolerate distress and his skills in coping with these feelings. For example, when the client is directing angry and verbally aggressive statements toward another person, rather than trying to talk him out of his feelings it may be more helpful to state, "I can see that you're very angry. This is a problem. What can you do with this anger? I'm glad to see you are keeping yourself in control. Maybe if you (alternative response), this would help." There should be continual, purposeful, and intense social reinforcement whenever D.J. is distressed but in control of his behavior, as this would represent a positive change in his ability to inhibit aggressive responding, even if he could not inhibit a paranoid thought. In addition, it would be helpful to have available a specific crisis plan for this client in the event that any significant psychosocial stressors occur (e.g., major loss). It would be important to provide D.J. with the alternative of a "day off" or a "vacation" from the routine, daily program activities in reaction to such stress before he exhibits a behavioral escalation, as well as communicating that the staff knows he may need some additional help in maintaining his self-control.

Note that the overall CPM and treatment plan would change as various instrumental outcomes are (or are not) achieved as a function of either treatment per se or inadvertent changes in his environment (e.g., major change in residential placement).

TRAINING

The following are crucial areas relevant to effective application of behavioral case formulation:

1. *Behavioral assessment.* A fundamental knowledge of the theory and procedures of behavioral assessment is crucial to conducting a functional analysis and behavioral case formulation. This involves a familiarity with the relevant literature concerning the process of understanding human behavior from a behavioral perspective, as well as the various behavioral assessment methods unique to this orientation (e.g., behavioral observation, behavioral avoidance tests, role-play assessments).

2. *Behavior therapy.* Similarly, a familiarity with the vast literature base regarding behavioral interventions is considered crucial to conducting a valid case formulation. A worthwhile starting point is the text edited by Bellack, Hersen, and Kazdin (1990).

3. *Psychopathology.* Fundamental knowledge of adult and child psychopathology is also considered essential. Familiarity with DSM-IV (American Psychiatric Association, 1994) is also considered advisable.

4. *Psychometrics.* The concepts of reliability and validity of any assessment procedure, be it objective or projective testing, behavioral observation, or a structured interview procedure, play an essential role in the accurate formulation of any patient's specific case. As such, a basic understanding of these issues is viewed as important parts of training in case formulation. Psychometric foundations of behavioral assessment are discussed in Cone (1996), Haynes and Wailalae (1994), Silva (1993), and in the special issue on research methods in the journal *Psychological Assessment* (1995, Vol. 7).

5. *Multivariate statistics.* In keeping with the planned critical multiplism tenet of our problem orientation, it is important to be able to understand various assumptions inherent in multiple causal modeling. Familiarity with path analysis or structural causal modeling is particularly useful.

6. *Problem-solving principles.* A basic familiarity with the general problem-solving model (Nezu et al., 1993), especially as it applies to clinical decision making and judgment (Nezu & Nezu, 1989, 1993, 1995), is particularly helpful.

7. *Clinical judgment.* Knowledge of research on the process and errors in clinical judgment is helpful. These issues are discussed in Nezu and Nezu (1989).

Having a basic knowledge in each of the above areas is a beginning point to learning this approach. However, as is the case with any skill, the key component is concerted practice. Although this approach is based heavily on the precepts of the scientific process, because of the ubiquity of human error (Nezu & Nezu, 1989), as well as the slipperiness of the "art" inherent in the *application* of anything scientific (see Nezu & Nezu, 1995), such practice is essential.

RESEARCH SUPPORT FOR THE APPROACH

The commitment to an empirical and scientific methodology is often cited as a major cornerstone of a behavioral approach to assessment and clinical interventions. In fact, this argument has been often used to support behavior therapy's clinical superiority over more traditional models. However, as noted in the beginning of this chapter, this empiricism was more evident in terms of developing and evaluating behavioral assessment and intervention strategies than in the process of translating these assessment data into case formulations and treatment implications. In fact, research has pointed to various discrepancies between behavior therapy as it is practiced and the empirical rigor with which its attempted validation is espoused in the literature. For example, Hay, Hay, Angle, and Nelson (1979) found that the reliability among a group of clinical interviewers concerning the identification of specific problem areas was low. Further, in a study by Wilson and Evans (1983), the reliability across 118 behavior therapists in selecting target problems was only modest. In addition, Felton and Nelson (1984) concluded that interassessor agreement regarding hypothesized controlling variables and the subsequent formulation of treatment protocols was poor.

It was in response to such disappointing revelations that the current models were developed (Haynes, Uchigakiuchi, et al., 1993; Nezu & Nezu, 1989). As such, the problem-solving model awaits empirical validation. However, a plethora of research exists underscoring the effectiveness of teaching individuals general problem-solving principles in order to improve specific problem-solving skills (Nezu et al., 1989). We hope that this chapter has engendered renewed clinical and research interest in this topic and has piqued some readers' curiosity regarding the relationship between behavioral assessment and treatment.

NOTES

1. One way of estimating consequences of various solutions is through functional analytic causal models, discussed later in this chapter.

2. A psychological assessment paradigm is an integrated set of principles, beliefs, values, hypotheses, and methods advocated by the adherents of an assessment discipline. It includes hypotheses about the best level of measurement precision, the causal variables that are most likely to affect behavior, the mechanisms that underlie causal and noncausal functional relationships, the role of assessment in the design and evaluation of treatment, and the best methods for obtaining assessment data. A psychological assessment paradigm also includes guidelines for clinical judgment based on assessment data (Haynes, 1996b).

3. An important component of many functional analyses is the identification of conditional probabilities for behavior problems—the identification of contexts and temporally proximal stimuli that are associated with an increased incidence, magnitude, or duration of the client's behavior problem. Assessment of conditional probabilities helps the clinician identify important causal variables and mechanisms.

4. In addition to delineating the manner in which various functional relationships exist, the FACM allows the behavior therapist to make mathematical estimates of the following aspects of these relationships. Because an explanation of how such mathematical estimates are conducted is beyond the scope of this chapter, the reader is referred to Haynes (1994) and Haynes, Uchigakiuchi, Meyer, Orimoto, and Blaine (1993).

5. We end here as the purpose of this chapter involves behavioral case formulation and not behavior therapy per se. For readers interested in how the problem-solving model is applied to the process of behavioral treatment planning, please refer to Nezu and Nezu (1989) and Nezu, Nezu, and Gill-Weiss (1992).

REFERENCES

Abel, G. G., Gore, D. K., Holland, C. L., Camp, N. L., Becker, J. V., & Rather, J. (1989). The measurement of the cognitive distortions of child molesters. *Annals of Sex Research, 2,* 135–153.

American Psychiatric Association (1994). *Diagnostic and statistical manual of mental disorders* (4th ed.). Washington, DC: Author.

Arkes, H. R. (1981). Impediments to accurate clinical judgment and possible ways to minimize their impact. *Journal of Consulting and Clinical Psychology, 49,* 323–330.

Bandura, A. (1977). *Social learning theory.* Englewood Cliffs, NJ: Prentice-Hall.

Barlow, D. H. (1980). Behavior therapy: The next decade. *Behavior Therapy, 11,* 315–328.

Barnett, P. A., & Gotlib, I. (1988). Psychosocial functioning and depression: Distinguishing among antecedents, concomitants and consequences. *Psychological Bulletin, 104,* 97–126.

Barrios, B. A., & Hartmann, D. P. (1986). The contribution of traditional assessment: Concepts, issues, and methodologies. In R. O. Nelson & S. C. Hayes (Eds.), *Conceptual foundations of behavioral assessment* (pp. 81–110). New York: Guilford Press.

Beck, A. T., Rush, A. J., Shaw, B. F., & Emery, G. (1979). *Cognitive therapy of depression: A treatment manual.* New York: Guilford Press.

Bellack, A. S., & Hersen, M. (Eds.). (1993). *Handbook of behavior therapy in the psychiatric setting.* New York: Plenum Press.

Bellack, A. S., Hersen, M., & Kazdin, A. E. (Eds.). (1990). *International handbook of behavior modification and therapy* (2nd ed.). New York: Plenum Press.

Benson, B. A., Rice, C. J., & Miranti, S. V. (1986). Effects of anger management training with mentally retarded adults in group treatment. *Journal of Consulting and Clinical Psychology, 54,* 728–729.

Cone, J. D. (1986). Idiographic, nomothetic and related perspectives in behavioral assessment. In R. O. Nelson & S. C. Hayes (Eds.), *Conceptual foundations of behavioral assessment* (pp. 111–128). New York: Guilford Press.

Cone, J. D. (1996). Psychometric considerations: Concepts, contents and methods. In M. Hersen & A. S. Bellack (Eds.), *Behavioral assessment: A practical handbook* (4th ed.). Boston: Allyn & Bacon.

De Maso, D. L., Eiraldi, R. B., Nezu, C. M., & Nezu, A. M. (1993, November). *Social Skills Role-Play Test.* Paper presented at the Annual Convention of the Association for Advancement of Behavior Therapy, Atlanta, GA.

D'Zurilla, T. J., & Nezu, A. M. (1982). Social problem solving in adults. In P. C. Kendall (Ed.), *Advances in cognitive-behavioral research and therapy* (Vol. 1, pp. 202–274). New York: Academic Press.

D'Zurilla, T. J., & Nezu, A. M. (1990). Development and preliminary evaluation of the Social Problem-Solving Inventory. *Psychological Assessment, 2,* 156–163.

Evans, I. M. (1985). Building systems models as a strategy for target behavior selection in clinical assessment. *Behavioral Assessment, 7,* 21–32.

Evans, I. [M.] (1993). Constructional perspectives in clinical assessment. *Psychological Assessment, 5,* 264–272.

Felton, J. L., & Nelson, R. O. (1984). Interassessor agreement on hypothesized controlling variables and treatment proposals. *Behavioral Assessment, 6,* 199–208.

Hawkins, R. P. (1986). Selection of target behaviors. In R. O. Nelson & S. C. Hayes (Eds.), *Conceptual foundations of behavioral assessment* (pp. 331–385). New York: Guilford Press.

Hay, W. M., Hay, L. R., Angle, H. V., & Nelson, R. O. (1979). The reliability of problem identification in the behavioral interview. *Behavioral Assessment, 1*, 107–118.

Haynes, S. N. (1986). The design of intervention programs. In R. O. Nelson & S. C. Hayes (Eds.), *Conceptual foundations of behavioral assessment* (pp. 386–429). New York: Guilford Press.

Haynes, S. N. (1992). *Models of causality in psychopathology: Toward synthetic, dynamic and nonlinear models of causality in psychopathology.* Boston: Allyn & Bacon.

Haynes, S. N. (1994). Clinical judgment and the design of behavioral intervention programs: Estimating the magnitudes of intervention effects. *Psicología Conductual, 2*, 165–184.

Haynes, S. N. (1996a). The changing nature of behavioral assessment. In M. Hersen & A. Bellack (Eds.), *Behavioral assessment: A practical guide* (4th ed.). Boston: Allyn & Bacon.

Haynes, S. N. (1996b). *Behavioral assessment: A functional approach to psychological assessment.* Manuscript submitted for publication.

Haynes, S. N., Blaine, D., & Meyer, K. (1993). Dynamical models for psychological assessment: Phase-space functions. *Psychological Assessment, 5*, 17–24.

Haynes, S. N., & O'Brien, W. H. (1988). The Gordian Knot of DSM III-R use: Integrating principles of behavior classification and complex causal models. *Behavioral Assessment, 10*, 95–105.

Haynes, S. N., & O'Brien, W. O. (1990). The functional analysis in behavior therapy. *Clinical Psychology Review, 10*, 649–668.

Haynes, S. N., Spain, E. H., & Oliveira, J. (1993). Deriving causal inferences in clinical assessment. *Psychological Assessment, 5*, 281–291.

Haynes, S. N., Uchigakiuchi, P., Meyer, K., Orimoto, L., & Blaine, D. (1993). Functional analytic causal models and the design of treatment programs: Concepts and clinical applications with childhood behavior problems. *European Journal of Psychological Assessment, 9*, 189–205.

Haynes, S. N., & Wailalae, K. (1994). Psychometric foundations of behavioral assessment. In R. Fernández-Ballestros (Ed.), *Evaluación conductual hoy.* Madrid: Ediciones Pirámide.

Hersen, M. (1988). Behavioral assessment and psychiatric diagnosis. *Behavioral Assessment, 10*, 107–121.

Hersen, M., & Bellack, A. S. (Eds.). (1996). *Behavioral assessment: A practical handbook* (4th ed.). Boston: Allyn & Bacon.

Hersen, M., Bellack, A. S., & Himmelhoch, J. M. (1980). Treatment of unipolar depression with social skills training. *Behavior Modification, 4*, 547–556.

Hersen, M., Eisler, R. M., & Miller, P. (1975). *Progress in behavior modification.* New York: Academic Press.

Hoberman, H. M., & Lewinsohn, P. M. (1985). The behavioral treatment of depression. In E. E. Beckham & W. R. Leber (Eds.), *Handbook of depression: Treatment, assessment, and research* (pp. 39–81). Homewood, IL: Dorsey.

Kanfer, F. H. (1985). Target selection for clinical change programs. *Behavioral Assessment, 10*, 107–121.

Kanfer, F. H., & Busemeyer, J. (1982). The use of problem-solving and decision-making in behavior therapy. *Clinical Psychology Review, 2,* 239–266.

Kanfer, F. H., & Schefft, B. K. (1988). *Guiding the process of therapeutic change.* Champaign, IL: Research Press.

Kazdin, A. E. (1985). Selection of target behaviors: The relationship of the treatment focus to clinical dysfunction. *Behavioral Assessment, 7,* 33–48.

Kazdin, A. E., & Kagan, J. (1994). Models of dysfunction in developmental psychopathology. *Clinical Psychology: Science and Practice, 1,* 35–52.

Kendall, P. C. (1985). Toward a cognitive-behavioral model of child psychopathology and a critique of related interventions. *Journal of Abnormal Child Psychology, 13,* 357–372.

Lazarus, A. A. (1980). *Multimodal Life History Questionnaire.* Kingston, NJ: Multimodal Publications.

Lochman, J. E., White, K. J., & Wayland, K. K. (1991). Cognitive-behavioral assessment and treatment with aggressive children. In P. C. Kendall (Ed.), *Child and adolescent therapy: Cognitive-behavioral procedures* (pp. 25–65). New York: Guilford Press.

Mash, E. J., & Hunsley, J. (1990). Behavioral assessment: A contemporary approach. In A. S. Bellack, M. Hersen, & A. E. Kazdin (Eds.), *International handbook of behavior modification and therapy* (2nd ed., pp. 87–106). New York: Plenum Press.

Mash, E. J., & Hunsley, J. (1993). Assessment considerations in the identification of failing psychotherapy: Bringing the negatives out of the darkroom. *Psychological Assessment, 5,* 292–301.

Nelson, R. O. (1988). Relationship between assessment and treatment within a behavioral perspective. *Journal of Psychopathology and Behavioral Assessment, 10,* 159–170.

Nezu, A. M. (1987). A problem-solving formulation of depression: A literature review and proposal of a pluralistic model. *Clinical Psychology Review, 7,* 121–144.

Nezu, A. M., & Nezu, C. M. (Eds.). (1989). *Clinical decision making in behavior therapy: A problem-solving perspective.* Champaign, IL: Research Press.

Nezu, A. M., & Nezu, C. M. (1991). Problem-solving skills training. In V. E. Caballo (Ed.), *Handbook of behavior modification and therapy techniques* (pp. 527–553). Madrid: Siglo Veintiuno de España Editores.

Nezu, A. M., & Nezu, C. M. (1993). Identifying and selecting target problems for clinical interventions: A problem-solving model. *Psychological Assessment, 5,* 254–263.

Nezu, A. M., Nezu, C. M., & Perri, M. G. (1989). *Problem-solving therapy for depression: Theory, research, and clinical guidelines.* New York: Wiley.

Nezu, A. M., Nezu, C. M., Saraydarian, L., Kalmar, K., & Ronan, G. F. (1986). Social problem solving as a moderating variable between negative life stress and depression. *Cognitive Therapy and Research, 10,* 489–498.

Nezu, A. M., & Ronan, G. F. (1985). Life stress, current problems, problem solving, and depressive symptoms: An integrative model. *Journal of Consulting and Clinical Psychology, 53,* 693–697.

Nezu, C. M., & Nezu, A. M. (1995). Clinical decision making in everyday practice: The science in the art. *Cognitive and Behavioral Practice, 2,* 5–25.

Nezu, C. M., Nezu, A. M., & Gill-Weiss, M. J. (1992). *Psychopathology in persons with mental retardation: Clinical guidelines for assessment and treatment.* Champaign, IL: Research Press.

Nezu, C. M., Nezu, A. M., & Houts, P. S. (1993). The multiple applications of prob-lem-solving principles in clinical practice. In K. T. Keuhlwein & H. Rosen (Eds.), *Cognitive therapy in action: Evolving innovative practice* (pp. 353–378). San Francisco: Jossey-Bass.

O'Brien, W. H., & Haynes, S. N. (1995). A functional analytic approach to the conceptualization, assessment and treatment of a child with frequent migraine headaches. *In Session, 1,* 65–80.

O'Donohue, W., & Krasner, L. (1995). Theories in behavior therapy: Philosophical and historical contexts. In W. O'Donohue & L. Krasner (Eds.), *Theories of be-havior therapy: Exploring behavior change* (pp. 1-22). Washington, DC: Ameri-can Psychological Association.

Ollendick, T. H., & Hersen, M. (1993). Child and adolescent behavioral assessment. In T. H. Ollendick & M. Hersen (Eds.), *Handbook of child and adolescent as-sessment* (pp. 3-14). Boston: Allyn & Bacon.

Pepper, S. C. (1942). *World hypotheses.* Berkeley: University of California Press.

Persons, J. B. (1989). *Cognitive therapy in practice: A case formulation approach.* New York: Norton.

Rosen, A., & Proctor, E. K. (1981). Distinctions between treatment outcomes and their implications for treatment evaluations. *Journal of Consulting and Clini-cal Psychology, 49,* 418–425.

Silva, F. (1993). *Psychometric foundations and behavioral assessment.* Newbury Park, CA: Sage.

Tversky, A., & Kahnemann, D. (1974). Judgment under uncertainty: Heuristics and biases. *Science, 185,* 1124–1131.

Wechsler, D. (1981). *Wechsler Adult Intelligence Scale—Revised.* San Antonio, TX: Psychological Corporation.

Weissman, A. N. (1978, November). *Development and validation of the Dysfunctional Attitude Scale.* Paper presented at the Annual Convention of the Association for Advancement of Behavior Therapy, Chicago.

Wilson, F. E., & Evans, I. M. (1983). The reliability of target behavior selection in behavioral assessment. *Behavioral Assessment, 15,* 15–32.

15

Case Formulation in Process-Experiential Therapy

RHONDA GOLDMAN
LESLIE S. GREENBERG

HISTORICAL BACKGROUND OF THE APPROACH

Our approach to case formulation emanates from a recently specified experiential approach to therapy referred to as process-experiential (PE) therapy (Greenberg, Rice, & Elliott, 1993). This model is informed by both humanistic–phenomenological theory (Rogers, 1951, 1957; Perls, Hefferline, & Goodman, 1951) and emotion and cognition theory (Arnold, 1960; Fridja, 1986; Pascual-Leone, 1984, 1991; Leventhal, 1984; Greenberg & Safran, 1987).

The Humanistic–Phenomenological Approach

A fundamental tenet underlying this approach is that the organism possesses an innate emotion-based system that provides an adaptive tendency toward growth and mastery; a corollary of this is that clients are viewed as experts on their own experience in that they have closest access to it. In the therapeutic hour, the therapist encourages the client to attend to momentary experiencing and nurtures the development of more adaptive functioning by continuously focusing the client on his or her experiencing. Growth in the client is constantly validated by focusing on adaptive needs and goals embedded in emotions and on the tendency toward adaptive flexibility (Greenberg et al., 1993; Rogers, 1957; Buber, 1960). Clients are consistently encouraged to identify and symbolize internal experience and bodily felt referents in order to create new meaning. Therapy is seen as facilitating conscious choice and reasoned action based on increased access to and awareness of inner experience and feeling.

In this view, the self is seen as an agent, constantly in flux, manifesting itself at the contact boundary with the environment (Perls, Hefferline, & Goodman, 1951). The person is constantly creating and synthesizing a set of internal schemes evoked in reaction to the situation, thereby reforming a "self-in-the-situation." Overly repetitive experiences of painful emotions across situations and occasions indicate lack of flexibility in the processing system and dysfunction; chronic enduring pain often represents rigid patterns of schematic activation and limited access to adaptive responses to situations. Psychological health is the ability to creatively adjust to situations and produce novel responses and experiences. The goal of treatment, therefore, is to overcome blocks to creative adjustment and to reinstate a "process of becoming."

PE therapy stresses the importance of self-acceptance and the ability to integrate various disowned aspects of self as well as the need for restructuring maladaptive emotional responses as a means of overcoming psychological dysfunction. Reowning involves overcoming the avoidance of disowned internal experience and disclaimed action tendencies and shifting from the negative evaluation of one's experience toward a more self-accepting stance. With the reowning of affect and associated action tendencies comes an increased sense of self-coherence and volition and the development of a sense that one is the agent of one's own experience. With the development of a coherent, agentic sense of self comes a greater sense of efficacy and mastery over one's psychological world.

In this approach, empathic attunement to affect and meaning is the therapist's primary medium of engagement. At all times, the therapist tries to make psychological *contact* with and convey a *genuine* understanding of the client's internal experience (Rogers, 1951, 1957). The therapist continually tracks what is important to the client throughout the session, constantly responding to what appears to be the client's central meanings. The approach involves the therapist actively entering into the client's internal frame of reference, resonating with the client's experience, and guiding the client's attentional focus to what the therapist hears as most crucial or poignant for the client at a particular moment (Rice, 1974; Vanaerschot, 1990).

The PE case formulation approach is very much embedded within the humanistic tradition, specifically client-centered and Gestalt therapy. Neither of these therapy theories, however, have developed a case formulation approach. Perls et al. (1951; also Perls, 1969) did not directly address the issue of case formulation but did identify interruptions to contact with self and other as boundary disturbances, or neurotic self-regulation. Interruptions such as projection, confluence, retroflection, introjection, and deflection were identified as producing current unhealthy functioning. Rogers (1951), on the other hand, worked with one universal formulation—that of incongruence between self-concept and experiencing. He was also opposed to most forms of assessment and wrote that "psychological diagnosis as usually understood is unnecessary for psychotherapy and may actually be detrimental to the therapeutic process" (p. 220). Rogers expressed concern about the "imbalance of power created when the therapist is in the position to diagnose, the possibility of an unhealthy dependency developing if the therapist plays the role of expert, and the possibility that diagnosing clients places social control of the many in the hands of the few" (1951, p. 224).

While we are largely in agreement with Rogers's concerns about expertness creating too great a power imbalance and interfering with the formation of a genuine relationship, we do hold the view that some form of formulation is beneficial. We believe that differential process formulations in our therapy help guide interventions and in so doing facilitate the development of a focus for treatment that ultimately enhances the healing process. The focus that develops is tantamount to a case formulation. Our particular approach to case formulation, however, stays very much within the bounds of the therapy tradition from which it emerges. In PE therapy, formulations are never performed a priori (i.e., based on early assessment), as we do not attempt to establish what is dysfunctional or presume to know what will be most salient or important for the client. We believe that what is most problematic, poignant, and meaningful best emerges progressively, in the safe context of the therapeutic environment. Like Rogers, we believe that assuming an authoritative position of deciding for ourselves on, or definitively informing clients as to, the source of their problems can (1) rupture the delicate interpersonal nature of the therapeutic bond, and (2) create situations wherein clients are prevented from discovering, through attention to their own emerging experience, that which is idiosyncratically meaningful and relevant to them—a powerful experiential learning process that is the key to change in this type of therapy.

Given this view, it is imperative in experiential therapy, that formulations be performed continuously on momentary experience or current states rather than being made about people as constants. Our major means of formulation are "process diagnoses," which indicate how people are currently impeding or interfering with their own experience. In relation to diagnoses, we believe that knowledge of certain nosological categories or syndromes can be helpful to experiential therapists but that they are best conceived of as descriptions of patterns of functioning rather than of types of people. Thus, for example, we prefer to think about anxious or obsessive processes rather than people.

Emotional Processing and Dysfunction

In this theoretical perspective, the organism is conceptualized as a complex self-organizing system that employs high-level information-processing structures, referred to as emotion schemes that tacitly apprehend patterns in situations and produce responses that create the organism's sense of being in the world (Greenberg et al., 1993; Greenberg & Paivio, 1997). Emotion schemes consist of a complex integration of perceptions, affects, needs, cognitions, and action tendencies that have developed from innate tendencies and responses to past experiences. In these past experiences, emotional reactions were encoded internally via three paths: *autonomically*, in terms of sensorimotor responses such as increased heart rate and a shrinking away in fear; *semantically*, in terms of such subjective meanings as "the image of my mother turning away from me"; and *conceptually*, in terms of such beliefs as "I am worthless." These together form an integrated scheme of self-experience in the world such as, in this instance, an experience of low self-confidence (Greenberg & Safran, 1987). In early formative years, syntheses of many schemes based on biologically adaptive primary emotions develop and continue to be currently adaptive. Some schemes that may have been adaptive in the person's early environment are now currently maladaptive (Greenberg & Safran, 1987; Greenberg & Korman, 1993) and are a source of emotional pain. Maladaptive schemes and the avoidance of pain associated with them constitute a primary source of dysfunction (Greenberg & Paivio, in press). Because of fears of annihilation in trauma, pain is often avoided, and when certain schemes that contain painful and traumatic memories are activated, the emotional material is often overwhelming and again avoided or the whole experience becomes dissociated. Such unresolved trauma results in a variety of emotional problems. Thus, much pathology comes from disowned emotional experience.

Past emotional learning thus influences present emotional processing styles and emotion regulation. In therapy, it is not essential to focus on content related to past experience. Although this might become a focus, PE therapy emphasizes increased awareness of present styles of self and affect regulation and a focus on current emotional processing. A focus on current client emotional states reveals important and relevant aspects of the personality.

Core maladaptive cognitive/affective schemes or organizing processes are seen as the underlying determinants that produce the dysfunctional feelings and meanings that people bring to therapy. Three major classes of determinants of emotional disturbances or barriers to healthy affect regulation have been delineated (Greenberg et al., 1993): (1) difficulties in symbolizing feelings, which results in confusion, self-alienation or general malaise; (2) the activation of maladaptive cognitive/affective emotion schemes that produce bad feelings and dysfunctional meanings such as feeling worthless, hopeless, or insecure (these prevent adaptive responding, influencing thought and action in maladaptive ways); and (3) the inability to integrate certain emotion schemes, resulting in splits between two opposing aspects of self (e.g., wishes and fears), or disowning (e.g., of anger) and dissociation from traumatic experience and memory. The goals of therapy, then, are to go beyond surface bad feelings, to access their determinants, and to restructure core maladaptive emotion schemes and/or integrate disowned emotional experience, as well as to enhance affect regulation and create new meanings.

A variety of therapeutic tasks, each designed to help resolve a particular type of processing difficulty, facilitate an ongoing focus on underlying dysfunctional emotion schemes that prevent healthy affect regulation and dysfunctional meanings. For example, evocative unfolding of problematic reactions helps people symbolize self-experience not previously symbolized. Unfinished business dialogues for resolving unfinished business help access maladaptive emotion schemes containing painful and disowned emotional memories and make them amenable to new information and reorganization. Two-chair dialogues for splits help clients to integrate opposing aspects of self to create a more unified sense of self (Greenberg et al., 1993).

CONCEPTUAL FRAMEWORK

Formulation involves a collaborative process of establishing a focus in the session and in the treatment as a whole. It involves the therapist making "process diagnoses," or formulations, of (1) what is occurring in the client at the moment and (2) how best to proceed with productive emotional exploration. This involves a moment-by-moment process of identifying the current determinants underlying the client's painful or uncomfortable experience and/or the means by which that experience is being interrupted. Formulation and intervention are, in the final analysis, inseparable, and both span the entire course of treatment. They also occur constantly at many levels. There is no discrete initial formulation or assessment phase. Instead, the therapist gets to know the client over time but never knows definitively what is occurring in the client. Formulation thus never ends.

Initially and throughout therapy sessions, the therapist is empathically attuned to the client's frame of reference, listening moment by moment for that which is currently most meaningful and poignant. It is through this coconstructive meaning-making expedition that therapists become apprised of how clients schematically organize their emotional world and eventually come to make process formulations. That is, through this continuing focus on the creation of meaning, markers arise that signal different types of cognitive/affective schematic processing problems. These markers inform the therapist on how to intervene differentially at different times. This is done by introducing therapeutic tasks that facilitate the working through of blocks to healthy meaning construction and affect regulation. Once in a mode of facilitating a particular task, the therapist is guided, both explicitly and tacitly by a preexisting map of how such tasks tend to unfold. These maps are formulations of optimal problem-solving processes. Rather than being instructional or thinking about the steps, the therapist attends, as fully as possible, to the client's momentary experience and, in response, makes miniformulations of how to facilitate experiential exploration through to resolutions of processing difficulties. Therefore, the therapist enters the client's meaning framework and intervenes at markers of dysfunctional schematic processing that interfere with adaptive responding. Over the course of therapy, continual work on these interferences forms a coherent thematic focus.

Moment-by-Moment versus Preliminary (A Priori) Formulation

We believe it is crucial to give priority to the person's experience in the moment, as this will reveal both the core pathogenic processes and how these are used to create meaning. A factual history taking conducted before therapy begins, or at the onset, does not provide the safe environment or the mode of experiential exploration necessary to allow feelings to emerge fully, thereby impeding the establishment of the true significance of the material. Material that emerges within a vivid, lively emotional context will reveal both that the material is important and what aspect(s) of it are of emotional significance. For example, factual information gathered about client "Joan's" relationship with her mother, without a discussion of feeling towards an evoked image of her mother, will yield less relevant information.

There is generally no need to plan a session focus; following the most salient phenomenology will lead to the most relevant material. Predictions or planning of particular contents to focus upon or the nature of underlying conflicts may only cause therapists to focus on their own agendas and miss the client's current state, thereby leading the therapy astray. Ultimately, the principle prevails that the client is the expert on his or her experience. In fact, proposing formulations as to underlying motivations or prescribing appropriate behavior is viewed as having the potential to block or disenable the client's experience from emerging. When clients feel understood and safe, they will reveal their inner experience, along with their manner of blocking it. This signals an opportunity for exploration. As this may be uncharted territory, the client and therapist together embark upon a meaning-finding and -making expedition.

The Therapeutic Relationship

Building the relationship is a primary goal of our approach to treatment and is the framework through which the formulation process occurs. The beginning stages of therapy are spent developing the relationship; the bond is continually monitored for the duration of therapy. A secure relationship is seen as curative in and of itself and as a necessary basis for further productive therapeutic work (Watson & Greenberg, 1995).

The relational context in therapy provides a secure bond that allows clients to access information in a manner that does not occur in an initial intake period. As a stable alliance is created, with agreed-upon goals and perceived relevance of task, clients will come to feel safer. This results in increased client participation, awareness, and disclosure. An egalitarian relationship is viewed as crucial in helping empower people. It is important that clients be active agents in the alliance-formation process, as this will engender their active participation, which is essential for successful treatment. In our view, problem definitions are always coconstructions that emerge from the relationship, rather than diagnoses imposed on clients. This establishment of a problem definition is tantamount to the agreement on treatment goals in the formation of the initial alliance (Bordin, 1994). This important aspect of the alliance involves the collaborative identification of core issues and the establishment of a thematic focus. In the establishment of the initial alliance, the initial tasks that the client needs to perceive as relevant to the treatment are the tasks of disclosure, exploration, and deepening of experience. Once engaged in these, the exploration for a focus begins.

Meaning and Poignancy

In each session, clients offer narratives that describe the impact of their world upon them. As therapists listen, they use the criteria of "meaning" and "poignancy" in establishing possible points of foci. Continually, the therapist is implicitly asking any or all of these questions: "What is the core meaning or message that she or he is communicating?" or "What is most alive?" or "What is being felt?" in the client narrative.

This dialogic process wherein the client and therapist together embark upon a meaning-making and -finding expedition is a crucial and distinguishing aspect of our approach to case formulation. Throughout the dialogue, the therapist refrains from applying a priori formulations and suspends judgments as long as possible on how healthy processing is being inhibited; the therapist does not want to constrain possible alternative emergent explanations. Furthermore, this attitude communicates that the therapist is not an expert on the client's experience and that the therapist is not interested in force-fitting the contents of the client's experience into any particular preexisting map or system. The therapist conveys respect for the client's system of making sense of his or her world and attempts to understand the client's overriding concerns. This focus on meaning is translated into an attempt to "see the world from the client's perspective," thereby conveying the attitude that the client's continuous symbolization of meaning will ultimately help the client access more flexible and adaptive methods for operating effectively.

The "poignancy" or vividness of how something is expressed reveals important information about the client's current mode of emotional processing. Poignancy is manifested in such nonverbal gestures as facial and vocal cues, sighs and pauses, and moments of emotional arousal. These are all crucial in signifying that certain content is more important than any other.

As the therapist reflects meaningful and emotionally laden material, the client in turn absorbs information and re-forms a view of his or her problems. The client's manner of creating meaning continuously provides windows into his or her system of synthesizing emotional schemes. By means of this process of attending to what is most live for the client, foci for treatment emerge.

Affective Problem Markers and Tasks

A focus on underlying determinants and the working through of maladaptive schemes is aided by the facilitation of client tasks that enable clients to explore and reintegrate previously disallowed or muted self-information. Particular affective problem markers and tasks may become increasingly more central as therapy progresses. Research has demonstrated that particular client in-therapy states are markers of particular types of dysfunctional processing that can be resolved in specific ways (Greenberg et al., 1993; Rice & Greenberg, 1984; Greenberg, Elliott, & Lietaer, 1994). A marker is defined as a verbal performance pattern that indicates some kind of problem. Markers signify particular types of affective problems that are currently amenable to particular interventions. The therapist therefore notices when a marker emerges and intervenes in a specific manner to facilitate resolution of that type of processing problem. The markers and the affective tasks that we have identified and studied are listed in Table 15.1 and are as follows:

1. Problematic reactions expressed through puzzlement about emotional or behavioral responses to particular situations indicate a readiness to explore by systematic evocative unfolding.
2. An unclear felt sense in which the person is on the surface of, or feeling confused and unable to get a clear sense of, his or her experience indicates a readiness for focusing.
3. Conflict splits in which one aspect of the self is critical or coercive toward another indicate readiness for a two-chair dialogue.

TABLE 15.1. Affective Markers, Tasks, and Resolution States

Marker	Task	End state
Problematic reaction point (self-understanding problem)	Systematic evocative unfolding	New view of self in-the-world-functioning
Absent or unclear felt sense	Experiential focusing	Symbolization of felt-sense; productive experiential processing
Self-evaluative split (self-criticism, tornness)	Two-chair dialogue	Self-acceptance, integration
Self-interruption (blocked feelings, resignation)	Two-chair enactment	Self-expression, empowerment
Unfinished business (lingering bad feeling re: specific other)	Empty-chair work	Forgive other or hold other accountable Affirm self/separate
Vulnerable (painful emotion related to self)	Empathic affirmation	Self-affirmation (feels understood, hopeful and strong)

4. Self-interruptive splits in which one part of the self interrupts or constricts emotional experience and expression indicate readiness for a two-chair enactment.

5. Unfinished business involving the statement of a lingering unresolved feeling toward a significant other indicates an opportunity for empty-chair dialogue.

6. Vulnerability in which the person feels deeply ashamed or insecure about some aspect of his or her experience indicates a need for empathic affirmation.

Markers of other important problem states and specific intervention processes that have been studied are alliance ruptures (Safran, Muran, & Samstag, 1994), misunderstanding events (Rhodes, Geller, Greenberg, & Elliot, 1992), and the creation of new meaning when a cherished belief has been disconfirmed (Clarke, 1989). Other more momentary cognitive/affective tasks that have been studied are the use of process suggestions to deepen levels of exploration (Sachse, 1990) and the use of specific types of interventions to influence the client's type of conceptual–perceptual processing (Toukmanian, 1986).

Session Focus and Emergent Themes

The formulation process involves the construction of in-session, process-diagnostic formulations that are made in response to the current material presented by the client. In each session, the therapist both follows and guides the client in a focused exploration of internal experience. In some sessions, this means continued exploration of momentary cognitive/affective processing, and encouraging awareness of internal experiencing. In other sessions, a marker might emerge that will lead to a formulation that it would be most productive to introduce a specific task. There is generally no definite plan that particular contents should be focused on in future sessions. In each session, the therapist waits to see what emerges for the client. As the self is seen to be reforming freshly in each moment, it is assumed that clients reorganize themselves differently each session, having reintegrated new information that may have emerged in the previous session and throughout the week. An underlying assumption of all therapeutic work is that clients have a tendency to work toward mastery in a facilitative environment. Thus, by closely attending to clients' current phenomenology, their efforts at resolving their problems and their blocks or interruptions to this will emerge.

While therapists do not direct content from one session to the next, therapists do facilitate a continuing focus on internal themes that consist of underlying emotional issues. For example, in one case, the therapy might repeatedly focus on feelings of insecurity and worthlessness. In another, unresolved anger may emerge as a focus. Focused empathic exploration and engagement in tasks often leads clients to important thematic material. Particularly, in successful cases, core thematic issues do seem to reemerge. Themes have been observed to fall into one of two or a combination of the following major classes: (1) problems in intrapersonal relations; or (2) problems in interpersonal relations (Goldman, 1995). Intrapersonal issues generally relate to self-definition and self-esteem, such as being overly self-critical, or perfectionistic, whereas interpersonal issues generally entail attachment and interdependence related issues such as feeling too dependent or vulnerable to rejection. Observations of these emergent themes support current theories espoused by Blatt, Quinlan, Chevron, McDonald, and Zuroff (1982) that problems arising as a result of developmental dysfunction are related to self-criticism or to dependence. It should be emphasized that in PE therapy, when statements arise that focus on either of these types of issues, therapists listen attentively, choosing only to respond to this information if it is poignant and alive. Again, manner is as important as content.

INCLUSION/EXCLUSION CRITERIA

Before PE therapy begins, a global assessment is conducted in which the client's appropriateness for this therapy is evaluated. If strong biological factors (i.e., a biochemical disorder) or factors that would deem the person more appropriate for marital or couples therapy are judged as being primary problem determinants, the client is considered inappropriate for this treatment. PE therapy is most suitable for dealing with moderate affective disorders or traumatic life events as well as interpersonal, identity, and existential problems. In addition, people who meet the following criteria are judged as not suitable for short-term PE treatment (16–20 weeks): high suicidal risk; long-term alcohol or drug addiction; three or more depressive episodes; psychotic conditions; and schizoid, schizotypal, borderline, and antisocial personality disorders. Long term PE treatment is not appropriate for schizoid, schizotypal, and antisocial personality disorders, as well as for psychotics. Beyond an initial assessment that the client satisfies the inclusion/exclusion criteria, that his or her problems are appropriate for individual psychotherapy, and that the client desires treatment, no other formal assessment is conducted. The person's ability to form an alliance is informally assessed at the outset and in an ongoing manner throughout PE treatment.

STEPS IN CASE FORMULATION CONSTRUCTION

The following four steps of PE case formulation are outlined below: (1) building of the therapeutic relationship; (2) assessment of the global style of processing; these are followed by the more specific phases of the formulation process involving (3) assessment of the momentary style of processing and (4) affective problem markers. Note that while these steps represent a sequence in which the formulation process occurs, the client and therapist will shuttle back and forth between the stages, depending on the demands of the therapeutic situation. Furthermore, the different aspects of formulation may occur simultaneously and over the course of the sessions. Thus, while the therapist is building the therapeutic relationship in the first few sessions, she or he may be making an assessment of the global style of processing. At any given point in a session, she or he may be assessing the momentary style of processing, and this in turn may affect the assessment of the global style of processing. In addition, depending on the needs of each particular client, more time may be spent on any of the stages. Each stage below will be illustrated with examples so that therapeutic situations can be identified that require further concentration at particular steps.

Building the Therapeutic Relationship

Building a stable alliance means both securing a therapeutic bond and establishing collaborative agreement to work. In the early stages, the therapist provides the relational conditions of congruence, empathy, and unconditional positive regard (Rogers, 1957) that are necessary to furnish such a safe working environment. The therapist listens to the client in a particular way, empathically entering the client's phenomenological frame of reference, using reflections of feelings and empathic exploration (Greenberg et al., 1993) to understand the client's meaning construction and reflect that which seems most poignant. This first step is necessary to allow the formulation process to emerge.

Through the empathic process, the client and therapist are continually negotiating the terms of the working relationship, clarifying what the problems are, and developing an agreement on the tasks, immediate goals, and responsibilities of treatment. In the initial stages, while the therapist may apply some of the steps of the PE case formulation this phase emphasizes making contact with and responding to the client and does not involve actively intervening.

Minimally, the first two sessions should be spent primarily focused on building the relationship. Throughout the course of therapy, however, the therapist continues to provide the relational conditions, as it is understood that productive exploration cannot occur without a trusting relationship. In addition, the therapist and client must have an ongoing implicit agreement on the tasks and goals of therapy. At times, therapists may sense or observe that they and their clients do not share a mutual understanding of the tasks and goals of therapy. This might be represented through the client's questioning the purpose or benefit of therapy, not wishing to engage in the cognitive/affective tasks, or missing sessions. It then becomes the therapist's responsibility to facilitate an explicit discussion in which tasks and goals are clarified and reestablished, and a safe environment is reinstated.

It should be noted that clients who present with a greater sense of fragility and/or difficulties with trust may require more sessions to secure a safe bond. Two sessions are a minimum requirement. Clients who have been victims of sexual abuse, incest, or extreme emotional abuse, for example, may require many more sessions of pure empathic responding in order to feel safe in the therapeutic environment.

The Global Style of Processing

Early in the therapy, the therapist makes formulations about the person's global processing style. The therapist assesses whether clients have the capacity to assume a self-focus and are able to turn attention inward to their experience. For this, therapists attend not only to clients' content but also to the manner and style in which they present their experiences. Attention is paid to *how* clients are presenting their experiences in addition to *what* they are saying. To aid therapists in reading such paralinguistic cues, they are trained to evaluate the following qualities (see Table 15.2): the client's vocal quality (CVQ) (Rice & Kerr, 1986) as well as his or her current depth of experiencing (EXP) (Klein, Mathieu, Gendlin, & Kiesler, 1969), and the concreteness, specificity, and vividness of language use.

Four vocal styles relevant to experiential processing have been defined: focused, emotional, limited, and external (Rice & Kerr, 1986). For example, a therapist will notice when a client's voice becomes more focused. This is an indication that the client's attentional energy is turned inward and the person is attempting to freshly symbolize experience. When a client's speech pattern is disrupted to some extent by emotional overflow, this is an indication that the client is actively experiencing and expressing emotions. This is classified as an emotional voice. Alternatively, a highly external voice, that is, one which has a premonitored quality involving a great deal of attentional energy being deployed outward, may indicate a more rehearsed conceptual style of processing and a lack of spontaneity. Although this may initially give an impression of expressiveness, the rhythmic intonation pattern conveys a "talking at" quality. It is unlikely that content being expressed in this voice is freshly experienced. A high degree of external vocal quality suggests that the person does not have a strong propensity to self-focus. Alternatively, a limited voice is characterized by a holding back or withdrawal of energy. This vocal quality is indicated by an effect of thinness and lack of energy that is more pronounced than in an inward or outward focus. This indicates tension and conscious control of what is being said and probably of what is being experienced (Rice & Kerr, 1986).

Clients who demonstrate none or little focused or emotional voice are seen as less emotionally accessible and needing further work to help them process internal experiential information. Clients with a high degree of external vocal quality need to be helped to focus inward, whereas those with a high degree of limited vocal quality need a safe environment to develop trust in the therapist and allow them to relax. Empathic understanding, explorations, and conjectures (Goldman, 1991; Greenberg et al., 1993) are used with all clients

TABLE 15.2. Steps of the PE Case Formulation Process

A. Building the therapeutic relationship
   1. Establish safe bond
   2. Implicit or explicit agreement on goals and tasks of therapy

B. Assessment of the global style of processing
   1. Client vocal quality
      a. Focused
      b. Emotional
      c. Limited
      d. External
   2. Client depth of experiencing
      a. Level 1: Impersonal
      b. Level 2: Superficial
      c. Level 3: Externalized
      d. Level 4: Direct focus on experience
      e. Level 5: Proposition about self from internal perspective
      f. Level 6: Forming new view of self
      g. Level 7: Continually expanding exploration of new views of self
   3. Concreteness versus abstractness
   4. Specificity versus generality
   5. Vividness of language use

C. Assessment of momentary cognitive/affective style
   1. Conceptual versus experiential processing
   2. Internal versus external processing
   3. Primary, secondary, or instrumental emotional responding

D. Affective problem markers
   1. Puzzlement about emotional or behavioral responses
   2. An unclear felt sense or confusion about experience
   3. Conflict splits in which one part of the self is critical or coercive toward another
   4. Self-interruptive splits in which one part of the self constricts emotional expression
   5. Unfinished business involving a significant other
   6. Expression of vulnerability

---

to explore what clients are experiencing, encourage a focus on bodily felt referents, and promote ongoing internal experiencing.

Another indicator of current capacity for self-focus is client initial depth of experiencing (Klein et al., 1969). The Experiencing scale (EXP) defines clients involvement in inner referents and experience from impersonal (level 1) and superficial (level 2) through externalized or limited references to feelings (level 3) to direct focus on inner experiencing and feelings (level 4), to questioning or propositioning the self about internal feelings and personal experiences (level 5), to experiencing an aspect of self from a new perspective (level 6), to a point where awareness of present feelings are immediately connected to internal processes and exploration is continually expanding (level 7). An example that would indicate level 4 experiencing might be the following:

CLIENT: When I saw him sitting across the room, I began to feel edgy. My stomach began to tense up. I started feeling so sad. I guess I kind of long for him. . . .

This indicates that the client is in contact with self-experience and is being associative and descriptive. Therapists are trained to know the different stages of EXP, and while they are not conceptually using the scale during therapy, this view of experiencing implicitly guides exploration. At any given moment a therapist can approximately identify at what level of EXP the client is functioning.

At this stage in the formulation process, the therapist is also listening to the following aspects of processing: (1) concreteness, such as how real or actual as opposed to abstract the material is manifested in the current moment or talked about in everyday life, and (2) specificity as opposed to generality, in terms of how the material uniquely relates to the client. For example, the statement "When she turned her head away from me, I felt unwanted and unloved" is concrete and specific, whereas the statement "It's depressing when I am ignored" is abstract and general. In addition, attention is paid to vividness of language use, such as the poignancy and liveliness of images and feelings that are conjured up by the material. A high degree of concreteness, specificity, and vividness of language use indicates a strong self-focus and high involvement in working. In summary, formulation at this global level involves evaluations of the nature of current emotional processing style and process diagnoses of how to best facilitate a focus on internal experiencing.

The Momentary Manner of Cognitive/Affective Processing

Formulations at this level involve assessments of the current manner of cognitive/affective processing and of how to intervene optimally from one moment to the next. They occur in both ongoing therapeutic interaction and when facilitating specific affective tasks. The therapist (1) assesses whether the client is processing primarily at an experiential or a conceptual and external level and (2) distinguishes different types of emotional expression.

Conceptual and external processing involves making an intellectual assessment about an object or situation outside of the self. An example of this type of processing is (said in an angry manner), "He is so dominant because he always wants to be in control," to which the therapist might respond "You are feeling pretty angry toward him." Conceptual processing is seen as useful at times in therapy, particularly after internal (and reflexive) processing has occurred. The internal mode of processing, however, is one that many clients are unfamiliar with and/or unable to achieve on their own, particularly in relation to painful or disowned feelings and experiences. It is also seen as necessary for productive exploration to occur.

To aid in formulation of momentary states, therapists are also trained to distinguish primary, secondary and instrumental emotional responses (Greenberg & Safran, 1987; Greenberg et al., 1993). Primary emotions are here-and-now direct responses to situations. Examples of primary emotions are sadness in relation to loss and anger in response to violation. Secondary emotions are reactive responses to more primary emotions or thoughts. They often obscure the primary generating process. Secondary anger, for example, is often expressed when the primary feeling is fear, or people may cry when their primary emotion is anger. Instrumental emotions are those expressions that are used to achieve an aim, such as expressing sadness to elicit comfort or anger in order to intimidate (Greenberg & Safran, 1989; Greenberg & Paivio, 1997).

The primary goal in differentiating emotional responses is to access the primary organismic emotional response that has not been acknowledged and must be incorporated. The therapist evaluates the nature of emotional expressions based on such nonverbal cues as vividness of language use, vocal quality, and facial and bodily expression, as well as on biological emotional responding, such as responses that occur in response to violation, threat, and goal attainment. For example, a person may express anger in a high-pitched airy tone, with a ranting quality (secondary feelings) that the therapist judges is actually overlaying hurt (primary feelings). The therapist might therefore say, "I hear that you feel very angry right now, and I imagine that inside you are feeling quite hurt."

Affective Problem Markers

This level of formulation involves the identification of affective problem markers. Manuals that guide the identification of six particular markers (see Table 15.1) have been specified and studied (Greenberg et al., 1993). An example of a verbal marker for a two-chair dialogue to resolve a self-evaluative split might occur as "Jim," a client, is talking about feeling like a failure in his work, saying "I'm just not good enough." The therapist would make a process diagnostic formulation that two parts of the self, an evaluative and an evaluated part, are operating and that it would be productive to implement a two-chair dialogue. An example of a marker for unfinished business might be client "Ellen" expressing sadness when she remembers her father forgetting her birthday when she was 8 years old.

APPLICATION TO PSYCHOTHERAPY TECHNIQUE

The different steps of formulation inform the therapist of what techniques to employ. Momentary interventions are implemented in response to assessments of the global style of processing and momentary cognitive/affective processing, and affective markers indicate the facilitation of affective tasks.

Momentary Interventions

Momentary interventions can take a number of different forms depending on the intention behind the response. There are three overall classes of responses in PE therapy that can be described in terms of "response intentions": (1) Empathic understanding, (2) Empathic exploration, and (3) Process directions. *Empathic understanding*, as it is carried out through various responses, seeks to communicate that the therapist grasps and appreciates the client's message. *Empathic exploration* responses are designed to facilitate client's self-search. These responses take a number of different forms, including exploratory reflections, exploratory questions, and empathic conjectures. *Process directions* address the flow and structure of the therapy session but not its content. The therapist does not give advice, but rather will suggest that the client try certain things within the session to facilitate present exploration and problem resolution. Different types of responses that fall within these three classes have been delineated and manualized (Greenberg et al., 1993; Goldman, 1991).

Different momentary formulations will lead to different momentary interventions. At a particular point in a session, an assessment of momentary cognitive/affective processing may indicate that a client is processing at a conceptual level. The therapist might attempt to reflect back the client's underlying feeling and meaning, focusing the person inward on internal experience. When clients are already processing at an internal level, therapists must decide how best to facilitate experiential exploration. At another time, the therapist may formulate, in an assessment of the global style of processing, that a client is processing at a low level of experiencing. The therapist may then choose to facilitate deeper experiencing, by conjecturing empathically as to what the client is presently experiencing. On the other hand, the therapist may choose to convey empathic understanding through an empathic reflection. Other formulations may induce the therapist to encourage self-reflexive questions about the nature of current internal experience.

Affective Tasks

Formulations of particular affective markers indicate the introduction of specific tasks. The stages involved in the resolution of affective tasks have been intensively analyzed and modeled. These models offer specific guidance to therapists on how to make appropriate momentary "process diagnoses," or assessments of current cognitive/affective states throughout the tasks. They also help therapists to determine at what point a particular intervention will facilitate further exploration and ultimately the resolution of the particular task (Greenberg et al., 1993).

For example, according to the model of the resolution of a self-evaluative conflict split, when a marker such as "I'm just not good enough" arises, the therapist would first ask Jim, the client, to put the evaluative side of himself in one chair and to make the other side feel like a failure. When an internalized self-critic is accessed, the therapist asks Jim to express some of the contempt or harshness of that critic—for instance, "You make me sick." Once the harshness of the critic has been accessed, the therapist will facilitate the dialogue by encouraging the expression of more specific criticisms: "You do not work hard enough. You are stupid." This work with the critic continues until such time as the underlying maladaptive emotion scheme of failure and inadequacy is accessed in the experiencing self. At this time the therapist makes another process diagnosis that it is necessary to express underlying feelings and therefore asks Jim to express feelings to the critic in the other chair (i.e., "I feel worthless when you say that, I feel like a nothing"). The therapist will continue to make such process diagnoses throughout the dialogue, facilitating the appropriate action at the appropriate moment. After accessing primary adaptive feelings, the therapist will encourage an assertion of needs toward the critic. Once the needs, on the one hand, and the values and standards underlying the criticisms, on the other, have been put in dialectical opposition, the therapist will continue to facilitate a shift or a softening of the critic. All these steps are viewed as helping the client to integrate the conflicting aspects of self (Greenberg et al., 1993). As is evident through this example, the facilitation of affective client tasks require therapists to make specific types of moment-by-moment formulations and interventions.

According to the model of resolution of an unfinished business dialogue, if Ellen expresses sadness remembering her father missing her eighth birthday, the therapist would ask the client to put her father in another chair (in imagination) and express feelings to him in an imaginary dialogue. When feelings of sadness have been accessed, deeper exploration may remind Ellen of other experiences of feeling abandoned and neglected by her father. The therapist would make a process diagnosis that it is necessary to express those feelings to her father in the empty chair. The schematic emotional memories of feeling neglected and abandoned, worthless and unlovable, would probably emerge. Momentary formulations of cognitive/affective processing allow therapists to differentiate feelings of blame and complaint into expressions of pure sadness and pure anger. Clients usually learn to interrupt such intense feelings in early life. After promoting the full expression of either one and/or the other, the therapist will facilitate an expression of the unmet need(s). Each step of this process is guided by formulations informed by the model that explicates what processing proposals to offer at what point to best facilitate the next step toward task resolution.

An affective marker such as client "Matt" reporting a puzzling outburst of anger toward a spouse would indicate the introduction of an evocative unfolding of a problematic reaction (see Table 15.1). Initially, the therapist would vividly evoke the scene in which the reaction occurred, and then help Matt determine the salient element(s) in the situation that triggered the reaction (e.g., his wife's scornful look). Next, the therapist would help Matt further explore his reaction of anger and attend to other associated feelings such as hurt and vulnerability. When such feelings have been sufficiently explored, Matt will likely begin to broaden his scope of understanding. At this point, clients tend to move from their idiosyncratic construal of the situation to a more general exploration of self. In this example, the client might understand how his reactive anger is accompanied by underlying vulnerability in different situations.

CASE EXAMPLE

"Jan" was a 44-year-old woman who entered therapy feeling depressed. Currently involved in her second marriage, she felt that the communication had broken down and the marriage was "on the rocks." She had left home at the age of 16. Home was a place where she remembered feeling overburdened with responsibility, underappreciated, and emotionally neglected. She soon entered her first marriage, in which she was emotionally and physically abused. After 6 years Jan left this marriage, leaving behind her two sons. She feared that taking them with her might put all of them into danger. Jan carried a great deal of grief over her decision to leave her sons with their father, in spite of presently being on good terms with them. The client had been screened for her appropriateness for short-term PE therapy of depression (16–20 sessions). She was currently displaying a number of somatic symptoms including indigestion and hives.

The Case Formulation Process

In the first sessions, the therapist was primarily concerned with establishing a therapeutic bond by demonstrating empathic understanding. By responding to "central meaning" and "poignant" feelings, she begins to create windows into internal experiencing. Following will be a description of how formulation begins to occur on a momentary basis, leading to the emergence of a thematic treatment focus.

In the following segment from the first session of therapy, the client describes her fear of losing control. The therapist listens empathically, validating painful feelings and slowly focusing on her manner of momentary cognitive/affective processing. The client's discussion of her fear of losing control later evolves into a central theme of Jan's need to be strong, perfect, and infallible. At this point, it is too early to identify a clear point of focus. Instead, the therapist makes momentary processing proposals that keep the client focused on current feelings. At times throughout the excerpts, commentary is provided to explain the therapist's response intentions and momentary interventions.

CLIENT: Well, part of me wants to ignore it all and pretend it is not happening; you see, I've always been the strong one you know who's in control of everything and I don't like these feelings.

THERAPIST: So it kind of feels like you shouldn't be like this. [Exploratory reflection]

CLIENT: I feel I'm letting myself down and people down; I cry so easily and I'm not in control of my emotions.

THERAPIST: Sounds like there's a lot of feelings in there. Why don't we explore some of that, 'cause I understand that there's a part of you that wants to curl up and kind of ignore it, but uh, since you are here I imagine there's a part of you that doesn't, that's aware that you're hurting and you need to talk.

It is apparent early on that this client's global style of processing is primarily an internal one. She often speaks in a focused or emotional voice, and when things feel painful she turns inward rather than becoming external and blaming. Also, from an early stage, she reaches level 4 on the EXP Scale. The therapist takes note that she has a strong capacity for self-focus and that a continued exploration at the edges of the client's internal feeling will likely lead to a deepening focus on emotional processing problems.

In the following sequence, the client describes what turns out later to be a central theme during therapy. At this point, however, the therapist has not apprehended the full significance of the client's issue (her difficulty seeing her self as weak, imperfect and vulnerable). The therapist hears the poignancy with which Jan states the problem, and the internal searching quality in her voice and manner of speech. The therapist also conveys an understanding of the *potential* pervasiveness of the issue in the client's life. The therapist and client engage in the coconstructive meaning-making process wherein the therapist shares her belief that Jan's lack of attention to feelings and needs has lead to a great deal of suffering. The therapist communicates that an exploration of Jan's feelings could lead to an alleviation of symptoms. Through this intervention, the therapist is establishing an implicit agreement to make core underlying maladaptive schemes a thematic point of therapy. Note that the therapist is attempting to deepen the focus of the therapy, not "point out" the client's problems. If this type of exploration is not fruitful, the therapist will follow that which is poignant and meaningful, knowing that the exploration will eventually lead to important material.

CLIENT: I guess over the years, I have this image of myself as superwoman, to be able to do everything, hold down a full-time job, do the cleaning, cook gourmet meals, do all the housework, drive my family around, be there for them when they need me.

THERAPIST: So that's why you are here then, to try to understand, you are aware of a lot of feelings, a lot happening in your life, you work very hard for everybody, you are there for your whole family, you are the one who should be working hard, sounds like a lot.

CLIENT: Well, I guess I put myself in that role, and maybe I'm not happy in it anymore and I don't know how to get out of it.

THERAPIST: Well I guess that's our job in here to explore together. . . . But I guess it says a lot about how much you have really suffered, sounds like your body and your emotional world inside, everything, has been really hurting . . .

CLIENT: Well part of me says give into it, and a part of me says there are people who are worse off than yourself.

THERAPIST: so because you haven't had to endure all the horrible stuff some people have . . . sounds like that is the same part that says you should be able to do everything, your work, your husband's work . . . there's a lot of *shoulds* there . . .

In the following few sessions, the therapist continues to follow the client's internal track, listening for emotional meaning and poignancy, and focusing on underlying determinants that could be causing her current suffering.

Session 2 was spent talking about an ongoing conflict Jan is having with her sister. Her sister will not speak to her, and Jan feels "slapped down." The therapist listens carefully, helping Jan to symbolize her feelings about the issue. While it is important for the therapist to understand Jan's concerns at this point, her conflict with her sister does not directly become a central theme of the therapy.

In Session 4, she reports censoring her desire to be more open with her husband, for fear of him laughing at her or changing the subject. The therapist recognizes the unfinished business and takes this opportunity to suggest an intervention wherein Jan can express her feelings to her husband in the empty chair:

CLIENT: I actually wanted to discuss it with my husband, how I felt, but I couldn't make myself do it. I can't talk to him yet about what's going on in here.

THERAPIST: You would like to be able to open up but it's kind of tough. I'm wondering if we could bring him in here, and you could talk to him, and we could help you with this kind of block or whatever it is you feel kind of apprehensive of. [Structuring the task]

As the dialogue progresses, the client expresses anger over feeling shut down, and lingering resentment over not feeling like her husband's top priority. Jan also begins to see that a part of her is actually prohibiting herself from being vulnerable with him and expressing feelings:

CLIENT: I feel this feeling coming over me of wanting to be in complete control, I feel she is very strong and independent. . . . I guess I have fought all my life to be independent and not be wishy-washy.

Later in the session, she realizes—

CLIENT: How can I be upset because somebody doesn't give me the things I want when I don't allow him to.

In some respects, this dialogue has helped her to crystallize one of her central themes: her tendency to undervalue her feelings and deny her needs.

In Session 6, Jan reports a recent family conflict over a Christmas dinner that her parents have canceled because of conflicts with their youngest daughter, Ann. Jan feels hurt and unappreciated, particularly by her mother—a marker of unfinished business. The therapist suggests having a dialogue with Jan's mother in the empty chair:

THERAPIST: What do you see, what does she look like? [Evoking the sensed presence of the significant other]

CLIENT: I don't see a happy women. She's always got a scowl on her face.

THERAPIST: What's happening to you? [Accessing client's initial feelings in response to significant other]

CLIENT: I feel like I'm going to break down and cry (*starts to cry*).

THERAPIST: Just let the tears come. What are you feeling right now, can you tell her? [Promoting expression of primary/adaptive feelings to significant other]

CLIENT: It hurts to see you so unhappy, it rubs off and it makes me unhappy too. I guess it hurts that I am second best, I guess because I am the oldest one, I'm supposed to be responsible for everyone so my feelings get pushed aside.

The dialogue helps Jan to consolidate what becomes a third and important theme throughout therapy: her need for approval, particularly from her mother. Later in the dialogue—

THERAPIST: What do you want from her? [Facilitating expression of unmet need to significant other]

CLIENT: I'd like you to acknowledge that I'm as lovable as I am.

THERAPIST: Let it come, let those tears come, tell her how much you are feeling now, can you speak from those tears and tell her how hurt you are. [Facilitating full expression of primary adaptive emotion to significant other]

CLIENT: I've been carrying this around for years and it's finally dawned on me, I've been trying for so many years to make you happy and do everything but no matter what I do it's never enough.

A retrospective content analysis of the therapy revealed that at this point three major themes had emerged although themes had not been formally identified. Two of them were intrapersonally related and one was more interpersonal in nature. They were as follows:

1. *A need to be perfect.* Jan felt that she had to be perfect in every respect in order to be lovable. Being perfect meant being independent and strong in her capacity as daughter, wife, sister, and friend. She felt bad about herself if she did not live up to these standards.

2. *Difficulty legitimizing feelings.* Jan did not value her own feelings and needs, and constantly put others before herself. She believed that feelings of vulnerability were signs of weakness and must be controlled. She had trouble disclosing her feelings and asserting her needs.

3. *An unmet need for approval and acceptance from her mother.* Jan still longed to be the "good little girl" who always did right by her parents. (This theme only became more fully fleshed out later in therapy.)

For Jan in particular, these three themes were highly interrelated but were also discrete and worked through via different types of affective interventions (see Table 15.1). While the therapist may have been aware early in treatment that important core material was emerging, she did not identify these as themes that demanded concentration throughout therapy. That is, the themes did not dictate the focus of the sessions that followed, although they did reemerge through a careful following of the client's ongoing experience. Each session was clearly informed by what happened earlier but was a fresh exploration of the client's current concerns and usually lead to the working through of the core underlying determinants embodied in the themes.

Applying the Formulation in Therapy

The resolution of these themes occurred through ongoing momentary interventions and affective tasks. The remaining sessions involved ongoing formulations of momentary cognitive/affective processing and affective tasks. Based on these formulations, the therapist performed appropriate momentary interventions and affective tasks.

In the next two subsections the process by which two of these themes reemerged will be described and the formulations that indicated particular affective interventions will be explicated.

Theme 1: Need to Be Strong, Perfect, and Infallible

In Session 10, Jan reported a current conflict with her husband in which she felt afraid to reveal her fears and wishes in relation to their financial situation. She does not want to confront him because she is afraid she will lose emotional control—break down and cry. She feels that she should be strong and independent, and resolve the problem within herself. The therapist formulates the marker for a two-chair dialogue and suggests putting the different aspects of herself into two separate chairs. The dialogue reveals a "strong" part of herself that feels the other part is weak for needing people (momentary therapist interventions are specified throughout sample transcripts):

THERAPIST: Tell her what you feel toward her. [Promoting awareness of self-criticisms]

CLIENT: You should be less needy, you are weak.

The other part of herself feels afraid and does not want to hurt her husband. She feels she needs his approval. A shift in the dialogue occurs after the client has accessed primary sadness about how alone she feels in the marriage and when the therapist encourages her to express her needs:

THERAPIST: What do you want from her [critic]? [Encouraging expression of need]

CLIENT: I want to be more like her, to feel more confident.

THERAPIST: What are you feeling like? [Facilitating negotiation]

CLIENT: I feel that the two sides have suddenly merged: it is as if the stronger person came over here and sat with me and said you're OK.

Later in the session she says to her critic in the other chair:

CLIENT: I'm not so scared anymore to confront the issues, I feel like stronger and like you are going to protect me.

Theme 2: Need for Approval from Her Mother

In Session 9, Jan talks about her guilt about leaving her two sons with her ex-husband, worrying that she "messed up their lives." Despite feeling that her sons have forgiven her, she feels unable to forgive herself. In Session 11, she works through the conflict in an empty-chair dialogue through which she confronts her mother's extreme disapproval of her decision:

CLIENT: Mom, I don't think we're ever going to see eye to eye—because you see it in a different light.

THERAPIST: Can you tell her how you feel? [Differentiating feelings to the significant other]

CLIENT: I feel that I've lived my life to please everybody else, and it's been very hard and I don't want to do it anymore, and maybe we should agree that your life has been hard and you will never understand how difficult it has been for me.

THERAPIST: Is there anything you want from her? [Facilitating expression of unfulfilled needs and expectations in regard to the other]

CLIENT: Don't expect so much from me anymore, 'cause I don't think I'm going to be able to deliver it.

THERAPIST: How do you feel saying that?

CLIENT: I don't feel so guilty anymore, that I can't jump everytime they want something. . . . It's been a real burden trying to live up to what everybody else thought of me and it's made me very sad.

In Session 13, Jan reports feeling more self-confident, in charge of her life, and able to make changes. She continues to report positive feelings for the duration of therapy. In Session 14, she reports standing up to her mother, not letting her push her around, and feeling more self-confidence in asserting her needs. In Session 15, she takes responsibility for trying to be "superwoman" and not allowing others to help her:

CLIENT: I put myself in the position of trying to protect and serve everybody. . . . I always felt I could be superwoman, that I could handle two full-time jobs, do all the housework.

THERAPIST: You were never going to show any vulnerability. [Exploratory reflection]

CLIENT: Yeah, I never asked for help.

Later in the session, she reports an awareness that she was the one devaluing her own feelings:

CLIENT: I felt like such a whiner, complaining and crying, but it was me discrediting my emotions. My feelings do count, they are legitimate, sometimes they may be foolish but that's OK.

Finally, in Session 16, she portrays a much more confident, self-valuing stance:

CLIENT: It's useless to think that way, and it's OK not to be liked by everybody, that's all right, I can't kill myself trying to please everybody. If I don't start looking after myself nobody is going to do it for me.

Case Summary

By the end of 16 sessions of therapy, Jan feels more self-assured and able to stand up for herself. She feels that her feelings and needs are legitimate and feels more entitled to express them. She feels that taking care of herself is as important as being liked by those around her, including her husband and family.

Jan showed improvement on all outcome measures that were used to assess a group of 17 clients who were administered PE therapy in a study of depression (Greenberg & Watson, 1993). Specifically, on the Beck Depression Inventory, her mean dropped from 30 before treatment to 5 at posttreatment (*SD* change = 4.36); on the Rosenberg Self-Esteem Scale, her mean scored moved from 25 to 37 (*SD* = 2.07); on the Inventory for Interpersonal Problems, her mean score dropped from 1.51 to 0.58 (*SD* change = 3.37); and on the Symptom Checklist 90-R, the Global Symptom index dropped from a mean of 1.79 to 0.33 (*SD* change = 4.5). Jan maintained these gains and even improved on some of these after 6 and 18 months.

TRAINING

Greenberg et al. (1993) specifies many of the techniques necessary to apply the case formulation method in a manualized form, including relationship-building techniques, empathic responding techniques, and steps involved in the facilitation of affective tasks. In addition, PE therapy trainees should learn the process measures mentioned previously in this chapter including the Client Vocal Quality (CVQ) Scale (Rice & Kerr, 1986), and the Experiencing Scale (EXP) (Klein et al., 1969). Such training helps the therapist to better assess the client's capacity for self-focus as well as improves the therapist's capacity for empathic attunement. The current chapter specifies the steps of the PE case formulation method in more detail than any other sources. The interested reader is, however, referred to sources such as Greenberg and Goldman (1988), wherein the training steps are more carefully outlined. Finally, demonstrations films of PE therapy have been published and are available (Greenberg, 1990, 1994).

RESEARCH SUPPORTING THE APPROACH

Various research studies support aspects of the method of case formulation described here. For example, recent research indicates that raters can reliably agree (kappa = .93) on client's level of vocal quality on 2097 two-minute segments of therapy tape, as well as on client depth of experiencing (*r* = .75) on 1170 two-minute segments of therapy transcript, thus supporting the notion that therapists can assess client's capacity for self-focus. In addition, studies indicate that raters can reliably distinguish markers for affective tasks such as unfinished business, two-chair conflict split, and problematic reaction points (Greenberg & Rice, 1991).

While PE case formulation does not involve a priori formulations, research has shown that in successful cases ongoing momentary formulations throughout sessions do result in particular themes emerging by the middle of therapy that form a strong focus of treatment, and that these themes relate to either intrapersonal or interpersonal issues, or both (Goldman, 1995). Research also indicates that focusing on these themes through engagement in particular affective tasks predicts resolution and is predictive of success in treatment. In a study by Singh (1994), for example, a self-report instrument was used to track the resolution of unfinished business with a significant other throughout 12–16 sessions of PE therapy and to relate repeated resolution to final outcome. Results showed that by Session 6 the degree of resolution reported by clients on postsession reports predicted decreases in symptoms and interpersonal problems as well as an increase in self-acceptance at termination and follow-up. By termination, the degree of resolution was also predictive of changes in perception of self as well as how affiliative clients felt toward the significant other with whom they had the unfinished business. Finally, empirical support has been documented for the efficacy of experiential therapy, and in particular of PE therapy that operates by the approach to case formulation articulated above (Paivio & Greenberg, 1995; Greenberg & Watson, 1995; Greenberg et al., 1994).

CONCLUSION

Case formulation in PE therapy is a moment-by-moment diagnostic process that leads to the identification of underlying determinants that are causing painful bad feelings. The case of Jan demonstrated how initially the therapist assumes a less active, nondiagnostic role, providing the relational conditions necessary to establish a bond and attain agreement to work. Through the course of sessions, by actively following the client's momentary meaningful experience, that which was most thematic for the client emerged and became focal. Through the ongoing formulation of affective markers and tasks, the client and therapist focused upon and reconstructed Jan's underlying maladaptive emotion schemes by symbolizing and integrating previously disowned experience. Thus, PE therapy helped Jan find more healthy and adaptive modes of functioning.

REFERENCES

Arnold, M. B. (1960). *Emotion and personality* (Vols. 1 & 2). New York: Columbia University Press.

Blatt, S.J., Quinlan, E. S., Chevron, C., McDonald, & Zuroff, C., (1982). Dependency and self-criticism: Psychological dimensions of depression. *Journal of Consulting and Clinical Psychology, 150*, 113–124.

Bordin, E. (1994). Theory and research on the therapeutic working alliance: New directions. In A. O. Horvath, & L. S. Greenberg (Eds.), *The working alliance: Theory, research, and practice* (pp. 13–37). New York: Wiley-Interscience.

Buber, M. (1960). *I and thou.* New York: Scribner's.

Clarke, K. M. (1989). Creation of meaning: An emotional processing task in psychotherapy. *Psychotherapy: Theory, Research, and Practice, 26*, 139–148.

Fridja, N. H. (1986). *The emotions*. Cambridge, England: Cambridge University Press.

Goldman, R. (1991). *The validation of the experiential therapy adherence measure*. Unpublished master's thesis, Department of Psychology, York University, Toronto, Ontario, Canada.

Goldman, R. (1995, June). *The relationship between depth of experiencing and outcome in a depressed population*. Paper presented at a meeting of the Society for Psychotherapy Research, Vancouver, British Columbia, Canada.

Greenberg, L. S. (1990). *Integrative psychotherapy, Part V: A demonstration with Dr. Leslie Greenberg*. Corona Del Mar, CA: Psychological and Educational Films.

Greenberg, L. S. (1994). *Process experiential psychotherapy*. Washington, DC: American Psychological Association Publications.

Greenberg, L. S., Elliott, R., & Lietaer, G. (1994). Research on humanistic and experiential psychotherapies. In A. E. Bergin & S. L. Garfield (Eds.), *Handbook of psychotherapy and behaviour change* (4th ed.). New York: Wiley.

Greenberg, L. S., & Goldman, R.N. (1988). Training in experiential therapy. *Journal of Consulting and Clinical Psychology, 56*, 696–702.

Greenberg, L. S., & Korman, L. (1993). Assimilating emotion into psychotherapy integration. *Journal of Psychotherapy Integration, 3*(3), 249–265.

Greenberg, L. S., & Paivio, S. C. (1997). *Working with emotions in psychotherapy*. New York: Guilford Press.

Greenberg, L. S., & Rice, L. N. (1991). *Change processes in experiential psychotherapy* (National Institute of Mental Health Grant 1R01MH45040). Washington, DC: U.S. Department of Health and Human Services.

Greenberg, L. S., Rice, L. N., & Elliott, R. (1993). *Facilitating emotional change: The moment-by-moment process*. New York: Guilford Press.

Greenberg, L. S., & Safran, J. D. (1987). *Emotion in psychotherapy: Affect, cognition, and the process of change*. New York: Guilford Press.

Greenberg, L. S., & Safran, J. D. (1989). Emotion in psychotherapy, *American Psychologist, 44*, 19–29.

Greenberg, L. S., & Watson, J. (1995, June). *Outcome data from the York Psychotherapy Experiential Therapy of Depression Project*. Paper presented at a meeting of the Society for Psychotherapy Research, Vancouver, British Columbia, Canada.

Klein, M., Mathieu, P., Gendlin, E., & Kiesler, D. (1969). *The Experiencing Scale: A research and training manual* (Vol. 1). Madison: University of Wisconsin Extension Bureau of Audiovisual Instruction.

Leventhal, H. (1984). A perceptual motor theory of emotion. In L. Berkowitz (Ed.), *Advances in experimental and social psychology* (pp. 117–182). New York: Academic Press.

Paivio, S., & Greenberg, L. S. (1995). Resolving unfinished business: Experiential therapy using empty chair dialogue. *Journal of Consulting and Clinical Psychology, 63*(3), 419–425.

Pascual-Leone, J. (1984). Attentional, dialectical, and mental effort: Toward an organismic theory of life stages. In M. L. Commons, F. A. Richards, & C. Amon (Eds.), *Beyond formal operations: Late adolescent and adult cognitive development*. New York: Praeger.

Pascual-Leone, J. (1991). Emotions, development, and psychotherapy: A dialectical-constructivist perspective. In J. D. Safran & L. S. Greenberg (Eds.), *Emotion, psychotherapy, and change* (pp. 302–335). New York: Guilford Press.

Perls, F. (1969). *Gestalt therapy verbatim.* Lafayette, CA: Real People.

Perls, F., Hefferline, R., & Goodman, P. (1951). *Gestalt therapy,* New York: Dell.

Rhodes, R., Geller, J., Greenberg, L. S., Elliott, R. (1992). *Interpersonal process recall of client selected misunderstanding events.* Paper presented at a meeting of the Society for Psychotherapy Research, Berkeley, CA.

Rice, L. N. (1974). The evocative function of the therapist. In L. N. Rice & D. A. Wexler (Eds.), *Innovations in client-centered therapy* (pp. 289–311). New York: Wiley.

Rice, L. N., & Greenberg, L. S. (Eds.). (1984). *Patterns of change: Intensive analysis of psychotherapy process.* New York: Guilford Press.

Rice, L. N., & Kerr, G. P. (1986). Measures of client and therapist vocal quality. In L. S. Greenberg & W. M. Pinsof (Eds.), *The psychotherapeutic process: A research handbook* (pp. 73–105). New York: Guilford Press.

Rogers, C. R. (1951). *Client-centered therapy.* Boston: Houghton Mifflin.

Rogers, C. R. (1957). The necessary and sufficient conditions of therapeutic personality change. *Journal of Consulting Psychology, 21,* 95–103.

Sachse, R. (1990). Concrete interventions are crucial: The influence of the therapist's processing proposals on the client's intrapersonal exploration in client-centered therapy. In G. Lietaer, J. Rombauts, & R. Van Balen (Eds.), *Client-centered and experiential psychotherapy in the nineties* (pp. 295–308). Leuven (Louvain), Belgium: Leuven University Press.

Safran, J. D., Muran, J. C., & Samstag, L. W. (1994). Resolving alliance ruptures: A task analytic investigation. In A. O. Horvath & L. S. Greenberg (Eds.), *The working alliance: Theory, research, and practice.* New York: Wiley-Interscience.

Singh, M. (1994). *Validation of a measure of session outcome in the resolution of unfinished business.* Unpublished doctoral dissertation, Department of Psychology, York University, Toronto, Ontario, Canada.

Toukmanian, S. (1986). A measure of client perceptual processing. In L. S. Greenberg & W. M. Pinsof (Eds.), *The psychotherapeutic process: A research handbook* (pp. 107–130). New York: Guilford Press.

Vanaerschot, G. (1990). The process of empathy: Holding and letting go. In G. Lietaer, J. Rombauts, & R. Van Balen (Eds.), *Client-centered psychotherapy in the nineties* (pp. 269–294). Leuven (Louvain), Belgium: Leuven University Press.

Watson, J. C., & Greenberg, L. S. (1995). The alliance in experiential therapy: Enacting the relationship conditions. In A. O. Horvath & L. S. Greenberg (Eds.), *The working alliance: Theory, research, and practice.* New York: Wiley-Interscience.

Index